A HISTORY OF
EDUCATION IN ANTIQUITY

A HISTORY OF
EDUCATION IN ANTIQUITY

BY

H. I. MARROU
Professor at the Sorbonne

TRANSLATED BY

GEORGE LAMB

SHEED AND WARD

FIRST PUBLISHED IN 1956
BY SHEED AND WARD LTD.
33 MAIDEN LANE
LONDON W.C.2
AND
SHEED AND WARD, INC.
840 BROADWAY
NEW YORK 3

This book is a translation of
Histoire de l'Education dans l'Antiquité,
3rd edition, Editions du Seuil, Paris.

PRINTED IN GREAT BRITAIN
BY PURNELL AND SONS, LTD.
PAULTON (SOMERSET) AND LONDON

CONTENTS

PART ONE

THE ORIGINS OF CLASSICAL EDUCATION
FROM HOMER TO ISOCRATES

PART TWO

CLASSICAL EDUCATION IN THE HELLENISTIC AGE

PART THREE

CLASSICAL EDUCATION AND ROME

NOTES

Figures between brackets refer to the Additional Notes, pp. 353–452.

The classical references accompanying the text make use of the current abbreviations taken, in most cases, from the *Oxford Classical Dictionary*. The reader will find an explanation of these references on pp. 453–460.

THE LINGUISTIC FRONTIERS OF THE ROMAN EMPIRE

In the map facing p. 256, the broken line marks the frontier between the Latin spheres of influence in the north and west and the Greek in the south, in the second century A.D. The dotted area shows the advance of Latin at the end of the third century. Asterisks indicate Roman colonies in which the Latin element was gradually absorbed by Hellenism. The mountainous regions marked are at an altitude of 3,000 feet or over. Where the place-names of antiquity have a modern equivalent, this is given in italics below the original name.

INTRODUCTION

SOME sort of apology may seem to be necessary to the world of scholarship for presenting it with this general study of a subject, by no means new, which already has a whole series of works of solid scholarship behind it (1). But these books are beginning to seem a little out of date, and in any case they are gradually disappearing under the dust accumulated by specialised study and the increasing mass of new findings; and it therefore seems necessary to attempt a general treatment of the whole subject, integrating all that is really valuable in the new acquisitions into a total synthesis.

This is all the more necessary because research has so far proceeded in an anarchic fashion, concentrating, sometimes excessively, on small sectors and working them to death, and neglecting others more worthy of its attention. The following effort at a treatment of the whole revealed these gaps all too clearly, and the reader will in fact find more new material in this book than I could have wished to incorporate; but I have often found myself obliged to deal with a whole section from scratch because I could not find enough material for my purpose in the work of my predecessors.

But in any case historical knowledge is only one aspect of human knowledge in general, and it is therefore essentially in movement and always provisional. Our ideas about man and his life and the world he lives in are in a continual process of transformation; every historical subject needs periodic revision—to be put in its proper place in the new perspective that has had to be adopted because the whole pattern of history has meanwhile been modified.

Finally, it is always useful to have at hand a brief account of any question of importance, at least as a basis for more detailed investigation. Students of history will be the first to realize this, but I have also had in mind the general educated public, which has a right to be acquainted with the results of scientific research. Learning is not an end in itself; it should become one of the sources helping to create the culture of our own day.

ANCIENT AND MODERN EDUCATION

The history of education in antiquity is not without relevance to our modern culture, for in it we can trace the direct ancestry of our own educational tradition. We are the heirs of the Græco-Latins, and everything of importance in our own civilization derives from theirs. Most of all is this true of our system of education.

At the end of this book, I shall explain how the declining life of the school of antiquity, persisting in some cases long beyond its time into the dark, barbarous days of the early Middle Ages, came to an end in the West at dates varying with the countries concerned. But the methods of the education of antiquity were revived at the time of the Carolingian Renaissance, when a renewal of study took place. This restoration, like all restorations, was clumsy and imperfect; nevertheless, the Carolingians genuinely sought, and in one direction undoubtedly achieved, a revival of the broken tradition.

As mediaeval civilization became increasingly more complex, Western Christendom, especially from the twelfth century onwards (2), was led to develop teaching-methods and institutions of a quite different and highly original kind. Yet even at the height of the thirteenth century the memory of the ancient models, and a desire to imitate them, continually haunted the minds of the men of the time, whose importance in the history of humanism has been underestimated for far too long.

But above all it was the Renaissance of the fifteenth and sixteenth centuries which left its mark on our education by its conscious, intentional return to the strict classical tradition. Today, to a much greater extent than is commonly realized, we are still living on the humanist heritage: to take but one example— French secondary education has, on the whole, retained the form given to it in the sixteenth century by the founders of the Protestant Academies and the Jesuit Colleges (3).

Our study will not, however, have the sole interest of helping us to know ourselves better by making us conscious of our origins. That in itself would be a worth-while achievement; for such an awareness is a means of escape, in so far as this is possible, from the bondage of historical necessity, liberating us from absolute dependence upon the tradition which upholds us and has made us what we are.

The fruitfulness of historical knowledge is to be found primarily in the dialogue which it generates within us between the Self and the Other. We are sufficiently unlike our forefathers for their education to appear to us as being largely in the category of the Other: there are many things in it, opposed either to our present practice or our future aspirations, which may give us a salutary shock. Thus the reader will be able to meditate at his leisure on the account given in this book.

Because this kind of dialogue is valuable, that does not mean that we are obliged to stop being ourselves; it is simply a means of acquiring culture, enlarging our perspective and stripping us moderns of that naïve self-sufficiency which prevents us from imagining that anyone could be different from ourselves. But though it may force us to think, it will not necessarily change our course of action: historical example merely compels us to test the validity and cogency of the reasons for our choices—it makes our decisions conscious ones. The sympathy which a historian must feel for his subject obliges me to appear as advocate for the ancient system of education—for we must understand before we pass judgment: but the reader must remember that I present him with it simply as an example to reflect upon, not as a model to be slavishly imitated.

The Curve of Educational Development

The period of time dealt with in this book stretches over a period of fifteen hundred years—in round figures, from 1000 B.C. to A.D. 500. This allows room for several complex stages of development. The subject is, however, more unified and more closely defined than we should expect, for the ancient Mediterranean world knew only one classical education, only one coherent and clearly defined educational system.

It is true that this did not appear at the beginning in its final, fully-developed form. It reached this only at a comparatively late date, which I place after the decisive contributions of the two great educators—Plato (d. 348) and Isocrates (d. 338). This need not surprise us. Education is a collective technique which a society employs to instruct its youth in the values and accomplishments of the civilization within which it exists. It is therefore a secondary activity, subordinate to the life of the civilization of which it forms a part, and normally appearing as its epitome. I say "normally", since irrational societies exist which impose on their youth an absurd education that has no relevance to life. In these cases any real introduction to the culture of the society takes place outside the official educational channels. The result is a certain time-lag. A civilization must achieve its true form before it can create the education in which it is reflected.

That is why classical education did not attain its own distinctive form until after the great creative epoch of Greek civilization. We have to wait until the Hellenistic era before we find it in full possession of its own specific forms, its own curricula and methods. Once it reached maturity, however, the inertia that is characteristic of all the achievements of civilization—and particularly of any phenomena connected with educational routine—enabled it to preserve its structure and method for many centuries without any important change. The extension of classical education beyond the boundaries of the Greek world to Rome, Italy, and the Latinized West, was to involve changes and adaptations of merely secondary importance—even though it was originally as completely unexpected and as staggering a phenomenon as the conversion of the Mediterranean world to Christianity. Again, the decay of ancient civilization is only to be detected in the educational field as a kind of sclerosis; and this further accentuates the impression it gives of stability.

Consequently, the record of the period we are about to investigate does not conform to the famous parabola shape—ascent, highest point of ἀκμή and inevitable decline—so dear to antiquity.[1] No doubt at the beginning of our enquiry we can trace an ascending curve, that of the development which took place from the tenth to the fourth century B.C. and brought classical education from birth to maturity (see Part I of this book); but this state of intrinsic perfection was not confined to a brief ἀκμή. Classical education took a long time to mature and receive its definitive character, but once this was reached it lasted for many centuries, throughout the Hellenistic era and beyond; and the infusion of new blood from Rome gave it a fresh lease of life. There was no decline in the curve: it split into two and then continued in two parallel lines, one going on indefinitely in the Byzantine East, the other existing in the Latin countries until it was brutally brought to an end by historical events—the barbarian invasions and the disappearance of the political framework of the Empire. Meanwhile, a new curve was already rising from below; and at the end

[1] Polyb., VI, 51.

of this book we shall see how, beginning from one small section of Christian society—the monasteries—a new course of development was rising which would in the end lead to a new type of education—that which was to dominate Western Christendom during the Middle Ages.

FROM THE NOBLE WARRIOR TO THE SCRIBE

To sum up this complex development in a simple formula, it might be said that the history of ancient education reflects the progressive transition from a "noble warrior" culture to a "scribe" culture (4). There are refined, mature civilizations, on which the legacy of the past, embodied in a written form, presses heavily, and whose education is in consequence dominated by the technique of writing. These are the "people of the Book"—*ahl el kitab*, as the Koran calls the Jews and Christians, with a respect not unmixed with astonishment. On the other hand, there are barbarian civilizations like Arabia at the time of the Prophet: in these civilizations the upper class is composed of an aristocracy of warriors, and education is therefore predominantly of a military kind: as such, it aims at training character and building up physical vigour and skill rather than developing the intelligence.

The whole history of ancient education constitutes a slow transition from the latter to the former type of culture. Its origins are to be found in a society still impregnated with the warrior spirit, which nevertheless managed to produce the central pivot around which the whole of Greek education was to be organized—and this was a book, Homer's *Iliad*, though it is true that it was entirely devoted to celebrating the deeds of heroes. As a result of this, there soon begin to be introduced into this culture elements which can not only be described as literary but even as bookish—even though the book concerned was for a long time sung or recited rather than read. On the other hand, we can detect much later remarkable survivals of these aristocratic, warlike origins, particularly in the prestige attached to physical culture and sport. It was not until long afterwards, when the Christian Faith decided to organize culture and education around the Book of Books—the Bible, the source of all knowledge and all life—that the literary man of antiquity finally became a scribe.

THE ORIENTAL SCRIBE

Until that time the history of classical education continued to a great extent to be at variance with that of the civilizations of the Near East which furnish us with the most characteristic examples of a "scribe" culture, the scribe being found in Egypt, Mesopotamia and Syria. We find echoes of this in the Sapiential Books of the Old Testament, especially in *Proverbs*, that handbook of moral education for the training of the perfect Civil Service clerk, whose aphorisms are a codification of the traditional wisdom of the cultural milieu in which the royal scribes of Israel lived between the tenth and seventh centuries B.C. (5).

These scribe cultures, of course, have taken very different forms at different times and places, but in this work it will be sufficient to consider them in general terms from two points of view, the technical and the moral. From the technical point of view, they emphasize the written word: the scribe is essentially a person who has mastered the technique of writing. We know the complexity, and as a result the practical difficulties, of the various systems of writing that were in use in Egypt and Mesopotamia, in which ideographic, syllabic and alphabetical elements were all juxtaposed. There were moreover added complications—involving in Egypt a simultaneous employment of different types of writing (hieroglyphic and hieratic, then demotic) and in Mesopotamia the use of different languages in the same cultural milieu (Sumerian and Accadian, and later Aramaic). It is a remarkable fact that the sign for *sesh*, which is Egyptian for "scribe", depicts all the tools used in writing—a calamus, a water-pot and a palette with two saucers, one for black ink, the other for red. In Hebrew, "scribe" is rendered *sopher*, a word which—like *sepher*, "a book"—is derived from *saphar*, "to write", "to count".

Socially the scribe was a civil servant: he put his knowledge of writing at the service of the civil administration. In Egypt this was essentially a kingly affair; in Mesopotamia it was at first, apparently, sacerdotal, but there too it soon came under the direction of the king. This was the scribe's fundamental importance, both historically as regards his origin and practically as regards his function. Contrary to the theories dear to romantic historians, it seems clear that writing was first invented and used, not to fix theological or metaphysical dogma in a rigid form, but for the practical needs of accountancy and administration (6). It was only later that it developed away from this utilitarian purpose and began to be put to more elevated use in matters of history and abstract thought; and even then the oriental scribe was still mainly the man who kept the accounts, looked after the archives, drafted orders, and, because he could be given commands in writing, was naturally entrusted with their execution.

Thus, from the social and political point of view, the scribes appear above the popular classes of peasants and manual workers as an upper class raised over the unorganized mass of serfs, and more or less directly sharing in the exercise of power. No doubt many of them had only a fraction of this power, but the constitution of these centralized, absolute monarchies was such that everyone had a fair chance: there were opportunities for the recognition of merit, and there was room for the exercise of patronage. Any scribe could hope that he might one day rise to the highest office in the State (such was the theory, at least: in fact, his hope was seldom realized. Not all Napoleon's soldiers finished up as Field Marshals!). This was a characteristic feature of the system: we shall see it appearing again at the end of the development of classical culture, in the bureaucracy of the late Roman Empire.

Hence the importance which the old oriental societies attached to education as the gateway to success. For the child, education was the means of entry into a privileged class. Certain Egyptian literary texts have handed down to us a vivid picture of the pride of caste that was displayed by the scribes. In the ninth or tenth dynasty (c. 2240–2060) we find the scribe Akhtoy trying to encourage his son Pepi to follow the thankless study of letters by painting a satirical picture of the thousand and one drawbacks there are in any kind of manual work, which he contrasts with the happy lot of the scribe, and the nobility of his lofty vocation. We find the same admonition again under the name of Amenemope, the principal royal archivist in the reign of Rameses II (1298–1232). These passages became classical: they have come down to us in the form of "selected passages" which enjoyed a long popularity. This gives us some idea of the importance of the feelings they expressed (7).

This high opinion of the scribe's art found symbolic expression in the idea that writing was a sacred activity, of divine origin and inspiration, placed under the patronage of a god, such as Thoth in Egypt, and Nabu, the son of Ea, the god of wisdom, in Mesopotamia (8).

THE EDUCATION OF THE ORIENTAL SCRIBE

We can dimly perceive the general outline, the curricula, the method and to a certain extent the history of the education which in the oriental civilizations imparted this culture to the young. There were schools for the training of the scribe (among the Jews this was the House of Instruction, bê(y)t midh^erasch),[1] the ruins of which Mesopotamian archaeologists claim to have discovered here and there—as, for example, in recent times, at Mari on the Euphrates. There, in the ruins of the palace destroyed by fire at the end of the second millennium, A. Parrot unearthed two classrooms which contained parallel rows of desks for two, three, or four pupils. Strewn on the ground he found a whole collection of school writing materials—baked-earth ink-stands, writing-tablets and shells (9).

The first thing the master taught his pupil was the correct way to hold the stylus or calamus, and how to print or draw the elementary signs. Then he gave him a model to copy and reproduce. The signs were simple at first, but they gradually became more and more complex. Then isolated words such as proper names were introduced, followed by whole phrases and more highly developed passages, including examples of letter-writing. Teachers' models and children's exercises have been found on papyri and writing-tablets (10).

The method of instruction was very elementary, and called for no initiative in the pupil: it depended for its effectiveness on his docility and therefore, as we might expect, made use of the most drastic corporal punishment, as did the classical education of a later date. The Hebrew word musar means both instruction and correction or chastisement. Here again the most vivid descriptions come from Egypt. "The ears of the stripling are on his back. He hears when he is being beaten." "You brought me up when I was a child," declares a grateful pupil to his master; "you beat me on the back and your teaching penetrated my ears" (11).

Side by side with the teaching of writing went oral teaching. The master read a text, commented on it, and then questioned his pupil about it; at a higher level there would be real discussions between the two (12). For it would be giving a false impression of oriental education to depict it as being strictly confined to technical and utilitarian instruction. The training of the scribe aimed higher: it professed to achieve a complete formation of mind and character and

[1] Ecclus., xli, 23.

to lead to what can only be called Wisdom—to use a fine word whose meaning we have lost and which the example of antiquity may help us to recover.

From Egypt a whole sapiential literature has come down to us. It was amassed over a long stretch of time, from the fifth to the twenty-fifth dynasty (twenty-sixth to eighth centuries), from the *Teachings* of Ptahhotep to those of Amenemope (13), whose long popularity is explained by the fact that they became educational classics. This Egyptian wisdom was, at least in the literary field, the source of the wisdom of Israel (14), and it had its equivalent in a parallel Mesopotamian tradition, which was to find a belated fulfilment in the *Wisdom of Ahiqar* (15). When considering this oriental wisdom we must not exaggerate its aims, or we shall be drawn by reaction into depreciating its real content. In principle it was only a practical worldly wisdom, first instilling decent manners into children and then teaching the art of how to behave in daily life, particularly in the dangerous life at court, where the scribe had his career to make; but thence it developed into a high moral code, full of elevated religious feeling. This was a noteworthy feature of oriental education; and it is this aspect of it which is related to classical education, which was later to show the same concern for the education of the whole man, for an ideal inner perfection.

Chronologically, however, there is a great difference between the two, for this oriental culture and scribe education date back to the very ancient past: they were fully developed as far back as the end of the fourth millennium B.C. In Egypt their origins are obscure, the reason being that they flourished on the Nile Delta, where the comparatively wet climate made it impossible for the papyrus to be preserved: the practice of writing and the full organization of the kingly government were already in existence when the Thinite monarchy was founded (first–second dynasties, circa 3200) (16). As regards Mesopotamia, we are luckier: the clay writing-tablets being indestructible, we are able to witness the joint origin of both writing and the scribe culture, and indeed of the education system itself, in the Jemdet-nasr period, i.e. contemporaneously with the first two Egyptian dynasties; and we can see all this more clearly still in the earlier period of Uruk III, when the system of writing, still wholly pictographic, is revealed in accountancy-tablets and in what may have been school exercises (17).

MINOAN AND MYCENEAN SCRIBES

It seems certain that in Crete and to some extent on the Greek mainland there had been a similar type of education in the great days of Minoan civilization. The archaeological data seem to indicate the existence of a strong monarchy, which Thucydides could still remember,[1] during the Middle and Later Minoan periods; and this must undoubtedly have possessed an administration of scribe officials.

These officials employed a system of writing of their own, which even now we are unable to decipher. But we can follow its formal development from a two-fold hieroglyphic stage to one in which it assumed a linear form, likewise of two

[1]Thuc., I, 4.

types. There seem to be survivals of this in the system of syllabic writing in use in Cyprus at the height of the classical era, and from this we can at least conjecture that Minoan linear writing was in part syllabic (18).

The existence of these scribes presupposes some kind of educational system and schools to train them; but no documents have been discovered that prove the existence of either (19). In any case, any knowledge we could gain of them would shed little light on the origins of Greek classical education, for between the two civilizations there was no real contact but only chronological sequence. No doubt, as we now know, the technique of writing, and consequently the scribe culture, lasted throughout the Mycenean period (Late Helladic 1400–1200), in a Greece which from that time onwards was peopled by Indo-Europeans, indeed by Hellenes (20); but the technique of writing and the scribe culture were both finally engulfed in the great upheaval which is generally described as the Dorian invasion. (Cyprus was, perhaps, an exception, but such an out-of-the-way place was of no importance.) We may leave the historians to argue over the various hypotheses concerning the ethnographical interpretation of this great phenomenon; it is sufficient for our purpose that the archaeological evidence proves that it happened. The Creto-Mycenean civilization perished in a great catastrophe.

Not everything perished, of course. It is customary nowadays—and reasonably so—to emphasize the Minoan and Mycenean survivals that are to be found in many fields of Greek civilization—in religion, in poetry, and in the plastic arts. But we must remember that what has survived is a few products of the civilization, a few isolated elements, not the systematic structure—the form—which gives a civilization its internal cohesion and spiritual value. In the dark ages which followed the great catastrophe (1000–700) there was certainly a quasi-barbaric period. But in it, after the break-up of the tradition, we can see signs of a new beginning, and Greek civilization begins to develop afresh.

Education is not an element that can be detached from one civilization and borrowed by another. It is the concentrated epitome of a culture and as such it is inseparable from the form of that culture, and perishes with it. And in actual fact Greek culture, under the stress of the Dorian invasion, reverted violently to a stage of barbaric warfare, after which Greek education bore no relation to that of Minoan times and was for many centuries to be utterly different from that of the oriental scribes. Its history, like that of classical culture as a whole, can only start with Homer.

PART I

THE ORIGINS OF CLASSICAL EDUCATION FROM HOMER TO ISOCRATES

CHAPTER I

EDUCATION IN HOMERIC TIMES

IT IS with Homer, clearly, that our history must begin. From him the Greek cultural tradition rises in an unbroken line and he supplies us with the oldest documentary evidence of any value about the education of antiquity. Moreover, the fact that he stands in the forefront of classical education encourages us to discover what precisely education can have meant for him at that early date (1).

THE HISTORICAL IMPORTANCE OF HOMER

Of course, a historian has to be careful when he mentions the name of Homer (2). He cannot refer to the "age of Homer" as a simple unity. The *Iliad* and the *Odyssey* appear as documents of a complex character, and in his analysis the historian must try to take into account the inherited tradition of legend and poetry and the poet's own specific contribution. He has to distinguish the broad composition of the work as a whole from the interpolation and revision and re-organization which philologists claim to have unearthed.

In so far as there seems to be any agreement on the question, which has been disputed to the point of exhaustion (3), there is a tendency to admit that the text in question was substantially in existence from the seventh century onwards. This is the text which it is thought that Hipparchus, at the end of the reign of his father, Pisistratus (d. 528–7), brought from Ionia to Athens, where it was officially adopted for the Panathenean rhapsody competitions.[1] With this as a starting point, the composition of the principal songs in the *Iliad* can be narrowed down to a date "which cannot be very much later than the middle of the eighth century" (4). The *Odyssey* appeared later. Assuming that this work may be regarded as that of a single poet, a real Homer, rather than the result of a collective effort of several generations of bards, a margin of at least a hundred years is needed to allow for the development of the highly advanced tradition evident in the style and language of the Homeric legends, and, out of all the dates proposed by ancient (5) and modern writers, this brings us to that calculated by Herodotus, who said that Homer (and Hesiod) lived "four hundred years before me, no more"[2]—i.e. about 850.

But it is not enough to date the epic as having been written between, roughly, 850 and 750; we have also to determine its precise value as a document (6). It is important to remember that Homer is a poet, not a historian; moreover, that he gives free reign to his creative imagination, since he sets out, not to describe scenes from real life, but to paint a picture of heroic deeds projected into a

---

[1] [Pl.] *Hipparch.*, 228b.   [2] Hdt., II, 53.

fascinating, far-off past, when not only gods but beasts could speak. Think of Xanthos, for example, one of Achilles' horses, prophesying to his master,[1] like Roland's horse in the *Petit Roi de Galice* of Victor Hugo—it is important not to exaggerate the naïve and primitive character of this work, which had so much mature experience behind it. All the same, Homer was not a Flaubert or a Leconte de Lisle, beset by archaeological scruples: his picture of the heroic age is a composite one, in which memories going back through nearly a thousand years' history are set one upon another. Certain references go back even beyond Mycenean times, to the days of Minoan greatness—as for example in the descriptions in the *Iliad*[2] of the dances of the youth of Cnossos and the acrobatics in the "theatre"—χόρος—of Daedalus, which was in fact destroyed during the catastrophe of 1400.

However, even though this picture may contain many anachronisms, in the main it must have taken most of its elements, not perhaps from Homer's own time (the aristocratic period in the history of the cities of Ionia) but at any rate from the period immediately preceding, the "Middle Ages" which came after the Dorian invasions (1180–1000). If we proceed carefully, and manage to eliminate all the more ancient or more recent matter, we can use Homer as a valuable source-book for the obscure times in which he lived.

HOMERIC CHIVALRY

I shall speak of the Homeric "Middle Ages", not because they are a comparatively unknown period coming between two others about which much more is known, but because the political and social structure of this ancient society presents strict analogies with that of our own Western Middle Ages. These analogies, of course, must not be pressed to the point of paradox, for history does not repeat itself; *omne simile claudicat*. I speak of Homeric chivalry, in the same way as one talks about "Japanese feudalism" (7). And it is primarily with our early Middle Ages, i.e. from the Merovingian period to A.D. 1000, that the comparison seems to be valid: society in Homer's time seems to have been very like Carolingian, pre-feudal Europe.

At the head of this society was the king. He was surrounded by an aristocracy of warriors, a veritable court, composed of a council of the greatest knights, old men—γέροντες—honoured for their age, whose experience made them invaluable in State councils and law courts; and then by a band of faithful young warriors—κοῦροι—who made up the nobility—or λαός—as opposed to the serfs—θῆτες—who composed the lower class or δῆμος. These κοῦροι (the equivalent of Hincmar's *pueri vel vassalli*) could either be the sons of princes, or of chiefs rendering service to the king of their country, or recruits drawn from amongst the bands of vagabonds and wandering soldiers of fortune. This society of the Hellenic Middle Ages was still very fluid and had hardly emerged from the period of the invasions. These κοῦροι lived at court—for were they not the king's companions, ἑταῖροι, eating at his table, supported by his levies and rents?

[1] *Il.*, XIX, 404–423.   [2] *Ibid.*, XVIII, 590–605.

This community life, this warrior-comradeship—whose influence on the subsequent course of education and morals we shall soon discover—lasted until the time when, in repayment for his loyal services, the faithful warrior was granted a domain, τέμενος, in fief. This domain, with the tenants necessary for its cultivation, was taken from the public lands. In its original form this grant was provisional, and at most lasted for life, until it was stabilized and made hereditary. Between the *Iliad* and the *Odyssey* we seem to see the vague outlines of a development similar to that experienced by Carolingian society: the nobility gained increasing control over their fiefs, and the royal power gradually declined as small manors arose on the outskirts of important villages; these later united to form the classical city—the Codrides might perhaps be described as the Capetians of Attica.

THE KNIGHTLY CULTURE

This is the fundamental fact underlying the original features of the educational tradition of classical Greece. Greek culture was originally a privilege reserved for an aristocracy of warriors. Here we see the culture in its nascent state; for these Homeric heroes are not brutal old soldiers, prehistoric warriors, as our romantic predecessors liked to think; in a sense, they are already knights.

Homeric society succeeded an old civilization whose refinements had not entirely disappeared. The young κοῦροι rendered their superior what can only be called "courtly service". Like the mediaeval squires, they served at table at royal feasts: "The κοῦροι fill the cups to the brim"[1] is a line so aptly descriptive of their rôle as cup-bearers that we find it repeated or interpolated in four other episodes.[2] And this was a noble service, quite different from that performed by mere servants—κήρυκες.

They served as a retinue: seven young men accompany Ulysses when he brings Briseis to Achilles.[3] They took part in sacrifices, standing by the side of the priest,[4] not only as carvers but also because they "sing the noble paean and dance in honour of the Preserver",

καλὸν ἀείδοντες παιήονα κοῦροι Ἀχαιῶν
μέλποντες Ἑκάεργον.[5]

Patroclus came to seek refuge at the court of Phthia, fleeing from Opontus, his fatherland, after accidentally killing someone. His own father, Menoetius, presented him to King Peleus. The latter welcomed him with kindness, and placed him at the side of his son Achilles, to whom he was later to render the noble service of equerry (θεράπων).[6]

Together with the religious ceremonies, the dominant feature of the life of these Homeric knights was sport. The games were sometimes free and spontaneous, mere episodes of daily life (the life of the nobility was already one of

---

[1]*Il.*, I, 463; 470.
[2]*Ibid.*, IX, 175; *Od.*, I, 148; III, 339; XXI, 271.
[3]*Il.*, XIX, 238 *seq.*

[4]*Ibid.*, I, 463 *seq.*
[5]*Ibid.*, I, 473-474.
[6]*Ibid.*, XXIII, 90.

elegant leisure) like the feast at the house of Alcinous,[1] which included sports (8), musical entertainments, dancing by the young Phaeaces, dancing with balls by the sons of Alcinous, the singing of the bard and the playing of the lyre. Achilles, retiring into his hut, found consolation in singing the heroes' exploits to himself, to the accompaniment of the melodious *phorminx*.[2] And also, perhaps, even at this stage, there may have been public debates and wordy jousts (9).

At other times, again, the games formed part of a solemn display, carefully organized and controlled—we need only think of the song Ψ in the *Iliad*, with its accompanying funeral games in honour of Patroclus. There was boxing (which had been a favourite sport with the Minoans) (10), wrestling, racing, jousting, putting the weight, archery, javelin-throwing, and above all chariot-racing,[3] which was always the noblest and most highly esteemed sport of all.

Clearly, these knights were no barbaric warriors: their life was a genuine court-life, a life of "courtesy", which involved a great refinement of manners—as witness, for instance, the tact displayed by Achilles as organizer and judge of the games,[4] and the sporting instinct of the champions and spectators—the boxer Epeios lifting his adversary Euryalus to his feet after punching him hard and knocking him out,[5] the Achaeans stopping Diomedes when the life of Ajax was in danger from his blows.[6]

This courtesy still characterized the heroes when they engaged in combat, even in the ritual insults which they hurled at each other as a prelude to action. It appeared in every kind of situation: what refinements of courtesy there are, for instance, in the relations between Telemachus and the suitors, despite the tension between them and the atmosphere of hate.

The atmosphere of refinement which surrounds the later of the two poems, at least—the *Odyssey*—seems to find its natural fulfilment in an attitude of the utmost delicacy towards women. The suitors are infinitely respectful to Penelope. We are told that old Laërtes refused to enjoy the slave girl Euryclea[7] in order not to arouse the jealousy of his wife. The mother of the family is absolute mistress of the house—think of Arete, queen of the Phaeaces; think of Helen at her home in Sparta welcoming Telemachus, guiding the conversation—"entertaining" in the modern sense of the word.

It is a life of courtesy, and also of *savoir-faire* (here we meet the oriental Wisdom again): how to act in polite society, how to react to unforeseen circumstances, how to behave, and above all how to speak—to appreciate the importance of all this one only needs to think of Telemachus at Pylos or Sparta, or Nausicaa faced with the shipwrecked Ulysses.

Such, in brief, is the ideal figure of Homer's "perfect knight". But a man did not become an accomplished κοῦρος by the light of nature. This culture, with its rich and complex content, presupposes the appropriate education, of the nature of which we are not left in ignorance. Homer is sufficiently interested in the psychology of his heroes to take care to tell us how they have been brought up, how they have been able to achieve such a flowering of chivalry: the heroic

---

[1] *Od.*, VIII, 104 *seq.*
[2] *Il.*, IX, 186 *seq.*
[3] *Ibid.*, XXIII, 261–897.
[4] *Ibid.*, 257 *seq.*
[5] *Ibid.*, 694.
[6] *Ibid.*, 822.
[7] *Od.*, I, 433.

legends contained stories about the education of Achilles which had been handed down from generation to generation—just like our mediaeval epic-cycles, which, for example, devoted a whole verse-chronicle to the *Enfances Vivien*.

CHIRON AND PHOENIX

The typical educator is Chiron, "the wise centaur".[1] A large number of legends appear to have gathered around his name. He not only brought up Achilles but many other heroes as well—Asclepius, the son of Apollo,[2] Actaeon, Cephalus, Jason, Melanion, Nestor. Xenophon[3] gives a list of twenty-one names. Here we need only mention Achilles: Chiron was the counsellor and friend of Peleus (it was to Chiron that Peleus owed, amongst other things, the fact that he had been successful in his suit for the hand of Thetis), and it was therefore only natural that the king should entrust his son to his care.

There is a great deal of literature and many monuments (11) showing Chiron teaching Achilles the knightly sports and exercises—hunting, horsemanship, javelin-throwing—courtly arts such as playing the lyre, and even surgery and pharmacopoea[4] (for his kingdom included the valleys of Pelion, rich in medicinal herbs)—a curious touch of encyclopaedic knowledge with a truly oriental flavour: it reminds one of the picture of Solomon's wide culture, painted by the Alexandrian author of the Book of Wisdom.[5] And there is no doubt that in both cases we have an idealized picture: the Homeric hero must know everything, but it must be remembered that he is a hero: it would be naïve to imagine that the average knight of old was a magic healer.

This last "fact" about Achilles and Chiron is the only one mentioned explicitly by Homer, but one episode in the *Iliad*[6] introduces us to another of Achilles' masters who was not so mythical as Chiron and who therefore helps us to gain a more realistic idea of what this knightly education may have been. I refer to the Phoenix episode (12). To aid Ulysses and Ajax in their difficult mission to Achilles, Nestor wisely arranges for this fine old man to accompany them, believing that he will know how to touch the heart of his old pupil—and indeed Achilles greets his "dear old father", as he calls him—ἄττα γεραιέ[7]—most affectionately.

To obtain a hearing, Phoenix finds it advisable to tell Achilles his whole life history, whence follows a long discourse[8] which, with the old man's wandering eloquence, is most illuminating for our present purpose. According to this account, Phoenix fled from his father's wrath because they were at odds over a beautiful girl they held captive, and came to seek refuge at the court of Peleus, who made him lord over the Dolopian marchland.[9] Peleus grew so fond of his vassal that he entrusted him with his son's education (again, a truly "mediaeval" touch) and handed him over while he was still a small child. We see Phoenix

---

[1] *Il.*, XI, 832.
[2] *Ibid.*, IV, 219.
[3] *Cyn.*, I.
[4] *Il.*, XI, 831–832; cf. IV, 219.
[9] *Ibid.*, 480 *seq.*

[5] Wisdom, vii, 17–20.
[6] *Il.*, IX, 434 *seq.*
[7] *Ibid.*, 607.
[8] *Ibid.*, 434–605.

take Achilles on his knees, cut up his food and feed him. "Just think of all the times you wet the front of my tunic when you spluttered your wine out all over me! Children are such trouble!"[1]

"I made you what you are," declares the old tutor, proudly.[2] For his rôle had not ended with Achilles' early childhood: he had been enjoined to look after him on his departure for the Trojan war, and to give the inexperienced youth all the help he needed. Nothing is more remarkable than the twofold mission with which Peleus charged him on this occasion. "You were only a lad; you knew nothing of warfare, which spares no one, nor of councils, in which men learn to shine. And so your father sent me with you: I was to teach you how to give good counsel and how to perform great deeds" (μύθων τε ῥητῆρ᾽ ἔμεναι, πρηκτῆρά τε ἔργων).[3] In these words are summed up the two ideals of the perfect knight: he is to be both orator and warrior, capable of serving his lord in the law courts as well as in war. In the *Odyssey*, again, we find Athena instructing Telemachus under the guidance of Mentes[4] or of Mentor.[5]

And so at the very beginning of Greek civilization we see a clearly defined type of education—that which the young nobleman received through the precept and the practice of an older man to whom he had been entrusted for his training.

SURVIVALS OF THE KNIGHTLY EDUCATION

For many centuries, indeed we might say almost to the end of its history, the education of antiquity was to retain many of the features which it received from its knightly and aristocratic origin. I am not referring to the fact that the most democratic societies of ancient times must seem aristocratic to us moderns because of the part played in them by slavery; I mean something more intrinsic. Even when these societies wanted to be democratic, and thought they were so (as did fourth-century Athens with its demagogic cultural policy—θεωρικόν— of bringing art within the reach of the people, etc.), they lived in a tradition which was noble in origin; and though their culture might indeed be shared in an egalitarian way, it none the less preserved the marks of its origin. It is not difficult to see here a parallel with the development of French and modern Western civilization, which has progressively extended to all social classes— and perhaps vulgarized—a culture whose origin and inspiration were indubitably aristocratic. French culture achieved its own proper form at the court and in the salons of the seventeenth century—every French child makes his first contact with poetry and literature through the *Fables* of La Fontaine, which were dedicated either to the Dauphin or (the twelfth book) to the Duke of Burgundy!

For this reason it is necessary to examine the content of Homeric education, and its ultimate fate, a little more closely. In it, as in all education worthy of the name, we can distinguish two aspects, one technical and the other ethical (the distinction is to be found as far back as Plato).[6] On the technical side, the child

---

[1] *Il.*, 488–491.
[2] *Ibid.*, 485.
[3] *Ibid.*, 442.
[4] *Od.*, I, 80 *seq.*
[5] *Ibid.*, II, 267 *seq.*
[6] *Leg.*, I, 643a–644a.

was prepared for, and gradually initiated into, a particular way of life. On the ethical side we find more than a set of moral rules: a certain ideal of existence is presented, an ideal type of Man—a warrior education may aim at producing either efficient barbarians or a refined type of "knight".

We have already dealt with the technical side—training in the use of arms, in sport and knightly games, in the art of music (singing and dancing and playing the lyre) and oratory; in good manners, in the ways of the world, and in wisdom. All these technical accomplishments are to be found in the later, classical, education, though only after an evolution whereby the more intellectual elements developed at the expense of the warrior element. Hardly anywhere save in Sparta did the latter remain primary, though it survived even in the peace-loving city of Athens as a liking for sport, and in that city's distinctively masculine style of life.

It becomes necessary to analyse this knightly ethic, the Homeric ideal of the hero, still further, and see how it survives into the classical period.

HOMER, THE EDUCATOR OF GREECE

At first sight its survival seems to be explained by the fact that throughout its history Greek literary education kept Homer as its basic text, the focus of all its studies. This is a fact of considerable importance, and one whose consequences Frenchmen find it difficult to imagine. For though we French have a number of "classics", we do not possess one classic *par excellence*, as the Italians have Dante and the English have their Shakespeare. And Homer dominated Greek education much more absolutely than Shakespeare did the English or Dante the Italians.

As Plato said,[1] Homer was, in the full sense of the word, the educator of Greece, τὴν Ἑλλάδα πεπαίδευκεν. He was this from the very beginning, ἐξ ἀρχῆς, as Xenophanes of Colophon[2] insisted as far back as the sixth century: consider the profound influence he had at the end of the eighth century in Boeotia—a still wholly peasant region—on the style of Hesiod, who began his career as a rhapsodist, reciting Homer. And the educator of Greece he remained: in the twelfth century, when in the Byzantine East the Middle Ages were at their height, Eustathius, Archbishop of Thessalonica, compiled a great commentary on Homer, drawing on the whole heritage of Hellenistic philology. There are many testimonies to the fact that every cultivated Greek had a copy of Homer's works at his bedside (as Alexander did during his campaigns); here I need only select one, from Xenophon's *Banquet*,[3] in which a certain Nicoratus says, "My father, wishing me to become an accomplished man [ἀνὴρ ἀγαθός] made me learn the whole of Homer, so that even today I can still recite the *Iliad* and the *Odyssey* by heart." Even when this has been said it remains true that the argument can be reversed, or at least works both ways: it was because the knightly ethic remained at the heart of the Greek ideal that Homer, as the outstanding interpreter of this ethic, remained the basic educational text-book.

---

[1] *Resp.*, X, 606; cf. *Prot.*, 339a.　　　　[2] Fr. 10.
[3] III, 5.

We must in fact reject any purely aesthetic explanation of the long favour he enjoyed. It was not primarily as a literary masterpiece that the epic was studied, but because its content was ethical, a treatise on the ideal. Indeed, as we shall see later, the technical content of Greek education underwent a profound development which reflected far-reaching changes in the civilization as a whole, and it was only Homer's ethics (together with his undying aesthetic value) which could have any lasting importance.

I am not suggesting, of course, that Homer's importance was always clearly and correctly understood throughout all those centuries. It is true that in the Hellenistic age we come across dense pedagogues without any sense of history or any ability to see the great changes in manners and customs that had gradually come about. They were determined to find in Homer all the elements of a religious and moral education that should still be valid in their day: with an ingenuity that at times became comic they attempted to extract from this fundamentally profane (13) epic a veritable catechism. Nor was this catechism to teach only (as in fact it did)[1] a theogony and the golden legend of gods and heroes, but also a whole theodicy, indeed a whole system of apologetics, a summarization of man's duties to the gods—more, a handbook of practical morality, illustrating precept by example, beginning with good manners for children. Nor was even that all: by a kind of allegorical exegesis Homer was used to throw light on philosophy itself.

But all this was mere foolishness: Homer's real educational significance lies elsewhere—in the moral climate in which his heroes act; in their style of life. No attentive reader can escape the pervasive influence of this atmosphere for long. From this point of view we rightly speak of "Homeric education", ὁμηρικὴ παιδεία: the education which the young Greek derived from Homer was that which the poet gave his own heroes, the education Achilles received from Peleus and Phoenix, and Telemachus from Athena.

THE HOMERIC ETHIC

The moral ideal was rather complicated. There is first of all the "cunning" type of person, whom we find a little embarrassing—πολύτροπος ἀνήρ, exemplified in the—to us—ambiguous figure of a Levantine adventurer—as Ulysses sometimes appears in the *Odyssey*. Here, as I have already pointed out, the good manners and *savoir-faire* of the Homeric hero meet the practical wisdom of the oriental scribe: the result is the art of knowing how to get out of any awkward situation! Our conscience, refined by centuries of Christianity, sometimes feels a slight uneasiness about this—think how complaisant Athena is, for example, when one of her dear Ulysses' lies turns out to be particularly successful.[2]

Fortunately this is not the most important thing. It is not the Ulysses of the *Return* but the pure and noble figure of Achilles who embodies the moral ideal of the perfect Homeric knight. This ideal can be defined in one phrase: it was

---

[1]Hdt., II, 53.   [2]*Od.*, XIII, 287 *seq.*

an heroic morality of honour. Homer was the source, and in Homer each succeeding generation of antiquity rediscovered the thing that is absolutely fundamental to this whole aristocratic ethic: the love of glory.

Its basis is that fundamental Hellenic pessimism which so impressed the young Nietzsche. The sadness of Achilles! (14) The shortness of life, the haunting fear of death, the small hope of consolation in the life beyond the grave! There was still no great belief in the possibility of a special destiny in the Elysian fields. And most people were destined for the shades—the mockery of the vague and uncertain shades. We know how Achilles himself regards them from his famous words from Hades to Ulysses, who has been impressed by the way in which the common shades respectfully make way for the shade of the hero. "Ah, do not try to gild death for me, Ulysses! I would rather be looking after some poor farmer's oxen than reigning here over the dead—over these wraiths."[1]

To this short life, rendered still more uncertain by the fact that they are warriors, our heroes are passionately devoted—with the kind of earthy attachment, the frank and unreflecting love, that is the typical feature of a certain kind of pagan soul. Nevertheless this life, however precious it may be, is not supreme; and they are ready, with courage and determination, to sacrifice it for something higher. In this respect the Homeric ethic is an ethic of honour (15).

The ideal value, to which even life itself must be sacrificed, is $\dot{\alpha}\varrho\varepsilon\tau\dot{\eta}$—an untranslatable expression, which it is ludicrous to call "virtue" unless into that simple word is compressed all that Machiavelli's contemporaries meant by virtù. Roughly speaking, $\dot{\alpha}\varrho\varepsilon\tau\dot{\eta}$ is "valour", in the chivalric sense of the word—the quality of the brave man, the hero. "He fell like the hero he was" —$\dot{\alpha}v\dot{\eta}\varrho$ $\dot{\alpha}\gamma\alpha\theta\dot{\partial}\varsigma$ $\gamma\varepsilon\nu\dot{\partial}\mu\varepsilon\nu\sigma\varsigma$ $\dot{\alpha}\pi\dot{\varepsilon}\theta\alpha\nu\varepsilon$—were words frequently used in honour of a warrior who had achieved his true destiny by giving his life. The Homeric hero lived and died in the effort to embody a certain ideal, a certain quality of existence, summed up in this word $\dot{\alpha}\varrho\varepsilon\tau\dot{\eta}$.

Now, glory, the renown recognized by those who know, the company of the brave, is the measure, the objective recognition, of valour. Hence the impassioned longing for glory, the longing to be hailed as the greatest, which was the mainspring of this knightly ethic. Homer was the first to represent this consciously; from Homer the men of antiquity received with rapturous applause the idea that life was a kind of sporting competition in which the great thing was to come first—the "agonistic ideal of life", which was first brilliantly described by Jacob Burckhardt and has since become recognized as one of the most significant aspects of the Greek soul (16). There can be no doubt that the Homeric hero and hence the actual Greek person of flesh and blood was only really happy when he felt and proved himself to be the first in his category, a man apart, superior.

This idea is certainly fundamental to the actual epic, which repeats the same sentiment in the same words, first putting it in the mouth of Hippolochus when he speaks to his son Glaucus, and next in Nestor's mouth when he tells Patroclus

[1] *Ibid.*, XI, 488 *seq.*

what advice Peleus had given his son Achilles. "Always be the best and keep well ahead of the others":

ἀιὲν ἀριστεύειν καὶ ὑπείροχον ἔμμεναι ἄλλων.[1]

It is from this tension of his whole being in pursuit of this one end that Achilles receives his tragic grandeur and nobility. He knows (for Thetis revealed it to him) that once he has vanquished Hector he is to die, but he advances to meet his fate with head proudly erect. He is not concerned with his country of Achaia or with the threatened expedition; his one aim is to avenge Patroclus and avoid disgrace. His one concern is his own honour. In my view this is not, however, any romantic individualism, however personal it may seem. This love of self—φιλαυτία—which Aristotle was to analyse, is not the love of the ego but of the *Self*, the Absolute Beauty, the Perfect Valour, that the hero longs to express in one Great Deed that will utterly astonish the great envious company of his equals.

To dazzle, to be first, the victor, to triumph, to prove one's worth in competition with others, to oust a rival before the judges, to perform the great deed—ἀριστεία—that will make one pre-eminent amongst men—the living, and perhaps even the dead—that is why a hero lives, and why he dies.

An ethic of honour, that can often seem strange to a Christian. It implies the kind of pride—μεγαλοψυχία—that is not the vice of the same name but the noble desire of one who aspires to be great, or, in the case of the hero, consciousness of a genuine superiority. It implies also rivalry, jealousy, that noble Ἔρις that inspires great deeds, whose praises Hesiod was to sing;[2] and hate, as the acknowledgment of proven superiority. Thus Thucydides makes Pericles say:[3] "Hatred and hostility are always for a time the lot of those who lay claim to rule over others, but to expose oneself to hatred for a noble cause is an excellent thing."

THE IMITATION OF THE HERO

The poet's function is to educate, and education means inculcating this high idea of glory. The aim of poetry is not essentially aesthetic but the immortalization of the hero. The poet, as Plato was to say,[4] "clothes all the great deeds accomplished by the men of old with glory, *and thus educates those who come after*." I have emphasized the last few words because they seem absolutely fundamental.

To understand Homer's educational influence one only has to read him and see what his method is, what he regards as proper education for his heroes. Their counsellors must set before them the great examples to be found in the old legends and so arouse the agonistic instinct, the competitive spirit. Thus Phoenix recommends conciliation by reminding Achilles of Meleager. "This

---

[1]*Il.*, VI, 208=XI, 784.   [3]II, 64.
[2]*Op.*, 17 seq.   [4]*Phdr.*, 245a.

is what we learn from the old heroes . . . I am reminded of that great achievement—τόδε ἔργον—a very old story. . . ."[1]

Athena again, in her efforts to awaken a desire for heroism in the immature, irresolute Telemachus, reminds him of Orestes' manly decisiveness. "Stop playing about and act your age. Think of the fame of god-like Orestes when he avenged his father and killed cunning Aegisthus."[2] In all, this event is referred to four times.[3]

This is the secret of Homer's education: the heroic example—παράδειγμα. At the end of the Middle Ages there appeared *The Imitation of Christ*; the Hellenic Middle Ages bequeathed through Homer to classical Greece the Imitation of the Hero. It is in this deep sense that Homer was the educator of Greece. Like Phoenix and Nestor and Athena he was always impressing on his hearers' minds idealized models of heroic ἀρετή; and at the same time the everlasting quality of his work gave tangible proof of the reality of the highest of all rewards—glory.

We know from subsequent history how well his lessons were learnt: his heroes haunted the Greek soul. Alexander (and, later, Pyrrhus) imagined himself, dreamed of himself, as a second Achilles; and there were many other Greeks who like him learned from Homer "to spurn a long dull life and choose instead a brief moment of glory"—a moment brief but heroic.

Homer was not the only person the Greeks listened to, of course. Each century added its own classics, and added something to the Hellenic moral ideal. One of the first people to do this was Hesiod, who introduced such valuable ideas as Right, Justice and Truth. Nevertheless Homer supplied the whole foundation of classical education, and despite sporadic attempts to shake off his tyrannical influence, his feudal ethic of the Great Deed remained unbroken through all the centuries of the classical tradition, to fire the hearts of all Greeks.

[1] *Il.*, IX, 524 *seq.*   [2] *Od.*, I, 296 *seq.*   [3] *Ibid.*, I, 30, 40; III, 306.

CHAPTER II

SPARTAN EDUCATION

SPARTA, being a special example of the Greek archaic culture, naturally forms the second stage of our history. There we can see how Homer's chivalric type of education persisted even when it was developing into something new. Sparta was essentially a military and aristocratic city, and it was never to go very far along the road towards what I have called "scribe-education". On the contrary, it made it a point of honour to remain semi-illiterate. Even when its meticulous legislation covered nearly everything, including marital relationships, its spelling, by a curious exception, was never made uniform. In this field, as inscriptions show, there was the most remarkably smug anarchy (1).

With Crete, which was conservative, aristocratic and military like itself (2), Sparta has a special place in the history of Greek education, and Greek culture generally. It enables us to see the old Greek civilization in its archaic state and in an advanced state of development, at a time when Athens, for instance, has practically nothing to teach us. Even as far back as the eighth century, art was flourishing in Laconia, and the seventh was Sparta's great age, reaching, in my opinion, its highest point—its ἀκμή, to use the Greek word—in about 600 (3).

For this sudden development was subsequently abruptly checked. After leading the march of progress, Sparta reversed its rôle and became the supreme example of a conservative city grimly holding on to the old customs that everyone else had abandoned. It became in the eyes of Greece itself a country of paradox, dismissed as scandalous, or passionately admired by Utopian theorists. The archaic "peplos", for instance, the robe open on the right side that was worn by the Lacedaemonian women, gave rise to malicious jibes from the more dirty-minded of the Athenians against "the women with the bare thighs".

In fact what the Greeks themselves regarded as the originality of Laconian (and Cretan) institutions and customs seems to have been simply a result of the fact that in classical times these countries still retained certain features of the old civilization which had everywhere else been lost. It was not the result of any special spirit, any particular Dorian genius, as Müller tried to make out with his racial theories, that have been so popular in Germany for over a century (4).

Unfortunately, the sources we have to rely on for any description of Spartan education are comparatively late. Xenophon and Plato only take us back to the fourth century, and their evidence is less explicit than Plutarch's and that supplied by the inscriptions, most of which only date from the first and second centuries A.D. Now Sparta was not only conservative but reactionary: in its determination to resist any natural development, to go against the current, to re-establish Lycurgus' "traditional customs", it was forced, from the fourth century onwards, into continual efforts at adjustment and restoration; and this led it to make many restorations of dubious validity, many false, pseudo-archaeological "integrations" (5).

It would be necessary to probe beneath the surface of these later changes to obtain any real idea of the old Spartan education as it existed between the eighth and sixth centuries, and especially as it appeared in the splendid period that followed upon the final submission of Messenia, after the stubborn revolt of 640–610 had been crushed. But we know very little about the education of this golden age, compared with what we know of its culture.

THE CULTURE OF SPARTA IN THE ARCHAIC ERA

We know something about its culture from two sorts of evidence—fragments from the great lyrical poets Tyrtaeus and Alcman, and the astonishing results of the excavations conducted by the British School at Athens, particularly at the sanctuary of Artemis Orthia (1906–1910). When we put these two complementary pictures together we see a Sparta that is very different from the usual picture of a harsh, barbarous city petrified in an attitude of morose distrust. On the contrary, in archaic times Sparta was a great cultural centre open to strangers, to the arts, to beauty, to everything it would later pretend to reject. It was then what Athens was not to become until the fifth century—the centre of Hellenic civilization.

ITS MILITARY AND CIVIC CULTURE

It is true that between the eighth and the sixth centuries Sparta was primarily a military state. By power of arms it had conquered and held a stretch of territory which after the annexation of Messenia (735–716) made it one of the largest states in Greece. Its military prowess gave it a prestige that remained unchallenged until the Athenian victories in the Persian wars. The importance of the military ideal in its culture appears in Tyrtaeus' elegies on war, which were beautifully illustrated in contemporary works of art—all glorifying the fighting hero (6).

We can therefore assume that in this archaic period Spartan education was already—or rather still—essentially military, and consisted of a practical and theoretical apprenticeship in the art of war.

But it must be realized that things had changed, technically and ethically, since the feudal days described by Homer. The Spartans were not brought up to be knights, but soldiers; the atmosphere was that of the city-state, not the castle.

Behind this transformation lay a technical revolution: battles were no longer won by single-handed encounters, as had been the case particularly in the old heroes' duels, but as a result of the clash of two lines of close infantry. Heavy infantry—made up of "hoplites"—now decided the result of battle. (Sparta

B

certainly had a special cavalry corps—but it seems to have been a kind of State secret police.)

This tactical revolution, as Aristotle realized with extraordinary insight,[1] had profound moral and social consequences (7). Whereas the old Homeric ideal of the knight as one of the king's troop had been profoundly personal, the new ideal was collective—devotion to the State—the πόλις—which became something it had never been in earlier ages, the focus of all human life, of all man's spiritual activity. It was the totalitarian idea: the πόλις was everything, turning citizens into men. Hence the profound feeling of solidarity between them, hence the enthusiasm with which they could devote themselves to the interests of their common land, ready to sacrifice themselves, who were mortal, for their city which was immortal. "It is a noble thing to be in the front of the battle and die bravely fighting for one's country,"[2] said Tyrtaeus, the finest spokesman of the new ethic (8).

It was a moral revolution, in fact, giving rise to a new conception of "virtue", of spiritual perfection, an ἀρετή very different from the Homeric quality of the same name. Tyrtaeus very consciously compares the new ideal with the old. "I should not consider a man worthy to be remembered, nor think highly of him, merely because he was a good runner or wrestler—even though he was as big and strong as the Cyclops, swifter than Boreus the Thracian, more handsome than Titho, richer than Midas or Cinyras, stronger than King Pelops, son of Tantalus; though his speech were softer than Adrastus' and he enjoyed every kind of fame—unless he was also valorous in arms, unless he could stand fast in battle.[3] . . . That is the true valour—ἀρετή—the highest reward that a man can obtain from his fellows. It is a good common to all, a service to the city and the people as a whole, when every man can stand firm on his two feet in the front line and rid his heart of all idea of flight."[4] (9)

It will be seen how energetically the new ideal subordinated the human person to the political collectivity. From now on the aim of Spartan education, as Jäger so happily put it, was to produce, not individual heroes, but an entire city of heroes—soldiers who were ready to give their lives for their country.

SPORTING FEATURES OF THE SPARTAN CULTURE

But it would be a good deal less than the truth to imagine that this education had already become a matter of learning the art of war and nothing more. It meant more than that. It still preserved many other features of its knightly origin, especially the delight in all kinds of riding, sports and athletics.

We have enough records of the Olympic Games to know what a high proportion of victories went to the champions from Laconia in these sports. Sparta's earliest recorded victory dates from the fifteenth Olympiad (720). Between 720 and 576, there were eighty-one known Olympic winners, and forty-six of these were Spartans. In the all-important running event, the "stadium race", twenty-one of the thirty-six known champions were Spartans

[1]*Pol.*, IV, 1297b, 16–25.   [3]Fr. 12, 1–10.
[2]Fr. 10, 1–3.   [4]*Ibid.*, 13–18.

(10). These successes were due to the excellence of their methods of training as much as to the physical qualities of the athletes. We know from Thucydides[1] that two typical innovations in Greek sporting technique were attributed to the Spartans—complete nudity, instead of the wearing of tight-fitting shorts, which had been the custom from Minoan times: and the use of oil for embrocation.

Sport was not for men only. There is evidence that even in the first half of the sixth century women were taking part in athletics—Plutarch was delighted about it:[2] it was apparently one of Sparta's curiosities in Roman times—for there are charming little bronzes showing girls running, holding up the hem of their short sports skirts with one hand (11).

MUSICAL FEATURES

Spartan culture was not merely a matter of physical training, however. Although it was not very "lettered" (12) it was not unacquainted with the arts. As in Homeric education, there was the essential Homeric element of music, which was central to the whole culture and acted as a link between its various parts, connected with gymnastics through dancing and through singing with poetry, the only form of literature known to archaic times.

Plutarch,[3] in his inquiry into the origins of Greek music—for much of which he seems to have depended on Glaucus of Rhegion (13)—tells us that Sparta was the real musical capital of Greece in the seventh and early sixth centuries. The first two schools—καταστάσεις—mentioned in his history are Spartan. The first, which produced Terpander, was noted for its vocal and instrumental solos and was in existence for the first two-thirds of the seventh century. The second "catastasis", which existed at the end of the seventh and the beginning of the sixth century, specialized more in choral lyrics and produced musicians like Thaletas of Gortyna, Xenodamus of Cythera, Xenocrites of Locres, Polymnestus of Colophon and Sacadas of Argos. These are now hardly more than names to us, but in their day they were quite famous. Better known are poets like Tyrtaeus and Alcman, who, being lyrical poets, were musicians as well. The fragments of their work that have come down to us show them to have been full of talent, and, indeed, genius.

The fact that most of these artists were foreign—for though it seems unlikely that Tyrtaeus was an Athenian, Alcman certainly seems to have come from Sardis—does not mean that Sparta had no original creative power in the arts but that she had considerable powers of attraction (as London attracted Handel and Paris Gluck). If creative artists and virtuosos flocked to Sparta, it was because they knew they would get the right audience there and have a chance of becoming famous. And here again we come across the new rôle being played by the πόλις: Sparta's artistic life—and its sporting life too—were given corporate expression in displays that were State institutions—the great religious festivals.

Early Sparta had a wonderful series of festivities throughout the year (14). When sacrifices were made to the city's tutelary deities there were solemn

[1] I, 6.   [2] Lyc., 14.   [3] Mus., 1134b. seq.

processions—πομπαί—like those of the Hyacinthia, in which girls in chariots and boys on horseback paraded to the accompaniment of singing. And there were all kinds of athletic and musical competitions. At the sanctuary of Artemis Orthia, for instance, boys of ten or twelve years of age took part in two musical competitions and a "hunting" game—κασσηρατόριον. A race was always a feature at the banquets held at the national Dorian festival, the Carnea. The Gymnopediae, organized by Thaletas, included recitals by two choirs, one of boys and the other of married men. Some of these displays take one by surprise. In the dances—β(α)ρυλλικά—in honour of Artemis, for instance, the performers wore queer, horrible old women's faces: the style of these masks is in certain respects reminiscent of Maori art (15).

Generally speaking, the festivals seem to have reached a high artistic level. There is a marvellous atmosphere of grace, poetry, youth, of playfulness and indeed roguishness (16) in the fragments which have been preserved of Alcman's *Partheneion*, incomplete though they are,[1] in which a chorus of girls describes in the most glowing terms the beauty of their chieftainesses, Agido and Hagesichora. And there is another fragment[2] in which their old teacher—such technical perfection needed a great deal of teaching, with trainers and masters—appears in a very tender and moving relationship with the young choir-girls. He laments the fact that his limbs are too old for dancing any more, and longs to become a bird, the κηρύλος, the male halcyon, which the female birds carry on their wings.

This is clearly something very different from the Laconian severity of classical times, from that Sparta whose one interest was war, which was a barracks for "men who were musketeers and Carthusians rolled into one", as Barrès said, quoting the Maréchal de Bassompière; very different, too, from the current idea of Sparta as the home of a barbarous utilitarianism in things in general, and a harsh, savage attitude to education.

The Great Refusal

But this wonderful early spring was followed by a disappointing summer. Most historians agree that Sparta's steady development came to an abrupt halt in about 550 (17). It began with a political and social revolution in which the aristocracy, perhaps led by the ephor Chilon, destroyed the popular risings that may have been caused by the second Messenian war, and at once set about the business of finding suitable means to maintain its power. Thus began the divorce between Sparta and the other Greek cities, which, on the whole, far from returning to any kind of aristocracy, were tending towards a more or less advanced form of democracy which was helped on decisively at this stage by the incidence of tyranny.

Sparta voluntarily petrified herself at the stage of development which had made her the leader of progress. After the annexation of Thyreatis (c. 550) she ceased to be a conquering nation. Politically, the ephors dominated the kings and the aristocracy dominated the people. There was an oppressive atmosphere

---

[1] Fr. 1.   [2] Fr. 26.

of secrecy and police tyranny that weighed upon the citizens—and of course
on foreigners too, who had previously been welcomed so hospitably. Now they
became suspect, and lived under the continual threat of expulsion—ξενηλασία.

With this went a gradual decline of culture. Sparta renounced the arts and
even athletics—because they were too disinterested, because they tended to
develop strong personalities. No more Laconian champions appeared in the
Olympic Games (18). Sparta became an out-and-out military barracks, a city
in the hands of a closed military caste that was kept permanently mobilized,
entirely absorbed in its threefold task of defence—national, political and social.

As a result of this new situation there developed the classical form of Spartan
education, traditionally ascribed to Lycurgus, though in fact we only get our
first glimpse of it with its own special organization and methods from Xenophon
at the beginning of the fourth century.[1] Already the conservative spirit was
beginning to react too far. This was especially marked in Xenophon's own
circle, the "old Spartans" centring round Agesilaus, who fought against the
moral laxity that always follows victory. This laxity had spread through Sparta
after its defeat of Athens in 404, which brought to an end the dreadful tension
of the Peloponnesian war. Claiming to represent the old traditional discipline
symbolized in the person of Lycurgus, these "old Spartans" opposed the new
spirit as exemplified for instance in Lysander.

Their influence went on increasing throughout the days of fourth-century
decadence, of utter collapse in the Hellenistic period, and in the lowly municipal
status to which Sparta was reduced in imperial times. The greatness of Lace-
daemon became no more than a memory, and Spartan education grew petrified,
exaggerating its peculiarities with an increasing despairing violence as its sense
of its own futility increased.

A STATE EDUCATION

In its classical form (19) Spartan education—or, to give it its technical name,
ἀγωγή—always had one clear aim—the training of the hoplites, the heavy infantry
who had been responsible for Sparta's military superiority, which survived
until they were outclassed by the tactical innovations introduced by Iphicrates
of Athens and the great Theban generals in the fourth century (20). Education
was entirely subordinated to the needs of the State and completely in the
State's hands. To have received ἀγωγή, to have been educated in the proper
fashion, was a necessary if not a sufficient (21) condition for the exercise of civic
rights. The law was exacting: it took an interest in children before they were
born. Sparta had a highly developed system of eugenics. As soon as a child
was born it had to be presented to a committee of elders at the Lesche or council-
hall. If it was not a fine-looking child, well-formed and healthy, it was not
accepted. Sickly and deformed children were thrown on to the Apothetes, the
dung-pit.[2]

The State condescended to delegate its powers to the family until the child
was seven. By Greek standards its education had not yet begun. Up to the

---

[1]Lac., 2.   [2]Plut., Lyc., 16.

age of seven a child was merely fit for "rearing"—(ἀνα)τροφή, an accomplishment at which Spartan women were traditionally expert: Laconian nurses fetched top prices in the market, and were particularly appreciated in Athens.[1]

But when the child was seven it was taken in hand by the State, and it was State property until the day of its death. Its education in the strict sense lasted until it was twenty. It was placed under the direct authority of a special magistrate, an absolute commissar of national education—the παιδόνομος— and then made to join various youth organisations, rather like the Boy Scouts in some respects, but still more like the totalitarian youth movements—the *Gioventù fascista* and the *Hitlerjugend*. Scholars even from the days of antiquity have always been interested in the highly complicated, picturesque language that was used to describe the yearly classes; here I shall confine myself to giving what after much consideration I have come to regard as the best hypothesis (22). The ἀγωγή lasted for thirteen years and was divided into three parts:

Eight to eleven: the "little boy"	ῥωβίδας (meaning unknown)
	προμικκιζόμενος (the very little boy)
	μικκι(χι)ζόμενος (the little boy)
	πρόπαις (the young adolescent)
Twelve to fifteen: the "adolescent"	πρατοπάμπαις (adolescent, first year)
	ἀτροπάμπαις (second year)
	μελλείρην (the future ephebe)
	μελλείρην (ditto, second year)
Sixteen to twenty: the ephebe (in Sparta, irene).	εἰρήν (first year ephebe) or σιδεύνας (?)
	εἰρήν (second year ephebe)
	εἰρήν (third year ephebe, or τριτείρην)
	εἰρήν (fourth year ephebe)
	πρωτεῖρας (senior eiren)

By the time he was twenty or twenty-one the young man had finished his training, but he had not yet satisfied the extremely exigent State, so he had to join the grown men's associations, beginning with the "ball-players"—σφαιρεῖς. It all sounds very much like the sequence Wolf Cub, Boy Scout, Rover, and indeed the analogy with the Scouts goes further, for Spartan boys were divided into units—ἴλαι or ἀγέλαι—like our wolf-packs or scout-troops, commanded by seniors, the twenty-year-old πρωτεῖραι, i.e. the senior ephebes.[2] The units were subdivided into small groups—βοῦαι—packs of six, or "patrols", and led by the smartest boy, who earned the coveted title of βουαγός—"patrol-leader"[3] (23).

The whole system of education was thus collective: children were simply torn from their families and made to live in community. And the process was progressive. During the first four years the "Wolf Cubs"—μικκιχιζόμενοι— only met for games and exercises. But at the age of twelve the "adolescent"

---

[1] *Ibid.*, *Alc.*, I.   [2] Xen., *Lac.*, 2, 5; 2, 11. Plut., *Lyc.*, 17.
[3] Hesych., *s.v.*

—πάμπαις—had to be made tougher, and was obliged to leave home and go to a boarding school—i.e. the barracks. He could not leave, even if he got married, before he was thirty.[1]

PRE-MILITARY INSTRUCTION

Having been thus called up, what did they learn? They learned to be soldiers: everything was sacrificed to that. The intellectual side of their education was immediately reduced to a minimum. "The Lacedaemonians consider it a bad thing for children to learn music and reading and writing, whereas the Ionians think it is shocking if they do not know these things": this was written in about 400, after the Spartan victory, by the unknown author of the Δισσοὶ λόγοι[2], a Dorian Sophist who had been one of Protagoras' pupils.

But it would be a mistake to take that absolutely at its face value. The Spartans were not entirely illiterate. According to Plutarch[3] they learnt at least "the necessary" in the matter of reading and writing. Some of the refinement that appears in Alcman was still to be found in "Laconism"—an affected sort of clipped speech useful for sharp retorts and biting irony:[4] and similarly they did not entirely lose touch with the old tradition that had produced Terpander and Tyrtaeus, but retained some sort of taste for music and poetry, adapted to educational purposes.[5]

Not, of course, that there was any question of practising the arts for their aesthetic value. Tyrtaeus' elegies were still the most popular songs in the repertoire,[6] but that was because of their moral tone and because they made good marching songs. Technically, the teaching of music seems to have declined a great deal from its excellence in the archaic period. There was no chance of its going "modern". The ephors are supposed to have condemned Phrynis (or was it Timotheus of Miletus?) for adding new strings to the standard lyre (24). Apart from choral singing the only music seems to have been military—a sort of regimental affair (the oboe is known to have played a part like that played by our trumpets and drums and kept the rhythm going) (25). "It was a dreadful but inspiring sight," says Plutarch[7] again, "to see the Spartan army marching to the attack to the sound of the oboe."

Everything centred round military training, so that physical education came first. But athletics, and sports like hunting,[8] were no longer part of an aristocratic way of life; their aim was simply to develop physical strength. Very soon the boy began to do real military training as well as gymnastics, learning how to move with others in formation, how to handle arms, how to fence and throw the javelin and so on.[9] The Spartan army was the only professional army in classical Greece—until the fourth century all the other city-states relied on improvised citizen armies; and it was universally admired for its skill in manœuvres, for it could suddenly change from formation in file to formation in line in perfect order, and do this just as faultlessly on the battlefield as on the parade ground.

[1] Plut., *Lyc.*, 16.
[2] II, 10.
[3] *Lyc.*, 16.
[4] *Ibid.*, 19.
[5] *Ibid.*, 21.
[6] Pl., *Leg.*, I, 629b.
[7] *Lyc.*, 22.
[8] Pl., *Leg.*, I, 633b.
[9] Xen., *Lac.*, 2.

A Totalitarian Morality

But soldiering demanded morale as well as technical skill, and education took this into account. In fact, the point is particularly emphasized in all our sources. The whole purpose of Spartan education was to build up character according to a clearly defined ideal—an ideal that has reappeared in all its savage and inhuman grandeur in the totalitarian states of twentieth-century Europe.

Everything was sacrificed to the safety and interest of the national community. The ideal was an absolute patriotism, devotion to the State carried to the supreme limit of death. The only standard of goodness was what served the interest of the city; whatever helped to increase the greatness of Sparta was right. Consequently, in relationships with foreign powers Machiavellianism was the rule, and in the fourth century there were to be some shocking examples of Machiavellianism from Spartan generals (26). The result of all this was that the young men who were being educated were taught to be crafty, to tell lies and to thieve.[1]

As far as internal affairs were concerned the aim was to develop a community sense and a sense of discipline. "Lycurgus," says Plutarch,[2] "trained citizens so that they had no wish to live alone and had lost even the capacity for doing so; like bees they were always united behind their leaders for the public good." In fact the citizen's fundamental and almost only virtue was obedience. The child was trained to obey in the most minute detail. He was never left to himself without someone over him. He owed obedience to all who were ranged above him, from the little βουαγός to the "paidonomos" (who by law had "whip-carriers"—μαστιγόφοροι—by his side ready to carry out his sentences).[3] The child was also obliged to obey any adult citizen he met on the road.[4]

This kind of public morality, which was a mixture of devotion to one's country and obedience to the laws, developed in an austere, ascetic atmosphere that was as typical of Sparta as it is of the modern States that have tried to imitate her. As Mussolini used to say, Spartan virtue demanded a "severe climate". Sparta was intentionally puritanical, consciously opposed to the refinements of civilization. Spartan educators aimed at teaching their pupils how to endure pain;[5] from the time they were twelve onwards the children had to learn how to live hard, and the barbaric harshness of their way of life increased as they got older.

They went around in poor clothes, hatless, with shaven heads and bare feet, and slept on a litter of reeds from the Eurotas, lined in winter with a padding of thistle-flock.[6] And they got very little to eat: if they wanted more, they were told to go and steal it.[7]

Manliness and fighting spirit were developed by way of beatings: hence the fights between gangs of boys at the Platanistas[8] or in front of the sanctuary to Orthia,[9] in which the educational value of Discord so much praised by the old

[1] Xen., Lac., 2, 6–8; Plut., Lyc., 17–18.
[2] Ibid., 25.
[3] Xen., Lac., 2.
[4] Ibid., 2, 10; Plut., Lyc., 17.
[5] Pl., Leg., I, 633bc.
[6] Xen., Lac., 2, 3–4; Plut., Lyc., 16.
[7] Xen., Ibid., 2, 5–8; Plut., Ibid., 17.
[8] Paus., III, 14, 8.
[9] Xen., Lac., 2, 9.

knightly ethic was taken very literally, not to say brutally. Hence too the krypteïa, which in the beginning seems to have been not so much a terrorist expedition against the helots as a campaign exercise designed to accustom the future combatant to the harsh life of ambushes and war (27).

THE EDUCATION OF GIRLS

So far we have been concerned with the boys. The girls too were brought up to be Spartans. Their education was rigidly controlled, with music, dancing (28) and singing occupying a less important place than gymnastics and sport.[1] The grace they had had in the archaic era was sacrificed to a crude utilitarianism. Like the women under Fascism, their first duty was to produce as many bouncing babies as possible, and all their education was subordinated to this one end. They had to learn "to put aside all delicacy and womanish tenderness" by hardening their bodies and appearing naked at feasts and ceremonies. The idea was to turn virgins into strapping viragos with no illusions about sentiment, who would mate in the best interests of the race.[2]

THE SPARTAN MIRAGE

This, then, is the famous education that so many moderns, and ancients too, have so much admired. It is difficult for a French historian, writing in 1945, to speak of it with complete detachment. From K. O. Müller (1824) to W. Jäger (1932), German scholarship lauded it to the skies as a product of the Nordic spirit possessed by the Dorians—the conscious embodiment of a racial, militarist, totalitarian policy—a model, miraculously before its time, of the ideal which from the time of Frederick II, Scharnhorst and Bismarck to the Nazi Third Reich, never ceased to inspire the German soul. Barrès was prevailed upon to follow their example and admire Sparta for being "a magnificent stud-farm". He described Greece as a "group of small societies concerned with the improvement of the Hellenic race". "Those Spartans had as the source of their vitality the surpassing excellence of their system of breeding" (*Le Voyage de Sparte*, pp. 199, 239).

This enthusiasm had had its precursors amongst the ancients (29); in fact we know Sparta primarily through the romantic, idealized picture of her presented by fanatical partisans, especially those who were to be found amongst her old enemies in Athens. Towards the end of the fifth century and throughout the fourth, the triumph of democratic tendencies became more pronounced and their hold more secure, and the party of old Right Wing aristocrats or oligarchs fell back into a surly, sterile opposition, the victims of a veritable neurotic introversion, projecting onto Sparta their own frustrated ideals. The modern historian finds it difficult to get at the truth about this "Spartan mirage". The Spartan bias prevalent in reactionary circles in Athens such as those in which Socrates moved was as strong as the French middle-class bias of "Popular Front" days in favour of the order and power of Mussolini's Italy.

[1] *Ibid.*, I, 4.   [2] Plut., *Lyc.*, 14.

LOST ILLUSIONS

When the historical truth has been so distorted by passion am I supposed to remain unmoved? Or shall I too allow myself to be carried away, and denounce the moral obliquity involved in this glorification of the Spartan educational system against all the teaching of sound history? To invert one of Barrès' phrases, I can easily dismiss the eulogies that Spartan education has received by saying that they "smack of the subaltern's outlook". The Spartan ideal was the ideal of a barrack-room sergeant-major.

I believe I am as conscious of Sparta's true greatness as most people, but I observe that she was great when she was beautiful and just, in those golden days when, in Terpander's words,[1] she nurtured "the valour of young men, the muse of harmony and that mistress of all that is great—justice with her generous ways"; when civic virtue and military might were perfectly balanced and there was a smile of humanity in the mischievous grace of its maidens and elegance in their ivory brooches. Sparta only began to grow hard when she began to decline.

Sparta's tragedy was that she matured too soon. She tried to make the first blessed moment of an early ἀκμή eternal, and grew rigid, glorifying in the fact that she was no longer subject to change—as though life were not essentially a matter of change, and death alone immutable! Everything in classical Sparta began from a refusal of life. In the first place, as we have seen, there was the aristocracy's egoistic reaction in refusing to extend civic rights to the combatants in the Messenian wars. As regards external affairs, Sparta was jealous of the growth of States or cultures more recent than her own.

Petrified in an attitude of refusal and defence, she was henceforth only capable of a sterile cult of her incommunicable difference from all others; hence her perverted desire—again repeated in modern Fascism—to set herself up against all the generally accepted customs and cut herself off from the rest of the world.

All the attempts to whitewash her have simply tried to camouflage a decadence that became more irremediable with each generation. Sparta conquered Athens in 404, but only at the cost of an inordinate effort that destroyed all her elasticity and exhausted her spiritual riches. The following centuries merely witnessed a gradual decline.

And, I repeat, it was as she declined that her education became increasingly and explicitly totalitarian. I do not regard ἀγωγή as a sure way to greatness, I denounce it as a sign of the radical impotence of a conquered people reduced to living on illusions about itself. Its inhuman eugenics go hand in hand with the increasing oliganthropy of a city with a declining birth-rate and a self-engrossed ruling class. All the unnatural efforts to produce hardy women produced in fact high-class adulteresses like Timaia, Alcibiades' mistress, or women of affairs like those who appeared in the third century, whose one interest was their own personal fortune and their property (30). And the military training! It grew progressively harsher and more brutal—and all the time it was losing its efficiency and its real purpose.

[1] Fr. 6.

Careful analysis of the sources shows that Spartan severity was not a legacy from the beginning; its severity was always on the increase. In the sixth century the Gymnopediae were accompanied by musical ceremonies; later, the nudity demanded of the children lost all its original ritual value and led to competitions to see who could best resist the terrible summer sun. In the beginning the sanctuary of Artemis Orthia had been the centre of harmless battles between two bands of children fighting for cheeses piled on the altar—no more than the sort of rag that takes place in French *grandes écoles* and English public schools. In Roman times—and not until Roman times—the same ceremony became the tragic ordeal of the διαμαστίγωσις, in which boys were submitted to a savage whipping, competing against each other sometimes to the death, before crowds of people who flocked sadistically to see them (31)—to such an extent that it became necessary to put a semicircular theatre up in front of the temple for all the "tourists" who came along. And when was this? It was in the Early Empire, when the Roman peace covered the civilized world, when a small professional army was all that was needed to keep the barbarians back beyond the strong Roman frontiers, when there flourished a civilization whose one ideal was a civilized, unified mankind, and when Sparta faded into oblivion, a peaceful little municipality in the disarmed province of Achaia!

CHAPTER III

PEDERASTY IN CLASSICAL EDUCATION

"I MUST now speak of pederasty, for it affects education," declared Xenophon[1] when he came to this subject in his analysis of the institutions of Sparta. They are words with which all must agree: for we are all aware of the place occupied by masculine love in Greek civilization (1), and its place was particularly important in the educational field. Nevertheless this subject, fundamental though it is, is seldom mentioned by the historian without an excessive circumspection, as though it were bound up with an unhealthy curiosity. And indeed certain modern writers have wasted a great deal of time in malignantly scrutinizing the ancient evidence relating to "love affairs with boys", confining their interest to the sexual aspect of the matter. Some have tried to represent ancient Greece as a perverts' paradise, but this is going too far: the very vocabulary of the Greek language (2) and the laws of most of the city-states (3) show that homosexuality was always regarded as something "abnormal". Others have tried to deceive themselves into making a case for pure pederasty, as opposed to carnal inversion; but this contradicts the most unequivocal evidence (4).

What then was the precise position? The question is, of course, a complex one, and to answer it we need to distinguish between the various levels of morality that existed at different times and places—for the peoples of Greece did not all react to pederasty[2] in the same way. We can imagine the difficulty which sociologists of the future will have when they try to decide what place adultery had in the lives of twentieth-century Frenchmen. Just as for us there is contradictory evidence from ancient times, so for them there will be evidence as diverse as the vaudeville at the Palais-Royal on the one hand and the spiritual writings on Christian marriage on the other.

But in any study of the phenomena of homosexuality the actual number of homosexuals in Greek society is of little interest except to the psychiatrist or the moral theologian. It is not there that the real human interest lies; it is to be found rather in the contemporary conception of love and in the place of love in the actual life of the times. For we must remember that since the twelfth century we have learnt to give love a deeper meaning than is conveyed by the word *libido*, in the biological sense of the term.

GREEK LOVE, A COMRADESHIP OF WARRIORS

For the historian it is enough to record that ancient Greek society found the most characteristic and the noblest form of love in the relation of passionate

[1] *Lac.*, 2, 12.   [2] Pl., *Conv.*, 182bd,

friendship between men, or more precisely between an adult man and an adolescent. (In theory the person loved, the "eromenos", was between fifteen and nineteen years of age.) It is quite understandable that such relationships should often have led to unnatural sexual intimacy: we need only refer to statistical evidence and remind ourselves of the weakness of the flesh. But, again, such behaviour was less important than the effect of this kind of feeling on the civilization as a whole.

The Jews of the time of the Machabees,[1] and the ancient Romans,[2] were right in thinking that pederasty, like the athletic nudity with which it was closely connected, was one of the distinguishing marks of Hellenism—one of the practices in which it contrasted most sharply with the "barbarians",[3] and hence in its own eyes one of the privileges establishing the nobility of civilized man.

Although no mention of pederasty seems to occur in Homer (5), I do not think we need hesitate to trace it back to quite early times (6). It was bound up with the genuine Hellenic tradition as a whole: German scholarship is mistaken in regarding it, as it frequently does, as a peculiarity confined to the Dorian race (7). In actual fact we encounter it quite as much elsewhere. The Dorian states may seem to have given it, if not a greater, at least a more official place; but this, I insist, was because the institutions of Crete and Sparta underwent an ossification which preserved them in an archaic form, and even at the height of the classical era they retained many characteristics of the military style of life as it had existed in the beginning.

In my opinion Greek pederasty was in fact one of the most obvious and lasting survivals from the feudal "Middle Ages". In essence, it was a comradeship of warriors. Greek homosexuality was of a military type. It was quite different from the inversion which is bound up with the rites of initiation and the duties of a priesthood. This type of inversion is now the subject of ethnological study in all the many forms in which it appears among "primitive" peoples inhabiting the most diverse parts of the earth (Australia, Siberia, South America and Bantu Africa); its purpose seems to be to enable the sorcerer to enter a magic world of supra-human relationships (8). It is not difficult to find parallels to the Greek type of love—parallels not far removed from us in space and time: the proceedings in which the Templars were involved; the scandals which broke out in the Hitler Youth movement in 1934; and the practices which I am told grew up during the last war in the lower ranks of certain armies.

In my view, love between men is a recurring feature of military societies, in which men tend to be shut in upon themselves. The exclusion—the utter absence—of women inevitably means an increase in masculine love—as for example in Moslem society—though here, it is true, we are under the conditions of an entirely different civilization and theology. The phenomenon is more accentuated in a military milieu, for here, with the glorification of an ideal made up of masculine virtues like strength and valour and loyalty, with the cultivation of a distinctively masculine pride, there goes a tendency to depreciate the normal love of a man for a woman. This sentiment of masculine pride was

[1]II Mach. iv. 9–16. [2]Ennius ap. Cic., Tusc., IV, 70. [3]Hdt., I, 135; Lucian, Am., 35.

forcibly expressed by Verlaine in two poems of *Parallèlement* in which, with shameless ardour, he celebrates the memory of his orgies with Rimbaud:

> . . . Peuvent dire ceux-là que sacre le haut Rite!

That "men's club", the Greek city, always preserved its memory of the original chivalry. Many customs and practices bear witness to the fact that love between men was very closely associated with *Kriegskameradschaft* (9). It was held in the circle around Socrates[1] that the most formidable army would be one composed of pairs of lovers, inspiring each other to deeds of heroism and sacrifice. This ideal was effectively realized in the fourth century in the élite corps formed by Gorgidas, which Pelopidas made into a "sacred battalion". To this battalion Thebes owed her brief greatness.[2]

There is a justly famous passage in Strabo[3] which enables us to recapture the characteristic atmosphere of this aristocratic conception of love between men. In Crete, we are told, the young man was the victim of what amounted to a veritable abduction on the part of his lover, and this moreover with the connivance of those around him. Thereupon the boy was introduced into the "men's club", $\dot{a}\nu\delta\varrho\varepsilon\tilde{\iota}o\nu$, by his abductor, and then he left with him and his friends for a two months' holiday in the country, celebrated with banquets and hunting. When this "honeymoon" was over, the young man returned and was solemnly fêted. He received from his lover, among other gifts, a suit of armour, and became his shield-bearer—$\pi\alpha\varrho\alpha\sigma\tau\alpha\theta\varepsilon i\varsigma$. Having been received into the Order of Illustrious Men—$K\lambda\varepsilon\iota\nu o i$—he was ready to take his full share in the noble life which he was thenceforth to lead, being accepted as an adult and taking the place of honour in the choirs and gymnasia. The point to notice is that this was the method of recruitment to an aristocratic military brotherhood. Strabo insists on the high social rank required of both the friends, and he adds, "In these relationships it is not so much beauty that counts as valour and good education."

As usual, our author throws a veil of modesty over the sexual side of this practice. The moderns on the other hand have been at pains to exaggerate it. They would have us believe that initiation and integration into this male community was not by way of the relationship taken as a whole but simply through the abnormal act itself, the masculine urge effecting the transmission of the warlike virtue from one male to another in a brutally material way (10).

In actual fact, this goes far beyond the evidence of the known texts; it is an example of the exaggeration tending towards obscenity of which modern sociologists are so often guilty when they deal with rites and legends they consider "primitive". Such hypotheses are matters for a little elementary psychoanalysis, which would soon reveal the unsuspected repressions tucked away in the souls of our scholars.

Whatever the truth about its origins, the practice of pederasty persisted as part and parcel of the customs and outlook of Hellenic civilization even when

---

[1] Pl., *Conv.*, 178e; Xen., *Conv.*, VIII, 32.   [3] X, 483.
[2] Plut., *Pel.*, 18.

Greece had on the whole given up its military way of life. We must now analyse its consequences in the sphere of education.

THE PEDERASTIC MORALE

In the first place, the Greek type of love helped to create the particular kind of moral ideal that underlay the whole system of Hellenic education. This ideal I began to analyse when I was discussing Homer. The elder's desire to stand out in the eyes of his beloved, to shine,[1] and the younger man's corresponding desire to show himself worthy of his lover, could not but strengthen in both that love of glory which was, moreover, extolled by the whole agonistic outlook. The amorous relationship was the chosen ground for affectionate emulation. Moreover, the knightly ethic was based on a sense of honour and reflected the ideal of a comradeship of arms. The tradition of antiquity is unanimous in linking the practice of pederasty with valour and courage.[2]

We must draw attention to an unexpected twist of fortune that helped to strengthen this feeling by bringing it from the military into the political sphere. This love between men was responsible for a great number of erotic crimes, as was to be expected in a tense atmosphere in which jealousy and masculine pride were so fiercely inflamed. We know from history, especially from that section of it which deals with the age of tyranny, how many tyrants were assassinated, and how many revolts were fomented against them by jealous lovers. "Many are the lovers," Plutarch tells us,[3] "who took issue with the tyrants over beautiful well-born youths." He cites the classical example of the Tyrannoctones in Athens, the conspiracy hatched in 514 against the Pisistratidae by Aristogiton and the boy he loved, Harmodius, who was also the object of the attentions of Hipparchus.[4] He recalls Antileon, who assassinated the tyrant of Metapontus and (or?) Heracleia, when he tried to take the handsome Hipparinos away from him. He also mentions the case of Chariton and Melanippus, who conspired against the tyrant Phalaris of Agrigentum.[5] There were many others (11). "The love of political liberty had not been enough to provoke an insurrection, but," says Plutarch, "as soon as the tyrants set out to seduce the boys they loved, the lovers rebelled, at the peril of their lives, as though it were a question of defending an inviolable sanctuary." The result was that these incidents, which in our law would come into the category of unnatural crimes, were in many cases the cause of national liberation, were celebrated as famous deeds in every way equal to the highest, and were set before the young for their admiration and imitation. In Greek thought[5] there was a strong link uniting pederasty with national honour and the love of independence and liberty.

MASCULINE LOVE AS A METHOD OF EDUCATION

We may go further. "Greek love" was to provide classical education with its material conditions and its method. For the men of ancient times this type of

[1]Xen., *Conv.*, VIII, 26; Pl., *Phdr.*, 239ab.
[2]Pl., *Conv.*, 182cd; Plut., *Erot.*, 929–930.
[3]*Erot.*, 929.
[4]Thuc., VI, 54–59.
[5]Ath., XVI, 602b.
[6]Pl., *Conv.*, 182bd; Arist., *Pol.*, V, 1313a, 41 *seq.*

love was essentially educative: καὶ ἐπιχειρεῖ παιδεύειν—"Its aim is to educate"—as Plato says.[1]

The establishment of a closed masculine community from which women were excluded had an educational significance, and in a certain sense derived from an educational impulse. For, although it exaggerated it to the point of absurdity and folly, it expressed a profound need: that which impels men to realise to the full all the tendencies that are most characteristic of their sex—the desire to become men in the fullest sense. The essence of pederasty did not lie in abnormal sexual relations. I have already mentioned how the Greek language expressed the disgust that was felt by Greek sensibility for the passive kind of inversion that is meant when Gide uses the word. Pederasty was primarily a form taken by sensibility and, indeed, an anti-feminine ideal of complete manliness.

This intra-sexual discipline found its own appropriate method of education. In this field as in so many others, so profound was the analysis carried out by the lucid Greek thinkers that it will be sufficient here to note the conclusions attributed to Socrates by both Plato and Xenophon. The relationship of passionate love was distinguished by Socrates from sensual desire, and indeed was regarded by him as its opposite. It involved an aspiration towards a higher perfection, an ideal of excellence—ἀρετή. I shall not deal with the ennobling effect which the consciousness of being admired might have on the older man, the "erastes": it is obvious that the educational aspect of the love relationship primarily concerned the younger partner, the adolescent.

The difference in their ages established between the two lovers a relationship of inequality at least as great as that which exists between an elder and a younger brother. The lover's desire to gain the boy's affection and shine before him roused feelings of ardent and active admiration in the latter. The older man was his hero, the higher type who was to be his model and to whose level he would try gradually to rise.

In the older man a complementary feeling developed. Greek tradition illustrates the Socratic theory with a wealth of symbolic stories: stimulated by the youth, the man would feel the stirrings of a vocation to teaching and, aware of the ennobling power of emulation, would become tutor to his beloved. We often see the Greek Eros represented as a mere aspiration of the soul, devoid of sensual desire, towards that which it longs to possess. On the lover's part, however, ancient love also involved a sharing of ἀγαπή through his desire to ennoble the beloved, his self-giving—in short, through a kind of spiritual paternity. This feeling, which Plato analysed in great detail,[2] becomes more comprehensible in the light of Freudian analysis: it is clearly the normal reproductive instinct, the passionate desire to perpetuate oneself in a being like oneself, which is frustrated by inversion and diverted and projected on to the plane of education. The educational activity of the elder appears as a substitute, a scornful Ersatz for fatherhood. "The object of love [i.e. inverted love] is to procreate and beget the sphere of the Beautiful."[3]

The love-relationship thus entailed, for the older man, the labour of teaching

[1] Conv., 209c.   [2] Ibid., 206be; 209be.   [3] Ibid., 206e.

which grew naturally out of his fatherly attitude; for the younger, an attitude of docility and veneration, which led to a growth in maturity. The relationship was maintained openly by daily association, personal contact and example, conversation, a sharing in the common life, and the gradual initiation of the younger into the social activities of the elder—the club, the gymnasium and the banquet.

I have undertaken this painstaking analysis of what is after all a dreadful aberration, because for the Greeks it was the normal mode, the standard type of all education. Παιδεία found its realization in παιδεραστεία. This seems strange to a modern, or at any rate to a Christian; but it must be realised that it was an integral part of the ancient system.

The family could not be the educational centre. The wife was kept in the background: she was considered fit enough to look after the baby, but no more: when the child was seven, it was taken out of her hands. As for the father, he was absorbed in public affairs, for we must not forget that we are speaking of what was originally an aristocracy; he was a citizen and a man of politics before he was head of the family. Read again Plato's curious remarks on this subject at the beginning of the *Laches*.[1] He shows us two fathers coming to consult Socrates about their sons' education: their own has been lamentably neglected. "We reproach our fathers for letting us have our own way during our youth because they were taken up with the affairs of others." These two men were in fact the great Aristides and Thucydides the son of Milesias, the aristocratic leader who opposed Pericles and was ostracized by the people of Athens in 443. And so it is not surprising that Plato should elsewhere declare[2] quite bluntly that the relationship of pederasty establishes between the two lovers "a union far closer"—πολὺ μείζω κοινωνίαν—than that which binds parents to their children.

Nor could the work of education be carried on at school. In the earliest times schools did not exist, and when they did come into being they always tended to be looked upon rather contemptuously, because the masters were paid for their services and the school itself existed merely to give technical instruction, not education. I should like to emphasize this fact for a moment. When we think of education we mean, in the first place, the schools: hence the sometimes excessive importance we attach to teaching-problems in modern society. This is a heritage and a survival from mediaeval times: it was in the monastic schools of the Dark Ages that a bond grew up between the schoolmaster and the spiritual director.

For the Greeks, education—παιδεία—meant, essentially, a profound and intimate relationship, a personal union between a young man and an elder who was at once his model, his guide and his initiator—a relationship on to which the fire of passion threw warm and turbid reflections.

Public opinion—and, in Sparta, the law[3]—held the lover morally responsible for the development of his beloved. Pederasty was considered the most beautiful, the perfect, form of education—τὴν καλλίστην παιδείαν.[4] Throughout Greek

[1] 179cd.
[2] *Conv.*, 209c.
[3] Plut., *Lyc.*, 18.
[4] Xen., *Lac.*, 2, 13.

history the relationship between master and pupil was to remain that between a lover and his beloved: education remained in principle not so much a form of teaching, an instruction in techniques, as an expenditure of loving effort by an elder concerned to promote the growth of a younger man who was burning with the desire to respond to this love and show himself worthy of it.

ARISTOCRATIC EDUCATION IN THE SIXTH CENTURY

This characteristic is all the more noticeable because education in the Greek classical period always preserved some of the aristocratic heritage of its earliest days. In the beginning, it developed in response to the needs of a wealthy class who lived in aristocratic style and had no need to provide their young men with any technical education that would enable them to earn their daily bread. And so it was primarily moral, consisting in the formation of character and the development of personality, with a background of polite society that was both sporting and worldly,[1] and proceeding under the direction of an elder and in an atmosphere of close friendship.

This is shown in action in the writings of Theognis of Megara, and his testimony is all the more valuable because of its early date—544, according to the ancient reckoning (12). He wrote elegies which were to be sung to the accompaniment of the flute[2] at the banquets held by the hetairias, or aristocratic clubs, and in a series of gnomic formulae they provide us with the poet's "Instructions" to his young friend, the noble Cyrnos, son of Polypais.

Even if we are obliged to disregard the more directly erotic content of the Second Book, which is apocryphal and of a later date, there is no doubt that the education which these elegies impart was inspired and coloured by the passion of love. "I shall give you good advice, like a father to his son," Theognis says indeed,[3] but the darker side of this fatherly affection is shown in the many tender reproaches, the anxieties felt by the jealous lover, the plaintive lamentations of the forsaken friend ("I mean nothing to you, you have deceived me like a little child")[4]—though, of course, exactly how much sensuality is implied in all this is a matter for argument (13).

The content of this teaching was entirely ethical: Theognis is conscious that he is handing on to his young friend the traditional wisdom of the aristocrats —'Αγαθοί—in matters of individual and political morality, just as he himself received it when he was young.[5]

SURVIVALS: RELATION OF MASTER TO PUPIL

When, later on, in different circumstances, there arose a different type of education more directly concerned with professional efficiency, it was still under the shadow of masculine erotic love that this high technical instruction flourished: no matter what branch was involved, it was carried on in the atmosphere of

[1]Xen., *Lac.*, 5, 5.   [3]I, 1049.
[2]I, 239–243.   [4]I, 254.
[5]I, 27–28.

spiritual communion that was created by the disciple's fervent and often passionate attachment to the master to whom he had given himself, whom he took as his model, and who gradually initiated him into the secrets of his science or art.

For a long time, the lack of proper educational institutions meant that only this one type of thorough-going education was possible—the type whereby a disciple was attached to a tutor who had honoured him by summoning him to his side, by electing him. Let us emphasize the *direction* of this vocation: it was a call from above, to one whom the tutor deemed worthy. For a long time the opinion of antiquity was to despise the teacher who made a business out of teaching and offered his learning to the first customer who came along. The communication of knowledge, it was believed, should be reserved for those worthy of it. In this, public opinion showed a profound sense of the high dignity of culture and its necessarily esoteric character—a sense which we in the West have lost but which still persists in the East—in Islam, for example, where the Platonic belief[1] in the superiority of oral teaching over the impersonality of the written word is still very much alive.

Obviously this passionate attachment very often degenerated into something murkier, something more carnal, to understand which, again, we need only to remind ourselves of the weakness of human nature. Chinese civilization, which had the same profound conception of cultural initiation, is also said to have encouraged homosexual relations between master and disciple, and also between disciples of the same master. But there is no need to leave Greece: historical gossip provides us with a fine enough array of famous lovers in the classical Pantheon alone.

Among philosophers it will be sufficient to mention Socrates, who, setting up as an expert in erotics, attracted to himself the flower of Athenian youth and bound them to him with the ties of amorous passion. But his is not an isolated example. Plato was the lover—and, it seems, not merely a "Platonic" one—of Alexis or Dion. For three generations the position of head of his Academy passed from lover to beloved; for Xenocrates loved Polemon, Polemon loved Crates and Crantor loved Arcesilaus. And this was not peculiar to Platonists: Aristotle was the lover of his pupil Hermias, the tyrant of Atarnea, whom he immortalized in a famous hymn; nor was it confined to philosophers, for the same relationship was to be found between poets, artists and scholars: Euripides was the lover of the tragic poet Agathon, Phidias the lover of his pupil, Agoracritus of Paros; the physician Theomedon the lover of the astronomer Eudoxus of Cnidus (14).

The Educational Work of Sappho

The Greek city was indeed a men's club; but, as Aristotle remarked with an engaging simplicity,[2] women nevertheless form one half of the human race. Just as, in every society that tolerates it, polygamy means a serious lack of balance, condemning part of the male population to celibacy or promiscuity, so any society that allows one of the sexes to form a closed autonomous fellowship

---

[1] *Phdr.*, 275ac. [2] Arist., *Pol.*, I, 1260b, 19.

must of necessity expect to see a similar fellowship, confined to the other sex, formed in opposition.

It is no secret—least of all to French readers brought up on Baudelaire (15) —that the aberration indulged in by the *femmes damnées* of Greece was woman's response to the frenzy of love between men. The same pattern was repeated in the field of education; indeed, judging by the remarkable evidence supplied by the work of Sappho of Lesbos—so utterly unexpected at such an early date (c. 600)—the feminine fellowship seems to have been in advance of its rival in so far as its social institutions were concerned—at least, such is the impression we gain from the few fragments of her work that have survived in the quotations of ancient grammarians and critics, or in mutilated Egyptian papyri.

These fragments seem to show that in Lesbos towards the end of the seventh century girls could receive a complete education, from the time they had out-grown childhood—which they spent at home under the authority of their mother —until they got married. This higher education took place within a community life, in a school, "the abode of the disciples of the Muses".[1] Juridically, this took the form of a religious fellowship, θίασος, dedicated to the goddesses of culture—a form that was also to be adopted by the schools of philosophy from the time of Pythagoras onwards. Here, under the direction of a mistress, whose typical representative Sappho has so magnificently described in her own self-portrait, the personality of these young girls was fashioned to conform to an ideal of beauty, aspiring to Wisdom.[2] From the technical point of view the school was the equivalent of an Academy of Music and Drama; it taught ballet dancing[3] (a heritage from the Minoan tradition), the playing of musical instruments[4]— especially the noble lyre[5]—and singing,[6] and the life of the community pro-ceeded to the rhythm of a whole series of festivals, religious ceremonies[7] and banquets.[8]

This remarkable educational system brought out the educative value of music, which was to remain equally important throughout the whole classical period; indeed it seems, even in Sappho's time, to have been the object of theological reflection—a fragment of hers[9] dealing with these questions clearly expresses the doctrine so dear to Greek thought, that immortality could be gained by the cult of the Muses.

Lesbian education was not merely artistic: the physical side was also cultivated. Without being Spartans, these refined Lesbian girls nevertheless took part in athletics, and Sappho herself proudly claimed the honour of having coached a champion runner.[10]

All this took place in a highly feminine atmosphere—indeed, if the feminine was not eternal, I should say in a very modern feminine atmosphere: I have in mind the importance that was attached not only to physical beauty but also to charm, coquetry, fashion.[11] And there were shrewd little sayings like "Don't ride the high horse when you are looking for a husband";[12] "A woman who does not even know how to lift her skirt to show her ankles!"[13]

---

[1] Saph., fr. 109.   [5] Fr. 103.   [8] Fr. 96.   [11] Fr. 45.
[2] Fr. 60.   [6] Fr. 11; 54.   [9] Fr. 58.   [12] Fr. 65.
[3] Fr. 140.   [7] Fr. 88.   [10] Fr. 62.   [13] Fr. 80.
[4] Fr. 93.

Finally—and here we return to the theme of the present chapter—this education, like the men's, was lit up by a blaze of passion that united mistress and disciple in bonds forged by its heat. Of this indeed we know more than we know about the actual education, which, after all, we can only perceive dimly through the overtones of Sappho's passion, as a faint echo heard through the agonized cries that sorrow wrested from her when marriage or faithlessness tore any of the girls she loved away from her. For her, there was no transposition on to the metaphysical plane, as there was for Plato, in whom pederasty became an aspiration of the soul to the Idea; her love remained entirely human, a burning desire. "O my Atthis, once again does Eros the limb-breaker torment me, Eros the bitter and sweet, the unconquerable one!—and you, tired of me, you fly to Andromeda."[1]

Here again the psychiatrist will be anxious to determine the extent of the ravages of misdirected sexual instinct, and will find himself faced by the same contradictory evidence. Even in antiquity there were doubts as to "whether Sappho had been a lewd woman",[2] and today she still has admirers who will maintain passionately that she was a woman of absolute virtue (16). But in this case it is not difficult to decide between these two extremes: the candour, indeed the immodesty, characteristic of feminine lyricism—Sappho has this in common with the Comtesse de Die and Louise Labbé—leaves us in no doubt as to the sensual character of her relationship with these girls. "Half the night is gone, time passes and I lie here all alone . . ."[3]—and there is all that jealous sobbing, which suggests far from spiritual passions.

We know of the Lesbian fellowship only because chance endowed Sappho's ardent soul with genius. But hers is not an isolated case. We know that in her own day she had competitors, professional rivals: Maximus Tyrius has even preserved for us the names of two of these "principals of young ladies' boarding-schools"—Andromeda and Gorgo.[4] For a long time afterwards, however, to judge by the available evidence, women's education was eclipsed by the dominance of the masculine element in Greek civilization, and it did not re-emerge into the full light of day until much later, only shortly before the Hellenistic age. When it did reappear, it showed itself particularly in those contests in which the agonistic spirit found expression, whose function, like that of the modern examination, was to sanction further study. At Pergamus, where in Greek and Roman times special magistrates were appointed as inspectors of women's education—they were called "superintendents of young ladies' behaviour"[5] —the girls competed in recitations and music and reading, just like the boys.[6] Elsewhere, particularly in the Aeolian Islands, their competitions did not simply imitate their brothers': there were specifically feminine subjects which perpetuated the spirit of Sapphic education. According to Theophrastus[7] there were beauty competitions in Lesbos and Tenedos and in other cities too, and also competitions in moral poise (if we may thus translate σωφροσύνη) and domestic science—οἰκονομία.

[1] Fr. 137.
[2] Didym. ap. Sen., *Ep.*, 38, 37.
[3] Fr. 74.
[4] *Diss.*, 24, 9.
[5] *Ins. Perg.*, 63b.
[6] *AM*, XXXVII, (1912), 277.
[7] Thuc. ap. Ath., XIII, 609e–610a.

CHAPTER IV

THE "OLD" ATHENIAN EDUCATION

I HAVE borrowed the expression ἡ ἀρχαία παιδεία from Aristophanes,[1] and I shall use it as he did to denote the type of education current in Athens in the first half of the fifth century, before the great changes that were made towards the end of the century by the Sophists and Socrates.

Although this earlier type of education was old-fashioned and even archaic in comparison with classical education in its fully developed form, it nevertheless represented a considerable advance in the general evolution from a warrior to a scribe culture. We are still far from the latter in its ultimate form, but already the decisive step has been taken—for in Athens, somewhere in the middle of the sixth century (the actual date is unfortunately not known), education lost its essentially military character.

According to Thucydides,[2] the Athenians were the first to abandon the old practice of going around the streets armed, and, putting aside their armour, to adopt a less violent and more civilized way of life. By so doing, their city, which had always remained somewhat outside the main stream of cultural development and been comparatively unknown, now for the first time came forward in her rôle as a leader of culture—a position which henceforth was to be peculiarly hers.

Originally there do not seem to have been any very noticeable differences in the level of culture and education in the different parts of Greece. In the seventh century we find everywhere the same civic and military ideal as we have seen in Sparta, the same total subjection of the individual to the community. For example, round about the year 650, at Ephesus, in "soft-living Ionia", the poet Callinus, in an endeavour to rouse his people, threatened by the Cimmerian invasion, gave utterance to the same sort of sentiments as had been expressed by Tyrtaeus in the Messenian war, as can be seen from the following passage: "It is a great and glorious thing for a man to defend against the enemy his country and his children, and the wife he espoused as a virgin. Death will come when the Fates decide; meanwhile, let every man, with sword aloft and heart beating high beneath the shield, fall into line when the battle begins. The whole people mourns a warrior who dies bravely; and if he lives, they honour him as a demi-god."[3]

EDUCATION NO LONGER MILITARY

A century or a century and a half later, the atmosphere had completely changed—in Athens, at least. Greek life and culture and education had become

---

[1] *Nub.*, 961.　　　　[2] I, 6.　　　　[3] Fr. 1, 6–11, 18–19.

36

predominantly civilian. Of course, the military element had not entirely disappeared: even omitting the glorious Persian campaigns, the incessant wars which the Athenian republic waged against its neighbours never failed to arouse the patriotism of the citizen-soldiers, or at least of those who came from the three wealthier classes—for in theory the *thetes* could not serve as hoplites because they could not afford the expensive equipment. Nevertheless, it seems clear that military training had ceased to play any important part in the education of the young Greek.

In this respect Athenian education, which was to be a model and inspiration to the whole of classical Greece, had quite different aims from those of later Sparta. In Athens children and young men were not regarded primarily as future hoplites and required to join up and keep in step for thirteen years; in fact, military training seems to have played so small a part in this "old education", that the historian, for lack of evidence, may justly doubt whether it ever existed.

Athens was later to develop a remarkable system of compulsory military training known as "ephebia", whereby its young citizens were obliged to do two years' service, between the ages of eighteen and twenty; but there is little evidence about it and it does not seem to have attained its full development until the end of the fourth century. There has been a great deal of discussion about the date of its first appearance; but this can hardly be placed earlier than the Peloponnesian War (431–404). A kind of ephebia may have existed before that time, but then the word could only have meant the coming-of-age ceremonies that marked the adolescent's entry into adult life—not the military training of classical times (1).

Apparently the new democratic tactic of using heavy infantry did not demand any very elaborate technical qualifications on the part of the soldier. Premilitary and para-military exercises were neglected. In Homeric times there had been tournaments like that between Ajax and Diomedes at the funeral games held in honour of Patroclus.[1] From these more or less mock battles the succeeding age had inherited a kind of contest called "armed combat"— ὁπλομαχία.

But this had become simply a competition, a matter of pure sport, and in any case it had hardly any connection with education. It is true that Plato devotes the whole of the *Laches* to a discussion of the part it could play in education; and Nicias develops the arguments in its favour,[2] stressing especially its value as a means of military training,[3] but it is easy to see that this is only a personal opinion, unsupported by general practice. Like European fencing from the time of the sixteenth century onwards, hoplomachy had become an art striving after formal perfection, with very little relation to actual fighting: dear old Herodotus in fact confesses somewhere how surprised he was to come across a fencing champion who had actually proved his valour on the field of battle.[4]

It was physical strength and bodily dexterity that gave the soldier whatever real advantage he might possess; and so, as Xenophon's Socrates explains in

[1] Hom., *Il.*, XXIII, 811–825.
[2] 181e–182d.
[3] 182a.
[4] VI, 92.

detail,[1] the only effective training for war came indirectly, through athletics and gymnastics generally. This fact undoubtedly helped to make physical training more popular and democratic; and we shall soon see how important this training was.

DEMOCRATIZATION OF THE ARISTOCRATIC TRADITION

In spite of this democratization Athenian education kept closely to its aristo-cratic origins, and in its principles and organization it remained an education for gentlemen: at the height of the democratic era Isocrates[2] could still remember a time when it had been the special privilege of an aristocracy wealthy enough to be able to enjoy its leisure. Indeed, as Plato insisted,[3] it would always tend to remain the privilege of an élite, since few were prepared to suffer the sacrifices it entailed and few could appreciate its advantages.

Even well on in the fifth century education was still mainly for the aristocracy, the great landed proprietors who had wealth and consequently a good deal of leisure, rather than the average Athenian who earned his humble livelihood as a peasant or a craftsman or a small shopkeeper. We can picture this aristocratic existence as the way of life, stripped of its war-like aspects, of the Homeric knight: it was essentially a fashionable sporting world.

One sport always remained the exclusive preserve of aristocratic families: horse-racing (including chariot-racing), which, together with hunting[4] or, as the Greeks called it, "cynegetics" (a word that reveals the part played in it by dogs), was, as it had been since Homer's time, the aristocratic sport *par excellence*, a liking for which was a characteristic of the "smart set". The second property-holding class in Athens was the Ἱππῆς—the knighthood. On the eve of Salamis it was the bit of his horse's bridle that Cimon, the leader of the old aristocratic Right Wing, solemnly went and consecrated to the goddess Athena.[5] The aristocratic families were fond of giving their children names compounded from "Hipp-" or "hippos": you may remember "Phidippides", the name that the self-made man in Aristophanes' *Clouds* coins for his son because his aristocratic wife insists: "She wanted a name with 'Hippo' in it, like Xanthippos or Char-ippos of Callippidos."[6] The incident is so vivid and significant for our present purpose that it is worth recalling. The mother dreams of a wonderful future for her son: "When you are grown up and drive your chariot to town like [your great-uncle, the illustrious] Megacles, wearing the long tunic of the racing charioteer . . .";[7] but the father bewails the results of the education Phidippides has had, to satisfy his mother's ambition: "He has long hair, rides a horse, drives a two-horse chariot and dreams about horses when he's asleep!"[8] In the fourth century Xenophon, who was a typical representative of the aristocratic class, thought it worth while to write three technical books, *On Hunting, On Riding,* and *The Cavalry Officer.*

Riding remained a reserved sport because it was expensive—as Phidippides'

[1] *Mem.*, III, 12.
[2] *Areop.*, 44–45.
[3] *Prot.*, 326c.
[4] Xen., *Cyn.*, 12.
[5] Plut., *Cim.*, 5.
[6] *Nub.*, 63–64.
[7] *Ibid.*, 69–70.
[8] *Ibid.*, 14–15; 25; 27; 32.

father discovered;[1] athletics, on the other hand, being less costly, became increasingly democratic. In earlier days only the nobility used to go to the gymnasiums: even at the beginning of the fifth century the pan-hellenic champions (whom Pindar praises for their ancestors as much as for their exploits) often came from noble families, because in the beginning they were the only ones who had the means, and also, perhaps, the gifts, for such pursuits. But even at that time the taste for sport was beginning to spread, and by the end of the century everyone in Athens was going to the gymnasium, just as all Romans under the Empire went to the baths. This caused great disgust to the old aristocrats,[2] who felt that with this "democratization" of sport everything of importance in the old culture had been degraded.

Athens became a real democracy (I have tried to emphasize the parallel between the way it developed and the development of modern Western Europe): by a gradual process of extension, its people not only won for themselves political privileges and rights and powers, but also gained access to the kind of life and culture and human ideals that in the beginning only the aristocracy had enjoyed. For when athletics passed from the "Knights" to "Demos", so did the whole Homeric ideal of "valour" and emulation and heroic deeds. The change from a military to a civilian way of life had in fact transformed the old ideal of heroism and reduced it to the level of a competitive sport. In this connection the writings of Pindar (521–441) are highly significant. His triumphal odes —ἐπινίκια—were written to celebrate the "valour" of the Greek champions, just as the Homeric epics had celebrated the deeds of the heroes. It was "valour" that was revealed in victory—the manifestation of an almost super-human type of ideal personality: the winner of the Olympic Games seemed worthy of the honour paid to the gods on Olympus when hymns are sung in their praise. This belief in the fundamental value of sporting ability as a sign of "valour" spread with the popularity of sport itself: Tyrtaeus[3] attacked it in the name of the city and Xenophanes[4] in the name of the philosophers' new ideal of spiritual and scientific wisdom; but in vain; and for a whole epoch it remained the ideal of all free men, the supreme ideal of Greek civilization.

First Appearance of the School

With the spread of this ideal, and of the culture which it inspired, the whole system of aristocratic education spread too, and became the standard type of education for every child in Greece. But while its subject-matter and general tendency remained the same, it was obliged, in the course of, and for the purpose of, the new popularization, to develop new institutions. The new education, intended for all free men, was necessarily of a collective character, and this led to the creation and development of the school. This was a decisive step: it is of paramount importance in the whole of the subsequent history.

The aristocratic poets Theognis and Pindar (2) faithfully reflect the scorn and suspicion with which the old nobility reacted to this development. Pindar was

----

[1] *Nub.*, 11 *seq.*
[2] [Xen.] *Ath.*, 2, 10.
[3] Fr. 12, 1–10.
[4] Fr. 2.

already concerned with the celebrated problem discussed by the Socratics, whether ἀρετή ("valour", not simply virtue) could be acquired by teaching alone. No doubt, he said, blue blood in itself had never sufficed to make a perfect knight: as the classical "paradigm" of Achilles and Chiron showed,[1] it would be absurd—ἄγνωμον—not to try to develop innate gifts by education.[2] But if ancestry was not a sufficient cause, it was at least, in the eyes of these aristocrats, these "good men"—Ἀγαθοί, as they proudly called themselves[3]—a necessary condition. In Pindar's view, education only makes sense if it is given to a nobleman, who has to become what he is. "Be the kind of man you know yourself to be."[4] The Wise Man is in the first place a person who knows many things by nature—φυᾷ. There is nothing but contempt for the self-educated, the μαθόντες, "those who know only because they have had lessons."[5]

But this contempt, and the vehemence with which it is expressed, are signs that the thing existed, that a growing number of the newly-rich were having their sons trained in arts and accomplishments that had originally been the jealously guarded privilege of the well-born.

In this kind of education, since it involved an increasing number of children, the system of individual tuition by a tutor or lover could no longer work. Some kind of collective instruction was inevitable, and I imagine it was the pressure of this social necessity that gave birth to the school. Private tuition did not disappear immediately; for a long time, as can be seen from Aristotle[6] and Quintilian,[7] educationists went on discussing the advantages and disadvantages of the two systems; but once corporate education had come into existence it soon came to be more generally accepted than the other, and we find Aristophanes recalling the "old education" that nurtured the glorious heroes of Marathon (men, therefore, who had reached adult age by 490),[8] and at the same time describing the city children, at dawn and throughout the day, on their way "to their teachers".[9]

PHYSICAL EDUCATION

Who were these teachers? The main feature of aristocratic culture was sport, and so, in the old educational system, physical training occupied the place of honour. The aim of this training was to prepare the child for athletic contests—racing, the discus, the javelin, the long jump, wrestling and boxing. To become adept in the finer points of these complicated sports it was necessary to have lessons from a competent teacher, a P.T. expert or παιδοτρίβης, who did his "coaching" on a sports ground, or palestra—παλαίστρα (the actual gymnasium was for adults).

This system of instruction must have been fully developed before the end of the seventh century, for at that time (at the Olympic Games of 632, in the old reckoning)[10] children's competitions made their first appearance in the great

[1] Pind., Nem., III, 57-58.
[2] Ol., VIII, 59-61.
[3] Theog., I, 28; 792; Pind., Pyth., II, 176.
[4] Pyth., II, 131.
[5] Ol., II, 94-96; Nem., III, 42.
[6] Eth. Nic. K., 1180b 7 seq.
[7] I, 2.
[8] Nub., 986.
[9] Ibid., 964-965.
[10] Paus., V, 9, 9; cf. Philstr., Gym., 13.

pan-hellenic games. These competitions gave official recognition to the physical education of the young, and therefore assumed it to be regularly organized throughout the whole of Greece (3).

MUSICAL EDUCATION

In the *Republic*,[1] Plato, describing the education of the "good old days", tells us that it was two-sided, comprising "gymnastics" for the body and "music" for the soul. From the beginning, as we have seen, Greek culture and hence Greek education had included, besides sport, an element that was spiritual, intellectual and artistic all at once. In Plato, music—μουσική—signifies the domain of the Muses in the widest sense; but in ancient education generally, music in the narrower sense of the word—i.e. vocal and instrumental music—came first in this category. Aristophanes has the children "marching in croco-dile" not only to the gymnastics teachers[2] but also εἰς κιθαριστοῦ, to the cither player or music master, "even if the snow is falling as thick as flour".[3]

The historian has to stress this to correct an error in perspective: as they appear in our own classical culture the Greeks were primarily poets, philosophers and mathematicians; and when we pay homage to their artistic genius we mean their architecture and sculpture. We never think of them as musicians. Our scholars and teachers pay less attention to their music than to their ceramics! And yet they looked upon themselves first and foremost as musicians.

Greek culture and education were artistic rather than scientific, and Greek art was musical before it became literary and plastic. It was "the lyre and sprightly dancing and singing" that summed up civilized life for Theognis.[4] Ἀχόρευτος, ἀπαίδευτος, as Plato says bluntly:[5] "Anyone who cannot take his place in a choir [i.e. as both singer and dancer] is not truly educated."

EDUCATION THROUGH POETRY

Even in this early period, however, a specifically intellectual, literary element begins to appear. But we are still a long way from "the peoples of the Book", for it is through songs that the teaching of doctrine is transmitted—songs, and poetry. Here, as always, the nature of the education that is given is made clear by the kind of culture to which it paved the way. Greek cultural life centred round the men's "club"—the Cretan ἀνδρεῖον, the Athenian ἑταιρεία: which meant the *conversazione*—λέσχη—the "banquet"—συμπόσιον: that is to say, the drinking party which followed the evening meal. This had its own strict rules and formal etiquette: each of the guests in turn received the myrtle branch that meant that it was his turn to sing, and the song "that zig-zags from one to another"—the σκόλιον—was the basic literary form around which the other artistic performances—dancing,[6] and musical interludes on the lyre or aulos—centred (4).

[1] *Il.*, 376e.
[2] *Ibid.*, 973 *seq.*
[3] *Ibid.*, 964.

[4] I, 791.
[5] *Leg.*, II, 654ab.
[6] Theog., I, 239–243; 789–792; Pind., *Pyth.*, VI, 43–54.

And so any child who wished to take his place one day at the banquets as an educated person had not only to learn a certain amount of Homer's poetry—which had no doubt quickly become a "classic"—but also to set about acquiring a repertoire of what were essentially lyrical poems.

Athens attached just as much importance as did Sparta to the moral quality of these songs and to their value as moral training: a considerable proportion of the songs were by the Gnomic poets, such as the author of the *Teachings of Chilon*, a few fragments of which have come down to us under the name of Hesiod. It was apparently for a group of Athenians, perhaps the aristocratic circle centring round Callias, that our collection of the elegies of Theognis was compiled, a collection which includes—besides the authentic poetry of the old poet of Megara—poems by other Gnomic poets, as well as the love poems in Book II.

But the truly Athenian poet, the man who, like Tyrtaeus in Sparta, embodied the nation's wisdom, was undoubtedly Solon (Archon, 594–593). He certainly had an educational aim in view when he composed his *Elegies*, which appeared in the form of moral injunctions to his fellow citizens.[1] It seems clear that he was looked upon as the national spokesman—consider, for instance, the way he was quoted in the law courts and the Assembly by any orator in need of authority, even by Cleophon[2] and Demosthenes.[3]

Solon's moral outlook, like that of Tyrtaeus, was grounded in the community life of the city, even though his emphasis was different from the latter's. His ideal was εὐνομία, the state of equilibrium required by justice. The danger which he sought to avert was no longer external but internal—inner dissension, social injustice, and the party passion that was jeopardizing Athenian unity (5). But it would be a mistake to regard his teaching as exclusively political. There is a real Solonian humanism which stresses the simple joys of existence that make life worth living in spite of everything, in spite even of death: "Happy is the man who loves children and horses, hunting-dogs and strangers . . ."[4] We find him singing the praises of wine and song and friendship—and love: through Solon there was instilled into the heart of every Athenian child the whole of the traditional aristocratic culture.

LITERARY EDUCATION

In all this we are, clearly, still far from any scribe education; nevertheless, writing had gradually been introduced, and it had spread so widely, and had come to be used so much in daily life, that in the end education was unable to ignore it. By the time of the classical era schools where the "three Rs" were taught were well-established institutions: the child no longer had two but three teachers: the pedotribe and the cither player, and also the γραμματιστής, "the teacher of letters", who was one day to become by synecdoche simply διδάσκαλος —the "teacher".

It would be interesting to try to date the first appearance of this third branch

[1] Fr. 4, 30.
[2] Ap. Arist., *Rh.*, I, 1375b 32.
[3] *De Falsa Legatione*, 255
[4] Fr. 12–14.

of learning—third in order of origin and, for a long time, third in order of value too. A great deal is made of some supposed legislation by Solon about the moral supervision of schools, but without going into the question of whether these laws were only attributed much later to that great law-giver (they are only known through allusions made to them in the fourth century) we can see that their provisions may quite easily—and perhaps more suitably—have applied to the palestra, rather than to the school of letters—γραμματοδιδασκαλεῖον.

The existence of the latter can only be conjectured indirectly from the fact that writing was in general use and some such school was needed where it could be taught. It is clear, for example, that since an institution like ostracism, which was introduced by Cleisthenes in 508–507, entailed a written procedure of voting, it required a knowledge of writing from the bulk of the citizens (6). There may still have been many illiterates in the Assembly, of course, like the one who is supposed to have asked Aristides to write his name for him on the piece of pottery that was used as a ballot-paper; and no doubt there were many others whose standard of culture was no higher than that of Aristophanes' butcher—"But my dear fellow, I know nothing about 'music' except how to read and write, and even that only so-so." Nevertheless there can be no doubt that from the time of the Persian Wars onward there existed a system of in-struction in reading and writing: thus, in 480, on the eve of Salamis, the Trez-enians, in their kindness welcoming the women and children who had escaped from Athens, engaged schoolmasters to teach them to read at their city's expense[1] (7).

THE IDEAL OF ΚΑΛΟΚΑΓΑΘΙΑ

Such was the old Athenian education—artistic rather than literary, athletic rather than intellectual: in the account in the *Clouds*, which we have already mentioned more than once, Aristophanes gives only eight verses[2] out of more than sixty[3] to the teaching of music; he says nothing about the teaching of letters. The remaining verses are concerned with physical education, and especially its moral aspects. This is a point to be emphasized: the education was in no sense technical; it was still designed for the leisured life of the aristocracy.

These Athenian aristocrats might be great landed proprietors or men of affairs, but nothing in their education prepared them for such activities. Let us return to that scene at the beginning of the *Laches* in which, as we have seen, Plato presents us with two Athenian noblemen consulting Socrates about their sons' education. We can easily imagine a similar scene today, with two fathers discussing whether their children should do Greek or mathematics when they get into the third form. Similar problems were soon to arise in Greece; but we have not yet reached that stage here: the only question discussed by our two Athenian fathers is whether the youngsters shall learn fencing or not.[4]

The guiding ideal of this old education was still an ethical one. It can be expressed in one word—καλοκἀγαθία—"being a man both beautiful and good."

---

[1] Plut., *Them.*, 10.
[2] *Nub.*, 964–971.
[3] *Ibid.*, 961–1023.
[4] *Lach.*, 179d.; 181c.

"Good"—ἀγαθός—signifies the moral aspect, which was essential, as we have seen, with the social and worldly implications which it had had from the very beginning. "Beautiful"—καλός—refers to physical beauty, with the inevitable "aura" of eroticism that had come to accompany it. And here I must try to explode the modern myth that Greek civilization achieved a harmonious synthesis between "racial beauty, the highest artistic perfection, and the most elevated flights of speculative thought" (8).

This ideal of a fully-developed mind in a superb body may not be entirely imaginary: it was at least in Plato's mind when he was creating his unforgettable young men—the handsome Charmides puzzling over the problem of moral perfection, Lysis and Menexenus gracefully discussing friendship. . . . But it must nevertheless be realized that if this ideal was ever achieved, it could only have been for a fleeting moment of unstable equilibrium between two opposite tendencies which could only grow at each other's expense. A time was to come when Greek education would be—like ours—essentially intellectual, under the influence of men like Socrates, who was ugly, and Epicurus, whose health was poor.

In the early period we are discussing at the moment, there is no doubt that the καλὸς κἀγαθός was primarily a sporting type. There may be a moral side to this education, but it is only realized in and through sport (as is clear from Aristophanes, who never separates the two), and its aim was to develop the body at least as much as the character. Much later, Plotinus used to say:[1] "Be always at work carving your own statue", and he meant this in a moral sense; but taken literally it could have been the motto of the old education. Remember how Plato introduces Charmides at the beginning of the dialogue that bears his name: "Everybody was looking at him as though he was a statue."[2] "What a handsome face he has! [εὐπρόσωπος]," cries Socrates. "But if he was naked he'd seem to you to have no face [ἀπρόσωπος]: he is so beautiful in every way [πάγκαλος]!"[3] "To have no face": this seems a strange way of putting it to us, accustomed as we are to looking on the face as the reflection of the soul; but it is symbolized by those expressionless athletes (the Discobolos for instance) whose features remain unmoved despite their most violent efforts.

This ideal, strange though it may seem to us, is nevertheless perfectly legitimate; that is to say, in itself it is quite consistent. There is nothing absurd in believing that physical beauty, the worship of the body, can be for some people a real reason for living, a way of expressing, indeed of fulfilling, their personality —after all, it has long been accepted as legitimate enough as far as women are concerned. In fact these young Greeks were honoured and courted and pampered and admired very much like our women of today (or yesterday). Their whole life was bathed, like any woman's, in the glow of their youthful successes, the lustre of their beauty (Alcibiades is a case in point).

Thus the ideal in itself is perfectly valid—but how brutal and uncomplicated, compared with the marvellous picture presented by Nietzsche and Burckhardt for example, and so many other neo-pagans of their school! No doubt these young men were strong and handsome, but in the pursuit of this single end they

---

[1] *Enn.*, I, 6, 9.   [2] *Chrm.*, 153c.   [3] *Ibid.*, 154d.

used up all their energies and all their will-power. It would be simple-minded (or sharp practice) to point to Plato's young men and forget the circumstances in which they appear. Socrates may go to the gymnasium to collect his disciples, but he goes there to drag them away from it and to submit them to the hard discipline of mathematics and dialectics.

Between the two types of training, the physical and the intellectual, there was not, as some would have us believe, any kind of mysterious secret attraction or pre-established harmony, but on the contrary the most radical hostility. Take, for instance, Aristophanes: what exactly is his pupil promised by the "Old Education" whose praises he sings? A strict morality, true, but also: "You will be as bright and fresh as a flower, spending your time in the gymnasium . . . you will go down to the Academy, and there, under the sacred olive trees, crowned with light reeds, you will run a race with a friend of your own age, to the scent of the yew tree and the white poplar that loses its leaves, enjoying all the delights of spring when the plane tree whispers to the elm. If you do what I tell you, and apply your whole mind to it, you will always have a powerful chest, a good complexion, broad shoulders, a short tongue, massive buttocks and a little rod. . . . But if you follow present-day practices"—and here Aristophanes explicitly attacks Socrates' teaching—"you will have a pale complexion, narrow shoulders, a pigeon-chest, a long tongue, bony buttocks and a big rod. . . ."[1]

If anyone is shocked by my choosing Aristophanes' coarse caricature rather than Plato's ideal figures, I reply that experience provides us with ample evidence of the truth of the picture presented by Aristophanes. For, after all, a man has only one nervous system, one fund of energy at his disposal, and that a small one; and we have learned, in Péguy's words, "that spiritual work is paid for by its own peculiar kind of inexpiable fatigue".

---

[1] *Nub.*, 1002–1019.

CHAPTER V

THE PEDAGOGICAL REVOLUTION OF THE EARLY SOPHISTS

THUS Athenians born in the decade 490–480—men like Pericles and Sophocles and Phidias, who, in politics and literature and the arts, brought classical culture to such a high level of maturity—had only had an elementary education, which as far as actual instruction is concerned was not much higher than the level of our present-day primary schools (1). This is a striking example of the inevitable time-lag between culture and education, a time-lag which is often increased by routine—the field of education being a preserve of the conservative outlook. Nevertheless, any really thriving civilization eventually becomes conscious of this gap and determines to bridge it. We know in fact that each new advance made by the Greek genius was soon followed by a corresponding endeavour to create an educational system that would disseminate it.

THE FIRST SCHOOLS OF MEDICINE

There is a great deal of evidence of this from the sixth century onwards. It was a time rich in great new enterprises. For example, there were the first schools of medicine, which appeared in Croton[1] and Cyrene[2] towards the end of the century, before the opening of the classical schools of Cnidus and Cos (2).

THE FIRST SCHOOLS OF PHILOSOPHY

But it is in the realm of philosophy that the effort to create a new type of education appears most clearly. The first physicists of the school of Miletus were pure scholars with no leisure for teaching. They were absolutely absorbed in their own creative efforts, and these isolated them from their contemporaries and made them appear odd. Their behaviour occasioned surprise and sometimes out-and-out disgust, but this was usually tinged with irony, and in kindly Ionia did not exclude a secret good-will—one remembers the case of Thales who fell into a well while he was studying the stars.[3]

But already Anaximander, and following him Anaximenes,[4] were giving written accounts of their teaching. In the next generation Xenophanes of Colophon no longer wrote, as they did, in prose—the law-maker's medium—but in verse, thus setting himself up in direct rivalry to the poet-educators, Homer and the Gnomics. This was his avowed intention: he used to address the cultivated audiences at the aristocratic banquets,[5] condemning Homer's

---

[1] Hdt., III, 129 *seq.*
[2] *Ibid.*, III, 131.
[3] D.L., I, 34.
[4] *Ibid.*, II, 2; 3.
[5] Fr. 1 (Diels).

immorality[1] and the traditional ideal of athletics,[2] and boldly—and indeed proudly—setting up his own new ideal of Wisdom in opposition.

Pythagorism eventually realized this educational aim in an institution adapted to the purpose—the school of philosophy. This, as we see it at Metapontus or Croton, was no longer a simple "hetairia" of the ancient type, with the master and his pupils all on the same level; it was a real school, taking charge of the whole man and forcing him to adopt a particular way of life. It was an organized institution, with its own buildings and laws and regular meetings— a kind of religious brotherhood devoted to the cult of the Muses and, after the death of its founder, to the cult of the apotheosized Pythagoras. And it set the type: modelled on it later were Plato's Academy, Aristotle's Lyceum and the school of Epicurus, and it was always to remain the standard pattern of the Greek school of philosophy (3).

THE NEW POLITICAL IDEAL

Nevertheless, it was not these specialized circles that produced the great revolution in teaching which was to put Greek education on the road to maturity; this occurred in the latter half of the fifth century and was the work of a group of innovators who have come to be known as the Sophists.

The problem that faced the Sophists, and which they succeeded in solving, was the fairly common one of how to produce capable statesmen. In their time this had become a matter of the utmost urgency. After the collapse of tyranny in the sixth century most of the Greek cities, and democratic Athens in particular, developed an intensely active political life; and exercise of power, the management of affairs, became the essential concern, the noblest, the most highly-prized activity in the eyes of every Greek, the ultimate aim of his ambition. He was still anxious to excel, to be superior and effective; but it was no longer in sport and polite society that his "valour"—his $\dot{\alpha}\varrho\varepsilon\tau\dot{\eta}$—sought to assert itself: from now on it expressed itself in political action. The Sophists put their talent as teachers at the service of this new ideal of the political $\dot{\alpha}\varrho\varepsilon\tau\dot{\eta}$:[3] the training of statesmen, the formation of the personality of the city's future leader—such was their programme.

It would be a mistake, however, to connect this undertaking too closely with the progress of democracy, and imagine that the Sophists' system was meant as a substitute, designed to meet the needs of a new class of democratic politicians, for the old hereditary aristocratic type of education. In the first place, Greek democracy went on recruiting its leaders from amongst the oldest aristocratic families for a very long time—think, for example, of the part played by the Alcmeonidae in Athens. Secondly, it is impossible to discern in the Sophists of the fifth century any definite political bias like that of the *Rhetores Latini* in Rome at the time of Marius: they had a wealthy clientèle, which generally included some of the newly-rich seeking "polish", like Aristophanes' Strepsiades; but the old aristocracy, far from resenting them, were eager to sit at their feet, as we can see from Plato's *Dialogues*.

[1] Fr. 11 *seq.*   [2] Fr. 2.   [3] Pl., *Prot.*, 316b; 319a.

c

The Sophists offered their services to anyone wishing to acquire the accomplishments needed for success in the political arena. Once again I refer the reader to the *Laches*: Lysimachus, the son of Aristides, and Melesias, the son of Thucydides, want their own sons to have the kind of education that will prepare them for political leadership,[1] and naturally, when the Sophists come and offer something more useful than fencing, they are quick to accept it.

Thus the revolution in education that has come to be known as Sophistry seems to have had a technical rather than a political origin: on the basis of a mature culture, these enterprising educators developed a new technique, a form of teaching that was wider in its scope, more ambitious and more effective than any previous system.

THE SOPHISTS AS EDUCATORS

The Sophists were active during the second half of the fifth century. There seems to be something rather artificial in the attempt that is sometimes made to parcel them out over two generations. In point of fact, their careers overlapped; Plato was able without any sense of anachronism to introduce the most famous of them to Socrates and Alcibiades at the house of the wealthy Callias in a famous scene in the *Protagoras*.[2] There was not much difference in age between the earlier and the later Sophists. The oldest, Protagoras of Abdera, must have been born in about the year 485, and Gorgias of Leontini, and the Athenian Antiphon (4) (of the deme of Rhamnus), who were almost as old, in about 480. The youngest, Prodicus of Ceos and Hippias of Elis, were born some ten years later and appear in Socrates' day—and Socrates, as we know, lived from 470-69 to 399 (5). Diverse in origin and itinerant from the necessities of their profession, they all, nevertheless, spent some time in Athens; and with them Athens became the crucible in which Greek culture was refined.

Every historian of philosophy or the exact sciences feels bound to devote a chapter to the Sophists. It is a chapter that is extremely difficult to write and rarely satisfactory (6).

It is not sufficient to say that we know very little about them. As our original sources we have only a few fragments and meagre doxographical notices—very slender evidence to set against the deceptive power of Plato's satirical portraits and parodies. Plato's treatment of the Sophists was always highly ambiguous and it has never been easy to grasp where invention and caricature and calumny begin and where they end. There is the further possibility that his representation of the conflict between Socrates and the Sophists was really a camouflaged form of his own struggle against his contemporaries, people like Antisthenes in particular.

The truth is the Sophists do not properly belong to either philosophy or science. They set in motion a number of ideas, some of them their own, some derived from others—Protagoras got his from Heraclitus, for example, and Gorgias his from the Eleatics or Empedocles—but strictly speaking they were not thinkers or seekers after truth, they were teachers. "The education of

[1] Pl., *Lach.*, 179cd.   [2] 314e-315e.

men"—παιδεύειν ἀνθρώπους—such, according to Plato,[1] was Protagoras' own definition of his art.

And indeed that was the only thing they had in common: their ideas were too heterogeneous, too vague and fleeting for them to belong to any school, in the philosophical sense. The only thing they had in common was their profession; and they deserve our respect as the great forerunners, as the first teachers of advanced education, appearing at a time when Greece had known nothing but sports-trainers, foremen, and, in the academic field, humble schoolmasters. In spite of the sarcasm thrown at them by the Socratics with their conservative prejudices,[2] I shall continue to respect them because, primarily, they were professional men for whom teaching was an occupation whose commercial success bore witness to its intrinsic value and its social utility.[3]

THE TEACHER'S PROFESSION

It is therefore a matter of some interest to study in detail the way in which they carried on their profession. They did not open any schools—in the institutional sense of that word. Their method, not unlike that of early times, might be described as collective tutoring. They gathered round them the youths entrusted to their care and undertook their entire training. This is generally reckoned to have taken three or four years, and it was agreed to by contract: the sum demanded by Protagoras was considerable—ten thousand drachmas,[4] and a drachma (approximately the equivalent of 2/-) was a qualified worker's daily wage. For a long time this was the standard practice, but prices began to fall rapidly and, in the following century, between 393 and 338, Isocrates was only asking a thousand drachmas,[5] and lamenting the fact that "blacklegs" were ready to carry on business at bargain rates of four hundred or even three hundred drachmas.[6]

Protagoras was the first to offer to teach for money in this way: there had been no similar system before. The result was that the Sophists did not find any customers waiting for them but had to go out and persuade the public to take advantage of their services: hence arose a whole publicity system. The Sophist went from town to town[7] in search of pupils, taking those he had already managed to catch with him;[8] to make himself known, to demonstrate the excellence of his teaching and to give a sample of his skill, he would give a sample lecture—ἐπίδειξις—either in a town through which he happened to be passing or in some pan-hellenic sanctuary like Olympus, where he could take advantage of the πανήγυρις, the international assembly that gathered there for the games. The ἐπίδειξις might be either a carefully thought-out discourse or a brilliant improvisation on some theme or other, a free debate on any subject

---

[1] Prot., 317b.
[2] Pl., Hipp. Ma., 281b; Cra., 384b; cf. Soph., 231d; Xen., Cyn., 13.
[3] Pl., Hipp. Ma., 282bc.
[4] D.L., IX, 52.
[5] [Plut.] Isoc., 837.
[6] Isoc., Soph., 3.
[7] Pl., Prot., 313d.
[8] Ibid., 315a.

chosen by his audience. This gave rise to the public lecture, a literary form which ever since those earliest days has been quite astonishingly popular.

Some of these lectures were open to anybody: Hippias, haranguing the crowd in the Agora, with the money-changers' table[1] quite close by, reminds one of the speakers in Hyde Park; others were for a select audience only, and had to be paid for even at this early stage:[2] indeed, unless we are being misled by the Socratic irony, there seem to have been different categories—publicity talks at an advertised price of one drachma, and technical lectures, at which the master contracted to give an exhaustive treatment of any scientific subject whatever, at fifty drachmas a seat.[3]

Naturally, this publicity was not carried on without some admixture of charlatanism. This is Greece, and long ago. In his efforts to impress his audience, the Sophist was not afraid to claim omniscience[4] and infallibility[5]— adopting a magisterial tone, a grave or an inspired manner, and pronouncing his decisions from a throne high up in the air;[6] sometimes, it seems, even donning the triumphal costume of the rhapsodist with his great purple robe.[7]

But these stage-effects were legitimate enough. The sarcastic criticisms they received from Plato's Socrates cannot outweigh Plato's own testimony to the extraordinary success this publicity achieved and the extent to which young people became infatuated with the Sophists. There is that scene at the beginning of the *Protagoras*,[8] in which young Hippocrates rushes to Socrates' house in the early dawn: Protagoras has just arrived in Athens and the great man must be visited without delay and be prevailed upon to accept him as an eventual disciple. This high estimation, which can also be traced in the profound influence that the great Sophists had on the best minds of their day—on men like Thucydides and Euripides and others—was not simply due to fashion and successful publicity-stunts: it was justified by the actual effects of their teaching.

THE ART OF POLITICS

We must now consider the content of this teaching. Its aim was to arm the strong character, to prepare him for political strife so that he would succeed in imposing his will on the city. This was apparently Protagoras' intention in particular: he wanted his pupils to be made into good citizens who could not only rule their own homes properly but also conduct affairs of state with the utmost efficiency. His aim was to teach them "the art of politics"—πολιτικὴ τέχνη.[9]

It was a purely practical aim: the "wisdom" and "valour" which Protagoras and his colleagues provided for their disciples were utilitarian and pragmatic, and they were judged by their concrete effectiveness. There was no time to waste in speculating, like the old physicists of Ionia, on the nature of the world

[1] *Hipp. Mi.*, 368b.
[2] *Hipp. Ma.*, 282bc; Arist., *Rh.*, III, 1415b 16.
[3] Pl., *Cra.*, 384b.
[4] *Hipp. Mi.*, 368bd.
[5] *Grg.*, 447c; 448a.
[6] *Prot.*, 315c.
[7] Ael., *N.H.*, XII, 32.
[8] 310a.
[9] 319a.

and the nature of the gods: "I do not know whether they exist or not," said Protagoras,[1] "it is a difficult question, and life is too short." The important thing was life, and in life, especially political life, knowledge of the truth was less important than the ability to make any particular audience, *hic et nunc*, admit the probability of any proposition whatsoever.

Consequently this education developed in the direction of a relativistic humanism: this seems to be expressed in one of the few genuine fragments that have come down to us from Protagoras—the famous formula, "Man is the measure of all things."[2] A great deal of mischief has been done by trying to give this a metaphysical significance, turning its author into the fountain-head of phenomenalist empiricism, a forerunner of modern subjectivism. Similarly, on the strength of the few echoes that have come down to us from the *Treatise on Not-Being* by Gorgias,[3] it has been suggested that Gorgias was a philosophical nihilist (7). This is a gross exaggeration of the meaning of the passages concerned, which were intended to be taken at their face-value: neither Protagoras nor Gorgias had any intention of creating a system; both were simply concerned to formulate a number of practical rules. They never taught their pupils any truths about being or man, but merely how to be always, and in any kind of circumstances, right.

DIALECTICS

Protagoras is said[4] to have been the first person to teach that it is possible to argue for or against any proposition whatsoever. His whole system of teaching was based on antilogy. Of his *Discourses in Refutation* we now possess only the famous first phrase quoted above;[5] but we find echoes of them in the *Double Reasons*—Δισσοὶ λόγοι—a dull catalogue of mutually conflicting opinions compiled in about the year 400 by one of his disciples.

This, then, is the first aspect of the Sophists' education: how to learn to win any kind of argument. Protagoras borrowed his polemical method and his rigorous dialectic from Zeno of Elea, but at the same time he emptied them of their profound and serious content and kept only the bare skeleton, from which, by a process of systematization, he formulated the principles of eristics, a debating-method that was supposed to confound any kind of opponent by taking points he had himself conceded and using them as a starting-point for further argument.

In their different ways, Aristophanes' *Clouds* and Thucydides' *History* furnish remarkable evidence of the prodigious effect that this system of education, which was so brazen in its cynical pragmatism and so astonishing in its practical effectiveness, had on the people of the time. Its historical importance cannot be over-estimated: the tradition inaugurated by Protagoras explains the predominantly dialectical tone that was henceforth to dominate, for better or for worse, the whole of Greek philosophy, science and culture. The sometimes

[1] Fr. 4 (Diels).
[2] Fr. 1.
[3] Fr. 1-5 (Diels).
[4] D.L., IX, 51.
[5] Fr. 1.

excessive use that the men of antiquity made of disputation as a means of discovery or proof, their facile over-confidence in it, their virtuosity at it—all this was part of the Sophist heritage.

They were not content simply to take this intellectual instrument ready-made from the Eleatics: they did a great deal to perfect it, to refine dialectical processes and explain their logical structure. Naturally, such an advance had its ups and downs: not all the weapons in the armoury of sophistry were made of the finest steel, and, since the end justified the means, they looked upon anything that seemed effective as good. Their eristic, being no more than the art of practical debate, tended to put convincing rational argument on the same level as tactical tricks that are sometimes little better than low cunning (we are, after all, in the country of Ulysses). Genuine reasoning gave way to audacious paradoxes, which their naïve hearers, still new to the game, could not distinguish from Zeno's arguments, which though equally paradoxical had genuine logic behind them. It was not until Aristotle came along that they learned to distinguish between false "sophistries" and valid inferences. Nevertheless, though this kind of sorting-out had to be done later, the *Topics* and the *Refutations of the Sophists* in the *Organon* are simply a classification, a restatement, of a great mass of material, much of which goes back to Protagoras and his followers.

RHETORIC

Besides the art of persuasion the Sophists taught the equally important art of speech, and in this too practical effectiveness was their sole concern. In modern times the spoken word has given way to the all-powerful written word, and this remains true even today, despite the great strides made by the radio and the gramophone. But in ancient Greece, and especially in its political life, the spoken word reigned supreme.

This was in a way recognized officially by the practice that was instituted in Athens well before 431[1] of delivering a prepared speech at the funeral of soldiers fallen in battle. But public speaking was not merely decorative: the democracy of antiquity knew only the direct method of government, and consequently it had most respect for the kind of politician who was able to impose his own point of view in the citizens' assembly, or in the various councils, as a result of his powers of speech. Eloquence was no less important in the law-courts: there was a great deal of litigation in Athens, both private and public—political trials, court enquiries into morality and the rendering of accounts, etc.—and here again the successful person was the one who could get the better of his opponent in front of a jury or panel of judges.[2] As Plato's Sophist, Polos of Agrigentum,[3] declares, skilful orators, like tyrants, can have anyone they dislike condemned to death, or to confiscation of their property, or to exile.

In this field too, the Sophists discovered that it was possible to develop and teach a particular technique for passing on the best lessons of experience in a condensed and perfect form: this was Rhetoric (8).

[1] Thuc., II, 34.   [2] Pl., *Hipp. Ma.*, 304ab.   [3] *Grg.*, 466c.

The master of rhetoric was Gorgias of Leontini, who is historically as important as Protagoras. Rhetoric indeed arose, not in Elis, nor even in Greece, but in Sicily. Aristotle attributed its rise to the sudden spate of proceedings for the recovery of goods that developed after the expulsion of the tyrants of the Theron dynasty at Agrigentum (471), and those of the Hieron dynasty at Syracuse (463), and the ensuing annulment of the confiscations which they had decreed. This helped to encourage eloquence in both politics and law, and Sicily's example is supposed to have prompted the Greeks to apply themselves with all their penetrating logic to this problem of effective speaking. Beginning with empirical facts, they gradually formulated general rules which when codified into a body of doctrine could serve as a basis for a systematic training in the art of public speaking. The first teachers of rhetoric—Corax and his pupil Tisias—appeared in fact in Syracuse, probably not later than 460; but the original founder is generally considered to be Empedocles of Agrigentum,[1] who taught Gorgias (9).

With Gorgias, rhetoric appeared fully-fledged, with its own method and principles and set forms, all worked out in minutest detail. The whole of antiquity lived on this achievement: even in the final decadence writers were still embellishing their meretricious art with the three "Gorgiac figures" which the great Sophist had formulated: antithesis, balance of clauses ($\iota\sigma\delta\varkappa\omega\lambda\alpha$) and final assonance ($\delta\mu o\iota o\tau\epsilon\lambda\epsilon\upsilon\tau o\nu$) (10).

We shall have occasion later to study this technique in detail. Once fixed, it never developed much further, except to become more precise and systematized. Here it will be sufficient to give a brief description of how rhetoric was taught from the time of Gorgias onwards. It was divided into two parts, theory and practice. First of all the Sophist instructed his pupil in the rules of the art: this was his $\tau\epsilon\chi\nu\eta$ (Tisias, if not Corax, had already produced this kind of theoretical treatise, and a few fragments of the similar work by Gorgias remain). In all essentials—as for example in the ground-plan of the judicial speech—the main outlines of classical theory seem to have been fixed by the time of the Sophists, although of course they had not then achieved the degree of detail that is to be found in treatises of Hellenistic and Roman times. In the fifth century the teaching of rhetoric was not so precise: the rules were very general and students soon got on to practical exercises.

The master prepared a model and gave it to his pupils to copy. Like the $\epsilon\pi\iota\delta\epsilon\iota\xi\iota\varsigma$, the sample lecture, the speech might have a poetical or a moral or a political subject. Gorgias transposed into his florid prose the mythological "panegyrics" that had been so beloved by lyric poets like Simonides and Pindar—the panegyric of Helen,[2] the apologia for Palamedes.[3] Xenophon has left us an account of a speech by Prodicus on the subject of Heracles at the cross-roads of vice and virtue;[4] Plato in the *Protagoras*[5] shows us Protagoras improvising on the myth of Prometheus and Epimetheus and again on the subject of justice; and in another dialogue,[6] through the mouth of Hippias,

---

[1] Arist., *ap*. D.L., VIII, 57.
[2] Fr. 11.
[3] Fr. 11a.
[4] *Mem.*, II, 1, 21–34.
[5] 320c–322a.
[6] *Hipp. Ma.*, 286ab.

we hear Nestor imparting instruction to Neoptolemus. There are also references to a eulogy of the city of Elis[1] by Gorgias. Sometimes a fantastic or paradoxical subject was used as an excuse for pure virtuosity, and the result was a eulogy of peacocks or mice. Other teachers preferred a more directly utilitarian approach: Antiphon for instance was only concerned with the eloquence of the law-courts: his *Tetralogies* give examples of all four speeches necessary in any given case—accusation, defence, reply and rejoinder. The cases were imaginary, but Antiphon also seems to have published real pleadings, which he composed as a logographer, so that they could be studied by his pupils.

These sample speeches were not only delivered to an audience; they were also put into writing so that the pupils could study them at their leisure.[2] Later they would be told to use them as models in compositions of their own, and in this way begin their apprenticeship in the art of rhetoric.

But an effective speech needs more than a mastery of form; it needs content —the ideas and arguments demanded by the subject; and so there was a whole branch of rhetoric devoted to *invention*—where and how to discover ideas. Here again the Sophists' analytical attitude enabled them to formulate a whole mass of ingenious rules, and they developed a complete method for extracting every possible topic from any given case—a method in which rhetoric joins hands with eristic and makes full use of its discoveries.

The Sophists had not been blind to the fact that many of their developments could be applied to different circumstances. Hence arose a number of standard passages, on, for instance, how to flatter judges, how to criticize evidence obtained by torture, and so on (in this way Antiphon composed a collection of *Exordiums* suitable for every occasion). Even more pat to the purpose were general reflections on topics of universal concern—justice and injustice, nature and convention. By skilful manipulation any subject could be reduced to the simple ideas that the Sophists' pupils knew all about in advance—the famous "commonplaces"—κοινοὶ τόποι—whose existence and fecundity the Sophists were the first to discover. And so they engaged on a systematic exploration and exploitation of these great themes: it was from them that ancient education, and consequently the whole of classical literature—Greek and Roman—derived their permanent taste for "general ideas", for those great moral themes of eternal import which, for good and for ill, form one of their most characteristic features, and which, despite the wearisome monotony and banality to which they so frequently led, were also responsible for their profound human value.

GENERAL CULTURE

But a grotesquely inadequate picture of the Sophists' education would be given by an exclusive insistence on these general and formal aspects of rhetoric and eristic. The perfect Sophist—like Plato's Gorgias[3] and Hippias[4]—had to be able to speak and hold his own on any subject whatsoever: this meant that his competence had to be universal, his knowledge had to extend over every

[1] Fr. 10.   [2] *Phdr.*, 228de.   [3] *Grg.*, 447c; 448a   [4] *Hipp. Mi.*, 364a; 368bd.

kind of specialized study. The Greeks had a word for it: he must have a "polymathy".

The Sophists varied in their attitude towards this aspect of culture, as I have suggested. Some seem to have had nothing but contempt for the arts and crafts and to have enjoyed using purely theoretical arguments against anyone who claimed to know anything about them;[1] whereas others proclaimed a universal curiosity and aspired—or seemed to aspire—towards every kind of knowledge. Hippias of Elis[2] is an outstanding example of this: Plato shows him boasting to the crowd of onlookers at Olympia that everything he was wearing was the work of his own hands: he had made the ring on his finger, engraved the signet, made his own massage-kit, woven his own cloak and tunic, embroidered his rich girdle in Persian fashion. . . . Modern scholars are divided about the real extent of this "polymathy", as to whether it was just a sham or genuine knowledge (11).

It is known from other sources that Hippias taught a system of mnemonics,[3] and some think that all this imposing learning meant no more in practice than providing the orator with the minimum amount of knowledge necessary to enable him to pose as an expert without ever getting caught out. This judgment seems rather harsh. Polymathy and mnemonics are two different things: the latter was retained in classical rhetoric as one of its five parts, and it had a purely practical purpose—to help the orator to learn his piece by heart. As for the former—we can of course have no idea how much technical knowledge Hippias possessed about the mechanical arts, or how much genuine interest Prodicus had in medicine;[4] but at least there is no doubt that Hippias was highly competent in all branches of science.

Plato vouches for this in mathematics;[5] and goes on to show Hippias[6]—unlike the more limited and utilitarian Protagoras—insisting that the young men in his charge should restrict themselves to a solid study of the four sciences that had been developed since the time of Pythagoras—and which were later to form the mediaeval Quadrivium—arithmetic, geometry, astronomy and acoustics (12). This is a fact worth emphasizing: the important point is not whether or not the Sophists contributed to the progress of mathematics—for Hippias was not alone in his interest: Antiphon worked on the squaring of the circle[7]—but the fact that they were the first to recognize the great educational value of these sciences and the first to incorporate them into a standard teaching-system. They set an example that was never to be forgotten.

Hippias showed the same lively interest in a variety of erudite studies: his own works included geographical tables (names of peoples),[8] "archaeological" tables (mythology, biography, genealogy),[9] and above all historical tables such as his catalogue of Olympic winners[10]—the first of a whole series of similar investigations and the beginning of scientific chronology in Greek history, of scientific history in the modern sense of the word. Finally, there was his more

[1] Pl., *Soph.*, 232d; 233b.
[2] *Hipp. Mi.*, 368bc.
[3] *Ibid.*, 368d.; Xen., *Conv.*, 4, 62.
[4] Fr. 4.
[5] *Prot.*, 315c; *Hipp. Ma.*, 285b; *Hipp. Mi.*, 366c–368a.
[6] *Prot.*, 318e.
[7] Fr. 13.
[8] Fr. 2.
[9] Fr. 4; 6.
[10] Fr. 3.

purely literary erudition, though here he was not alone—a reader of the *Protagoras*[1] might consider Prodicus the specialist in this field, with his passion for synonyms and his remarkable exegesis of Simonides—but in fact all the Sophists engaged in literature with the same enthusiasm.

This last fact had such important consequences that it is worth while inquiring how it came about. We often find that when they start discussing literature the argument soon degenerates into a quibble about some tiny point of language or thought—for example, we find Protagoras remarking that Homer uses the imperative mood where the optative would be expected,[2] and that Simonides contradicts himself from one verse to the next[3]—and so one is inclined to wonder whether the Sophists studied the poets simply to show off their brilliance in argument. For apart from the field of general ideas, which was soon exhausted, poetry supplied the only material in contemporary culture that could be treated in this way.

But even if this was their attitude in the beginning, it was not long before the Sophists deepened their method of approach and turned the criticism of poetry into a special kind of mental exercise, a way of studying the relationships between thought and language: in their hands the study of poetry, as Plato makes Protagoras say,[4] became "the most important part of the whole of education". Here too they were pioneers, for, as we shall see, classical education was to enter wholeheartedly along the way which they had opened up, the way taken by every literary culture since. When we see Hippias comparing the characters of Achilles and Ulysses,[5] we seem to be attending one of our own literature classes and hearing one of those endless comparisons between Corneille and Racine which French children have been making ever since the time of Mme de Sévigné and Vauvenargues.

Thus, even though many of the early questions raised about literature were simply an excuse for dialectical fireworks, they soon led the Sophists and their pupils to study the structure and the laws of language seriously: Protagoras composed a treatise "On Correctness of Diction"—'Ορθοέπεια,[6] Prodicus studied etymology, synonymy and precision of language;[7] Hippias wrote about sound and syllabic quantities, rhythm and metre.[8] In this way the Sophists laid the foundations of the second pillar of literary education, the science of grammar (13).

THE HUMANISM OF THE SOPHISTS

This rapid review will have given some idea of the many innovations which the Sophists introduced into Greek education. They opened up a number of different avenues, of which some were explored more than others, and of which none was explored right to the end. They were pioneers who discovered and set in motion a whole series of new educational tendencies, and though they did not advance far in any one direction themselves, from their time onwards the general

---

[1] 337a *seq.*; 358a *seq.*
[2] Arist., *Poet.*, 1456b 15.
[3] Pl., *Prot.*, 339c.
[4] *Prot.*, 338d.
[5] *Hipp. Mi.*, 364c *seq.*
[6] Pl., *Phdr.*, 267c.
[7] *Cra.*, 384b.
[8] *Hipp. Mi.*, 368d.

direction was fixed, to be followed later. Their fundamental utilitarianism would in any case have prevented them from penetrating to the depths.

But we must not be too ready to blame them for this, for their distrust of over-specialization was one of the noblest and most lasting characteristics of the Greek genius: its sense of reasonable limits, of human nature—in a word, its humanism. The child and the adolescent should study, "not to become experts but to educate themselves"—οὐκ ἐπὶ τέχνῃ, ἀλλ᾽ ἐπὶ παιδείᾳ.[1] The Sophists' best pupils, Thucydides and Euripides, agree with Gorgias that philosophy is a good thing, but within limits, only to the extent that it helps to form the mind and leads to a proper education.[2]

This was a bold solution of a difficult problem, for there is a fundamental antinomy between scientific research and education. If a young mind is made a slave to science and treated merely as an instrument in furthering scientific progress, its education suffers, becomes narrow and short-sighted. But if on the other hand too much emphasis is laid on the open mind, on a purely humanistic culture, there is a danger of superficiality and unreality. This problem has still not been settled (14): it was certainly not settled in the fifth century B.C. when against the solution offered by the Sophists there arose the stubborn opposition of Socrates.

THE SOCRATIC REACTION

Any account of the educational movement of the fifth century would be incomplete if it omitted to mention this other great original spirit, whose thought was no less fruitful than the Sophists'. Paradoxically, the exact nature of his thought is very difficult to ascertain, for whilst our sources are abundant, and whilst they all agree in emphasizing its importance, they do everything they can to obscure its nature and make it impossible to grasp: this is true of the caricatured presentations of it in the comedy of the time—in Aristophanes and Eupolis and Amipsias (15)—and in pseudo-biographical renderings like Plato's; and Plato was probably Aristotle's only source. Even honest Xenophon, tame and pedestrian as he is, has not always been accepted as reliable (16).

Fortunately, there is no need for me to tackle this problem, with all its formidable complexity, here; it will be sufficient to discuss the comparatively simple matter of Socrates' contribution to this problem of education, first raised by the Sophists. He belonged to their generation, and he too, in his own way, was an educator.

I shall not be so rash as to dogmatize about the precise nature of his teaching: I confess that I find myself slightly shocked by the recklessness of the kind of historian who boldly engages to correct the distorted picture given in *The Clouds* by means of a few glimpses of the Cynical School of Antisthenes and then goes on to conclude that the school round Socrates was populated exclusively by scholars and ascetics (17). But, lacking the confidence to paint such a decided picture, one may nevertheless hazard the guess that in major matters Socrates must undoubtedly have appeared as the critic and rival of the great Sophists

---

[1] Pl., *Prot.*, 312b.   [2] *Grg.*, 485a; Thuc., II, 40, 1; Eur. *ap.* Enn., *Fr. Sc.* 376.

ranged against him by Plato. And, by and large—any attempt to go into the matter in detail would mean getting lost in a maze of argument—his objection seems to reduce itself to two main points.

In the first place, Socrates appears as the mouthpiece of the old aristocratic tradition; politically, he seems to be "the centre of an anti-democratic clique" that includes people like Alcibiades and Critias and Charmides. When he charges the Sophists with being too exclusively concerned with political *virtù*, with effective action, and thus in danger of relapsing into an attitude of cynical amoralism, he takes his stand on the traditional values, first among which, in the matter of education, was ethics, "virtue" in the distinctively moral sense which it has acquired in modern times (as a result, in fact, of the Socratic teaching).

Again, because the Sophists had too high an opinion of the value of their own teaching and too much faith in its infallibility, Socrates—who was less commercially-minded than they were—harked back to the doctrine of the old masters, that education was primarily a matter of gifts and of discovering a simple method of developing them—a conception that was at once more natural and more serious. As we have seen, the famous problem debated in the *Protagoras*— "Can virtue be taught?"—had already been discussed by the great aristocratic poets Theognis and Pindar, and the tentative or at least somewhat qualified solution which Plato represents as having been Socrates' own was the very solution that those poets had suggested as the only one consonant with the noble tradition of which they were the representatives.

Secondly, faced with the fundamental utilitarianism of the Sophists' education, the narrow anthropomorphism which sees every branch of study as an instrument, a means to increased power and efficiency, Socrates asserted the transcendent claims of Truth. Here he comes forward as heir to the great Ionian and Italic philosophers, to that mighty effort of thought directed with such high seriousness towards the unravelling of the mystery of things, the mystery of the nature of the world and Being. This great effort Socrates now redirected, preserving its strict integrity, from things to man: it is by Truth and not by any power-technique that he will lead his pupil to ἀρετή, to spiritual perfection, to "virtue": the ultimate aim of human education is achieved by submitting to the demands of the Absolute.

This two-fold opposition should not be exaggerated, of course: it was not so great that the two attitudes could not be confused, as can be seen in Aristophanes, and as the trial in 399 proved all too tragically. Socrates and the Sophists came under the same head as daring innovators, leading the youth of Athens along new paths. One must go further: the Sophists had awakened so many different ideas, and between them taken up so many different attitudes, that Socrates was not equally opposed to them all. His moral gravity and his acute sense of the inner life brought him close to Prodicus (as their contemporaries realized, indeed); and although Hippias's "polymathy" with its erudite pretentiousness was utterly remote from Socratic "ignorance", nevertheless in their search for the living springs of knowledge the two were united in a single, continuous, indefatigable pursuit of unshakable truth.

The tracks cross and become misleading. It was the great achievement of the generation to which both Socrates and the Sophists belonged to put a large number of ideas—some of them contradictory—into circulation: to plant in the soil of the Greek cultural tradition a number of seeds that promised to be highly fruitful. But at the moment all this varied luxuriant growth was intertwined: it was to be the task of the succeeding generation to sort it out and to select those elements which could be combined into a coherent and definitive system.

It is no exaggeration to say that in the field of Greek education the Sophists accomplished a veritable revolution.

INTELLIGENCE VERSUS SPORT

With the Sophists Greek education finally forsook its knightly origins. If they were not yet exactly scribes they were already scholars. As seen from the outside by Aristophanes, they seemed to be the possessors of a mysterious wisdom, a technical knowledge frightening to the ordinary man and overwhelming for their pupils, who are described emerging from their "thinking shop" —φροντιστήριον—lean, pale, and stupefied.[1] Xenophon, though less inclined to caricature, is no less outspoken: he is fiercely critical of the Sophists' education at the end of his treatise On Hunting[2]—a sport dear to the "old education" and of great value as a direct preparation for war.[3]

Thereafter, Greek education became predominantly a matter of the intellect and ceased to emphasize the value of sport. Not that sport disappeared: it went on for centuries; but it began to decline and fade into the background. This change in educational values was all the more marked because technique became increasingly important not only in the matter of learning but in sport too; so that the gap between the two kinds of training grew wider and wider.

I have already mentioned the place of honour occupied by sport in the earliest Greek culture. This exaggeration of its importance proved fatal to it. As in our own day, the universal interest in sporting affairs, the glory of being a champion and the feverish desire to win great international competitions, led to the development of professionalism, and this gradually put an end to "amateur athletics". Because of the terrific competition, only highly-specialized experts could expect to be chosen, and for these, sport was simply a job, and a narrow one at that (18).

In their efforts to improve they developed special techniques, special training, special diets: the trainer Dromeus of Stymphalus (the Olympic long-distance champion in 460 and 456) discovered the advantages of meat as a training-diet.[4]

Sport became a commercial racket. In Pindar's time pan-hellenic champions had often come from the greatest aristocratic and even from reigning families; from the time of the Peloponnesian War onwards they were nearly all professionals, recruited increasingly from the rural and least civilized districts, Arcady and Thessaly. Often they were coarse and brutal men, utter strangers to the noble ideals of the early aristocracy. Even their "sporting feeling"

---

[1] Nub., 184–186.   [2] Cyn., 13.   [3] Ibid., 12.   [4] Paus., VI, 7, 3.

became dubious, like that of our modern professionals; and just as the latter can be bought by clubs whose one aim is to win, so we find the runner Astylos of Croton, as far back as 480, induced by the tryant Hieron to let himself be classified as citizen of Syracuse.[1]

And so on the one hand sport became a specialized pursuit, whilst on the other the Sophists demanded greater efforts from their pupils on the intellectual plane. The unstable equilibrium which in the last chapter I suggested as a fleeting possibility was henceforth destroyed. There would always be sport in Athens, but it was no longer the main object of youthful ambitions. The youths who, with the enthusiasm of adolescence, flocked to Protagoras[2] before the sun was up, and then, like Phaedrus, went off after his lecture into the fields to meditate on the words of his ἐπίδειξις,[3] could no longer raise any enthusiasm for athletics. And if they did not show the same indifference to worldly success, a brief visit with Plato or Xenophon into the select circle of an aristocratic banquet is enough to show how far, within the unchanging framework of the "symposium", the content of the highest Greek culture had been transformed since the time of old Theognis. The intellectual, scientific, rational element had become, and was to remain, predominant.

---

[1] *Ibid.*, VI, 13, 1.   [2] Pl., *Prot.*, 310a *seq.*   [3] *Phdr.*, 227a.

CHAPTER VI

THE MASTERS OF THE CLASSICAL TRADITION

I. PLATO

THE generation of Socrates and the great Sophists, a generation so fruitful in ideas but so inchoate and confusing, was succeeded by a new generation destined to bring Greek education to maturity. This education had long been arrested at the archaic stage of its development, and uncertain of its future. It now achieved that final Form which remained intact through all later developments and was the hallmark of its originality to historians.

This decisive achievement was accomplished at the beginning of the fourth century—in point of fact, during the decades 390 and 380—and it was essentially the result of the work of two great teachers, Plato (427–348) and Isocrates (436–338). The former opened his school in 387; the latter, in 393.

Not that these two men (or any others of their time) introduced many changes in the institutions and technical methods of education; all they did was to single out the best of their predecessors' and perfect them. Their principal achievement was of a much more profound character; it was the discovery, made once and for all, of the main categories of advanced culture, both in their own thought and in that of antiquity. And in making this discovery, they found that they had also discovered the main principles of education.

The first fact to notice is that the cultural ideal of antiquity was two-fold. Classical civilization was not restricted to one type of culture or one type of education; it was torn between two rival forms between which it never managed to make up its mind. One was philosophical and its protagonist was Plato; the other was oratorical and its protagonist was Isocrates.

It would be an over-simplification, and indeed quite wrong, to regard Plato as Socrates' heir and Isocrates as the Sophists', and to turn their rivalry into a mere repetition of the dispute that had taken place in the previous generation. The situation was in fact more complex, and the network of contending influences more intricate: this is shown by the original position adopted by the Lesser Socratics—Phaedon of Elis, Euclides of Megara, Aristippus of Cyrene, and Aeschines and Antisthenes of Athens.

THE LESSER SOCRATICS

Although little is known about them, the Lesser Socratics prove that Platonism cannot be unreservedly identified with pure Socratism. For they were disciples of Socrates too—and fervent disciples, though Antisthenes, for example, was also the pupil of Gorgias.[1] Their teaching is stamped with the seal of the

[1] D.L., VI, 1.

Master; like Plato, they wrote "Socratic Dialogues"; and it is not impossible that they were more successful than Plato in preserving some of the authentic features of their master's quizzical outlook.

It is not part of my purpose to study the philosophical aspect of their thought here (it is known to have had a considerable influence, opening the way, by its criticism of Platonism and Aristotelianism, to the Hellenistic schools of Stoicism and Epicureanism). I am here only interested in their contribution to the development of educational ideas (1). On the whole, they occupy a curious intermediate position between Plato and Isocrates, a position that in some respects brings them closer to the Sophists than to Plato's Socrates.

With the exception of Phaedon of Elis, who was older than the rest and had old-fashioned ideas (his school was a philosophical school of the old Ionian type), they were all, like the Sophists, professional teachers—no longer itinerant, of course: their schools were normally established in cities and took their names from them—Megara, Eretria. But they were still obliged to give advertizing lectures to attract customers (2): the technical term used to describe their activity was σοφιστεύειν—"to play the Sophist".[1] Like the Sophists they taught by contract, and in return for a fixed sum undertook to educate an adolescent for two or more years (3).

But as with Plato, and, of course, Socrates, their guiding ideal was wisdom —σοφία—rather than practical efficiency. Like good Socratics they emphasized the moral aspect of education, the development of the personality and the inner life. With them we gradually move away from the political ideal which had originated in the environment of the ancient city: in their view individual development, self-realization, was not only the aim of their professional activity but the goal of all human endeavour. This is the ethic of the παιδεία, which, as we shall see later, set the tone for all subsequent Hellenistic civilization.

But when we inquire more closely into the matter of technique, we find once again that they come closer to the Sophists and Isocrates. Leaving aside the purely philosophical issue, we must remember what a formidable battery of dialectic the schools of Megara and Elis-Eretria and Antisthenes' school of Cynic philosophy were able to bring up against Plato's conceptual dogmatism. These Lesser Socratics went in for a great deal of discussion, and they thus helped to create that typically Greek atmosphere in which vehement and often bad-tempered argument is the general rule and in which no new idea can be put forward without the protection of heavy defensive fire—a stultifying atmosphere which undoubtedly prevented the full flowering of the mystical tendency latent in early Stoicism.

This kind of argumentativeness—or, to use a more appropriate term, this eristic—aggressive and predominantly negative though it was, undoubtedly played a part of the utmost importance in their teaching, and here it was more valuable than in polemics. In the technique of reasoning they reached unprecedented heights of virtuosity. Euclides is second only to Zeno of Elea as a dealer in paradoxes: he is the author of many famous arguments on various

[1] *Ibid.*, II, 62; 65.

themes—the liar, the horned, Electra, the veiled, the "Sorites", the bald.[1] . . .
For all the Lesser Socratics, dialectic seems to have been the foundation of
mental training, and in this they were following in Protagoras' footsteps; but
was Socrates himself such a stranger to the idea of disputation as a mental
exercise? What about Plato's early dialogues, so lacking in positive content?

This education was of a highly developed formal type, and hence little concerned with the detailed elaboration of specific doctrinal truths. Nor was it to
any extent "scientific", in the modern sense of the word. Either, like Antisthenes,[2] it deliberately rejected the sciences—particularly mathematics—or, as
Aristippus[3] did, it tolerated them, rather contemptuously, so long as they
remained in their place "below stairs" as preparatory disciplines. It was an
education whose dominant tone was literary, devoted to the study of language
and commentaries on the poets—even though, like the Cynics, the Lesser
Socratics could not resist larding the latter with philosophical and moral asides
(ὑπόνοιαι). But they did not merely practise this kind of allegorical or ten-
dentious exegesis; they studied the classics for their own sake: the pupil of
Aristippus went to the theatre as a well-informed critic.[4]

All these are interesting features, and together they make up a colourful and
delicately-shaded picture which reveals the complexity of the scholastic world
at the beginning of the fourth century, when so many rival programmes of
education were courting public favour. But although the Lesser Socratics can
contribute much to the enrichment of our ideas on Greek education (a subject
which should not be too hastily schematized), they were not, in themselves, of
great significance. Their very ambivalence was ultimately a sign of a lingering
archaism. Neither in importance nor in historical interest can they compare
with the two great masters whom we are now about to study.

PLATO'S POLITICAL CAREER AND IDEALS

First I shall deal with Plato as the founder of a predominantly philosophical
type of culture and education (4)—though his main object was political, not
philosophical; but history records many such tricks of fate. In his admirable
"Letter VII" (5), written about 353-2 when he was seventy-five years old,
Plato gives us a touching revelation of the dreams of his youth, and admits his
disillusionment. "A long time ago, when I was a young man, I wanted, like
so many others, to devote myself to politics as soon as I became my own
master."[5] In his outlook he was not in advance of his time: the fourth century
had already witnessed the break-up of the narrow framework of the city-state
and the first flowering of that personalism which was to achieve its triumph in
the Hellenistic era; and already many of his fellow-disciples, such as Aristippus
and Antisthenes, were proclaiming themselves "citizens of the world"; but he
himself remained a man of the old city-state.

Both his own personal temperament and the cultural heritage of the circles

---

[1] *Ibid.*, II, 108.   [3] *Ibid.*, II, 79
[2] *Ibid.*, VI, 11.   [4] *Ibid.*, II, 72.
[5] *Ep.*, VII, 324c.

from which he sprang bound him to the ideal of the preceding century, which saw in political ἀρετή the supreme object of human striving. Everyone knows the set-back which Plato's ambition received from the final defeat of the reactionary aristocracy to which he belonged. His cousin Critias and his uncle Charmides would willingly have given him their support; but they were forced to retire from public life, discredited by their collaboration with the Tyranny of the Thirty (404–403), which the old Athenian Right Wing, aided by the disaster of the Peloponnesian War, had hoped to use as its instrument in the restoration of its power. Democracy was reborn, and gained permanent ascendancy. It soon (399) took upon itself the death of Socrates. In the new Athens there was no longer any place for a man of Plato's ideas and connections. He sought employment for his energies elsewhere, and in 398 went to Syracuse. It seemed that there his task would be easier, since to realize his theories of government it would only be necessary to convert one man,[1] the all-powerful "Archon of Sicily", Dionysius the Elder, Tyrant of Syracuse (413–367)[2]—not the hydra-headed Demos. However, this one man wanted not a Mentor but flatterers, as Aristippus was to prove at the Court of Dionysius II.[3] This first sojourn at Syracuse was a failure and almost brought Plato to a tragic end. He then resigned himself to the life of an ordinary private individual and in 387 opened the Academy; but it was clearly with regret that he left the real city to take refuge in theory and Utopia. Political problems were continually before his mind, from the time when he was writing the *Republic*, which was finished about 375, until his death in 347, when he had finished his *Politics* and was engaged upon the *Laws*. Nor would he ever be content to remain a mere theorist. To the very end he was ready to respond to every call to action. Twice, around 367[4] and 361,[5] he returned to Syracuse to repeat his experiment, this time with the son and successor of Dionysius the Elder, but again without success and to the accompaniment of the same personal peril. Later, his advice helped his pupil and friend Dion to overthrow Dionysius the Younger.[6] Then in 353–2 he aided Hipparinos and the parents and friends of Dion in their successful attempt to avenge Dion's assassination.[7]

In all this he was helped by his pupils, for the Academy was a school not only of philosophy but also of political science: it was a seminary that provided councillors and law-givers for republics and reigning sovereigns—Plutarch[8] gives a list of the statesmen Plato helped to produce, and they were to be found in every part of the Hellenic world: Dion of Syracuse, Python and Heraclides (the liberators of Thrace), Chabrias and Phocion (the great Athenian generals), Aristonymos the law-giver of Megalopolis in Arcadia, Phormion of Elis, Menedemus of Pyrrha, Eudoxus of Cnidus, Aristotle of Stagira, and, lastly, Xenocrates, adviser to Alexander. But even this long list is incomplete, for we must at least add Callipus the murderer of Dion of Syracuse, Clearchus the Tyrant of Heraclea in Pontus and his opponent Chion; Euphraios, who was adviser to Perdiccas III of Macedonia before he became the champion of democracy

---

[1] Cf. *ibid.*, 328c.
[2] *Ibid.*, 326a seq.
[3] D.L., 11, 66–67.
[4] *Ep.*, VII, 328c seq.; 340b seq.; *Ep.* XIII.
[5] *Ep.* VII, 330c seq.; *Ep.* II–VI.
[6] *Ep.* VII, 350b seq.
[7] *Ep.* VII–VIII.
[8] *Adv. Col.*, 1126 A.

and independence in his native city of Oreos in Euboea;[1] Erastus and Coriscus, who governed Assos and were the allies of Hermeias of Atarneus: perhaps even Hermeias himself.[2] Occasionally we catch a glimpse of the mysterious bond which united the pupils of the Academy[3] and made it into a kind of fraternity of political technicians who were able to take concerted action at any time, and thus played an important part in the history of the period, as for example at the time of Dion's return to Syracuse in 357.[4]

The guiding ideal of Plato's activity and teaching should not be dismissed too summarily as having been behind the times. It is true that it had the common good of the city as its object and end, but with Plato we are far from the age of Callinus or Tyrtaeus: he does not stress military valour but the civic virtues of political life. In this connection there is a remarkable passage in the *Laws*,[5] in which Plato expressly disowns the military ideal of ancient Spartan education (6). To appreciate the full force of this passage we should remember that Tyrtaeus—like Xenophanes, though from a different standpoint—had extolled the ideal of the patriotic hoplite as against the knightly ethic of individual deeds of valour.[6] Plato gives an exact quotation of this passage, but only for the purpose of refuting it in its turn: "To die in battle standing firm on both feet, as Tyrtaeus says, is to open the gates to a flood of mercenaries" (here Plato is very much a man of his time, an inhabitant of that fourth century in which mercenaries were becoming all-important) (7). "And what sort of people are these mercenaries? Insolent fellows, thieves, men of violence: brutes devoid of reason!"[7] The noblest ἀρετή found its true expression not in war against foreigners but in political struggle, amongst seditions, conspiracies, revolutions —in short, amongst everything signified by that ambiguous, typically Greek term στάσις, which Plato here contrasts with πόλεμος.

But there is more to it than this. Plato was less concerned with the education of the ordinary citizen than with the problem of how to train political technicians, experts in political affairs who could act as advisers to kings or as leaders of the people. It may be that this was an aristocratic prejudice; but it was a remarkable anticipation of what was in fact to become the normal mode of effective political action after the triumph of Macedonia, when the system of absolute monarchy was imposed on the whole Hellenised world. The rôle played under Plato by the Academy as nursery of counsellors-of-state was later assumed by the Stoic schools at the beginning of the Hellenistic era, from the generation of the Diadochi onwards: examples of this are Perseus or Aratos at the court of Antigonus Gonatus, and Sphairos as advisor to Ptolemy Evergetes and Cleomenes of Sparta. History gives many examples of such overlapping: something that seems to be a survival from a past that is dead and gone turns out to be a pointer to the future.

[1] Ath., XI, 506 E; 508 D.
[2] Pl., *Ep.* VI.
[3] *Ep.*, VII, 350c.
[4] Plut., *Dion.*, 22.
[5] I, 628e–630c.
[6] Tyrt., Fr. 12.
[7] *Leg.*, I, 630b.

THE SEARCH FOR TRUTH

Nevertheless Plato's work in the sphere of education itself was of much greater historical importance than the political rôle he had intended it to play. Opposing the Sophists because they were too exclusively concerned with immediate practical results, Plato built his system of education on a fundamental belief in truth, and on the conquest of truth by rational knowledge.

The true statesman, the ideal "king" whom it was Plato's purpose to train, was to be distinguished from his counterfeits by the possession of "Science",[1] an immediate, rational knowledge of government,[2] in the technical sense which the word ἐπιστήμη bears in Plato's Greek—genuine knowledge based on reason, as against δόξα, vulgar opinion.

But this "royal knowledge" could be enjoyed just as easily by a man who, instead of a real city, had only his family and household to govern.[3] Furthermore, the same criterion—the possession of truth—would distinguish the true orator from the Sophist,[4] and the true from the false physician,[5] and of course the true philosopher.[6] And so the type of education envisaged by Plato for the training of the political leader was one of universal range and value. In any field of human activity whatsoever, the only worthy ideal for a man of culture was that which led him to seek the truth and the possession of real knowledge. The whole of Plato's thought is dominated by this great idea. We find it expressed most clearly in the famous reply in the *Hippias Major*:[7]

> Perhaps, Socrates, this distinction will escape our opponent.
> That may be so, Hippias; but, by the dog, it will not escape the man to whom above all others I should be ashamed to talk nonsense and use a great many words for the purpose of saying precisely nothing.
> Who is this man?
> Myself—Socrates, son of Sophroniscos: I could no more bring myself to make a casual unverified assertion than I could to believe that I knew something of which in fact I knew nothing.

Plato's criterion was not success but truth: hence the supreme value of true knowledge based on rigorous demonstration, of which the prototype is geometrical truth (the example given in the *Meno*). This theme recurs throughout Plato's work: the *Protagoras*, and even the early Socratic dialogues, show us that Plato regarded knowledge, the science of the Good, as the prerequisite of ἀρετή, spiritual nobility, even if he did not identify the two. In the Seventh Book of the *Republic*,[8] the famous myth of the Cave proclaims the liberating power of knowledge, which redeems the soul from that uncultured state—ἀπαιδευσία— which the *Gorgias* had already denounced as the greatest of evils.[9]

Plato did not merely dream about this "scientific" education: for close on

[1] *Pol.*, 259b.
[2] *Ibid.*, 292b.
[3] *Ibid.*, 259bc.
[4] *Phdr.*, 270a seq.
[5] *Ibid.*, 270b.
[6] *Soph.*, 267e.
[7] 298b.
[8] 514a seq.
[9] 527e.

forty years (387–348) he disseminated it amongst the groups of disciples who gathered around him at the Academy.

ORGANIZATION OF THE ACADEMY

In modern times there has been a great deal of dispute about the organization of the Academy. It has been asked whether it was an "Association for the Advancement of Science", or on the other hand an establishment for higher education (8). But this dispute seems rather pointless. The fervent realism of the Platonist school and the naive outlook of ancient times make it impossible to transpose into this environment the modern idea of science as a discipline undergoing perpetual change and making continual progress. Science already exists, ready-made, outside us, in the world of Ideas; and the problem is how to acquire rather than how to create it. It is not until Aristotle's time[1] that we find the distinction—so strongly emphasized in modern times by Max Scheler —between Science on the one hand and the Learning of the schools on the other. There was no separate teaching system for handing on this new Platonic knowledge, still pulsing with the life of fresh discovery; the teaching coincided with the method of research.

All the evidence of the *Dialogues* shows Plato as a supporter of active methods: his dialectical method was the exact opposite of passive indoctrination. Far from instilling into his disciples the finished results of his own efforts, Plato's Socrates likes to set them to work to find out for themselves both the difficulty of the given question and then, after a progressive clarification of the issues, the means of surmounting it. The Academy was therefore in fact both a School of Higher Studies and at the same time an educational establishment.

We have recently begun to obtain some idea of its structure. The Academy was a strongly built institution. It was not a commercial enterprise but a confraternity or sect, and all its members were closely united in the bonds of friendship. There was still an emotional if not an amorous link between master and pupil. Juridically, like the Pythagorean sect, it was a religious association— θίασος—a brotherhood dedicated to the Muses (9) and, after his death, to the apotheosised Plato—a wise precaution, soothing the susceptibilities of a bigoted democracy ever ready to accuse the philosophers of impiety (10), as the proceedings against Anaxagoras (432) and Diagoras and Protagoras (415) had shown— not to mention the action taken against Socrates (399) and still to be taken against Aristotle (between 319 and 315) and Theophrastus (307). The cult took the form of festivals, arranged with the utmost care in a series of sacrifices and banquets. The Academy was a sanctuary consecrated first to the Muses and then to Plato himself; it was situated in the shade of the sacred wood dedicated to the hero Academos, in a lonely and secluded spot in the northern environs of Athens near Colonus. Plato had chosen it not for its convenience (we are told that it was a rather unhealthy spot)[2] but for its religious associations (11). For it was a holy place, made famous by many legends which were used as an

---

[1] *Part. An.*, 639a seq.
[2] Ael., *V.H.*, IX, 10; Porph., *Abst.*, 36, 112; Bas., *Hom.*, XXII, 9.

excuse for regular funeral games. It was close to a number of sanctuaries consecrated to the infernal gods Poseidon, Adrastes and Dionysus. The land dedicated to Academos was at the end of a straight road that started from Athens at the Dipylon and was itself given a religious appearance by a double row of tombs and commemorative monuments. The sacred wood proper must have consisted only of a small clump of trees in the midst of a highly complicated network of buildings, for side by side with the consecrated ground which encircled the temple and altars and was loaded with votive monuments, were sports fields surrounded by colonnades. It was in one of these gymnasiums[1] that the Master carried on his teaching, seated in the centre of an "exedra"[2] (12).

Nevertheless we should not imagine this teaching as having been excessively magisterial. Besides lectures, a prominent place was given to the kind of friendly conversation that went on during the drinking parties—συμπόσια. These, judiciously used, remained for Plato one of the essential elements of education.[3] Life at the Academy meant in fact a kind of communal life between master and pupil, and possibly a collegiate organization (though it is not certain whether all lived together in an adjoining building).

Unfortunately we know more about the juridical status of this school, its site and even its furnishings (such as the mural pictures used for the illustration of dichotomic classification) (13) than we do about its daily activities. There are only a few pieces of evidence, such as the amusing picture painted by the comic poet Epicrates, showing the young Platonists hammering out the definition of the pumpkin,[4] and Aristotle's remarks on the direction taken by Plato's oral teaching in his old age.[5] But these would not give us a clear picture of the content of Platonic education without the additional evidence of the detailed educational schemes that is to be found in the great Utopian proposals of the *Republic* and the *Laws*.

UTOPIA AND THE FUTURE

Needless to say, I am not claiming that within the narrow framework of the Academy Plato systematically put into practice the plans which he elaborated with all the freedom of a theorist in these two great works; he himself insisted that the fulfilment of his educational ideal was dependent on a reorganization of the State. And so the front-rank place which I am assigning to Plato in the history of education is not due solely to the actual educational work that he did at the Academy; it was his thought as a whole, even in the paradoxical form in which he intentionally presented it, that exercised so profound an influence on the education of antiquity.

His thought was not in any case completely Utopian, even in its paradoxes, for these contained many prophetic anticipations. To make this point a little clearer, let us say that these paradoxes show a recognition of the profound

---

[1] Epicr. *ap.* Ath., II, 59 D, 10.   [3] *Leg.*, I, 41cd; II, 652a.
[2] D.L., IV, 19.   [4] *Ap.* Ath., II, 59 D.
[5] *Metaph.*, VI–VIII.

aspirations of the Greek spirit, which the institutions of the following era were in large measure to fulfil. Let me give two examples of this.

First, we have Plato's fundamental requirement: education, he said, should be a State concern, with the teachers chosen by the city and controlled by special magistrates.[1] In his own time this ideal was hardly realized anywhere except in aristocratic cities like Sparta; elsewhere, education was optional and treated as a purely private affair. But, as we shall see, a system similar to that recommended in the *Laws* was to be widely adopted in Hellenistic Greece. Another seeming paradox was his demand for strict equality in the education of boys and girls[2]—parallel education, not co-education: from the age of six the two sexes were to have different teachers and classes.[3] This was a reflection of the development taking place in the outside world—the emancipation of women in the fourth century. Here again we have an anticipation of the Hellenistic era.

But—let me repeat—whether we think of it as Utopian or as prophetic, Plato's theory of education needs to be studied for its own sake, and as a whole.

THE TRADITIONAL ELEMENTARY EDUCATION

The crowning point of Plato's educational system was reached with the higher philosophical studies, which were reserved for an élite of special gifted individuals. They presupposed as their basis a solid preliminary training, which Plato describes in Books II and III of the *Republic* as that given to the military aristocracy of the φύλακες. This training is described again in the *Laws*, in greater detail and with particular reference to the requirements of Greek civilization at the time. This "preparatory education"—προπαιδεία[4]—did not profess to provide genuine knowledge: its purpose was simply to give human beings the means of reaching it as a result of a harmonious development of mind and body. At the same time it set them on the road to it and prepared them for it by ingraining good habits in them. It is worth noticing that Plato did not think it necessary to provide a curriculum of his own for this first stage of education. He prefaces his account of it with these words, which he puts into the mouth of Socrates:[5]

Then what will this education be like? It seems difficult to discover a better one than that which our forefathers adopted—gymnastics for the body and "music" for the soul.

And indeed it is the "old" Athenian education as depicted by Aristophanes[6] that the *Laws*[7] so graphically describe, with children going to school together at dawn in the charge of their pedagogues. The fact that Plato thus made the traditional Greek education the basis of his own was extremely important in

[1] *Leg.*, VI, 754cd; 765d; VII, 801d; 804c; 813e; 809a.
[2] *Resp.*, V, 451d–457b; *Leg.*, VII, 804d–805b; 813b.
[3] *Ibid.*, 794c; 802e; 813b.
[4] *Resp.*, VII, 536d.
[5] *Ibid.*, II, 376e; cf. VII, 521de.
[6] *Nub.*, 961 *seq.*
[7] VII, 808d.

the development of the classical tradition, for it greatly strengthened its continuity and homogeneity. On the one hand the philosophical culture, instead of breaking with the earlier education, was seen to be a continuation and enrichment of it; on the other, this earlier education came to function as the common denominator between the philosophical culture and its rival, the rhetorical culture of Isocrates; thus they appeared as two species of the same genus, two branches of the same tree.

It was Plato's wish that the first years of childhood should be spent by boys and girls playing educational games[1] together under supervision in a kind of kindergarten;[2] for Plato, as for all other Greeks, education proper did not begin until the child was seven, and then it was made up of gymnastics for the body and "music"—i.e. spiritual culture—for the soul (this division, first made in the *Republic*, was repeated in the *Laws*).

As regards gymnastics, Plato spoke out violently[3] against the competitive spirit,[4] which, as I have remarked, was already wreaking havoc on sport in his day. He aimed at restoring it to its original purpose as a preparation for war; and for this reason the branch of pure athletics in which he was chiefly interested was wrestling,[5] the immediate preparation for combat. Of course the list of games that together made up physical education included other sports: there were the usual foot races, sprinting and so on;[6] but Plato also introduced fencing and heavy and light infantry fights[7] and, generally speaking, insisted on the exercises being of a military nature[8]—intended for women as well as men, for the Platonic city had women-soldiers—archery, throwing the javelin, slinging, marching, manoeuvres, camping. To this standard training he added the aristocratic sport of riding (compulsory for the girls too) and its normal accompaniment, hunting[9]—all these being archaic features deriving immediately from the most ancient aristocratic tradition. But there is one point that forecasts the Hellenistic institutions of the future: all this pre-military training is to be given in gymnasiums, in public stadiums and riding-schools under the direction of professional instructors paid by the State.[10]

There was another archaic feature—the endeavour to give back to sport its true educational value, its moral significance, so that it should have an equal share with intellectual culture in the formation of character and personality.[11] But here again archaism and "modernism" were closely connected: Plato's conception of gymnastics included the whole field of hygiene, with rules about the proper ordering of daily life and particularly about diet—a favourite subject in the medical literature of his day. The influence of medicine on Plato's thought was profound, at least equal to that of mathematics (14), and Greek medicine, by a remarkable process of development which can be traced through the fifth and fourth centuries, had come to believe that its fundamental object was not the immediate treatment of sickness but something much wider:

[1] *Leg.*, I, 643bc.
[2] *Ibid.*, VII, 793e–749b.
[3] *Ibid.*, 795d–796d.
[4] *Ibid.*, 796a, d; VIII, 830a.
[5] *Ibid.*, VII, 795d–796a; VIII, 814cd.
[6] *Ibid.*, 832d–833d.
[7] *Ibid.*, 833d–834a.
[8] *Ibid.*, VII, 749c; 804d–806c; 813b; VIII, 829e; 833cd.
[9] *Ibid.*, VII, 823c; 824a.
[10] *Ibid.*, 804cd; 813e.
[11] *Resp.*, III, 410c–412a.

the maintenance of health by a proper mode of life. Thus there came to be a close connection between the doctor and the sports-trainer, symbolized in Herodicos of Selymbria, who carried on the two professions at once.[1]

Under the heading of gymnastics the *Laws* also include dancing, which, as it was inseparable from choral singing,[2] belonged to music too. Plato discusses at great length how it should be taught and practised:[3] he gives it a place in competitions and festivals, side by side with the solemn processions in which young people took part.[4] Here again he emphasizes its educational value: dancing is a way of disciplining and bringing under the harmony of a law the natural tendency of every young human being to get rid of its energy by means of violent movement,[5] and it is thus a direct and highly effective way of promoting moral discipline.[6] This again is an archaic feature: the excellent saying quoted above,[7] "We shall look upon anyone who cannot take his place in a choir as uncultured", reminds one of the pederastic *graffiti* in Thera, according to which there is no better way of praising a beautiful boy than to describe him as a "splendid dancer"—ἄριστος ὀρχ(h)εστάς.[8]

However, the place that Plato gives in his discussion to the genuinely intellectual aspects of culture shows clearly that physical education was even then taking second place. Hellenic culture was gradually moving away from its knightly origins and developing in the direction of literature. This transformation was of course not yet complete: music, in the special sense that the word had then, always had a place in education[9] and for Plato it was a place of honour—κυριωτάτη,[10] so that children were to be taught by their music-master—κιθαριστής—how to sing and how to play the lyre.[11] Loyal to the old traditions, Plato was prepared to pass strict laws to ensure that the arts went on being taught in the old way, remote from all the innovations and disintegrating tendencies of "modern" music which were supposed to encourage all manner of degeneracy and lawlessness and immorality.[12] For here, as always, Plato's whole effort was dominated by moral considerations.

But already music proper—"singing and melody"[13]—was beginning to give way to letters—λόγοι,[14] γράμματα.[15] The child must first learn to read and write,[16] then embark on the classics, either the full works[17] or as found in anthologies[18] (this is the first time that history records the use of "selected passages", which were to have such a long and successful career). Besides the poets, who had previously been the only authors who were studied, Plato includes prose writers.[19] And there were to be competitions and musical games to test the study of literature.[20]

With regard to the authors, we know that Plato was violently critical of the poets who in his own time were considered classics—especially Homer; but

[1] *Ibid.*, 406ab; *Prot.*, 316e; *Phdr.*, 227d.
[2] *Leg.*, II, 654b.
[3] *Ibid.*, 653d *seq.*; VII, 795e, 814e–816d.
[4] *Ibid.*, 796c.
[5] *Ibid.*, II, 653de.
[6] *Ibid.*, 654a–655b.
[7] *Ibid.*, 654ab.
[8] *IG*, XII, 3, 540, 11.
[9] *Resp.*, III, 398c–403c.
[10] *Ibid.*, 401d.
[11] *Leg.*, VII, 812be.
[12] *Ibid.*, II, 656ce; III, 700a–701c.
[13] *Resp.*, III, 398c.
[14] *Ibid.*, II, 376e.
[15] *Leg.*, VII, 809b.
[16] *Ibid.*, 810b.
[17] *Ibid.*, 810e.
[18] *Ibid.*, 811a.
[19] *Ibid.*, 809b.
[20] *Ibid.*, VIII, 834e–835b.

his criticism went beyond the tragic poets to the part played by myths generally in the traditional education of Greek children. His criticism first appeared in the Second and Third Books of the *Republic*,[1] was continued at a deeper level in the Tenth Book[2] and then repeated in the *Laws*.[3] We should not allow its paradoxical form to conceal from us how closely it belongs to the very essence of Plato's teaching.

Plato condemned the poets because their myths were lies giving a false picture of the gods and heroes and one that was unworthy of their perfection. The poet's art, being a product of illusion, was pernicious because it was inconsistent with Truth—to which all education should be subordinated—and because it distracted the mind from its proper end—the attainment of rational knowledge. By his vigorous contrast between philosophy and poetry,[4] and by breaking with the settled tradition that Homer was the basis of all education, Plato put the Greek soul in a dilemma: should education remain fundamentally artistic and poetical, or become scientific? Every educator since has had to face this problem, and it has never received any final solution, our own education still being divided between the opposing claims of "science" and "the arts".

We know that on the whole Greek civilization did not agree with Plato's condemnation of Homer and refused to accept the radical changes which he suggested:[5] a severe censorship—by expurgation, correction, and, if necessary, re-writing—of the offending texts. Plato's own work bore witness against him: are not his dialogues models of magnificent poetry, shunning no artistic device, and even using myths to instil conviction by a kind of quasi-magical incantation? And Plato himself was the first to realize this. "We are poets too", he cries boldly, challenging the tragedians,[6] and half-seriously, half-jokingly, proposes to adopt his own *Laws* as a school text-book.[7]

But this is not all: every page of his *Dialogues* gives striking proof of the extent to which his own personal culture had been nourished by and had profited from the traditional teaching of poetry; quotations from Homer and the lyric and tragic poets came spontaneously to his pen and were used to express his deepest thoughts, not only illustrating but supporting them. By his use of this poetry Plato disproves his own case and shows how advantageous and fruitful it could be for the philosophic mind.

Nevertheless this criticism of his must not be regarded as a mere freak. It may not have succeeded in getting Homer banished from the city, any more than Rousseau's criticism in *Emile* drove La Fontaine out of French schools; but it too became part of the tradition, as a question-mark, a challenge, a temptation; and every succeeding generation, every scholar since, has had to face up to it again.

[1] 377a–392b.
[2] 595a–608b.
[3] VII, 810c–811b.
[4] *Resp.*, X, 607b.
[5] *Ibid.*, III, 386c; 387b; *Leg.*, VII, 801d–802b; cf. VIII, 829de.
[6] *Ibid.*, VIII, 817b.
[7] *Ibid.*, 811ce.

THE ROLE OF MATHEMATICS

In the μουσική Plato unexpectedly introduces a third order of studies,[1] or at least enlarges its scope to such an extent that the whole educational structure is transformed. This is mathematics. For Plato this was not, as it had been for Hippias and others, a subject to be reserved for the later stages of education; it could exist at every stage, even the most elementary.

From its very first beginnings, of course, the primary school had been obliged to give some elementary instruction in arithmetic—counting one, two, three,[2] learning about whole numbers and probably also about the duodecimal fractions used in Greek metrology—for these came into everyday language and everyday life. But Plato went much further: to arithmetic proper, which for the Greeks meant the study of numbers, he added λογιστική,[3] exercises in arithmetic, λογισμοί, based on concrete problems of real life or business, which we may imagine to have been the equivalent of the profit-and-loss sums which we make our own children toil over (15). Similarly, in geometry he introduced simple practical applications such as the measurement of lengths and areas and volumes,[4] and in astronomy the minimum of knowledge needed for the use of the calendar.[5]

All these innovations were of immense importance for the future of teaching. Plato tells us[6] that they were copied from Egyptian practices, with which he may easily have been acquainted, if not directly, at least through his pupil Eudoxes of Cnidus, a mathematician who had studied in Egypt;[7] and problems of this sort did in fact figure in the syllabuses of the scribes' schools, as the discovery of mathematical papyri has shown (16).

And so all children were to be obliged to study mathematics, at least at this elementary stage. They were to be taught them from the beginning of their school life[8] in the form of games[9] and with immediate reference to the practical affairs of life, to the art of war[10] and commerce,[11] and agriculture, and navigation.[12] No one who wanted to be looked upon as "a man[13] rather than as a pig being fattened up for market"[14] could afford to be without this minimum of mathematical knowledge.

But the essential point is that the function of these mathematical studies was not simply to provide technical training: however practical they might be, they nevertheless had a much deeper function.[15] Fully accepting, and enlarging, Hippias's teaching, Plato asserted the supreme educational value of mathematics, and maintained that no other subject was in this respect comparable with it:[16] mathematics awakened the mind, developed its speed and liveliness and its memorizing powers.

Everyone could derive benefit from it: these exercises in applied mathematics

[1] Resp., VII, 721c seq.; Leg., V, 747b; VII, 809c.
[2] Resp., VII, 522c.
[3] Ibid., 522e; 525a; Leg., VII, 809c; 817e.
[4] Ibid., 818e; 819cd.
[5] Ibid., 809cd.
[6] Ibid., VII, 819bc.
[7] D.L., VIII, 87.
[8] Resp., VII, 536d.

[9] Ibid., 537a; cf. Leg., VII, 819b.
[10] Resp., VII, 522ce; 525b; 526d.
[11] Cf. ibid., 525c.
[12] Ibid., 527d.
[13] Ibid., 522e.
[14] Leg., VII, 819d.
[15] Ibid., 818c.
[16] Ibid., V, 747b.

sorted out the best pupils and encouraged them in their natural quickness to learn, but even the slower, more stubborn ones were gradually roused from their torpor, and improved, and became quicker to learn than they would have been by nature.[1] This is an original and profound observation. Unlike many of his successors (ancient and modern), who maintain that literature is the only subject that everyone can learn, mathematics being reserved for the fortunate few who have a bent for it, Plato claims that anyone can learn mathematics because the only thing that is needed for it is the reasoning faculty, a thing that everybody possesses.

This is true at this elementary stage at least, though only a few specially gifted minds will be able to complete the study of mathematics,[2] and these will have to be carefully chosen.[3] We must stress the historical importance of this idea of selection, which is still the basis of our own competitive system of examinations. Plato believed that mathematics provided the test for the "best minds",[4] the people who would one day be ready to study philosophy:[5] mathematics would discover their learning ability, their perceptiveness, their powers of memory, their capacity for hard work despite the aridity of such gruelling study.[6] And in the very process of being selected, the future philosophers would at the same time be undergoing training and preparation for their future work. The essential element in this "preparatory education"—προπαιδεία—was mathematics.[7]

Hence the syllabus and the very definite state of mind to be adopted for this branch of study: it should be remembered that the Seventh Book of the *Republic*, which deals with mathematics, opens with the myth of the Cave.[8] Mathematics is the main instrument for the "conversion" of the soul and the interior re-formation that will awaken it to the true light of day and enable it to contemplate, not "the shadows of real objects", but "reality itself".[9]

To achieve this desirable end it was necessary to order the study in such a way as to free the mind from the bonds of sensory knowledge and enable it to rise to the apprehension of the Intelligible, the only ultimate reality, the one absolute truth. According to Plato, this philosophical orientation should affect the teaching at an early stage:[10] he did not want the simple calculation to be confined to practical matters like buying and selling, etc., but—as he believed—like the educational games of the Egyptians,[11] to lead to a higher degree of abstraction, to the idea of odd and even, the idea of proportion and so on. "Logistics" was merely to be an introduction to "arithmetic" proper—i.e. the science of numbers—and this in turn was to lead to a sense of intelligible reality. Plato gives us a remarkable example of this kind of teaching: from a consideration of elementary facts—the first three numbers—his thought ascends and reflects upon the abstract notions of units and size, conceptions eminently suitable for "facilitating the soul's journey from the world of becoming to the world of truth and essence".[12]

[1] *Resp.*, VII, 526b.
[2] *Leg.*, VII, 818a.
[3] *Resp.*, VII, 503e–504a; 535a.
[4] *Ibid.*, 526c.
[5] *Ibid.*, 503e–504a.
[6] *Ibid.*, 535cd.
[7] *Ibid*, 536d.
[8] *Ibid.*, 514a.
[9] *Ibid.*, 521c; 532bc.
[10] *Ibid.*, 525cd.
[11] *Leg.*, VII, 181bc.
[12] *Resp.*, VII, 525c.

In the matter of the curriculum, Plato, like Hippias before him, followed the traditional Pythagorean quadrivium of arithmetic,[1] geometry,[2] astronomy[3] and acoustics.[4] Plato was anxious to include in his teaching the results of the most recent scientific discovery, and so he completed it by adding cubic geometry, which had just been discovered by the great mathematician Theaetetus and which indeed the Academy, through Eudoxus, was to help to develop. But much more important was the need to purify one's idea of these sciences: they were to eliminate every remnant of sense experience and become purely rational —one might almost say, matters of *a priori* reasoning.

For example, take the case of astronomy (17): it should be a mathematical science, not a science of observation. For Plato the starry heavens, with all their splendour and the regularity of their ordered movements, were still no more than a sense-image, having the same importance for the genuine astronomer as a geometrical figure—even one drawn with the utmost accuracy by the most skilful artist in the world—has for the genuine geometrician; that is to say, no importance at all; for the genuine geometrician works in the abstract on the intellectual form.[5] Plato's astronomy was a combination of uniform circular movements, but its aim was not simply—as Simplicius, who was still too empirical in his approach,[6] thought—"to save appearances", i.e. explain observed phenomena; on the contrary, its aim was to discover the actual calculations used by the Demiurge in the formation of the world.

Rising above all utilitarian considerations, Plato assigned to mathematics a rôle which was above all propaedeutic: its purpose was not to store the memory with useful knowledge but to create a "well-developed head", i.e. a mind capable of receiving intelligible truth, in the way that in geometry an arc is said to be capable of having a given angle formed upon it. It is impossible to overestimate the immense historical importance of this doctrine, which marks a decisive step in the history of education; for Plato here introduces nothing less than the actual theory, and indeed the specific syllabus, of what can only be called secondary education.

Plato was quite consciously opposed to the simple—or shrewd—optimism of his predecessors the Sophists, who confidently offered the highest culture "to the first comer"—ὁ τυχών[7]—without bothering about his aptitudes or his previous training, the resulting failures—which, as Plato sadly remarks, were not without an adverse effect on philosophy itself[8]—being sufficient proof of their error. The philosophers of the future must be both prepared and at the same time tested: Plato was the first to stress this fact, which has since become a commonplace for all educators. The distinctive thing about his own scheme of studies was the important place given to mathematics. As we have seen, he did not underestimate the educational value of literary, artistic and physical education. These all had an important part to play, impressing a kind of rhythm and grace upon the whole personality. But this was not comparable in effect to the part played by the exact sciences, the first accessible type of true

---

[1] *Ibid.*, 521c seq.
[2] *Ibid.*, 526c seq.
[3] *Ibid.*, 527c seq.
[4] *Ibid.*, 530d.
[5] *Ibid.*, 529de.
[6] *In Coel.*, II, 12, 488; 493.
[7] *Resp.*, VII, 539d.
[8] *Ibid.*, 535c; 536b.

knowledge, a direct introduction to the higher philosophical culture which, as we know, is based on the search for rational Truth.

THE CYCLE OF PHILOSOPHICAL STUDIES

Because of the historical interest of this curriculum, it is important to be quite precise about the chronological order of the various stages of the course of studies which Plato imposed on his future philosopher (18). Coming after the "kindergarten" stage (from three to six), and the "primary-school" stage (from six to ten), these "secondary" studies were to last from ten to seventeen or eighteen.

To judge by his actual words, Plato seems to have wished to divide this latter period into three sections of three years each—literature from ten to thirteen, music from thirteen to sixteen, and finally mathematics—a scheme which no doubt many science teachers would be delighted to adopt today. But Plato may only have meant that such was to be the dominating feature of each period: just as gymnastics is continued from infancy to adulthood, so mathematics would begin in the primary school and continue without interruption, until at the end of the course it was the major occupation of the little group of pupils brilliant enough to profit by it.

At seventeen or eighteen years of age, the strictly intellectual studies were to be interrupted by two or three years of "compulsory gymnastic service"[1]—a clear allusion to the contemporary custom of ephebia, which in Athens, for example, imposed two years' compulsory military service upon young citizens. "During this time," says Plato,[2] "it is impossible for them to do anything else: fatigue and sleep are the enemies of all study"—a pertinent observation which I recommend to certain enthusiasts for physical education who are rather too keen to claim the great philosopher as their patron. Education in the broader sense, of course, was never interrupted: military service, and the actual ordeal of war—an ever-present possibility for a Greek city—provided great opportunities for the training and testing of character. Like all classical educators, Plato emphasized the importance of moral factors, and he took this military experience into account when, from the already restricted group of his aspirants to philosophy, he chose those who on their demobilization at the age of twenty were available for the more advanced studies.[3]

And then the higher education really began. But there was no question of going straight on to philosophy. For ten more years the student went on with the various sciences, but at a higher level; so that by developing a wider viewpoint,[4] by co-ordinating[5] and combining the various branches, the mind gradually developed the faculty to detect the unity behind their mutual relationships, the nature of the fundamental reality from which they all derived.

Only when the student was at the end of this course of higher mathematics, and after a final selection, could the genuinely philosophic method, the method

---

[1] Ibid., 537b.
[2] Resp., VII, 537b.
[3] Ibid., 537ab.
[4] Ibid., 537bc.
[5] Leg., VII, 818d.

of dialectics, be embarked upon—and this enabled its user, now emancipated beyond sense knowledge, to attain to the truth of Being. And here again there were many precautions. For it was not sufficient for these minds to have been made, and proved themselves, "well-balanced and steadfast"—κοσμίους καὶ στασίμους[1]; only gradually would they be initiated into the rewarding but highly dangerous art of dialectic—five more years would be needed before they were ready to take full possession of the instrument that alone could lead to complete truth.[2] In this again we see the determination that true philosophy should be spared the misfortunes brought about by Sophist imprudence.

Such was the long course of study envisaged by Plato. And even now the training of the philosopher was not absolutely complete: for fifteen years he would have to take part in the active life of the city, to add to his experience and complete his moral training by struggling against temptation. Only at the age of fifty would those who had survived and surmounted all these trials finally arrive at their goal: the contemplation of pure Goodness.[3] As Malraux says in *La Condition Humaine*, "It takes fifty years to make a man . . ."

We can well understand why, to describe his educational method, Plato is so ready to employ the expression "a long way round"[4] μακρὰ or [μακρότερα] περίοδος (19). Culture[5] is something very different from the "gardens of Adonis", which flowered in eight days and faded as quickly;[6] like the art of the true peasant it is a serious work that needs deep ploughing, carefully chosen seeds and continual hard labour. And here we come upon one of the fundamental demands of Platonism. Eight centuries later, when St. Augustine described his own similar scheme of philosophic culture, he adopted the same curriculum (mathematics and dialectics) and he made the same demand: *aut ordine illo eruditionis, aut nullo modo*—"either follow this long itinerary or renounce everything."[7]

THE GREATNESS AND THE SOLITUDE OF THE PHILOSOPHER

Nevertheless, this was all rather terrifying, and in one sense absurd. Such a curriculum was a challenge to the practically-minded Athenians, who had not been fully converted by the Sophists' propaganda that a high degree of technical skill was necessary for intellectual work to be done properly. Nowhere in Thucydides' account does Pericles venture to praise the Athenian people for its taste in intellectual culture without straightway adding, "but without going to excess"—that is, without reaching that state of refinement which traditional wisdom regarded as "softness", a disquietening symptom of decadence: φιλοσοφοῦμεν ἄνευ μαλακίας.[8]

For in the last resort the practical educational problem for fourth-century society was how to bring up its various sections, and Plato's ambitious and difficult schemes left this concrete problem unsolved, his sole concern being to select and train a small group of philosopher-rulers who could take over the

---

[1] *Resp.*, VII, 539d.
[2] *Ibid.*, 537d; 539de.
[3] *Ibid.*, 539e–540a.
[4] *Resp.*, IV, 535d; VI, 503e–504a; *Phdr.*, 274a.

[5] Plut., *Lib. Educ.*, 2b.
[6] Pl., *Phdr.*, 276 B.
[7] *Ord.*, II, 18(47).
[8] Thuc., II, 40, 1.

reins of government for the good of the State. But Plato himself had few illusions about the possibility of this kind of effective seizure of power: it seemed to demand such an improbable conjunction of physical and mental strength as to be—and he was the first to realize it—well-nigh miraculous (20).

If it is true, as seems to be generally recognized, that the *Republic* was finished about the year 375, before the Master's last two voyages to Sicily and the final failure of his attempts to establish philosophy on the throne of Syracuse, then it follows that he foresaw—and, so to speak, constructed *a priori*—the philosopher's necessary failure even before his own final discomforture. Returning—and this time for his own benefit—to Callicles' sarcasms in the *Gorgias*,[1] he shows us this great soul, too pure for effective action, thrown defenceless into a world given over to injustice and too corrupt to trust him: if he attempts to reform the State he is sure to perish as a failure. And so the philosopher can only renounce such a useless ambition and turn "to the city he bears within himself", πρὸς τὴν ἐν αὐτῷ πολιτείαν[2]—a marvellously profound saying, the last word (if there ever is a last word), full of bitter resignation, of the great Platonic wisdom.

When he wrote the *Gorgias*, he may not have reached this point and renounced the will to power which had been the inspiration of his youth (there seems to be a suggestion of approval in his highly spirited and life-like picture of the immoral but effective politician Callicles). But now the die has been cast, and he knows that the philosopher, who is led essentially by an ideal of inner perfection, is beaten before he starts. He will always be a misfit, a stranger to politics and to the world; absorbed in transcendent thought, he will always seem powerless, a figure of fun like Thales gazing at the stars and falling into a well. And yet he alone is free. . . .[3]

In the end, Plato perceived the truth about his own nature. His teaching became concerned with one man only, or at most a small group of men gathered together in a school, a closed sect, a cultural oasis in the midst of a vast social desert. The Wise Man shall spend his life "cultivating his own garden"—τὰ αὑτοῦ πράττων[4]—the Wise Man, for Platonism had now achieved a personalist type of wisdom. Thus Plato's thought, set in motion in the first instance by the desire to reinstate the totalitarian ethic of the ancient city, finally rises far above it and lays the foundations of what will remain the personal culture of the classical philosopher.

[1] 486ac.
[2] *Resp.*, IX, 591c.
[3] *Tht.*, 173c–176a.
[4] *Resp.*, VII, 496b; cf. 500d.

CHAPTER VII

THE MASTERS OF THE CLASSICAL TRADITION

II. ISOCRATES

THUS, in his pursuit of inner perfection, the philosopher retreated into a heroic solitude. But what in the meantime was to become of the actual city? Must it be left to the bad shepherds? Platonism, aiming too high, had left this problem unsolved. Such at least was Isocrates' opinion. Isocrates' own teaching had an immediate and in a sense a quite prosaic objective—the formation of the intellectual elite which Greece needed *hic et nunc* (1).

When Plato and Isocrates are studied consecutively Isocrates necessarily gets left in the shade and is more or less sacrificed to his brilliant rival (2). In every possible respect—in power of attraction, radiance of personality, variety of temperament, depth of thought or in art itself—Isocrates is not in the same street as Plato: his work seems flat and monotonous, his influence superficial and even pernicious. . . . But the educational historian, and indeed any kind of historian, is obliged to react against the disdain felt by the philosopher and the scholar (the reader will realize that this piece of special pleading is made from a sense of professional duty and against my own inclination).

It is true that from the time of Cicero[1] to our own day (Burnet, Barker, Drerup, Burke, Mathieu) Isocrates has not lacked supporters, some of whom have even gone so far as to bestow upon him the title "Father of Humanism" (3), which in my opinion is something of an exaggeration; for one is entitled to expect a deeper and wider definition of humanism, something less academic, less scholarly, something a little more virile and exacting than his rather flabby and florid, his slightly enervating Atticism. But there is no doubt that Isocrates has one claim to fame at least, and that is as the supreme master of oratorical culture, the literary kind of education that was to become the dominant feature of the classical tradition—despite the dialectical tension created at the very heart of that tradition by the permanent opportunity of choice that had been opened up by the critical philosophy. On the whole it was Isocrates, not Plato, who educated fourth-century Greece and subsequently the Hellenistic and Roman worlds; it was from Isocrates that, "as from a Trojan horse",[2] there emerged all those teachers and men of culture, noble idealists, simple moralists, lovers of fine phrases, all those fluent, voluble speakers, to whom classical antiquity owed both the qualities and the defects of its main cultural tradition.

And not only antiquity: as I have suggested in the opening pages of this book, in so far as the three Renaissances returned to the classical heritage, in so far as this tradition has been perpetuated in our own teaching methods, it is to

---

[1] *De Or.*, II, 94.   [2] Cic., *ibid.*

Isocrates more than to any other person that the honour and responsibility belong of having inspired in our Western traditional education a predominantly literary tone. Indeed, as we endeavour to reconstruct the figure of this old Athenian teacher we shall all find a kind of profile emerging of one or other of our old high-school professors, the man to whom we owe so much, sometimes all that we essentially are, and of whom we have such touching memories, even if these are sometimes tinged with irony.

Herein lies Isocrates' real greatness: his historical importance is such that there is no point in arguing about his weaknesses and limitations. But it must be repeated that there can be no question of attempting to make him Plato's spiritual equal. He was not a philosopher. Nevertheless, we must not blame him for having claimed so constantly and so eagerly the title of φιλοσοφία, φιλοσοφεῖν (4), for he had a strict right to it: in the mouth of a fifth-century Athenian, as we have seen in Thucydides,[1] for example, these words simply evoked in a general way the ideas of disinterested intellectual activity and culture; Isocrates was justified in objecting to the beautiful appellation, "the friend of wisdom", being adopted by Plato and narrowed down to describe only himself. It remains true that there was nothing of the philosopher about him in the sense in which the word has been understood ever since Plato's time.

He was not a "hero of thought". Tradition relates[2] that the Athenians had a siren sculptured symbolically on his tomb in honour of the "perfection of his culture"—εὐμουσία: homage that was well deserved but very much less than the kind of apotheosization, the quasi-divine worship which Plato received from his more fanatical disciples. Isocrates' life and thought and work unfolded on a much humbler level than the imposing drama that centred around Plato; he remained much nearer to the average Athenian intellectual—to the average man.

ISOCRATES' CAREER

Isocrates was essentially a teacher of oratory, and he taught this for nearly fifty-five years (393–338). Before embarking upon this career he had been, from about 403–402 to about 391–390, a "logographer", a writer of law-court speeches; and from 380 onwards he combined with teaching a certain amount of writing as a political publicist.

It is necessary to emphasize in passing the historical importance of this latter activity. By developing a kind of writing that had been introduced in the first place by the early Sophists, Isocrates was the real creator of the "set speech"; in his hands this λόγος ἐπιδεικτικός ceased to be, as it had been for the Sophists, a means of advertisement, a specimen copy of oratorical skill; it became an instrument of action, especially political action, a means whereby the thinker could put his ideas into circulation and act through them upon his contemporaries. From the time of Isocrates onwards this literary category, the public lecture, assumes the decisive importance which it is to have throughout Hellenistic and Roman culture and thus on the way in which teaching developed. Isocrates' part as an initiator extends to details: his *Evagoras*, a funeral oration

---

[1] II, 40, 1.   [2] V. Isoc., 178–182.

on the King of Cyprus (c. 365), the father of his pupil and friend Nicocles, is the first known example of a prose oration over a real person: Isocrates, who was not afraid to set himself up as a rival to Pindar,[1] hoped to take over a category which had previously been the special preserve of lyric poets. His example was quickly and enthusiastically copied, to such an extent that in the Hellenistic age the oration became one of the most popular branches of literature and as a result came to have a special place in education.

Because of certain personal deficiences Isocrates did not in fact deliver his set speeches himself; he published them. They were works of art which took a long time to ripen—with the result that they very often smell of "midnight oil"; the *Panegyric* is said to have taken ten or fifteen years to compose (5). But they are always presented in the form of real speeches—even when the speech is entirely fictitious, like the one *On Exchange*, in which Isocrates pretends to call upon the clerk of the court,[2] refers to the water in the water-clock used to measure how long a speech took,[3] etc. In this way he helped to raise oratory to the level of a literary art and, on the other hand, preserve that influence of the spoken word on literature which, helped by the custom of reading aloud, was to remain one of the dominant features of Greek literature.

As for his actual teaching, Isocrates always remained vitally concerned with practical effectiveness; as he himself explains,[4] he produced either teachers like himself—and this is one of the permanent features of our own classical tradition, that the best pupils in our literature classes are chosen and brought up to be teachers themselves—or expert debaters—ἀγωνισταί: or else—and these were his particular province—men of culture, people with a good sense of judgment, able to take part quite naturally in any sort of discussion: as will be seen, he was chiefly concerned with the average cultivated Athenian.

All his pupils, whether they intended to become professionals or remain merely private individuals, learned first of all to speak well. If Plato's education is based ultimately on the idea of Truth, that of Isocrates relies on the virtues of speech—or perhaps it would be better to say, of the Logos, for it is quite clear that for him speech was already a Word. If you read the hymn to the λόγος which appears in his *Nicocles*[5] and is reproduced word for word some fifteen years later (353) in the *Antidosis*,[6] you will find him saying that speech is the thing that distinguishes men from animals; the basis of all progress in law, art and mechanical invention; the means whereby man achieves justice, gives a voice to fame, promotes civilization and culture. In all this Isocrates was simply giving systematic form and moral justification to the taste for oratory, which, as I have already said, had come to occupy such an important place in Athenian life: its power had become quite tyrannical in politics and law, and now, thanks to Isocrates, it was managing to invade the field of literature too. From this time onwards, all culture, all the education of antiquity, tended more and more—once again, to the extent that it managed to overcome the philosopher's objection—towards this one ideal, the orator's ideal, the ideal of "good speaking"—τὸ εὖ λέγειν.

[1] Isoc., *Ant.*, 166.
[2] *Ant.*, 29.
[3] *Ibid.*, 320.
[4] *Ibid.*, 204.
[5] 5-9.
[6] 253-257.

It will be remembered that this had been the great Sophists' ideal. At first sight there can be no doubt that Isocrates, who was their pupil, seems to do no more than continue their teaching. Tradition—no doubt under the influence of Plato's *Phaedrus*[1]—has it that he was also a disciple of Socrates;[2] but it seems more likely that his acquaintance with Socrates was only indirect, by way of books, although there is no doubt that Socrates' example, upon which he reflected more and more deeply as the years went by, had an influence on his thought which it would be difficult to exaggerate (6). His real teachers were the Sophists Prodicus and, even more, Gorgias,[3] whom he joined in Thessaly, where, far from Athens, he spent the terrible years from 415–410 to 403 (7). Here again, no doubt, it would be wrong to suggest that this filiation accounts for everything: Isocrates was not afraid to criticize his master's alleged "philosophic nihilism",[4] and later on we shall discuss the new alignment which finally took the subject matter and the methods of his teaching in quite a new direction. Nevertheless, in a general sense it can be said that from the purely technical point of view Isocrates simply continued the teaching of the Sophists.

Like the Lesser Socratics he was a professional teacher: he opened a school in Athens, or at least near Athens, close to the Lyceum, the gymnasium in which Aristotle was later to establish himself[5] (8). His school was open to everybody and had none of the characteristics of a closed sect like the Academy;[6] it was a school one paid to enter[7]—as with the Sophists, the money was paid in advance for a complete course of study which lasted three or four years,[8] the charge being a thousand drachmas.[9] Prices, it is known, had gone down considerably since the time of Protagoras and were always in danger of going down further as a result of competition,[10] but this did not prevent Isocrates from making his fortune, helped, it is true, by the generous gifts showered upon him by his pupils—by Timotheus, for example, and Nicocles.[11] There seems no doubt that in the year 356 he lost a lawsuit about an "exchange of goods",[12] which proves that he was recognized by the tribunal as being one of the twelve hundred richest citizens in Athens, who, by the law of Periandros, were responsible for the trierarchy. This gives some idea of the success of his school—he is supposed to have had no less than a hundred pupils[13]—a success, of course, of which he was outrageously vain, as can be seen by the way he describes his pupils rushing down from all the remotest districts of the Greek world—Sicily and the Euxine—at great expense, and with great difficulty, to attend his lessons in Athens.[14]

SECONDARY EDUCATION

The education imparted by Isocrates was a kind of higher education which came at the end of adolescence as the crowning-point of a course of preparatory

[1] 278d–279b.
[2] *V. Isoc.*, 8.
[3] [Plut.] *Isoc.*, 836e; D.H., *Isoc.*, I.
[4] *Helen*, 3; *Ant.*, 286.
[5] *V. Isoc.*, 116–117.
[6] Isoc., *Ant.*, 193.
[7] [Plut.] *Isoc.*, 837e; *V. Isoc.*, 40–41.

[8] Isoc., *Ant.*, 87.
[9] [Plut.] *Isoc.*, 837e; *V. Isoc.*, 43.
[10] Isoc., *Soph.*, 3.
[11] [Plut.] *Isoc.*, 838a.
[12] Isoc., *Ant.*, 5.
[13] [Plut.] *Isoc.*, 837c; D.H., *Isoc.*, I.
[14] Isoc., *Ant.*, 224; 226.

studies, but to these he makes no more than a passing allusion, evidently supposing them to be far too well known to deserve further mention.

For the same reasons as Plato and in almost the same words, he accepts with approval the old traditional education dating back to archaic times, but adds the main innovations in teaching which had been introduced since:[1] his education was thus addressed to the complete man, body and soul—physical training and mental culture going forward together, as two interlocking and balanced forms of discipline.[2]

Whereas for the historian Plato is rendered somewhat suspect by his Utopian reforming activities, Isocrates is a much more reliable witness to current educational practice: one can feel, for instance, by the way in which he refers so briefly to the preliminary elementary education that he looks upon it as something that was very widely established. About gymnastics, the pedotribe's business, he tells us nothing; his "philosophy"—i.e. mental culture, Plato's "music"—is a much more narrowly intellectual matter than Plato's; that is to say, it includes very little art or music in the strict sense.[3] Its basis was grammar,[4] which meant the study of the classics. It is a pity that Isocrates never fulfilled his promise[5] to express his mind on the subject of "poetry and education"; all that is known[6] is that he was highly critical of the way in which other teachers dealt with Homer and Hesiod, the difference of opinion no doubt concerning questions of method, not (as with Plato) the principle itself; for Isocrates advised Nicocles[7] "not to neglect any of the best poets"—or indeed any of the "Sophists", by which he probably meant the philosophers. He also recommended an interesting addition, "the knowledge of the past, of events and their consequences".[8] This was doubtless a reflection of the progress of contemporary culture, which had taken into its field the work of the historians and elevated Herodotus and Thucydides to the rank of classics.

To these literary studies Isocrates added mathematics, and here his dependence on Plato is clearly evident, unless they are both simply echoing the spontaneous practice of their generation. He advises his future pupil to spend some time on the subject of mathematics,[9] which he praises, like Plato, for its formative value: being abstract and difficult, it is a subject that accustoms the mind to sustained effort, gives it exercise, and sharpens it.[10]

But, and here he differs from Plato, Isocrates adds to this "intellectual gymnastics, which is the preparation for higher culture"—γυμνασία τῆς ψυχῆς καὶ παρασκευὴ φιλοσοφίας[11]—a further subject which he calls "Eristics"—the art of debate as taught by means of the dialogue,[12] and which may be regarded as dialectics, or, in more general terms, philosophy.[13] This branch of study, which for Plato was the crowning-point of the highest culture, jealously reserved for minds of the highest quality which were prepared for it by a probationary period lasting many years, is here relegated contemptuously to the level of a

[1] *Panath.*, 26.
[2] *Ant.*, 180–185.
[3] *Ibid.*, 267.
[4] *Ibid.*
[5] *Panath.*, 25.
[6] *Ibid.*, 18–25.
[7] *Ad Nic.*, 13; cf. 42–44.
[8] *Ibid.*, 35.
[9] *Ant.*, 268; *Panath.*, 26–27; cf. *Bus.*, 23.
[10] *Ant.*, 265.
[11] *Ibid.*, 266.
[12] *Ibid.*, 261.
[13] *Ibid.*, 268; *Panath.*, 26–27.

mere secondary subject: Isocrates, with ironical references to people who go on studying it into their maturity,[1] regards it as suitable only for the young, and even then only on condition that they give a limited time to it and thus run no risk of their wits running dry or giving out[2]—that is to say, run no risk of getting to the bottom of it.

THE TEACHING OF RHETORIC

His young people had in fact little time to lose, for his higher education was awaiting them, an education which meant, essentially, learning the art of oratory. Whereas for Plato, as can be seen from the *Phaedrus*, rhetoric was no more than a simple form of applied dialectics, for Isocrates it was an art in its own right, and indeed the supreme art.

Isocrates' rhetoric was a very different thing from rhetoric even as it appears in Gorgias; from the very beginning of his career[3] he had been a harsh critic of the formal rhetoric that appeared in the handbooks—τεχναί—whose authors treated it over-confidently as a perfect machine that was bound to function without fail, no matter what the mental ability of the person applying it. Isocrates, very sensibly, reacted against the outrageous optimism of this kind of formal teaching and insisted on the need for practice, the need for innate gifts, personal qualities (some of which he so cruelly lacked): inventiveness, capacity for work, memory, voice, tact. . . .[4]

Nevertheless his teaching did indeed rest on a theory, elementary though it was: the systematic exposition of what he called ἰδεαῖ—the general principles behind composition and elocution. But, wiser in this than his successors in the Hellenistic age, he reduced this initiation to a minimum and got rid of all the details.[5] The thing that is still discussed—and was being discussed even in antiquity[6]—is whether he himself ever published a proper formal treatise, a τεχνή (9).

Very soon his pupils started practising, doing exercises that involved the simultaneous use of elements which had first been studied in the abstract, and this was done according to the requirements of a given subject.[7] The pupil was not left to his own devices: the essential part of his apprenticeship was the study and criticism of first-class models. As an inheritor of the oldest tradition, Isocrates adapted to literature the fundamental ideas of Homeric education: "example" and "imitation"—παράδειγμα, μίμησις. By doing this he in his turn inaugurated a tradition, and one which was to last: this classical idea of the imitation of literary models now has a long history behind it.

But it was necessary to substitute for the old poets new models which would be more immediately useful to orators. In Isocrates' school the basic texts are in point of fact the master's own masterpieces. There is something slightly embarrassing in the thought of this old teacher smugly quoting and commenting on his own works.[8] Sometimes, however, he does us the favour of introducing

[1] *Ibid.*, 28–29.
[2] *Ant.*, 268.
[3] *Soph.*, 19.
[4] *Ibid.*, 10; *Ant.*, 189–192.
[5] *Soph.*, 16.
[6] *V. Isoc.*, 149; [Plut.] *Isoc.*, 873e.
[7] *Ant.*, 184.
[8] *Ibid.*, 195.

us right into his seminary,[1] where we can listen to him delivering his *Discourse* to a few intimate friends, and we know that he has spent years over the work: its structure is examined and there is a general discussion about the best way of bringing it to a conclusion. . . .

His teaching was practical and realistic: Isocrates' aim was to get his pupils to do the work themselves, to share in the work of creation. In this way he gradually enabled them to discover the ideal that lay behind his art—an ideal carried out by old teachers of rhetoric, century after century, right down to our own day, and which was the kind of writing that is easy to read and, on the surface, easy to understand, but in which the attentive reader will discover endless felicities, interlaced as it is with innumerable allusions to history and philosophy, and full of illustrations and embellishments.[2]

Its Educational Value

Though the aim of this teaching was, like the Sophists', mastery of speech and expression, Isocrates' eloquence was very far from being irresponsible and indifferent to its actual content; its aim was not mere success. Isocrates was undoubtedly concerned to rebut the philosophical objection to oratory voiced by Socrates in the *Gorgias*, and he endeavoured to load his art with a content of real values; his eloquence was not amoral—it had, in particular, a distinct civic and patriotic purpose.

For a proper understanding of his importance it must be remembered that Isocrates was fighting a battle on two fronts: he was not only opposed to Plato and with him all the other Socratics—notably Antisthenes: he was also anxious to distinguish himself from the Sophists' real successors—people like Alcidamas, for example (10), who, like Isocrates, was a pupil of Gorgias, but an out-and-out practitioner entirely concerned with success, with the effectiveness of the spoken word as it was used in the assembly or the tribunal; a great expert on improvisations—αὐτοσχεδιαστικοὶ λόγοι—with nothing but sarcasm for those who like Isocrates spent a long time and much labour on their speeches. "They are poets," he would say,[3] "not Sophists"—by which he meant, they are literary types, not men of action.

But, as I have said, Isocrates was no mere dreamer. Like Plato he was very definitely a man of his time, and his time was that fourth century that witnessed the change-over from the collective ideal of the old city to the more personal ideal which was to be the distinguishing feature of the following age. He too had a sense of political vocation, but his was stifled—not, like Plato's, for historical and social reasons, but from quite different causes—his weak voice, his lack of assurance and a kind of neurotic shyness which has been described as agoraphobia. He too diverted this ambition of his on to teaching, making it his task to raise men who would one day be capable of achieving his own ideals of good government.

His success on this level was even greater than Plato's: like the Academy, only even more so, his school was a centre for the formation of men of politics. To

---

[1] *Panath.*, 200; cf. *Phil.*, 17 *seq.*   [2] *Panath.*, 246.   [3] Alcid., *Soph.*, 1.

his pupils Isocrates was a master in the full sense of the word. His school must not be imagined as a vast auditorium crowded with attentive listeners: from what we know it is easy to estimate (11) that he never had more than nine pupils present at once and that on the average there were five or six, of whom only three or four were hard at work. This gives some idea of the kind of intimate atmosphere that surrounded the relationship between the master and his students. Isocrates took full advantage of this, and had upon his disciples the kind of deep personal influence without which no genuine teaching activity is possible. In this he was as successful as was Plato at the Academy: we know from his own words that the community life that was lived in his school was so attractive to his pupils that they sometimes found it difficult to tear themselves away after they had finished their studies.[1] Timotheus dedicated a statue of his master to Eleusis, "in honour not only of his great intelligence but also the charm of his friendship".[2]

This was indeed the characteristic atmosphere in which Greek education was conducted, so it is not surprising to find that, like Socrates before him, Isocrates was suspected of corrupting youth[3]—his influence was as profound as that! This can be clearly seen in the case of Timotheus himself and again in the case of Nicocles, the petty king of Salamis in Cyprus: the bond lasted far beyond their student days and continued throughout the whole of their lives.

And then, what a list of successes he had! One can see the old man going proudly through his school's honours list, enumerating his most brilliant pupils, dating back to his earliest days:[4] well-known politicians whom, he said, Athens had honoured with golden crowns—Eunomos, Lysitheides, Calippos, Oneter, Anticles, Philonides, Charmantides,[5] and above all the outstanding pupil, the pride of the school, his beloved Timotheus (the son of Conon) the great *strategus*, whom Isocrates looked upon as the embodiment of his ideal and with whom he maintained an active collaboration, always being ready to put his pen at the service of his pupil's politics.[6] And there were many more, as we can see from old biographies:[7] leaving aside men of letters—the tragic poet Theodectes, the critic Asclepius, the "atthidographos" Androtion, philosophical historians like Theopompus and Ephorus—the great names of Athenian political oratory were there on his list: Hyperides, Isaeus, Lycurgus. Even Demosthenes longed to be enrolled as one of his pupils and was only prevented, it is said, by poverty.[8] Isocrates might well be proud of his work; at the end of his career he had in a sense realized his dream: he had been the educator of a new political group and thus helped to provide his city with the leaders whom it needed to achieve the difficult task with which it was faced: the national revival, upon which it had been engaged since the defeat in 404, and the recovery of its position as a great power, a position which it was determined not to renounce.

Isocrates' life, of course, like everyone else's, ended on a note of failure: despite their brilliance, his pupils had not realized his ideal absolutely. His political ideas are known (12). In home affairs he represented what might be called

---

[1] *Ant.*, 87–88.
[2] [Plut.] *Isoc.*, 838 D.
[3] *Ant.*, 30.
[4] *Ibid.*, 87 seq.
[5] *Ibid.*, 93.
[6] [Plut.] *Isoc.*, 837 C.
[7] *Ibid.*, 837 CD; *V. Isoc.*, 99–105.
[8] [Plut.] *Isoc.*, 837 D.

the "new Right Wing Party", the enlightened aristocracy: this meant learning, from the hard lessons of defeat, and from the experience of the subsequent generation, to renounce any seditious attitude of opposition and to agree to a reconciliation with the progress of democracy—not without the hope of limiting the ravages of the latter, even at the cost of a certain amount of demagogy on its own part. This was the policy which in fact triumphed for a moment at the time of Euboulos, but it seems fair to say that in the long run it failed.

Isocrates' apparently ambiguous position as regards foreign affairs was the result of one fundamental preoccupation: the ideal of pan-hellenic unity. His aim was to put an end to the fratricidal wars which had been setting the various cities in Greece at each other's throats ever since the time of the Peloponnesian War, and to solve the problem of peace. But however necessary this solution was, it was never reached—any more than today—which makes fourth-century Greece so like our own anguished times. Isocrates was quite consistent about his own solution: it was to unite all the Greeks in the common task of opposing the barbarians. But unity seemed to him to necessitate some kind of "conductor", and it was in the search for this "hegemony" that he manoeuvred this way and that, inclining, like the good patriot he was, first to his own dear Athens,[1] then to Jason of Pheres, Dionysius of Syracuse, Archidamos of Sparta,[2] and even perhaps Nicocles of Salamis;[3] then towards Athens again,[4] and finally towards the person who was in fact to prove victorious, Philip of Macedon.[5] Isocrates' support of Philip of Macedon seems at first sight utterly incongruous, and it was generally regarded as a betrayal of the national cause. Undoubtedly there was a certain amount of illusion and simple-mindedness in it, but Isocrates was not a traitor: there is a tradition—and if it were true it would be beautifully symbolic —that he died of grief at the news of the defeat at Chaeronea. . . .

The Humanism of Isocrates

But here we are only interested in Isocrates' political ideals because of their intimate connection with his ideals of teaching and culture. What, in the first place, was the basis of his profound sense of Greek unity? Not community of race alone, though A. Aymard has proved beyond all doubt, in *Mélanges V. Magnien* (Toulouse, 1949, pp. 3-9), that Isocrates held this community as a condition, though not the sole condition, for bearing the name of Hellene. And W. Jäger had already pointed this out in *Paideia*, vol. II, pp. 79-80. None the less, although Isocrates' political attitude presupposed a common ideal of "freedom and autonomy", this was simply one particular aspect of a far more universal ideal, a whole theory of man. It was not only race—though race came into it—but the mind that made a Greek: "The people we call Greeks are those who have the same culture as ours, not the same blood."[6]

Here again we get the feeling that we are on the edge of a new epoch and a new world: in this very explicit attitude the whole ideal of Hellenistic times is already fully expressed—the idea of culture as the supreme good. Isocrates goes

---

[1] *Panath.*
[2] *Arch.*
[3] *Ad Nic; Nic; Evag.*
[4] *Panath.*
[5] *Phil.*
[6] *Panath.*, 50.

further: no doubt this national culture is the work of the Greeks as a whole, of history as a whole, of all the Greek cities, but it is pre-eminently the work of Athens—"the school of Greece", as Isocrates, following Thucydides,[1] loved to repeat:[2] its true greatness is to be found in its superior culture.[3] Hence Isocrates' political attitude; for an Athens that was a prey to demagogues, the enemy of its own best sons, the élite responsible for its culture and hence its glory—such a degenerate Athens would not be the real Athens: it would have nothing left to defend; it would not be worth defending (13).

Thus Isocrates' cultural ideal and the education which it demands may have seemed comparatively frivolous to us at the beginning—for is not his "philosophy" essentially "philology", a love of fine words?[4] Nevertheless, they end by transcending themselves in a magnificent ideal whose value is universal; for language—λόγος—is, as we know, the Word that turns a man into a Man, the Greeks into a civilized people with the right to impose themselves—as in fact, as the result of Alexander's great deeds, they were to impose themselves—on a barbarous world which is theirs to conquer and subjugate because of their own superiority. Here we get some idea of the tremendous distance that separates the Sophists' formal rhetoric and cynical pragmatism from Isocrates' grave and upright kind of education. In Isocrates' thought, and in his teaching, form and content are inseparable.

Even supposing that, to begin with, an orator has a purely literary ambition—if he really wants to compose a work of art, if he wants to be great, and interest and move his hearers, he will not be able to manage on frivolous or trivial subject-matter: he will need to choose a subject that has a certain amount of depth, is human, fine and elevated, with a universal interest.[5] Here again we find the tendency—this time with a reasonable justification—which I have already pointed out as one of the most characteristic features of the classical tradition: the gradual amplification of a subject in the direction of what is universal, towards general ideas, great and noble feelings; a tendency which in the end wreaked havoc on the language by helping to produce all those empty commonplaces which have disfigured so many of the works produced by classical academicism. But here we are only at the beginning of the process, and in Isocrates it appears as a remarkable progress, enlarging the orator's horizon and elevating his ambitions, opposed not only to the pure virtuosity of the Sophists but also to the pedestrian profession of the logographer,[6] with his lawcourt speeches devoted to sordid private interests. Isocrates is on the side of the "political" speech, which is able to interest a vast public because it treats of subjects with a universal human interest.

Not only that, but this kind of training has also a moral value. Assuming, again, that the orator's only aim is to succeed, and persuade, and create a fine work of art—he will naturally be led to choose (so says the old master,[7] with his candid and upright mind) subjects which are most in conformity with virtue. Further still, he will necessarily be led to transmit the virtue of his words

[1] Ant., 295–297.   [4] Ibid., 296.
[2] Thuc., II, 41.   [5] Ibid., 275–276; cf. 46; Phil., 10; Panath., 246.
[3] Ant., 293–299; 302.   [6] Ant., 46.
                        [7] Ibid., 277.

into his behaviour, his life; for the orator's entire personality is embodied in his speeches,[1] and the personal authority which is conferred upon his words by a virtuous life gives them more weight than they would have if they were the result of the highest possible art and nothing else.

Thus in the hands of Isocrates rhetoric is gradually transformed into ethics. There is no question, of course, of his sharing what he believed to be the illusion under which the Socratics laboured—that is to say, that virtue can be learned as a kind of knowledge:[2] nevertheless he is convinced that mental application to any subject worthy to be treated is a sure way of contributing to the development of character and the moral sense, to nobility of soul: "True words, words in conformity with law and justice, are images of a good and trustworthy soul."[3] With his gradual, imperceptible shift from literature to life (believing as he did that habits of morality developed in the one must necessarily pass into the other),[4] with his naïve idealism, his unlimited confidence in the power of words —we are a million miles away from the agonizing problems which have arisen today around the subject of language—Isocrates appears as the original fountainhead of the whole great current of humanist scholarship.

ISOCRATES VERSUS PLATO

We have moved a long way from philosophy, especially Plato's philosophy. Isocrates' attitude towards Plato and the scheme of education upon which Plato's philosophy was based, reminds one of Pascal's summary dismissal of Descartes: 'Dubious and useless!'' To understand this, of course, we must put ourselves on the level which Isocrates was determined never to forsake, the level of daily life and practical efficiency. Plato's idea was to subject his pupils to an enormous series of studies, so complex and so difficult that most of the candidates fell by the wayside—and he did all this under the illusion that he could lead us to perfect knowledge. But in the affairs of everyday life no knowledge is possible in Plato's sense of the word—$\dot{\epsilon}\pi\iota\sigma\tau\dot{\eta}\mu\eta$: the knowledge that is rational and demonstrable.[5] Let us take any concrete problem: the question will be what to do, and what to say. There will never be any theoretical knowledge precise enough to tell us this. The "genuinely cultivated" man—$\pi\epsilon\pi\alpha\iota\delta\epsilon\nu\mu\dot{\epsilon}\nu o\varsigma$—says Isocrates, is the kind of person who has a gift for "hitting upon" the right solution—$\dot{\epsilon}\pi\iota\tau\nu\gamma\chi\dot{\alpha}\nu\epsilon\iota\nu$—or at least the solution that is most nearly right, the best in the circumstances—$\kappa\alpha\iota\varrho\dot{o}\varsigma$: and this is because he has the right "opinion" —$\delta\dot{o}\xi\alpha$.[6] This latter word, which was dismissed contemptuously by Plato, means for the more modest Isocrates the limit of what can in practice be achieved, the only kind of ambition that man can realize.

If knowledge is unattainable, what point is there in giving oneself so much trouble and making so many pretensions for such an uncertain result? According to Plato himself, philosophical knowledge is useless because the philosopher has no actual reasonable city to apply his ideas to and so is condemned to fall

---

[1] *Ibid.*, 278.
[2] *Ibid.*, 274; *Soph.*, 21.
[3] *Nic.*, 7.
[4] *Ant.*, 277.
[5] *Ibid.*, 184.
[6] *Ibid.*, 271; *Panath.*, 30–32.

back upon an ideal city, a dream world which he bears within his own soul—for in the real city he is, inevitably, as we have seen, an object of ridicule, a failure, fit only to be persecuted—and done to death.

Isocrates himself chose as his particular province something that was a good deal more practical, and also a matter of urgent necessity: he educated his pupils for life, particularly political life, preferring to teach them to be able to form sensible opinions about things that were useful rather than spend their time in hair-splitting about points that were utterly useless[1]—things like duplicating the cube and how to find the place of the Angler in the dichotomic classification of beings.[2] There is no point in attempting to mount into the heaven of Ideas or in playing about with paradoxes: for the purpose of living properly what we need is not new and surprising ideas but established good sense, traditional wisdom.[3]

The "Spirit of Finesse" and the Geometric Spirit

Fundamentally, the difference between Isocrates and Plato was the difference between Pascal's two kinds of mind—the sensitive mind—the "spirit of finesse"—and the geometrical. The things that Isocrates tried to foster in his disciples were—ability to make decisions, an intuitive grasp of the complexity of human affairs, and a perception of all the imponderable factors which help to direct one's "opinion" and make it a just one. Literature—the art (not the science) of speech—is the best instrument for sharpening the faculty of judgment. The instrument is not in itself sufficient, a certain gift is needed too, for in this field of reality—moral, human reality—there can be no infallible system ensuring that any mind will get the right result simply because it is rational. There was nothing more absurd in Isocrates' view than the Socratics' attempt to turn "virtue" into a kind of knowledge, a science like mathematics, that could be taught.[4]

And here it is necessary to go a little more deeply into the question of the connection which we have said exists between rhetoric and morals, and to discuss in much greater detail the intimate bond that we believe the art of oratory creates between form and content. These, we said, are inseparable; and this is so because the effort to find the right expression demands and develops a sensitivity of thought, a sense of different shades of meaning, which it is difficult to express in conceptual ideas, and even, sometimes, impossible. This idea will be familiar to anybody who has read Valéry or Bremond: there are things that a poet feels and makes you feel at once, and which no amount of science can ever fathom. The result is that an "oratorical" kind of education, which in appearance is entirely a matter of aesthetics, whose one aim is to create "wizards with words", is in fact the most effective way of developing subtlety of thought.

"The right word is a sure sign of good thinking."[5] This idea, which is absolutely fundamental to Isocrates, has a depth, and implications, which possibly he himself never suspected—he would have needed to be endowed with still more of the sensitive mind, to have been less prosaic, more highly aware of the genuinely poetic values of artistic prose; and he would then have been able

---

[1] *Helen*, 5.
[2] Cf. Pl., *Soph.*, 218e seq.
[3] Isoc., *Ad Nic.*, 41.
[4] *Soph.*, 21; *Ant.*, 274.
[5] *Nic.*, 7 = *Ant.*, 255.

to quote Plato against himself, and oppose to the uncompromising scientific nature of his theory his actual practice as a writer. We know how, in Plato's hands, myth, poetry, pure art, express their own values, by means of psychological preparation, the rhythm of his dialogue, the art that lies in a phrase—in a word, even. Is it not through these rather than by the dry and dusty labours of his dialectic that Plato expresses the essence of his teaching, all that is finest and most delicate—indeed, all that is truest—in it?

The Two Columns of the Temple

Such are the two fundamental types of education, the two rival streams of development, which Plato and Isocrates set before Greek education, before what was to be the classical tradition. For the purposes of exposition I have been obliged to a certain extent to heighten the opposition between them. In actual fact the two types of teaching were contemporary and ran parallel with each other; they did not always stand over against each other as rivals and adversaries.

It would be extremely interesting—though in the present state of our knowledge it is in fact impossible—to describe the history of their interaction upon each other. This would probably prove very complex and involved (14). And it may have varied. They both had other opponents. There were other kinds of rhetoric besides Isocrates': he was opposed, for instance, to the pure sophistry of Alcidamas. There was other philosophy besides Plato's: the "Eristics" whom Isocrates combated may have been chiefly Antisthenes and the thinkers of Megara. Between the two party leaders there may easily have been alliances in the face of a common enemy—a common front of Dogmatics against the dissolvent criticism coming from the school at Megara, and indeed of "Ideologues"—apostles of high culture—against the narrowness of political realists.

It must be remembered particularly that such tactical combinations were undoubtedly reinforced by a number of reciprocal influences. Isocrates seems to be under Plato's influence when he gives such a high position to mathematics and philosophy in his preparatory culture. Again, there seems to be a kind of concession to Isocrates on Plato's part, in his recognition of the legitimacy of literary art in the *Phaedrus*, which is in fact a manifesto in favour of philosophical rhetoric, which the young Aristotle, as a *privat dozent* of rhetoric, was given the task of teaching in the Academy itself (15).

Thus there was not only rivalry between the two; there was emulation; and this is important for what followed. In the eyes of posterity philosophic culture and oratorical culture did indeed appear as rivals, but they also appeared as sisters, having not only a common origin but similar ambitions that could at times be confused. As we have said, they were two varieties of the same species, and the conflict between them enriched the classical tradition without disturbing its unity. By the door of the sanctuary which we are now about to enter there arise on either side, like two pillars, like two sturdy Atlantes, the figures of these two great teachers, "balancing and as though answering each other" —ἀντιστρόφους καὶ σύζυγας.[1]

---

[1] Isoc., *Ant.*, 182.

Part II

CLASSICAL EDUCATION IN THE HELLENISTIC AGE

CHAPTER I

THE CIVILIZATION OF THE "PAIDEIA"

AT this point we reach the very heart of our subject, and our study of the education of antiquity now becomes truly rewarding. For the aim of any historical enquiry is not so much the enumeration of stages of development as the analysis and synthetic understanding of its subject-matter, as the latter is found in its mature form, with all its values fully developed. It was only in the generation following Aristotle and Alexander the Great that education assumed its classical and definitive form; thereafter it underwent no substantial change. It is true that there was some further development (to which, for lack of sufficiently detailed documentary evidence, it is difficult to assign dates), but this was little more than the completion of a process that had been going on from the very beginning, the fulfilment of tendencies already present.

In later centuries classical education lost many further vestiges of its original aristocratic character, even though it was always to remain an integral part of aristocratic life; physical culture became less and less important (though this decline did not take place without occasional opposition and delay). Intellectual culture correspondingly advanced, but its artistic and especially its musical side finally yielded precedence to literature. While still retaining its essentially moral character, education became more and more dependent on books, and in consequence took a more scholastic turn. The school came to the forefront and developed its institutional character, gradually taking the place of the spontaneous or organized youth club, with its characteristic atmosphere of more or less amorous relationships between older and younger members. The transition to a scribe education had finally been accomplished.

But here again this development was simply the unfolding of characteristics present from the beginning. Although the gymnasium, as the sporting-centre, remained the symbol of the final phase of education, although it is not until the late Roman Empire that we find schoolboys using as models for their writing, maxims like "Letters are the beginning of wisdom"—'Αρχὴ μεγίστη τοῦ φρονεῖν (or, τοῦ βίου) τὰ γράμματα[1]—nevertheless, this outlook, which was only gradually realized in practice, had in principle existed all along. Aristotle had expressed it clearly:[2] reading and writing, he tells us, play a leading part in education because, in addition to their practical utility in professional, family and political life, "they are the means of acquiring many other types of knowledge" and in consequence form the basis of all education.

When we say "classical education" we really mean "Hellenistic education". This became the education of the whole Greek world, when the latter achieved

---

[1] *PBouriant*, I, 169; Crum, *Epiph.* II, 615; Preisigke, *SB*, 6218.
[2] *Pol.*, VIII, 1338a, 15-17, 36-40.

some sort of stability after the exploits accompanying Alexander's conquests and the hazards of the wars of succession following his death. It remained in use throughout the Mediterranean world for as long as the latter could be termed "ancient", overlapping the strictly Hellenistic age and lasting into the Roman era.

It must be said at once that there was no strictly autonomous Roman education, any more than there was any autonomous Roman civilization. Italy—and, through her, the whole of the Latinized West—was absorbed into the sphere of Hellenistic civilization, which German scholars, with useful precision, therefore describe as the *hellenistisch-römische Kultur*. It is true that there were some distinctively Latin characteristics, but these were only secondary features and did not form a separate civilization. Roman education, which we shall study in Part III of this book, was only an adaptation of Hellenistic education to Latin circumstances. In the Greek countries to the east, the Roman conquest and the replacement of the dynasts by the "king-people", first in the person of an all-powerful pro-consul and later in the form of the emperor-god, had no serious influence on civilization, or on cultural life, or, in particular, on educational tradition.

It is true that a careful chronological grouping of the epigraphical and papyrological data shows that certain educational innovations appeared in the Imperial epoch, but these concerned only small details which, even taken all together, would not be sufficient to impart a specifically different character to Roman education. Furthermore, throughout the eastern half of the Mediterranean world, Hellenistic education continued unchanged and without a break for the whole of the Roman era, and even beyond; for, as we shall see later, the triumph of Christianity did not lead to the educational revolution that one might expect; the classical system of education stretched throughout the whole length of Byzantine history.

THE PRESENT STATE OF THE QUESTION

Thus we reach the very heart of our subject. And here, unfortunately, the fact that this period has been so little studied makes the task of describing it very difficult. A work like the present one depends upon the results of a considerable amount of earlier painstaking investigation; but far less attention has been paid to Hellenistic education than to that of the previous era and to the later Roman education (1). Not that the materials are lacking; on the contrary, there is a superabundance of them: besides the literary sources, which include a great number of essays and handbooks on education, there is a wealth of epigraphical material that is important for the study of established institutions like schools and competitions; there is also the invaluable evidence brought to light by the Egyptian excavations, whose papyri and *ostrakca* and writing-tablets (2) give us an intimate picture of school-life, which we can study at first hand in school-books and exercises. All this material is easily accessible, and most of it has already been assembled, but so far it has not received the attention it deserves. And so the following account must necessarily seem premature, to say the least, and all I can hope is that its inevitable imperfection will stimulate someone more competent than I am to undertake the task of remedying this regrettable deficiency (3).

This state of affairs gives us some idea of the anarchic way in which scientific research goes on: whatever value there may have been in the works on the Hellenistic age that appeared after its importance was first realized by Droysen, we have had to wait until quite recently for any satisfactory treatment of its civilization (4). If during all the intervening time it had been favoured with a tenth part of the energy that has been expended in France on subtle refinements concerning the definition of purism in the Golden Age of Pericles—and in Germany on the virtues of archaism and Dorianism—and in Italy on the pursuit of some chimera concerning the cultural autonomy of the Latins—we should not now be obliged to deplore this serious gap in our knowledge of the past, our own Western tradition.

I repeat, for it is a point that must be grasped: if antiquity has fertilized our whole European tradition, if the Archaism and Atticism that have been alternately so highly praised, and the genuine Roman spirit that came later, have affected such a long line of generations, it is to the extent that their own particular contributions were accepted and integrated and passed on by the classical tradition; and the classical tradition received its Form from Hellenistic civilization and was synthesized—and, so to speak, symbolized—in Hellenistic education.

EDUCATION THE HEART OF HELLENISTIC CIVILIZATION

But even without these long-term considerations this education still merits the attention of the historian; its importance in the history of the Hellenistic period is so great that it must be placed at the very centre of any genuine picture of its civilization.

Attention is commonly drawn to the abrupt change of scale entailed by the conquests of Alexander in the area covered by Hellenism; its eastern frontier suddenly retreated over two thousand miles, from the fringe bordering the Aegean on the one side to the Syr-Daria and the Indus on the other; and the stakes of war were now vast empires, not just a few feet of olive-groves in the insignificant plains of Lelantos or Crissa.

Against this immensely enlarged background, the traditional framework of the ancient city broke up, or at least retreated into the background. It is true that the Greek type of city continued to exist; in fact there were more of these cities than ever: everywhere, except in Egypt, Alexander's successors carried out a hellenizing policy by establishing or developing urban centres on the Greek model. It is also true that there was still an active "political" life, even in the sphere of external relations; in the Hellenistic era there were still wars between cities, there were still treaties and alliances—we even find two rival cities having recourse to the arbitration, not of the sovereign, but of a third city. The Hellenistic kingdom remained, in fact, as a superstructure; its administrative machinery tended to be reduced to a minimum and then incorporated, wherever possible, into the already existing institutions of the city. We shall find the same tendency much later in the Early Roman Empire.

Nevertheless, this city-activity had little more than a local significance (of vital importance, of course, to its members); the city was simply a "home town", it was no longer the fundamental category, the supreme norm, of thought and culture.

Nevertheless, in spite of appearances, and sometimes, even, despite its own requirements, it was not the monarchical state which succeeded it; for, lacking all organic character, and uncertain of itself, divided and re-united by the hazards of war or dynastic ambition, the State was the plaything of Fortune—*Τύχη* (who became the great goddess, eclipsing the old deities of the city state)—with none of the moral authority required for imposing any fundamental discipline of the kind that gives a meaning to life and the world in which man lives. The Hellenistic "Wise Man" thought himself, and claimed to be, *κοσμοπολίτης*— "a citizen of the world" (5), rather than a subject of the Lagids or Seleucids; but this term (at least until the heyday of the Roman Empire) was negative, it meant simply going beyond the bounds of the city, rather than being any positive affirmation of the concrete unity of mankind—an idea which remained unthinkable.[1]

The real heir of the ancient city was not, as is often said, with a slight suggestion of contempt, the individual, but the human person, who, liberated from the corporate conditioning and totalitarian pressure of city life, now becomes conscious of himself, of his capacities and needs and rights. Henceforth the norm and justification of all existence are to be found in man—man considered as an autonomous personality in his own right, achieving the realization of his being—beyond the self, perhaps, but certainly through the self, and without ever renouncing his own individuality. To a greater extent than any who went before him, Greek man had regarded himself as the centre and "measure of all things", and in Hellenistic times this humanism became conscious of its personalist claims. For Hellenistic man the sole aim of human existence was the achievement of the fullest and most perfect development of the personality: just as the "coroplast" modelled his little figures of clay and decorated them, so must each man have as his basic task the modelling of his own statue. I have already quoted the words of this well-known saying; they were uttered, in later times, by Plotinus. But the idea underlies the whole of Hellenistic thought. To make oneself; to produce from the original childish material, and from the imperfectly formed creature one may so easily remain, the man who is fully a man, whose ideal proportions one can just perceive: such is every man's life-work, the one task worthy of a lifetime's devotion.

But what is this but the principle behind all education, pushed to its furthest limit and made absolute? *Παιδεία* is here no longer the technique by which the child—*παῖς*—is equipped and made ready early in life for the job of becoming a man; by a remarkable extension of meaning, *αὔξησις*—the same word, in Hellenistic Greek—is made to denote the results of this educational effort, pursued beyond the years of schooling and lasting throughout the whole of life, to realize ever more perfectly the human ideal. *Παιδεία* (or *παίδευσις*)

---

[1] Tert., *Apol.*, 38, 3.

comes to signify "culture"—not in the sense of something active and preparational like education, but in the sense that the word has for us today—of something perfected: a mind fully developed, the mind of a man who has become truly man; it is a striking fact that when, later, Varro and Cicero had to translate παιδεία into Latin, they used the word *Humanitas*[1] (6).

This transfiguration of what was originally a very humble idea of education had its reflection in the sphere of corporate life. The unity of this Greek world, which had been extended to cover the οἰκουμένη—"the inhabited universe", i.e. the world of civilized men, men worthy of the name—was now less racial than ever. Isocrates had already recognized this, but it became even more obvious in the Hellenistic era, when the Greek world included and assimilated so many foreign elements—Iranian, Semitic, Egyptian. Nor was there any political unity, for political unity scarcely survived Alexander's death. Unity could only come from sharing a single ideal, a common attitude towards the purpose of existence and the various means of attaining it—in short, from a common civilization, or rather, culture.

Here I must repeat that in French, as in English, this world "culture" has a pronounced personalist tinge; in accordance with the spirit of the French language it means the exact opposite of any collective idea of civilization: French *culture* is not by any means the same thing as German *Kultur*. Now it was exactly this ideal of personal life—and not necessarily any particular form of social organization such as the city—that all Greeks had in common. Although the city, with all its characteristic institutions, still provided the best conditions for the full development of civilized life, it was no longer a necessary condition, because there were Greeks living the Greek way of life outside the confines of organized cities, in the χώρα, for example—the "lowlands" of Egypt. Between the Greeks of Greece proper, and those who had emigrated all over the vast area between the Libyan desert and the steppes of Central Asia, and the recently hellenized barbarians, unity came from a common devotion to a single ideal of human perfection, from the fact that they had all received the same kind of upbringing devoted to the same end—the same education, in fact.

Wherever the Greeks settled—in the villages of the Fayum, where the Ptolemies organized a military colonization,[2] in Babylon,[3] in far-off Susiana[4]— one of their first tasks was to set up their own institutions, their educational establishments—their primary schools and gymnasiums. For education was a matter of primary importance to them: they were isolated in a foreign land, and their chief concern was to enable their sons, despite the influence of the surroundings, to preserve the distinguishing marks of the Hellenic character—the thing they clung to more than anything else. Classical education was essentially an initiation into the Greek way of life, moulding the child and the adolescent in accordance with the national customs and submitting him to a particular style of living—the style that distinguished man from the brutes, Greeks from barbarians.

[1] Gell., XIII, 16, 1.
[2] *Aeg.*, XI (1930–31), 485.
[3] *SEG*, VII, 39.
[4] *Ibid.*, 3.

When we enquire how the Greeks expressed our idea of civilization, in its abstract sense, we come across the remarkable fact that here again, by a further extension of its meaning, they used the word παιδεία (παίδευσις). So expressive is this word that if I were asked to describe the distinctive character of Hellenistic civilization, I should define it as the civilization of παιδεία—coming between the civilization of the ancient city—the πόλις—and the civilization of the City of God—the Θεόπολις, i.e. the Christian civilization that covers the late Roman Empire from Constantine's time onwards and the Western and Byzantine Middle Ages.

As proof of this is the increasing importance, in Greek thought, of ideas about education. As we have seen, Plato and even Aristotle[1] looked upon education as a part—and a subordinate part—of the problem of politics; but Hellenistic philosophers usually deal with it in a separate treatise, περὶ παιδείας or περὶ παίδων ἀγωγῆς; following the example of Aristippus[2] there are Theophrastus[3] and Aristoxenus[4]—pupils of Aristotle: the great Stoics and champions of Hellenism—Cleanthes,[5] Zeno[6] and Chrysippus[7]—and others like Clearchus of Soloi[8] and Cleomenes.[9]

To the men of this age individual culture of the kind imparted by classical education seemed "the most precious boon ever granted to mortal men". These words from Plato[10] were quoted by Menander,[11] and for eight centuries[12] were to go on being repeated, into the far-distant days of the pagan Libanius,[13] and St. Gregory Nazianzen,[14] true heirs of the Hellenistic ideal.

Individual culture was the greatest of all goods—in a sense, the only good. There is a characteristic story about the philosopher Stilpo, whom Demetrius Poliorcetes wished to indemnify after the capture of Megara for any losses he had suffered during the pillage. On being asked to draw up an estimate of the damage, Stilpo replied that he had lost nothing that belonged to him, for no one had taken his culture—παιδεία—from him: "he still had eloquence and learning"—λόγος, ἐπιστήμη.[15]

The Religion of Culture

This is why we also find amongst the epitaphs on so many funeral monuments, bas-reliefs and statues, references to the intellectual attainments of the deceased. Either by their own express wish or on the initiative of their families they are represented as having been men of letters, orators, philosophers, amateur artists or lady-musicians (7).

These monuments were not, as it was once believed, necessarily raised to professional intellectuals such as teachers, artists or writers: we know that in most cases they were dedicated to private individuals whose professional activity

[1] Pol., VII–VIII.
[2] D.L., II, 85.
[3] Ibid., V, 42.
[4] Ibid., VIII, 15.
[5] Ibid., VII, 175.
[6] Ibid., VII, 4.
[7] Quint., I, 11, 17.
[8] D.L., I, 9.
[9] Ibid., VI, 75.
[10] Leg., I, 644b.
[11] Monost., 275.
[12] Plut., Lib. Educ., 8 E.
[13] Or., LII, 13.
[14] Or., XLIII, 11, 1.
[15] D.L., II, 115; cf. Plut., Lib. Educ. 5 F–6 A.

took them into quite other fields—medicine or the army or business. But all, no matter what their profession, wanted one thing to be recorded on their tombs—the fact that they had won the friendship of the Muses, had possessed the one incomparable treasure, a cultured mind.

The knowledge that has been gained from these monuments has given us a clearer insight into a great number of curious beliefs widely held at the time, all expressing in their own way the same metaphysical exaltation of cultural values.

Hellenistic civilization attached so much importance to these values that it could only conceive of supreme happiness as the life of the artist or the man of letters. In this refined form, the eternally happy life enjoyed by the souls of the heroes in the Elysian Fields is represented as a time spent in the supreme delights of art and thought: in an eternal spring, among meadows speckled with flowers and watered with running streams, are "discussions for the philosophers; theatres for the poets; dancing; concerts; discreet conversation round the banquet table": thus speaks the unknown rhetorician who, in the first century B.C., wrote the pseudo-Platonic dialogue *Axiochos*.[1]

Thus cultural life came to be looked upon as a reflection and a foretaste of the happy life enjoyed by the souls blessed with immortality—and not only that, but as the means of obtaining it: mental labour and the pursuit of science and art were a sure means of cleansing the soul from the stains of earthly passion and freeing it from the restricting bonds of matter. After devoting his whole life to the service of the Muses a man could confidently count on their patronage when he came to die; for they would summon him into their presence and lead him into the astral spheres along with all those other souls who on earth had been similarly prepared for that great honour.

This curious doctrine of immortality as a thing merited by culture is very old; it appears very clearly in the death of Pythagoras, to whom Metapontus and Croton paid the divine honours which until then had been reserved for heroes who had founded or saved cities. In the classical epoch apotheosis by way of culture remained the privilege of exceptional persons, great scholars, founders of sects—as we have seen, after Pythagoras, Plato received this honour. But in Hellenistic and Roman times the practice spread widely; apotheosization came to be regarded indeed as something quite commonplace, and from that time onward it was only natural that every poet, every thinker, every artist, every man of letters, every disciple of the Muses, should aspire to it; they could all claim the splendid title of μουσικὸς ἀνήρ—"a man of the Muses"[2]—i.e. a man sanctified and saved by those goddesses.

This kind of mysticism was not of course professed by all the men of letters with the same consciousness and the same intrepid faith, but to some degree it affected the culture of them all: παιδεία—a thing divine—a heavenly game, a nobility of soul, was invested with a kind of sacred radiance that gave it a special dignity of a genuinely religious kind. In the deep confusion caused by the sudden collapse of ancient beliefs, it was the one true unshakable value to which the mind of man could cling; and Hellenistic culture, thus erected into an absolute, eventually became for many the equivalent of a religion.

[1] [Pl.] *Ax.*, 371cd.   [2] *IG*, XIV, 2000.

CHAPTER II

THE EDUCATIONAL INSTITUTIONS OF THE HELLENISTIC AGE

IN ITS most highly developed form, Hellenistic education consisted of a complicated course of studies which began when the pupil was seven and went on until he was about twenty. For a description of its various stages there is no better system than that employed by Hippocrates—so long as we ignore his passion for symmetry: we know how, from the time of Pythagoras to the days when the Fathers of the Church developed their complicated biblical allegories, the men of antiquity loved to speculate on numbers. Hippocrates,[1] we are told, divided human life into eight periods of seven years each: education took up the first three periods, and these were thus allocated: παιδίον—"small child" (up to seven years of age); παῖς—"child" (from seven to fourteen); and μειράκιον—"adolescent" (from fourteen to twenty-one). Aristotle used on the whole a similar system, and his description of it gives us the best idea of its actual content.

Up to the age of seven the child stayed at home and was looked after by the womenfolk: the Ancients—who were not interested in the child as such, being concerned only with the ultimate aims of education—took little interest in this first stage, and in fact they did not look upon it as part of παιδεία in the proper sense of the word at all. The school period began when the child reached the age of seven and in theory lasted until he was fourteen (Aristotle is not so precise: he says until puberty, ἥβη); thus it was more or less the equivalent of our primary-school education. The following period culminated in a course of civic and military training known as the ephebia. In some places circumstances were exceptional: in Egypt, for example, because it was a colony, the ephebia began when the child was fourteen; in Sparta it lasted throughout adolescence; but generally speaking it was not reached until the end of the third period, and in most cases it only lasted a year—very occasionally it lasted two years and it could even go on for three, but even then it always took place between the eighteenth and twentieth year.

Between the boy's primary-school days and the ephebia there was thus a period for which, in the "old" education, no provision had been made. It was an unsettled time, a "difficult" age, in which he tended to get involved in unsavoury love-affairs. But in the Hellenistic age these years of adolescence were put to good use and devoted to those "other studies"—ἄλλοις μαθήμασι, as Aristotle put it[2]—which Plato and Isocrates had both considered essential. These were the equivalent of our secondary-school education: they aimed at providing a solid background for the higher education that was to follow.

[1] Poll., II, 4; Censorinus, XIV, 3-4; Arist., *Pol.*, VII, 1336a-23-24; VIII, 1338b 39-1339a 8.
[2] *Pol.*, VIII, 1339a 5.

This higher education took place at the same time as the ephebia; not that the essentially sporting education that the ephebes received in the gymnasium could be compared to our university education, but within the precincts of the gymnasium there developed for youths of ephebic age a real higher education, technically excellent and, like our own system today, including a number of specialized subjects that ran concurrently and between which there was a certain amount of healthy rivalry: rhetoric, philosophy and medicine.

Finally, in certain privileged centres—first in Alexandria, then in Pergamus, and later, under the Empire, in Athens—there appeared, as a sort of crowning-point of the whole system, establishments like the Museum, where the most highly qualified men of the day engaged in research, and gathered young disciples around them to form genuine institutes of higher learning.

Naturally, only the favoured few—those with enough money, as well as enough brains—covered the whole course; to the great majority only the elementary stages were open; though in principle this classical education was a free man's privilege, nevertheless young slaves were sometimes admitted (1). As for the girls, from now on they went to primary and secondary schools just like the boys, and sometimes—and not only in Sparta—to the palestra and gymnasium. The Hellenistic notion of the ideal woman was very different from that of Xenophon's Isomachos. This is how the latter gentleman describes his chosen spouse, the girl who had delighted his heart:[1] "She was only fifteen when we were married. She had lived a very sheltered life, and knew that it was her job to be neither seen nor heard. What more could I want? She could weave, spin, make her own clothes and look after her spinning-girls. And no flightiness—her parents had seen to that. Excellent, eh?"

PUBLIC INSTRUCTION

In the Hellenistic era, education stopped being a matter of private initiative and became, generally speaking, subject to official control. This was something new, at least on such a large scale. It is true that Aristotle[2] makes it a legislator's strict duty to legislate on education—νομοθετητέον περὶ παιδέιας—but in this the great philosopher was speaking prophetically (2), for in his own time[3] any system of "public instruction" under the control of the State was a peculiarity of "aristocratic" states like Sparta and Crete, whose totalitarian tendencies we have already mentioned (3). To the men of Hellenistic times, however, legislation on school affairs had become the normal thing, one of the necessary attributes of the civilized State—hence their surprise when in Republican Rome they came across an archaic stage of development in which education was still outside the control of the State.[4]

EDUCATION A MUNICIPAL CONCERN

But it is time to get down to a few facts. In the first place, the State in this connection is the city, the municipality, not the kingdom. The Hellenistic

[1] Xen., Œc., 7.
[2] Pol., VIII, 1337a 33; cf. 11; X, 1180a 24 seq.
[3] Ibid., IV, 1300a 4-6.
[4] Polyb ap. Cic., Resp., IV, 3.

kingdom was not, like the late Roman Empire, totalitarian; in a sense it was a "liberal" State which reduced its responsibilities to a minimum and possessed only such machinery as was absolutely essential; it was quite prepared to decentralize wherever possible and entrust the public services to the municipalities: this was particularly so in the case of educational institutions.

We occasionally find a Hellenistic monarch intervening in the administration or the policy of some particular school, but only privately, as a "benefactor" or patron. It was only in the time of the Roman Empire that the sovereign began to interfere in this field as a legislator, and even then, as we shall see, this was in the first place mainly in order to remind the municipalities of their duties, not to take their place.

Egypt is in a way the exception that proves the rule. We know how late municipal institutions were in developing in that country; apart from Alexandria, Lagid Egypt had only two or three real cities—Naucratis, Ptolemaïs and possibly Paraetonion. But even here the characteristic institutions connected with Greek education—the schools and gymnasiums—which had entered the country with Hellenism and were to be found everywhere, were not the king's responsibility; nor were they left to commercial private enterprise: or at least this is quite certain in so far as the gymnasium, the chief corner-stone of the educational system, was concerned. As far as we know, the gymnasiums in Lagid Egypt seem to have been administered and financially maintained by associations, perhaps of "old boys"—οἱ ἐκ τοῦ γυμνασίου.[1] Now whenever, in any given locality, there was also an organization made up of the Greeks living in that district (as for example in the garrison posts, where the Greek soldiers formed a πολίτευμα), the two associations became very closely related. Even more striking is the fact that even when no such organization was in existence in the first place, the gymnasium seems to have formed a centre around which some such para-municipal and, later, quasi-municipal structure could crystallize and gradually expand. The full development did not come until much later, but by the time of the Roman Empire the Egyptian gymnasium had relinquished its status as a private association and assumed that of a public institution; so that the practice was uniform throughout the Greek world (4).

The municipal character of these educational institutions makes it difficult to give a comprehensive account of the subject that would be both brief and accurate. We know what a passionate attachment the Greeks had to the ideals of liberty and autonomy. The Hellenistic cities could not even agree on a common calendar; it is therefore hardly likely that they would be able to pursue a uniform educational policy. They almost seem to have taken a delight in complicating matters: the same titles often signified different offices in different cities, whilst in other cases the same kind of function was performed by officials bearing different titles.

And so we must proceed with care. To begin with, it is not true that education simply became a State concern in every Hellenistic city. Since it was a matter of general interest the State could not be indifferent to it and therefore, almost

[1] APF, II, 528, 26; SEG, VIII, 504; 531; 694.

everywhere, it was an object of the city's attention; but not always to the same degree, nor in the same way at the different degrees.

Of all the educational institutions the ephebia was the most official, and indeed it was the only one which always remained a public institution. It was extremely widespread, and it appeared wherever Hellenism took root, or tried to take root. In point of fact the Athenian ephebia is the only one we know much about, but it seems almost undoubtedly to have been the model for that of the other Hellenistic cities, so that we can take it as typical of the rest.

THE ATTIC EPHEBIA

However it originated, and whenever it first appeared—a matter about which there is some dispute—the Attic ephebia seems to have been an adaptation of Spartan military training to the requirements of a democratic régime. It was a way of producing soldier-citizens, with the emphasis on the soldier. There is evidence of its existence from about 370[1] onwards, but it did not receive its final form until much later, immediately after the defeat of Chaeronea (338), as the result of a law for which Epicrates[2] seems to have been responsible and which was passed between 337 and 335. Our knowledge of it is derived from certain inscriptions which show that it was functioning regularly from 334–333 onwards,[3] and from Aristotle's detailed description of it,[4] as he saw it round about the year 325 (5).

It seems to have been then almost identical with the compulsory military service demanded by modern States. Each year, on the basis of the civilian records, the *demes* drew up a list of the young men who were about to attain their civic majority, i.e. eighteen. This list was submitted to the Boulè for checking and revision, and when their claims to the enjoyment of civic rights had been duly verified, the young conscripts were enrolled, placed under a corps of specially chosen officers, and embarked upon two years' military service. The first of these was spent in barracks at the Piraeus, and here they received physical and military instruction; during the second they practised campaign manœuvres, discharged garrison duties at fortified posts on the frontier and fulfilled the functions of a militia. The ephebes were fed by the State and wore a uniform:[5] this consisted of a large hat—πέτασος—worn with the hair cut short, and a black chlamys (changed to white—for religious ceremonies at least—thanks to Herod Atticus, A.D. 166–168).[6]

Thus the Athenian ephebe was primarily a young soldier; but not entirely—for the fourth-century ephebia also included a kind of civic novitiate, a system of moral and religious training in preparation for the full exercise of the rights and duties of citizenship. Unfortunately, in the present state of our knowledge it is difficult to decide what elements are traditional, deriving from a dim and distant past, and what are moralizing innovations introduced by the reform group that centred round the orator Lycurgus. The ephebes began their period

[1] Aeschin., *Amb.*, 167.
[2] Harp., s.v.
[3] *IG²*, II, 1156.
[4] *Ath.*, 42.
[5] Poll., X, 164.
[6] Philstr., *V.S.*, II, 1, 550; *IG²*, II, 2090; 2606.

of service with an official pilgrimage to the principal sanctuaries of the city:[1] at the end of their first year, when they became real soldiers, they received their arms and swore the famous oath:

I shall not dishonour these sacred arms, nor shall I abandon my comrades in battle; I shall fight for the gods and for hearth and home, and I shall not leave my country smaller, but rather [I shall leave it] greater and stronger than I found it, either by my own efforts or in company with my comrades. . . .[2]

The oath continues with a remarkable political statement (the stress on democracy was certainly recent if, as seems the case, the oath was in the main archaic in origin):

. . . and I shall submit to whosoever has authority [over me and exercises it] with wisdom, and I shall obey the existing laws and those that the wisdom of the rulers may enact.

(The text given by Stobaeus[3] states more precisely "and those that the people enact by common consent"):

. . . and if anyone should attempt to subvert them I will not tolerate it, but I will fight for them,[4] either by myself, or in company with my comrades; and I shall venerate those whom my fathers venerated. [Be] my witness— Agraulos, Hestia, Enyo, Enyalios, Ares and Athena Areia, Zeus, Thallo, Auxo, Hegemone, Heracles, my country's frontiers, its cornfields, its barley, its vines, olives and fig-trees!

But there was a tragic irony in all this. For Athens developed this meticulous organization for recruiting her national army just when Philip's victory and Macedonian hegemony had ended Hellenic independence and the free city. As happens so often in the history of human institutions, the ephebia did not reach perfection until for all practical purposes it had lost its *raison d'être*.

We know how international politics destroyed the hopes of a national revival that had sustained the reforming zeal of Lycurgus (337–326): after the disaster of the "Hellenic" war (322) it was clear that Athens, and indeed all the other cities of Greece proper, would be no more than pawns on a diplomatic chessboard, on which the rival ambitions of the kings who succeeded Alexander would jostle and clash. She would occasionally know the ephemeral joys of this or that "liberation", but in fact this would mean no more than a change of master. Athens was to go on gravitating like a satellite in the sphere of influence of one or other of the Hellenistic monarchs until, with the rest of the Eastern world, she fell under the domination of Rome.

With the loss of independence any civic army lost its point too: Athens— or at least the Piraeus, which held a key-position—was often garrisoned by foreigners. The ephebia, as described above, ceased to function regularly; but it did not disappear: instead, by a paradoxical development, an institution that had been intended to serve the army and democracy was transformed, in the

---

[1] Arist., *Ath.*, 42.
[2] *BEHE*, 272, 302–3.
[3] XLIII, 48.
[4] Stob., *ibid*; Poll., VIII, 105–6.

new aristocratic Athens, into a peace-time college where a few rich young men could be initiated into the refinements of polite society.

THE DECLINE OF THE EPHEBIA IN THE HELLENISTIC ERA

The inscriptions enable us to set out the stages of this decline. From 269–268,[1] perhaps even from 306–305—that is to say, less than thirty years after Epicrates' law[2]—the period of service was reduced to one year. It was no longer compulsory: as a result of which, during the years 334–333 and 327–326 the annual contingent for the whole of Attica seems to have been between five and six hundred; in 305–304 the effective force was no more than four hundred, and in 269–268 it fell to the figure of thirty-three.[3] In the following year it sank even further: it was twenty-nine in 249–248,[4] and a little later, in 244–243,[5] it had become as low as twenty-three. But this must have been the result of exceptional circumstances, for later on we find it rising: there were a hundred and seven ephebes in the years 128–127[6] and the number went on increasing; it reached a hundred and forty-one in 119–118[7] and became fixed between a hundred and a hundred and forty for several generations (6).

But this force was not made up exclusively of young Athenians: after 119–118 foreigners were admitted as ephebes[8] (7), a fact which clearly shows that it had entirely lost its original national exclusiveness. These foreigners seem at first to have been the sons of rich Syrian and Italian merchants living in Delos, but it was not long before admission ceased to be confined to members of resident colonies in Attica or its dependencies: young men came from the cities of Asiatic Greece, from Syria, from Thrace, even from the Euxine, Cyrene and Rome, to complete their education—if not, strictly speaking, their studies— attracted by the wonderful city's great reputation for refinement, and in particular by its college of ephebes. This latter had become highly "select", and clearly it was something of a snob school. It reminds one of English university colleges in the nineteenth century: like them, it was designed for the wealthier classes and had no higher ambition than that of teaching them how to enjoy their leisure.

For a long time, no doubt, the college retained traces of its original military and civic purpose. Foreigners were not admitted on the same footing as actual Athenians; in the lists they were described as "also present" and put on a supplementary register—ἐπέγγραφοι—and they were not allowed to compete. Military training was still given: in 123–122 we find the ephebes boasting that they had resurrected an old catapult, which had been lying forgotten in some corner of the arsenal, so that they could take up artillery exercises again;[9] in 102–101 they gave themselves a pat on the back for having carried out campaign manœuvres "a little more frequently than usual"—πλεονάκις;[10] but the fact that these are referred to as exceptional events proves that nothing serious was

[1] *IG²*, II, 665.
[2] *Ibid.*, 478.
[3] *Ibid.*, 665.
[4] *Ibid.*, 766.
[5] *Ibid.*, 681.
[6] *Hesp.* (1935) IV, 74, 75.
[7] *IG²*, II, 1008, 55.
[8] *Ibid.*, I, 112–127.
[9] *IG²*, 1006, 34–5; 81.
[10] Dittenberg., *SIG*, 717, n.18.

involved. The staff of military instructors (teachers of the javelin, archery, artillery, etc.) was reduced to one, the fencing master; and he was very much of a minor figure (8).

On the other hand the part played by the gymnastics master—the "pedo-tribe"—grew more and more important, and he became an increasingly pro-minent and highly esteemed personage. From the second century A.D. onwards his office was conferred on him for life, and his duties became so heavy that he had to have an assistant, the "hypo-pedotribe" (9). He was clearly the linch-pin of the whole college, responsible for all that was most essential in the training of the ephebes. In the Hellenistic and Roman era, in fact, the Athenian ephebia—which went on functioning until A.D. 262–263 or 266–267[1]—had become simply a Higher Institute of Physical Education.

It remained nevertheless a college to which the gilded youth of Athens and elsewhere came to receive the finishing touches of their education; and thus it perpetuated, for a restricted circle at least, the fundamental characteristics of the most ancient type of Greek education. For these youths, as for their far-off predecessors in Homeric and aristocratic times, sport was still the foundation of all advanced culture, the hallmark of polite society, and consequently the basis of all education.

Nevertheless, times had changed: important though it was, sport no longer had an exclusive place in education. In the second century B.C., side by side with physical education, there appeared a genuinely intellectual form of teaching which aimed at giving the ephebes at least a smattering of literature and philo-sophy. We shall be examining this general culture later. Its standard was not very high: the ephebia existed for the benefit of young men who had no need to work for their living and so were not interested in achieving a high standard of technical excellence in any of the fields of science and intellectual study.

Much more important in the eyes of the ephebes than the simple popular lectures which were all that the school provided were the friendships they made, the social experience they gained in this small community—for it was organized like a miniature city, with an assembly, elected magistrates,[2] debates, voting, and so on. This was another survival from the original ephebia, which had aimed at providing an apprenticeship in civic affairs; but these parliamentary games, reminiscent of the French Conférence Molé-Tocqueville took place in a highly aristocratic atmosphere—an atmosphere which became increasingly characteristic of Athenian municipal life, especially in the Roman era—and thus, like everything else in the ephebia, they had simply one object: the per-petuation of the aristocratic way of life.

THE EPHEBIA OUTSIDE ATHENS

The ephebia was to be found in more than a hundred Hellenistic cities all over the Greek world, from Marseilles in the west to the Euxine in the east (10), and everywhere it had the same features as the Athenian. There were occasion-ally slight local variations: thus in certain Dorian cities, where the new insti-

[1] IG², II, 2245.   [2] Ibid., 2130.

tution could be combined with an old local tradition, the ephebes had a different name: just as they were called eirenes in Sparta, so in Cyrene they were known as τριακάτιοι[1] and in Crete as ἀπόδρομοι or ἀγέλαοι.[2] Their training, which usually lasted a year, might last two: in Cyzicus,[3] this was exceptional, but in Apollonis[4] normal; whilst in Chios it seems to have lasted three years[5] (11).

As in Athens, we frequently come across more or less distinct traces of the original ephebia—for example, in an obscure corner of Achaea, in Pellene, it was still remembered under the Empire that service in the ephebia had once been a necessary condition for the full rights of citizenship.[6] Often the ephebes took part as a body in the processions,[7] sang hymns to the gods[8] and generally played a part in the official religious life of the city (12). Until the end of the third century at least, military exercises were still a part of the normal curriculum, as can be seen from the events in the competitions,[9] and the lists of instructors.[10]

Nevertheless, on the whole it may be said that, as in Athens, so in all other places, the Hellenistic ephebia had become aristocratic rather than civic, sporting rather than military. In spite of appearances, its characteristics were very much the same, both in the old Hellenic cities of Greece proper or Asia Minor and in the new countries in which Hellenism appeared as a colonizing power. Sometimes one gets the impression that there was a fairly close connection between the gymnasium and the army, but this link always seems to have been indirect (13)—the ephebia was certainly not organized for the purpose of training soldiers; but as the great Hellenistic kingdoms preferred to recruit their mercenaries from amongst the Greeks (or Macedonians), many former ephebes eventually took up a military career, whilst, conversely, the garrisons were little Greek centres where the children naturally went to the gymnasium (this was particularly the case in Egypt) (14).

Encompassed by barbarism, these Greeks were not so much interested in the ephebia because it could prepare their sons for a career—in the army, for example—as because it provided an initiation into the Greek way of life, above all to athletics, its most characteristic feature. And, as one of the elements of Hellenism in these "colonial" countries, the ephebia also encouraged the growth of an aristocracy. This can be clearly seen in Roman Egypt, where the process that had begun in the time of the Ptolemies reached its full development: there, the ephebia had become an official institution, part of the new municipal organization (15), and its function was to initiate young Greeks into the life of sport, which was the only thing that would make them truly civilized and set them apart from the natives—the Αἰγύπτιοι ("Copts")—who were

---

[1] Hesych., s.v.; *AI* (1930), III, 189.
[2] Ar. Byz., *Onom.*, 429; Dittenberg., *SIG*, 527, n.6.
[3] *CIG*, 3665, 11.
[4] *BCH* (1887), LXXXVI, no. 6, l. 4.
[5] Dittenberg., *SIG*, 959.
[6] Paus., VII, 27, 5.
[7] *IG Rom.*, IV, 292; Dittenberg., *SIG*, 870, 885.
[8] *F. Eph.*, II, no. 21, 525.
[9] Dittenberg., *SIG*, 958, 245.
[10] *Ibid.*, 578, 21-24.

despised as barbarians. For this reason it began when they were fourteen[1] and on the threshold of adolescence. But even though (as seems likely) the ephebia in the strict sense lasted only one year, they felt its effects for the rest of their lives: ten or fourteen years later they would still be grouped together as old boys of the same class—αἵρεσις[2] (16). It was only as members of a privileged aristocracy that in official declarations certain Greeks were able to have the words "old gymnasium boys"—ἀπὸ γυμνασίου, ἐκ τοῦ γυμνασίου[3]—put after their names, and their sons' names (17). And so some parents with an eye to the future took the precaution of getting their sons' names down for the ephebia well in advance, when they were seven, or three,[4] or even only one[5] (18).

As an element in Hellenism the ephebia was at the same time a powerful hellenizing force: anyone who had received a Greek education was a Greek. When the high priest Jason decided to introduce Hellenism into Jerusalem his first step was to organize a body of ephebes from amongst the young noblemen and get them to wear a *petasos* and then do exercises in the gymnasium.[6] Wherever Hellenism went, the ephebia went too; wherever it was slow in taking root, the ephebia too was slow to appear—in the cities of far-off Paphlagonia[7] it did not appear until the end of the second century. The ephebia lasted as long as the ancient way of life itself: in A.D. 323, when Constantine had finally defeated his last enemy Licinius, and when for more than fifty years the Athenian ephebia had ceased to be written about, ephebes were still to be found in Oxyrrhyncus.[8]

THE EPHEBIC MAGISTRATES

The integration of the ephebia into the official framework of any city followed logically from the nature of the ephebia itself: it took concrete form in the magistrates who were appointed to control and supervise and cover the general administration of the college. Of these the most frequently mentioned is—typically—the "master of the gymnasium"—γυμνασίαρχος (19)—who was always a very important person and sometimes "the foremost man in the city".[9] He was chosen—for reasons which we shall soon appreciate—from amongst the most influential and above all the most affluent of the citizens. In Roman Egypt at least, and not only in the main provincial towns but in Alexandria itself, to be a "gymnasiarch" was one of the highest of municipal honours (20).

Known to have existed in more than two hundred cities, this kind of office may safely be looked upon as having been universal; for gymnasiarchs were found not only in the actual cities, but in the small urban centres of Central Egypt, in provincial towns and even simple villages (21). Even when the actual word was not used (and even when it was used but had a different meaning) the office still existed; this was so in Athens, where it was filled by a magistrate called the κοσμήτης—the "guardian of order".

---

[1] Wilcken, *Chrest.*, 143; 146.
[2] *Ibid.*, 141, 142; *BSA*, VII (1929), 277, 3.
[3] *PFior.*, 79, 24; *POxy.*, 2186.
[4] *PTeb.*, II, 316.

[5] *BGU*, 1084.
[6] II *Mach.*, iv, 9, 12, 14.
[7] *IG Rom.*, III, 1446.
[8] *POxy.*, 42.

[9] *IG*, XII, 5, 292.

This exalted personage was assisted by an adjutant, the "hypo-" (or, less frequently, the "anti-") "gymnasiarch". In the same way, in Athens one, and sometimes two, "hypo-" (or "anti-") cosmetes were installed besides the cosmete. In the fourth century the administration of the ephebia was also guaranteed by the introduction of a committee of "controllers of wisdom"—σωφρονισταί—ten in number, elected on the basis of one to a tribe. This committee disappeared at some unknown date in the Hellenistic period, but it began to function again under the Empire, and at this later period it consisted of six *sophronists* with as many "hypo"-sophronists. In the more densely populated and highly-organized cities the number of gymnasiums increased by their being split up for different age groups, and so the office was repeated: above the gymnasiarchs in charge of each separate establishment was a "gymnasiarch general" with jurisdiction over all the others (22).

The gymnasiarch ruled from on high; he did not actually teach. The ephebes were looked after by an expert known as the "pedotribe" in Athens and the "cosmete" in the Egyptian gymnasiums. This person often had a subordinate officer who took direct charge of the young conscripts: he was "the master of the ephebes"—ἐφήβαρχος, ἀρχέφηβος, ἐφηβοφύλαξ— and he was sometimes chosen from amongst the ephebes themselves. The gymnasiarch was therefore a kind of director-general, or rather the principal of the ephebia.

I must apologize for going into such detail, but perhaps I have enabled the reader to gain some idea of the solicitude which the Hellenistic cities continued to display for this institution even after it had lost its original military purpose and become an instrument of higher education. But although, because of its origin, the ephebia was the most thoroughly State-controlled of all the educational establishments, the others were not always considered unworthy of official attention. In quite a large number of cities—particularly in Asia Minor, which under the Empire was to become the centre of the Greek world—we find a special magistrate in charge of the lower schools; he was called the "pedonomos"—παιδόνομος—but this title did not designate a general superintendent of the youth of the city, as it did in Sparta, but simply an inspector of primary and secondary schools. He was below the gymnasiarch in the honours list, but he fulfilled functions in his own sphere which were similar to those performed by the gymnasiarch in the ephebia: the epigraphic charters of the schools in Miletus and Teos,[1] for instance, show that he used to preside over the choice of masters and settle any argument that arose concerning them. The job could become so onerous that more than one pedonomos might be necessary: there were several of them in Miletus and Priene and Magnesia ad Meandrum. Where co-education was the rule, as in Teos,[2] their authority extended over girls' education too; otherwise the girls had their own inspector (known in Pergamus,[3] and perhaps in Smyrna too[4], as the "officer responsible for the behaviour of the girls"—ὁ ἐπὶ τῆς εὐκοσμίας τῶν παρθένων)—except where

[1] Dittenberg., *SIG*, 577; 578.
[2] *Ibid.*, 578, 9.
[3] *AM* (1912), p. 277; *Ins. Perg.*, II, 463.
[4] Robert, *Et. Anat.*, 56, 19.

E

they were under the jurisdiction of "gyneconomes", as in Magnesia ad Meandrum[1] (23).

ABSENCE OF STATE SCHOOLS

One would have thought that since the State was so concerned with the proper functioning of educational establishments it would have taken on their direction and upkeep itself. Hellenistic scholars have projected this logical attitude into the past and attributed[2] the institution of free compulsory schooling to the old law-giver Charondas of Catana, conveniently confusing him for their purpose with his colleague Zaleucus of Locres (24). Unfortunately there was an obstacle to the application of this strict logic, and that was the city's economic structure, which generally speaking had remained archaic and was consequently very shaky. It had neither the resources nor the administrative apparatus that would have enabled it to take direct charge of public education. Normally only the ephebia—once again, because of its origin—and the gymnasiums dependent upon the ephebia were endowed and maintained by public authority (25). As for the more elementary schools, they were originally, as we have seen, private concerns, and they usually remained so.

But the growing sense of the social importance of education suffered under this neglect, and a practical solution was found by appealing to the generosity of private individuals and asking them to supply financial backing for a matter of common concern. This was an appeal to the "benefactor"—Εὐεργέτης—a title of great renown, much sought after by sovereigns and granted to private individuals in many special honour-decrees. The practice was erected into a system, and became characteristic of Hellenistic and Roman civilization; its decline meant the end of the old liberal, personalist civilization. When patriotism and the desire for fame no longer sufficed to move an impoverished bourgeoisie to such acts of generosity, the State (i.e. the Empire) was obliged to introduce coercive measures to combat this shirking of municipal responsibility; and its demands, which grew daily more exacting, set the Roman world on the road to the totalitarianism of the Late Empire.

SCHOOL FOUNDATIONS

A system known as "evergetism" materialized, characteristically, in the shape of "foundations" by which a private individual gave the city enough capital to provide income for the upkeep, or at least the improvement, of some particular public service. These foundations were of all kinds: for the repair or construction or maintenance of public monuments, for the expenses of religious ceremonies, and so on (26). We know of at least four whose object was the establishment and endowment of elementary and secondary schools.

Towards the end of the third century a certain Polythrous gave his own city of Teos a sum of thirty-four thousand drachmae, which was invested at about eleven and a half per cent and so gave an interest of nearly four thousand

---

[1] Dittenberg., SIG, 589.   [2] Diod. Sic., XII, 12.

drachmae: this was to be used for teachers' salaries, in accordance with the terms of the foundation charter, which specified the nature of the staff and their rate of pay.[1]

Similarly, in 200–199 Eudemos of Miletus left his native city the sum of sixty thousand drachmae, which, when invested in the State Bank at ten per cent, yielded an interest of six thousand: a little more than half of this—three thousand three hundred and sixty drachmae—again went in teachers' salaries, and their status and payment were again fixed in great detail; the remainder was used to defray the costs of various sacrifices.[2]

The other two foundations came from princes, acting not as sovereigns within their own kingdoms but as private individuals in foreign states (and not without an eye to propaganda): in 160–159 (27) the city of Delphi appealed to the rulers of Pergamus for financial aid,[3] and the future Attalus II, who was already sharing the throne with his brother Eumenes II, gave a sum of eighteen thousand drachmae "for children's education".[4] This amount, invested at seven per cent, must have brought an interest of one thousand two hundred and sixty drachmae, and this was used to pay the "masters"—παιδευταί.

At about the same time, or a little before, Eumenes II had offered the people of Rhodes a gift of twenty-eight thousand *medimnae* of corn, so that its value in cash could be used to pay the city's teachers—a gift which Polybius reproached the Rhodians for accepting at the cost of the nation's pride and independence.[5]

The inscriptions in Teos and Miletus (which are as detailed as could be wished for) tell us not only how many teachers there were, and what their duties were, but also how they were selected. In Miletus, apparently, they were elected annually by the citizens' assembly from candidates who had given their names to the "pedonomos".[6] In Teos it was the same, except that the military instructors were taken on by the pedonomos and the gymnasiarch personally, and then their choice was confirmed by the people's assembly.[7] In Miletus the founder—the "benefactor"—maintained an interest in the schools he had endowed, taking part personally, and after his death in the person of his eldest son, in the procession prescribed by the charter,[8] which took place every five years; nevertheless, he did not interfere in the administration: there was nothing like the part played by "trustees" in the school and university foundations of Anglo-Saxon countries; as can be seen, these Hellenistic foundations resulted in the creation of schools that genuinely existed for the people, and were completely in the hands of the city.

But however striking and original they may have been, it would be going too far to present these "foundation schools"—*Stiftungsschulen*—as the main feature of Hellenistic education. We only have these four examples altogether, and they all belong to the same period (200–160). And it is very likely that as a result of neglect or lack of money the schools even in these four cities finally faded away into insignificance.

[1] Dittenberg., *SIG*, 578.
[2] *Ibid.*, 577.
[3] *Ibid.*, 671.
[4] *Ibid.*, 672, 4.

[5] Polyb., XXXI, 31, 1.
[6] Dittenberg., *SIG*, 577, 25 *seq.*
[7] *Ibid.*, 578, 7 *seq.*; 22–23.
[8] *Ibid.*, 577, 57 *seq.*; 73–75.

PRIVATE SCHOOLS

However that may be, in our account of school institutions pride of place must undoubtedly go to the private schools, which functioned on a strictly commercial basis, the teacher receiving fees from his pupils. The documentary evidence about them is quite consistent and artless, both in the case of literary schools like the one described so picturesquely in the mime of Herondas,[1] and in the case of establishments of physical education like the "palestras", which were named after their proprietor or "manager"—Timeas' palestra[2] and Antigenes' palestra[3] in Athens, Staseas' palestra, Nicias' palestra, and the palestra run by the two Nicorati, father and son, in Delos.[4]

Normally—let me repeat—only the ephebia was under State control: an official secondary school like "Diogenes' College" in Athens—Διογένειον —was exceptional (28). This, as it existed under the Empire at least, was a State school for young men who were preparing for the ephebia; their instruction was both physical and intellectual, and it was tested by examinations held under the supervision of a *strategus*.[5] The teaching staff and the servants were classed with those of the ephebia proper, and their names appear after theirs in the inscriptions.

LITURGIES AND MAINTENANCE FOUNDATIONS

However, even for the proper functioning of the official ephebia, the city frequently had recourse to the generosity of the wealthier citizens, and this appeal to the private pocket had to a certain extent been recognized in Greek public law by the institution of payments which were known as "liturgies". This practice spread considerably in the Roman-Hellenistic period.

The time came—particularly in Athens—when "gymnasiarch"—in Athenian language, "cosmete"—no longer meant the magistrate in charge of the ephebia, but a wealthy citizen who paid to keep the institution going for a year—he might even be an ephebe. Even when the gymnasiarch was an actual magistrate the "liturgical" element was not necessarily absent by any means. Theoretically the city allotted him a fixed sum, but it was an understood thing that it relied upon him to add any extras that were necessary out of his own pocket—either for out-of-the-ordinary things like repairs to an old gymnasium or the construction of a new one, or even the normal running costs for equipment and maintenance and teachers' salaries.

Thus the great thing was that the gymnasiarch should be not only one of the most distinguished but also one of the richest and most generous citizens: money came first—that is why the gymnasiarchy might be conferred on the same dignitary for several years in succession, or bestowed for life on some willing "benefactor", or even made hereditary. The holder's personal qualifications

---

[1] Her., *Did.*
[2] Dittenberg., *SIG*, 67, 60–62; *IG²*, II, 957, 47.
[3] *Ibid.*, 958, 60.
[4] Durrbach, *Choix*, 117.
[5] Plut., *Quaest. Conv.*, 736d.

mattered little. A woman could share the honour—and also the financial obligation—with her husband or her son. Sometimes she could receive the actual office. Sometimes, for the same reason, this might fall to a baby because it was the heir to a great fortune (29).

Here, too, private foundations came to the financial aid of the institution: some simply helped the gymnasiarch in a general way to fulfil his obligations in a manner befitting his office; others—the most numerous—were specially set aside for his heaviest item—the embrocation oil used in athletics. We know of twenty such cases between the third century B.C. and the second century A.D. (30).

THE GAMES AND THE FESTIVALS: OFFICIAL SANCTION

Though the city's financial weakness prevented it from taking direct control of all educational activities, it still made its presence felt and brought the education of youth under some kind of regulation by means of the games and competitions it organized, both athletic and musical. These games, which formed an integral part of the city festivals, had such a high reputation that they provided an effective substitute for examinations—in fact, at the risk of a certain anachronism, we could define the Hellenistic system as one of independent schools (except for the "public foundation" schools) plus State examinations.

The same function of providing a moral sanction for education by integrating it with the official life of the city was fulfilled when children, and, as we have seen, the ephebes, took part in religious processions and in sacrifices offered to the gods of the city. Their presence was required by law, in Tamynae in Euboea, for instance,[1] and in Amorgos:[2] indeed it is only in this respect that we can find any equivalent to our modern legislation on compulsory schooling.

One of the major responsibilities of the magistrates specially concerned with education—the gymnasiarchs and pedonomes—was to organize these processions and see that the young people who took part in them behaved in an orderly and dignified way that would do the city credit. In so far as we can reconstruct the school calendar as it must have existed in Hellenistic cities, the most striking thing is the number of "holidays of obligation"—not "holidays", but days on which official ceremonies took place—in which the young people—the school-children and the ephebes—took part in displays that were both civic and religious, the equivalent of the great "rallies" which have been reintroduced in our own day by the various totalitarianisms (31).

[1] *IG*, XIII, 9, 154.　　　　　　　　　　[2] *IG*, XII, 7, 515.

CHAPTER III

PHYSICAL EDUCATION

LET us now turn to the actual content of this education. As I have already pointed out in my discussion of the ephebia, gymnastics may have ceased to play a preponderant part in the education of the young Greek, but they were still the most characteristic part, at least at the beginning of the Hellenistic period. As in the very earliest times, athletics was still one of the primary distinguishing marks of the Greek way of life as against that of the barbarians. If you had found yourself amongst the Jews in Jerusalem around 175 B.C. you would have discovered that adopting "the customs of the goyim"[1] meant, chiefly, doing exercises in the nude on a sports-ground.[2] Wherever Hellenism took root, gymnasiums and stadiums and all the rest of the paraphernalia appeared—from Marseilles[3] to Babylon[4] and Susa,[5] from Southern Egypt[6] to the Crimea;[7] and not only in the great cities but in tiny colonial villages like those in the Fayum.[8] To the Greeks, sport was not merely a pleasant form of relaxation; it was a highly serious business, involving a whole complex of affairs concerned with hygiene and medicine, aesthetics and ethics.

Thus physical training remained an essential part of the process of initiation into civilized life—that is to say, of education: hence its predominant place in the ephebia, which was the highest rung on the educational ladder. But it does not seem to have been confined to the lordly youths of the ephebia, or, with them, to have been given only on the threshold of adult life. It will be remembered that from the earliest times there had been athletic competitions and consequently some sort of physical education for children; but it is difficult to know when exactly this education began. Fortunately, the Hellenistic era is richer in documentary evidence than those earlier times, and we can be considerably more precise in our statements.

In the first place, it is certain that children of secondary-school age were given a training in sport. This was obviously the case in Egypt, for there, as we have seen, they went to the ephebia when they were fourteen. But it was the same elsewhere: in Pergamus the children had a separate gymnasium from the adults and the *neoi* and the ephebes:[9] Lapethus[10] had a special children's gymnasiarch; in other cities—in Eretria,[11] for example, and Attaleia[12]—the general gymnasiarch kept an eye on the children too. They could enter for competitions almost

---

[1] I Mach., i, 15.
[2] II Mach., iv, 9–14.
[3] IG, XIV, 2466.
[4] SEG, VII, 39.
[5] Ibid., 3.
[6] Ibid., VIII, 531.
[7] IOSPE, II, 299; 360; IV, 459.
[8] Aeg. (1930–1), XI, 485 seq.
[9] Gal., San. tu., II, 1; 12. Ins. Perg., 467, 7.
[10] IG Rom., III, 933.
[11] Dittenberg., SIG, 714.
[12] IG Rom., III, 777; 783.

everywhere—in Chios,[1] in Teos,[2] in Larissa,[3] in Tamyna in Euboea[4] and, of course, in Athens itself.[5] These were local competitions for the youngsters, not the great pan-hellenic meetings where nearly all the competitors were professional athletes who had been specializing since they were children.[6]

In these competitions, however, we frequently find several categories of children: in Thespiae there seems to have been a distinction between seniors —πρεσβύτεροι—and juniors;[7] in Larissa,[8] Oropos[9] and other places,[10] between younger children and older ones described as "beardless"—ἀγένειοι; in Coronea[11] and Chalcis[12] between "children"—παῖδες—and "wholly children" —πάμπαιδες. It seems reasonable to conclude from this that children took part in gymnastics at quite a tender age (1). Not only in Sparta, where *mikkik-hizomenes* of nine or ten years old competed in the games (2), but throughout the Greek world, physical education accompanied literary education from the time the child was seven or eight: for this the convergent testimony of the very varied evidence is most striking—there are epigraphical charters from the schools in Teos and Miletus,[13] literary references,[14] inscriptions on tombs,[15] and a mass of sculptured monuments all pointing to the same conclusion (3).

Similarly, in the Hellenistic age Sparta was no longer the only city in which girls received physical education on the same footing as boys—except, of course, for training for professional athletics[16]—for in Chios, for instance, not only did the girls receive the same sports training as the boys, but they practised with them on the same sports-grounds.[17] There seems to have been something similar in Teos,[18] and to a more restricted extent in Pergamus too.[19]

In Hellenistic times, therefore, physical education was given to a public as vast as it was various. But the actual training does not seem to have varied much according to age or sex: all that we are told is that the children's exercises were lighter—κουφότερα[20]—than the ephebes' and that the girls' events were easier than the boys': at Olympia, for example, the women's race, known as the "Heraia", was run over a track that was one-sixth shorter than the men's.[21]

PHYSICAL EDUCATION AND SPORT

We can therefore content ourselves with a general analysis of this training, and ignore the differences between that which was given to young children and that which was given to the ephebes. On the whole, the spirit and the organization behind physical education were the same in the Hellenistic era as they were in the preceding age. Being a heritage from archaic times, Greek gymnastics had become fixed in their definitive form very early on, and they were not

[1] Dittenberg., *SIG.*, 959.
[2] Michel, 897.
[3] Dittenberg., *SIG*, 1058-9.
[4] Michel, 897.
[5] Dittenberg., *SIG*, 667, n.9; *IG²*, II, 957-964.
[6] *PCairo-Zenon*, I, 59060; *PSI*, 340, 23 *seq.*
[7] *IG*, VII, 1765.
[8] Dittenberg., *SIG*, 1058.
[9] Michel, 889.
[10] *IG*, XIV, 738.
[11] Michel, 893.
[12] *Ibid.*, 896.
[13] Dittenberg., *SIG*, 577; 578.
[14] Tel. *ap.* Stob., 98, 72; [Pl.] *Ax.*, 366a.
[15] *Rev. Phil.* (1909), XXIII, 6.
[16] Dittenberg., *SIG*, 802 A.
[17] *Ath.*, XIII, 566e.
[18] Dittenberg., *SIG*, 578, 14; cf. 9.
[19] *Ins. Perg.*, 463 B; cf. A.
[20] Arist., *Pol.*, VIII, 1338b, 40.
[21] Paus., V, 16, 3.

affected much by any of the later developments in Greek civilization. It is true, as I mentioned in connection with the Sophists, that from this time onwards there was a great deal of professional sport, which became further and further removed from amateur sport and consequently from school sport; it is also true that from the time of Herodicus of Selymbria to the time of the Roman physicians, the science of hygiene was becoming both more exact and more exacting, and laying claim to the whole field of physical education (4). Nevertheless, physical education remained true to its own tradition. It had little interest in any methodical scientific development of the body; as we shall see later, there were exercises approximating to the modern "Swedish drill", but for a long time they remained secondary and subordinate. As in archaic times, physical education was essentially a sporting affair, dominated by a noble spirit of emulation and competition, and preparing first the child, then the adolescent, to take part with distinction in sports meetings composed of a limited and traditional number of "events".

Other sports were in a quite different category. Even in the democratic fifth century, it may be remembered, riding contests were confined to aristocratic circles, to a minority of great landowners; and riding continued to form part of the education of this class during the Hellenistic era. Considering the snob-value assumed by the Athenian ephebia, it is not surprising to find that in the inscriptions referring to it, which date from 47–46 to 39–30 B.C.,[1] riding is placed on the same level as gymnastics and weapon-training. As in high English society today, children learned to ride at an early age, as young adolescents,[2] or even—as the physician Galen was not afraid to advise[3]—whilst they were still children, no more than seven (5).

We naturally think of the Greeks as a seafaring people, and so it comes as a surprise to find that they hardly went in for swimming sports at all. Of course they could all swim—"He can neither read nor swim" was a common way of describing a nitwit[4]—but that is not the same thing as treating it as a sport. Only in one place do we know that swimming competitions took place—or perhaps it was diving: the word κόλυμβος is ambiguous: this was at the sanctuary to Dionysius of the Black Shield, near the small town of Hermione in Argolis[5] (6).

Rowing regattas were more frequent: there were boat races at the Panathenic Games,[6] in Corcyra (7) and, at least from the time of Augustus, in Nicopolis;[7] in the Hellenistic[8] and Roman[9] era, the Athenian ephebes took part in dinghy races on the waters of Salamanos and Mounyhia. I think that the comparative lack of prestige from which these sports suffered was a legacy from early times. Most of the Greeks had become seafaring people, but they had not been so in the beginning—their far-off ancestors had come from the north, from the

[1] IG², II, 1040, 29; 1042, ab 21; c.9; 1043, 21.
[2] Tel. ap. Stob., 98, 72; Lucian, Am., 45.
[3] San. tu., I, 8.
[4] Pl., Leg., III, 689d; Suid., III M, 989.
[5] Paus., II, 35, 1.
[6] IG², II, 2311, 78.
[7] Steph. Byz., s.v. Actia.
[8] Dittenberg., SIG, 717, n.11.
[9] IG², II, 1996, 9; 2024, 136; 2119, 223; 2130, 49; 2167; 2208, 146; 2245.

continent, and it was from the knightly tradition introduced by these invaders that the sporting element in aristocratic culture directly derived; it was not particularly affected by any relics of the predominantly maritime Minoan civilization which the invaders had succeeded in displacing around the shores of the Aegean.

Greek physical education, therefore, was primarily concerned with athletics—athletics pure and simple. There were various types of ball games: a variety of fives—ἀπόρραξις—throwing the ball—φαινίνδα (in the Roman era there was ἁρπαστόν—ball in a triangle, ball in the air);[1]—and even a sort of hockey played with a crooked stick (8); but these were normally played by the younger athletes,[2] along with other sports, and they were looked upon as amusements, like knuckle-bones,[3] or at the most as exercises—it is not surprising to find a physician devoting an entire treatise to their hygienic value.[4] But they were not proper sports: they never became really popular like our modern rugby football or baseball. We never find them included in any of the Games, either the great pan-hellenic meetings or the ordinary municipal ones. The programme had never varied since the sixth century, and it determined the character of the whole teaching of sport: the list is a familiar one—running, jumping, throwing the discus, throwing the javelin, wrestling, boxing and all-in wrestling.

I will now endeavour to give a brief description of each of these sports, comparing and contrasting them with modern athletic exercises, which, as will be seen, they sometimes resemble but from which they can sometimes be very different (9).

RUNNING

First of all, running. The Greeks had no obstacle or cross-country races: all their racing took place on a straight flat track. The characteristic event was the "stadium" race—στάδιον (we might call it the "furlong"), which was not only the most popular but also to some extent the sporting event *par excellence*—the winner gave his name to the Olympiad. The same word—στάδιον—was used for the race itself, the course over which it was run, and the distance covered; the latter was six hundred feet, but as the standard foot was not the same in all cities, this represented a variable length of about two hundred and ten yards. The Olympic "stadium" was about this length, the one at Delphi about one hundred and ninety-four yards, the one at Pergamus about two hundred and thirty, but this was exceptionally long. The "furlong" was the shortest race. This seems strange to us, for although we run it ourselves, we generally look upon the hundred yards as the real test of speed. Their technique was rather different from ours, too. They did not practise the kneeling start, for instance: Greek runners started from a standing position, with their bodies bent forward and their feet very close together. To avoid congestion on the track when there were a great many competitors, they had "heats" and a final, as we do.[5]

[1] Ath. I, 14f–15b; Poll., IX, 103–107.
[2] Men. *ap*. Plaut., *Bacch.*, 428.
[3] Poll., IX, 103–107
[4] Gal., *Parv. pil.*
[5] Paus., VI, 13, 2.

Then came the longer races. There was the "double furlong"—δίαυλος—
twice round the course, or rather, as we shall see in a minute, "there and back"
—which in Olympia would be four hundred and twenty yards, very nearly the
same as our quarter-mile. The four-lap race—ἵππιος—was not so common. On
the other hand, long-distance races—δολιχός—of seven, twelve, twenty, and,
in Olympia, twenty-four laps (nearly three miles), were run everywhere. But
here is the surprising thing: all these races, whatever their length, took place on
the same standard course of one "lap", and therefore involved—like their horse-
racing—the use of two-way tracks. When the runner reached the end he turned,
probably round a post set up on the starting or finishing line (this point is not
absolutely clear). Thus in this respect their athletics were utterly different from
ours.

Most of the games also included an arms-race—ὁπλίτης—in which the
runners wore a helmet and carried a shield (after 450, greaves were no longer
used). The distance varied from city to city: it was two furlongs in Olympia
and Athens, four in Nemea, and perhaps a little more in Platea (where the rules
were particularly severe—full armour, etc.).[1] Torch races were popular too—
but these were not exactly athletics in the strict sense of the word.

Long Jump

In Greek athletics there was only one kind of jump—the long jump. There
was no high jump, no pole-vaulting; and the standing long-jump came only
into training. And here again their way of doing it was different from ours.
The run was shorter and slower. The athlete had a firm take-off—βάτηρ—
(probably at the starting-line) and landed on carefully levelled ground—σκάμμα.
The jump did not count unless his footprints showed clearly in the soil, and
this excluded slides, falls, and even (apparently) landing with one foot in front
of the other.[2] But the most striking feature was that the athlete held a stone
or bronze "dumb-bell"—ἁλτῆρες—in each hand while he made his jump:
these were round, and could be either hollowed out so that they were easy to
hold, or solid with a handle; in weight they might be anything from two pounds
to ten. They were supposed to help to balance the arms, in much the same
way as in our own standing long jump today.

Throwing the Discus

Unlike our discus, which is made of wood ringed with iron, the Greek discus,
from the end of the fifth century onwards, was made of bronze. It seems to
have been heavier than ours (which weighs about three lb.) although the examples
which have come down to us vary considerably and belong to different types,
their weights being about three lb., four and a half lb., six lb. or nine lb. There
is even one of twelve and a half lb., but this may have been a votive discus and
had no connection with those in general use. No doubt the type that was used
was different in different places and at different times, and also according to

[1] Philstr., *Gym.*, 8.   [2] *Ibid.*, 55.

who was using it: the lightest are the oldest—sixth century B.C.—and the children's discus was naturally lighter than the adults'.[1]

The actual throw seems to have differed considerably from the style that was adopted when this event was revived at the first modern Olympic Games meeting, held in Athens in 1896. There has been a great deal of argument about it, in archaeological as well as sporting circles: the question is how to interpret the various sculptured monuments that exist, the vases and paintings and statues, the standing Discobolus of Naucydas and above all the famous bronze of Myron which—since we now have only marble copies of it, and these damaged or clumsily restored—has been responsible for many a wild hypothesis.

The base—$\beta\alpha\lambda\beta\ell\varsigma$[2]—was not, as with us, a circle; it was only bounded on the front and sides, and this gave the athlete more room. The throw had to be made in a certain definite direction; as in the case of the long jump, the starting-line of the running track was no doubt used again as a $\beta\alpha\lambda\beta\ell\varsigma$. The thrower held the discus in both hands, lifted it to the level of his head and then, pressing it tightly against his right forearm with his hand, he brought this arm down violently behind him, his head and body turning and following the movement. All the weight of the body rested on the right foot, which acted as a pivot; the left foot and the left arm were simply used to keep the balance. Then came the fling: the force of it did not come from the arm but from the sudden straightening of the thigh and the bent body. The discus had previously been rubbed with sand to prevent it from slipping.

THROWING THE JAVELIN

Throwing the javelin was not only a sport; it was useful in hunting and fighting. In athletics, however, the one idea was to throw it as far as possible in a certain direction; whereas for its more utilitarian purposes the thrower practised by aiming at a horizontal target drawn on the ground. The sports-javelin, which was the length of the body and as thick as a finger, had no point, was weighted at the end and seems to have been extremely light.[3]

The method of throwing was again quite different from ours today. Something vaguely like a catapult—$\dot{\alpha}\gamma\kappa\dot{\nu}\lambda\eta$ (Latin: *amentum*)—was used: the same sort of thing is used today, especially in New Caledonia, where it goes under the name of an *ounep*. It was a leather thong a foot to eighteen inches long, which was wound round the shaft of the javelin near to its centre of gravity and ended in a loop in which the thrower inserted the first two fingers of his right hand. The value of this kind of catapult or sling—which doubles or trebles the length of the throw, as you can easily discover if you try it out—was two-fold: on the one hand it made the javelin rotate, and thus (like the barrel of a modern rifle) kept it flying straight; and on the other hand it lengthened, so to speak, the thrower's arm and outstretched fingers (this was the great aim: javelin-throwers always had very long fingers).[4] As with the discus, the throw was

---

[1] Paus., I, 35, 3.
[2] Philstr., *Im.*, I, 24.
[3] Lucian, *Anach.*, 32.
[4] Philstr., *Gym.*, 31.

preceded by a little spring and a general tensing of the body, the trunk and head following the right arm as it was thrown back as far as it could possibly go.

WRESTLING

Wrestling enjoyed perhaps even greater popularity than running: there is fairly clear evidence for this in the fact that the word παλαίστρα, which, strictly speaking, meant a "ground for wrestling"—πάλη—was used both for the sports field and the school for physical education. Wrestling in the proper sense, i.e. standing wrestling—ὀρθή or σταδιαία πάλη—took place on ground that had been broken up with a pick in the same way as for the jump. The athletes were paired off after drawing lots, and the wrestler's object was to throw his opponent to the ground without falling himself—if he did the throw was not counted. It did not matter how the opponent landed—he could fall on his back or his shoulder or his hip—but it was not enough merely to bring him to his knees. There were three rounds to a match. Tripping seems to have been allowed, but not leg-holds: the only holds permitted were on the arms, the neck and the body.

These five events—flat race, long jump, throwing the discus, throwing the javelin and wrestling—made up that part of the Games known as the *pentathlon*, which decided who was to be crowned as the best all-round athlete. In modern times there has been a great deal of controversy about the order of the events and the rules of placing, but it seems certain that the flat race came first and wrestling last, and the general opinion is that the winner had to come first in at least three of the five events.

BOXING

At the beginning of the fourth century "hard bandages"—ἱμάντες ὀξεῖς or σφαῖραι—were substituted for "soft bandages"—ἱμάντες μαλακώτεροι—for boxing. These "hard bandages" were a kind of glove—or rather mitten, for the fingers were left uncovered—and were probably made of leather. They covered the wrist and most of the forearm, and were fastened below the elbow by a sheepskin band. The fingers were kept in place by a supplementary bandage of three or five strips of hard leather held in position by laces.

The boxing of antiquity was somewhat different from the boxing of the present day.[1] There was no ring, and this meant less clinching; on the other hand there was more scope for tactics and for foot-work. There were no rounds. The fight went on until one of the competitors was exhausted, or admitted defeat by raising his arm. The pace was consequently much slower than in modern boxing. As in the bare-fist matches in eighteenth-century England, blows were aimed chiefly at the head;[2] and this meant a high guard and extended arm. We are told that there was a champion in the reign of the Emperor Titus who could keep his guard up for two whole days and tire his opponent out without letting him land a single blow.[3]

[1] Theoc., 22.   [2] Philstr., *Gym.*, 9.   [3] Dio Chrys., *Or.*, XXIX.

ALL-IN WRESTLING ("PANCRATIUM")

Finally we come to the most violent and brutal event in ancient athletics—the "pancratium", which is usually described as a combination of boxing and wrestling but which was, in fact, very different from either; it was more like all-in wrestling. The aim was to knock one's opponent out or to make him raise one of his arms as a sign that he gave in. Anything was allowed—not only the usual boxing punches and wrestling holds but kicks in the stomach, twisting the arms and legs, biting, strangling, etc. The only thing that was disallowed was putting your fingers in your opponent's eyes or nose or mouth.

Usually, after a few passes, the two adversaries rolled onto the ground locked together, and went on fighting there until the match was over. The holds were very different from those used in ordinary wrestling and were known as κύλισις or ἀλίνδησις.

It was thus a fairly brutal kind of sport, and the finishing touch was that it was fought out on ground that was not only dug up with a pick but watered, so that the contestants floundered and slid and rolled about until they were soon covered in mud from head to foot.

THE TEACHING OF GYMNASTICS

Such was the kind of physical education given to children and adolescents in the Hellenistic age. The person in charge of it was a highly specialised teacher who, though he retained the old name "pedotribe"—παιδοτρίβης—was much more than a P.T. instructor. He was a genuine educator, and besides athletic ability he needed to have a profound knowledge of the laws of hygiene and of all the rules and prescriptions about the development of the body that had been amassed by Greek medical science—the effects on the body of different exercises, the kind of diet and training that suited different temperaments. The physical training of the young gained a great deal from the scientific study of gymnastics that had accompanied the rise of professionalism.[1] To get some idea of the refinement and precision attained by the Greek analytical genius in this sphere, one needs to read Philostratus' detailed analysis of the qualities required for each particular exercise. The pedotribe did not, presumably, go to such lengths as the professional trainer (generally known as the "gymnast"—γυμναστής),[2] but he could not afford to disregard the new discoveries and managed to incorporate them in his own teaching.

It was a highly organized system of instruction, forming a complete whole. When the pedotribe did not receive a monthly salary, as in the "State" schools in Teos and Miletus,[3] he made an agreement with the parents for a fixed sum to cover the whole course—in about 320 B.C. this sum was somewhere round a hundred drachmae.[4] We do not know as much about the pedotribe's methods of teaching as we do about the literature teacher's, but the little we do know suggests that they were very similar. They were not simply a matter of copying

[1] *Gym.*, 28–42.
[2] *Ibid.*, 14; Gal., *San. tu.*, II, 9.
[3] Dittenberg., *SIG*, 578, 14; 577.
[4] Ath., XIII, 584c.

and practising. The Greeks always tried to rise above the purely empirical level, and in this matter their love of clear thinking obliged them to subject the different movements involved in the various athletic exercises to a close and detailed scrutiny. As in the field of literary education, this led to highly elaborate theories which the master passed on to his pupils in the form of instructions.[1]

The thing we know most about is the way wrestling was taught. The pedotribe used to teach the different positions or "figures"—σχήματα—in turn, and then the wrestler would use them in the actual match. In a papyrus dating from the second century A.D. we have a fragment from a master's handbook which enables us to watch a wrestling lesson being given to two pupils:

> Get up close to him and put your right arm round his head!
> You, put your arms round him!
> You, get hold of him from underneath!
> You, move forward and hug him!
> You, get hold of him from underneath with your right arm!
> You, put your arms around him where he has got hold of you from underneath and bring your left leg up to his side!
> You, push him away with your left hand!
> You, change your place and clasp him!
> You, turn round!
> You, catch hold of him by the testicles!
> You, bring your foot forward!
> You, get hold of him round the waist!
> You, throw your weight forward and bend him backwards!
> You, bring your body forward and straighten up: [pounce] on him and give him as good as you get! . . .[2]

I have ventured to translate this passage (10), which is in fact very obscure. Hellenistic Greek had an extraordinarily rich vocabulary of technical terms for teaching purposes and its secrets are difficult to fathom, but it was so familiar to the average cultivated reader that it could be used by pornographic authors in their blunt descriptions of the various stages of sexual intercourse.[3]

LOOSENING-UP EXERCISES

The same passion for analysis had also led the pedotribes to produce a whole system of loosening-up exercises for the benefit of their pupils. They were meant to be a kind of indirect preparation for the athletic events themselves, and here again Greek teachers showed tremendous analytical acumen and inventive skill. The list of exercises grew continually in the course of the centuries and reached its height in the second and third centuries of the

---

[1] Th., *Char.*, 7.
[2] *POxy.*, 466.
[3] Lucian, *As.*, 8–10; *Anth.*, XII, 206.

Christian era.[1] It included hiking; running thirty yards or so; running round a circular course; running backwards and forwards; running and skipping with the feet hitting the buttocks (the women of Sparta's favourite exercise);[2] kicking the legs in the air; various movements of the arms—χειρονομία;[3] not to mention more complicated exercises like rope-climbing and games with balls and hoops.[4]

It is easy to understand how these exercises developed. Many of them originated quite naturally as a by-product of athletics, and then, by a natural transition from means to ends, became things in their own right. Thus the need to prepare loose ground—σκάμμα—for wrestling or jumping meant that the athlete had to use a pick—as a matter of fact the pick was part of the equipment: it is often shown in fifth-century vase-paintings of the games. Finally it was recognized that wielding a pick was good exercise and so it became one of the "violent exercises" for strengthening the muscles.

In the same way boxers' training led to the development of arm exercises— keeping the arms stretched out, remaining on guard a long time with clenched fists, keeping the arm up with someone trying to force it down, and so on.[6] Hence too the use of a punch-bag—κώρυκος—a leather bag filled with small seeds or sand that hung down from the ceiling at chest height. This was not only used by the pugilists but by the all-in wrestlers too: they practised by letting it swing back onto their heads or bodies so as to improve their balance.[7]

Training for the long jump led to the development of exercises carried out in a stationary position, e.g. with dumb-bells,[8] and soon quite a number of exercises grew up which were similar to those we have nowadays: trunk forward bend, right hand to left foot, then the other way round—and so on.[9]

The specifically Greek feature about all these exercises was the fact that they were performed to the sound of an oboe. Attached to each establishment was an *auletes*, whose job it was to provide a rhythmic accompaniment to the athletes' movements—and, curiously, he not only played for the loosening-up exercises but for the various events of the *pentathlon* too (11).

By the end of this process the scope of Greek gymnastics had in a way been doubled: side by side with the purely sporting technique which had existed from the very beginning, there had grown up a complete system of health exercises that are very reminiscent of the "analytical method" of nineteenth-century Swedish drill. Our information about this comes mainly from the medical literature of the Roman era, but it would be a mistake to think that it was only used by physicians for health reasons—though it did serve this purpose: walking on tip-toe[10] was prescribed for ophthalmia and constipation, running

[1] Lucian, *Anach.*, 4; Gal., *San. tu.*, II, 9–10; Antyll. *ap.* Orib., VI, 22; 35.
[2] *Ibid.*, VI, 31.
[3] *Ibid.*, VI, 30.
[4] *Ibid.*, VI, 26; 32. Gal., *San. tu.*, II, 9.
[5] *Ibid.*, II, 9–10.
[6] *Ibid.*, II, 9, 141.
[7] Philstr., *Gym.*, 57; Sor., I, 49; Antyll. *ap.* Orib., VI, 33.
[8] Philstr., *Gym.*, 55; Antyll. *ap.* Orib., VI, 34.
[9] Gal., *San. tu.*, II, 10, 145.
[10] Antyll. *ap.* Orib., VI, 21, 9.

for gonorrhoea,[1] swimming for dropsy.[2] But we have Galen's own word for it that this side of gymnastics was devised to meet the educational needs of youths from fourteen years onwards, and possibly even younger.[3]

THE CARE OF THE BODY

Greek athletes always performed in the nude. This remained one of the most striking differences between the Greeks and the barbarians. As we have seen, it had been the rule ever since the eighth century.[4] It is surprising that the abandonment of small shorts as worn by the Minoans should have been regarded as a technical improvement: complete nudity is not such a great advantage from the athletic point of view, and it may have its disadvantages! (12).

They had nothing on their feet, even for jumping and running. Their track was a great deal softer than ours, of course: the ground was cleared, loosened with a pick, flattened and covered with a thick layer of sand[5] so that the foot would sink in.[6] This is another case in which Greek athletics differed from ours.

And the athletes had nothing on their heads, as a rule, even under the burning summer sun,[7] though some of the more delicate ones wore a curious little cap, made from dog-skin, apparently,[8] and tied by a lace under the chin—very much like the bonnet worn by French peasants in thirteenth-century Gothic sculptures (13).

But perhaps the most characteristic feature of Greek gymnastics was the practice of rubbing the body with oil. Here again it is the medical writing of the time that we must consult to get some idea of the importance attached to this practice, and the detailed precision of its rules. The body was massaged all over in a lukewarm room before each exercise. After a preliminary dry rub carried out with only moderate vigour, the oil, which took the place of our embrocation, was applied—rubbed in with the bare hand, gently at first, and then more vigorously (this varied according to the child's age, of course).[9] And then, in complete contrast, there was the "apotherapeutic" massage, which came after each exercise and was supposed to get rid of fatigue and relax the muscles, just as the first massage had loosened them up.[10] This apotherapeutic massage was just as complicated and the oil was just as important. In fact oil was one of the main items of any decent gymnasiarch's expenditure, and every young athlete carried a small bottle of it in his kit.

This general practice of massaging with oil was adopted mainly for hygienic reasons; only to a very secondary degree were other considerations involved, such as making the skin slippery and in consequence more difficult to hold in the all-in wrestling.[11] In actual fact the use of oil was followed by another stage

---

[1] Antyll. *ap.* Orib., VI, 22, 3.
[2] *Ibid.*, VI, 27, 2.
[3] Gal., *San. tu.*, II, 1, 81; II, 2, 91.
[4] Paus., I, 44, 1.
[5] *BCH* (1899) XXIII, 566, 5 *seq.*
[6] Lucian, *Anach.*, 27.
[7] *Ibid.*, 16.
[8] Poll., X, 64.
[9] Gal., *San. tu.*, II, 2; 3, 7 (= Orib., VI, 13).
[10] Gal., *ibid.*, III, 2 (= Orib., VI, 16; cf. 17–20).
[11] Lucian, *Anach.*, 28.

in the treatment which had the opposite effect. For after he had been duly massaged, the athlete would cover himself with a thin layer of dust which he sifted through his fingers over his skin[1]—and indeed some writers tell us that the object of this was to make the hold on the body in wrestling more secure by making the skin less slippery.[2] But more often it was reasons of health that determined this practice too, for the dust was said to regulate the flow of perspiration and protect the skin from the weather (did they mean the sun's rays or the cold wind?).[3] Here again we find a carefully graded system with precise rules. Galen seems to have regarded the use of dust as too harsh a treatment for the very young.[4] Philostratus enumerated five different kinds of dust, each with its own distinctive properties: mud dust was a detergent; pottery dust caused perspiration (although according to Lucian dust prevented too much sweating); asphalt dust gave warmth; black or yellow earth dust was excellent for massage and for feeding the skin, and the yellow had the additional advantage of imparting a shine to the body and making it pleasant to look at.[5] So as soon as the exercises were over, the athletes needed a thorough clean-up, beginning with a good scrape with a bronze curry-comb—στλεγγίς:[6] and when we try to imagine, in the words of J. M. de Hérédia,

the naked athletes under the clear Greek skies

we should do well to take the somewhat idealised renderings of the neo-classical poets with more than a grain of salt, and see them instead in the heat of the sun, and standing in a dust-raising wind,[7] their greasy skins covered with a layer of coloured earth—not forgetting the blood-stained all-in wrestlers rolling in the mud. . . .[8]

In the centre paraded the pedotribe. He was not naked, but clad impressively in a purple cloak[9] to emphasize the autocratic nature of his teaching (though with a shrug of the shoulders he could throw off his *himation* and give any demonstration he considered necessary). His authority was reinforced by the curious mark of office that he carried—a long forked stick which he used not so much to indicate or rectify the position of a limb as to administer vigorous correction to a clumsy pupil or anyone caught cheating or attempting foul play in the course of a match (14). When we come to deal with the schools for reading and writing we shall see how brutal the old education was; so that a school of gymnastics could hardly be expected to show any particular squeamishness on this point.

GYMNASIUMS AND PALESTRAS

As for the school itself, we sometimes find it called a palestra, sometimes a gymnasium. The two words were certainly not synonymous, but in Hellenistic

[1] Philstr., *Gym.*, 56.
[2] Lucian, *Anach.*, 2; 29.
[3] *Ibid.*, 29.
[4] Gal., *San. tu.*, II, 12, 162.
[5] Philstr., *Gym.*, 56; cf. 42.
[6] *Ibid.*, 18.
[7] Lucian, *Am.*, 45.
[8] Lucian, *Anach.*, 1–3.
[9] *Ibid.*, 3.

usage the various meanings were so inextricably intertwined that modern scholarship has given up the attempt to make any sharp distinction between them (the reader may remember that similar difficulties are caused by titles like "cosmetes", "gymnasiarch" etc.—it is a mistake to think that Hellenistic Greek was a uniform language: the meaning of the words varied at different times and different places). Sometimes the palestra is described as the children's school and the gymnasium as the place where the ephebes and adults performed; sometimes it is a private school, and the gymnasium the municipal institution. I am more inclined to look upon the relationship between them as that between the whole and the part, the gymnasium being the whole, made up of the palestra—i.e. the practice-ground with all its equipment—and the actual running track or *stadion* (15).

Whatever we call them, palestras or gymnasiums, there were so many of them in the Hellenistic world that they have provided a rich harvest for archaeological excavations, and what is particularly fortunate is that they are all of a highly uniform type, so that they help to explain each other, especially in the light of a commentary on them in a chapter of Vitruvius,[1] not to mention epigraphical evidence like the inventory we have of a gymnasium in Delos.[2]

As a typical example we may take the lower gymnasium in Priene, whose excavation has been completed and the results published in a most satisfactory manner. It dates from the second century B.C. (before 130), and its lay-out, which is quite clear, is very characteristic, with none of the disfigurements that are to be seen in gymnasiums constructed later under Roman influence (16).

The Priene gymnasium is in the southern part of this small city, immediately above the rampart. It stands on a terrace, and is surrounded by a strong wall built into the side of the steep hill on which Priene stands. The entrance, to which steps and columns give a monumental effect like that of the Propylaea, opens out on to a terraced street. On the west is a courtyard, roughly square, facing east and surrounded by porticos; this is what we shall call the palestra proper. It is between thirty-seven and thirty-eight yards long (about a hundred feet: a little less than the model described by Vitruvius). This court-yard formed the sports-ground on which most of the exercises were carried out: the soil must have been dug up and covered with sand.

The entrance to the palestra was on the west side; north of the entrance was an "exedra" between two columns; on the south were three rooms which, following the epigraphical inventory of a gymnasium in Delos,[3] I take to have been dressing-rooms—ἀποδυτήριον. In perfect keeping with Vitruvius' rule, the northern portico has a double depth with two rows of columns "to protect the interior from squalls when the south wind blows up". It was behind this portico, up against the hill, that the most important buildings stood: they must have had an upper storey, of which nothing is left, but on the ground floor are five rooms, and the purpose of two of these is quite clear (17).

First of all, in the centre, is a splendid room, wider than it is long (about thirty feet by twenty), with a high ceiling and an opening through two columns. Its walls are faced with rich marble to a height of ten feet. High up on the wall

[1] Vitr., V, 11.   [2] *BCH* (1930), LIV, 97–98.   [3] *Ibid.*, 97, l. 123; 125.

at the far end is a row of pilasters with an arcade in the middle over the statue of a draped standing figure—no doubt some city-benefactor who had been specially generous to the gymnasium. This is obviously the ephebeum mentioned by Vitruvius—i.e. the ephebes' common-room and lecture-hall: there are hundreds of scratchings on the wall made by the ephebes: "This is so-and-so's place, son of so-and-so."[1] There is always a room like this, and always in the same place; in the splendid gymnasiums of the Roman era, like the one in Pergamus for example, it had developed into a little semicircular theatre with steps leading up to it. The one in Priene seems to have been called "the ephebes' exedra", according to an inscription[2] that describes the dedication of two figures of Hermes that were put up as part of the decoration: such figures, and statues, the gifts of generous donors, were in fact usually put up to decorate the palestra and its porticos (17).

The north-west corner of the portico opened on to the cold baths, the *frigida lavatio—λουτρόν—*mentioned by Vitruvius. In the Roman era hot baths were added, and these quickly spread, to such an extent that in Latin countries they became the really important thing and the palestra took second place. But Priene dates from much earlier times, and has the kind of simplicity that is to be seen in fifth-century vase-paintings: along the shorter wall, at chest height, ran a trough, into which a number of lion's heads shot streams of water—a system that reminds one of the primitive washing facilities that can still be found in so many of our own barracks and old schools. The high quality of the mouldings and the lion's heads may have added to the appearance, but it can hardly have made the place any more comfortable.

As for the other three rooms, these must be the three annexes also described by Vitruvius. The only question is, which is which? As I see it, the room to the right of the ephebeum must be the *coryceum*—the room with the punch-bag (the only exercise practised indoors); and the other two rooms the *elaeothesium*, the oil-store, and the *conisterium*, the sand- and dust-store—all these things, it will be remembered, being necessary for the care of the skin. The room in the north-east corner (the *conisterium*?) is obviously bigger than the other, and that, I should think, is where the massaging was done—in the shade, as prescribed by the physicians.

In the same north-east corner of the palestra is a small door leading to the running-track, which was also used for the discus and javelin, and perhaps for the long jump as well. Because of the slope of the hill there are three distinct levels. On the lowest, five yards down from the palestra, is the actual track itself—the στάδιον or δρόμος—about twenty yards wide and two hundred and ten yards long. Unfortunately, no traces have been found of the finishing-line, and so we cannot tell what its exact length was. But we are able to study the arrangements at the starting-line. The excavations have brought to light the remains of two different ones, one of which must have been installed after the other. The simpler and better preserved one is on the inside, and has eight bases, upon each of which a pillar must have stood. Between these pillars, at the start of the race, the runners took up their positions, with their feet touching

---

[1] *Ins. Priene*, 313.   [2] *Ibid.*, 112, l. 114-115.

a double line drawn in the sand; in the longer races they had to go round these pillars—so it is supposed—and then set off down the straight. The second was further to the west and seems to have been more monumental, but the state in which it was discovered is so bad that one cannot speak with any certainty about it. Possibly, as at Olympia and Epidaurus and Delphi, the starting-line was actually a stone one set in the ground, with each runner's position again indicated by pillars; and perhaps in this more advanced type of arrangement the signal for the start was not a shout from the herald but the opening of a barrier.

To the north, higher up, was the spectators' "enclosure"—twelve rows of steps extending for only a third of the length of the track; if these were not enough, the spectators had to make do with wooden seats or the natural slope of the ground itself. Conditions here only allowed for one block of steps; the more usual plan, when the stadium was built on flat ground or in a valley, was two lines of steps joined by semi-circular ones—σφενδόνη.

Finally, right at the top, level with the entrance, was a portico twenty-five feet wide and as long as the stadium, with an exit at the north-east corner. This was a covered track—ξυστός—which enabled the runner to practise in bad weather and which could also be used for walking or resting in, in the shade.

THE DECLINE OF GYMNASTICS

This brings us to the end of our brief account of the physical education of old, its events, methods and conditions, which, by ancient and modern historians alike, have been acclaimed as the distinctive feature of the education of those days. But though sport continued to occupy a prominent place in education, in the first centuries of the Hellenistic era, at least, it must be realized that it had lost its earlier vitality: it was a heritage of the past, looked upon with reverence, no doubt, but no longer essential to the culture of the future. Hellenistic physical education remained static, in fact, showing very little change from that of previous centuries; the only notable development, as we have seen, were the "Swedish" health exercises. It made no further progress. It was faced with the competition of the professional athletes, and technically the sport learned in the schools could not bear comparison with the professionals', which started giving its champions specialized training from the time they were children and achieved a higher standard of performance all round. But the main cause of the decline of athletics was, as we shall see, the development of other "subjects", especially literature. This had become the really dynamic element in the culture of the day, and it tended to monopolize the whole of the young people's time and energy and interest.

My own opinion is that athletics slowly lost the prestige and importance they had originally had in Greek education. This is of course difficult to prove satisfactorily, especially in the matter of dates for the early stages of the decline, though it is worth reading what Xenophon said about Jason of Pheres (375 B.C.) in *Hellenics*, VI, 1, 5. I do not think, however, that it can be seriously doubted—though I am aware that my statement would not be allowed to pass unchallenged by the specialists. But in these matters an apparent continuity often conceals new developments. In the last years of the second century A.D., we still find Termessos in Pisidia arranging contests for school-children in jumping, racing, "pancratium" and wrestling (18). The inscriptions[1] give lists of winners just like those of four centuries earlier that are to be found here and there all over the Greek world, particularly in Ionia.

This conservative tradition was particularly tenacious in certain districts and amongst certain sections of society. For example, in the colonial centres in the Egyptian countryside the Greeks were so anxious to remain distinct from the barbarians around them that they clung to their athletics as an infallible sign of Hellenism, truer and easier to recognize than any ties of blood. The same thing was true in the wealthy aristocratic circles, particularly in Athens and Asia Minor, which from this time onwards provided all the pupils for the ephebia. In Asia Minor, to judge by some of the numismatic and epigraphic documents of the Imperial age, it sometimes seems as though nothing had changed since the time of Pindar: the winners of the great games are still being loaded with honours; they still seem to come from the noblest and wealthiest families, and the latter continue to bathe in the reflected glory of their successes ... (19).

On the other hand, we have the literary evidence, which frequently gives us quite a different picture of these champions. Admiration for their performances, it cannot be denied, mingles with contempt for them as individuals. They did not all come from the "plutocracy" by any means. Many of them came from the slums—uncultured brutes whose arduous physical training prevented any sort of spiritual or intellectual development at all.[2] The barbarous athletic types depicted in the art of the Roman era[3] show how far the original ideal of a perfect balance between mind and body had been forgotten.

Before we can form any opinion on the effect of these conflicting tendencies we need to take a bit of a jump to the end of the classical era. In the Greek-speaking countries the classical literary education persisted after the triumph of Christianity, but the physical education disappeared completely. As we have already seen, A.D. 323 was the last date at which ephebes appeared in any sporting events[4]—in Oxyrrhynchus in Egypt. The last mention of a gymnasiarch occurs two generations later, in 370, also in Oxyrrhynchus.[5] At about the same date, St. Basil refers for the last time to the gymnasiums,[6] and Himerius to the palestras;[7] somewhat later—shortly after 400—Synesius writes of a pedotribe.[8] These are only brief references, and they hardly conjure up a picture of a flourishing institution. This is not a misuse of the argument *a silentio*, for we have detailed evidence of the type of life led by Greek students in the fourth century A.D. and we know a great deal about their occupations and pastimes. And sport, in the strict sense of the word, was conspicuous by its absence. Of course, like all young people they played open-air games—ball games, etc.[9]

[1] *TAM*, III, 1, 201–210; 4.
[2] Plut., *San. pr.*, 133bd; Gal., *Protr.*, 13 *seq.*
[3] *RPGR*, 280–283.
[4] *POxy.*, 42.
[5] *Ibid.*, 2110.
[6] *Ep.*, LXXIV, 448a.
[7] *Or.*, XXII, 7.
[8] Syn., *Ep.*, XXII.
[9] Lib., *Or.*, I, 22.

—but these were simply pastimes: their education was completely intellectual, and athletics had no place in it.

No one denies that physical education was quite dead in the Christian era and that its death had been a natural one, unaccompanied by any violent revolution—history would have told us if there had been anything of the kind. It had simply died of old age. The attitude of Christian moralists and apologists seems to confirm this view. There would have been so much that they could have objected to in ancient gymnastics—its immodesty, its sexual immorality, its vanity. And yet, strange to relate, they do not seem to have done so. It is true that the Fathers of the Church have many pages dissuading Christians from the passion for athletics, but the remarkable fact is that their criticism is directed against sport as a spectacle, against professional sport, not against any kind of amateur sport. For example, St. Gregory Nazianzen, writing to his great-nephew Nicobolus somewhere between 384 and 390, denounces the frivolity of people who waste their time and money at the stadium or the palestra or the circus;[1] but this criticism is simply one of many, and they are all directed against shows of one kind or another—the bloody combats in the amphitheatre,[2] the indecent mimes in the theatre.[3] This had also been the attitude of the second- and third-century apologists, Tatian[4] and Tertullian.[5] It was as a form of entertainment, not as a system of education, that athletics presented a problem for the Christian conscience.

That professional sporting events played an important part in Greek life throughout the Early Empire, and until late in the fourth century, is shown by the remarkable number of metaphors taken from sport that are to be found in Christian writers from St. Paul[6] to St. John Chrysostom (20); but this persistent vogue could quite easily coincide with the decline of gymnastics as a form of education for the young. In our own days we can see the same thing—a contrast and even an opposition between sport as a spectacle and sport as a part of education. The young people of France are passionately fond of all kinds of sport, and yet many people competent to judge do not consider it to play a role of first-class importance in their education.

---

[1] *Carm.*, II, 11, 4, 154–157.
[2] *Ibid.*, 149–153.
[3] *Ibid.*, 157–162.
[4] Tat., 23.
[5] Tert., *Spect.*, 11; cf. 5–10; 12: [Cypr.] *Spect.*, II, 2–4.
[6] I Cor. ix, 24–26, etc.

CHAPTER IV

ARTISTIC EDUCATION

TRADITIONALLY, artistic education meant instruction in music, but music was not the only one of the fine arts taught at school. Greek education, reflecting, as we should expect, the development of culture as a whole, also included the plastic arts by introducing drawing-lessons into its syllabus (1).

DRAWING

Drawing made its first appearance in liberal education in Sicyon in the fourth century under the influence of the painter Pamphilus, one of Apelles' teachers,[1] and from Sicyon it spread to the whole of Greece. For Aristotle it was still only an "extra" subject which a few pupils took in addition to the normal curriculum of literature, gymnastics and music;[2] but a century later, in about the year 240, the drawing teacher—ζωγράφος—was a regular member of the teaching staff,[3] and the subject he taught—ζωγραφία—figures as one of the subjects in the school examinations that were being held in Teos[4] and Magnesia ad Meandrum[5] in the second century B.C.

Little is known about this subject. The child learned to draw (with charcoal) and no doubt also to paint on a board made of box-wood.[6] The words ζωγράφος, ζωγραφία—literally, "drawing from a live model"—seem to indicate—and it would be only natural—that the human figure was the chief model. Although we should not place too much reliance on the etymological sense of a term that had become hackneyed, it is nevertheless true that bodily beauty is the thing to which Aristotle is referring in that valuable passage[7] in which he tries to define the proper function of the drawing lesson—whose purpose, he says, is in no sense practical but the refinement of the sense of sight and the feeling for line and form.

In theory, right up to late Roman times, the plastic arts had an acknowledged place in advanced education.[8] When Porphyry relates the history of Pythagoras, he takes it for granted that he had had drawing lessons.[9] But we have not enough evidence to be sure that instruction in drawing was always given. Probably, having come on the scene so late, and having been unable to establish itself firmly in the educational scheme, the new subject was unable to withstand the competition of the various literary subjects which were then rising rapidly in importance—as I shall show later.

[1] Pliny, *HN*, XXXV, 77.
[2] *Polit.*, VIII, 1337b 25.
[3] Tel. *ap.* Stob., 98, 72.
[4] Michel, 913, 10.
[5] Dittenberg., *SIG*, 960, 13.
[6] Pliny, *HN*, XXXV, 77.
[7] *Polit.*, VIII, 1338a 40 *seq.*
[8] Vitr., I, 1; Gal., *Protr.*, 14; Philstr., *Gym.*, 1.
[9] *V. Pyth.*, 11.

Music battled much longer, and much harder—but then music, as we have seen, belonged to the very essence of the old Greek cultural tradition.

INSTRUMENTAL MUSIC: THE LYRE

In Greek culture—and therefore in Greek education—music was at least as important as gymnastics. To take instrumental music first: in the fifth century, to judge by the delightful genre paintings that are to be found on vases signed Douris, Euphronios, Hieron and Euthymedes (2), the young Athenians learned to play both the instruments which were essential to ancient music—the lyre, and the *aulos* (which should not be translated, as it so often is, as "flute"; it was an oboe) (3).

Later, the *aulos* became unpopular in Athens—there is a well-known story describing how young Alcibiades refused to learn it because he said it made him screw his face up[1]—but it was not given up at once by the rest of the city! It was still being taught in the fourth century,[2] when Aristotle expressly excluded it from his educational theory,[3] and although it may have persisted longer in districts like Boeotia, where it was a kind of national instrument, Hellenistic education seems on the whole to have followed Aristotle. One obscure remark to the contrary by Strabo[4] is nothing compared with the significant silence of the epigraphic winners' lists; the *aulos* was entirely absent from school examinations in the second century B.C.

From then on, the only instrument taught was the lyre—Terpander's old seven-stringed lyre; music teachers were very conservative, and they had not adopted the technical improvements and harmonic refinements which the "modern" school of composers had made in the great concert cithern (4). The lyre was an instrument with open strings, like our harp, and, because of the small number of its strings, it had a very limited range. It was played either with the fingers or with a *plectrum* made of shell like the one used for the modern mandoline. These necessitated two playing techniques that were sufficiently different to form two separate subjects in the examinations, as we can see from the second-century winners' lists which have been found in Chios[5] and Teos,[6] in which a careful distinction is made between ψαλμός (playing with the *plectrum*) and κιθαρισμός (playing with the fingers).

To tell the truth, we know very little about how music was taught at this time. There was a special teacher for music—only rarely[7] did the same person teach literature as well. The instruction seems to have been entirely practical. Greek musical theory had been very advanced from the time of Aristoxenus of Tarentum, and was in fact one of the finest achievements of the Greek genius (5), but there was a wide gulf between theory and practice. The theory of music was a science, part, since the time of Pythagoras, of the *corpus* of the mathematical sciences: we shall find it again there, but in a context quite foreign to any teaching of music as an art (6).

[1] Plut., *Alc.*, 2; Gell., XV, 17.
[2] Xen., *Mem.*, I, 2, 27.
[3] *Polit.*, VIII, 1341a 18.
[4] I, 15.
[5] Dittenberg., *SIG*, 959, 10.
[6] Michel, 913, 6–7.
[7] Eup., 10–11; Quint., I, 10, 17.

Indeed it is not even certain that the pupil was obliged to learn to read music (7). According to fifth-century vase paintings, at least (8), the teacher, with his lyre in his hand, and the pupil, holding his by his side, seem to have sat face to face, the master playing and the pupil first listening and then trying to imitate him as best he could. The teaching was thus done by the "direct method", without anything being written down—*ad orecchio*, as they say in Naples, where even in our own day—in the 'thirties of this century, to be precise—I saw a teacher using this very method to teach the piano to people who could not read. The fact that Greek music was melodic made it easier to memorise than ours, and strange though it may seem there is really nothing extraordinary about it— right up to our own times all Arab music has been handed on by memory in just the same way.

CHORAL AND ACCOMPANIED SINGING

Besides learning to play, the young Greeks also learned to sing—in fact the two frequently went together, for, unlike the *aulos*, the lyre could be played and sung to by the same person. The school examinations in Teos[1] and Magnesia ad Meandrum[2] in the third century A.D., included a test in "accompanied singing"—κιθαρῳδία—as well as a lyre solo.

But the main thing was choral singing, which from the musical point of view was extremely simple. Vocal polyphony being unknown, the choirs sang in unison, or in mixed choruses at an octave interval[3], and moreover were always led by an instrument, usually the *aulos*.

These choirs were required for the many religious ceremonies in which the city's official worship found expression—and great care was taken in organizing the citizens, adults and children, to take part in these ceremonies in fifth- and fourth-century Athens (9). They took place at the time of certain feasts—the Dionysia, the Thargelia, the Panathenaea—and were accompanied by inter-tribal competitions. Each tribe was represented by its own choir, formed by some rich citizen—the *choregos*—and trained at his expense. This onerous duty —the *choregia*—was considered a great honour, and more than one successful *choregos* sought to immortalize his victory by erecting a monument over the bronze tripod on which he had received his prize. (Here again we find the same love of glory, the same rather ostentatious pride, which is so characteristic of the Greeks.) A number of these graceful "choregic" monuments have lasted right up to our own day, the best known being the one erected by Lysicrates in 335–334:

Lysicrates, son of Lysitheides, of the deme of Kikynna, being choregos, the Akamantis tribe was the winner in the children's competition. Oboe: Theon. Teacher: Lysiades of Athens. Choirmaster: Euainetos.[4]

In the Hellenistic era, however, with its stress on the proper performance and high artistic quality of the ceremonies, these choirs were in many cases no

[1] Michel, 913, 8.
[2] Dittenberg., *SIG*, 960, 9.
[3] Arist., *Pr.*, XIX, 918a 6 *seq.*; b 40.
[4] Dittenberg., *SIG*, 1087; cf. 1081 *seq.*

longer composed of amateurs specially recruited for the occasion from the body of the citizens—they sometimes even had their names perpetuated in inscriptions[1]; their duties would be entrusted instead to troupes of professional artists—τεχνῖται—members of the colleges or syndicates which had sprung up in Greece in Alexander's time. Thus, when in 138–137 the city of Athens revived the fourth-century practice of sending an official delegation or "theoria", known as the *Pythaïs* (10), to Delphi, the official delegation included the usual chorus of young children.[2] At the next Pythaïs, in 128–127, we find the same "Pythaist children"[3] present, but their rôle has become a silent one, and the paean in honour of the god is sung by a chorus of thirty-nine professionals,[4] part of the large troupe of Athenian τεχνῖται—sixty in all—which accompanied the delegation on this occasion and whose brilliant performance at the ceremonies was acclaimed by the whole of Delphi.[5]

The words and music of two of the hymns sung to Apollo on this occasion have been discovered inscribed on the walls of the Athenian Treasury,[6] so that we are able to form some idea of the value of their performance.

Nevertheless, either because of religious scruples, or a conservative attachment to old customs, or merely from reasons of economy (11), these choruses were still sung in many places by the young people of the city, and there is considerable evidence that they continued to be so from the third and second centuries B.C. right up to Roman times. In a few rare cases there were choirs of ephebes, as in Ephesus in A.D. 44[7] and in Athens in A.D. 163–164,[8] but generally the choirs were composed of younger boys, as in Delphi and Delos[9] in the third century B.C., in Arcady in the second[10] and in Pergamus[11] and Stratonicea[12] at the time of the Emperors. There were also girls' choirs—in Magnesia ad Meandrum in the second century B.C.[13]—and mixed choirs, as for example, in the second century again, in Teos[14] (where the girls danced as well).[15]

We have already seen how important it was for school-children and members of young men's clubs to take part officially, as a matter of social duty and legal obligation, in the religious ceremonies, and we shall soon see what a large place these festivals had in the school calendar. It is clear, therefore, that the ceremonies played a considerable part in the education of Hellenistic youth. But it does not necessarily follow that choral singing was one of the main subjects of the curriculum. Considering the very elementary character of the music, regular teaching would hardly be necessary: the children chosen for the choir could simply be put under a singing master—χοροδιδάσκαλος[16]—for a few rehearsals—it would not take him long to prepare them. To return to the Pythaïs of 138–137: the Athenian boys were conducted by Elpinikios and

---

[1] *Ibid.*, 1091.
[2] *F. Delph.*, III, 2, 11.
[3] *Ibid.*, 12.
[4] *Ibid.*, 47, 9.
[5] *Ibid.*, 47.
[6] *Ibid.*, 137, 138.
[7] *F. Eph.*, II, 21, 53 *seq.*
[8] *IG²*, II, 2086, 30.
[9] Dittenberg., *SIG*, 450; Michel, 902–904.
[10] Polyb., IV, 20, 5.
[11] Arstd., XLVII K, 30.
[12] Robert, *Et. Anat.*, 29.
[13] Dittenberg., *SIG*, 695, 29.
[14] Michel, 499, 8–12.
[15] Robert, *Et. Anat.*, 19.
[16] Dittenberg., *SIG*, 450, 5.

Cleon,[1] who were not teachers in the strict sense but lyre-players who appeared ten years later at the next Pythaïs[2] as members of the professional troupe.

DANCING

Choral singing, it must be remembered, was closely bound up with dancing: the Greek word χορός referred to both. In actual fact the two things varied in importance according to circumstances—according to the place and the festival and the type of celebration: sometimes the singing was more important, as in the dramatic choruses, and then the dancing was reduced to a few grave concerted movements; whereas at other times, as in the "hyporchema" at Delos,[3] the dancing was the essential thing—it was a *danse aux chansons*, as French peasants say, the best dancers interpreting the melody while the rest of the chorus simply sang it. Naturally, the Greeks had a whole repertoire of dances that were performed to music (12).

But dancing, like singing, does not seem to have occupied a very important place in Hellenistic education. We can regard it, I imagine, as having had more or less the same position as school play-acting has in modern education—that is to say, it does not go down on the official curriculum but is rehearsed out of school hours for a particular performance. We can find no evidence of any proper teaching of dancing except in very out-of-the-way cases, as in Arcady[4] at the time of Polybius and, later still, in Sparta[5] under the Empire.

Here, as is not surprising, culture still had an archaic flavour—we have already seen how close, from Homer to Plato, was the relationship between dancing and the old aristocratic tradition. And in these two districts customs seemed to develop away from the new liberal tendencies. Some of the steps of this gradual regression can be observed. In the fourth century the programme of the Panathenean Games included competitions in martial or "Pyrrhic" dancing with separate contests for men, youths and children;[6] at the end of the second century, according to Aristocles,[7] this Pyrrhic dancing had gone out of fashion not only in Athens but in every Greek city except—again—Sparta, where it was obstinately preserved because it was bound up with the maintenance of education as a preparation for military life.

By the time of the Empire, apart from a few local exceptions—in Ionia, for example, where Dionysiac dancing remained in favour among the aristocracy[8]—dancing had been eliminated from liberal culture and become a mere "show", very popular, but something which no man of the world would ever think of doing himself: he left it to professionals, admiring their talents but despising them as persons.[9]

---

[1] *F. Delph.*, III, 2, 11, 20–22.
[2] *Ibid.*, 47, 15; 14.
[3] Lucian, *Salt.*, 16.
[4] Polyb., IV, 20, 5.
[5] Lucian, *Salt.*, 10.
[6] *IG²*, II, 2312, 72–74.
[7] *Ap.* Ath., XIV, 631 A.
[8] Lucian, *Salt.*, 79.
[9] *Ibid.*, 1–2.

DECLINE OF MUSIC IN CULTURE AND EDUCATION

This was part of a wider process which affected not only dancing but music as a whole. Music was a heritage from archaic times, and as such it appeared in Hellenistic culture as a recessive and not a dominant characteristic; the result being that it had difficulty in keeping its place in the educational world as a suitable school subject: and we see it gradually losing ground, like gymnastics, as the study of literature moved from strength to strength. The dates tell their own tale. The epigraphic winners' lists in Chios and Magnesia and Teos,[1] from which we have taken our references to music as a subject in school examinations, date from the second century at the latest, but even then the decline had begun—as we can see if we read the school charter drawn up by Polythrous, which lays down how schools were to be organized in Teos in the second century: music, it is clear, was no longer on the same level as literature and gymnastics, as it had been in the good old days.

The rules of this charter show that to do the teaching in all the schools there were three teachers of literature, two for gymnastics, but only one for music.[2] It is true that he got particularly good pay—700 drachmae a year, whereas his colleagues only got between 500 and 600: he was a specialist, but something of a man apart. For instance, he did not teach all the age-groups, but only the older boys, for their last two years at school and then at the ephebia. Whilst they were at school he taught them the two ways of playing the lyre—with and without *plectrum*—and also "music"—τὰ μουσικά—which may mean either mathematical theory or singing; and when they became ephebes he taught them music only.[3] And so in Teos the boys only learned the lyre for two years altogether—which almost certainly would have seemed very unsatisfactory two or three centuries earlier.

This state of affairs was general. In a similar charter drawn up by Eudemus in Miletus there is no mention of any music lessons at all. In Athens in Hellenistic and Roman times only the "mellephebes"—i.e. the boys at the College of Diogenes who preferred to go on to the ephebia—learnt music;[4] and even then it may only have been its mathematical aspect. Music had no place in any of the ephebes' many examinations—in which, as we shall see, the study of literature had become as important as athletics.

The same sort of thing happened in music as in gymnastics: technical progress meant specialization, and this in its turn meant a kind of divorce from the general culture and education. In archaic times, say until the early years of the fifth century, there was a perfect balance between music—which was still technically undeveloped, and grave, and simple—and culture and education; but this was suddenly shattered when great composers like Melanippides, Cinesias, Phrynis and Timotheus[5] introduced complicated rhythms and harmony which demanded corresponding improvements in the make of the instruments. Under their influence Greek music soon became so complex, and required

---

[1] Dittenberg., *SIG*, 577; 578; Michel, 913.
[2] Dittenberg., *SIG*, 578, 9; 13; 15.
[3] *Ibid.*, 578, 16–19.
[4] Plut., *Quaest. Conv.*, IX, 736 D.
[5] *Ibid.*, *De Musica*, 1141 D–1142 A.

such an elaborate technique, involving years of constant practice, that the
average amateur could not possibly tackle it and had to leave it to a handful of
specialists. This process, which began towards the end of the fifth century,
continued throughout the fourth, despite attacks by some conservative critics
in Athens[1] and Sparta who resented the "corruption" of taste; and the split
was complete by the beginning of the Hellenistic age, when, as we have seen,
a corporation of professional musicians—the τεχνῖται we have already met in
Delphi—established a monopoly and looked upon the average cultured music-
lover as someone whose job it was simply to listen—just as in sport the amateurs
were absolutely swamped by professionals.

This raised a serious problem for the teaching of music: should it—could it
—attempt to follow, even from afar, the development of this "modern" art?
And if it refused, would it not be failing in its job, which was to initiate children
into the living culture of their time? Thanks to Aristotle, who devoted almost
the whole of the Eighth Book of his *Politics*[2] to these problems, we can realize
what a burning question this was for the teachers of the time.

Aristotle's own solution was very subtle. Just as physical education, he said,
far from trying to breed champions, should aim at the child's harmonious
development,[3] so musical education should renounce any idea of teaching
students to compete with professionals[4] and simply aim at training intelligent
amateurs, who would only study the technical side of music in so far as such
immediate practical experience helped to develop their taste.[5] This shows considerable insight, and many musicians would readily agree with it today (13),
for the genuine amateur is the person who not only goes to concerts and listens
to the radio or the gramophone but actually makes music by playing the piano or
the violin—even though he never becomes a virtuoso.

But, like so many educational theorists, Aristotle did not manage to translate
his profound theories into concrete fact, and so they remained stillborn. Nor
were his successors in Hellenistic times any more successful. What was required
was for the teaching of music to break with routine, renounce the fanatical
tradition which confined it within the old narrow limits—it dated from the time
of Lympus in the seventh century—and endeavour to reflect, however tardily,
and however many adaptations were necessary, the progress of the music of
the time. In our own day children are taught easy pieces by Ravel or Honegger
when they are quite young, and in this way they grow accustomed to the new
language of modern music. But Aristotle and the teachers of Hellenistic times
were stubborn conservatives and would do nothing of the kind, and the teaching
of music remained fixed on its archaic foundations. No wonder the life went
out of it!

But it was not only from the technical point of view that the tradition handed
down by Plato and Aristotle proved archaic in its effect. It also helped to
perpetuate ingenuous ideas about the efficacy of music as a moral agent, a
personal and social discipline.[6] Throughout the Graeco-Roman period the

[1] Aristox. *ap.* Ath., XIV, 632a.
[2] VIII, 1337b, 29 *seq.*; 1339a, 11 *seq.*
[3] *Ibid.*, 1338b, 38 *seq.*
[4] *Ibid.*, 1341b, 9–19.
[5] *Ibid.*, 1340b, 20–40; cf. 1339a, 35*seq.*
[6] Plut., *Mus.*, 1140 B *seq.*

same edifying stories were repeated of how, by a mere change of mode or rhythm, Pythagoras had managed to cool the erotic ardour of an intoxicated young man;[1] how Pythagoras again[2]—or perhaps it was his disciple Cleinias[3]— or Empedocles[4]—or some other great musician of bygone times, Damon perhaps[5] —used to get rid of his bad temper by playing the lyre; and so on, and so on. The heroes of the Trojan war had even managed to keep their wives faithful while they were away fighting by choosing the right musician.[6]

These ideas had been developed into a whole body of doctrine about the different emotional and moral values, the *ethos*, of the various modes—the Dorian, the Phrygian, etc. (14), and here again, faithfully following Plato's[7] and Aristotle's[8] example, the whole Graeco-Roman tradition from Heraclides Ponticus onwards never stopped laying down the law about the virtues of the various modes—the manliness, the gravity, the majesty of the Dorian, the arrogant pomposity of the hypo-Dorian, the excitability of the Phrygian, the funereal solemnity of the Lydian, the voluptuousness of the hypo-Lydian. . . .[9]

This was all quite absurd, of course—a bit like our own idea at the end of the eighteenth century that a minor key was always sad and moving. The expressiveness of any note or key depends on the way it is habitually used—it is sociological rather than strictly musical (as when plainchant is said to be Catholic and polyphony Protestant). But absurd though this doctrine was in the Hellenistic age, it had not always been so; it had had some sense in archaic times, when the mode, or rather the canon—νόμος[10]—(15) as it was in those times, had still not been artificially restricted to a certain type of scale but was embodied in a number of typical works. These were legitimately regarded as classics and they had in common not only the same possibly highly original harmonic structure but also the same style, and often the same social purpose— so that it was quite legitimate to credit them with certain characteristic moral values. But in the Hellenistic age it had become simply a matter of words. Music had moved away from the old traditions. The modal scales had changed tremendously: the different modes had been confused and lost their own particular expressiveness. Not only that, but the actual words had frequently changed their meaning so much that it could not be certain that any of the old ethical definitions could properly be said to apply to any of the modes in existence at the time. It was thus not so much a body of doctrine as a series of legends, and very often childish legends at that. For the virtues of the various modes were not confined to ethics: taking Theophrastus' word for it, Athenaeus gravely informs us that all that is needed to cure an attack of sciatica is to play a tune in the Phrygian mode on the *aulos* above the affected part.[11]

This growing paralysis of musical pedagogy, the ever-widening gap between school music and the living art, explains why the musical side of Greek educa-tion, which had been one of its really original and attractive features, gradually

---

[1] Sext. Emp., *Math.*, VI, 8.
[2] Sen., *Ir.*, 3, 9.
[3] Ath., XIV, 624a.
[4] *Schol.*, Hermog., 383.
[5] Gal., *Plat. Hipp.*, IX, 5.

[6] Sext. Emp., *Math.*, VI, 11.
[7] *Resp.*, III, 398d *seq.*
[8] *Pol.*, VIII, 1340b 1 *seq.*; 1342a 30 *seq.*
[9] Plut., *Mus.*, 1136 C *seq.*; Ath., XIV, 624 D *seq.*
[10] Plut., *Mus.*, 1133 BC.

[11] Ath., XIV, 624 AB.

declined during Hellenistic times. The only places where it seems to have persisted were conservative regions like Laconia, Arcady and Achaea, and here it was simply another sign of the ossification of these cities, which remained outside the main cultural stream.[1] Here and there, of course, there were a few signs of its survival—as late as A.D. 163–164 we find the Athenian ephebes learning to sing hymns in honour of the divine Hadrian under the direction of a chorus master.[2] Nevertheless, on the whole, it is true to say that music tended to disappear from liberal education. This does not mean to say that it disappeared from Greek culture; on the contrary, it was more popular than ever;[3] but it is one thing to listen to it, quite another thing to play it. Increasingly it was left to professional virtuosos, and these, like the dancers, were regarded with mixed feelings. They were admired for their talent, and they were well paid, but at the same time they were despised. They were not usually seen in polite society, amongst educated people. Their manners may not have been as suspect as those of theatre-folk, but the fact that they worked for money put them outside the pale: they were tradespeople—βάναυσοι. This disdain, which Aristotle had already voiced in the strongest terms,[4] became more and more clearly marked as the Graeco-Roman period wore on. When the Alexandrian wits nicknamed Ptolemy XII (80–51 B.C.) "Auletes", they were not being very nice to him: the word suggested something of the mountebank. How far we have moved from the time when the self-made Themistocles disgraced himself at table by being unable to perform on the lyre when it came to his turn. . . .[5]

Gymnastics and music were the two archaic elements in Greek education, and both were declining in the Hellenistic age. Education was becoming predominantly literary; it is in the school of literature that we shall see it at its truest and liveliest.

[1] Plut., *Mus.*, 1142 E; *Pol.*, IV, 20, 5.
[2] *IG*², II, 2086, 30.
[3] Ath., XIV, 623 E *seq.*
[4] *Pol.*, VIII, 1339b, 9–10; 1340b, 40 *seq.*
[5] Cic., *Tusc.*, I, 4.

CHAPTER V

THE PRIMARY SCHOOL

EDUCATION proper—παιδεία—did not begin until the child was seven and was sent to school. Until then he was merely "brought up"—(ἀνα)τροφή—"reared" at home[1] by women, by his mother in the first place, but chiefly—in all the reasonably well-off families—by his "nanny"—τροφός—who, according to the purists, was different from the nurse proper—τίτθη.[2] Both were[3] usually slaves,[4] but, occasionally,[5] freewomen,[6] and the nurse stayed with the family, tenderly regarded by her foster-child, until she died[7] (1).

ABSENCE OF INFANT SCHOOLS

In a sense, of course, the child's education began in these early years (2). He was introduced into social life and shown how to behave, how to be well-mannered and polite, and also given some kind of moral discipline—some of the "nurses" used to check the child and try to develop his will by means of strict rules, and by treatment that, considering his age, was extremely harsh.[8]

As regards intellectual matters, these nursery years were devoted to learning the language. The more careful educators, like the Stoic Chrysippus, insisted[9] on the need for choosing nursemaids whose purity of speech was such that the child ran no risk of catching faulty habits which would later need to be cured.

In these early years, too, he began to learn something about his own culture. Like any child today, he entered the enchanted world of music by hearing cradle-songs—βαυκαλήματα; he came into contact with "literature" through his nurse's tales—animal stories (there were all Aesop's fables, for instance), tales of witches—terrifying figures—μορμολύκεια—like Mormo, Lamia, Empusa or Gorgo . . . there were all kinds of stories. In so far as the old traditional religion lasted into Hellenistic times, this was the age at which myths and legends about the gods and the heroes were taught. But there was no effort to systematize all this into a regular course of learning.

These early years were in fact primarily a time for play, and from the literature of the time, the vase-paintings and terra-cottas, and toys found in tombs, we can get some idea of the games played by Greek children. They were indeed the same old games on which children always expend their bursting energy, discovering with delight their marvellous faculty of movement and the tricks they can get up to because of it, and copying the grown-ups in their own juvenile

---

[1] Arist., *Pol.*, VIII, 1336b 1; [Pl.] *Ax.*, 366d.
[2] Eust., *Il.*, VI, 399.
[3] *IG²*, II, 9079; 9112; 12996.
[4] *Ibid.*, 12563.
[5] *IG*, IV, 3553b.
[6] *IG²*, II, 5514; 7873.
[7] [Dem.] *Everg.*, 52 *seq.*
[8] Tel. *ap.* Stob., 98, 72.
[9] Quint., I, 1, 4; Plut., *Lib. Educ.*, 3 E; 4 A.

way. Then, as always, they had rattles, dolls (some of them jointed ones), rocking-horses, little carts, cups and saucers for their dolls' dinner-parties, small gardening tools, and balls and especially knucklebones for games of skill.

This is all quite ordinary, and the Greeks did not look upon it as important; it was merely παιδιά—"childishness". The Ancients would have laughed their heads off if they could have seen our infant-school and kindergarten specialists, Froebel or Signora Montessori, gravely studying the educational value of the most elementary games. In Greece, of course, there were no infant-schools. These did not appear until quite recently—out of the barbarous womb of the Industrial Revolution, when the employment of women in factories meant establishing day-nurseries, so that mothers could be "free" to respond to the sound of the factory whistle (3). In antiquity the family was the centre of the child's early education.

I know that the Greeks had a few serious people among them too. Their philosophers worried about time lost in these early years. Plato wanted to make children's games an introduction to the professions,[1] and even to science.[2] He wanted children to go to school earlier—at the age of six instead of seven.[3] Aristotle[4] went one better and said five. Chrysippus[5] went two better and said three. There was no time like the present, apparently, for these theorists! Fortunately these were advanced opinions which the average family recognized as such, and went on its own sweet way.

The old way of life went on unmoved, and throughout antiquity children were left to develop in the most delightfully spontaneous manner; their instincts were given free range; they grew up in an atmosphere of freedom. The general attitude towards them was one of amused indulgence—it was all so unimportant! To educate children for themselves alone, for the sake of their childishness, as our modern educators are determined to do, would have seemed to the Ancients absolutely pointless.

When the child was seven, school began. Communal education had long been the rule, and in the Hellenistic age it was only the sons of kings who could have private tutors, like Alexander.

THE GOVERNOR OR PEDAGOGUE

Nevertheless, a small private element remained. Among the people who helped to train the child we must include the "pedagogue"—παιδαγωγός—the family servant whose job it was to take the boy to school and bring him home again each day (4). This seems a humble enough occupation: he was simply a slave who had to carry his young master's belongings, or a lantern to light his path—sometimes even the child himself if he was tired (there are many delightful terra-cottas showing him doing this).

But there was also a moral aspect to his duties. If the child had to be accompanied, this was because he needed protecting against dangers to be met with

---

[1] *Leg.*, VI, 793e.
[2] *Ibid.*, VIII, 819bc.
[3] *Ibid.*, I, 643bc.
[4] *Pol.*, VII, 1336a 23–24; b 35–37.
[5] Quint., I, 1, 16.

F

in the streets—and we know what they were. The pedagogue kept a continual watch over his charge, and this often came to be resented in adolescence as an unbearable tyranny.[1] Naturally, in spite of his servile status, and the lack of respect from which he all too often suffered,[2] he did more than supply this merely negative protection; he trained the child in good manners and helped to mould his character and morals. Indeed the "pedagogue" was entrusted with the actual moral education of the child, as distinct from the technical instruction imparted by the various teachers—to which he often made his own contribution as a kind of monitor, making the child learn his lessons, etc. Thus he carried into Hellenistic middle-class life the part played in the days of the Homeric heroes by the "tutor". His importance is reflected in his actual name: in Hellenistic Greek παιδαγωγός often loses its etymological sense of "slave companion" and begins to take on the modern meaning of the word "pedagogue"—someone who is an educator in the full sense of the word (though he remained distinct from the "master" whose work it was to impart learning).

THE SPREAD OF PRIMARY SCHOOLS

Language also reflects what is from now on the major importance of literature in education. When the word "master"—διδάσκαλος[3]—is used without qualification, it is the master who taught reading who is meant—the γραμματίστης, γραμματοδιδάσκαλος;[4] and the "school"—the διδασκαλεῖον— is the place where he teaches.

These schools existed throughout the Hellenistic world. There had been many of them in Greek cities in the preceding era, but now they appeared wherever Hellenism took root. When the Ptolemies established a cleruchy of soldier-workers to colonize the lands reclaimed from the desert at Fayum, there immediately sprang up, even in the smallest rural centres, not only palestras and gymnasiums but these primary schools too (5). Papyri show that although the knowledge of writing was not universal in these parts, it was fairly general, even outside the ranks of the ruling class (6)—and this was in a colony where the Greeks were a tiny minority, lost amongst the barbarian masses.

In regions that were completely Greek it seems to have been the normal thing for all freemen's children to go to school; this is clearly implied by the school laws in Miletus and Teos.[5] In Teos it was laid down that the girls should be taught in exactly the same way as the boys[6]—a remarkable advance on the previous age, and one which appears to have been fairly widespread: some of the terra-cottas found in Myrina and Alexandria portray little schoolgirls at work (7). In a considerable number of the cities in Aegeus and Asia Minor we even find a flourishing system of secondary education for girls. This was all well before the Roman era, when in Egypt the "strategus" Appollonius was told when to buy a "reading book" for his little daughter Heraïdous because she needed it for school.[7]

[1] Plaut., Bacch., 422–423; Ter., Andr., I, 24 seq.
[2] Plut., Lib. Educ., 4 A; 12 A; Pl., Lys., 233ab.
[3] Her., Did.
[4] Tel. ap. Stob., 98, 72.
[5] Dittenberg., SIG, 577; 578.
[6] Ibid., 578, 9.
[7] PGiessen, 85.

SCHOOL BUILDINGS

We have no very precise information about the kind of buildings that were used as primary schools. As for a long time used to be the case with us, and is still the case in Moslem countries, they probably had any old room, not one specially designed as a school-room. One room was all they needed. Some have said that there was also a waiting-room, which the pedagogues used as a kind of common-room, but this seems doubtful; (8) the pedagogues probably stayed in the school-room itself and sat on one side, as they are represented as doing even on fifth-century vases.

We know more about how this room was furnished. It was all extremely simple. There were a few chairs, a θρόνος[1]—an armchair with slanting legs, in which the master himself sat pontificating—and backless wooden stools—βάθρα[2]—for the pupils. There were no tables; their stiff writing-tablets enabled them to write on their knees. As usual with furniture in those days, artistic decoration was considered more important than utility or comfort. Our sources of information, which have so little to say about the equipment of these schools, leave us in no doubt that they were decorated in a way befitting a sanctuary of the Muses, with images of these "revered goddesses",[3] or masks of the kind used in the theatre or at Dionysiac feasts,[4] hanging on the wall.

STATUS OF THE MASTER

It was in a room like this that the master held his class. He generally took the whole class himself—in pre-Roman times it was unusual for there to be an "assistant-master"—ὑποδιδάσκαλος[5] (9)—or older pupils acting as monitors. As for the master himself, the low esteem in which he was held in ancient society comes as a surprise to anyone used to seeing teaching regarded with the respect and honour it receives—or is supposed to receive—in our own society.

Throughout antiquity the teaching profession remained a humble, somewhat despised occupation—it could be thrown up against Aeschines[6] and Epicurus,[7] for instance, that their fathers had been reduced to it. Like the Victorian school-mistress or governess, the teacher of old was essentially a man of good family who had gone down in the world—a political exile, a wanderer without a land of his own, "whom poverty has reduced to teaching";[8] a tyrant who had lost his throne, like Dionysius of Syracuse.[9] Remember Lucian's kings who are stripped of all their wealth in Hades and compelled to sell salt or old boots or become school-teachers.[10] "He's either dead or else he's teaching somewhere," some wag says about someone who is missing.[11]

Why this contempt? In the first place—except in cities like Miletus or Teos, where the schools were municipally owned, and the master, being elected by the

[1] *Anth. Pal.*, IX, 174, 5.
[2] Pl., *Prot.*, 315c; 325e; Dem., *Cor.*, 258.
[3] Her., *Did.*, 97; 71 E; Ath., VIII, 348 D.
[4] Callim., *Epigr.*, 48.
[5] D.L., X, 4.
[6] Dem., *Cor.*, 258.
[7] D.L., X, 4.
[8] Ath., IV, 184 C.
[9] Cic., *Tusc.*, III, 27; Trog. Pomp., XXI, 5.
[10] Lucian, *Menipp.*, 17.
[11] *FCG*, IV, 698, 375.

citizens' assembly, had some of the dignity of a public official—because school-teaching was a trade, in the servile commercial sense, because it meant running after customers and asking for money—discreditable features in the eyes of the Greeks, who remained, despite any other changes, essentially aristocratic at heart.

Teaching was a paid job—and, what was worse, it was badly paid (10). The most detailed documentary evidence about this is to be found in the epigraphical school-charters in Miletus and Teos. In Miletus a teacher got forty drachmae a month,[1] in Teos five hundred drachmae a year (11)—i.e. a normal year: it was a bit more, of course, when there was an extra month in the year.[2] In both cases this was slightly higher than the pay of a skilled workman, which was usually a drachma a day, but the difference was not sufficient to give the teacher any appreciably higher standard of living.

And then again he did not always get paid regularly. Miletus and Teos were exceptional: teachers' salaries were guaranteed by the money that came in from a "foundation"—they went down on the city's budget and were paid out of the city treasury according to certain definite rules. But everywhere else teachers had to run the risk of dealing with private customers. In theory they were paid at the end of each month[3] like the municipal teachers in Teos and Miletus, but parents short of money sometimes made them wait, and there were always Scrooges—like the one in Theophrastus who tried to economize by keeping his son away from school during the month "Antistherion", on the pretext that as holidays took up so much time during that month there were not enough school days left to warrant the expense.[4]

But the fundamental reason for the contempt in which the teaching profession was held was that it required no special qualifications. Nowhere was it thought necessary for school-teachers to undergo professional training like that given in our modern teachers' training colleges. The school laws in Miletus, which contain so much valuable detail, show how teachers were elected: no qualifications were required, and all that the electors were bound in conscience to do was to choose "those most capable of dealing with children".[5] Except for moral assurances about good character and honourable conduct (12),[6] it seems that no guarantees were demanded: technically, anyone who could read was considered capable of setting himself up as a teacher—he simply had to remember what he had learnt at school.

All this was a result of the very elementary and routine character of teaching in those days, as we shall soon see: attention was focused entirely on the needs of the adult, and any problems concerning children—their particular psychology, their needs and demands, etc.—were more or less ignored.

But I do not wish to draw too dark a picture. However badly paid they may have been, the teachers in Miletus, at least, were slightly better off than their colleagues in the gymnasiums, who only got thirty drachmae a month.[7] And scorned though it was, the profession was so obviously useful that it occasionally

---

[1] Dittenberg., *SIG*, 577, 52–53.
[2] *Ibid.*, 578, 11; 20–21.
[3] Her., *Did.*, 8–11.
[4] Th., *Char.*, 30.
[5] Dittenberg., *SIG*, 577, 43–49.
[6] *Ibid.*, 775, 4.
[7] *Ibid.*, 577, 51.

received a certain amount of official encouragement. In the third century B.C., for instance, the city of Lampsacus granted schoolmasters fiscal immunity,[1] while Ptolemy Philadelphus exempted them from the salt tax.[2] And, finally, there are monuments which show that their old pupils sometimes went on feeling gratitude and respect towards them—as, for example, the epitaph on the old master in Rhodes who died after teaching for fifty-two years (13).[3]

THE SCHOOL AND EDUCATION

Nevertheless, in contrast with our modern ideas there can be no doubt that school-teaching was not properly appreciated. I wish to emphasize this fact, for it is important for a proper understanding of school life and the organization of schools at this time. Schools did not play the all-important part in education which they were to play in the Middle Ages.

The schoolmaster was only responsible for one small section of children's education—the mental side. He did not really educate his pupils. Education means, essentially, moral training, character-training, a whole way of life. The "master" was only expected to teach them to read—which is a much less important matter.

The connection between elementary education and moral training, which seems so natural to us today, is a heritage from the Middle Ages—to be more precise, from monastic schools, in which the same person found himself obliged to unite two quite distinct rôles—that of the school-teacher and that of the spiritual father. In antiquity the schoolmaster was far too insignificant a person for any family to think of giving him the responsibility of educating its children, as it so often does today.

If anyone other than the parents was ever given the job, it was the pedagogue, who was only a slave, no doubt, but who was at least one of the family. Through his daily contact with the child, and his example—whenever possible—and at any rate by his precepts and the careful watch he kept over him, he made a far greater contribution to his education, especially his moral education, than the purely technical lessons provided by the schoolmaster.

It is not difficult to appreciate the importance of all this. It means that there is a great difference between our own problems and those of ancient times. For us the cardinal problem in education is the school. There was no comparable problem for the Ancients. For example, in one of the innumerable treatises "On the Education of Children" which the Graeco-Roman age produced, one which has come down to us as having been written by Plutarch (14), surprisingly little space is devoted to actual school questions. There is a eulogy on general secondary education as a preparation for philosophy;[4] a eulogy on books as "the instruments of education";[5] allusions to the gymnasium[6] and the value of a good memory;[7] but apart from the passages in which the author has felt obliged to explain his literary theories,[8] the rest is devoted entirely to the moral

[1] SAWW (1910), CLXVI, 1, 46.
[2] PHal., I, 260.
[3] IG, XII, 1, 141.
[4] Plut., Lib. Educ., 7 CD.
[5] Ibid., 8 B.
[6] Ibid., 11 CD.
[7] Ibid., 9 DE.
[8] Ibid., 6 C–7 C.

atmosphere which should surround education. And this is not so much a matter of instruction in the strict sense as of the formation of character, and for this the school was not recognized as being important. We shall come across the same facts when we come to the problem of religious education as posed by Christianity.

TIME-TABLE OF CLASSES

But let us take a look at the school of antiquity from the inside. In theory as we know, the child was supposed to attend three schools at once—the reading and writing school, the music school and the gymnastics school. But, as we have already seen, music was now hardly more than a second subject. As regards the other two, from what we know at present it is not clear how the school-work was divided between them during the day. The most likely solution seems to me to be as follows (15).

The school day began very early, shortly after daybreak[1]—in fact in winter the child had to go to school by the light of a lantern carried by the pedagogue. (This is a favourite scene with the "coroplaths"). At the beginning of the Hellenistic age, when physical education still had the place of honour it had had at the beginning, the child went straight to the palestra and spent the morning there. He then had a bath and went home for his lunch, and in the afternoon he went to school for his reading lesson. But as the result of the growing importance of letters, an additional lesson gradually came to be introduced, and the child then began the morning with this. At first it may have been no more than a private lesson with the pedagogue at home, but then it began to take place at school and soon became the most important lesson of the day. The physical education was pushed on to the end of the morning and given less and less time, until—at least in the Latin districts—it disappeared altogether.

SCHOOL CALENDAR

The Greek calendar made no provision for any weekly day of rest such as was adopted by Roman society under the influence of Judaism in the first century A.D. Nor were there, properly speaking, any school holidays. There were days off for the various civic and religious festivals, municipal and national, and also for special school occasions. As these festivals occurred rather irregularly, whenever a large number of them came together they were in fact rather like our holidays—as was the case with the month "Anthesterion", as we have seen, in Athens. This was a matter of local patriotism, of course: every region, every city, had its own particular calendar. In Miletus the children were given a day's holiday on the fifth of each month, in honour of their generous benefactor Eudemus;[2] in Alexandria, in the third century B.C., the schools closed on the seventh and twentieth of each month in honour of Apollo.[3] These were not the only holidays; if we studied the whole calendar we should find many more.

---

[1] Tel. *ap.* Stob., 98, 72.   [2] Dittenberg., *SIG*, 577, 76–9.
[3] Her., *Did.*, 53–55.

Here, for example, is what might be called the academic calendar for the city of Cos in the middle of the second century B.C. It is for the month "Artemision", and includes the following festivals and examinations, when, apparently, classes were suspended:[1]

4th: Festival in honour of Poseidon.

5th: *Ephebes' Sports.*

6th: Procession in honour of the deceased King Eumenes II of Pergamus.

7th: Festivals at the Sanctuaries of Apollo Cyparissios and the Twelve Gods.

Children's Sports.

10th: Festival instituted by Pythocles in honour of Zeus Soter. (Pythocles was probably one of the city's benefactors, and perhaps a special school benefactor, like Eudemus in Miletus and Polythrous in Teos.)

11th: *Ephebes' Sports.*

12th: Festival at the Temple of Dionysus.

15th: Festival at the Temple of the Delian Apollo.

19th: Procession in honour of the Muses.

25th: *Ephebes' Sports.*

26th: Procession in honour of the reigning king, Attalus II (or III).

29th: *School Examinations* (16).

This made a total of eight festivals, and, for the children, two examination days. In the preceding month they were not so lucky: they only had six festivals and one examination day.

Besides these official holidays, each child had his own special holiday on the occasion of any particular family festival—his birthday; the day his hair was cut to mark the end of early childhood; similar days for the rest of the family; important events like marriages and so on.

It would be interesting to know the average number of pupils to a class, but as we do not know the actual number of school-children in any city it is not much use being told that Miletus, for example, had four schoolmasters[2] and Teos three (who also had to teach in the secondary school).[3] The pupils were divided into different classes by the "paidonomos",[4] and since the law allowed for the teachers' objecting to being given "an excessive number of children",[5] no doubt they preferred small classes. This sounds quite modern. We may go further. Much of the evidence seems to show that this education was much more in-dividualistic than ours. It is significant that there was nothing like our "black-board" (17)—that outstanding symbol of collective teaching.

[1] Dittenberg., *SIG*, 1028.
[2] *Ibid.*, 577, 50.
[3] *Ibid.*, 578, 9.
[4] *Ibid.*, 578, 19–20.
[5] *Ibid.*, 578, 32.

CHAPTER VI

PRIMARY EDUCATION

THANKS to all the valuable records—the papyri, the writing-tablets, the *ostraca* —which the dry soil of Egypt has yielded up to our investigations, we can form a very exact picture of the kind of work that went on in Hellenistic primary schools. Excavations in the *kom* of *sebahk*—i.e. heaps of refuse found at the entrances to various towns or villages that have been excavated—have revealed a number of school writings buried in what seem to have been old waste-paper baskets: exercises, exercise books, and—a recent discovery—a primary-school text-book in almost perfect condition (1). These things give us a very good idea of what the school life was like.

The aim was quite simple: it meant learning the three R's,[1] plus a certain amount of "learning by heart". Let us begin with reading, which was a rather grotesque affair. The poor child was a long time getting there!

THE READING LESSON

There was nothing comparable to our "reading by wholes", nor was any effort made to arouse the child's interest by giving him little sentences like "The cat sat on the mat" once he had learnt the necessary letters. Hellenistic schools despised such humble exercises. Its method was based on a purely rational *a priori* analysis of the thing to be learnt, in complete indifference to any of the learner's—i.e. the child's—psychological problems. Learning proceeded from the simple to the complex, from the part to the whole. Any other procedure would have seemed absurd—as it seemed later to St. Augustine.[2] Hence the first thing to be learned was the alphabet; then syllables, then words, then sentences, and finally continuous passages.[3] One stage was not tackled until all the problems in the preceding stage had been fully dealt with—which meant spending a long time on each.[4]

THE ALPHABET

The children began with the alphabet. They learned the twenty-four letters one after another, not, as we do now, by their sounds, but by their names (alpha, beta, gamma, delta, and so on) and apparently without knowing what they looked like.[5] But they were soon given a written alphabet with capital letters arranged in columns,[6] and this they would recite—or probably chant—

[1] Poll., IV., 18.
[2] August., *Ord.*, II, 7 (24).
[3] D.H., 52.
[4] *Ibid.*, *Comp.*, 25.
[5] Quint., I, 1, 24.
[6] *ABSA* (1905–1906), XII, 476, 38. Bataille, *Deir el Bahari*, 185.

in chorus. From the fifth century, four lines of verse were used, containing the whole of the alphabet: "There are alpha, beta, gamma and delta and eta and also zeta."

> ἔστ᾽ ἄλφα, βῆτα, γάμμα, δέλτα τ᾽, εἶ τε, καὶ
> ζῆτ᾽ ἦτα, θῆτ, ἰῶτα, κάππα, λάμβδα, μῦ,
> νῦ, ξεῖ, τὸ οὗ, πεῖ, ῥῶ, τὸ σίγμα, ταῦ, τὸ ὗ
> πάροντα φεῖ τε, χεῖ τε, τῷ ψεῖ εἰς τὸ ὦ.[1]

Thorough work—no wonder they were proud and thankful when they "knew their letters"—γράμματα γιγνώσκειν! And no wonder a kind of religious awe surrounded these first "elements"—στοιχεῖα! (The letters of the alphabet, it must be remembered, were used as figures and musical notes as well). As samples of this religious awe, the historian will note with interest the strange belief that the letters of the alphabet were symbolic of the "cosmic elements", the seven vowels being associated with the seven notes of the scale and the seven angels presiding over the seven planets; they were thus used to make charms and amulets, for since they had the marvellous power to reveal man's thoughts they must be full of a mysterious magic potency (2).

It was not till Roman times that any attempt was made to help beginners to learn these first elements. It is said, for instance, that Herod Atticus had a dim-witted son who could never remember the names of the letters of the alphabet. His father, in desperation, finally hit upon the idea of having twenty-four young slaves of the same age as his son brought up with him, and naming each after one of the twenty-four letters.[2] This was the kind of whim only a millionaire could indulge, and Latin teachers introduced innovations of a more practical kind—movable wooden letters, alphabetical cakes, and so on.

In Roman times it was not enough to know the alphabet from alpha to omega. It had to be learned backwards, from omega to alpha[3] and then both ways at once, $A\Omega$, $B\Psi$, ΓX . . . MN.[4]

THE SYLLABLES

Having cleared the first hurdle, the pupil went on to syllables; and, with the same passion for system, he was taught a complete list of them, in their proper order. No words were attempted until all the syllables had been combined in every possible way.[5] The simplest came first: βα, βε, βη, βι, βο, βυ, βω . . .; γα, γε, γη . . . up to ψα, ψε, ψη, ψι, ψο, ψυ, ψω;[6] and these apparently[7] were not simply pronounced according to their sound but by the name of each individual letter first and then as joined together—thus: beta-alpha-ba; beta-ei-be; beta-eta-be. . . .

---

[1] Ath., X, 453 D.
[2] Philstr., VS II, 1, 558.
[3] Wessely, Studien, II, LVI: Iren., I, 14, 3.
[4] JHS (1908), XXVIII, 121, 1; cf. Quint., I, 1, 25.
[5] Ibid., I, 1, 30.
[6] PGuér.Joug., 1–8; UPZ I, 147, 1–18.
[7] Ath., X, 453 CD.

The pupil then passed on to three-letter syllables, made up of different combinations of letters. The oldest method we know of—it dates from the fourth century B.C.[1]—involved putting a consonant—ν, for example, or β or λ or ϱ or σ—after each of the syllables in the preceding table. This gave: $\beta\alpha\nu$, $\beta\varepsilon\nu$, $\beta\eta\nu$, $\beta\iota\nu$, $\beta o\nu$, $\beta\upsilon\nu$, $\beta\omega\nu$; $\gamma\alpha\nu$, $\gamma\varepsilon\nu$, $\gamma\eta\nu$ . . . up to $\psi\alpha\nu$, $\psi\varepsilon\nu$, $\psi\eta\nu$, $\psi\iota\nu$, $\psi o\nu$, $\psi\upsilon\nu$, $\psi\omega\nu$.[2] Or, conversely, the first consonant could remain unchanged, and this would give: $\beta\alpha\beta$, $\beta\varepsilon\beta$ . . ., $\beta\alpha\gamma$, $\beta\varepsilon\gamma$ . . ., $\beta\alpha\delta$, $\beta\varepsilon\delta$. Or the same consonant could come both before and after each vowel, and that gave $\beta\alpha\beta$, $\beta\varepsilon\beta$, $\beta\eta\beta$ . . ., $\gamma\alpha\gamma$, $\gamma\varepsilon\gamma$. . . . Then it began to get really complicated: $\beta\varrho\alpha\varsigma$, $\beta\varrho\varepsilon\varsigma$ $\beta\varrho\eta\varsigma$ . . ., $\gamma\varrho\alpha\varsigma$, $\gamma\varrho\varepsilon\varsigma$. . . .[3]

WORDS

When the syllables had finally been mastered the children went on to words; and here again it was a case of a step at a time. First of all came the monosyllables. Some of the lists given in school papyri[4] are rather strange, for not only do they include ordinary everyday words, but some quite rare ones, and even words whose meaning seems to have been unknown to the Ancients themselves, such as $\lambda\acute{\upsilon}\gamma\xi$ (lynx), $\sigma\tau\varrho\acute{\alpha}\gamma\xi$ (drop), $\varkappa\lambda\acute{\alpha}\gamma\xi$ (howl), $\varkappa\lambda\acute{\omega}\psi$ (thief), $\varkappa\nu\acute{\alpha}\xi$ (meaning unknown—milk? itch?). These seem to have been specially chosen for their difficulty of pronunciation, like our "gnome" and "pneumonia", for instance.

Here again we are at the opposite pole from present-day ideas about education: the aim was not to make things easy for the child but to give him the hardest things first, in the belief that once those were mastered the rest would follow of its own accord.

Then came two-syllable words—$'O\nu\acute{o}\mu\alpha\tau\alpha$ $\delta\iota\sigma\acute{\upsilon}\lambda\lambda\alpha\beta\alpha$[5]—then words of three, four and five syllables, with the syllables separated as in our modern primers:

$K\acute{\alpha}\sigma : \tau\omega\varrho$ $'O : \delta\upsilon\sigma : \sigma\varepsilon\acute{\upsilon}\varsigma$ . . .

$\Lambda\acute{\varepsilon} : \omega\nu$ $'A\nu : \tau\acute{\iota} : \lambda o : \chi o\varsigma$ . . .

$"E\varkappa : \tau\omega\varrho$ . . . $\Lambda\varepsilon : o\nu : \tau o : \mu\acute{\varepsilon} : \nu\eta\varsigma$ . . .[6]

This list is not made up of words that were in everyday use: it consists entirely of proper names, mainly Homeric ones. There were other lists of gods and rivers and months of the year.[7]

Perhaps all this was some kind of remote preparation for reading the poets, but the general impression is that these words were chosen because they were so difficult to say—hence, as in the case of the monosyllables, the choice of rare outlandish words, chosen rather as we would choose a word like "antidisestablishmentarianism" to find out whether someone was drunk: words like

[1] *IG²*, II, 2784.
[2] *PGuér.Joug.*, 9–15.
[3] *Ibid.*, 16–18; *UPZ*, I, 147, 19–29.
[4] *PGuér.Joug.*, 27–30; *PBouriant*, I, 1–12.
[5] *PGuér.Joug.*, 67.
[6] *Ibid.*, 68–114; *PBouriant*, I, 13–140; *JHS* (1908), XXVIII, 122, 2.
    PGuér. Joug., 38–47; 58–66; 19–20.

κναξζβίχ, apparently the name of an illness,[1] and φλεγμοδρώψ, whose meaning is unknown but which was probably a medical term too. Rare words like these were even made up into phrases, as absurd as they were unpronounceable, each phrase containing all the twenty-four letters of the alphabet used once only:

$$\beta\acute{\epsilon}\delta\upsilon\ \zeta\grave{\alpha}\psi\ \chi\theta\grave{\omega}\mu\ \pi\lambda\tilde{\eta}\varkappa\tau\rho\upsilon\upsilon\ \sigma\varphi\acute{\iota}\gamma\xi.$$ [2]

According to Quintilian[3] the technical term for such gibberish was χαλινοί— "bridles" (of the tongue), or "muzzles". Children were trained to say them as quickly as possible because they were supposed to help pronunciation and eventually get rid of any "faults of speech".

TEXTS AND ANTHOLOGIES

At last the time came when they were allowed to read short continuous passages. In the earlier of these, as in ours today, the words were split up into their separate syllables; later on, ordinary texts were used. It was not so easy for the child to read these as it is for our modern child today, because the Greeks used a *scriptio continua* in which not only was there no punctuation but even the words themselves were not separated from each other.

Apart from the matter of the syllables there seems to have been no effort to grade these exercises: if we turn to any third-century manual we shall find isolated words immediately followed by selected passages from Euripides or Homer.[4] We may well be surprised by such extraordinary teaching-methods, that presented the child with such difficulties at such an early stage in his career. The only parallel I can think of is to be found in our classical music: ancient collections for beginners, such as Bach's *Little Clavier Book for Wilhelm Friedemann Bach* or Rameau's *Pieces for the Clavichord*, begin with a "first lesson" obviously meant for beginners, but then immediately go on to pieces that soon become really difficult.

Next came a certain amount of selected poetry. As our knowledge of papyri of the time increases, we find that the same pieces keep on recurring, both in the school anthologies and in authors' quotations. Tradition, or rather routine, had fixed the famous passages once and for all, and these were learned by one generation after the other, forming a basis of poetic knowledge common to all educated men; rather like "O to be in England", Wordsworth's "Daffodils", and so on, in English. For example, there was a passage from the comic poet Straton, the words of a ridiculous cook with a Homeric turn of speech, who reminds one of the hero in Aldous Huxley's *Brave New World*, who speaks in Shakespearean fashion. This passage was selected for inclusion in a third-century[5] elementary reading book less than eighty years after it was written; five centuries later, Athenaeus is still quoting it,[6] and it is the only quotation from Straton he knows. Obviously, it was the only passage that had survived! (3).

---

[1] Clem., *Strom.*, V, 8, 357.
[2] Wessely, *Studien*, II, XLV, 2. Bataille, *Deir el Bahari*, 187.
[3] I, I, 37.

[4] *PGuér.Joug.*, 115–139.
[5] *Ibid.*, 185–215.
[6] Ath., IX, 382 C.

The child read aloud, of course: throughout antiquity, until the late Empire, silent reading was exceptional. People read aloud to themselves, or, if they could, got a servant to read to them (4).

RECITATION

Closely associated with reading was recitation: the selected passages were not only read aloud but also learnt by heart,[1] and it seems that beginners at least used to recite in a sing-song manner, syllable by syllable: "Com-ing through, ray by ray, A-pol-lo, the mor-ning sun. . . ."[2]

Thus were children taught to read: when one compares the school manual dating from the end of the third century B.C. that has been edited by Guéraud and Jouguet with any of the Coptic schoolbooks of the fourth century A.D., one is struck by the extraordinary similarity of the methods employed: with more than five centuries between them, the procedure is the same in both cases.

Innovations were few. Word-lists and selected passages came to be presented alphabetically, for instance. A more interesting innovation—if we could be sure that it was recent—was the insertion of short one-line sentences after each word in the word-lists, and then whole passages of an elementary nature, like the fables by Babrios[3]—rather than plunging the pupil immediately into difficult continuous passages.

BOOKS, EXERCISE-BOOKS AND WRITING-TABLETS

It is easier to understand why these short pieces were introduced when we remember that they were also used to teach writing—which in any case for practical reasons could hardly be separated from reading because of the very nature of the old books. The modern book, the *codex* made up of sheets of paper bound together, only appeared at the time of the Roman Empire and was at first only used to produce compact editions of very long works—hence the eager welcome it received from Christians, who could use it for their Scriptures (5).

Before that, books had simply been rolls of papyrus, which were both fragile and awkward to handle. If we take the valuable school manual edited by Guéraud and Jouguet, for instance, and gradually unroll it, we find that it begins with the simplest kind of lessons—syllables, and probably even the alphabet—and at the end has become an anthology of really difficult pieces of poetry. It must have taken several years to get through. Now materially it is simply a fragile strip of papyrus about nine and a half feet long, made up of sixteen sheets—κολλήματα—joined end to end (6). Can you imagine it in the hands of a clumsy, careless schoolboy, who has to keep on rolling and unrolling it on the wooden rods at each end? One has only to think of the martyrdom endured by our own stoutly bound class-books today! For this reason I am convinced that this particular manuscript is not, as the learned editors would have it, "a schoolboy's book", but on the contrary "a teacher's copy", a hand-

---

[1] Callim., *Epigr.*, 48.   [2] Her., *Did.*, 30-36.   [3] *PBouriant*, I, 157 *seq.*

book containing a series of model passages for the children to study. In the early stages he would have to copy them out for them, but as soon as they could write they could start copying them for themselves, and later take them down from dictation. It was thus to everyone's advantage that reading and writing should be taught together.

This is indeed exactly what happened[1]—and that is why our "teacher's copy" is the only one of its kind: all the other school documents that have been found in Egypt and Palmyra are in fact pages of writing, not the remains of reading books.

The materials the children used were of various kinds. Their first writing-tools, equivalent to our slates, were single, double or multiple wooden boards; when there was more than one, the various parts were joined together either by hinges or by a single piece of string passed through a hole.[2] Each board had a waxed surface inside a hollow frame,[3] and the pupil wrote on this with a pricker whose other end was rounded and was used as a rubber. Often boards were used that could be written on in ink.[4] The pen was made from a reed that was split and pointed, and the ink, which was solid like our Chinese ink, was made into a powder and watered down beforehand by the master or a servant.[5] In this case a small sponge was used as a rubber.[6]

It seems equally certain that papyrus was used in schools—either in single sheets or in broadsheets sewn together with string to make exercise books.[7] But papyrus was always comparatively expensive and scarce (7), so that even though both sides were used in schools fragments of pottery were often used too—the *ostraca* which are so well represented in our collections. At first sight it may seem odd that these queer fragments should have been employed for such a purpose, but they were commonly used even outside school for making rough copies on, and even for private correspondence—which must have been rather awkward.

WRITING

Writing was taught in the same way as reading. There was the same indifference to psychology, the same progression from the simple to the complex, from single letters via syllables and words to short sentences and continuous passages.

We have no detailed evidence about the kind or kinds of writing that were taught.[8] There was a cursive script. There was also a system of writing by capitals, the letters being very carefully written at regular intervals in a kind of chessboard pattern. This kind of writing was called στοιχηδόν, and no doubt it was for drawing the necessary squares that a curious ruler was used.[9] This

[1] Sen., *Ep.*, 84, 2.
[2] *POxy.*, 736.
[3] *JHS* (1893), XIII, 293 *seq*; *ABKK* (1913), XXXIV, 211 *seq*.
[4] *JHS* (1909), XXIX, 29–40.
[5] Dem., *Cor.*, 258.
[6] *Anth. Pal.*, VI, 295, 2; 65, 7–8; 66, 7.
[7] *PBouriant*, I.
[8] *Schol. Ar., Ach.*, 686.
[9] *Anth.*, VI, 63, 2.

was made of two strips joined at right angles, and it appears from the fifth century onwards in vase paintings of school scenes.

The master began by teaching the child to draw the letters one by one. There were no preliminaries—no "pot-hooks", for instance: the child was taught to write the actual letter straight away. The lesson seems to have gone something like this.[1] The master would draw one of the letters, probably very lightly—like the letters written with dotted lines in writing books—and then, before he let the child try it by himself, take his hand and make him go over it, so as to give him the "feel" of the letter.[2] Once the child had learned how to do it he would go on practising, repeating the same letter for a line or a page at a time.[3]

After the letters came the syllables—judging by the clumsy, childish way in which lists of syllables have been found copied out.[4] Then came single words. The master would draw initials in alphabetical order on an ostraca and the child would add the rest of the word, racking his brains to find nouns or other words ending in -ous:

$$| \ldots \; Ο\mathring{\text{η}}ς \; | \; Πούς \; | \; {}^\prime Ρωμαίους \; | \; Σοφόνς \; | \; Ταύρους \; | \; {}^\prime Υιούς[5]$$

Then came short sentences, which the master would write first and the child would copy—once, twice, or several times. Anything would do as a "model sentence"—ὑπογραμμοὶ παιδικοί, as Clement of Alexandria called them: the address on a letter,[6] or the absurd twenty-four-letter χαλινοί mentioned above,[7] might be used, for instance. But from the second century A.D. onwards, at least (8), short passages which might be described as more literary in character were used—aphorisms—χρεῖαι—commonly attributed to Diogenes, and a whole stock of short maxims—γνῶμαι μονόστιχοι—supposedly the work of Menander.

The texts chosen are sometimes surprising. Some are quite in keeping with the circumstances: "Work hard, my lad, if you do not want a whipping!"—Φιλοπόνει, ὦ παῖ, μὴ δαρῇς[8]—and the one already quoted: "The learning of letters is the beginning of wisdom." Some of Diogenes' aphorisms may be regarded as amusing, and they may have managed to bring a smile to some poor scholar's face as he laboured at his dreary toil. "Seeing a fly settle on his table, he said, 'Even Diogenes feeds parasites!'" But what is one to think of fierce or filthy observations such as these? "Seeing one woman giving advice to another, he said, 'The asp is buying poison from the viper'"; and (the Greek outrages all standards of propriety): "Seeing a Negro defecating, he said, 'Hullo, a split cauldron!'"[9] The Ancients were not unacquainted with delicacy, and the fact that it was needed when dealing with children,[10] but they had a rather different idea of it from ours.

The teacher's "literary" instruction had one simple objective: to teach the

---

[1] Pl., *Prot.*, 326d.
[2] Sen., *Ep.*, XCIV, LI.
[3] Ziebarth, No. 48.
[4] Wessely, *Studien*, II, LV, LIX.
[5] *JHS* (1908), XXVIII, 124, 4.

[6] Wessely, *Studien*, II, L; LVII.
[7] Clem., *Strom.*, V, 8, 357.
[8] *PBerl.Erman-Krebs*, p. 233.
[9] *PBouriant*, I, 141–166.
[10] Arist., *Pol.*, VII, 1336b, 12–17.

child to read and write. He had none of the "encyclopaedic" pretensions that are sometimes deplored in modern primary-school teaching. Even elementary exercises like grammar and composition were reserved, as we shall see, for the secondary school at the earliest: the primary school did not consider itself qualified to teach Greek, since it was a living language and best acquired in the daily commerce of life.

COUNTING

The mathematical syllabus was not at first much more ambitious. It was limited to counting—i.e. learning to say and read numbers, the cardinals[1] and the ordinals.[2] The Greeks used the letters of the alphabet as figures, adding on the *digamma*, the *koppa* and the *sampi* to make twenty-seven signs—three series of nine signs each—one for the units, one for the tens and one for the hundreds.[3] These were taught at the same time as the syllables.[4]

At the elementary school too, I imagine (9), the child learnt to count on his fingers. This was something very different from what we mean by that expression: it was a real art with strict rules which enabled the two hands to indicate any whole number from 1 to 1,000,000. The last three fingers of the left hand indicated the numbers 1 to 9, according to the extent that they were bent towards the palm. Tens were indicated by the relative positions of the thumb and first finger of the same hand. The right hand was used in the same way—first finger and thumb, last three fingers—to indicate hundreds and thousands. Tens and hundreds of thousands were indicated by the position of the left or right hand in relation to the chest, navel or thigh-bone. A million was indicated by the two hands locked together. We have quite forgotten this system nowadays, but it had an immense vogue in the West even in the schools of medieval times, and it is still employed in the Moslem East today. Known to have been in everyday use in the Mediterranean world from the time of the early Roman Empire, it may have first appeared much earlier, in the last centuries before Christ.

After whole numbers came a list of fractions—which again were learned as names and as symbols—fractions of an *arour* or a drachma:[5] $\frac{1}{8}$ was written CXX (half an *obol* and two *chalci*); $\frac{1}{12}$ was written X (one *chalcus*), etc.[6] As the use of these concrete units shows, we have passed from pure arithmetic to systems of measurement, for the existence of which there is ample evidence in papyri dating from the second and third centuries A.D., which contain metrological tables[7]—lists of multiples and divisions of the foot, for instance.[8] But all this was an introduction to the affairs of practical life rather than mathematics proper.

[1] Ziebarth, No. LI; *JHS* (1908), XXVIII, 131, 16.
[2] *Ibid.*
[3] *PSI*, 250; Preisigke, *SB*, 6215.
[4] *PGuér.Joug.*, 21-6; *ABKK* (1913), XXXIV, 213; 218.
[5] *JHS* (1908), XXVIII, 132, 17.
[6] *PGuér.Joug.*, 235-42.
[7] *POxy.*, 1669 v.
[8] *PRyl.*, II, 64.

Thus at the beginning of the Hellenistic age school arithmetic did not amount to much. The third-century manual to which I have so often referred contains nothing else except a list of squares,[1] which may simply have been intended to take the list of numerical symbols up to 640,000. It is only on a papyrus of the first century B.C. that we find, after a series of calculations of squares ($2 \times 2 = 4$, $3 \times 3 = 9$, $4 \times 4 = 16$), practical exercises on the fractions of a drachma like the ones that were done later in Latin schools at the time of Horace:[2]

$\frac{1}{4}$ drachma $= 1\frac{1}{2}$ obols; $\frac{1}{12}$ drachma $= \frac{1}{2}$ obol; $\frac{1}{4} + \frac{1}{12} = \frac{1}{3} \ldots$ [3]

After this come more complex calculations which make one wonder whether this papyrus, which seems to be a school one, does indeed come from a primary school. Only in the Coptic era, in the fourth and fifth centuries A.D., do we find any writing-boards that we can be quite sure belonged to young children, and these have really elementary addition tables: "8 (and) 1 : 9; 8 (and) 2 : 10; 8 (and) 8 : 16; 2 (times) 8 : 16; 8 (and) 7 : 15; 7 (and) 8 : 15."[4] And even in this period, whenever we find any arithmetic exercises that rise above this rudimentary level, the speed and perfection of the writing show that they are the work of adults and not of children[5] (10).

Strange though it may seem at first, it is nevertheless quite clear that addition, subtraction, multiplication and division—comparatively simple operations, which we inflict on our children while they are still quite young—were, in antiquity, far beyond the horizon of any primary school. The widespread use of calculating-tables and counting-machines (11) shows that not many people could add up—and this goes on being true to a much later date, even in educated circles.

BRUTALITY OF DISCIPLINE

Plato, it will be remembered, maintained that a child was old enough to learn to read when it was four, but Hellenistic teaching seems to have lagged behind somewhat. In A.D. 234 it was still not extraordinary for a nine-year-old child to be incapable of writing his name:[6] one such was no mere country bumpkin, for at the age of forty he was "comarch" of the district.[7] We come across children of ten or thirteen in 265 who are said to be still "learning their letters".[8] This seems to show the psychological defects of the methods employed.

As in the schools in the ancient East, teaching remained rudimentary. Teachers had no idea how to make learning easy for their pupils except by spoon-feeding them, in the way modern educationists detest. Tradition having decided what was to be taught—we have already seen how—the teacher's job was simply to go on repeating the same thing over and over again until the child saw the light. To deal with what he deemed to be insubordination he had one method to fall back on, and he never failed to make use of it: corporal punishment.

Apart from fear, the only psychological motive for learning was emulation, which, as I have already attempted to explain, was a potent influence on the

[1] PGuér.Joug., 216–34.
[2] Hor., P., 325 seq.
[3] PSI, 763.
[4] Preisigke, SB, 6215.
[5] Ibid., 6220–6222.
[6] PFior., 56, 22.
[7] Ibid., 2, 150.
[8] Wessely, Studien, II, 27, 5; 7.

Greek soul. But, curiously enough, of all the competitions that Hellenistic cities and their wealthy benefactors so richly endowed, very few were open to primary-school pupils (another sign of the low esteem in which these schools were held). Even the competitions in writing[1] and reading[2] mentioned in the winners' list in Pergamus and Teos and Chios seem from the context to have been for boys or girls of "secondary-school" age (12). Almost the only competitions for younger children were the "Muses' Games" at the sanctuary of Orthia in Sparta, in which young mikkikhizomenes of nine or ten years of age took part and received the laurel crown (13).

The characteristic figure that stayed in the memory of the men who had been educated at these little schools was not the ἀγών and its noble rivalry, but the terrible schoolmaster, stick in hand, inspiring terror. Here is how Herondas draws up his sketch of a school. Coccalos is a lazy little boy who has played truant; so his mother takes him to his master Lampriscos to be punished. The poet's realistic talent leaves us in no doubt as to what happened in cases like this: the culprit is hoisted on to the back of one of his school-fellows, and the master himself comes in.

"Where is my hard leather strap, the bullock's tail I use to beat rebellious boys? Give it to me before I lose my temper!"

And Coccalos cries out, "Oh, no, Lampriscos, by the Muses and the life of your [daughter] Coutis, please don't use the hard strap! Beat me with the other one instead!"[3]

Education and corporal punishment appeared as inseparable to a Hellenistic Greek as they had to a Jewish or an Egyptian scribe in the time of the Pharaohs; it was therefore only natural that in their translation of the Hebrew *mûsar*, which meant both "education" and "chastisement", the Alexandrian translators of the Scriptures should use the Greek word παιδεία, which thus ended up by meaning simply "punishment." The association of ideas was lasting—as witnesses to which, ignoring Abelard and Montaigne, I need only mention two figures of barely a century ago: Béranger and Stendhal.

No doubt as the Graeco-Roman period wore on there was a certain growth of sensitivity, and the conscience of these Ancients began to feel a few qualms: Chrysippus[4] is said not to have disapproved of corporal punishment—which is proof at least that he regarded it as a problem, or that it was regarded as a problem by the people around him. Under the Empire the Romans began to lose some of their original severity and show a desire for less brutal teaching-methods, giving children little presents, such as cakes, as a reward for their efforts. But any progress that was made was moral rather than educational: it was the inhumanity, not the inefficiency of "orbilianism" that was criticized, and there was thus little change in the actual teaching. None of the schools of antiquity ever shared our illusions about "teaching without tears." They had their own motto: "No progress without painful effort"—μετὰ λυπῆς γὰρ ἡ μάθησις.[5]

[1] AM (1910), XXXV, 436; 20; Michel, 913b, 4.
[2] AM (1912), XXXVII, 277b, 7; Dittenberg., SIG, 959, 8; Michel, 913a, 3; 6; b3.
[3] Her., Did., 59–73.
[4] Quint., I, 3, 14.
[5] Arist., Pol., VIII, 1339a, 28.

CHAPTER VII

LITERARY STUDIES AT SECONDARY SCHOOL STANDARD

THERE was a special teacher for each of the three stages—primary, secondary and higher—of literary education: after the primary-school teacher—the "grammatist"—γραμματιστής—came the "grammarian"—γραμματικός—who in his turn was succeeded by the "rhetor"—σοφιστής or ῥήτωρ. The theoretical distinction between them did not always work out in practice, however; in the "colonial" countries the educational system may not have been fully developed, but even elsewhere the same teacher might have two sets of pupils—this apparently was the normal situation in Rhodes, the great university city in the first century B.C., where Aristodemus of Nysa, for example, taught rhetoric in the morning and grammar in the afternoon[1] (1).

There is also a general law to be kept in mind: educational syllabuses tend to become increasingly top-heavy as the years go by, with the result that subjects gradually sink—they begin by being "advanced" and end by being "ordinary" or even elementary. When a civilization enjoys a long uninterrupted development, each generation adds something new to its culture, and as this becomes more and more complex and more and more difficult to assimilate, parallel changes become necessary in teaching syllabuses. The new subject-matter is at first absorbed by the higher education, which is the immediate reflection of contemporary culture, but as this cannot expand beyond a certain point, it is soon obliged to unload some of its material upon the lower grades.

This is often resented by the lower grades as illegitimate, an unwarranted invasion of their territory; but it is nevertheless inevitable. The same thing can be seen happening today: primary-school education has puffed itself up with "encyclopaedic" pretensions which it has taken from the secondary schools, and the secondary schools in their turn have taken over what used to be advanced science and philology. Something of the same sort seems to have taken place in the Graeco-Roman period: the grammarians ended up by annexing part of the rhetors' field, whilst the grammatists may possibly have encroached on the grammarians.

We are all familiar with the spectacle of parents pushing their children as quickly as possible up the examination ladder at the risk of endangering their full mental development, and we find the little Greek schoolboy displaying the same apprehension as the modern boy at the prospect of the gigantic course of study towering ahead of him as he is forced to embark earlier and earlier on exercises that had formerly been left to a later stage. We often hear people complaining that school-work is becoming too heavy. The Ancients had the same experience: it is an inevitable consequence of the progress of culture.

[1] Strab., XIV, 650.

As we are faced with a continuous process it is difficult to give any precise dates to the various stages (all our Latin sources[1] tell us is that the grammarians' "usurpation" of the rhetors' dominion had been an accomplished fact from the middle of the first century B.C.); so that any account of the literary education imparted at the secondary-school stage is bound to be a bit hazy. It is impossible to say definitely when exactly it began or how long it lasted.

Roughly, then, it may be said that any child who wanted to go on beyond the primary-school stage went to the secondary school as soon as he could read and write fluently. There he was taught by the grammarian—generally known in Greek as γραμματικός,[2] sometimes as φιλόλογος,[3] and even, in certain philosophical circles of a Cynical persuasion, as κριτικός.[4] The specific object of his teaching, its chief matter—there were others, as we shall see—was an elaborate study of the classical poets and classical writers generally: this was his proper sphere, distinguishing his kind of "grammar" from that of the primary-school grammatist.

THE CLASSICS

In spite of all Plato's efforts, the higher Hellenistic culture remained faithful to the archaic tradition and based itself on poetry, not science. As a result of this, education was not so much concerned to develop the reasoning faculty as to hand on its literary heritage of great masterpieces. I have often had occasion to use the word "classical" in connection with both culture and education. Perhaps I should explain what exactly is meant by this word.

As something essentially *classical*, Hellenistic civilization was the opposite of those revolutionary, innovating cultures that are propelled forward by a great creative drive. It rested essentially upon the peaceful possession of an already acquired capital. It is a mistake to say, as is often said by its detractors, that it "was born with its head back to front", looking back to the past. It is not autumnal, tormented with nostalgic regrets for a vanished spring. On the contrary, it looks upon itself as firmly established in an unchanging present, in the full blaze of a hot summer sun. It knows what mighty reserves it possesses, what past masters it has. The fact that these appeared at a certain moment of time, under the influence of certain historical forces, is unimportant; what matters is that they exist and can be re-discovered in the same way, again and again, by each successive generation, can be recognized and admired and imitated. A classical culture can be defined as a unified collection of great masterpieces existing as the recognized basis of its scale of values.

The Hellenistic age carried its official canonization of the classics to great lengths. The educational tradition had produced lists of typical great men— legislators, painters, sculptors and inventors.[5] These lists eventually came to be codified, probably by people connected with the university in Pergamus,

---

[1] Cic., *De Or.*, III, 108; Suet., *Gramm.*, 4; Quint., II, I, 1.
[2] L & S, s.v.; cf. Philo, *Congr.*, 148.
[3] Dittenberg., *SIG*, 714, n.2.
[4] [Pl.] *Ax.*, 366e; Sext. Emp., *Math.*, I, 49.
[5] *APAW* (1904), II, 1; *POxy.*, 1241.

perhaps in the middle of the second century B.C. (2), and thus the "canon" was established: ten Attic orators, ten historians, ten painters, ten sculptors; poets, philosophers, physicians. . . .

The same canonizing tendency led to an attempt to select from the—sometimes vast—body of work produced by these great writers, the books most worthy of inclusion in the educational scheme: the influence of these "selections" on our manuscript tradition has frequently been stressed (3). Of the forty or forty-four comedies by Aristophanes which were known to the Ancients we have only the eleven which a certain grammarian, Symmachus, edited about A.D. 100 as "selected plays" for school classes. Similarly, out of all the enormous numbers of plays by Aeschylus and Sophocles we possess only seven that were chosen for teaching purposes (the selections from Aeschylus were made under Hadrian, those from Sophocles may have been much later). These symbolic numbers were popular: were there not Seven Wise Men of Greece, Seven Wonders of the World, Seven Liberal Arts? The same service was performed for lesser authors by anthologists, who could fix the memory of a writer for centuries by including a certain extract from his writings (4).

Thanks in the first place to the papyri, which are as useful in this case as in the matter of primary-school education; thanks also to the school library catalogues found in literary works[1] and inscriptions,[2] we can reconstruct the list of classical authors studied by the grammarians.

HOMER

In the forefront, of course, and dominating all the rest, stands Homer. Throughout the Hellenistic period his popularity never wavered. There is abundant proof of this—Alexander the Great, taking his carefully guarded, piously regarded *Iliad* with him on all his campaigns; the towns lost in the remotest corners of the Greek world—Marseilles, Sinope, the cities of Cyprus —which had their own special editions of the *Iliad* made in proof of their loyalty to the Greek heritage when they were faced with or surrounded by barbarians (5). As long as Greek culture lasted, Homer was its dominating figure. We shall see this demonstrated most strikingly when we come to the Byzantine Middle Ages—to which, it must be remembered, we owe the preservation of all the Homeric scholarship of antiquity.

The gigantic figure of Homer loomed on the horizon from primary-school days.[3] "Homer was not a man but a god" was one of the first sentences that children copied down in their handwriting lessons;[4] when they were learning to read, as we have seen, they would have to puzzle out lists of names which brought Homer's heroes one after the other before their eyes; among their first continuous passages were selected lines from the *Odyssey*,[5] solemnly headed by the word ἔπη—"epic verse".[6] Thus it was bound to be considered a great privilege to start on a comprehensive reading of the poet's entire work: a mother who asked

---

[1] Ath., IV, 164 BD.
[2] *IG*² II, 2363.
[3] Plut., *Alc.*, 7.
[4] *JHS* (1893), XIII, 296.
[5] *PGuér.Joug.*, 131–9.
[6] *Ibid.*, 130.

the teacher how her son was getting on felt a thrill of pride when she was told, "He is studying the sixth"—τὸ ζῆτα—i.e. canto Z of the *Iliad*.[1]

From the soil of Egypt, papyri, writing tablets and ostraca have come forth containing hundreds of fragments from Homer. There are very few that do not contain something from him. Not all, of course, come from schools—it is difficult in practice to decide which do (6)—but the number of those we can be certain about is large enough to show the place Homer had in the education of Greek Egypt.

The same papyri also show how interest varied regarding different parts of the master's enormous output. The philosophers considered the *Odyssey* the more important of the two books; men of letters and, at first, the schools, preferred the *Iliad*. The papyri contain two or three times as many extracts from the *Iliad* as from the *Odyssey* (7). In theory, probably, the epic was studied canto by canto,[2] but some books were more popular than others and these recur far more frequently than the rest—the first cantos of the *Iliad*; cantos X and Ω, which even today are published separately as school-books; and a few special sections like the duel between Paris and Menelaus and the description of Achilles' shield.

THE OTHER CLASSICS

Homer was not the only epic poet who was studied at school, however; there were also Hesiod (who was sometimes learnt at the primary school too),[3] "Orpheus" and the moderns—Choerilus, who wrote an epic on the Persian Wars, and particularly Apollonius of Rhodes, whose *Argonautica* seems to have been very highly thought of. And there were others (8).

As in archaic times, lyric poets played an essential part in education: the old masters were still being studied—Alcman, Alcaeus, Sappho, and of course Pindar—but in Hellenistic times more recent authors like Callimachus and the Epigrammatists were included. Fragments of the complete works of these poets have been found, but it seems clear that they were mainly known through anthologies. In theory their lyrics were written for singing and so should have been studied along with music, but already it was being considered sufficient if they were simply declaimed.[4]

Finally there were the plays. Aeschylus and Sophocles had a place on the school syllabuses, but they were utterly over-shadowed by Euripides, the great master of classical tragedy. His opposite number among the comic poets was Menander, who was not supplanted by Aristophanes until the days of the Later Empire. Aristophanes' popularity, though it was long in coming, was so complete that in the medieval manuscripts Menander does not appear at all: it is only the papyri that have begun to restore him. Here again, along with the great names, the schools had other authors like Epicharmus—not to mention the *minores*, fragments of whose works are to be found in collections of "selected passages".

[1] *POxy.*, 930, 15.
[2] *Ibid.*

[3] *JHS* (1893), XIII, 302.
[4] Dittenberg., *SIG*, 1059, II, 47.

Poetry was supreme because it was to be found at the very origin of Greek culture, but Hellenistic schools also had a place for prose, though very much down the scale. The prose writers were mainly historians—Herodotus, Xenophon, Hellanicus and, above all, Thucydides. Aesop and his fellow-fabler Babrius belonged rather to the primary school.

Naturally, any cultured man worthy of the name had also read the orators, among whom Demosthenes held pride of place, even above Isocrates; but apparently the grammarians were not allowed to deal with them—they seem to have been left to the rhetors, and so formed part of the higher education.[1]

To sum up: the four main pillars of classical culture were Homer—especially the *Iliad*—Euripides, Menander and Demosthenes. But there was nothing exclusive about these four: the schools of antiquity were perhaps even more open than our own to second-class writers, and even to "the moderns".

LEARNED PHILOLOGY AND EDUCATION

Let us now examine how these classics were studied. A school is a microcosm in which the macrocosm of culture is reflected, and the teaching of literature was naturally affected by the prodigious development of philology, which is one of the outstanding features of Hellenistic culture. I must deal with this subject in some detail.

The influence of the great Alexandrian critics—Zenodotus, Aristophanes of Byzantium and Aristarchus—on culture generally, and especially on schools, must not be exaggerated. All the manuscripts of the *Iliad* and the *Odyssey* show that their advice went unheeded, except for a slight effect upon our Vulgate and the papyri (9). The Greek literary tradition was particularly conservative and hidebound, and it resisted all the efforts of the learned men at the Museum to introduce "cuts"—"atheteses" of the lines which they considered should be expurgated.

As for their literary criticism, its influence on educational practice was equally slight; some traces of it may possibly be found in the "scholia" of our manuscripts and papyri,[2] but it was too exclusively critical, too "scientific", to be of much use to the grammarian.

Of far greater importance than Alexandrian scholarship was, in my opinion, the work of the Stoic school, which, especially after Chrysippus, was very much concerned with teaching the study of Homer. Its influence came mainly through the philological schools that rivalled Alexandria—Pergamus and, later, Rhodes. Crates of Mallus and Panaetius are more worthy of a place in the gallery of great classical teachers than Aristarchus (10).

Steadfast conservatives, determined above all things to integrate the whole Greek heritage into their culture, they were less concerned to expurgate Homer for the sake of some abstract principle or other than to explain the accepted text that was already in existence. Instead of looking for verses they could find fault with or interpolations to reject, they made a continuous effort to understand, to justify, a particular episode or a particular detail, even if it meant using all the

---

[1] Cf. Quint., II, 5.   [2] *POxy.*, 1086–1087.

resources of dialectic. This had a profound and lasting effect upon classical teaching—for our own high-school pupils are still trained to use all kinds of intellectual gymnastics to justify bits of padding by Corneille or Molière, and discover dark meanings and hidden "beauties" in them.

PLAN AND METHOD OF STUDY OF THE AUTHORS

But let us see how the method worked. The children did not go straight to the poetry; first, they were given a summary—ποιητικὰς ὑποθέσεις[1]—the story of the whole epic[2] or a particular canto,[3] or the outline of a play or speech; these played the same part in the schools of antiquity as, for instance, Lamb's *Tales from Shakespeare* can play today. The teacher seems to have used wall-pictures too, miniature bas-reliefs showing the main episodes of heroic legend, with captions and short summaries to identify the characters and scenes. Our museums have half a score of these Iliac Tables, representing not only the *Iliad* but other legends like those included in the Theban cycle and the Twelve Labours of Hercules (11).

As for real interpretation, this took a long time to pass beyond the tentative gropings of practice and take on a scientific form. In the first-century (B.C.) handbook by Dionysius Thrax—whose importance I shall endeavour to describe later—the grammarian's work is still divided rather haphazardly under a number of different headings, and it was not till about the beginning of the Christian era, after Dionysius[4] and before Quintilian,[5] that the final classical definition of his task emerged.[6] According to this, the grammarian's treatment of an author had four stages: criticism of the text, reading, exposition and judgment—διόρθωσις, ἀνάγνωσις, ἐξήγησις, κρίσις.

I have explained the διόρθωσις elsewhere (12): it was the equivalent of our "textual criticism"—though this is not a very accurate translation, as the actual "correcting" was a good deal less systematic and strict than the modern ecdotic operation has become in the hands of Lachmann or Havet or Quentin. And for the old grammarian, of course, its purpose was entirely practical. Today, printing enables an unlimited number of identical copies of a book to be produced, and the task of establishing the critical text can be left to a specially qualified scholar; but in antiquity everything existed in manuscript, and this was such a fluid medium that in a manner of speaking there were hardly ever two copies alike—with the result that the first thing that had to be done in class was to compare and check the master's and the pupils' copies.

READING AND RECITATION

All this, however, was merely introductory; the proper study of the authors only began with the "expressive reading".[7] Here again it was because the books were in manuscript that this kind of exercise, which seems to us so elementary,

[1] Plut., *Aud. Poet.*, 14 E.
[2] *PRyl.*, I, 23.
[3] *PAchmim*, 2; *PErlangen* 5 (*PErl.* 3 R); *cf. PSchwarz*.
[7] Dion. Thrax, 2.
[4] Dion. Thrax, I
[5] Quint., I, 4, 3.
[6] *Schol.*, Dion. Thrax, 10, 8.

had to appear at secondary-school level. The words were not separated, and the absence of punctuation made reading much more difficult that it is today; the words had to be divided—and this could not always be done without ambiguity: the phrases and sentences had to be found, questions had to be distinguished from plain statements by the tone of voice, and lines had to be made to scan according to the laws of prosody and metre.

A proper reading, therefore, required an attentive study of the text; it needed to be thoroughly prepared; and there are sometimes traces of this kind of preparation in the papyri—we can see where the boy has used strokes to separate lines and words (13) and cut up words into syllables for the sake of the scansion.[1] The aim, Dionysius Thrax tells us,[2] was an expressive declamation which should take account of the sense of the text, the rhythm of the verse and the general tone of the work (heroic for tragedy, realistic for comedy, etc.). Plays, and even the epic too, were probably read in dialogue form: this is suggested by the references to characters in the papyri. (Bérard has rightly drawn attention to these, but they may simply be a sign of the normal practice in schools, and not, as he would have it, typical of the originals.)

Such a close study of the text made memorization easy: everything seems to indicate that under the grammarian, as in the primary school, the text was learnt by heart and reading followed by recitation. Recitation was a special item in the programmes of several official competitions organized by Hellenistic cities as a kind of examination system. In Teos in the second and first centuries B.C. children of secondary-school age took part in competitions for reading and reciting Homer—each competitor taking up the text at the point where his predecessor had left off[3]—and in recitations from the poets—tragic, comic and lyrical; the latter probably being sung.[4] In Larissa, on the other hand, there were competitions in the spoken declamation of the lyric poets, both classical and modern.[5] In Chios the boys competed for prizes for reading and solemn declamation of Homer;[6] as the girls did in Pergamus, with the addition of elegiac poetry.[7]

EXPLANATION OF THE TEXT

But most of the work was devoted to the explanation of the text—ἐξήγησις—to such an extent that ἐξηγητής sometimes became almost synonymous with γραμματικός.[8] This work was divided, as it is today, into literal explanation and literary explanation.[9]

First of all it was necessary to understand the actual meaning of the text, and in the case of the poets, particularly Homer, the difficulties were considerable, because of the special archaic language they used, Greek poetry having its own vocabulary. And so the schoolboy's first task was to "prepare" the passage or, as the Greeks put it, his "word for word" list—ὀνομαστικὸν Ὁμήρου.[10] He

[1] PH (1905), 146, 2.
[2] Dion. Thrax, 2.
[3] D.L., I, 57.
[4] Dittenberg., SIG, 960, n.1.
[5] Ibid., 1059, II, 13, 47.
[6] Ibid., 959, 8; 9.
[7] AM (1912), XXXVII, 277.
[8] L & S, s.v.
[9] Schol., Dion. Thrax, 10, 9.
[10] POslo, 12.

did this as school-children make their own vocabularies today, in two columns: on the left were Homer's words, on the right the modern equivalent:

Α 1	Πηληϊάδεω	παιδὶ τοῦ Πηλέως
	Ἀχιλῆος	τοῦ Ἀχιλλέως
2	οὐλομένην	ὀλεθρίαν
	ἥ	ἥτις
	μυρία	πολλὰ
	Ἀχαιοῖς	τοῖς Ἕλλησι
	ἄλγεα	κακὰ
	ἔθηκεν	ἐποίησεν[1]

He studied the construction and the cases and translated poetic expressions and difficult words into his own language with the help of dictionaries, of which a few fragments have come down to us.

It was the poets' special vocabulary, technically known as "glosses"—γλῶσσαι —that caused most trouble.[2] In antiquity an educated man was in the first place, and sometimes essentially, someone who knew that πίσυρες was "Homeric" for τέσσαρες—"four"—that ῥιγεδανός meant "frightful [death]", βῆσσα or ἄγκος "a deep ravine".[3] This was one of the ways in which scholarship affected the literary culture and literary education which it was soon to dominate.

But the study of the language of the classics was not confined to lexicography: morphology also claimed attention—increasingly, as the strange mania developed for meticulous research into Attic forms of speech and their substitution for words in everyday use. This led on to turns and figures of speech, the manner of expression proper to poetry. A great deal of erudition, authentic or otherwise, was also devoted to etymological research: λύχνος—"a lamp"—for example, was said to derive from λύειν τὸ νύχος "to blot out the night"; προσκεφάλαιον—"a pillow"—meant literally "that which is placed under the head", from πρός and κεφαλή.[4]

After form came content—or, as the Greek grammarians put it, after the γλωσσηματικόν, the ἱστορικόν.[5] "Stories"—ἱστορίαι—meant anything mentioned by the poet—persons, places, times and events.[6] A pedagogy that was at once childish and pedantic had multiplied divisions and sub-divisions just as it felt like it—Asclepiades of Myrlea, for example, in the first century B.C., divided tales into true, possible and imaginary, and then divided the true ones into characters (gods, heroes, men), times, places and actions.[7]

The reader will remember the part played in the primary-school reading lessons by lists of proper names taken from literature—names of gods, heroes, rivers, etc. This was an early and perhaps intentional preparation for the

[1] *ABKK* (1913), XXXIV, 220; *PBerl. Erman-Krebs*, 232; *POslo*, 12; *PHombert-Préaux*.
[2] Dion. Thrax, 1; *Schol.*, Dion. Thrax, 10, 9.
[3] Sext. Emp., *Math.*, I, 78; 59.
[4] *Ibid.*, I, 243-244.
[5] *Schol.*, Dion. Thrax, 10, 9.
[6] Eust. *ap.* Dionys. Per., p. 81.
[7] Sext. Emp., *Math.*, I, 253.

exposition of the classics; for the emphasis continued to be laid on words rather than on ideas and feelings—an educated man and even a well-taught child was expected to know who such and such a character was, or what such and such a place was that was mentioned by the poet: "Brilessos and Arakynthos are mountains in Attica, Akamas a headland in Crete".[1] Two samples of a catechism about Homer have been discovered. They are both in the same book and are in question and answer form; they were both found written on the same page of a copy of Dionysius Thrax's treatise on grammar.[2]

Q. Which gods were favourable to the Trojans?
A. (*In alphabetical order*) Aphrodite, Apollo, Ares, Artemis, Leto, Scamander.
Q. Who was the King of the Trojans?
A. Priam.
Q. Who was their general?
A. Hector.
Q. Who were their counsellors?
A. Polydamas and Agenor.
Q. Their soothsayers?
A. Helenus and Cassandra, Priam's children.
Q. Their heralds?
A. Idaeus, and Eumedes the father of Dolon; and Dolon himself. . . .

This was how Homer was studied "historically". About history in the modern sense, the history actually written by the historians, we know very little, but it is a remarkable fact that on the one occasion we do find any indications about it, these too are a matter of words. Inscribed on one of the walls of the Hellenistic gymnasium in Priene there is, amongst other things, a list of fifteen famous characters in Spartan history, introduced by the words τῶν ἐφόρων—"[names] of the ephors"; and this includes, without any attempt at order, the king Cleomenes, the poet Tyrtaeus, Lysander, Gylippus, etc. The writer has obviously put down the names of all the Lacadaemonian heroes he could think of, for as for ephors, there is only one amongst the whole fifteen—Brasidas.[3]

Interest centred round mythology rather than history, round the poets' innumerable legends, with their endless array of heroes. This was called "genealogy",[4] because the mythical descent of the heroes did in fact count for a great deal, just as it did in strictly historical prose writing.[5] But something more was involved. Culture and education were being invaded by scholarship on all sides. It was essential, for example, to know the names of all the persons who had been restored to life by the art of Asclepius;[6] to know that Heracles was bald when he came out of the sea-monster which had swallowed him for a moment when he was trying to rescue Hesione from it. . . .[7]

The philosophers—Sextus Empiricus for example—were to make a great deal

---

[1] Sext. Emp., *Math.*, I, 258.
[2] *PSI*, 19; *PSchwartz*.
[3] *Ins. Priene*, 316a.
[4] Sext. Emp., *Math.*, I, 253.
[5] *Ibid.*, 258.
[6] *Ibid.*, 261.
[7] *Ibid.*, 255.

of fun of this mania for learning, which was indeed a bit absurd; and as the centuries rolled on, the reason why it was a good thing to study the poets became more and more hazy in the Greek consciousness until, from the time of Plutarch[1] to the time of St. Basil,[2] the question had become simply a subject on which to exercise one's skill. As so often happens, the means had become an end: the study of the classics had become an object in itself, and no one quite knew why it was so important to be acquainted with them.

MORAL ASPECT OF THE STUDY OF THE POETS

In theory, the crowning-point of all this learning was "judgment", literary criticism—"the finest flower of the grammarian's art."[3] But this did not mean that its primary purpose was aesthetic; it was the rhetor rather than the grammarian who studied the classics, in the hope of discovering the secrets of their style—so that he might borrow them for himself. The grammarian's object was ultimately moral, and he was thus in the main stream of the old tradition, with its search for heroic examples of "human perfection" (to try once again to translate ἀρετή) in the annals of the past.

But as time went on the Ancients seem to have become less and less aware of the sublimity that was supposed to lie behind all this learning of Homer. The feeling for pure poetry was stifled by an excess of erudition. Hellenistic teachers tried to give a rational form to the lessons in wisdom which they expected their pupils to learn. This kind of well-meant bowdlerization is usually fatal: any tampering with great poetry for scholastic purposes inevitably results in mediocrity. I remember a school edition of *Hamlet* in which the earnest editor openly attempted to prove to his young readers that the real hero of the piece, the person whom Shakespeare intended to set before us as a model, was the virtuous, the moral, the *successful* Fortinbras!

From the poets, especially Homer, Hellenistic teachers tried to extract a fully articulated moral code. The prime movers in this endeavour were the Stoics. In their hands Homer became "the wisest of poets", a romantic Wise Man, intentionally concealing under the veil of myth a complete and detailed body of doctrine, the meaning of which could be discovered by investigating his allegories (14). Ulysses, who symbolizes the Wise Man, escapes from the Sirens, and thus teaches us to flee from temptation, both physical and spiritual. . . . All this had a rather puerile side: however much sententiousness there may have been in classical literature generally—especially as a result of the many well-intentioned interpolations (15)—there were far too many things in the divine Homer that offended the refined moral sense of the "moderns". But they did not let this defeat them: in the end they always managed to make him castigate vice, punish impiety and give virtue its due reward. If we cannot be bothered to read Eustathes' long-winded commentary, there is always Plutarch's naïve treatise "On the Way in which Young Men should read the Poets": if Homer[4] shows us the lewd adulterer Paris forgetting all about the fighting and

---

[1] Plut., *Aud. poet.*, 14 D *seq.*
[2] Bas., *Hom.*, XXII.
[3] Dion. Thrax, 1.
[4] Hom., *Il.*, III, 447.

going to bed with Helen in the middle of the day, this is obviously so that he can pour scorn on such goings-on![1]

But these crude endeavours were something quite apart from the essence of Hellenistic education. It was not for lessons with such a dubious value as this that the classics were studied so religiously; the main reason was because an acquaintance with the poets was looked upon as one of the first attributes of an educated man, one of the highest cultural values. We have only to glance through the pages of the ancient authors to realize how real and all-pervading was the presence of the poets in the lives of well-read men. In conversation, in private correspondence, in the serious situations of life that call for "famous sayings", always and everywhere the right word could be found—it was expected, welcomed, regarded as indispensable! Classical culture did not know any romantic need to make all things new, to forget the past and be original; it was proud of its inherited wealth, proud of its pedantry, proud of being what our modern pedantry—whose only sign of progress seems to be that it has replaced literary scholarship by technical science—would call the victim of a culture complex.

THE SCIENCE OF GRAMMAR

But from the first century B.C. the teaching of "grammar" in secondary schools ceased to be confined to poetry; and though the latter did not lose its pre-eminent position, it began to be supplemented by what was called "technique"[2]—which meant the methodical study of the elements of the language: what we call "grammar", in fact.

This introduction of grammar into education is an outstanding example of education's natural tendency to reflect the progress and development of culture. Grammar was one of the last conquests achieved by Greek science—the fruit of a long-sustained effort, which began, as we have seen, with Protagoras, and continued in the schools of Plato and his successors (the Stoic contribution, especially from Chrysippus, being particularly noteworthy). Its final flowering is one of the great glories of Hellenistic culture, and admirably presents the reflective temper of the time, which was critical rather than creative. It was only, in fact, at the beginning of the first century B.C. that grammar became recognized as a science—when Dionysius Thrax, one of the shining lights of the schools in Rhodes, produced his famous book on the subject—Τέχνη—which codified the results of all previous research.

We must not exaggerate the value of this book. The Greeks were not as successful in analysing the structure of language as they were in developing Euclid's geometry and Pythagoras' acoustics—indeed grammar is one of the few fields in which they have been surpassed by other peoples—and Dionysius did not approach the incomparable profundity of Sanskrit grammar, which, as is well known, has had a considerable influence on modern philology. Nevertheless, this little treatise—it is only a few pages long—was extraordinarily successful. It was immediately adopted for educational purposes as the basic text-book,

---

[1] *Aud. poet.*, 18 F.
[2] *Schol.*, Dion. Thrax, 6, 20; Quint., I, 9, 1; Sext. Emp., *Math.*, I, 91 *seq.*

and thereafter it was continually being re-copied,[1] re-edited, furnished with
appendices, "scholia", commentaries, not only throughout Roman times but
for long into the Byzantine period—not until the twelfth century was it replaced
by a kind of question and answer catechism—Ἐρωτήματα; and even in this,
though the matter was presented differently, the substance remained the same.
Indeed, its influence has extended beyond the Greek-speaking world. Leaving
aside the paradoxical uses to which it was put in Syriac and Armenian, this
work by Dionysius Thrax, by way of Varro and Remmius Palaemon, led on to
Latin grammar, and hence still further in place and time, right up to our own
day. It is worth remembering that French grammar, as taught in French
primary schools, is simply a bastard form of the old Rhodian τέχνη, gradually
vulgarized through two thousand years of use. We often hear it said that our
teaching of grammar is too formal and unpractical. This takes us right back
to its origin, for grammar was not in the first place intended to help with teaching, it was not supposed to help children to grasp the mechanics of their mother
tongue; it was an advanced science, on the level of our general linguistics, and,
as befitted a Greek science, it was purely speculative and theoretical.

Dionysius' grammar is essentially an abstract and wholly formal analysis
of the Greek language, taking it to pieces and resolving it into simple elements,
which it then carefully defines and classifies. His treatise does not take long
to summarize; it is indeed so bare an outline that a modern reader is surprised
and perhaps slightly misled by it—he may feel inclined to wonder how such
meagre fare could have satisfied so many people's curiosity for so long.

After a few general definitions of things like grammar, reading, etc.,[2] the
following elements are dealt with one after the other: letters (vowels and consonants—long, short and mixed vowels; diphthongs, mute consonants, etc.),[3]
syllables (long, short and medium: a syllable could be long in eight ways—
three from its nature, five from its position, etc.).[4] Then came the essential
part of the subject, the eight parts of speech: noun, verb, participle, article,
pronoun, preposition, adverb and conjunction.[5] Only the first two were given
any detailed treatment, which in any case never went beyond definitions and
classifications. In the case of the noun, for example, the following items were
treated in succession: the three genders, the two kinds (primitive words and
derived words—seven varieties of the latter), the three forms (simple words,
compound words and double-compound words), the three numbers, and the
five cases; then the nouns were classified again, into twenty-four classes—
proper nouns, appellatives, adjectives, etc.[6] The verb in its turn was divided
into eight categories—mood, voice, kind, figure, number, person, tense and
conjugation.[7] The other parts of speech were treated much more briefly,
though still in the same formal manner;[8] all that Dionysius could find to say

---

[1] PSI, 18; PSchwartz; cf. PAmh., II, 21; POslo, 13; PIanda., 83a; Aeg. (1939), XIX, 211.
[2] Dion. Thrax, 1–5.
[3] Ibid., 7.
[4] Ibid., 8–10.
[5] Ibid., 11.
[6] Ibid., 12.
[7] Ibid., 13–14.
[8] Ibid., 15–20.

about the prepositions, for example, after briefly defining them, was "There are eighteen prepositions—six monosyllables (which cannot be transposed), and twelve disyllables".[1]

That was all. Dionysius' grammar was all analysis and no synthesis; hence its total lack of anything like syntax. Later centuries added nothing except for a few general ideas about prosody[2] and metre,[3] and a table of the full conjugation of a regular verb ($\tau \acute{\upsilon} \pi \tau \omega$). These additions seem to have been made between the third and fifth centuries A.D.

It is in the third century A.D. that practical exercises in morphology appear on school papyri: there is a writing-board, for instance, that has the verb $\nu \iota \varkappa \tilde{\omega}$ on the back, meticulously conjugated into all the forms (voice, tense, person and number) of the optative and participle.[4] We should expect this to be a primary-school exercise at the latest, but when we turn the writing-board over we find it taken up by the declension of a "chria" of Pythagoras—a type of exercise we shall have occasion to study later, and which certainly came into the grammarian's sphere. For this reason I think we should look upon similar exercises dating from the second or third to the sixth century as having been part of secondary-school education—exercises like the declension of a noun with its adjective,[5] conjugations,[6] the classification of verbs according (more or less) to their meaning, with the cases they govern.[7] Of course it is not impossible that in the long run all these percolated into primary-school education as a result of the general tendency of educational techniques to extend gradually downwards from the highest levels to the lowest.

PRACTICAL EXERCISES IN COMPOSITION

Along with these exercises in morphology, and the study of literature and the theory of grammar, went elementary exercises in composition;[8] these completed the grammarian's course.

In theory the rhetor was the person who taught the art of speaking (and writing, for the Ancients looked upon the two things as inseparable). Before Hellenistic students of rhetoric began composing proper speeches, they were put through a series of carefully graded "preparatory exercises"—$\pi \varrho o \gamma v \mu \nu \acute{\alpha} \sigma \mu \alpha \tau \alpha$. But the familiar percolation took place here too: as the more advanced rhetoric became increasingly technical and more and more exacting, it became a matter of necessity for higher education to hand preparatory exercises over to the secondary school and so, by force of circumstances, they were "usurped" by the grammarian. The rhetors, of course, did not take this lying down—though the Latin rhetors who came at a much later stage of educational development did not stand on their dignity quite so much—but the Greek ones never gave up the whole field of the $\pi \varrho o \gamma v \mu \nu \acute{\alpha} \sigma \mu \alpha \tau \alpha$ to their humble rivals, and only allowed them the most elementary portions.[9]

[1] Dion. Thrax, 18.
[2] Dion. Thrax, Suppl., I.
[3] Ibid., III.
[4] JHS (1909), XXIX, 30 seq.
[5] ABKK (1913), XXXIV, 219.
[6] POxy., 469; Wessely, Studien, II, LVIII.
[7] JHS (1909), XXIX, 32 seq.
[8] Quint., I, 9, 1; 3.
[9] Ibid., I, 9, 6; II, 1, 1.

These προγυμνάσματα were in fact a weighty set of exercises, found in a meticulously codified form in the wordy manuals of Imperial times, like the ones by Hermogenes and Theon of Alexandria (second century) and Aphthonius (fourth century). The list that the boys had to follow was always the same: fable, narrative, "chria", aphorism, confirmation (or refutation), common-places, eulogy (or censure), comparison, ethopeia (or prosopopeia), the "thesis", and finally the discussion of law. But the last four stages have brought us to the threshold of the speech proper, and in any case we have already been in the school of rhetoric for a long time. Only the first five stages—three in the case of Theon, who grouped "chria", aphorism and confirmation together—seem to have formed a normal part of secondary-school education.

We are surprised to find them so elementary—we have children doing similar exercises in primary schools when they have only been there a short time. But after all that has gone before, the reader will not be surprised at the gap between teaching then and teaching now.

To begin at the beginning: the "fable" was simply a short composition in which the child wrote down a little story that he had just read or had told to him. Although the word "paraphrase" was used in those days,[1] I hesitate to employ it here, for there was absolutely no question of explaining it; the aim was to reproduce the story as exactly as possible. Here is an example—a late one (fourth-fifth century)—found on a papyrus in the Fayum.[2]

"A son who had murdered his father 'was afraid of being caught by the law, and so he fled to the desert.'" (The child has in this case remembered a verse from the original and put it down word for word). "And going over the mountain he was chased by a lion. And with the lion chasing him he climbed up a tree. And seeing a dragon leap on to the tree that could climb up it . . . And fleeing from the dragon he fell down. Wicked people cannot escape from God. 'God will bring the wicked to judgment.'" (Another line written down from memory: it was a saying attributed to Menander.[3])

As can be seen, this first exercise did not call for any great imagination; all the child had to do was to put the verse into prose. The next exercise, "narrative", did call for a little more imagination, but very little. The narrative was not made up by the child himself, as it would be today; he was simply told a "story" and then asked to repeat it in his own words—repeat it, not develop it: these little stories took up no more than ten lines, and of the qualities they were expected to show the manuals never fail to mention brevity, along with clarity, verisimilitude and correctness.[4]

For Hellenistic teachers, meticulous, finicky as they were, showed tremendous enthusiasm and put all their power of analysis into these apparently insignificant exercises. The narrative, which was only a few lines long, had not only to possess the four qualities mentioned above but to introduce six elements—agent, action, time, place, manner and cause[5]—and choose between five

---

[1] Rhet. Gr., II, 62, 10 (Theon).
[2] [Babr.] 437.
[3] [Men.] Monost., 14.
[4] Rhet. Gr., II, 79, 20; 83, 14 seq. (Theon), 22, 11 (Apht.).
[5] Ibid., II, 78, 16 seq. (Theon); 22, 9 seq. (Apht.).

genuses[1] and three or four species[2]—mythical, poetical, historical or civic. The papyri contain a few examples of historical narrative—Alexander's letter to the Carthaginians,[3] a supposed letter from Hadrian to Antoninus—a reference to very recent history, this, for the papyrus it is written on dates from the second century.[4]

But usually the narratives were from poetry, and closely connected with the literary study of the classics. The teacher would describe the subject of a poem or play, and thus have a ready-made story that the children could try to put into their own words; and so we find little Egyptian schoolboys writing a few lines on the story of Philoctetes, or Aeneas, or Achilles;[5] Iphigenia in Aulis,[6] Adrastus and his daughters,[7] Lycurgus the son of Dryas,[8] Patroclus saving Eurypylus.[9]

One stage higher, and we come to the "chria"—χρεία—what we should call a fable—attributed to some famous person like Aesop[10] or Anarcharsis[11] or Pythagoras, or some sage of antiquity; amongst the moderns, Diogenes was by far the most popular. There was the same meticulous classification: the "chria" might refer either to a symbolic action or to a historic saying—or to a combination of both. Although brevity was still the rule,[12] the pupil now began to be allowed to develop his subject-matter—the actual subject was given in a couple of lines, and his "answer" might fill a small page.[13] But how tentative he had to be: he could only advance one step at a time, guided by strict rules to which he was bound to adhere in each section. Suppose he was given the following:

"Isocrates says, 'The roots of education are bitter but the fruits thereof are sweet.'"

This had to be treated in its proper order in eight paragraphs (κεφάλαια):

1. Introduction to Isocrates and a eulogy on him.
2. A paraphrase of his aphorism in three lines.
3. A brief defence of his opinion.
4. Proof by contrast, refuting the contrary opinion.
5. Illustration by analogy.
6. Illustration by anecdote—borrowed from Demosthenes, for example.
7. Quotations from old authorities in support—Hesiod, etc.
8. Conclusion: "Such is Isocrates' excellent saying about education."[14]

I shall not describe in detail the exercises that followed: the aphorism—γνώμη—which was almost the same as the "chria" except that it was anonymous (this is a simplification—there were in fact four differences!);[15] the confirmation or refutation of an opinion or myth. . . . It is enough to have given some idea

[1] *Rhet. Gr.*, II, 5, 1 *seq.* (Herm.)
[2] *Ibid.*, II, 4, 27 *seq.* (Herm. J.); 22, 5 *seq.* (Apht.).
[3] *JHS* (1908), XXVIII, 130.
[4] *PFay.*, 19.
[5] *JHS* (1908), XXVIII, 128-9; *PTebt.*, 683r.
[6] *ASFNA* (1868), III, XLVIII *seq.*
[7] *POxy.*, 124.

[8] *PSI*, 135.
[9] *POxy.*, 154.
[10] *O. Wilcken*, II, 1226.
[11] *BCH* (1904), XXVIII, 201.
[12] *Rhet. Gr.*, II, 61, 22 (Herm.).
[13] *Ibid.*, II, 23, 19 *seq.* (Apht.)
[14] *Ibid.*, II, 23, 14 *seq.* (Apht.).

[15] *Ibid.*, II, 96, 24 (Theon).

of the system. A modern reader is struck by the excessively meticulous, legalistic, dogmatic character of these exercises. This becomes all the more noticeable as we go higher up the scale, until in the teaching of rhetoric proper it becomes the dominant feature.

This was the very essence of classicism—the antipodes of modern romanticism, with its systematic search for originality. The schoolboy of antiquity was not obliged to be original: all that was required of him was that he should learn to write and criticize according to certain rules. He had first to learn what these rules were, therefore—and that meant learning by heart the three qualities, the six elements, the nine headings. Which took time!

But the ancient school knew how to make haste slowly. No new step was ever taken until there had been a long stay on the level beneath: the pupil could take his time, especially as the grammarian had to train him in language as well as composition. This accounts for the curious practice of getting him to go through all the cases and all the numbers of the words that occurred in the short passages upon which each fable[1] or narration[2] or chria[3] was based—an exercise so extraordinary that one finds it hard to believe the theoretical writers who mention it. But there is no doubt that it was practised: an Egyptian writing-board shows us a schoolboy dutifully declining a chria based on Pythagoras. First, in the singular:

"The philosopher Pythagoras, having gone ashore and started giving language lessons, advised his disciples to abstain from flesh meat. We are told that the opinion of the philosopher Pythagoras was . . ." and so on—the genitive case following the nominative. "It seemed good to the philosopher Pythagoras . . ." (dative). "They describe the philosopher Pythagoras as saying . . ." (accusative and infinitive construction). "O philosopher Pythagoras!" (vocative). Then, scorning all logic, this had to be repeated in the dual number: "The [two] Pythagorases, philosophers . . ." and then in the plural: "The Pythagorases, philosophers, having gone ashore and started giving language lessons, advised their disciples . . ." and so on for all the different cases.[4]

This was verbal gymnastics all right, even if it wasn't highly intellectual! Here again one feels the dead weight of these teaching methods, tolerable only because syllabuses were so limited and the cultural horizon more limited still, compared with teaching today.

[1] *Rhet. Gr.*, II, 74, 22 *seq.* (Theon.)
[2] *Ibid.*, II, 85, 28 *seq.*
[3] *Ibid.*, II, 101, 3 *seq.*
[4] *JHS* (1909), XXVIII, 30 *seq.*

CHAPTER VIII

SCIENCE

BUT literature was not the only subject on the secondary-school syllabus. Both Plato and Isocrates, it will be remembered, agreeing for once, supported Hippias's contention that the study of mathematics was an excellent training for the mind.

THE TEACHING OF MATHEMATICS

There are various indications that this advice did not go unheeded in the Hellenistic age.

When, in about the year 240 B.C., Teles tried to describe the trials of human life,[1] it was the teachers of arithmetic and geometry—ἀριθμητικός, γεωμέτρης —that, together with the riding master, he chose as being typical of the secondary-school stage of education, sandwiched between the primary school and the ephebia. We have the same picture again, two centuries later, from the author of the Axiochos.[2]

A list of the winners of school competitions in Magnesia ad Meandrum in the second century B.C. mentions an examination in arithmetic;[3] and, since this occurs along with examinations in drawing, music and lyric poetry, it puts mathematics in the category of secondary-school education. Again, at the Diogeneion college in Athens (1), according to Plutarch,[4] the (future) ephebes learnt geometry and music at the same time as letters and rhetoric; whilst in Delphi in the first century B.C. lectures were given in the gymnasium by an astronomer.[5]

The evidence, however, as can be seen, is rather meagre, and it will be necessary to inquire whether this is not in fact a sign of how little interest was taken in practice in the natural sciences.

THE IDEAL OF ΈΓΚΥΚΛΙΟΣ ΠΑΙΔΕΙΑ

Theoretically, at least, the principle was never in any doubt: in the ideal syllabus of a good "general education"—ἐγκύκλιος παιδεία (2)—the Hellenistic Greeks always put the mathematical sciences on the same level as language and literature.

We find frequent allusions to this term, ἐγκύκλιος παιδεία, in the writers of Graeco-Roman times. This has nothing to do with anything "encyclopaedic", which is an entirely modern idea—the word itself only came into existence in

[1] Ap. Stob., 98, 72.
[2] [Pl.] Ax., 366e.
[3] Dittenberg., SIG, 960, 17.
[4] Quaest. Conv., IX, 736 D.
[5] BEHE, 272, 15.

the sixteenth century (3). The word "encyclopaedia" evokes a picture of universal knowledge, and however elastic it may have been, ἐγκύκλιος παιδεία never claimed to embrace the totality of human knowledge; it simply meant, in accordance with the accepted meaning of ἐγκύκλιος in Hellenistic Greek, "the usual everyday education received by all". For this reason I suggest "general education" as a suitable translation.

This general education always remained difficult to pin down. It seemed to alternate between two ideas—one, the general culture of the educated gentleman, with no particular reference to teaching but including all the different stages, "prep. school, public school and university", and, of course, home background; and the other the basic learning, the "propaedeutic", the προπαιδεύματα,[1] that prepared the mind for the more advanced stages of education and culture; in other words, the ideal secondary education. This latter was particularly the philosophers' idea of it—both the ones who condemned ἐγκύκλιος παιδεία as being useless as a basis for philosophical culture—Epicurus,[2] and all the different varieties of Sceptic[3] and Cynic[4]—and those who insisted that it was essential, as did most of the schools[5]—especially, after Chrysippus,[6] the Stoics.[7]

Consequently the boundaries of such a syllabus were not very clear. Taken in the perfective aspect of the word "culture", it tended to absorb not only philosophy but various technical subjects too—medicine, architecture, law, drawing and military art (4)—which varied according to the personal predilections of the authors concerned. But essentially, in the restricted sense in which it was used by the philosophers, it always meant the seven liberal arts which the Middle Ages were to take over from the schools of late antiquity. These seven liberal arts, which were finally and definitely formulated in about the middle of the first century B.C., between the times of Dionysius Thrax and of Varro, were made up of the three literary arts, the Carolingian *Trivium*—grammar, rhetoric and dialectic: and the four mathematical branches of the *Quadrivium*—geometry, arithmetic, astronomy and theory of music—the traditional division since the time of Archytas of Tarentum,[8] if not Pythagoras himself (5).

The many school text-books that have come down to us from Hellenistic times (6) give us a clear idea of the way in which young Greek students embarked on these subjects. Although great progress was made in science in Graeco-Roman times from Archimedes to Pappus and Diophantus, the dominant feature of the period was an attempt to complete and bring to maturity the labours of the generations that had followed Thales and Pythagoras, when Greek science had reached a perfection of form which it was never to surpass.

GEOMETRY

Geometry was the Greek science *par excellence*, and Euclid (*c.* 330–275 B.C.) was its master. His *Elements* are famous: directly or indirectly they have been

[1] Phil., *Congr.*, 9: Orig., *Greg.* i.
[2] D.L., X, 6.
[3] [Ceb.]
[4] Sext. Emp., *Math.*
[5] D.L., II, 79; IV, 10; V, 86–88; IV, 29–33.
[6] *Ibid.*, VII, 129; cf. Quint., I, 10, 15.
[7] Sen., *Ep.*, 88, 20.
[8] Archyt., fr. I.

behind all the geometry taught not only to the Greeks but to the Romans and Arabs and us moderns as well. Until recently English schoolboys were using as their geometry text-book a translation of the *Elements* that differed little from the original work.

The book is therefore so well known that there is no need to embark on any lengthy analysis of its contents and method. Essentially it is a sequence of theorems with their attendant proofs based on a number of original definitions and αἰτήματα (a term covering what we nowadays divide into axioms and postulates). As many others have done before me, I must emphasize the logic of the proofs, their strictly rational character: geometrical reasoning is concerned with purely intellectual figures and proceeds with an extreme distrust of anything relating to sense experience. Unlike modern teachers of mathematics, Euclid, to escape the theoretical difficulties raised by the Eleatic criticism of the notion of movement, avoids as far as possible the processes which we know as rotation and superposing. Thus in order to demonstrate that in an isosceles triangle ABC the angles ABC and ACB are equal, a fundamental property which we can easily prove by similar triangles, Euclid has to go a long way round. He extends AB and AC to D and E, so that BD = CE and then joins BE and CD so that ABE = ACD and BCD = BCE . . . , etc.[1]

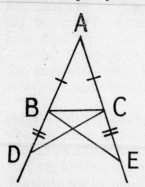

Intimately bound up with this synthetic method of having a series of interlinked proofs was what was called analysis, i.e. problems, particularly problems of construction. The *Elements* open with a typical example—to construct an equilateral triangle on a given base.[2] The methodological importance of these problems was considerable (only Platonists like Speusippus, inveterate a-priorists, thought fit to question it),[3] for construction proved the real existence of the particular figure involved. We still use the method Euclid generally followed—i.e. we assume the problem to be solved and then by ἀπαγωγή reduce it to propositions that have already been established. The history of Greek science is dotted with problems which, after the elementary matter of duplicating the square had been solved, raised great and even insurmountable difficulties—duplicating the cube, for example, trisecting an angle and squaring the circle.

These problems were purely speculative, of course; practical applications involving numbers, calculations of surfaces and volumes, did not belong to geometry but to subjects like geodesy or metrics. And these had a place in education too; a few text-books about them have come down to us—there are some by Hieron of Alexandria written in the second century A.D. for instance[4] —and then there are papyri with actual examples of the exercises that pupils had to do;[5] but this kind of education was only for future practitioners—

[1] Euc., *Elem.*, I, pr. 5.   [3] Procl., *In Eucl.*, I, p. 77, 15 *seq.*
[2] *Ibid.*, I, pr. 1.   [4] *Geom., Geod., Stereom.*
          [5] *P.Ayer* (*AJPhil.*, 19, 1898), 25 *seq.*; *Mizraim* (1936), III, 18 *seq.*

surveyors, contractors, engineers, masons; being technical instruction, it did not form part of a liberal education and remained outside the realm of mathematics proper.

ARITHMETIC

The same applies to arithmetic: it was the theoretical science of numbers, and so, following Plato's advice, it disdained real-life problems like those set in modern primary schools—profit and loss, buying and selling: antiquity honoured the great Pythagoras for having been the first to raise arithmetic above a squalid commercial level.[1]

Because it lacked the necessary symbols, Greek arithmetic was unable to reach the same level of universality and perfection as Greek geometry. As we have already noted, the Greeks used letters for numbers, there being three groups of nine signs each, one group for the units, one for the tens and one for the hundreds; when an iota was added underneath on the left, this meant thousands. Theoretically, therefore, the system provided for all whole numbers from 1 to 999,999.

This was all right for practical purposes, but it meant that there was no way of writing anything from a million upwards, and it was far less flexible than the Arabic system we use today, which depends upon the actual position of the figures. (Incidentally, though Arabic, this system also existed in the Maya civilization.) The Greeks in fact did not like writing down any number higher than 100,000—unlike the Indian mathematicians of the fourth and fifth centuries A.D., who loved speculating on enormous numbers, like 1,577,917,828, which would have made the Greeks shudder with the fear of $\check{\alpha}\pi\varepsilon\iota\varrho o\nu$, the terror of infinity. A more serious disadvantage was that this notation was unable to express fractions or surds. It was in geometry that Greek mathematics carried the study of dimensions furthest—as can be seen particularly in Book X of Euclid's *Elements*, which is devoted to irrational sizes.

Greek arithmetic, therefore, must be regarded as the science of $\dot\alpha\varrho\iota\theta\mu\acute{o}\varsigma$ in the strict sense, i.e. as the science of *whole* numbers. Here again Euclid's *Elements*[2] give us a very useful idea of the matter, but the text-book which had the greatest historical influence was the *Introduction to Arithmetic* by Nicomachus of Gerasa (about A.D. 100). This was immediately adopted by the teaching fraternity, written about at great length, and translated into Latin (and later into Arabic). Its influence was so great that arithmetic took the place of geometry as the basis and the most important part of mathematics.

What were studied, then, were the properties of whole numbers, first odds and evens, then different kinds of evens—even evens (such as 2^n), even odds (2 multiplied by an odd number) and odd evens, $2^{n+1}(2m + 1)$. From a different standpoint, a distinction was made between prime numbers and the product of prime numbers, and the products of prime numbers with common factors; between equal and unequal numbers; multiples and sub-multiples;

---

[1] Stob., I, 19, 2.   [2] Euc., *Elem.*, VII–IX; cf. II.

superpartials and subsuperpartials (i.e. numbers of the form $\frac{m+1}{m}$), etc. Then there were ratios and means, arithmetical, geometrical, and harmonic, the latter being defined by the relationship $\frac{a}{b} = \frac{m-a}{b-m}$ . . .

Along with all this, which seems to go into such curious detail but is nevertheless quite a legitimate part of mathematics, went even stranger investigations into the qualitative and aesthetic properties of numbers. I do not mean the classification of compound numbers (i.e. numbers which are the product of several factors), which had begun with Pythagoras and which, as can be seen in Nicomachus, was developed in Hellenistic times to a high degree of precision —planar numbers (the product of 2 factors) and solid numbers (the product of 3 factors), the former including square, triangular and rectangular numbers (divided into heteromeceis of the form $m(m + 1)$ and promeceis, $m(m + n)$, ($n = 1$), and the latter being cubic, pyramidal and parallelipipedic, $m^2(m + 1)$, etc. These names were perfectly reasonable: since the Ancients regarded the (whole) number as a collection of units, monads, represented by material points, it was quite proper to study the ways in which they were associated and so link arithmetic with geometry.

I should like to say a word about the introduction of aesthetic and sometimes moral values, that can be seen for example when the expression "a perfect number" is used to describe a number like 28, which is equal to the sum of its aliquot parts ($28 = 1 + 2 + 4 + 7 + 14$), and when 220 and 284 are called "friendly numbers"—φίλιοι—because each is equal to the sum of the aliquot parts of the other ($220 = 1 + 2 + 4 + 71 + 142$ and $284 = 1 + 2 + 4 + 5 + 10 + 11 + 20 + 22 + 44 + 55 + 110$). Then there were the speculations, sometimes disarmingly childlike, on the marvellous properties of the first ten numbers, the "decade" on which the whole series of numbers is based. The Ancients went into raptures over the virtues of unity, the primary source of all things, individual, immutable, never losing its nature however much it is multiplied ($1 \times 1 = 1$); the "perfection" of the number three, the first to have a beginning, a middle and an end, each represented by a one ($1 + 1 + 1 = 3$); the balance and power of the quaternary—the τετρακτύς: $1 + 3 = 2 \times 2 = 4$, and the sum $1 + 2 + 3 + 4 = 10$; thus the quaternary engenders the decade. . . . Naturally, a symbolic value came to be attached to each of these first numbers. The Pythagoreans used to swear by the quaternary, "the source of eternal nature".[1] The figure One, the monad, was regarded with mystical adoration: "In her resides all that is intellectual and uncreated; she is the nature of Ideas, she is God, the Mind, the Beautiful, the Good and every intellectual essence. . . ."[2] The number Seven was Athena, the goddess who was no one's mother and no one's daughter—for seven is the only number that cannot produce any of the other numbers of the decade and cannot be produced by them.[3] It was also Ares, Osiris, Chance, Opportunity, sleep, speech, song, Clio and Adrastes as well.[4] But enough!

---

[1] [Pyth] V. Aur., 47–48.
[2] Theon Sm., Arith., 40.
[3] Theon Sm., Arith., 46.
[4] Nicom. ap. Phot., Bibl., 187, 600 B.

All this sort of thing came from the old Pythagorism, but the Greeks never managed to disentangle their ideas about numbers from these qualitative elements. Nicomachus of Gerasa, who wrote the *Introduction to Arithmetic*, also devoted a whole book to this "arithmology", this theology of numbers— his *Theologoumena arithmetica*; all that remains of it is an analysis by the patriarch Photius,[1] which goes into it in some detail; but there are echoes of it in several treatises of later Roman times.[2]

MUSIC

From Pythagoras too derived the third of the mathematical sciences, the science of the numerical laws governing music. There is a great deal of writing at various intervals between Aristoxenus and Boethius that enables us to develop a very clear idea of the extent of the knowledge that was gained in this field (7). The science of "music" had two parts—intervals, and rhythm. The first— harmonics, or canonics—analysed the numerical relationship between the different intervals of the scale: $\frac{2}{1}$ signified the octave, $\frac{3}{2}$ a fifth, $\frac{4}{3}$ a fourth, $\frac{5}{4}$ and $\frac{6}{5}$ major and minor thirds, and so on; $\frac{9}{8}$, the difference between a fifth and a fourth $(\frac{3}{2} : \frac{4}{3} = \frac{9}{8})$, measured the major tone. The theory was extremely advanced: to register the subtle harmonies which Greek musicians called χροαί, one had to measure a twelfth of a tone.

All these numerical relationships can be found today in treatises on acoustics, but they describe the different "wave frequencies" of each sound. The Ancients had no direct way of measuring the frequency of sound vibrations, but they managed to do so indirectly by measuring the length of the vibrating string or sounding pipe on a monochord (the length being inversely proportionate to the frequency of the vibrations). The discovery of the relationships between the various lengths was one of the greatest achievements of Greek science, and it is understandable that not only the Pythagoreans but all the thinkers of antiquity were absolutely fascinated by it; for they had managed to connect numbers, definite and indeed simple numbers like 2, $\frac{3}{2}$, etc., with subjective impressions and aesthetic values—proper intervals, harmonies (the octave, the fifth, etc.). How could anyone doubt after this that number was the key to the Cosmos and the whole universe based on it?

Less complicated numerically, but no less exact and no less fruitful, was their investigation into rhythm. Rhythm is created by combining different sound durations, and so it can be reduced even more easily than melody to simple combinations of arithmetical values—equals, doubles, "sesquialternates"—just as we speak of "binary" and "ternary" rhythms today. But Greek rhythm— in both music and poetry—was not made up like ours by taking a particular length—the breve—and dividing and then sub-dividing it, but by adding indivisible units to each other—Aristoxenus' "primary time"—χρόνος πρῶτος —a more flexible system than our rather feeble "four in a bar", and one which

---

[1] *Ibid.*, 187, 591 *seq.*
[2] Anat., *Dec.*; Theon Sm., *Arith.*, 37–49; [Iambl.] *Theol. arith.*; August., *Mus.*, I, 11(18)– 12(26).

was able to produce far more powerful and complex rhythms. Here again the Greek genius for lucid inquiry created an imperishable monument—κτῆμα ἐς ἀεί—which has become part of our Western heritage—as will be realized when it is remembered that it was by studying the remaining fragments of Aristo-xenus' *Elements of Rhythm* that Westphal was able to produce such a profound and illuminating analysis of the rhythms in the *Well-Tempered Clavichord* (8).

ASTRONOMY

Although it developed later, Greek mathematical astronomy too performed some remarkable feats, especially in the Hellenistic period, from Aristarchus of Samos (310–250) and Hipparchus (end of the second century B.C.) to Ptolemy (second century A.D.): the results were collected and given some sort of order in what we may call its *Summa*—the thirteen books of Ptolemy's *Almagestes* (9).

This great work, which was to become quite famous during the Middle Ages not only in the Latin West but in the Byzantine East and Islam, was used as a text-book sometimes—in the neo-Platonic school in Athens under the Late Empire, for instance—but for the early stages of astronomy the Greeks generally used less ambitious books like the Stoic Geminus of Rhodes' *Intro-duction to Phaenomena* (first century B.C.), and the work by Aratus, to which I shall be returning later. Geminus's book was short and unpretentious; it opened with an account of the Zodiac and the constellations, went on to describe the heavenly body, the earth's axis, the poles, the circles (Arctic, Tropic, the Equator), day and night, the months, the phases of the moon, the planets, and ended with a calendar showing the times of the rising and setting of the stars, with quite a few numerical details on the way.

It was not the only book of its kind. We know by name, or possess the re-mains of, a whole series. Some have been found on papyrus—the elementary treatise in twenty-three columns on the *Papyrus Letronne I*,[1] for instance, which is a summary of the principles of Eudoxus, as can be seen from the title, Εὐδόξου τέχνη, which is an acrostic.

Of the four branches of mathematics, astronomy was the most popular, the one that aroused most curiosity. It was not a purely theoretic interest, for it was inseparable from the increasing popularity of astrology in Graeco-Roman society—in fact the terms "astrology" and "astronomy" seem to have been more or less interchangeable: a genuine scholar like Ptolemy could put his name not only to an authentic treatise on astronomy like the *Almagestes* but also to a book on astrology, his well-known *Tetrabiblos*. But there is no indication that astrology had got into the schools, or that it figured on the syllabus of liberal education.

DECLINE OF SCIENTIFIC STUDIES

As can be seen, there is no difficulty about knowing what science was taught, and how it was taught, in the Hellenistic age. The difficulty is to know who benefited from it.

[1] *NEMBN*, XVIII, 2, 25–76.

Theoretically, according to Plato and Aristotle, and according to the Hellenistic formula ἐγκύκλιος παιδεία, mathematics was bound to be included in any truly liberal education. The question is, was this so in practice? Who was supposed to be taught mathematics—everybody, or a specialist élite? Did it form part of secondary-school education—as it was supposed to, in theory—or was it entirely for the more advanced students?

This question is not easily answered. The reader cannot fail to have been struck by the paucity of the evidence adduced at the beginning of this chapter. Of course more data could be added—biographical and bibliographical scraps about a few writers and others. Diogenes Laertius, for instance, describes how the philosopher Arcesilaus was educated, and that brings us to the middle of the third century B.C.[1] As we should expect, his education had a solid literary foundation: he was an admirer of Pindar; his day began and ended with a reading of Homer; he himself wrote poetry and literary criticism. But he also studied mathematics, and we are told the names of his teachers—Autolycus, the musician Xanthus, and the geometer Hipponicus. What is more illuminating still: we are told that he studied under the first two of these *before* he decided which of the two rival branches of advanced learning he intended to go on with —philosophy or rhetoric. This means that in the case of Arcesilaus mathematics formed part of what we today would call the secondary-school period.

Nicolaus Damascenus, a historian who lived in the time of Augustus, tells us in a passage of autobiography[2] that first of all he studied grammar, then rhetoric, music and mathematics, and, last of all, philosophy. The physician Galen, who was born in Pergamus in A.D. 129, likewise tells us, in an interesting treatise which he called *My Own Writings*, that in his youth he studied not only grammar, dialectics and philosophy—subjects he later wrote about at great length[3]—but geometry, arithmetic and its practical applications (logistics).[4]

Probably there is more evidence of the same kind, but I do not think that it would make any substantial difference to the general picture. It seems clear that as the Graeco-Roman period advanced the sciences gradually gave way more and more to literature. I ask those of my readers who are Greek and Latin scholars to decide; is it not clear from the classics of this era that Hellenistic culture was predominantly literary in character and had little room for mathematics? It follows that mathematics played very little active part in the formation of the mind.

Indeed, on the educational level I do not think it can be denied that in the end literature practically eliminated mathematics from the secondary-school syllabus. Mathematics went on being studied, of course; but the people interested in the subject—mathematical specialists, or philosophers for whom mathematics was an indispensable preliminary—got no new recruits from the secondary schools. The result was that it had to be included in the higher education.

Significantly, at the beginning of the second century A.D., a certain Theon of Smyrna felt obliged to write a summary of mathematics in five books—

---

[1] D.L., IV, 29–33.
[2] *Ap.* Suid., III, p. 468.

[3] Gal., *Libr. propr.*, 11–18, pp. 39–48.
[4] *Ibid.*, 11, p. 40.

arithmetic, plane geometry, stereogeometry, astronomy and "music"—and he entitled it *Mathematical Knowledge Useful for the Learning of Plato:* as he himself explains at the beginning,[1] many people who wanted to study Plato had never done any mathematics even when they were children.

The evidence supplied by the neo-Platonists of the Late Empire is even more significant. They were too faithful to the *Republic* not to insist on the necessity for a "preliminary purification" of the mind—προκαθαρσία—by mathematics; but the young people who came to sit at their feet had had a purely literary training, so that science had to be taught inside the school itself (10). Proclus, for instance, as we know from the biography by Marinus of Neapolis, spent many years studying science. His early training had been purely literary— grammar and rhetoric[2]—and only after his conversion to philosophy did he embark on mathematics, which he studied under Hero while he was studying Aristotle's logic under Olympiodorus.[3]

ARATUS AND THE LITERARY STUDY OF ASTRONOMY

There is one particularly significant example of this invasion of science by the literary grammarian. As I have already pointed out, astronomy was the most popular of the sciences, but when we come to examine the way it was taught in Hellenistic schools (11), we find that this was not based on either of the elementary hand-books on astronomy which I have already mentioned but on a poem of 1,154 hexameters by Aratus of Soli, written *c*.276–274 B.C. and entitled *Phaenomena* (for the second part,[4] on Prognostics, should be included).

This poem became tremendously popular in scholastic circles all over the place, as can be seen from commentaries, "scholia", translations, not to mention painting: in Hellenistic art Aratus is the Astronomer just as Homer is the Poet (12). And yet Aratus was not a scientific astronomer; he was essentially a philosopher and man of letters, one of the wits at the court of Antigonus Gonatas, and all he did was put two prose works into verse and join them together —Eudoxus of Cnidus' *Phaenomena* and Theophrastus' mediocre Περὶ σημείων. And in this form Aratus' poem has no mathematics in it, no numbers, and only a few brief remarks about the heavenly body, about its axis and the poles.[5] The important part of the poem is its detailed "realistic" descriptions of the shapes traditionally associated with the constellations—Perseus[6] bearing his wife Andromeda on his shoulders, stretching his right hand towards the bed where his mother-in-law Cassiopeia is lying, raising a cloud of dust as he moves rapidly forward (a reference to the mass of stars in this part of the sky). There is the same anthropomorphism in the description of the rising and setting of the constellations,[7] which follows a brief account of the planets and circles of the heavenly body.[8] There are errors in his observations: as Hipparchus mentioned in his commentary,[9] Aratus does not realize that there are seven stars, not six, in the Pleiades (the smallest is difficult to see).[10] In the second part, the

---

[1] Theon Sm., *Arith.*, 1.
[2] Marin., *V. Procl.*, 8.
[3] *Ibid.*, 9.
[4] Ar. Sol., *Ph.*, 733 *seq.*
[5] *Ibid.*, 19–27.
[6] *Ibid.*, 248–253.
[7] *Ibid.*, 559–732.
[8] *Ibid.*, 454–558.
[9] *In Arat.*, I, 6, 12.
[10] *Ph.*, 254–258.

Prognostics, the errors are more serious, and perpetuate many popular superstitions.

The "popular" nature of the work was increased by the way in which it was studied in Hellenistic schools. Although some mathematicians and astronomers —Attalus of Rhodes and Hipparchus, in the second century B.C., for instance —did not consider it beneath their dignity to write about it, usually it was left to the grammarians, and from the scientific point of view their remarks were limited to a sketchy introduction to the globe—definitions of the axis, the poles and circles (arctic, tropical, equatorial, ecliptic)—for which they might use a model of the heavenly body; but this treatment was nevertheless not very advanced mathematically, so far as can be judged from the *scholia* that still exist. Their treatment of the poem was primarily literary, and spent itself on etymology and above all on the mythological legends suggested by Aratus' descriptions.

This brings us to an essential point. It was thanks to Aratus that astronomy had such a prominent place in secondary-school syllabuses, and the result was that astronomy appeared as something essentially literary, a literary explanation of a text. And—in spite of some resistance from the mathematicians[1]—the grammarians, the teachers of letters, seem to have succeeded in eliminating geometers and other scientific specialists almost completely. Mathematics no longer had any place in education—except for a few odd remarks mentioned in passing in some commentary or other, or in the form of extremely sketchy introductions written by a few grammarians with a smattering of science, like Mnaseas of Corcyra. We have this gentleman's epitaph: it proudly tells us that he had not only written commentaries on Homer,[2] but also taught astronomy[3] and geometry.[4]

As a result of this process, classical education developed in the Hellenistic age what was to be one of its essential features. For nothing is more characteristic of classical tradition—as we can see from the influence it has had and still has on our own education—than the predominance of literature and the dislike of mathematics as a basis for general education. Mathematics may be respected and admired, but it is for the experts, it demands a particular vocation.

This feature appears for the first time in Hellenistic times; henceforth Hippias and Plato, and even Isocrates, are far behind us. Mathematics, as I have already said, continues to flourish and progress as a science, continues to be widely studied, if not widely taught—we can see from the papyri how far it spread in Egypt, for fragments of Euclid's *Elements* have been found in Oxyrrhyncus and the Fayum,[5] along with treatises on the science of music[6] and astrononomy[7] and problems in geometry. But it is, from now on, a subject for specialists: mathematics no longer has any real place in the common culture, nor in that deep layer that unites all the different branches of the culture of any epoch and provides the adolescent with his first real training—secondary school education.

[1] *Schol.*, Ar. Sol., 19; 23.
[2] *IG*, IX, 1, 880, 6–8.
[3] *Ibid.*, 8–9.
[4] *Ibid.*, 9–13.
[5] *POxy.*, 29; *PFay.*, 9.
[6] *PTebt.*, 694; *PReinach*, 5; *POxy.*, 9; 667; *PHibeh*, I, 13.
[7] *PLetronne*, 1.

CHAPTER IX

HIGHER EDUCATION

I. LESSER FORMS

As IS only natural, the more advanced stages of education were less uniform than the lower; the latter supplied a general foundation, and above this arose several rival higher stages that suited different vocations and attracted young students in varying degrees. One of the first forms that we are able to study was found within the ephebia.

THE EPHEBE'S GENERAL CULTURE

As the Hellenistic ephebia ceased to be merely or even mainly a form of compulsory military service, intellectual culture came to be included more and more in its curriculum. The physical side remained essential, as we have seen, but it was no longer everything. The rich young men who went to the college wanted to be properly prepared for the life of the fashionable society to which they belonged, and the cultivation of the mind could no longer be left out. And so along with the sport there grew up lessons, lectures and auditions—σχολαί, ἐπιδείξεις, ἀκροάσεις (1).

These took place in the gymnasium itself, in a room built in the form of an "exedra"—Vitruvius' "ephebeum"—opening out on to the northern portico of the palestra. The architects were more particular about this room than any other: in Roman times it was enlarged and steps were added, so that it became a tiny but real indoor theatre, like the ones in Pergamus, Ephesus, Epidaurus and Philippi (2). Even in Hellenistic times, as can be seen from second[1] and first-century[2] inscriptions, it had ceased to be a genuine common-room; it was known as the ἀκροατήριον—the "auditorium" or lecture hall.

These studies were an integral part of the syllabus. There is a series of inscriptions dating from 122–121 to 39–38 B.C. in which we can see the "ecclesia's" pronouncements in honour of the ephebes of any given year: the young men (or their cosmetes) are congratulated for their diligence in attending "the courses of lectures given by the grammarians, philosophers, rhetors and others."[3] Similar lectures are known to have taken place outside Athens more or less everywhere—in Sestos,[4] for example, and Pergamus[5] and Perga.[6]

---

[1] Robert, *Et. Anat.*, 74 *seq.*
[2] *IG Rom.*, IV, 1703.
[3] *IG*² II, 1906, 19; 20; 64; 1028, 85; 1029, 21–2; 1030, 31; cf. 1039, 17; 18; 47; 1042 b 19–20; c 7–8; 1043, 20; 43.
[4] Michel, 327, 74 *seq.*
[5] *AM*, 1908, 380, 14, 376, 11–15; 1907, 279, 9; 1910, 404, 8.
[6] *SEG*, VI, 725.

They had a very wide syllabus, and it can only be described as "advanced" in the sense that the ephebes had got beyond secondary-school age and went to the ephebia after they had finished their secondary schooling, for one of the purposes of these lectures was to complete the literary culture which was absolutely central in Hellenistic secondary school education (3). Not only were there in Athens γραμματικοί, teachers of letters, whose job was to teach the classics, but in Delphi,[1] Priene[2] and Eretria it is explained more precisely that the man in question was a ὁμηρικὸς φιλόλογος, i.e. a philologist concerned exclusively with Homer.[3] This work of criticism was rounded off with occasional recitals of poetry[4] and music.[5] There seems to have been far less mathematics; I can only think of the instance I have already mentioned of the Roman astronomer who went and lectured at the gymnasium in Dephi[6] in the first century B.C. Physicians lectured in the gymnasiums more frequently—in Elatea, in Perga and in Seleucia at least.[7]

But naturally the main subjects were the two that were most typical of advanced education—philosophy and rhetoric. We have seen that both were mentioned together regularly in Athens, but they were also found elsewhere—a philosopher is known to have lectured to the ephebes in Haliartus[8] and rhetors to have taught in Delphi[9] and Eretria.[10]

The difficulty is to know at what level these subjects were taught and how seriously they were taken. To judge by the documents that mention them, it was customary to make use of the services—often given freely—of a strolling lecturer who happened to be in the city: he was asked to give the ephebes one or more talks and was then repaid by being given some sort of official recognition or honorary title. Nothing is more characteristic of Hellenistic civilization than this category that included wandering poets, artists, philosophers, rhetors and specialists in hygiene, who went from city to city, from one end of the Greek world to the other, armed with fine speeches and sure of an enthusiastic reception (4). The "lecture" became the most vital form of literature, the one which to a modern historian seems most highly characteristic of the originality of the culture of the time. Indeed it becomes impossible to draw a line between the lessons that were given to young students and lectures to adults living in polite society.

But besides these casual visiting lecturers, who would often only give one performance, there also seem to have been, according to the documents, proper teachers. These were engaged by the gymnasiarch,[11] often at his own expense, and had the same status in the gymnasium as the military instructors;[12] they taught continuously throughout the year (5). If this was really so, then there was a proper system of teaching, of a more effective kind than anything that could be supplied by "popular" lecturers who just happened to come along.

The ephebes also had their own libraries—we know in particular of the

[1] Dittenberg., *SIG*, 739.
[2] *Ins. Priene*, 112; 113.
[3] Dittenberg., *SIG*, 739
[4] *F. Delph.*, III, 1, 273.
[5] *SEG*, II, 184.
[6] *BEHE*, 272, 15.
[7] *SEG*, III, 416; *SAWW* (1916), CLXXIX, 6, 54, 5–9; 55, 34–5.
[8] *IG*, VII, 2849.
[9] *BEHE*, 272, 13 *seq.*
[10] Dittenberg., *SIG*, 714.
[11] *Ibid.*, 714 (and n.2).
[12] *Ibid.*, I. 9.

Ptolemeion in Athens, which the ephebes both supplied with books and maintained themselves. In the second and first centuries B.C. each annual class seems to have been obliged to provide a batch of a hundred volumes,[1] which in the years between 47 and 42, for example, consisted of works by Homer and Euripides.[2] By great good luck we have a catalogue of this library, though unfortunately it is somewhat damaged: I have already had occasion to quote from it, for first on its list were the works of the classical poets, Aeschylus, Sophocles and the other tragedians, and commentaries on them: the comedian Menander was also there, as well as orators and historians like Demosthenes and Hellanicus, and some philosophers—for instance Euclides of Megara's *Dialogues*.[3] But there were similar libraries here and there all over the Greek world (6)—in Teos,[4] for example, and in Cos, where there are three inscriptions that refer to libraries, probably the same one in each case. This was attached to the gymnasium,[5] and it was built and furnished with books by a number of generous donors, some giving a fixed sum of two hundred drachmae, others giving a batch of a hundred volumes as well.[6] This library too had a catalogue, part of which remains in an inscription:[7] classification seems to have been by subject-matter—philosophy, politics and rhetoric—with each of these sections arranged in alphabetical order according to the authors' names. The titles which still survive show that the books were of a high technical standard; there were dialogues and political treatises by Demetrius of Phalera, Hegesias of Magnesia, Theopompus; and a book on rhetoric in four volumes by Theodectes of Phaselis. . . .

Final proof that these subjects were sometimes, at least, taken with absolute seriousness, and did not consist entirely of "popular" lectures, is to be found in the fact that official competitions were held in them. In Priene in the first century B.C. there was a generous gymnasiarch who organized competitions "on subject-matter connected with philology"—and, of course, in gymnastics too.[8] In Athens at the end of the second century A.D. most of the festivals that were held at the end of the ephebic year included two literary competitions, which took place before the sporting contests—a prose "eulogy" and a "poem"; both, it seems, composed in honour of the god, hero or emperor whose festival was being celebrated (7).[9]

But we must be careful not to exaggerate the evidence: even in the Athens of those days sport came first in the ephebia's honours-lists; elsewhere—and, at all other times, in Athens itself—sport was practically the only thing that was competed about. When there were any other competitions, they were moral, not intellectual. Take, for example, the ephebic games instituted about 125 B.C. by the gymnasiarch Menas in his city of Sestos on the Hellespont,

---

[1] *IG*[2] 1029, 25; 1009, 8; 1041, 23; 1043, 50.
[2] *Ibid.*, 1041, 24.
[3] *Ibid.*, 2363.
[4] *SEG*, II, 584.
[5] *RF*, 1936, 40; cf. 1935, 219.
[6] *BCH* (1935), LIX, 421.
[7] *RF*, 1935, 214 *seq.*
[8] *Ins. Priene*, 113, 28–29; 114, 21.
[9] *IG*[2], II, 2119, 131–133; 177; 189; cf. 2115, 46–47; 2116, 12.

which are typical of a fair number of cases that were to be found throughout the Greek world, from Marseilles in the west[1] to Heraclea[2] in Pontus in the east (8). Besides the usual military and athletic contests there were three others—for "good conduct", "fondness for work" and "vigour"—εὐταξία, φιλοπονία, εὐεξία[3]—but there was nothing really intellectual about these.

When they are seen in their proper perspective, therefore, the subjects we have been discussing tend to disappear into the background. And when one remembers the fashionable, frivolous atmosphere of the Hellenistic ephebia, and then remembers that the ephebes were only there for a year, one can easily imagine that the general cultural level was not very high. There was an immense range of subjects—literature, rhetoric, philosophy (not to mention the sciences) —and the ephebe could only have acquired the merest smattering, the rudiments. At best, he ended up as a jack-of-all-trades—and master of none.

THE MUSEUM AND HIGHER SCIENTIFIC EDUCATION

At the other end of the scientific scale we find a type of teaching that reached a very high technical level. This was at the Museum in Alexandria. The Lagid monarchy had founded a remarkable organization for scientific research (9) in its capital city at the end of the reign of Ptolemy I Soter (323–285).[4] As it was under royal patronage· it attracted not only poets and men of letters into the city, but the most eminent scholars of the day—geometers, astronomers, physicians, historians, critics and grammarians. These "museum pensioners" —οἱ ἀτελεῖς σιτούμενοι ἐν τῷ Μουσείῳ—lived in community, close to the Palace.[5] They had no taxes to pay and no other duties to perform, and they lived at the king's expense in luxurious conditions, with a "promenade", "exedras" for their discussions, and a vast dining-hall where they took their meals together. *Odium philologicum* is no new thing, and nobody familiar with any modern university will be surprised to learn that this corporate life was not entirely free from dialectical tension: which caused a certain amount of amusement in the city. "In this populous Egypt of ours," wrote Timon in his *Satirical Poems*, "there is a kind of bird-cage called the Museum where they fatten up any amount of pen-pushers and readers of musty tomes who are never tired of squabbling with each other."[6] Functionaries appointed by the king looked after the scholars' material needs so that they should have nothing to worry about and could devote all their attention to their studies. They had wonderful facilities for their work—Botanical and Zoological Gardens, and their world-famous Library with its annex, the Serapeum, a library unique in the history of antiquity for the number and quality of its books: the catalogue drawn up by its third librarian, Callimachus, between 260 and 240, contained a hundred and twenty thousand volumes (10).

The Museum was obviously a remarkable institution, but it had not appeared out of the void; it was simply a vaster and more official form of the kind of philosophical community created by the early Pythagoreans and copied by the

[1] *IG*, XIV, 2445.
[2] *BCH* (1898), XXII, 493, 12; 15–17.
[3] Michel, 327, 83.
[4] Plut., *Non posse suav.*, 1095 D.
[5] Strab., XVII, 793–794.
[6] Ath., I, 22 D.

Academy, the Lyceum and, at a later stage (306), by the Garden of Epicurus: the actual name—*Μουσεῖον*—had been used by the schools centring round Plato and Aristotle, which, as we have seen, were regarded as fellowships of the Muses. If, as seems likely, Ptolemy Soter established the Museum on the advice of Demetrius Phalerius, who took refuge at his court in 294, the Lyceum must have had a direct influence on the Alexandrian Museum, for Demetrius was the pupil of Aristotle's first successor, Theophrastus.[1]

The Museum was essentially a centre for scientific research, not advanced education: the scientists and scholars supported by the Lagids were not obliged to give any lectures. Nevertheless, they did teach. Good is self-diffusive, and knowledge has a natural tendency to spread: this is generally recognized to be one of human nature's fundamental characteristics. It was particularly strong in the Greeks who, as we have seen, even introduced a master-pupil attitude into their conception of love. We know that the scholars in the Museum did in fact attract disciples, and accepted and educated them (11): it is traditional, for instance, that grammarians like Dionysius of Alexandria and Apion had been *pupils* at the Museum, the former under Aristarchus and the latter under Apollonius.[2] And the teaching was so effective that it produced not one but several rival schools in each subject: we read of Aristarchians and Aristophanians in philology and the schools of Herophilus and Erasistratus in medicine.

The difficulty is to decide how big the student public was for whom this higher education was intended. Perhaps it grew up gradually. In the early stages the Museum was undoubtedly an academy rather than a university, so that the university side must have developed in the centuries that followed; for at the end of the third century A.D. Alexandria, like Athens, had professorial chairs in all the main branches of philosophy, and we know that in about the year 279 a Christian scholar, Anatolius, who was later to become Bishop of Laodicea, was promoted to the chair of Aristotelian philosophy (12). In the fourth century Alexandria was a great university city, particularly famous for medicine, and it attracted students from far and wide—from as far away as Cappadocia, as we know from the case of Caesarius, the brother of St. Gregory Nazianzen:[3] the best way for a doctor to impress his patients was to let them know that he had studied at Alexandria.[4]

It may of course be questioned whether this university activity had any connection with the Museum, for there is no absolute proof that it had. Not that the Museum disappeared: the imperial treasury carried on the work of the Lagid kings of Egypt, and the Museum certainly continued to exist—though confined to the Serapeum from Aurelian onwards—right up to the destruction of the famous sanctuary by the patriarch Theophilus in 391 (13). And the semantic development of the word *Μουσεῖον* undoubtedly seems to show that under the Empire it had become a centre of higher education.

As a matter of fact inscriptions reveal the existence of other Museums outside Alexandria (14) which functioned as universities. This was clearly so in Ephesus where, in the second century A.D., there was a faculty of medicine with pro-

[1] D.L., V, 75; Strab., IX, 398.
[2] Suid., s. vv. (II, 1173; I, 3215.)
[3] Greg. Naz., *Or.*, VII, 6, 2; 8, 3.
[4] Amm. Marc., XXII, 18; cf. 16–22.

fessors who had the characteristic titles of "physicians of the Museum", "masters at the Museum"—οἱ ἀπὸ τοῦ Μουσείον,[1] οἱ περὶ τὸν Μουσείου παιδευταί.[2] About Smyrna we have fewer details, but the fact that the Museum there had a jurist for its president at least once, suggests that the record office had developed into a school of law,[3] as it did later in Beirut. Finally, μουσεῖον is used in the fourth century by rhetors like Libanius[4] and Themistius[5] to mean simply a school.

Nevertheless at the beginning, in the time of the Ptolemies, the teaching activity of the Museum was still not properly established. It could only have been an esoteric type of teaching, largely archaic in character, a more or less individual kind of tuition which a master was willing to give a small group of specially chosen disciples whom he considered worthy to receive the revelation of his superior knowledge.

LACK OF ANY REAL TECHNICAL EDUCATION

Between these two extremes, the superficial education of the ephebia and the advanced work done in the various faculties at the Museum, were the ordinary forms of higher education. It comes as a surprise to a historian to discover that except for medicine there were no regular courses of study to prepare anyone for any of the professions. To take the case of law: we know that professional barristers—συνήγοροι—even if not solicitors—νομικοί (there is no evidence for them before Roman times)—were already in existence, especially in Ptolemaic Egypt. They were officially recognized by the law, which limited their field of operations (excluding them for example from fiscal tribunals)[6] and imposed a special tax on them, the "barristers' tax"—συνηγορικόν.[7] But there is no record of any law schools having existed anywhere; the teaching of law was to be one of the innovations introduced under the Roman Empire. One can only assume that barristers and jurists were trained like apprentices and attached themselves to someone already in practice (15). The same absence of documentary evidence forces us to the same conclusion in the case of all the other technical experts—the engineers (civil and military), surveyors and sailors who are so familiar in Hellenistic society and yet so strangely absent from its education. These may of course have been the people who did the exercises in geometrical and arithmetical calculus which have been found on papyri and which do not seem to have formed part of the regular secondary-school education;[8] but we cannot find any record of any higher centres of education in which these subjects were regularly taught. The technician, like the scientist, learned his job in a very simple, archaic way, the way of personal relationship between master and pupil, craftsman and apprentice.

[1] JOAI (1905), VIII, 135.
[2] F. Eph. II, 65; III, 68.
[3] IG Rom., IV, 618.
[4] Lib., Or., LXIV, 112.
[5] Them., Or. XXIV, 303 A (Hard.).
[6] PAmh., 33.
[7] UPZ, 172.
[8] PSI, 186; 763; ABKK (1916), XXXVII, 161–170.

THE TEACHING OF MEDICINE

To a certain extent this was still true of medicine, which we know much more about because it was more widespread and better organized. Greek medicine had made great progress and it played a big part in Hellenistic life. Besides private physicians there were public physicians maintained by the city or the kingdom, and these formed a real "health service" directed by master-physicians—ἀρχίατροι (16). This meant that a great number of specialists had to be trained, and there are in fact records of many schools of medicine not only in Alexandria but here and there throughout the Greek world. The old schools at Cnidus and Cos were still in existence—the latter indeed experienced a revival in the first century B.C. that went on increasing until the time of the Julio-Claudians (17)—and others grew up, so that in the second century A.D. there were schools in Smyrna, Laodicea, Ephesus and, the most famous of all, in Pergamus, where the school that had grown up around the celebrated sanctuary to Asclepius surpassed even the famous Cos, once made glorious by Hippocrates.

Thanks to all the writing about medicine that has come down to us we can get some idea (18) of the kind of teaching that was given in these schools. First and foremost amongst the actual writings was the *corpus* attributed to Hippocrates, though much of it was written later. This was to all intents and purposes complete by the beginning of the third century B.C., and it became the medical bible. To this must be added the no less considerable work of the physicians of Roman times—especially Galen (or Soranus) who collected the work of many centuries. A mere glance at these voluminous works is sufficient to show the Greek genius for teaching in full play: their medicine was a genuine "art"—a τέχνη—a body of doctrine that had developed practical rules into a system. There is no better evidence of the lengths to which this mania for systematization could go than the short Hippocratic treatises on deontology, i.e., the physician's attitude towards his patients. There is the curious treatise *On the Right Way to Behave*, for instance—περὶ εὐσχημοσύνης—(which a German scholar translated as *Über den Chic*). This contains a great deal of advice, of extreme psychological subtlety, on how to behave in the sick-room, with rules carefully catalogued so that the student will find them easier to remember. "Upon entering, remember (i) how to sit down: (ii) how to arrange your attire"—the flowing drapery required special attention: the physician should not thoughtlessly take too much off.[1] He was also to remember to be dignified, brief, calm, etc.[2] There is advice about visiting,[3] about the patient's psychology;[4] there are the *Precepts*, with remarks on the question of fees—"Don't broach the subject too soon"[5]—and consultations—colleagues may be called in for consultation in difficult cases, but there should be no squabbling in public and another physician's opinion should never be criticized.[6]

All this elaborate technical teaching was given in a very undeveloped, archaic

---

[1] HPC, Hab., 7 (IX, 236).
[2] Ibid., 12 (IX, 238 seq.).
[3] Ibid., 13, (240.)

[4] Ibid., 14 (Ibid).
[5] Ibid., Praec., 4-5 (IX, 254 seq.).
[6] Ibid., 8 (262 seq.).

way, however. When we speak of medical schools in Hellenistic Greece we mean a few teachers in a city, with a number of pupils under them. To speak of a "faculty" in Alexandria, Cos, etc., as is so often done, is only permissible if this term is used to mean a corporate organization uniting the various teachers. This was particularly the case at the Museum in Ephesus under the Empire, when the physicians formed a syndicate—συνέδριον—and had a yearly medical competition. The president of the contest was called the "physicians' gymnasiarch" (!); it lasted two days and had four parts: surgery, instruments, thesis and problem. Beginners were not eligible, only the most highly qualified doctors—the ἀρχίατροι[1]—which gives some idea of the lengths to which the Hellenes' agonistic spirit could go. But it would not be correct to speak of a "faculty" at Ephesus, if this is supposed to mean a properly organized centre of higher education in which a body of specialist teachers share the various branches of the curriculum.

The actual conditions were far more humble. The study of medicine in Graeco-Roman times still meant getting in with a practising physician and doing one's apprenticeship under him. No doubt this included theory, which meant reading and studying the classics—i.e. Hippocrates—and discussing the principles of biology and medical treatment; in fact a great deal of time was spent (or lost)[2] on this preliminary work, for the argumentative atmosphere of Hellenistic philosophy had invaded medicine, and the rival sects—Dogmatics, Empirics, Methodics, Pneumatics—made dialectical onslaughts on each other and tore each other to pieces.

But the teaching of medicine proper was mainly clinical. There was not much study of anatomy—this was always the weak point in ancient medicine— and dissection was comparatively rare, a matter of advanced research that never came into teaching; judging by a fragment of a text-book in question-and-answer form that has come down to us on a papyrus,[3] theory was reduced to a minimum and the main thing was practice. The physician would go on his rounds with his pupils and they would examine the patient with him and after he had finished;[4] gradually one of them would rise to be his assistant and then his "locum"—he would be left by the bedside to watch how the patient got on and what effect the treatment had;[5] he would be given deputies. . . . It was a slow process, of course—only charlatans like the Empiricists claimed to train anyone in six months.[6] Galen studied for eleven years—though he was un-usually conscientious: not satisfied with one teacher and one school, he had three teachers one after the other in his native city of Pergamus, and then went on to Smyrna, Corinth and Alexandria (19). But it was effective, for the student absorbed not only knowledge but the teacher's entire experience. This personal element compensated for the lack of institutionalism as compared with our training.

[1] JOAI (1905), VIII, 128, 5; 7.
[2] Pliny, HN, XXVI, 11.
[3] PGen., 111 (APF, II, 2).

[4] Mart., V, 9; Philstr., V.Ap., VIII, 7.
[5] HPC, Hab., 17 (IX, 242).
[6] Gal., Met. med., I, 83; X, 5; 19.

CHAPTER X

HIGHER EDUCATION

II. Rhetoric

BUT the physician was nevertheless a specialist, a technician, and though in "Hippocrates" and Galen we find the true and interesting and thoroughly modern idea that a subject like medicine, if it is properly studied to its depths, can become a perfect and entirely self-sufficient manifestation of the highest culture—the physician becoming himself a "philosopher"[1] and the physician-philosopher being a demigod[2]—nevertheless this was not the generally accepted view in Hellenistic times. The pure technician was not normally regarded as a man of culture. Galen himself, who was very keen to appear as an all-round man, lets us know that he had studied other subjects besides medicine: after a hard secondary schooling—which, remarkably, had even included mathematics—he went on to philosophy before he started on medicine, and then he studied the two together. In Smyrna, for example, he was studying medicine under Pelops at the same time as he was attending lectures on philosophy by the Platonist Albinus. Besides his own art he never lost his interest in grammar and logic. . . .[3]

The thing that really showed whether a man was cultivated or not was not whether he had studied science or medicine—things that only interested a narrow range of specialists—but whether he had received either of the two rival and allied forms of advanced education which were still the most widespread and characteristic—the two forms of culture typified by Plato and Isocrates: the philosophical and the rhetorical.

RHETORIC—THE QUEEN OF SUBJECTS

Of these the dominant member was unquestionably the second, which left a profound impression on all manifestations of the Hellenistic spirit. For the very great majority of students, higher education meant taking lessons from the rhetor, learning the art of eloquence from him.

This fact must be emphasized from the start. On the level of history Plato had been defeated: posterity had not accepted his educational ideals. The victor, generally speaking, was Isocrates, and Isocrates became the educator first of Greece and then of the whole ancient world. His success had already been evident when the two were alive, and it became more and more marked as the generations wore on. Rhetoric is the specific object of Greek education and the highest Greek culture.

[1] Gal., *Med. phil.; Protr.*, 14. [2] *HPC, Hab.* 5 (IX, 232).
[3] Gal., *Libr propr.*, 11 *seq.*

A historian's first reaction is one of surprise: at first sight it seems strange that the prestige attaching to the art of oratory should have survived the social conditions that had produced it and brought it into the foreground; for, as we have seen, it was the political conditions of the fifth century, especially in the democratic cities, that lay behind the development of eloquence and oratorical technique. But in the Hellenistic age, the free autonomous city was a thing of the past, and political conditions centred round absolute monarchy. The orator seemed to have had his day. From now on the man who counts in politics is the court adviser, who knows how to gain his master's confidence and, through him, influence the government. A number of Hellenistic intellectuals tried their hand at this game; for a short time, as I suggested when I was dealing with the Academy, it seems to have been one of the Stoics' specialities. . . .

Of the three "kinds of speech" which had been recognized in theory since the time of Aristotle—the deliberative, the judicial and the epideictic—the two former had not completely disappeared, but they had been relegated to the background as a result of the decline of the city system; deliberative assemblies went on existing, but except in special emergencies—as for instance in times of political disturbance, when the city might side with one king against another—the matters discussed had become unimportant except from a municipal point of view. Again, there were still tribunals, but here too, though the proceedings occasionally had a political aspect, they were only concerned with matters of local interest; they were not, as they had been in the sixth or fifth century, the nerve-centre of life and civilization. The only kind of speech that had survived and was flourishing was the last of the three, "epideictic" eloquence, or the eloquence of the set speech—in something more approximating to decent English, the art of the lecturer.

This had not merely survived, it had developed, and it was now in a thriving condition, seeping into all the neighbouring subjects and invading everything. We have already come across it in the gymnasiums, where even astronomers and physicians had to be lecturers. What else could be expected in literature, then? Reading was done aloud, so that there was no borderline between the written and the spoken word; the result was that the categories of eloquence were imposed on every form of mental activity—on poetry, history and even (as we shall see later on) philosophy. Hellenistic culture was above all things a rhetorical culture, and its typical literary form was the public lecture.

By a curious reversal of fate, the orator's artistic prestige was ultimately to invest him with a certain political importance. In Roman times, whenever a city produced one of these artists-in-words, and he turned out to be a successful professional lecturer, it was glad to have him as its spokesman—not merely at public ceremonies like the festivals and the games—that was only a matter of set speeches and comparatively unimportant—but in far more weighty matters. If the city got into trouble with the king, or the province with a neighbouring province, it would naturally choose him as its ambassador (20)—not only because he was the best person to plead its cause, the most persuasive arguer (that would have been the attitude in Demosthenes' time), but also because his personal authority as an orator, an authority deriving from the universal prestige accorded to his art, ensured, *a priori*, that he would be received with attention, goodwill and respect. Experience proved that this was a fair bet. This curious phenomenon is characteristic of Graeco-Roman culture; many examples of it are to be found dotted here and there throughout the centuries, right to the end of antiquity (21).

But we must be careful not to stand this matter on its head and mistake the effect for the cause: rhetoric did not lie at the root of Hellenistic culture as a primary, paradoxical fact and so burst forth naturally into flower in the field of education. On the contrary, it was secondary and derivative. The primary fact is that ever since the time of Isocrates and the Sophists, and in spite of all the political and social revolutions that had taken place, eloquence had been the main cultural objective, the crown and completion of any liberal education worthy of the name.

There are gaps in our knowledge, and it is not easy to reconstruct the history of the old schools of rhetoric (22), but we know enough to be able to say that the tradition was never broken. From the time of Isocrates, rhetoric was always, in practice, accepted as the normal means to the highest flights of education.

Why? You may say, routine, for teaching is not exactly a happy hunting-ground for innovators—things are inclined to go on long after their original *raison d'être* has disappeared into the mists of oblivion. But the exceptional popularity of rhetoric in the schools of old needs something more direct to explain it, and I believe that this exists—in Isocrates' remarkable teaching about the Word. Learning to speak properly meant learning to think properly, and even to live properly: in the eyes of the Ancients eloquence had a truly human value transcending any practical applications that might develop as a result of historical circumstances; it was the one means for handing on everything that made man man, the whole cultural heritage that distinguished civilized men from barbarians. This idea underlies all Greek thought, from Diodorus Siculus[1] to Libanius.[2] Is it surprising, therefore, that rhetoric should have remained at the heart of all their education and all their culture?

Παιδεία! The essential ambiguity of this word is worth remembering. It meant both education and culture. And this helps to explain a characteristic feature of Graeco-Roman civilization which we moderns tend to regard as a symptom of decadence (23)—the scholastic character of the literary life. As I have said, Hellenistic culture was primarily a lecturers' culture, and the public speeches which so delighted the men of letters were not substantially different from the scholastic exercises in rhetoric which we shall be examining shortly. We may smile at these good people "who never get tired of going to their rhetoric classes," and this "literature for teachers and good boys" may tend to make us yawn, but in so far as it represented the victory of the Word, it acquired the value of an absolute and became in a way an end in itself. Nothing finer was imaginable, and our clear-cut distinction between "culture" and "education" grew fainter and fainter.

[1] I, 2, 5-6.   [2] *Ep.*, 369, 9.

THE PRACTICE OF RHETORIC

We can get a very clear idea of what was involved in the teaching of this highly esteemed subject. When a youth had finished his literary studies he would leave the grammarian for a specialist in eloquence, a rhetor—σοφιστής, ῥήτωρ (24). Rhetors were everywhere, in every self-respecting city; as we have seen, a wealthy patron provided the ephebes in Eretria with one.[1] There were more of them, and more high-class ones, in the great "university" centres that attracted foreign students. It might happen, as in the case of medicine, that a student determined to know his subject thoroughly would go from one teacher to another, but the principle of a personal relationship between teacher and pupil—a principle dear to antiquity—still held good, and a group of disciples centring round the same master was often described poetically as a chorus or a "thiasos" or a fraternity—χορός, θίασος, ἀγέλη, φρατρία—so that the spiritual bond that united them had an almost sacred character (25).

The actual content of the teaching had changed little since Isocrates' time; it had simply gone on developing along its own lines in the direction of an ever greater technical perfection. This appears clearly in the first of its three parts —which were: theory, study of models, and applied exercises.

Isocrates, it will be remembered, would have liked to reduce this first part— the theory—to a minimum, but his views on this point had been ignored. Even Aristotle's *Rhetoric* introduced new distinctions and new definitions. Aristotle imagined that his great synthesis, based as it was upon a systematic enquiry into all the books that had ever been written on the subject—the Συναγωγή τεχνῶν[2]—would standardise the way it was taught, but it did nothing of the kind: with each successive generation the teaching grew more and more complicated, until it ended up with those exhaustive and exhausting tracts that dumbfound any casual reader of the collections of the *Rhetores Graeci*.

Since rhetoric disappeared from our own secondary-school education, we have so completely forgotten what this sort of codification of rhetorical processes could lead to that we find it difficult to imagine just how far the analytical spirit characteristic of the Greeks had penetrated into this field (26). In a sense this is unfortunate, for our ignorance of this kind of study, which was so familiar to all the men of antiquity, makes classical literature much more difficult to appreciate: a great many things in the Greek and Latin authors that escape us or astonish us explain themselves quite easily when they are seen against this educational background.

We have already seen signs in the grammarian's teaching of an almost morbid tendency towards systems and rules, and this tendency was given full rein in the special field of eloquence. Rhetoric began with classifications and definitions: the first thing any student had to do was to learn a whole new technical vocabulary and acquaint himself with all the unexpected ramifications of the analytical approach. There were five parts: invention, arrangement, elocution, memorising and action.

"Invention" provided a number of ingenious methods for obtaining new

[1] Dittenberg., *SIG*, 714.   [2] Arist., fr. 136–141 (Rose).

ideas, founded on the celebrated theory of "places"—τόποι—intrinsic places, extrinsic places, etc. The theory went into great detail, with model answers that could be applied to any kind of question, any kind of subject-matter, any kind of approach.

To give the reader some idea of the refinements to which it could go, I shall give an example of the eulogy—ἐγκώμιον. As we know, this came into the category of introductory exercises—προγυμνάσματα—and seems to have been the first branch of his subject that the rhetor was determined not to surrender to the grammarian. It was also, as we have seen, the essential literary test in the ephebia competitions in Athens under the Empire. But it was much more than a school exercise—there was no sharp distinction, as I have already said, between "school" and "life". It was an essential part—together with the "consolation"—of the funeral oration, a literary genre that had many different variations, all of which were highly popular. But it was also a literary genre in its own right, and one that was often practised; a number of public meetings —including the most famous: the Panathenaean, the Pythian, the Isthmian— included eulogy competitions in either prose or verse: they made their first official appearance in the first century B.C. and became more and more popular under the Empire (27).

Suppose a certain person, living or dead, real or mythical, is to be eulogised. According to the theory, there will be thirty-six definite stages, divided and subdivided as follows:[1]

I   *Exterior Excellences*
  (a) Noble birth (εὐγενεία)
  (b) Environment
        1. Native city
        2. Fellow citizens
        3. Excellence of the city's political regime
        4. Parents and family
  (c) Personal advantages
        1. Education
        2. Friends
        3. Fame
        4. Public service
        5. Wealth
        6. Children, number and beauty of
        7. Happy death (εὐθανασία)

II   *Bodily Excellences*
        1. Health
        2. Strength
        3. Beauty
        4. Bubbling vitality and capacity for deep feeling (εὐαισθησία)

[1] *Rhet. Gr.*, II, 109 *seq.* (Theon).

III *Spiritual Excellences*

(a) Virtues
   1. Wisdom
   2. Temperance
   3. Courage
   4. Justice
   5. Piety
   6. Nobility
   7. Sense of greatness

(b) Resultant Actions

   (A) As to their objectives:
      1. Altruistic and disinterested
      2. Good, not utilitarian or pleasant
      3. In the public interest
      4. Braving risks and dangers

   (B) As to their circumstances:
      1. Timely
      2. Original
      3. Performed alone
      4. More than anyone else?
      5. Few to help him?
      6. Old head on young shoulders?
      7. Against all the odds
      8. At great cost to himself
      9. Prompt and efficient

All this was absolutely basic, and other sections might be added—how highly eminent men had thought of him; all the striking deeds he would undoubtedly have done if he had not unfortunately died; where possible, a cunning pun or two on his name—Demosthenes, for instance, was very "well-named" "the strength of the people"—τοῦ δήμου σθένος; or references to other famous men with similar names, or the names he might have been given—Pericles, the Olympian. . . .

It will be seen that models like this could be very useful to a budding orator, but it is also clear that it must have been very difficult for both teacher and pupil to cope with a whole series of these *vade-mecums*—especially as the "invention", though it went into the utmost detail, did not by any means put the other four sections in the shade. The "arrangement", for instance, meant the plan, which usually had six parts—the Exordium; the Narrative; the Division; the Argument; the Digression; the Peroration—each having its own rules. The "elocution" gave advice on style—on the need for grammatical accuracy, brilliance (by the use of images, figures of speech, etc.), rhythm (here Gorgias came in, and the highly subtle theory of rhythmic "clausulae") and suitability (hence the three "modes"—restrained, medium and sublime). Then came "memorization", which was usually based on a system of associating visual images. In practice this played a great part in oratory, though in theory the great thing was "improvization";[1] but improvisation in both literature and music is always greatly helped by a well-stocked memory—as anyone will soon find out if he wants to develop a "hot" technique in playing jazz. Finally—"action", the actual delivery, the way to regulate the voice and say the words, above all the way to give point to the words by making the right gestures. The Greeks, we must not forget, were a Mediterranean people, and they were not afraid of mimicry, even of a vehement kind. And here again the thing that most strikes the modern reader is the lavish detail of all the advice. Gesture was codified as much as everything else, and "hand-play"—χειρονομία (28)—was an absolute language in itself, hardly equalled anywhere else in the world except possibly in the plastic art of India. "Admiration is expressed by turning the hand slightly towards the sky, closing the fingers one after the other, little finger first, and then by repeating this movement backwards, opening the hand and returning it to its original position. . . ."[2]

The danger of all this—a danger that Hellenistic teaching did not avoid—was that the technique would seem so perfect that it would come to be looked upon as infallible. With such an arsenal of rules and formulas and prescriptions behind him, with every possible aspect of every conceivable speech nicely docketed, the rhetor might—and often did—imagine himself to possess a sure and certain method that would always function perfectly and enable him to teach any pupil, however ungifted, the secrets of his great art.

The theory was of course balanced by the study of model passages that beginners were expected to admire and imitate. Like Isocrates, and the Sophists before him, professors of eloquence loved to give their pupils their own productions to work on, especially when, as at the time of the Empire, they were themselves great orators, and not only teachers but famous lecturers. Nevertheless tradition was so strong, even in this field, that it tended to fasten upon certain typical masterpieces that were universally admired. Rhetoric, like poetry, had its own "canon", its fixed list of authors—the Ten Attic Orators (29), whose influence on the transmission of manuscripts was just as tyrannical as that of the Tragic Poets. The study of these great speeches, and perhaps of the historians too, who had also produced some first-class examples of the art of oratory, certainly does not seem to have been left to the grammarians, or, at least, not entirely: it was under the rhetor that one "read" oratory and history; and the actual expounding, which the teacher would generally leave to an assistant,[3] was probably less concerned with literary criticism and the scholarly approach than with the study of oratorical methods and the application of technique.

In the different schools each master had his own particular classic, whom he regarded as the embodiment of his own ideal of eloquence; one might prefer Demosthenes, another Lysias, because he was so polished and yet so restrained. . . .

Unfortunately it has to be said that the teaching was not always such as to get the most out of this subject. From the time of Dionysius of Halicarnassus

---

[1] Philstr., VS, I, 25, 537.   [2] Quint., XI, 3, 100.   [3] Ibid., II, 5, 3.

onwards schools of rhetoric tended increasingly to imitate the great Attic writers of the Golden Age. This imitation was done consciously and more and more thoroughly as time went on. But when we try to define what the orators of Imperial times, the masters of what is generally known as the Later Sophistry, meant by "Atticism" (30), we are surprised and somewhat disillusioned to find that they were not so much interested in the literary side as in the grammar; they were less concerned to recreate the style and taste of the great Athenian writers than to get back to the vocabulary, the morphology, the syntax of classical language as it had existed in a "pure" state in the past, by cutting out everything that had come into the language of literature during Hellenistic times. Only words or forms of speech that had already been used in the classics were to be employed,[1] and you always had to be able to quote a recognized classic in self-defence.[2] Even as early as Lucian, this was seen to have its ridiculous side: "Take a score of Attic words, fifteen at a pinch. Practise how to pronounce them so that you are never lost for a [Attic] word. Sprinkle liberally on your speech . . . Make a list of terms not in general use, found only in the oldest authors, and pelt everyone you meet with them."[3] To us, accustomed as we are by the study of linguistics to a view of language as something constantly evolving, this attempt to turn back the clock, to separate language from life, inevitably seems absurd; but it was a natural consequence of the classical ideal of perfection as something that had been fixed once and for all, something that could be rediscovered but never surpassed.

After the theory and the imitation of good models came part three—applied exercises. The rhetor took up where the grammarian had left off and conducted his pupil through the rest of the graduated "preparatory exercises"—προγυμνάσματα—each of which had its own highly detailed code of rules. We have already had a sample of how the eulogy was dealt with: its opposite, the reproach, was treated in the same way. Then followed, in this order, the *comparison* (example: compare Achilles and Hector),[4] the *ethopeia* (example: Niobe mourns over her dead children):[5] the *description* (example: the Alexandrian Acropolis):[6] the *thesis*, a discussion on a topic of general interest (the classical example[7] was the famous question "Should one marry?" and the rhetorical variations on this theme were to find their way into treatises on virginity composed by the Fathers of the Church long before Rabelais got to work on it), and the *legal tenet*, which meant defending or attacking a point of law—for instance: "It is forbidden to kill an adulterer caught in the act."[8]

These latter exercises approximated very closely to real speeches delivered in the law courts or the assembly, and to these at last the student finally came, still relying, of course, on a whole series of "hints" and rules and analysing the different aspects and elements and varieties of every type of speech. Here again I can only give an indication of the incredible complexity of this system of teaching: one is absolutely stupefied, for instance, by the degrees of abstraction that could be reached in considering "the state of the case"—στάσεις—one of

[1] [Arstd.] *Rhet.*, II, 6.
[2] Philstr., *VS*, II, 8, 578.
[3] Lucian., *Rh. Pr.*, 16; cf. 20; *Lex.*, 16.
[4] *Rhet. Gr.*, II, 43, 7 (Apht.).
[5] *Ibid.*, 45, 20.
[6] *Ibid.*, 47, 9.
[7] *Ibid.*, 50, 5.
[8] *Ibid.*, 54, 4.

the fundamental points in preparing a legal speech. Did the accused commit murder? This was a question of fact—"the conjectural state of the case". Is this murder a crime? This was the state of "definition". And so on. Different schools distinguished one, or two, or three (the classical position) or four, or as many as nine "states of the case".[1] The different kinds of set speech were also studied and systematized, the rhetor supplying his pupil with model wedding speeches, birthday speeches, funeral speeches, ambassadors' speeches, farewell speeches. . . .[2]

The most characteristic thing about all this teaching of rhetoric was that it gradually forgot all about its original aim, which was to prepare the would-be orator for real life by teaching him how to compose speeches that he would actually need for serious occasions. The chief place was taken up by imaginary speeches that scholars still insist on calling "declamations", because that was the word the Latin rhetors used to translate the technical term μελέται. It is worth noticing that this kind of school speech, which deliberately turned its back on life, first appeared at the time of Demetrius of Phalera,[3] who was master of Athens, as deputy to Cassander of Macedonia, from 318–317 to 307 (31)—that is to say just when the loss of political liberty deprived genuine eloquence of any real significance. The eloquence of the schools went on, but bereft of its aim and object, with the result that it became an end in itself and organized itself accordingly.

These "exercises"—which is what μελέται really means—were of two main varieties, the "controversy" and the "suasion" (though since the vocabulary of classical rhetoric has fallen into such oblivion I doubt whether these terms will be much use to anyone).

First let us consider the legal speeches—ὑποθέσεις δικανικαί—in Latin, controversiae. These were supposed to provide a practical apprenticeship in forensic eloquence: young barristers are usually given a chance to compose imaginary speeches before they are sent out to face a jury in a real case. But while the fifth-century Sophists tried to get as near as possible to the actual conditions of a law court—as we can see in the case of Antiphon—the Hellenistic rhetors presented their pupils with cases that were not only imaginary but absolutely fantastic, centring round ridiculous points that meant applying bizarre laws specially made up for the purpose, with nothing but tyrants and pirates and abductions and rapes and disinherited sons in unlikely situations, reminding one of the romantic and equally unreal plots that the New Comedy —they were contemporaries: Menander was a friend of Demetrius of Phalera —loved to wallow in. Perhaps you would like some examples (32). The law condemns to death any foreigner who dares to climb on to the city ramparts. During a siege a foreigner climbs on to the ramparts and by his valour helps to repel the enemy. Should he be condemned, in conformity with the letter of the law?[4] Again: a philosopher manages to persuade a tyrant to commit suicide and then claims the reward promised by the law for the death of a tyrant:

[1] Quint., III, 6.
[2] *Rhet. Gr.*, III, 331 *seq.* (Men.), 339; 412; 418; 423; 430.
[3] Quint., II, 4, 41.
[4] *Rhet. Gr.*, II, 140, 30 *seq.* (Herm.).

has he a right to it?[1] A young man who has been disinherited studies medicine and later cures his father, who has gone mad and been given up as hopeless by his own physicians. The father in gratitude restores his son's rights of inheritance. Later, the young physician refuses to treat his stepmother, who has also gone mad; whereupon he is disinherited for a second time. So he appeals to the judge.[2] It really looks as though Hellenistic teachers made a deliberate attempt to turn their backs on life—unlike our own, who are so determined to bring the school into contact with real life. These improbable subjects—ἄδοξοι —says the rhetor Favorinus of Arles with great satisfaction, in the second century A.D., are very useful in arousing the imagination, sharpening the wits and accustoming the mind to difficult cases.[3]

The same tendency can be observed in the second category of μελέται, the "suasions" (which in Greek—as distinct from Latin—schools were preferred to controversies). These were deliberative, not legal—συμβουλευτικὸν γένος: but again the subjects they dealt with, instead of being taken from contemporary life, were given an imaginary historical or mythological background—the Ancients did not distinguish between history and mythology: ancient thought did not include the modern—or Christian—category of historicity, the importance of time; it was concerned with the pictorial or emotional value of a story, not with whether it was actually true. For example, if it was a question of trying to make up an ambassador's speech—πρεσβευτικὸς λόγος—this would be modelled on the speech by Agamemnon's envoys to Achilles in canto I of the Iliad.[4]

The same applies to political eloquence: Solon might be imagined asking for the repeal of his laws after Pisistratus had adopted a bodyguard;[5] or it might be the Athenian people discussing whether they should send reinforcements to Nicias during the Sicilian expedition,[6] or Demosthenes offering himself as an expiatory victim after the disaster at Chaeronea.[7] But of all the history of Greece the Persian wars supplied the most popular themes for discussion: "You must concentrate on Marathon and Cynegeirus; without them you'll get nowhere! Fly over Mount Athos, walk across the Hellespont, let the sun be darkened by the arrows of the Persians . . . tell us about Salamis, Artemisium, Plataea." This is Lucian's Master of Rhetoric speaking,[8] and of course it is a joke, but the reality certainly deserved his sarcasm—listen to the ridiculous way in which the rhetor Polemon, for instance (second century A.D.), describes the legendary valour of Cynegeirus, the Athenian hoplite who was at the battle of Marathon and tried to hold off a Persian ship with his right hand,[9] then— and the rest is purely imaginary and not in Herodotus' account[10]—after his right hand was cut off, with his left, and then in the end with his teeth. "Cynegeirus was the first person ever to engage upon a naval battle without leaving solid ground. . . . Each of his limbs was the scene of violent battle. . . ."[11] And later:

[1] Rhet. Gr., II., 153, 18 seq. (Herm.).
[2] Lucian, Abd.
[3] Gell., XVII; 12.
[4] Arstd., LII D.
[5] Philstr., VS, I, 25, 542.
[6] Arstd., XXIX–XXX D.
[7] Philstr., VS, I, 22, 522; 25, 542.
[8] Lucian, Rh. Pr., 18.
[9] Hdt., VI, 114.
[10] Trog. Pomp., VIII, 9.
[11] Polem., I, 5–6.

"O king," said the Persians, "we have met men of steel, who do not care if their hands are cut off—their right hands are as strong as whole ships."[1] There was a whole repertoire of such stories, and once they had been accepted they were handed down from one generation to another in the schools, right to the end of antiquity.

This description, brief though it is, may have given some idea of how complicated the study of rhetoric was, with its continually increasing burden of new rules and regulations. It is not surprising that it took so many years to reach the end of it. In the fourth century A.D. two students—St. Basil of Caesarea and St. Gregory Nazianzen—went from Cappadocia to Athens to complete their rhetorical studies: one stayed four years, the other five, perhaps even eight (33). The truth is that there was no end to the study of rhetoric. As I have said, there was no boundary between the schools and the life of letters —a man of letters went on composing declamations—μελέται—all his life, and the transition from school exercise to public lecture took place imperceptibly; in fact it is known that the most famous orators amongst the Later Sophists were not ashamed to go on doing school exercises, including even the most elementary kind, the eulogy. Naturally, to show how bright they were, they chose the most unlikely subjects: Lucian wrote a eulogy on a fly,[2] Dionysius of Prusa a eulogy on a parrot,[3] Favorinus on quartan fever (34).[4] But besides producing actual works of literature like these, any Hellenistic man of letters would go on practising declamation as a student, so as to keep his hand in and keep on form: they went on declaiming year after year, until they were old men, until they were in their graves. Philostratus solemnly describes how, when the great Sophist Polemon was dying, he gave orders that he should be carried to his tomb before he had drawn his last breath. The tomb closed on him, and as his household lamented his passing he was heard to cry out in a loud voice: "Give me back a body and I will declaim again!"[5]

We find it difficult to understand this sort of enthusiasm. For us moderns, rhetoric means artificiality, insincerity, decadence. Perhaps this is simply because we do not understand it and have become barbarians ourselves. Rhetoric, it is true, had its own system of rigid conventions, but once these had been recognized and assimilated, the artist had complete freedom within the system, and when he had mastered the various processes he could use them to express his own feelings and ideas without any loss of sincerity. Far from hindering originality or talent, the restrictions enabled very subtle, polished effects to be produced. Rhetoric must be seen in comparison with other conventional systems that have applied to other arts in other periods—the laws of perspective, the laws of harmony in Bach and Rameau and right down to Wagner, the laws of verse: until the Symbolists came along, French poets were perfectly willing to submit to rules that were just as strict and arbitrary as the rules of rhetoric, and they did not seem to suffer from them unduly.

Rhetoric gave the Ancients a system of formal values that supplied prose with

[1] *Ibid.*, 15.
[2] Lucian, *Musc.*
[3] Philstr., *VS*, I, 7, 487.
[4] Gell., XVII, 12.
[5] Philstr., *VS*, I, 25, 544.

its own aesthetic; this ran parallel with the poetic aesthetic, and it was no less valid (35).

But it must also be recognized that, apart from its intrinsic value, such a system, open to all educated people, and peacefully installed at the heart of a tradition that was passed down for centuries from generation to generation, meant a common standard, a common denominator between all types of intelligence, uniting writers and public, the classics and the "moderns", in mutual understanding and harmony. Modern humanists, who have been perverted by the anarchy of Romanticism, consider all this a mistake and deplore the resulting monotony of ancient literature. But when you think of the present disorder, our lack of any common doctrine—which is putting it mildly, for today the unity of language itself is being questioned—it is impossible not to look back sometimes with nostalgia to classicism and its marvellous unity.

Not that one can forget the complaints that can be levelled against rhetoric: like any culture whose ultimate aim is purely aesthetic, it can be charged as being essentially vain, hollow and frivolous. And these criticisms are already to be found in the old tradition itself, formulated by its old rival—philosophy.

CHAPTER XI

HIGHER EDUCATION

III. PHILOSOPHY

PHILOSOPHY was a minority culture for an intellectual élite prepared to make the necessary effort. It meant breaking with the usual culture, whose general tone, as we have seen, was literary, rhetorical and aesthetic. It meant even more, for Hellenistic philosophy was not only a special kind of intellectual training, it was also an ideal of life that claimed the whole man. To become a philosopher meant adopting a new way of life—one that was more exacting morally and demanded a certain amount of ascetic effort. This manifested itself in dress, food and behaviour: the philosopher could be recognized by his cloak, which was short and dark and made of coarse cloth—the τρίβων.[1] The Cynics pushed this break with society to such a point that it became self-contradictory and scandalous: they never washed, never had their hair cut, wrapped themselves in rags and lived on alms like beggars, claiming to be outside ordinary polite society (36). But this was only an extreme statement of what was recognized to be a general principle: everyone knew that philosophy implied an ideal of life (37) that was opposed to the ordinary culture and presupposed a deep sense of vocation, indeed a conversion.

This is not too strong a word: the Ancients were very fond of the story about young Polemon, who burst into the lecture-hall after an orgy while he was still drunk and had a crown on his head. The philosopher Xenocrates was discussing temperance, and he went on speaking so persuasively and so affectingly that Polemon renounced his life of debauchery, fell in love with philosophy and later succeeded his master as director of the Academy.[2] Hipparchia, again, was a rich and beautiful young woman who came from the aristocracy: she gave up everything to study under Crates[3]—for though women neither welcomed nor were welcomed by the schools of rhetoric, they were no strangers to philosophy, and such vocations, though not very common, were not exceptional (38). Often, when this "conversion" to philosophy took place—and it has an amazing likeness to our own idea of religious conversion (39)—the break with rhetoric was particularly emphasized. The classic case is that of Dionysius of Prusa in A.D. 85; when this renowned Sophist was about fifty-five, Domitian sent him into exile, and his trials and tribulations were such that he experienced a profound moral transformation, renounced the vanities of Sophistry and adopted the austere way of life of the militant philosopher. . . . (40).

Hence the importance in philosophical teaching of the "exhortation"—λόγος προτρεπτικός—an inaugural lecture that tried to gain converts and attract

---

[1] Dio Chrys., XXXII, 22.   [2] D.L., IV, 16.   [3] Id., VI, 96.

young people to the philosophic life. This had been instituted by Aristotle: his *Protrepticus*,[1] addressed to Themison, Prince of Cyprus, was often imitated, beginning with the Epicureans[2] and ending with Cicero, whose *Hortensius* first converted a young African rhetor later to be known as St. Augustine.[3]

THE TEACHING OF PHILOSOPHY

For there was a proper system for teaching philosophy. It had three main forms—first, the more or less official teaching given in the actual "schools", i.e. by each separate sect. These schools were organized as confraternities; they were founded originally by one master, whose teaching was carried on from one generation to the next by a "head"—the σχολάρχης—who was duly appointed by his predecessor: as Plato had chosen his nephew Speusippus to succeed him, so Speusippus chose Xenocrates, who chose Polemon, who chose Crates. . . . Similarly, Aristotle left the Lyceum to Theophrastus—and Aristoxenus was very much annoyed about it. We can follow the succession—διαδοχή —in the four greatest schools almost without a break right through the Hellenistic period and to the end of antiquity (41). All these schools were centred in Athens, but they sometimes had daughter houses elsewhere.

Secondly, there were isolated teachers working on their own account in some city in which they had established themselves. Epictetus, for instance, who had also been driven from Rome by Domitian, settled in Nicopolis in Epirus, opened a school and was soon drawing pupils who themselves settled there (42). Following the example of Athens, other cities finally succeeded in putting this teaching on a permanent basis—we have seen it happening already in Alexandria and we shall come across it again in Constantinople, if not in Rome; but this was later, at the end of the third or during the fourth century A.D.

Finally there were the wandering philosophers—popular lecturers, or rather preachers, who got up at street corners or in the market-place and harangued the casual or curious bystanders, hurling challenges at them and exchanging backchat with them (whence arose the famous practice of the *diatribe*) (43). The Cynics were specialists at this sort of thing, but many of the Stoics flirted with Cynicism and copied them. I only mention this third class as a reminder, for obviously these tub-thumpers can hardly be looked upon as professors of the higher learning. Most people looked down on them with suspicion, and they were often in difficulties with the police, and though they may have helped a few of their listeners to realize their vocation for philosophy they gave no regular course of instruction.

The teaching of philosophy was many-sided, and it gradually got more technical. Students were supposed to have finished their secondary schooling before they embarked on it, but the various sects were not all equally strict on this point: Epicureans and Sceptics pretended not to mind, whereas those who insisted on a basis of mathematics were obliged, as this science declined, to teach it themselves, though it was foreign to philosophy proper. This happened, as we have seen, in the case of the neo-Platonists at the end of the period.

[1] Arist., fr. 50–61 (Rose); *POxy.*, 666. [2] *PHerc.*[2], X, 71–80.
[3] August., *Conf.*, III, 4(7).

H

The study of philosophy proper began simply enough. All the schools began in the same way, with a few general ideas about the history of philosophy. Greek students, like the students of today, learned that thinking had begun in Ionia with the great "physicists", that Thales had maintained that all things came from water, Anaximander from the unbounded, Anaximenes from air, and Heraclitus[1] from fire—and, again like the students of today, they did not know much more about these people than that. They learned these rudimentary facts from entirely unoriginal text-books that were simply copied again and again—modern scholars are endeavouring to trace the history of this "doxographical" tradition, which began with Theophrastus and came to an end with the collections of Arius Didymus and Aetius, fragments of which are to be found in Plutarch, Stobaeus and the *History of Philosophy* which was supposed to have been written by Galen (44).

Then came a course, still fairly general, on the school's own doctrine: thanks to Apuleius[2] and Albinus,[3] for example, we can get some idea of the way in which the scholarch Gaios introduced his students to Platonism in Athens in about A.D. 140. This Apuleius was conscientious: he also wrote an account of the course of peripatetic philosophy that he was attending at the same time.[4] This should not cause any astonishment, nor is there any need to drag in any reference to the general eclectic tendency of Graeco-Roman times to explain it, for the matter was still comparatively elementary and there was no question of any profound adhesion to any particular school, nor even, necessarily, any conversion to philosophy. Some idea of the various philosophical doctrines was simply part of one's general culture: as can be seen in Galen's case, it could be quite the normal thing to make some sort of contact with the four main traditions of Hellenistic philosophy one after the other.

It was only after this that the school's real teaching began. This also had two sides to it. In the first place it meant studying the school's own classics— to begin with, of course, those by the original founder—Plato, Aristotle, Epicurus, or (in the Stoic school) Zeno or Chrysippus. As the rhetors expounded their canon of orators, so the philosophers "read"—i.e. expounded and analysed— *classical* works (45); and here too the typically Hellenistic love of erudition sometimes swamped everything else, so that philosophy too was in danger of becoming philology—to quote Seneca.[5]

But there was a second side to this teaching, and this was more personal and more alive, for the teacher would give his own unbiassed view of philosophy and thus share his own opinions and his wisdom with his students (46). These lectures were not all of a piece, nor were they all intended for the same kind of audience. They might be "open", for the philosophers also "declaimed", like the rhetors—lectured to the general public—or they could be "closed"; but to judge by the literature that seems to reflect this kind of teaching[6] they must not be imagined as a planned course that gradually developed into a mighty system,

[1] Plut., *Plac.*, I, 531d *seq.*; Stob., I, 10.
[2] Apul., *De dog. Plat.*
[3] Albin., *Isag.*; *Epit.*
[4] Apul., *Mund.*
[5] Sen., *Ep.*, 108, 23-24.
[6] Epict.; Plot.; Herm. Tr.

like the *Lebens- und Weltanschauungen* produced by Hegelian professors in nineteenth-century Germany. The talks were much freer and more intimate, and might arise out of a point of philosophy or an incident in daily life or a passing question, and so lead on to matters of doctrine. And then—and these were perhaps the most important part of the teaching—there were the personal conversations between the master and his disciple, either alone or in the company of a friend and colleague. The personal tone of the old education, which I have stressed again and again, here comes out particularly clearly. The philosopher was expected to be much more than a teacher; he was expected to be "guide, philosopher and friend", and the essence of his teaching was imbibed, not from the lofty eminence of his chair, but in the common life that he shared with his disciples: more important than his words was the example he set,[1] his inspiring virtues and living wisdom. The result was that the pupil became attached—often passionately—to his master, and the master felt a corresponding affection for the pupil: it was in philosophic circles that the great archaic tradition of the educative *eros*, the source of all virtue, survived longest.

Theoretically, a philosopher's training had, in all, three parts: logic, physics and ethics—i.e. a theory of knowledge, a doctrine about the physical world, and a system of morality. This division seems to have been introduced by Xenocrates and Plato's early disciples,[2] and it was accepted unquestioningly by all the schools. But this does not mean that they were all equally concerned with the various parts. The more the Graeco-Roman period advances, the more important the moral aspect becomes, until it is the essential if not the only object of the philosopher's speculation and activity and whole life. His aim is to define and conquer and possess and pass on a *personal* Wisdom: a certain weakening of interest in disinterested speculation results from a corresponding strengthening and deepening of conscience and moral disquiet. The fundamental problem is henceforth concerned not so much with Truth as with Wisdom—the truth of a doctrine being simply a necessary means, not the ultimate object of the effort of thought. Hellenistic philosophers were searching for the final End implied and demanded by the nature of man—the Sovereign Good which, once possessed, fulfils all the aspirations of man's nature and brings him happiness. Everything else either disappeared before this fundamental preoccupation or took its importance from its relation to it.

And this end, this good, this happiness, concerned the human Person in all his uniqueness. The Hellenistic philosophers tended, even more than Plato— who, as we have seen, fell back in the end upon a purely inward city—towards a strictly personalist point of view. Not that they lost interest in political and social problems, of course; they were still counsellors, right-hand men to kings and political leaders; but even here their attitude was more personalist—they wrote tracts *On Kingly Power*[3]—περὶ βασιλείας—rather than *On the Republic*.[4]

---

[1] Poll., IV, 40.
[2] Sext. Emp., *Math.*, VII, 16.
[3] Cf. L. Delatte, *Les Traités de la Royauté d'Ecphante, Diogène et Sthénidas*, Paris-Liège, 1942 (*Bibl. de la Fac. de Philos. et Lettres de l'Université de Liège*).
[4] *POxy.*, 1611, 38 *seq.*; *RF* (1935), 215, 29; Dio Chrys., I–IV, LXII; Syn., *Regn.*, 1053 *seq.*

But the philosophers directed many more consciences than the consciences of their kings.

One final point. There was not one Hellenistic philosophy, there were a number of rival sects, all at each other's throats. The only way a doctrine could make any headway was under cover of a powerful barrage of dialectic, refuting its opponents' claims and mounting a vigorous counter-attack. The fact has often been pointed out by historians of philosophy: polemic was very important —sometimes too important—in the literary activity of the various schools. A strained, rather cantankerous, controversial atmosphere is highly characteristic of Hellenistic philosophy, and this has tended to discredit its findings in the eyes of many people: we have only to read Lucian[1] to see how philosophy went down in people's estimation as a result of the distressing spectacle of all these rival claims and passionate mutual refutations.

RIVALRY BETWEEN PHILOSOPHERS AND RHETORS

For we must not forget that the philosophers not only fought amongst themselves, they had to line up against their rivals, the rhetors. It would be quite wrong to imagine that Hellenistic culture and its advanced education were shared out peacefully between two parallel forms, and that young students chose rhetoric or philosophy just as the students of today get their school certificate and then go on to arts or science. On the contrary, they were two hostile cultures, and they fiercely disputed each other's right to existence.

This argument went on throughout Graeco-Roman times, following the example set by its two great founders, Plato and Isocrates (47); and after each period of calm it flared up again more violently than ever—just think of the Epicureans' onslaught against Nausiphanes, who had inherited the old confusionism of the Lesser Socratics, and the girding of loins that went on amongst the second-century philosophers, Critolaus, Diogenes, Carneades, etc., when they rose up against the weakening of the metaphysical spirit that had affected their immediate predecessors. It was the same old quarrel. In the second century B.C. the champions of a rhetorical culture revived the word "Sophist" and proudly claimed it for themselves, emphasizing their descent from Socrates' great adversaries. Scopelianus proclaimed himself a follower of Gorgias;[2] Aelius Aristides—with an intrepidity explained by his self-conceit—valiantly declared war on Plato.[3] This went on for generation after generation, and it is so fundamental that I seem to see traces of it, either clear or implied, wherever the classical tradition persists or reappears—in semi-barbarous Gaul in the fifth century, when Sidonius Apollinaris is balanced by Claudius Mamertinus, or in the twelfth-century Renaissance, when Abelard's philosophical culture is opposed by St. Bernard's literary humanism (48).

This persistent struggle was one of the main causes of the predominantly dialectical trend in Hellenistic culture—using the word "dialectical" in its modern sense. The opposition between the two hostile forces caused a creative tension, an influence that worked both ways, and, as always happens in the

---

[1] Lucian, *Herm.*   [2] Philstr., *VS*, I, 21, 518.
[3] Aristd., XLV–XLVII D.

course of a prolonged struggle, the two adversaries ended up by taking a good deal of colour from each other.

As had been the case with Isocrates, rhetorical culture was not completely shut off from philosophy: the Sophist too had his σοφία. The wiser men of letters like Dionysius of Halicarnassus (49) were disturbed to see rhetoric narrowing itself down to an empty formal technique, a mere matter of rules, and tried to brighten it up with a few general ideas; with the result that philosophy in this sense sometimes came to be included amongst the liberal arts— the ἐγκύκλιος παιδεία.[1] We have seen already that it came into the syllabuses of the ephebia.

Again, when the philosophical apparatus became too top-heavy with technicalities—as happened from time to time—then rhetoric stepped in to defend the rights of humanism and, as Isocrates had done earlier, set up against the abstract philosopher, hag-ridden with syllogisms, the ordinary decent chap, with his common sense and primal truths and average intellectual equipment. For the rhetor did not despise general ideas or human moral problems. His teaching was full of them. The doctrine of "invention" laid great stress on those precious "commonplaces", those universal sayings about justice and injustice, happiness, life and death, that were so useful to the orator because they opened the way to a treatment of fundamental themes. Even at the elementary stage of the "preparatory exercises"—προγυμνάσματα—the student was taught how to handle great problems by being made to discuss "theses" of general interest, and rhetoric thus invaded the domain of moral philosophy so thoroughly that the philosophers finally objected and said they were the only people who should discuss "theses". So said Posidonius in the course of a celebrated debate with the rhetor Hermagoras.[2] Rhetors, he said, should be content with "hypotheses", i.e. concrete subjects on particular cases, legal cases for instance; they should forget all about general ideas (50).

To balance matters, the philosophers did not pretend to be entirely above rhetoric. Since the time of Aristotle no one had questioned its validity, no one had attempted to follow Plato's example in the *Phaedrus* and set up a special philosophical rhetoric. The philosophers looked upon the art as a practical technique that was quite legitimate in its own way and had a perfectly proper place in culture as a preliminary study, like grammar or mathematics; and they had no compunction about teaching it, as Aristotle himself had done, first at the Academy and then at the Lyceum. Aristotle did not include rhetoric as part of philosophy proper, however. The Stoics did; they claimed it as an integral part of their logic, which was the first of the three stages into which they divided philosophy (51).

But the influence of rhetoric went much further than this. Its victory had been so complete, and left such a deep impression on Hellenistic culture as a whole, that the philosophers were affected by it much more insidiously. It is never possible for people to isolate themselves completely from the surrounding

[1] Vitr., I, I (3–10); Gal., *Protr.*, 14; Philstr., *Gym.*, 1; *Gram. Lat.*, VI, 187 (M. Vict.); *Schol. Dion. Thrax*, III, 112.
[2] Plut., *Pomp.*, 42.

civilization, with its various categories of thought, its mediums of expression, its fashions, its manias; and whether they admitted it to themselves or not the Hellenistic philosophers were rhetors themselves. They too "declaimed", and taught their pupils to declaim. They too knew all the rhetorical processes, and used all the rhetorical tricks—as soon as you start reading them you can see how thoroughly imbued they are with the language of Sophistry: just think of Seneca or Epictetus, for example! The phenomenon was widespread, and it affected the men of science too: even the great Galen was a Sophist at times.

The influence of rhetoric was so profound that it led to the appearance of certain mixed forms of culture that are not easy to classify: a slight cooling of metaphysical fervour, a slight increase of literary talent, and we have an ambiguous type in which the old ideal of the early Sophists seems to appear in all its integrity again—in the third-century Arcesilaus and Lycon the Peripatetic, and the first-century Philo of Larissa, who was to have such a profound influence on Cicero's idea of the "perfect orator" (52). The more time goes on, the more complete becomes the triumph of rhetoric, and the more the philosopher loses his philosophical integrity: even after their "conversion", Dionysius of Prusa and Favorinus of Arles still seem more sophistical than philosophical. How is one to describe Maximus Tyrius, or the Latin Apuleius, or the later Themistius, Julian the Apostate, even Synesius of Cyrene? There was not only hostility between the two types of culture, but an inextricable interweaving, knitting the classical tradition into an ever-closer unity.

HISTORICAL GEOGRAPHY OF THE HELLENISTIC SCHOOLS

The preceding sketch may perhaps seem rather too static to be historical, but the fact is that this whole long period, which began with Alexander and went right through Roman times, is not one which shows any signs of evolution in the proper sense of the word—i.e. a gradual transformation ending in a complete renewal. There are many changes, but no alteration in the basic structure. During the long summer of Hellenistic civilization we can only discover in a very limited sense anything that bears a resemblance to what some biologists describe as the "evolution" of the human species: the type is present from the beginning and remains substantially the same, and all we see is the blossoming of certain tendencies present in a rudimentary form at the beginning, and the gradual regression of certain organs whose fate was in fact settled at the start. Gymnastics and music gradually lose ground—but it was clear from the time of Plato that they were bound to disappear. Meanwhile rhetoric becomes technically more and more complicated—more and more itself, in fact. . . .

It might not be out of place to attempt to complete the picture with a few chronological facts and a brief description of how the main centres of advanced education were distributed geographically. In the actual Hellenistic period there were no real universities (the word only ceases to be anachronistic in the fourth century A.D.); but there were some towns in which teachers were more numerous and more highly thought of, and so had more students.

The first of these was of course Athens, which remained to the end a lively centre of intellectual activity. Even when she had finally lost all her political independence and all her political importance she never became a provincial town like the rest: she was still glorious Athens, mother of the arts and sciences and literature; never merely a museum-piece, living in the after-glow of a glorious past, visited only for the sake of her monuments, but a living centre of learning, where an uninterrupted tradition had preserved a climate exceptionally favourable to the work of the mind.

She had a few gentle ups and downs, of course. In the beginning she was the great centre for philosophy. Here all the main "schools" were established, scholarly and religious brotherhoods—beginning with the Academy, which was set up in 387. The Lyceum was opened in 335 but only became properly organized later, when the special favour shown to it by Demetrius of Phalera enabled it to overcome the legal difficulties that Aristotle and Theophrastus had encountered because they were aliens. The democratic reaction in 307–306 gave it some cause for alarm, but the repeal of the law of Sophocles of Sounion early in 306 finally removed the threat which philosophy had been under for so long from popular bigotry, and in the same year Epicurus was finally able to set up his Garden in Athens. In 301–300 came the Stoic school under Zeno. These were the four main official sects; the other philosophies—Cynic, Sceptic, etc.—also developed in Athens (53).

From the end of the fourth century B.C. onwards philosophy began to attract many students from outside: two of the four main schools had been founded by foreigners, and always had a number of foreigners amongst their members, from the director downwards. It was not until the end of the second century B.C. that an Athenian—Mnesarchos—was installed as head of the Portico.

But in Roman times students were also attracted to Athens by the fame of its schools of eloquence. In the first century B.C. these were not properly established—though Cicero took advantage of the six months he spent there in his youth to "declaim" under the direction of a "quite well-known"—*non ignobilem* —old master, Demetrius the Syrian (it is worth noting that this gentleman had come from such a long way away).[1] Under the Empire the fame of these schools increased, reaching its highest pitch at the time of Secundus and especially Herod Atticus in the second century A.D. (54). From then on, to the end of antiquity, Athens was one of the main centres of the Later Sophistry.

The other great centre of learning was of course Alexandria. I have already described its Museum, which was founded round about the year 280, but this was only one manifestation of the intense intellectual activity which very quickly developed in this, the capital city of the Lagids. Within the Museum, and all around it, teachers of every variety offered their services not only in philosophy and eloquence but in all the other branches of knowledge, especially, as we have seen, in medicine. From this point of view Alexandria was even more illustrious than Athens itself, and apart from one or two brief crises it preserved its vitality throughout the Hellenistic age and right up to the end of antiquity—it is not such a mistake as some have thought to identify "Hellenistic" with "Alexandrian" in the matter of civilization. Alexandria appeared

---

[1] Cic., *Brut.*, 315; Philstr., *VS*, I, 26, 544 *seq.*

as the intellectual metropolis in the earlier part of our period particularly, at the time of the Diadochi and the first generation of Epigoni, when the rest of the Hellenic world, including Greece herself, was being ravaged by war and revolution, and when, under the wise administration of the Ptolemies, Egypt was the only country enjoying peace and security—so that it became as it were the conservatory of Greek culture in time of peril, and ultimately, when the time was ripe, the source of its renewal.

In the second half of the second century there seems "to have taken place, throughout the Greek world, a general renascence of learning"—ἐγένετο οὖν ἀνανέωσις πάλιν παιδείας ἁπάσης—to borrow the words of Athenaeus,[1] following the historians Menekles of Barca and Andro of Alexandria. The persecutions by Ptolemy VIII Physcon (146-145 to 116) drove many people from the cultured class in his capital city into exile, and this literally "filled islands and cities with grammarians, philosophers, geometricians, musicians, drawing masters, gymnastics masters, physicians and every other kind of expert" —this is a pretty good list of the various sides to Hellenistic culture—"all reduced by misfortune to teaching the subjects wherein they excelled; and thus they helped to educate many distinguished men".

In fact, in the second and first centuries B.C., schools seem to have prospered in the whole of the Aegean basin, especially on the coast of Asia Minor, which came to be looked upon as the home of ornamental eloquence, and the term "Asianism" to be used to describe the perfect style—brilliant, affected, inflated, flashy (55). When we try to place the main centres of this activity on the map, the first place we have to find is Pergamus, where the Attalid kings developed such a marvellous library that it eventually put even the great Museum library of Alexandria in the shade. But it was mainly in places outside their own realms—in Athens and Delphi and Rhodes and so on—that these kings developed their policy of cultural evergetism and appeared as the patrons of university education (56).

From the end of the second century the most active and flourishing university centre was Rhodes. Since the Roman victory had forced her to give up her hegemony of the Aegean, which had once brought her greatness and riches— her place as the greatest international port was taken by Delos—Rhodes found new fame in the renown of her schools—grammar schools (as we have seen, it was at Rhodes that grammar reached its maturity with Dionysius Thrax); schools of philosophy—made illustrious by Posidonius, one of the masters of middle-period Stoicism and one of the great names in ancient thought (though his importance, especially in the field of education, has perhaps been exaggerated a little by modern scholarship); and, above all, schools of rhetoric (57). To Rhodes came the Romans of the first century B.C., beginning with Cicero and ending with Tiberius, to learn the secrets of great oratory, for they knew that in Rhodes they were sure to find the best teachers—like the rhetor Molon, Cicero's teacher, whom his pupil praised so enthusiastically[2]—and the genuine tradition: the rhetors in Rhodes seem to have managed to avoid any excessive "Asianist" pathos and to have had a "healthier"[3] idea of eloquence, one that

---

[1] Ath., IV, 184 B.C.   [2] Cic., Brut., 316.   [3] Ibid., 51.

approximated more closely to the Attic ideal—their favourite model was the calm, dispassionate Hyperides (58).

Under the Empire it was Asia proper, the mainland province, that took the lead. Culturally, this province long lagged behind, as a result of the plundering and devastation, the shameless exploitation it had suffered at the hands of the politicians and financiers of the Republic, and then the ravages of war—the wars of Mithridates, the civil wars from Sulla to Antony. But with Augustus came peace, order and justice, and with them came prosperity, and the province became the richest, the happiest and the most cultured part of the Empire. From the end of the first century A.D., and throughout the second—the golden age of the Antonines—Asia was the best place for Greek culture and for learning any advanced subject. First Cos, as we have seen, and then Pergamus and Ephesus, developed prosperous schools of medicine, and though philosophy did not enjoy the popularity it had in Athens, there was plenty of brilliant eloquence: from Nicetes to Aelius Aristides, Asia was the home of the Later Sophistry and Smyrna its undoubted capital (59)—and, if the whole of Ionia was worthy to be described as a sanctuary of the Muses, Smyrna was its cardinal point, like the bridge of a lyre.[1] But in fact there were schools of higher learning throughout the Roman East: and the whole area had the same enthusiasm.

Later—in the fourth century—this learning seems to have tended to become more concentrated; at any rate a few particular centres then came to the fore— Alexandria; Beirut (for Roman law); Antioch; Constantinople, the new capital; and of course the perennial Athens. People like to talk about the "universities" in these places, and by this time it is not too much of an anachronism.

The great influx of students, some of whom came from distant provinces, gave these places a typically "Latin Quarter" atmosphere of rowdy, lawless, carefree, frivolous youths, who got into trouble with the police,[2] wasted their time playing ball games,[3] were mad on horse-racing and other shows,[4] and had a weakness for feeble practical jokes—preferably on their teachers when they couldn't be seen, according to Libanius.[5] And of course there was some sexual immorality. Nevertheless we must not paint too black a picture of these students of the Late Empire; besides the wasters there were sober and virtuous youths there too—St. Gregory Nazianzen and St. Basil in fourth-century Athens,[6] and Zacharias Scholasticus and Severus of Antioch in fifth-century Beirut,[7] left entirely edifying memories behind them.

And on the whole the young men there were studious, passionately fond of their subjects and the men who taught them, and quick to take sides in all their quarrels and enmities—which meant more rags and high jinks.[8] The result was that they came to be grouped under their own special teachers—each one had his "chorus" of faithful, not to say fanatical, disciples—and also according to where they came from, rather after the fashion of the "nations" in the universities of Western Europe in the Middle Ages.[9] There was thus a real,

---

[1] Philstr., *VS*, I, 21, 516.
[2] Cf. *Cod. Theod.*, XIV, 9, 1; *Just.*, *Omnem*, 9–10.
[3] Lib., *Or.* I, 22.
[4] *Ibid.*, I, 37–8.
[5] *Ibid.*, LVIII.
[6] Greg. Naz., *Or.*, XLIII, 19–22.
[7] Zach., *V. Sev.*, p. 13 *seq.*; 46 *seq.*
[8] Lib., *Or.*, I, 19.
[9] Eunap., *Proh.*, 488.

organized student life with its own private conventions—beginning, of course, with the ragging of "freshmen"[1] (60).

On the other hand, as we shall see, the State had a very direct hand in the appointment and organization of the teaching body: the Late Empire State was something of an octopus, well on the way to totalitarianism. But by then a very different kind of civilization had arisen, one that had nothing in common with the civilization of Hellenistic times.

[1] Greg. Naz., *Or.*, XLIII, 16.

CLASSICAL HUMANISM

WE have now examined the main elements in the education of classical Greece. With the help of the historical background outlined in Part I of this book, the reader will have had no difficulty in plotting each new point of technical development in its proper position relative to the previous points. He will have seen how residual characteristics, like gymnastics and music, which had originated in the old aristocratic education, quickly became recessive; how others that appeared later—such as the study of language and literature—came to the fore, and in doing so grew more complex and more widely differentiated—indeed, were utterly changed; how the art of oratory abandoned its original practical preoccupations for the more aesthetic values of formal eloquence, only to discover a new kind of political function and political value in doing so. . . .

Does this mean that our work is ended as far as the Hellenistic period is concerned, and that all we have to do now is to pass straight on to the generations that came after, and study the last stages of this evolution?

HISTORY AND VALUE

History is not merely a monotonous series of events, linked together one after the other throughout inexorable time. It is not enough to know that Hellenistic education took on a certain form as a result of certain antecedent happenings and as a prelude to certain further happenings. There needs to be a pause for consideration: Hellenistic education is not simply something that has passed away, it has *been*—it has *had being*—and we cannot consider ourselves to have finished with it until we have made some attempt to ponder its essence and understand its values.

And it is worth it; for this education was not merely a transitory form, one moment in a continuous evolution; it was the stable, mature Form in which the whole educational effort of antiquity was realized. The climax of seven centuries of creative effort, it was like the flat top of a curve, a long level stretch lasting many generations, during which its educational methods peacefully enjoyed undisputed authority.

It stretched through space as well as time. As we shall soon see, what is called Roman education was on the whole merely an extension of Hellenistic education to the Latin or Latin-speaking regions in the West. But we can go further and say that Hellenistic education has a significance that extends beyond antiquity and even beyond history itself. It is probably not generally realized that what we call classical culture, i.e. the culture that was handed down by tradition or rediscovered by the various "Renaissances" in the Byzantine East and in Western Europe, is the culture of Hellenistic times. And the most important point of all is that this culture does not merely belong to the past as a spent force whose greatness is over and done with: in a sense, it has not merely existed, but is ever-present and ever-living at the heart of our own thought— as an ideal transcending all its actual manifestations, a stronghold of eternal values.

This does not mean, of course, that I should claim that the classical ideal can be the standard for every possible kind of education and that we must all imitate it. In the first place, I am not at all sure about this, and secondly, any such opinion is out of place in a work of history. All I mean is that the ideal is still with us, either as a model to be copied or as an error to be avoided; it still exists, at least for educated people who have been able to appreciate and understand it, as an Idea which modern thought must be either for or against; contact with it is always rewarding, whether we accept it unquestioningly or resist the temptation to do that and subject it to our own rational analysis.

For this reason the present work will only be satisfactorily accomplished when it has managed to give a clear idea of the values that in their various ways were spread abroad by this classical Form of education. I expect the philosophical reader will want me to give a word to describe the essence of this education: I suggest that we use the old word *humanism*, however overworked it has been: properly explained, it can still be of use. For the ideal at which Hellenistic education aimed can certainly be described as humanistic from many different points of view, all of which are quite legitimate.

MAN NOT CHILD THE STANDARD

In the first place the whole aim of this education was the formation of adults, not the development of the child. There is no point in being led astray by etymology. I know quite well that $\pi\alpha\iota\delta\epsilon\iota\alpha$ contains the word $\pi\alpha\tilde{\iota}\varsigma$. But this needs to be translated as "the treatment to which a child should be subjected" —to turn him into a man. As we saw, the Latins happily translated $\pi\alpha\iota\delta\epsilon\iota\alpha$ as "humanitas".

Hence, as we have seen in passing, the utter absence of, the utter lack of interest in, child psychology; hence the absence of anything approximating to our infant schools; hence the abstract analytical character of all the "exercises"; hence the barbaric severity of the discipline. Nothing could be more unlike the modern "progressive school" methods than the system of education that was practised in ancient Greece.

But the moderns should not be in too much of a hurry to crow about this and dismiss the Greeks' attitude as outmoded ignorance. In a culture as refined as theirs, and which in so many other fields has given so much evidence of great creative genius, such apparent ignorance must be regarded as deliberate, the expression of an implicit, perhaps, but nevertheless a quite definite rejection of what it did not include.

One cannot feel confident that if the Greeks could have known the endeavours that psychology and education have been making ever since *Emile* was written to adapt themselves to the child and the special characteristics of his mind they would have responded with anything but amused surprise. What is the point, they seem to say, of concentrating on the child as though he were an end in himself? Apart from the few unlucky children who are condemned to a premature death, the only point of childhood is that it leads to manhood, and the proper object of education is therefore not any slobbering child or awkward adolescent or even an up-and-coming young man, but Man, and Man alone; and the only point of education is to teach the child to transcend himself.

THE WHOLE MAN

Classical Greece wanted education to concern itself with the whole man, and here for a change we find it in agreement with the modern outlook, which also insists that education and training should be "general", in reaction against the over-emphasis on "instruction", i.e. development of the intellectual faculties only. Yes, said the Greeks, the whole man, body and soul, sense and reason, character and mind.

First the body: the old ideals of chivalry had left such a profound mark on the Greek tradition that at the beginning of the Hellenistic era, at least, a liking for physical education was still the most distinctive characteristic of Greek culture as opposed to that of the barbarians. No doubt for a long time—from the time of Xenophanes of Colophon in the sixth century, at least, as we have seen—ancient thought had been aware of the antinomy between the contradictory and in themselves totalitarian demands of body and mind, and in actual fact such equilibrium as existed between the two was always rather precarious; but there is a difference between what is actually achieved and what remains as the essential ideal, and it is the latter that I am concerned with here. And there can be no doubt that ancient thought never renounced its ideal—which slowly became more and more unrealizable in practice—of a complete man who developed both sides of his nature equally—his bodily powers, and his mental powers.

The classic expression of this ideal was given in the words of a Latin poet who was writing as late as the second century A.D.: "We should pray for a sound mind in a sound body."

Orandum est ut sit mens sana in corpore sano.[1]

And though the emphasis on sport, as in the case of the professional athlete, was sometimes severely criticized, this was not so much the result of a prejudice in favour of pure intellectualism as a consequence of the traditional ideal of a complete man whose faculties were harmoniously balanced—an ideal that was denied by specialized training, whose one aim was to produce track-champions.

This aspiration towards human wholeness was equally apparent in the school syllabuses. In theory (and here again it must be remembered that we are simply describing an ideal) Hellenistic education was never prepared to renounce

---

[1] Juv., X, 356.

its artistic side; it even tried to keep pace with the increasing specialization of culture by adding drawing to the music it had inherited from Homeric times.

In the same way, "general culture"—the ἐγκύκλιος παιδεία that aimed at supplying the intellectual basis of any really educated mind—endeavoured to combine the advantages of a grounding in both literature and mathematics.

This longing for human wholeness is nowhere more evident than in the violent conflict that went on between the two rival forms of higher culture—rhetoric and philosophy. Both derived equally and essentially from the old culture: the dialogue between the two—which could be so bitter and tense—is its chief characteristic. We must realize that Hellenistic man would hesitate before making the difficult choice: the decision would not be made without some feelings of regret and an attempt to synthesize the two.

As we have seen, each of these two hostile forms of culture was continually trying to appropriate some of its rival's undeniable prestige: from Plato to Themistius[1] philosophers had always insisted that Truth could not afford to dispense with the Muses, while rhetors at the time of the Later Sophists claimed like Isocrates before them that the honourable title of philosopher was the name that should be given to their ideal orator.

There was more in this than a desire for compromise, more than the selfish aim of attracting customers by adopting the good points of a rival firm. Between these two poles of the old culture there was a dialectical tension at once pathetic and fruitful; another manifestation of ἀγών—rivalry, noble discord. The orator and the philosopher could not do without each other; neither could give up what was really the other's aim and object. The Greek wanted to be both artist and sage—a man of letters, refined, charming, a maker of fine phrases, and a thinker familiar with all the secrets of man and the universe, able to establish them with geometrical accuracy and to deduce from them a rule of life. For Man included all this, and any kind of choosing meant self-mutilation.

It has to be confessed that the realities of daily life generally gave the lie most cruelly to this paradoxical and, in a way, this desperate longing: the technical progress that went on in every branch of Greek cultural life in Hellenistic times shattered the limits that are ultimately imposed upon the human person by his nervous system and his brief span of life. The old civilization already knew something of the difficulties that confront our own monstrous civilization, whose colossal constructions no longer exist at the human but at the planetary level—where is the physicist today who can claim to know all about physics? Hellenistic man was already beginning to be torn between that aspiration towards totality which we with our bad Greek call the "encyclopaedic" tendency, and the need, no less essential to humanism, to preserve culture as something human, within the limits of some sort of personalism.

As we have seen, the only kind of Hellenistic education that succeeded in combining gymnastics, music, letters, science and art—i.e. the education that was provided by the aristocratic ephebia—only managed to do so by substituting for real knowledge a frivolous, superficial smattering of knowledge that was no more than a caricature of any genuine humanism. But the fruitfulness of

[1] Them., *Or.*, XXIV, 302d–303a, Syn., *Dion.*, 4, 1125a.

any ideal is not to be judged simply by the comparative proliferation of its practical achievements: the nostalgia and disquiet and regret that remain in the depths of the heart after the perfect ideal has been glimpsed—and then so imperfectly realized in practice—are also a kind of presence. Even though Hellenistic man never in fact became a total being, nevertheless he never forgot that such was his ideal, and he never willingly gave it up.

PRIMACY OF MORAL CONSIDERATIONS

On one level at least this humanistic desire for an all-round education was always realized—i.e. on the all-important level of morals. Classicism was not content with producing a man of letters or an artist or a scientist: it aimed at producing a man—i.e. someone whose way of life conformed to some ideal standard. And in this respect it is a very useful model for us moderns; for our own educational system, with its increasing secularization since the time of the Reformation and the Counter-Reformation, has finally lost all sense of this.

When the Greeks spoke about "the training of the child"—τῶν παίδων ἀγωγή—what they really meant was essentially moral training.

Very significant in this respect is the semantic development whereby from the Hellenistic period onwards the word "pedagogue" gradually changed its meaning until it came to have its modern sense of "educator". The fact is that the humble slave who was known as the "pedagogue" was a more important person as regards the training of the child than the schoolmaster. The schoolmaster was simply a technician, and he only affected a limited area of the child's intelligence; but the pedagogue was with the child all day, he taught him how to behave, how to be a good boy, how to get on in life, in society—all more important things than knowing how to read. We have made the school the decisive factor in education; for the Greeks the decisive factor was the surroundings in which the child grew up—the family, with its servants and friends.

The same preoccupation with moral values can be seen in the more advanced stages of education. The grammarians who expounded Homer, the rhetors who taught the art of speaking, insisted in season and out of season on their authors' moral virtues, on the moral value of doing their exercises: not to speak of the philosophers, who at this stage of Greek culture were not so much concerned with the inmost nature of the universe and society as with the practical inculcation of an ethical ideal—a system of moral values and a way of life in conformity with it.

Hence the idea that any kind of advanced education involved a deep and absolutely personal bond between teacher and pupil, a bond in which, as we have seen, emotion, if not passion, played a considerable part. This explains why there was such a scandal when the early Sophists began to commercialize teaching; there were no real centres of higher education like those great emporiums of culture, the modern universities. School, for the Greeks, meant an enthusiastic little band of pupils centring round a well-known teacher and growing more deeply united as time went by as a result of living a more or less communal life and developing more and more intimate personal relationships.

Man as Such

The object was the whole man, but man as man, not in any special form or any special part. It is worth noting in passing that in Hellenistic schools sexual discrimination tended to disappear. In the earlier days, it will be remembered, this discrimination was very marked: Sapphic education arose in opposition to the masculine education that was so strongly characterized by pederasty. But from now on girls were normally brought up in the same way as their brothers —though not always so logically as to result in the strict co-education that existed in Teos[1] and Chios.[2]

The Man as Opposed to the Technician

Classical teaching was chiefly interested in the man himself, not in equipping technicians for specialized jobs; and it is this, perhaps, that most sharply distinguishes it from the education of our own time, which makes it its first aim to produce the specialists required by a civilization that to a quite fantastic extent has been invaded by technology and split up into fragments.

The old civilization thus presents us with a challenge, and this cannot be explained away by glib references to its aristocratic origins. It is undoubtedly true that the Greeks' slave system enabled them to identify man—i.e. the "free" man—with the aristocratic man of leisure, who was relieved by the labour of others from performing any degrading work, and had every opportunity for indulging in a life of elegant leisure and spiritual freedom.

But, I say again, the contingent forms of history are the bearers and embodiment of values that transcend them. Let us try to "understand", rather than explain away: the more difficult this turns out to be, the more fruitful it becomes. And once again it must be insisted that ancient thought deliberately refused to set out along the path that modern civilization has been rushing along so blindly.

It had no use for technique. It was not unaware of the possibility of technical development; it simply rejected it. Its one aim was to form the man himself, the kind of man who would ultimately be ready for anything but had no special bias in any particular direction.

Only medicine, because it had a more immediate social relevance, and was thus the first to split off as a separate autonomous branch of learning, managed to develop its own particular type of training. And even so the physicians seem to have been continually dogged by an inferiority complex. From Hippocrates to Galen they go on saying: "The physician is a philosopher as well." They had no desire to remain walled up within their own particular culture; they longed to join in with the general culture on a genuinely human level; and for this they did not rely on their technical training but, as can be seen in Roman times in the case of Galen, they tried to be educated men like all the others, men who knew their classics, men who could speak like rhetors and argue like philosophers.

[1] Dittenberg., *SIG*, 578, 9.   [2] Ath., XIII, 566e.

It is from the Ancients that we have inherited our ideas of a "general culture"—which, as we have seen, is one of the meanings of the ambiguous term ἐγκύκλιος παιδεία. Classical education flattered itself that it could provide a standard training in all subjects for every type of student. It aimed at developing all his potentialities without mutilating a single one, so enabling him to fulfil to the best of his ability whatever task should later be imposed upon him by life or the demands of society or his own free choice. Ideally such an education was supposed to result in a kind of indeterminate human product of very high intrinsic quality, ready to respond to any demand made upon it by the intellect or circumstance—καιρός. The Ancients were very much alive to the value of this kind of latent potentiality, which was never better described than in a lyrical passage by Julian the Apostate, in which the traditional "Hellenism" is contrasted with what he believed was the barbarism of the Christians. Any gifted person, he says,[1] who has received a classical education, is capable of great things in any direction: he can take the lead in science or politics, just as easily as he can become a man of war, an explorer or a hero: he comes down amongst men like a gift from the gods. . . .

This education embraced all subjects, and could be embraced by all types; since it was concerned with everything, it was suitable for all. It was thus a powerful factor in promoting unity amongst men. Hence what seems at first sight its surprising emphasis on the idea of Speech—Λόγος: its predominantly literary tone. The Word was regarded as the prime instrument of any culture and any civilization, the best means of ensuring contact and communication between men; for it broke through the enchanted circle of solitude in which any specialist inevitably tends to be enclosed as a result of his very accomplishments.

Once again, this is the true humanism—this emphasis on the social aspect of culture, on the danger inherent in any activity that tends to be self-enclosed and aloof from the ordinary intercourse of daily life. Here we reach the really profound reason why the ancient tradition rejected Plato's great idea of making mathematics the centre of all education. No doubt mathematics was entirely a matter of reason, and reason was common to all men, and so mathematics must seem a suitable subject for everyone to learn; but as soon as it rose above the most elementary stage most minds found the barren, abstract climate in which mathematics really existed quite unbearable. Plato himself seems to have admitted this when he emphasized the great sorting-out value these difficult sciences had.

A Literary as Opposed to a Scientific Humanism

When it was not just a small group of rulers that had to be educated, but the upper section of a whole society, it was better to remain on a more modest, more concrete level, and concentrate on words and literature, on those general ideas and grand and noble sentiments that the classical tradition loved and regarded as by far the best meeting-place for the generality of good minds.

[1] Jul., C. Galil., 299 E.

Of course it did not give up mathematics completely—it hated giving up anything—but the only side of mathematics that it took much notice of was the formal side, the early training: ideally, the four mathematical sciences only went on to secondary-school level in Hellenistic education; more advanced science was a speciality, something for which a special vocation was needed, and like every kind of specialization it needed to have a watchful eye kept on it in case it began to stray beyond the proper human bounds.

I repeat, for it is a matter of some importance: ultimately, in the eyes of posterity, it was Isocrates who carried the day, not Plato: the culture that arose out of classical education was essentially aesthetic, artistic and literary, not scientific. Homer remained the "educator of the Greeks". The philosophers had failed in their attempt to drive him out of the State, and in the end they gave up trying: it was no use trying to put Euclid in his place.

The higher levels of intellectual life were only opened by poetry. Poetry was like a marvellous instrument that could cast a spell over men's souls, and in some unknown way give their hearts a kind of intuitive knowledge of truth and beauty and goodness. It provided a sort of experience that was infinitely varied, subtle, complex, something far above the strict proofs and pure concepts of geometry. It was a product of the sensitive mind, and this, in the eyes of the humanists, was far more important than the geometrical mind. Classicism regarded the educated man as someone whose cradle-songs had been Hector's farewells and the tales told in Alcinous' house; someone who had discovered the reality of human passion and the depths of the human heart in some "chorus-ending from Euripides" or a tale by an historian; someone who had thus had some sort of psychological experience, some refining of his sense of moral values, of what is real and possible—of what Man is, and what the life of Man.

VALUE OF TRADITION

Poetry has its own proper power, and it matters little at the moment that Hellenistic teachers often failed to realize that it is thus its own best justification —they often found it difficult to explain why Homer was so important in education, and their efforts to turn him into a model moralist or orator are pathetic. Fortunately poetry is able to do without their well-meaning "explanations". These were often rather comic; the essential thing is that the tradition was preserved intact.

For in the last resort classical humanism was based on tradition, something imparted by one's teachers and handed on unquestioningly. This, incidentally, had a further advantage: it meant that all the minds of one generation, and indeed of a whole historical period, had a fundamental homogeneity which made communication and genuine communion easier. This is something we can all appreciate today, when we are floundering in a cultural anarchy. In a classical culture all men have in common a wealth of things they can all admire and emulate: the same rules; the same metaphors, images, words—the same language. Is there anyone acquainted with modern culture who can think of all this without feeling a certain nostalgia?

Undifferentiated Polyvalence

But to return to the technical side of the matter: the classical ideal both preceded and transcended any specialized technical considerations. It preceded them because once the mind had been trained it was pure power, completely free, ready for any demands that might be made on it.

Hellenistic education—as, I hope, I have made quite clear—made provision for the kind of professional training that an apprentice receives from a master who takes him on as his assistant. But the classical mind regarded such a narrow focusing of the mental powers as a handicap: it was considered self-evident that the main thing was to become a person of intelligence, someone with insight and good judgment. As for a profession, that was something to be learned as quickly as possible: anyone with any intelligence could soon learn to turn his hand to anything practical.

And the classical ideal transcended technical considerations: an educated man began by being human, and even if he became a highly qualified specialist, he had to do his best to remain human. Here again the contrast with our own attitude is instructive; for we are obviously suffering from swollen ideas about technique, and we may perhaps learn something from the Greeks' insistence that any specialized activity needs to be guided by human considerations.

There is a terrible tyranny at the heart of technology. Any particular technique tends by its own inner logic to develop exclusively along its own line, in and for itself, and thus it ends by enslaving the man whom it should serve. It is only too clear today that science can make scientists inhuman, biology can make doctors forget that it is their duty to cure people, and political science turn doctrinaire politicians into tyrants. The classics tell us again and again that no form of government, no branch of knowledge, no technique, should ever become an end in itself: since they are created by man, and supposed to serve man, they should always, no matter what their results, be subordinated in the way they are used to one supreme value: humanity.

Beyond Humanism

The effectiveness of an ideal is not a matter of logic, and it is not easy to give a blueprint of the essence of classicism, for it did not in actual fact embody a single idea—indeed one of the great merits of its "sensitive mind" was its insistence that it is dangerous to push any idea too far, that practical achievement must be hedged in by conditions.

It never, for example, actually repudiated the old totalitarian ideal that had motivated the ancient city—i.e. the absolute dedication of the individual to society—though in fact it certainly went beyond this. What remained of this ideal helped to give a certain amount of ballast to the rather nebulous idea that classical education had of man, and at the same time it served as a kind of bridge and introduction to the new totalitarian civilization which was to arise in the Spätantike, the Late Empire, and in Byzantium. Historians of civilization are continually coming across this curious phenomenon of superposition, whereby things left over from an earlier stage turn out to be the basis for future developments.

Nevertheless, on the whole, there was upon classical humanism a profound imprint of the personalist ideal that characterized the Hellenistic period when classicism assumed its full Form. Classical education aimed at developing men as men, not as cogs in a political machine or bees in a hive.

It was the distinctive tendency of the Hellenistic mind to make man the supreme value—the free man, of course, the wealthy, cultured man whom education had developed to his full stature and παιδεία had brought to *humanitas*. Free, utterly free, faced by the crumbling walls of his city and abandoned by his gods, faced with a world with no end to it and an empty heaven, Hellenistic man looked vainly for something to belong to, some star to guide his life—and his only solution was to turn in upon himself and look there for the principle of all his actions.

This can be regarded—and rightly—as a narrowing of perspective, and dangerous. There is something slightly alarming in the fact that the chief aim of classical humanism was to produce men of taste, men of quality, men of letters and artists; in the fact that it cultivated almost exclusively those powers of the soul that need an endless refinement of inner experience, delicate pleasures, dainty living. Undoubtedly this is what classical education led to, particularly in Hellenistic times.

But the point is that the historical conditions of the period—political, economic, social and technical conditions—did not really know what to do with the admirable human capital with which it had thus been so well provided. I must repeat that classical education supplied the *materia prima* for a higher human type than had hitherto been known, a type capable of anything—if only it could have discovered something, or someone, to devote itself to. When it failed to do this, failed to transcend itself, classical humanism turned inwards in search of an immanent perfection and became absorbed in an egoistic aesthetic contemplation, which may well seem frivolous and futile to people who belong to a more severe or more ambitious culture. And this was often the case during the Hellenistic period.

But the value of this system was not limited to its first historical achievements, which were merely empirical and contingent. Classical humanism was able to lead to—and did in fact lead to—a higher kind of greatness, by putting itself at the service of a higher cause, to which the human person was willing to consecrate himself and thus find fulfilment in self-transcendence. For classical humanism was not necessarily a closed system turned in upon itself. Even in antiquity, as we shall see in the next part of this History, there were two remarkable examples to disprove this. First, classical education put itself at the service of the State, the State of Rome in which the old city ideals burst forth again in a civilization still Hellenistic; and then later, when the Empire became Christian, it put itself at the service of God.

Part III

CLASSICAL EDUCATION AND ROME

CHAPTER I

THE OLD ROMAN EDUCATION

BEFORE we can embark on any study of Roman education we have to go back a little—chronologically, perhaps not as far back as 753 B.C.: I don't suppose the reader will expect me to be as clever as Plutarch[1] and describe the education that was current in the time of Romulus—but at least as far back as the sixth century. In the realm of ideas we have to go back still further, for in its whole spiritual development Rome lagged behind Greece by at least two centuries. On the whole it evolved along similar lines, but it took more time over it, and the result was perhaps less far-reaching.

ROMAN ORIGINALITY

The difference between the Romans and the Greeks arose in the first place because two different stages of development were anachronistically brought into contact with each other. What is commonly known as "Roman" virtue was simply the moral outlook of the old city-state. To this the Romans of Republic times—hardy, unbending types, hardly better than barbarians—remained loyal, in contrast to the Greeks of the same time—men who were highly developed intellectually, highly civilized—perhaps a little over-civilized, though to me they do not seem degenerate so much as enfranchised, emancipated from the old totalitarian ideal and ethically at the personalist stage of the παιδεία.

The originality of Rome, as distinct from that of Greece, was partly the result of this survival of archaism. And Rome was never to emancipate herself entirely from the collective ideal whereby the individual is completely in the hands of the State—not even when in all her customs she had grown far away from it. She always looked back to it nostalgically. She was always making efforts to return to it. One has only to think of all the attempts at moral rearmament that were going on under Augustus when Horace was writing:

Dulce et decorum est pro patria mori[2]

"It is a lovely and a splendid thing to die for one's country"—which re-echoes the inspiration that had animated Tyrtaeus of Sparta and Callinus of Ephesus six centuries earlier.

But Roman civilization was not simply Greek civilization all over again: it was archaic in its own way. In the early centuries it had grown up independently on the fringe of the Greek world and was only superficially affected by it, and in so far as anything of this primitive stage persisted—as it did, even

[1] *Rom.*, 6.   [2] *Carm.*, III, 2, 13.

after Latin culture had been more or less absorbed into the Hellenistic civilization—Rome continued to be opposed to Greece. This was particularly true in
education: right to the end Latin education remained in some ways different
from classical Greek education, despite the fact that it modelled itself on it
very closely; and this was because to a certain extent it preserved some of the
features of the old original Roman education—which we shall now examine (1).

A Peasant People

It can be summed up in a few words. When you look to its origins you find
that it was an education, not for knights, as in heroic Greece, but for peasants.
By its "origins" I mean the end of the sixth century—there is no point in going
back any further, for all we are concerned with are the immediate origins that
were consciously remembered and so had an effect on tradition (2). At about
the end of the sixth century, therefore, we find the city of Rome, and its culture,
in the hands of a rural aristocracy, landed proprietors who farmed the land
themselves—a very different kind of class from Homer's military aristocracy or
the Indo-European aristocracy that, according to comparative philology, existed
at the dawn of history.

This rural character might easily have been obliterated by the Etruscans,
who turned Rome into a town, and a very busy town too; but the expulsion
of the kings and the establishment of the Republic (509, 508 or 503) seems to
have been a victory for the rural aristocracy over the urbanizing elements (3)
and so to have consolidated the power of the original peasantry. This was
maintained by the continual incursion of Italian families who were gradually
integrated into the old nobility and bound it more and more closely to the soil,
preventing it from becoming too urbanized—there were Sabine elements,
beginning with the Claudii in the sixth century,[1] then Latins, Etruscans, Cam-
panians. . . .

This dominance of the rural element is to be found everywhere—in names,
for instance. Latin patricians dropped compound names like "Eteocles" or
"Dumnorix" that the old Indo-European aristocracies had been so proud of,
and developed a *tria-nomina* system instead, in which we can often see a reflection of the peasant's down-to-earth attitude—unimaginative first names like
Primus, Quintus, Decimus; Lucius, Manius, Marcus ("born at dawn", "born
in the morning", "born in March"), and realistic surnames recalling their
work in the fields—Pilumnus (from the corn-pounder), Piso (from *pisere*, to
pound), Fabius, Lentulus, Cicero (from the bean, the lentil, the chick-pea).[2]

Indeed the whole Latin language seems like the language of peasants (4).
So many of the words that later developed a wider meaning began by being
technical agricultural terms: *laetus* was first used to describe well-manured
ground, *felix*, the fertility of the soil, *sincerus*, honey without beeswax, *frugi*,
the profits, *egregius*, a beast separated from the rest of the herd—yet these came
to mean "joy", "happiness", "truthfulness", "virtue" and "fame". *Putare*
meant "to prune", then "to mark a stick with notches", then "to calculate",

---

[1] Suet., *Ti.*, 1.   [2] Pliny, *HN*, XVIII, 10.

before it finally came to mean "to think". And then there are all the country sayings and proverbs that reflect the absolute genius of the language with their blunt unpretentiousness and earthiness.

In the same way Roman building developed on the model of the peasant's primitive farmhouse (5). The centre piece was a rectangular hut, which in time became the *tablinum*—the room of honour. At the front was the *atrium*, the old farmyard—it was never entirely covered in. At the back, the grand peristyle found in Pompeian houses was nothing more than the old kitchen garden, decked out with all the tricks of Hellenistic architecture.

A Peasant Education

This explains the highly original characteristics of the earliest Roman education; it was a peasant education adapted for an aristocracy. To understand its essentials, we have simply got to look at the way our own young village people are educated today. The chief thing that education means to them is being initiated into a traditional way of life. As soon as a child begins to "take notice", in all his games, for instance, he tries to imitate his elders' actions, behaviour, work. When he gets older he takes his place amongst the grown-ups, and sits there quiet and reserved, listening to the old ones talking about the rain and the fine weather and the day's work, about man and beast—and thus he grows into a whole body of wisdom. He begins to do odd jobs in the fields, goes along with the shepherd or the ploughman, sometimes takes over their job from them—and feels mighty proud when he does so.

The Custom of the Ancestors

This is the kind of thing we must have in mind when we try to imagine the old Roman education. Its fundamental idea, the thing it was based on, was respect for the old customs—*mos maiorum*—and to open the eyes of the young to these, to get them to respect them unquestioningly as the ideal, as the standard for all their actions and all their thoughts, was the educator's main task.

The early Greeks were not unfamiliar with this idea—we have come across it in Theognis.[1] But it will be remembered that when he refers to "the Wisdom that he had learned from the Best Ones when he was still a child" he has a polemical purpose in mind, for he was a desperate conservative reacting violently against a new spirit. In Rome, tradition always had a much stronger position; it was always revered unquestioningly—there was something slightly contemptuous in any reference to *res novae*, "innovations" and "revolution"— they all meant the same thing in Latin. "The strength of Rome," wrote Cicero, echoing Ennius,[2] "is founded on her ancient customs as much as on the strength of her sons"—

Moribus antiquis res stat Romana virisque

[1] Theog., I, 27.   [2] *Resp.*, V, 1.

And again, unlike the wisdom of Theognis's aristocratic clubs, the *mos maiorum* was more than a system of ethics and an aristocratic code: it included every aspect of human activity—including the technical skills.

FAMILY EDUCATION

The basis and backbone of this education was the family. Legal historians love to emphasize the Roman family's strong constitution—the sovereign authority that was invested in the *paterfamilias*, the respect that was accorded to the mother—and nowhere is this more evident than in the matter of education. In the eyes of the Romans the obvious place in which children should grow up and be educated was the family. Even under the Empire, when it had been the custom for a long time to educate children together in schools, they still went on, as we can see in Quintilian,[1] discussing the advantages and disadvantages of the two systems; and it was not always the old one of keeping the child at home—*domi atque intra privatos parietes*[2]—that was given up.

How different from Greece! The contrast is clear from the child's earliest years. In Rome it was not a slave but the mother herself who brought up her child,[3] and even in the greatest families she considered it an honour to stay at home so that she could do her duty and be as it were a servant to her children.

The mother's influence lasted a lifetime—hence the symbolic value of the famous tale that was handed down about Coriolanus. Coriolanus had revolted against Rome and was advancing upon the great city at the head of the Volsci. Ambassadors came out from the Roman people and pleaded with him, and they were followed by the city's priests, but despite their entreaties Coriolanus remained inflexible. Finally his mother appeared and upbraided him; and he yielded.[4] The story may have been a myth, but it expressed a genuine feeling. We know the part played in their sons' lives in historical times, in the second and first centuries B.C., by Cornelia the mother of the Gracchi, Aurelia the mother of Caesar, and Atia the mother of Augustus, all of whom brought up their sons to become leaders of men.[5]

When the mother was unable to do her job properly, a governess was chosen to look after the children, and she was always a relative, a woman of experience whom all the family respected, and a person who knew how to maintain an atmosphere of severity and a high moral tone[6]—even when the children were playing games.

From the age of seven onwards the child ceased, as in Greece, to be entirely in the hands of the women, but in Rome he came under his father. This is absolutely typical of the Roman system of teaching. The father was looked upon as the child's real teacher, and even later on, when there were proper teachers, they were still supposed to behave more or less like fathers.[7]

While the girls tended to remain at home with their mothers, industriously spinning wool and doing the housework—this was still the custom when the

[1] Quint., I, 2.   [4] Livy, II, 40, 5-9.
[2] *Ibid.*, I, 2, 1.   [5] Tac., *Dial.*, 28, 6.
[3] Tac., *Dial.*, 28, 4.   [6] *Ibid.*, 28, 5.
                    [7] Quint., II, 2, 4.

austere Livia was bringing up Augustus's grand-daughters[1]—the boys went off with their father, right into the "curia" even when the senate was sitting in secret,[2] and so they saw all sides of the life ahead of them, learning from his precepts and still more from his example.[3] The young Roman aristocrat, in his toga edged with purple—*praetextatus*—took part like the Greek κοῦρος in the great feasts, singing[4] and serving at table—but he was with his father, not his lover.[5]

It was with a strong sense of duty that the Roman *paterfamilias* applied himself to his job as an educator: he was a very different figure from the careless and incompetent Greek fathers who appear in the pages of Plato's *Laches*. There is an excellent chapter in Plutarch describing the care Cato the Censor took over his son's education:[6] Plutarch shows what an eagle eye he kept on his progress, how he taught him all his subjects, and he emphasizes the gravity and the respect for the child that he showed throughout.

Maxima debetur puero reverentia

Juvenal was to write later.[7] This was one of the fundamental features of the Roman tradition.

The elder Cato of course was a reactionary, and he always had an eye on the publicity-value of his activities, but in his admirable enthusiasm for his son's education, the son "whom he wished to be his masterpiece, formed and set in the mould of perfect virtue",[8] he was not alone. There was his contemporary Paulus Aemilius,[9] who had "philhellenic" tendencies that made him one of the "modern" school compared with the traditional Cato; there was Cicero, who kept the same watchful eye on the education of his son and nephews;[10] there was Augustus.[11] In fact this is one of the ways in which the old traditional families can be recognized—like the Cassii in the time of Tiberius.[12]

EDUCATION FOR PUBLIC LIFE

When the boy was about sixteen, this home education came to an end. There was a ceremony to mark the beginning of the next stage: he took off his toga edged with purple and any other marks of childhood and put on the *toga virilis* instead. He was now a citizen. But he had not finished his education. There was his military service, and before that, usually, a year spent in "preparing for public life"—*tirocinium fori* (6).

And now, unless there was some exceptional reason,[13] it was not his father who took him in hand but some old friend of the family who had had experience of politics—someone rich in years, experience and honours. Cicero, for instance, describes how his father put him under Q. Mucius Scaevola Augur, the

[1] Suet., *Aug.*, 64, 4.
[2] Gell., I, 23, 4.
[3] Pliny, *Ep.*, VIII, 14, 4–5.
[4] Non., I, 107–108, s.v. *Assa*.
[5] Plut., *Qu. Rom.*, 272c.
[6] *Ibid.*, *Cat. Mai.*, 20.
[7] XIV, 47.
[8] Plut., *Cat. Mai.*, 20 (42 Amyot).
[9] *Ibid.*, *Aem.*, 6.
[10] Cic., *Att.*, VIII, 4, 1.
[11] Suet., *Aug.*, 64, 5.
[12] Tac., *Ann.*, VI, 21(15), 3.
[13] Pliny, *Ep.*, VIII, 14, 6.

son-in-law of Laelius, one of the last survivors of the great generation of the Gracchi: young Cicero went everywhere with him, not missing any opportunity that came his way to learn from him: *fierique studebam eius prudentia doctior*.[1] This gentleman was a great lawyer,[2] and it was through being present at his consultations that Cicero first began to study law—a service he was later to pass on to several of his young friends, Caelius, Pansa, Hirtius, Dolabella.[3]

Theoretically the *tirocinium fori* was supposed to end after a year and the young Roman was supposed to go off to the army, but politics was far too serious a matter for it to come to an end as quickly as that. The young aristocrat went on following a successful politician around—who might be his father,[4] but was usually someone else. Cicero, for example, remained with Scaevola Augur until the old man's death—which occurred after the year 88 B.C., possibly in 84, and Cicero, who was born in 106, must have been wearing the *toga virilis* since 90–89. Even then he did not consider his education to be complete, for he transferred himself to one of his first master's cousins, Scaevola Pontifex Maximus (d. 82).[5]

It was the same with military service. The first year was spent in the ranks: a potential leader had first to learn to obey, and in any case it would always be to the advantage of his political career if he was wounded or did something striking in battle. Young Scipio, for instance, the future Africanus, saved his father the consul when he was wounded at the battle of the Ticinus.[6] But in actual fact the young aristocrats were not treated like ordinary conscripts, for they had tutors to look after them,[7] and in any case they very soon left the ranks to become staff officers—*tribuni militum*—either as the result of being elected by the people or by being nominated by the general-in-chief (7).

Having become a staff officer, the young Roman aristocrat completed his training under some well-known man for whom he had the utmost respect and veneration—so that the atmosphere was very different from that in ancient Greece, where all the heat and light came from homosexuality. One is also struck by the continual emphasis on the value of old age, with its experience and wisdom; Rome would have rejected even more violently than Greece one of our modern habits—"fascist", some would call it—of adoring the virtues of youth and despising the authority of the elders.

The Roman Moral Ideal

When we come to examine the content of this old system of education, we find, in the first place, a moral ideal; the essential thing was the development of the child's or the young man's conscience, the inculcation of a rigid system of moral values, reliable reflexes, a particular way of life. On the whole, as I have said, it was the old city-ideal, and meant sacrifice, renunciation, absolute devotion to the community, the State; it was the Greek ideal at the time of Callinus and Tyrtaeus.

[1] Cic., *Lae.*, I.
[2] *Ibid.*, *Brut.*, 306; *Leg.*, I, 13.
[3] Quint., XII, 11, 6.
[4] Pliny, *Ep.*, VIII, 14, 6.
[5] Cic., *Lae.*, I.
[6] Livy, XXI, 46, 7–8.
[7] Cic. *ap.* Serv., *Aen.*, V, 546.

The striking feature about the Roman ideal is that it was never questioned: neither in the tradition nor in the corporate memory is there the slightest trace of any rival that the city-ideal had to overcome before it could establish itself— nothing like the Homeric ideal of individual heroism, for instance, that had meant distinction and fame in ancient Greece. Not that the Roman soul was indifferent to glory, but its heroism never had any particular individual character; it was always strictly subordinated to the public good and the public safety, as though this was its one aim.

The Roman hero, whatever his name—Horatius Cocles, Camillus, Menenius Agrippa, Octavius Augustus—was the man who, by his courage or wisdom, and in the face of great difficulties, saved his country when it was in danger—a very different type of person from the rather wild and imaginative Homeric hero, a deserter like Achilles, for instance, who brought the Achaean army to the verge of destruction simply through sulking, and only returned to the fight to avenge a personal loss, the death of a friend. *Salus publica suprema lex esto*,[1] said the Romans: the country's interest should set the supreme standard for valour and virtue.

In practice, the young Roman's moral education, like the Greek's, was fostered by many examples of this kind of virtue, which were put before him so that he could learn to admire them; but these were taken from the nation's history, not from heroic poetry. Many were in fact mythical, but this does not matter: they were presented, and received, as historical fact.

THE FAMILY IDEAL

This brings us back to the dominance of the family in education. Roman culture always remained aristocratic: the old patricians were followed by a new *nobilitas* just as eager to build up great family traditions; and the hardening of the oligarchy in the second century B.C. and the aristocratic reaction on the establishment of the Empire had through the centuries the effect of strengthening this particular characteristic, which was another distinctively Latin feature as compared with Greek "democracy".

The young aristocrat was brought up to respect not only the national tradition, which all Romans shared in, but his own family traditions too. We know how proud the great houses were of the magistrates they had given to the curia under the Republic, and how they displayed this to all and sundry in their great funerals, in which effigies of their forefathers were carried in procession, and their fame was celebrated along with that of the dead person in the funeral oration.[2] One can easily see what a great influence this would have on any child, when each day his eyes could not fail to light upon the glorified *imagines* set up in the family "atrium", nor his ears to hear the endless stories about them; unconsciously at first, but very consciously later on, he was induced to model his outlook and behaviour on a certain ideal which was, so to speak, the hallmark of his family.

Each of the great Roman houses had its own more or less fixed attitude to

[1] Cic., *Leg.*, III, 8.   [2] Polyb., VI, 53-54.

life, its own way of reacting to circumstance: the Claudii were traditionally proud, the Iunii inflexible, the Aelii Tuberones and the Quinctii austere; in politics a Cassius was expected to be "democratic", a Manlius to be aristocratic. Modern criticism has rather tended to fasten on these traditional attitudes as having been responsible for the way in which, throughout the history of the Republic, a certain kind of action is supposed to have been anticipated, or repeated—sometimes more than once (8). My own opinion is that this is not quite so certain as it appears to be—for there seems to be no reason why an ardent desire to conform to an ideal type of conduct should not have inspired individuals separated by several generations to repeat some great exploit hallowed by time.

Let us take an example. An heroic act known as *devotio* was by tradition attributed to three different people named P. Decius Mus. The father in 340, the son in 295 and the grandson in 279 were all supposed to have secured victory in a decisive battle by "vowing" themselves—and, with themselves, the enemy army—to the infernal gods. The Ancients themselves were not quite sure about the third sacrifice; but the moderns go further and only admit one (9).

Now, I am not in a position to establish the historicity of any of these sacred acts of suicide, of course, but the words that Livy attributes to the second Decius when he is preparing to follow his father's glorious example seem to me psychologically true:[1] "Why should I hesitate to follow the family destiny? It has fallen to our house to provide the sacrificial victim when our country is in danger. . . ." Similarly with regard to the third: Dio Cassius[2] tells us that on the eve of the battle of Asculum many were convinced that Decius would follow his father's and grandfather's example, with the result that Pyrrhus—who was a prudent man—is supposed to have informed the Roman generals that he had made arrangements so that Decius should not go to his death.

The fact that such stories were known in Rome proves at least that such feelings were very real. We should not minimize the importance of this inherited, consciously accepted, consciously re-lived system of values—in proof of it, in the full light of history, we have, contemporary with Cicero himself, Cato and Brutus wanting to be, feeling themselves to be, the heirs and imitators of their forefathers—Cato the Censor, and the remote, real or imaginary Brutus, the first consul. I described the old Greek education as an imitation of heroes in the Homeric style; Roman education was an imitation of one's ancestors.

ROMAN PIETY

More a city and family matter than the Greek system, Roman education was possibly more religious too. Here again we must realize the absence of anything behind the Latin tradition comparable to Homer's epic, which was so mature, so "modern" and in a sense so irreligious—Spengler would have said

---

[1] Livy, X, 28.　　　[2] Dio Cass., XL, 38 = Zonar., VIII, 5.

"secular". The Latin feeling for religion had something more naïve about it—perhaps something more profound, too.

Rome never admitted anything that smacked of Machiavellianism into its public affairs, as Sparta did, for instance. One ought to be ready to do anything for one's country, but not everything was permissible—nothing that went against justice or morality or the law. Consider, for example, the minute precautions that surrounded the ritual declaring war: the fetial priests advanced to the enemy frontier and called upon the gods and the power of right to witness the justice of the Roman cause: Rome only made war to obtain her rightful due. . . .[1]

Of course I am not suggesting that Roman politics were always as pure as that, but after all hypocrisy is the tribute that vice pays to virtue, and in point of fact there was never a time when Roman education did not signal out as examples to be followed men of honour who had put divine right before their country's immediate interests: the incorruptible Fabricius, for example, handing over the traitor who had intended to poison him to King Pyrrhus;[2] the heroic Regulus returning to Carthage to be tortured because he had urged the Senate to reject the peace proposals that the Carthaginians had entrusted him with (10)[3].

Roman patriotism itself believed that it was essentially religious. "It is by obeying the gods, O Roman, that you will rule the world," says Horace.

Dis te minorem quod geris imperas.[4]

And before Horace, Cicero had gravely explained that Rome surpassed all other peoples in piety, in watching for signs from the gods, in faith in the gods' providence[5] (11).

This kind of religion included a good deal of formalism. "To be attentive to the will of the gods" meant watching with the utmost care for all the signs —the flight of birds, the victims' entrails, the sweating bronze—which showed the good will of the gods or their mysterious anger. "Piety" meant, essentially, scrupulous observance of all the traditional rites: there was a rather sordid element of narrow self-interest in it, a calculating eye for returns.

THE PEASANT VIRTUES

This may well be regarded as a further aspect of the practical, down-to-earth, peasant character of early Rome. It is found in other spheres. The virtues that the old education aimed at developing were the peasant virtues—hard work, frugality, severity. Any Roman child would hear denunciations of luxury and its corrupting influence, and eulogies of the indifference to self shown by old consuls and dictators like Cincinnatus, who used to cultivate the soil with their own hands, and had to be dragged from their ploughs when the senate voted them chief magistrate.[6]

---

[1] Livy, I, 32, 6–14.
[2] Gell., III, 8.
[3] Cic., Off., III, 100.

[4] C. III, 6, 5.
[5] Har. Resp., 19.
[6] Livy, III, 27, 7–10.

I am not forgetting that the Greeks too looked upon luxury as one of the signs of the "softness"—τρυφή—that brings men and cities to destruction (12), but the Greek ideal, with its sober moderation, had none of the crudeness of the peasant outlook that can see no difference between thrift and avarice. There was nothing in the Roman tradition to compare with the blatant generosity— so good for one's prestige—that is to be found in Homer's heroes, and again in the medieval *cortezia* in the Troubadours' poetry, and even, perhaps, in the "potlatch" of our sociologists. A glance at the elder Cato's treatise on agriculture is enough to show this permanent single-minded determination not to waste anything: "Give your slaves less to eat when they are ill,[1] don't waste your winter evenings[2] or rainy days,[3] sell all your surplus and all your refuse, sell your old chariots, your scrap-iron, your slaves when they get too old or too ill . . ."[4]

So we pass from ethics to technics. Being predominantly practical, the old Latin education could not imagine any kind of moral training as being separate from real life and its responsibilities. There was no question, as in old Hellas, of preparing for the aristocratic life, in which great deeds of sport or war alternated with periods of elegant leisure. The Roman ideal was the ideal of the *paterfamilias* responsible for the proper ordering of his patrimony.

PHYSICAL EDUCATION

This appears very clearly in their attitude to physical training (13). In Greece physical education from the time of Homer onwards had tended to draw further and further away from its original military aim and to concentrate more and more on sport only, with plenty of performances and competitions. The old Romans would have none of this. Not that, being soldier-farmers, they despised the body; but in this field as in others education was strictly utilitarian. Plutarch gives a list of the things the elder Cato and his son taught: fencing, throwing the javelin, sword-play, vaulting, riding, the use of every kind of weapon; boxing, how to endure great cold and heat, how to swim across a cold fast-flowing river.[5] One of the poets' favourite pieces of description was that of the young men doing their military exercises on the Field of Mars, galloping around in the sun and the dust and then plunging into the Tiber.[6]

There was no sport, as we understand it. The Latin *ludus* meant either training, or a game, and unlike the Greek word ἀγών it did not really include any idea of competition. The reader may remember the rustic junketings so charmingly described by Virgil:[7] shepherds throw the javelin with an elm for their target, wrestle with a great deal of vigour in a rustic palestra. . . .

No doubt as time went on the *ludi* became ceremonies, more official, more

---

[1] Cato, *De Agri Cultura*, 2, 4.
[2] *Ibid.*, 37, 3.
[3] *Ibid.*, 39, 2.
[4] *Ibid.*, 5, 7.
[5] Plut., *Cat. Mai.*, 20.
[6] Hor., *Carm.*, I, 8, 4 *seq.*; III, 12, 7 *seq.* Cf. Virg., *Aen.*, VII, 162–165; IX, 606; Veg., I, 10; Varro *ap.* Non., I, 1558, s.v. *Epiphippium.*
[7] G., II, 529–530.

solemn than they had been in the early days; but they seem to me to have been not so much competitions as exhibitions, with plenty of opportunity for vanity as well as the desire to shine and get talked about.[1]

No doubt, too, as far as the young aristocrats were concerned, physical education was not always simply a matter of military training; as we shall see, in the early Empire young Romans had clubs rather like ephebia where they did physical exercises that had very little to do with preparing for the army. But the thing that must be stressed—it is so often overlooked—is the fact that Roman sport developed in a highly original way.

Greek sport was based on the pure athletics of the palestra and the stadium; the Romans, on the other hand, always preferred the circus and the amphitheatre. As regards the circus: riding was the favourite aristocratic sport, as it was in Greece, but in Rome it was not so much a matter of racing as of the armed "march past"; jumping—not unknown in Hellenistic Greece: the Tarentini specialized in it[2]—a tournament with complicated movements known as *ludus serpentis*,[3] and above all the *ludus Troiae*, an exercise that went back to Etruscan times and had a great revival from the time of Sulla onwards, especially under Augustus.[4]

Besides the circus there were the fights that went on in the amphitheatre, and these, however extraordinary it may appear, were not confined to men who were professionals or slaves or men condemned to death. Fencing was taught by the gladiators,[5] and it was included in the most refined type of education, as we know from the case of Titus.[6] There were mock fights, which were probably not dangerous. But that was not all, for in the amphitheatre young men of the best families would be seen taking part in the "hunts"—*venationes*[7]—i.e. fighting against wild animals—bears[8] and lions.[9] Perhaps Commodus was not such an exceptional fellow after all. . . .

THE OCCUPATION OF LANDED PROPRIETOR

There was nothing really intellectual about this old Latin education. The intellectual element came later, under the influence of Greece. A young Roman only learnt what every good landed gentleman should know—i.e., in the first place, husbandry. He had to know how to make his land pay; which meant that even if he did not work it himself he had to know how to manage it, how to superintend his slaves and advise his tenant or bailiff.

The place given to agriculture is another original feature of Roman culture. I am not forgetting that Xenophon wrote his *Oeconomicus* and that Varro began his treatise on agriculture with a list of about fifty Greek writers on the subject;

---

[1] *CIL*, IV, 1595; XII, 533, 16.
[2] Steph. Byz., s.v.; Dionys. Per., V, 376.
[3] *CIL*, IV, 1595.
[4] Suet., *Caes.*, 39, 4; *Aug.*, 43–5; Dio. Cass., LIII, 1, 14; Livy, 26, 1. Festus, 504, 11 L.
[5] Juv. III, 158.
[6] Dio. Cass. LXVI, 15, 2.
[7] *Ibid.*, LXVII, 1, 2; Suet., *Dom.* 4, 11.
[8] *CIL*, XXII, 533, 7–8.
[9] Fronto, *M. Caes.*, V, 22(37); 23(38).

I

but in Greek literature generally it had nothing like the importance that it had in Latin, century after century, for writers like Cato, Varro, Virgil, Columella, Gargilius and Palladius.

This was indeed one of the absolutely fundamental features of the Latin tradition, and it is not easy to estimate how much the famous Roman realism was indebted to it for its depth of experience and open-mindedness. It is a mistake to follow the usual idea of Roman agriculture too closely: people have been too fond of quoting from the second part of Cato's old treatise,[1] where all his advice—about the innumerable medical virtues of the cabbage, for instance[2]—is lumped together. The *De Agri Cultura* was not entirely a matter of superstitious folklore. Its tone was very "modern". It was a book about the new rural economy in Italy after the conquest, and it dealt with the stock-breeding and orchard-cultivation—the growing of olives and vines—that were taking the place of the old corn-growing, which could now be done in the provinces—in Sardinia, Sicily, Africa.

The Roman aristocracy managed on the whole to adapt itself very successfully to the new developments in economic conditions and to take full advantage of all the innovations introduced into agriculture by Hellenistic and Carthaginian experts.[3]

Compared with the Greeks, the Roman aristocrats seem less like great overlords than like squires, gentlemen farmers. They did their best to teach their sons everything that a country gentleman should know, besides husbandry. There was a Roman "encyclopaedic" tradition, very different from Hippias' "polymathy" (14), consisting of practical applications, not "objective" curiosity.

Thus the Romans were interested in medicine, not like the Greeks of the fourth century onwards, who had certain ideals about the human person, but mainly, as Cato shows, so that they would know how to look after their slaves properly and so increase the amount of work they could do.

The "encyclopaedic" tendency took the form of various collections of textbooks put together by erudite polygraphers; the most typical, perhaps, is the collection made by A. Cornelius Celsus, who in the reign of Tiberius published his *Artes* in twenty books, dealing successively with husbandry, the art of war, rhetoric, philosophy, medicine and law (15).

The rhetoric and philosophy had been introduced from Greece; the rest was the Romans' own genuine capital. Much practice had brought the art of war to a high technical level: it was normally learned by actual soldiering, first in the ranks and then as a staff officer.

The importance of law in the Roman civilization needs no emphasizing. Unlike Greek justice—especially the Athenian variety—which was based on a few simple laws, and whose general tendency was towards equity rather than law, Roman justice always seems very formalistic. It involved a most complex system of prescriptions, and with their great feeling for tradition the Romans attached much importance to judgments already given, the whole body of

---

[1] Cato, *Agr.*, 56 *seq.*   [2] *Ibid.*, 156–157.
[3] Varro, *De Re Rust.*, I, 1, 10; Pliny, *HN*, XVIII, 22.

precedents known to jurisprudence. Hence the teaching of law necessarily played a great part in education.

The Law of the Twelve Tables was learnt by heart in childhood—Cicero could still remember this custom.[1] Later, as we have seen, the young aristocrat received a genuinely professional training from an experienced practitioner when he was doing his *tirocinium fori*: he studied public law as well as private law, for a knowledge of rules and precedents was just as important in politics as in the law-courts.

Together these various elements made up a kind of culture and education that were typically Latin. There is a strikingly succinct picture of it—and it is an excellent example of the plainness and sobriety of Roman eloquence before it came under the Greek influence—in Pliny's account of the funeral oration[2] delivered by Q. Caecilius Metellus Macedonicus in the year 221 at his (grand)-father Lucius's funeral (16). Lucius had twice been consul, and had also been master of the cavalry, dictator, *triumphator* and *Pontifex Maximus*: "He had gained possession of the ten supreme goods that Wise Men spend their lives looking for: he had been a great soldier, an excellent orator, a gallant general; he had been responsible for great undertakings, he had been first magistrate; he possessed the highest wisdom, he had been foremost amongst the senators, he had made a great fortune by honest means, he had left many children behind him and he had been famous in the State."

[1] Cic., *Leg.*, II, 59.   [2] Pliny, *HN*, VII, 139-140.

CHAPTER II

ROME ADOPTS GREEK EDUCATION

THUS in the beginning Rome had her own tradition of teaching. Yet Latin education eventually took quite a different direction; for Rome found herself induced to adopt the forms and methods of Hellenistic education.

ROMAN CIVILIZATION AND HELLENISTIC CIVILIZATION

This was a particular example of the fundamental fact that dominated the whole history of Roman civilization: a genuinely autonomous Italian civilization had no time to grow up, because Rome and Italy were snatched up into the civilization of Greece. After running rapidly through the various stages that separated their comparative barbarism from the precocious level of culture reached in Hellas, they showed a remarkable facility of adaptation and quickly assimilated the Hellenistic culture. This fact was so striking that even the Ancients themselves were aware of it—as will be realized by recalling Horace's famous line: "Captive Greece took captive her savage conqueror, and brought civilization to barbarous Latium:"

> Graecia capta ferum victorem cepit et artes
> intulit agresti Latio.[1]

There was not a Hellenistic civilization on one side and a Latin civilization on the other, but, as the Germans with their customary pedantry so conveniently put it, a *hellenistich-römische Kultur*. It is only legitimate to speak of Latin culture in a secondary sense, as a particular variety of this single civilization. In education, for example, the distinctive contribution made by Roman sensibility, the Roman character and the Roman tradition, only appear as slight alterations of detail, or as trends that sometimes tended to favour and sometimes tended to inhibit certain aspects of the Greek attitude towards education.

STAGES IN GREEK INFLUENCE

The various stages of this process of integration need to be dated. Though, as we shall see, the full technical development of Roman education did not arrive until the end of the first century B.C., in the main it had been completed in the second century as the result of the conquest of the Greek countries of the East, which has been called "the spiritual revolution of the second century" (1). But this was merely the finally decisive and particularly fruitful phase of a process of integration that had begun much earlier.

[1] Hor., *Epist.*, II, 1, 156.

The process went back in fact to the very beginnings of Rome as a town. Rome was situated on the fringe, the very edge, of the Greek world, for the nearest Greek town was on its doorstep, at Cumae, which had been founded a little earlier than Rome, between 775 and 750 (2), and spread its influence on the surrounding countryside. Thus Rome had never been completely free from contamination by Hellenism. It was influenced, first indirectly through the Etruscans, who had received so much from the Greeks—right up to the fourth century, Etruscan education continued to attract the sons of the Roman aristocracy[1] (3)—and through the Campania, which had also at a very early stage been profoundly hellenized, and which had a considerable influence on Latin districts from the sixth century onwards (4), and then directly, partly in the fifth century, but mainly in the fourth, as a result of the influx of Greek or hellenized elements amongst the Roman populace. From then on Greek influence was everywhere—in religion (5), in art,[2] even in the actual structure of the city ramparts; for the wall known as "Servius's", said to date from 378, has signs of a close connection between Rome and Syracuse[3] (6).

The movement received a new impetus after the year 340, when Rome joined up with Oscan Campania, which had been subject to Hellenistic influences for so long (7). We know enough about that "Hellenistic town", pre-Roman Pompeii, to be able to glimpse something of its system of education. Its young aristocrats formed the "Pompeian young guard"—the VEREIIA PUMPAIIANA[4]— which was obviously modelled on the Hellenistic ephebia and had a magnificent palestra in pure Greek style as its centre (8); and these, as we know, were the kind of institutions that always marked the planting of Hellenistic culture in barbarian lands (9).

Greek influence went on increasing as Rome extended its empire. What was left of Greater Greece surrendered at Tarentum in 272. Sicily was conquered between 241 and 212. From 214 onwards, and especially from 200, there was the long series of Eastern wars that ended with the annexation of Macedonia in 168 and of Greece in 146. Finally, and perhaps most important of all— for Asia was rich and flourishing, far more influential than Greece herself, which was by now utterly devitalized—the kingdom of Pergamus was annexed in 132. From then on the Roman Empire was a bi-lingual state that included within its boundaries a whole sequence of provinces in which Greek was the spoken language. Historians rightly insist on the profound effects that this invasion of Hellenism had on Rome; nowhere were they more considerable than in the field of intellectual culture, and hence in education.

For the Greek civilization that Rome finally discovered in the second century was no longer the sensitive plant, impossible to transplant, of the old πόλις civilization; it was the cosmopolitan Hellenistic civilization that was used to being sent abroad—had it not reached the furthermost parts of Turkestan and the heart of India? Since it had succeeded in taking root in Egypt and Mesopotamia and Iran—all countries with an ancient culture of their own—how could it fail to conquer the Italians, who were still new to such things and had

[1] Livy, IX, 36, 3; cf. Cic., *Div.*, I, 92.
[2] Pliny, *HN*, XXXV, 154.
[3] Livy, VI, 32, 1.
[4] Conway, I, 42.

already been prepared for it by previous penetration—these Romans with their intelligence and their capacity for looking after number one? It was not long before they had a pretty shrewd idea what they could get out of a mature and highly developed culture like the Greeks', especially when they compared it with their own indigenous culture, which had lagged behind at such a comparatively archaic stage of development.

Even by the year 312 the celebrated censor App. Claudius Caecus seems to have modelled himself on Hellenism,[1] and by the second century it was quite normal to find Roman politicians speaking to the Greeks in their own language, not only fluently but with considerable style—the father of the Gracchi, who was censor in 169, made a speech to the people of Rhodes which was still remembered in Cicero's time,[2] and Crassus Mucianus, during his mission to Asia in 131, performed his duties as judge with the help of five Greek dialects that he knew perfectly[3] (10). The Roman aristocracy looked upon Greek as being primarily an international language, the language used in diplomacy, the language of their enemies in the East, who were soon to be their subjects.

But they very soon realized that there was another and wider advantage to be gained from adopting Greek culture. Its main object was the mastery of rhetoric, and because of her late development, second-century Rome gave the spoken word the same high place that it had in fifth-century Athens. In Rome, as in the Greek democracies, a politician had to know how to get on the right side of the crowd, how to influence the voting in the assembly, how to inspire the troops, how to harangue a tribunal.

It was not long before some of the shrewder Romans learned from the Greeks[4] what increased efficiency an ambitious, high-class politician could gain from a knowledge of rhetoric. The first Latin orators with a Greek training behind them seem to have appeared at the time of Cato the Censor (234–139),[5] though Cicero, who was in a better position to judge than we are, makes M. Aemilius Lepidus Porcina, who was not consul until 137, the first artist in the spoken word worthy to be mentioned in the same breath as the Attic orators.[6]

From rhetoric, and the literary education upon which it was based, Rome gradually went on to discover all the other aspects of Greek culture. When we hear Polybius blandly explaining how useful astronomy can be to generals on their campaigns because it enables them to regulate their armies' rate of progress,[7] we seem to hear an echo of the learned discussions that went on in the enlightened circles in which Scipio Aemilianus grew up, when the young aristocrats got their education from listening to the talk between their Greek masters and friends.

But it would be unfair to imagine this society as having been made up of boorish country squires whose only concern was their own immediate interest (11). They were not insensitive to the genuinely human values that made up the noblest and most generous side of Greek culture. No one could doubt the sincerity or depth of the philhellenism that appeared in men like the first

[1] Cic., *Tusc.*, IV, 4.
[2] Cic., *Brut.*, 79.
[3] Quint., XI, 2, 50. Val. Max., VIII, 7, 6.
[4] Cic., *De Or.*, I, 14.
[5] *Ibid.*, *Brut.*, 77–81.
[6] *Ibid.*, 96.
[7] Polyb., IX, 15.

Africanus—especially Flamininus, the victor at Cynoscephalae (197), and Aemilius Paulus, the victor at Pydna, and of course the men of the next generation in the remarkable circle that gathered around Aemilius Paulus' son, Scipio Aemilianus (12). There were many stories about the latter—in particular one of how he saw Carthage burning and began musing over its destruction, and was then seized with a sad foreboding at the thought that a similar fate could befall his own city.[1] Such feelings are not those of a barbarian or a country yokel—especially when it is remembered that to express them Aemilianus quoted Homer:[2]

The day is coming when holy Ilium will be destroyed, with Priam and the people of Priam of the good ashen spear. . . .

And it was again a line from Homer[3] that came instinctively to his lips when he heard of the death of his brother-in-law, the revolutionary tribune Tiberius Gracchus:[4] "He that would imitate him, let him die like him!"

In these circles the greatest figures in Greek science rubbed shoulders with the highest Roman nobility—the historian Polybius, the philosopher Panaetius. And do I need to mention the influence that Posidonius had on the society of his time a little later?

This philhellenism was not confined to a small group of aristocrats: the whole of Rome was full of it, as can be seen from the great welcome that was given in the theatre to plays that were built on the Greek model, with Greek stories and Greek characters. But even if we confine ourselves to the aristocracy, we can estimate the extent of the intelligent interest shown by the youth of Rome in the most sublime aspects of Greek culture, by the enthusiastic welcome they gave Hellenistic lecturers who came to Rome on diplomatic missions and then gave "auditions"—ἀκροάσεις—just as they would have done at home. So did the Stoic critic Crates of Mallus,[5] ambassador to the king of Pergamus, in 159 (13); so did the Athenian envoys, the philosophers Carneades, Diogenes of Babylon and Critolaus,[6] in 154. "It was like a wind sweeping through the city . . . people could talk about nothing else"[7]—to such an extent that Cato hurriedly got the Senate to publish a decree of expulsion against them for arguing—"men who had such glib tongues that they could get anyone to believe whatever they liked."

For this invasion by Greek scholarship, though it was welcomed by most people with enthusiasm, met with violent hostility from one section of opinion that was strongly imbued with the traditional spirit and a sense of national pride. These "old Romans", represented by Cato the Censor, who is still for us today their best spokesman, criticised Greek culture for carrying the poisonous germs of "softness" and immorality.

The Senate's decree of 154 was not the first of its kind. In 173 the Senate

[1] App., Pun., 132; Diod. Sic., XXXII, 24.
[2] Hom., Il., VI, 448.
[3] Ibid., Od., I, 47.
[4] Plut., Ti. Gracch., 21.
[5] Suet., Gram., 2, 1.
[6] Pliny, HN, VII, 112; Gell., VII, 14, 8.
[7] Plut., Cat. Mai., 22.

had banished two Epicurean philosophers, Alcius and Philiscus;[1] in 161, a general proclamation ordered all philosophers and rhetors to be banished.[2]

Something of this opposition always remained, as we can see in Juvenal,[3] though in his case it was hardly more than bad temper, a very understandable reaction against the smugness and exaggerated nationalism of the *Graeculi*. It hardly appeared publicly except in the form of a rather hypocritical kind of false modesty on the part of those Roman politicians who pretended to be ashamed of a Hellenism that they were riddled with; even Cicero, for instance, could still pretend in the *Verrinae*[4] that he did not know the name of Polycletus—as, two generations earlier, the great orators Crassus and Antonius had thought it better for publicity "if one of them pretended to despise the Greeks and the other not even to know them", whereas they both knew them very well.[5]

In actual fact, by the middle of the second century Hellenism had triumphed in senate circles. Not only the half-baked intellectuals whom Cato had various digs at,[6] but all the most serious-minded people, took a pride in being able to speak Greek. Cato himself, who gave his son such pathetic advice to avoid Greek literature and Greek medicine,[7] found it necessary at the end of his life to learn Greek and read Thucydides and Demosthenes:[8] perhaps he had not been so ignorant of it as he had tried to make out, even earlier.[9]

GREEK EDUCATION IN ROME

Thus the Roman aristocracy adopted Greek education for its sons. Teachers were already to hand amongst the great numbers of slaves that conquest had provided—the oldest known example being Livius Andronicus, a Greek from Tarentum who was taken to Rome as a slave after his city had been captured in 272 and later freed by his master after bringing up his children.[10] Roman society was very generous about emancipating its slaves—it thus did something to redeem the barbarous way it chose to obtain them.

Very soon, besides the private tuition that was given in the houses of the great, public teaching of Greek began to be given in genuine schools: Andronicus himself taught *domi forisque*—he was both tutor and schoolmaster.[11] As well as freedmen who had set up on their own account there were slaves whose teaching abilities could be exploited by their owners: a slave who could teach was a good investment (as Cato knew)[12] and fetched top price in the market.[13] Not all the teachers began as slaves: Ennius was born in an allied city in Messapia. As soon as it was known that there were people in the capital anxious to learn their language, the Greeks came along to take advantage of it: in about the year 167, says Polybius, there were a large number of qualified teachers in Rome.[14]

The Roman families, who wanted their children to have the best education

[1] Ath., XII, 547 A.
[2] Suet., *Gram.*, 25, 1; Gell., XV, 11.
[3] III, 60-108.
[4] *Verr.*, IV, 5.
[5] Cic., *De Or.*, II, 4.
[6] *Ap.* Macrob., *Sat.*, III, 14, 9; Polyb., XXXIX, 1.
[7] Pliny, *HN*, XXIX, 14.
[8] Cic., *Sen.*, 3; Plut., *Cat. Mai.*, 2.
[9] *Ibid.*, 4, 18.
[10] Hier., *Chron.*, 187 a.
[11] Suet., *Gram.*, I, 1.
[12] Plut., *Cat. Mai.*, 20.
[13] Pliny, *HN*, VII, 128; Suet., *Gram.*, 3, 3.
[14] Polyb., XXXI, 24.

they could get, did all they could to give them a first-class training in Greek. This can be seen in the case of Aemilius Paulus, who engaged a whole staff of special Greek teachers[1] for his sons and offered them the use of the valuable library that had belonged to King Perseus and been taken from booty seized in Macedonia.[2] Then there was Cornelia, the mother of the Gracchi, who is described in a famous anecdote as proudly awaiting her two sons' return from school.[3] She supervised their lessons herself and secured the most highly qualified teachers for them: her elder son Tiberius had the famous Diophanes of Mytilene[4] as his teacher of eloquence and the Stoic Blossius of Cumae as his philosophy teacher and director of conscience.[5]

We must not be surprised to find a Roman mother playing such a part. Greek culture was open to women too. This Cornelia held an absolute "salon" attended by all the best minds in Greece,[6] and it was not the only one. Sallust found it quite normal that Sempronia, mother to the Brutus who murdered Caesar, should be "equally versed in the Greek and Latin literatures".[7]

In their search for a thoroughly Greek education, young Romans began to want more than they could get from the teachers who were to be found or could be prevailed upon to come to Rome, and so they started going to Greece to finish their education, doing their studies along with the Greeks themselves. In 119–118 Romans were allowed to enter the Athenian ephebia,[8] and, more significantly still, they began to attend lectures given by the philosophers and rhetors in the greatest university centres in the Greek world—Athens and Rhodes. The young Cicero did this,[9] and so did his contemporaries.[10]

ADAPTATION TO THE LATIN SPIRIT

In the first excitement of discovery, these young Romans clamoured for everything connected with Greek culture. Aemilius Paulus supplied his sons not only with teachers of Greek language and literature—grammarians, sophists and rhetors—but with Greek painters, Greek sculptors, Greek grooms and Greek huntsmen.[11] The plastic arts had taken a back place in Greek education, of course; but Aemilius Paulus wanted his sons to have the very best of everything, so that there was no side of humanism with which they were unfamiliar.

There was something of a craze for music, for the singing and dancing that had always been so characteristic of Greek life,[12] but the nation soon reacted against this in the name of all that was Roman and "serious". Scipio Aemilianus[13] only mentions schools of music and dancing so that he can castigate the

---

[1] Plut., *Aem.*, 6.
[2] *Ibid.*, 28.
[3] Val. Max., IV, 4, pr.
[4] Cic., *Brut.*, 104.
[5] Plut., *Ti. Gracch.*, 8; 17; 20.
[6] *Ibid.*, *C. Gracch.*, 19.
[7] Sall., *Cat.*, 25, 2.
[8] *IG*, II², 1008.
[9] Cic., *Brut.*, 307; 312; 315–316.
[10] *Ibid.*, 245.
[11] Plut., *Aem.*, 6.
[12] Macrob., *Sat.*, III, 14, 7; 10; Cic., *de Or.* III, 87; *Pis.* 22.
[13] *Ap.* Macrob., *Sat.*, III, 14, 7.

young people of his day for liking such an unseemly and immodest art, which may be all right for mountebanks but is definitely not the thing for free-born children who will one day be senators. People soon came to see that such pleasures were rather unsavoury, and should be left to rakes and wastrels:[1] they were quite beneath the dignity of any well-born Roman.[2]

Music—well, it was all right for girls, as an "accomplishment";[3] but even then music was liable to be received with the typical Roman frown: Sallust, describing Brutus's mother, who found herself mixed up in Catilina's rather shady circle, says that she could dance and play the lyre "rather better than one would expect from a decent woman"—*elegantius quam necesse probae*.[4]

This exactly expresses what seems to have been Roman society's final attitude: the various branches of the art of music had been accepted as an integral part of any culture, essential in any decent high society, but as things to be watched rather than as things to be performed by amateurs (14). The natural result was that music and dancing tended to be abandoned, or at least neglected, in liberal education,[5] without being actually proscribed, for from Augustus to Severus choirs of boys and girls from aristocratic families went on copying the Greek custom of singing together at solemn festivals, especially the centenary games.[6] More significant still is the part played by music[7] and the plastic arts[8] in the lives of the emperors. There is a great deal of conflicting evidence about this, and any attempt to discuss it here would be out of place, but it seems clear that in the first and second, and the fourth and fifth, centuries A.D. art was held to be essential to an emperor's education, and, as we know (15), the emperor was the ideal man.

OPPOSITION TO ATHLETICS

The Roman reaction against athletics was perhaps even more decisive, though the Greek παιδεία cannot be imagined without them. The Romans never took to athletics; they looked upon them as something exclusively Greek,[9] and unlike the Oscans of Campania they decided against them. We have already seen how Roman sport developed in its own way in the associations for youth that came into existence under the Empire, circus and amphitheatre taking the place of stadium and palestra.

In Sicily in 204, the first Scipio Africanus was doing his best to dress like a Greek and do his exercises in the gymnasium, but this may have been to get on the right side of the Sicilians, and in any case he caused considerable scandal.[10] His example was not followed. Athletic competitions became very popular in

---

[1] Cic., *Cat.*, II, 23; Sen., *Controv.*, I, pr. 8.
[2] Nep., *Epam.*, I, 2.
[3] Ov., *Am.*, II, 4, 25 *seq.*; *Ars Am.*, III, 311 *seq.*
[4] Sall., *Cat.*, 25, 2.
[5] Quint., I, 12, 14; cf. Mart., V, 56.
[6] Hor., *Carm. Sec.* 6; cf. *Carm.*, IV, 6, 31; Catull., 34, 2; Dessau, 5050, 147 *seq.*; *Aep* (1932), 70, 58–9; 84.
[7] Suet., *Tit.*, 3, 2; *Ner.*, 20, 1; *Cal.*, 54, 1; cf. Tac., XIII, 3, 7; S.H.A., *Hadr.*, 14, 9; *Helag.*, 32, 8; *Alex. S.*, 27, 7; 9.
[8] Tac., *Ann.*, XIII, 3, 7; Suet., *Ner.*, 52; S.H.A., *Hadr.*, 14, 8; *M. Aur.*, 4. 9; *Alex. S.*, 27, 7.
[9] Vitr., V, 11; Strab., V, 246.
[10] Livy, XXIX, 19, 12.

Rome—they were included in the games from 186 B.C.[1] onwards and increased in number under the Empire (16)—but, even more than was the case with music, as shows given by professional performers. Nero in particular tried to get members of the aristocracy to appear in the stadium,[2] but the only response, except for a few rare cases, was a storm of opposition.[3]

If physical exercise came into the life of Rome at all it was as a matter of hygiene, ancillary to the use of steam baths. Architecturally the Roman "palestra" was subsidiary to the *thermae*, which, compared with the Greek original, had developed out of all proportion to the actual arrangements for sport. As for the Roman "gymnasium", it was simply a pleasure garden—a "Culture Park" (17).

The Romans reacted to Greek gymnastics very much like the "barbarians": their sense of modesty was shocked by its nudity, and they regarded homosexuality—which centred round the gymnasium—as something that Greek civilization should be ashamed of, not proud of.[4] Besides their sound moral principles, their sense of the deep seriousness of life was opposed to the Greek love of sport, for it seemed to them a purposeless and useless kind of activity. Roman Republicans had no time for elegant leisure: Polybius, congratulating his young friend Scipio Aemilianus on his truly royal love of hunting—which as a good Achaean gentleman and spiritual brother to Xenophon he himself shared —observed that most of the other young Roman nobles had no time for it because they thought of nothing but law and politics[5]—i.e. their duties as citizens.

Thus in the two matters of art and sport the Roman national spirit set up its own distinctive reaction, and helped to correct the otherwise all-conquering tendency to adopt Hellenistic education as a whole. But it is worth remembering that music and gymnastics, which had been such characteristic features of the old Greek education, were already receding in Greece itself in the last few centuries B.C. Like all regressive cultural characteristics they were kept going by force, but they no longer had enough vitality to assert themselves and "catch on". Thus even in Greece music and sport both tended to become matters for professionals and specialists to perform, and the general public to listen to or watch. This was the only way in which Hellenistic music and sport were really alive, and it is highly interesting that this was the way in which they penetrated into Roman culture and life. But as regards their being part of a liberal education, their tattered prestige had become far too feeble even in their own country for them to be able to have any effect on the Latins.

BIRTH OF LATIN SCHOOLS

Greek influence on Roman education was even more far-reaching than we have seen it to be. There were two sides to it. In the first place the Roman aristocrats

---

[1] *Ibid.*, XXXIX, 22, 2.
[2] Tac., *Ann.*, XIV, 20; 47, 4.
[3] *Schol.*, Juv., IV, 53.
[4] Ennius ap. Cic., *Tusc.*, IV, 70; Pliny, *HN*, XV, 19; Tac., *Ann.*, XIV, 20, 5–6; Plut., *Qu. Rom.*, 274 (*C.D.*); *Cat. Mai.*, 20.
[5] Polyb., XXXI, 25.

brought up their children Greek fashion, to be, in fact, to all intents and purposes, educated Greeks, but at the same time, along with this foreign education, they provided a parallel course of study that was exactly modelled on the Greek system, but in Latin; so that side by side with the schools in which Greek subjects were taught arose a parallel series of Latin schools—primary, secondary and higher. These new schools appeared at a different period and in different historical circumstances in each case; the primary school in the seventh and sixth centuries, secondary schools in the third century, and the advanced schools not until the first.

PRIMARY SCHOOLS

The origins of the primary school went very far back into the past. Plutarch says that the first man to open a fee-paying school was a certain master named Sp. Carvilius, a slave who had been freed by the consul in 234,[1] but, if there is any truth in this, it can only be on the public and commercial side. The highly coloured passages in Livy which are supposed to describe primary schools of a classical type in Rome in 445 (449)[2] and among the Falisci shortly after 400,[3] cannot of course be taken seriously, but nevertheless there is no doubt that an elementary teaching of letters must have been current in Rome long before the fourth century.

Since the teaching of letters is essentially bound up with writing, both must have gone back to the Etruscan period of Rome in the time of the kings. The Latins are known in fact to have taken their alphabet from the ancient Etruscans. Now, by an unexpected stroke of luck, we have some idea of the methods used in Etruscan primary education—we have direct documentary evidence about it older than anything we have about Greece. There is a charming ivory writing-tablet (18) from Marsigliana d'Albegna that dates from about 600 B.C., and engraved on the top border of the frame is an absolutely complete archaic alphabet that was obviously meant to be copied by the pupil practising on the wax part of the tablet underneath. We have seven more examples of these model alphabets, dating from various times during the seventh century, and one of them is accompanied by a syllabary: clearly, Etruscan teaching went through the same stages as Greek, and there can be no doubt that the Etruscans took their teaching methods, as well as the secret of writing, from their first Greek masters (19).

By analogy we can assume that the same methods were used in elementary Latin education at the same period. On the famous Praeneste golden clasp there is an inscription engraved in Etruscan fashion from left to right. It reads:

MANIOS : MED : PHE PHAKED : NUMASIOI

"Manius made me for Numerius."[4] This shows that writing—and hence the teaching of writing—was quite common in the seventh century—and not only

---

[1] Plut., *Qu. Rom.*, 278 E.
[2] Livy, III, 44, 6; cf. D.H., XI, 28.
[3] Livy, V, 27.
[4] *CIL*, I², 3=Dessau 8561.

in Rome, the bridgehead of Etruscan influence beyond the Tiber, but in the rest of Latium too, even at this early stage.

SECONDARY EDUCATION

Latin "secondary" education appeared much later, in the middle of the third century B.C. It is not really surprising that it should have had to wait so long. Greek secondary education centred round the great poets, especially Homer, and as Rome had no national literature it could hardly have any similar type of education. Hence this paradox, which has perhaps not been sufficiently emphasized: Latin poetry came into existence so that teachers should have something to argue about, probably as a result of national pride, for Rome would not have gone on being satisfied for long with an education that was given solely in Greek.

The first Latin poet, Livius Andronicus of Tarentum, was the first teacher of Latin literature, and he was also the first teacher of Greek to teach in Rome. He translated the *Odyssey* into Latin, using an old Latin metre, the saturnian. The translation was very literal, line by line: αI, "Tell me, O Muse, of the man of a thousand tricks", was rendered as

Virum mihi Camoena insece versutum.[1]

But it must not be imagined that the idea behind this translation was to help young students to learn Homer's Greek. Andronicus regarded it as a text that he could expound—*praelegebat*—just as though it was a Greek classic.[2]

Of course this was not the only source of early Latin poetry (20), but for a long time Latin poetry did in fact preserve this strange—to us—characteristic of being closely bound up with the need to give some sort of body to the secondary-school syllabus. Two generations later, Ennius, who was half Greek too, went on expounding, along with the Greek authors, his own poems, which were no sooner written than they became "classics".[3]

Soon—apparently by the time of the Gracchi, at the latest—this kind of teaching had become autonomous and had been taken up by teachers known as *grammatici Latini*, the Latin equivalent of the grammarians responsible for Greek; but for a long time it was hampered by the poor reputation and slight cultural value of the texts that had to be expounded. Old Andronicus remained on the syllabus,[4] fighting valiantly for top place with Ennius, but they were both small beer compared with Homer! We can assume[5] that in about the second century the Latin comic poets were included too—it was hardly possible for such reinforcements to be despised. And in any case it would have been only fitting to include the writers who set out to copy Menander—who was already on the Greek grammarians' syllabus.

But it was only in the time of Augustus that Latin secondary teaching took on its final form and emerged as a serious rival to Greek—when, not long after the

---

[1] Gell., XVIII, 9, 5. [3] *Ibid.*
[2] Suet., *Gram.*, I, I. [4] Hor., *Epist.*, II, I, 70–71.
[5] Cf. Gell., XV, 24.

year 26 B.C., a freedman of Atticus, whose name was Q. Caecilius Epirota, had the hardihood to choose "Virgil and the other new poets",[1] as the authors he would deal with—the first, no doubt, being Horace. From then on, as long as the ancient schools lasted—that is to say, until darkness descended over Europe with the barbarians—the programme remained unchanged: there were the comic writers, especially Terence, and the great Augustan poets with Virgil towering above them; and these formed the foundation of Latin literary culture. Henceforth, an educated Roman was a man who knew his Virgil, as a Greek knew his Homer, as a treasury of wisdom and beauty buried in the depths of his memory, lines of which came back to him whenever he needed to express, or insist on, or stand up for, any feeling or idea.

As for the other side of secondary education, the study of language, it naturally did not become known in Rome until after it had been invented by Dionysius Thrax in Rhodes. The first Latin treatise on the new science seems to have been the *De Grammatica*, which was *Lib.* I of Varro's *Disciplinarum libri*—and Varro lived between 116–27 B.C. (21).

HIGHER EDUCATION: THE LATIN RHETORS

Higher education, in its main form, rhetoric, did not appear in Rome in any Latin form until the first century B.C., and even then it did not settle down without difficulty. The first school for Latin rhetors was opened in 93 by L. Plotius Gallus, one of Marius's supporters,[2] but in the following year it was closed again by edict of the aristocratic censors, Cn. Domitius Ahenobarbus and L. Licinius Crassus,[3] as being an innovation contrary to the customs and traditions of the ancestors.

There was undoubtedly a political motive behind this (22), but it would nevertheless be a mistake to regard it as being prompted solely by the hostility of aristocratic censors against anything that came from the rival party. The whole spirit of the new school was disturbing to the conservatives. We get a clear idea of Plotius' kind of teaching from an anonymous manual called *Rhetoric Dedicated to Herennius*, which was written between 86 and 82 by one of his pupils.

It reveals a highly "modern" type of education, very different from the classical rhetoric taught in the Greek schools. Although it is obviously based on this—especially on Hermagoras—the author dislikes the multiplicity of rules,[4] and wishes to bring teaching closer to real life: for the traditional subjects for declamation—Orestes and Clytemnestra[5]—he substitutes themes taken from the Roman life of the day, questions of maritime law or the law of inheritance;[6] above all, discussions on contemporary political issues such as, "Should the quaestor Cepion be convicted for opposing the corn law instituted by the tribune Saturninus?"[7] "Should the murderer of the tribune P. Sulpicius"

---

[1] Suet., *Gram.*, 16, 2.
[2] *Ibid.*, 26 (Cic.); Sen., *Controv.*, II, pr. 5; Hieron., *Chron.*, 88a.
[3] Suet., *Gram.*, 25, 2; Gell., XV, 11; Cic., *de Or.*, III, 93–94; Tac., *Dial.*, 35.
[4] [Cic.] *Her.*, I, 1.
[5] *Ibid.*, I, 17; 25; 26.
[6] *Ibid.*, I, 19; 20; 23.
[7] *Ibid.*, I, 21.

(who was killed in 88 on Sulla's orders)[1] "be pardoned?" Then there were the Senate's deliberations during the Social War (91–88) on whether to grant citizens' rights to the Italians:[2] or the tragic death of Tiberius Gracchus . . .[3]

Not all the subjects were taken from such burning questions of the day, of course, nor was the argument always presented from a point of view favourable to the *populares*—a good rhetor had to know how to plead both for and against: but there is no doubt that the school's general atmosphere was affected by its founder's political attitude.

A further point was involved, for the traditional teaching of rhetoric, because it was given in Greek and demanded years of hard study, was very much up the conservatives' street: if they could forbid the teaching of Latin rhetoric they could ensure that only the sons of rich aristocrats reaped the benefit of this magical art of speech in the struggles in the forum; whereas the Marianist school of L. Plotius Gallus offered more or less the same thing at reduced rates to any young man of the people who wanted to get on.

THE WORK OF CICERO

Having thus been thwarted by the edict of Ahenobarbus and Licinius Crassus, the teaching of Latin eloquence did not revive until the end of the century, as a result of the work that Cicero had been engaged upon—paradoxically, for Cicero himself had been brought up as an aristocrat, and so had had no connection with Latin eloquence but only with Greek (23).

From motives that were genuinely patriotic, and throughout his long career, this great orator devoted a great deal of effort to the task of ensuring that his art could be pursued in Latin. In the first place there were his own speeches, which were actual models that young Latins could study and imitate, far more profitably than the Attic masterpieces. Then there were his treatises, which carried on the work begun by Plotius and his school, by supplying the technical material that made the Greek theorists unnecessary: the early *De Inventione*, which was simply his master Molon's teaching adapted to Latin; the *Divisions of Rhetoric*, and great treatises on aesthetics and history like the *De Oratore*, *Brutus*, *Orator*.

Cicero may have been the very first in this field—we know that he had young disciples to whom he disclosed the secrets of his art—but at least it seems certain that from the time of Augustus (24) rhetoric was taught in Latin as well as in Greek.

Cicero's philosophic work, from the *De Republica* to the *De Officiis*, had the same aim as his rhetorical work: to create in Latin a technical language that could be used to "popularize" Greek thought: once that had been done, it was possible to set about introducing a genuinely Roman teaching of philosophy.

PHILOSOPHY REMAINS GREEK

But Cicero's influence on philosophy was much less fruitful than it was on eloquence. There never was any Latin school of philosophy, no doubt because

---

[1] [Cic.] *Her.*, I, 25. [2] *Ibid.*, III, 2. [3] *Ibid.*, IV, 55.

there were only a few people keen enough not to be put off by the preliminary difficulty of the language.

There was indeed such a thing as Roman philosophy—in the first place mainly "Pythagorean", then Epicurean under the Republic, Stoic under the Empire and neo-Platonist between the third and fifth centuries; and after Cicero there were philosophers who thought and wrote in Latin. But there were many who came from typically Roman families who nevertheless wrote in Greek—the Sextii, Cornutus, Musonius, the Emperor Marcus Aurelius. More significant still, even those who wrote in Latin had done their studying in Greek; this is clear in the case of Seneca (25) and Apuleius.[1]

SCIENCE ALSO REMAINS GREEK

The same thing will be observed in the case of advanced science, which also remained entirely Greek. As regards mathematics, the only new developments the Latins made were in architecture and surveying (26), which were technical rather than scientific subjects—though surveying was done in a highly original manner, as the curious literature that makes up the *corpus* of the *Agrimensores* shows. We may if we choose regard this—as the Latins themselves did[2]—as a sign of their practical outlook, their lack of interest in research for its own sake; but it must not be forgotten that science played only a small part in Hellenistic education, and that it was taken up by an even smaller minority of specialists than philosophy. What point would there have been in having special Latin teaching for a few exceptional vocations? The language obstacle did not come into it, and in any case what was the object of studying science or philosophy if not to discover a Truth that transcended language?

ROMAN MEDICINE

Medicine was the only branch of learning that really came to be at home in Rome—but not until comparatively late. Under the Republic and throughout the Early Empire the professional teaching of medicine was still given in Greek. Latin treatises on medicine, like Varro's or Celsus's, were simply part of the general knowledge that every true *paterfamilias* was supposed to possess—as I have already explained. There was indeed official instruction in medicine, given by the physicians who controlled the public health service—*archiatri* (27) (the name, like the thing itself, had come from the East)—but this was given in Greek.

It was only in the Late Empire, in the fourth and especially the fifth centuries, that medicine (and the veterinary art) began to be written about in Latin, and even then it was chiefly a matter of translations from Greek (28). This late development was a result of a natural social reaction—society cannot do without doctors—to a phenomenon to which we must now turn our attention: the decline of Greek studies, which was soon followed by the utter neglect of Greek in the West—the characteristic feature of the cultural history of late antiquity.

[1] *Flor.*, 20.   [2] Cic., *Tusc.*, I, 5.

CHAPTER III

THE LANGUAGE QUESTION: GREEK AND LATIN

THUS from the time of Horace[1] onwards an educated Roman was proficient in the two languages, Greek and Latin—*utriusque linguae*, as they said (1). This is a fact worth noting, for Roman classicism thus prepared the way for modern forms of humanism that are based on a second language, a cultural *lingua franca* which is used to transmit a tradition generally recognised as having an essential superiority over all others, and therefore to be imitated.

The Latins always respected Greek culture as having been the source of their own spiritual development.[2] One may even go so far as to say that they never quite lost a slight inferiority complex about it:[3] for instance, they were always[4] deploring the "poverty" of their own language compared with the magnificence of Greek.

The Romans were the first to use a foreign language systematically to increase their mastery over their own. Like our own schoolboys, young Romans did translations from Greek into Latin and *vice versa*;[5] they "compared" Cicero and Demosthenes,[6] Homer and Virgil[7]—"comparison", σύγκρισις, it will be remembered, was one of the *progymnasmata* to the study of rhetoric: from Varro[8] to the Later Empire[9] Latin grammarians went on "comparing" the two languages, thus preparing the way for the modern "comparative grammar of Greek and Latin" (2).

In fact we are here at the origin of the methods used in our own classical education; and we have the Latins to thank for them. Hellenistic humanism had always refused to give foreign languages any place in its educational system—they were "barbarians". The Greeks, unlike the Latins, knew and felt their culture to be autonomous, *sui generis*.

Of course, from Polybius to Plutarch there were occasional Greeks who took a sympathetic, intelligent interest in Roman affairs, but they were specialists, cultural liaison officers, not average representatives of Greek culture.

Their attitude—a mixture of ignorance and disdain[10]—was natural enough under the Republic, when there was hardly any Latin culture worth speaking of and Rome was simply a foreign power, an enemy, an all-conquering tyrant; but it did not change appreciably even under the Empire, when the Greeks had lost most of their resentment at having been conquered (3) and had begun, like the

---

[1] *Carm.*, III, 8, 5.
[2] Quint., I, 1, 12; Pliny, *Ep.*, VIII, 24, 4.
[3] Virg., *Aen.*, VI, 847 *seq.*; Lucr., I, 832; cf. 139.
[4] *Ibid.*, III, 260; Pliny, *Ep.*, IV, 18.
[5] Quint., X, 5, 2–3; Pliny, *Ep.*, VII, 9; Suet., *Gram.*, 25, 5.
[6] Quint., X, 1, 105 *seq.*
[7] Juv., VI, 436; XI, 180.
[8] Varro, *De Ling. Lat.*, V, 96 *seq.*
[9] Macrob., *Diff.*; *Gram. Lat.*, IV, 566 *seq.* (Serv.).
[10] Cic., *De Or.*, II, 77.

Italians and the peoples of Western Europe, to feel themselves an integral part[1] of one great country stretching from end to end of the civilized world: a world now identified with the city of Rome.[2]

THE ROMAN WORLD BILINGUAL

The Roman Empire did not bring any linguistic unification to correspond to the dual movement of political and cultural unification—one coming from Rome, the other from Greece—that had welded the two halves of the Mediterranean world into such a powerful unity; it remained divided into two zones of influence centring round its two cultural languages. The line between them can be seen on the map, (4) running through comparatively uncivilized countries in which Greek and Latin either took the place of the local language or were at least superimposed upon it. There was no particular encroachment of one into the other, except that Greater Greece and Sicily tended to be Latinized, whereas the colonies that Rome had developed so profusely in the Greek-speaking districts along the *Via Egnatia* soon returned to Hellenism (5).

The fact is that Greek culture had such tremendous prestige that the Roman State never made any serious attempt[3] to impose Latin on its Eastern subjects. Roman administrators never had any use for the barbarian languages—Celtic, Germanic, etc.—but they even gave Greek a kind of official sanction, for acts and decrees and edicts about the Eastern provinces were translated and promulgated in Greek (6). From Claudius to the Late Empire,[4] the Imperial Chancellery had two separate departments for correspondence, one controlled by the procurator *ab epistulis Latinis*, the other by the procurator *ab epistulis Graecis*. Not that Greek ever came to be regarded as the equal of Latin, which was the "national language"—πάτριος φωνή—even in Justinian's day.[5] Magistrates were obliged to use Latin for all their work,[6] and this "old law" died hard[7]— only under Arcadius were judges authorized to give sentence in Greek[8]—but in fact Roman officials could understand Greek and speak it, and they found it better to do without interpreters, so that, in the East, the cross-examination of witnesses, and the court proceedings generally, were carried on in Greek.[9] To give one case by way of example: an inscription recently published[10] has provided a complete account of a trial held in Antioch by the Emperor Caracalla on May 27th, 216: the title—and the sentence, of course—were in Latin, but during the actual proceedings everyone—from the Emperor downwards— spoke Greek. Nevertheless, the importance of Latin in the court-rooms of Egypt increased in the fourth and fifth centuries.[11]

[1] Arstd., XXVI K.
[2] Rut. Namat., I, 63 *seq.*
[3] Contra: Val. Max., II, 2; Aug., *Civ. Dei*, XIX, 7.
[4] *Not. Dign., Or.,* 17.
[5] Just., *Nov.,* VII, 1.
[6] Val. Max., II, 2, 2.
[7] Lydus, *Mag.,* III, 68; cf. II, 12; III, 42.
[8] *Cod. Just.,* VII, 45, 12.
[9] Val. Max., VIII, 7, 6; Suet., *Ti.,* 71.
[10] *Syria* (1942–1943), XXIII, 178–179.
[11] Cf. M. Norsa, *Miscellanea G. Mercati, VI,* Vatican, 1946 (*Studi e Testi,* 126), pp. 112–113.

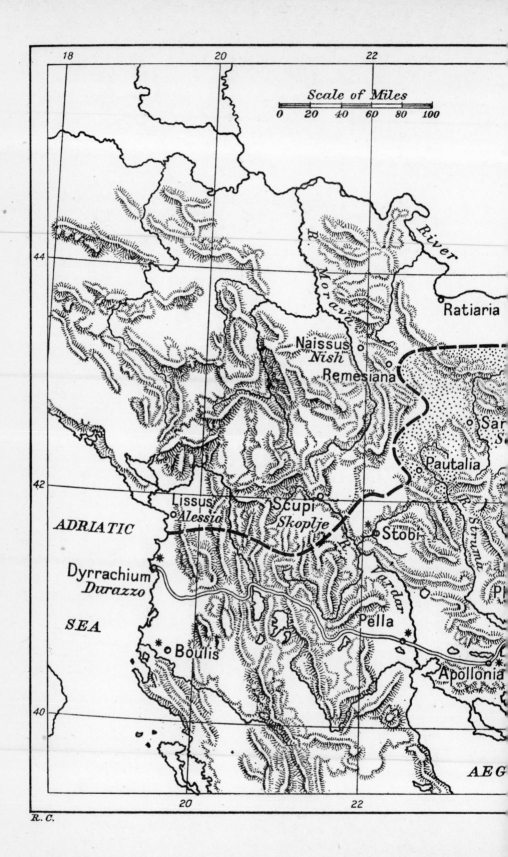

Scale of Miles

0   20   40   60   80   100

18   20   22

River

Ratiaria

R. Morava

Naissus
Nish
Remesiana

Sar
S.

Pautalia

Lissus
Alessia

ADRIATIC

Scupi
Skoplje

Stobi

R. Struma

R. Vardar

Dyrrachium
Durazzo

SEA

Pella

Boulis

Apollonia

AEG

R. C.

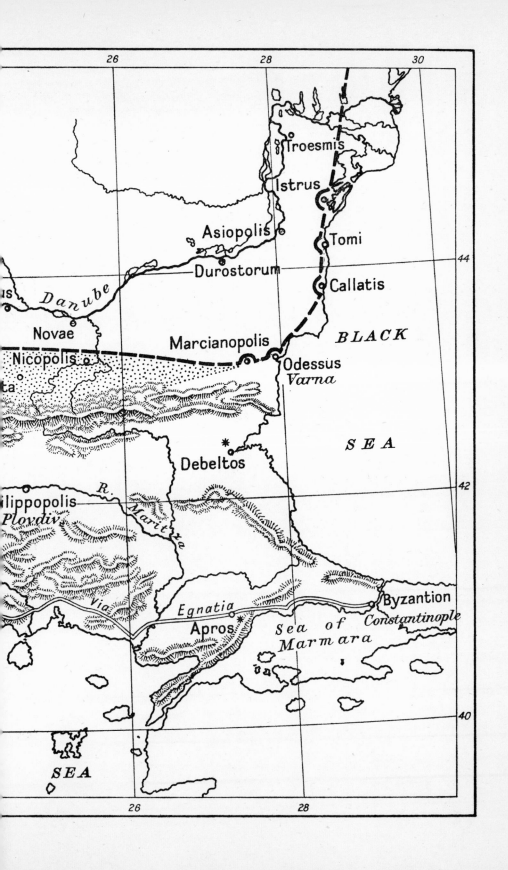

The only completely Latin thing was the army, where the staff was Latin and so was the language. In the Greek East, the civil administration recruited a considerable proportion of its men on the spot—not only the subordinates but most of the procurators of equestrian rank too.

FEW GREEKS LEARN LATIN

It is not surprising, therefore, that the Greeks should have been in no hurry to learn Latin. The only exceptions were the people who came from the small aristocratic élite that as a special favour from the emperor was admitted to the Senate—men like Herod Atticus, who even went to Rome to learn Latin in the home of a friend of the family, the consul P. Caluisius Tullus, maternal grandfather to Herod's future pupil the Emperor Marcus Aurelius.[1] And then there were those who were going in for the army or high administrative careers —though most of the Greeks who went into the civil service were local officials in the Eastern provinces and they spent all their lives there: if they went away— that is to say, if they got on exceptionally well—they almost invariably went to some office in Rome (7).

The men of letters living in Greek-speaking regions who took any interest in Roman literature[2] were few and far between. Latin had never been included in their scheme of liberal education, and they always regarded it as something technical, necessary mainly for the one truly Latin branch of learning—law.[3]

A few examples could perhaps be quoted from the first century A.D.[4] onwards, of young Greeks who took up Latin in the hope of getting some sort of official position, but there were very few of these until the Severi dynasty came into existence in the third century and, in the person of Julia Domna, the East was raised to the purple. Then many lawyers arose who were of Greek origin— Papinianus, Ulpianus, etc.: there were many young men like the future St. Gregory Thaumaturgus and his brother, who left their native province of Cappadocia in about the year 239 and went to Beirut to be educated because it had become the centre for Latin law students.[5] This tendency increased under the Late Empire. It is no accident that all the school papyri written in Latin that have been found in Egypt date from the fourth and fifth centuries: there is a great deal of evidence to show that by that time many parents in the East were encouraging their sons to take up this kind of career[6]—a rhetor like Libanius was disturbed by the competition he met with from the Latin schools in Rome or Palestine (i.e. Beirut).[7]

This was not simply caused by the development of the State bureaucratic machine. Diocletian and his successors seem to have made it their conscious policy[8] to familiarize the East with the "national language" so as to create a spirit of unity that would still further strengthen the Empire. With the foundation of Constantinople, a lasting centre of Latin culture and the Latin language was set up in the heart of the Greek-speaking part of the Empire (8), and it is

[1] Fronto, *M. Caes.*, III, 2.
[2] Gell., XIX, 9, 7.
[3] Greg. Thaum., *Pan.*, 5, 1066 B.
[4] Philstr., *VA*, VII, 42.
[5] *Pan.*, 5, 1066 C.
[6] Chrys., *Adv. Opp.*, III, 5.
[7] Lib., *Or.*, I, 214; XLIII, 5; XLVIII, 22; XLIX, 27.
[8] *Ibid.*, I, 234.

in fact in the fourth century that we begin to come across Latin writers who originate from the East—higher civil servants like Claudian of Alexandria[1] and Macrobius,[2] and army officers like Ammianus Marcellinus of Antioch.[3]

But this progress was purely relative, and it soon came to an end. By the end of the fourth century Greek had taken the place of Latin in the Beirut law schools. By the time of Justinian, as we can see from his *Novellae*,[4] the emperors had decided to do their normal legislating in Greek. The Empire had become an Hellenic Empire.

GREEK IN ROME

Meanwhile, in Latin-speaking districts, the bilingual system of education instituted in the second century B.C. had never been challenged, and it lasted in theory as long as the ancient tradition itself. It was always understood that any educated person worthy of the name must have been brought up on Homer and Menander. This was so in Gaul in the time of Ausonius;[5] it was still true in Sidonius Apollinaris' day, and he was not born until about 430 (9); in Africa, it was true for St. Augustine, and it was true for St. Fulgentius of Ruspae, who was born in 467.[6] The only question for the historian—and it is not an easy one (10)—is to decide how genuine this Hellenism was, and how deep it went at different periods.

Let us go back to the beginning. We know that the Greek culture of a man like Scipio Aemilianus was the real thing: in his day, being educated meant knowing Greek. Throughout the second century this emphasis on Greek went on increasing, as is well shown by Cicero's *Brutus* which is simply a monotonous catalogue of the orators of the past.[7] In the nineties an educated Roman could speak Greek as well as his own language.[8] There were even snobs who pretended to despise[9] their own language, and it had long been the fashion for Roman writers to write in Greek, especially history.[10]

THE GREEK OF CICERO

And then comes Cicero, in whom Latin Hellenism reaches its perfection. Cicero not only knew Greek perfectly, but he had assimilated all the Greek culture of his day. In Athens and in Rhodes he had studied rhetoric and philosophy as deeply as any Greek.[11] His culture was profound, not a superficial veneer, not an affectation. He translated Aratus,[12] Plato[13] and some of the orators.[14] He could declaim in Greek like a Sophist.[15] He carried on part of his correspondence in Greek[16]—his private letters are full of Greek words and Greek quotations, so that in his prose Greek and Latin become "the perfect

[1] *Carm. min.*, XIX, 3.
[2] *Sat.*, pr. 11.
[3] XXXI, 16, 9.
[4] Just., *Nov.*, VII, 1.
[5] *Protr.*, 46.
[6] Ferrand., I.
[7] *Brut.*, 107, 167.
[8] Cic., *De Or.*, II, 2–3.
[9] *Ibid.*, *Brut.*, 247.
[10] Polyb., XXXIX, 1.
[11] Cic., *Brut.*, 304–316.
[12] *Ibid.*, *Arat.*
[13] *Ibid*, *Tim.*
[14] *Ibid.*, *De Or.*, I, 155.
[15] *Ibid.*, *Brut.*, 310; 315.
[16] Plut., *Cic.*, 24.

consort, dancing together". One feels that he thought in Greek, and that he was writing to men like himself, who could appreciate his subtleties. He often uses Greek for finer shades of meaning that Greek alone, with its rich vocabulary, can express. He also uses it to add variety, and for an occasional joke. If he sometimes seems to overdo it, this is because Greek for him forms part of a homely kind of Latin—it appears most plainly in his most intimate letters— that he can use in a sort of literary game that he loves playing because it involves using his—and every other educated man's—favourite language: as in his private notebook a Frenchman of our own day—Charles Du Bos, for instance, or V. Larbaud—will use English, or, better still, as a German in the time of Baron Grimm would use French. And the result is a living language, with nothing bookish about it—in fact Cicero is himself the only witness to many of the Greek words he uses—words he borrowed from the vocabulary of the contemporary κοινή (11).

THE DECLINE OF GREEK

It seems to me quite clear that Cicero came at the top of the curve; after him, with the beginning of the Empire, the knowledge of Greek in Rome began to decline. This was inevitable, considering the way Latin culture itself was developing.

Until Cicero's time there had been no sort of equality between the two languages—on one side there was Ennius, on the other Homer, and Greek was thus essential for any real culture. But after the school reform carried out by C. Caecilius Epirota, the position was different. As soon as Latin revealed that it was just as capable as Greek of transmitting the highest cultural values, the two languages met, in a sense, on equal terms.

Thus after the work of Plotius Gallus and Cicero it was no longer essential to go to Greek to learn all the marvellous secrets of oratory; in fact, studying the Greek theory of rhetoric meant doing double work.

And a child's time and capacity are limited: how could a Latin boy be expected to get on with the Greek classics as well as a boy in the East, when they took up, at most, half of his syllabus and the Greek boy did nothing else? Henceforth, being educated meant, to a Latin, knowing Virgil and Cicero. Something similar has been happening to us since the seventeenth century: as Greek declined before the onset of Latin, so Greek and Latin have been giving way to "modern languages". From the teaching point of view it is not practical to try to keep two languages going at once. Experience in certain modern countries (12) confirms the view of Ausonius' own grandson, Paulinus of Pella. At the beginning of the fifth century he wrote, with an engaging simplicity: "To have to learn two languages at once is all right for the clever ones and gives excellent results; but for an average mind like mine such dispersion of effort soon becomes very tiring."[1]

That Greek did decline in the face of Latin cannot be doubted: by the time of the Late Empire the wonderful unity of Graeco-Roman culture had gone,

[1] P. Pel., 81–84.

and from then on there were two distinct Mediterranean cultures—a Latin culture in the West and a Greek culture in the East. The difficulty is to fix the stages of this decline and particularly to detect its first symptoms—and this is a real difficulty, for on the surface nothing had changed: Roman schools never abandoned the teaching of Greek. What has to be studied, therefore, is the quality of the teaching, and the value of its results.

But unless I am mistaken, even at the end of the first century some signs of weakening may be discerned in Quintilian. I know that he insisted on the study of Greek,[1] and that he himself knew it well; that he knew all about the technical side of Greek rhetoric, and all the ins and outs of its vocabulary (13) —as he needed to, for that was his particular speciality. He also knew his classics—Homer and others[2]—and could quote them whenever he needed to. But he did this a good deal less frequently and naturally than he quoted from Virgil or Cicero—they were his real authors, the ones he remembered without effort, the ones to whom his mind went instinctively. Quintilian's humanism was beginning to be academic rather than humanistic; it was a good deal less profound than Cicero's.

We should not overestimate the speed of the decline. In 97, two years after Quintilian's death, there were fifty-two competitors for the Greek poetry prize at the third Capitoline Games, and among them were Romans, including the child prodigy Q. Sulpicius Maximus, who at the age of eleven contributed a poem on Phaeton, which is absolutely dreadful but does at least show that he knew the language.[3]

A generation later, with Pliny the Younger, we enter a society in which Greek is still highly esteemed (14). Pliny's friends were educated men *utraque lingua*, who knew both languages;[4] they composed Greek epigrams,[5] wrote Greek history books[6] and were always quoting Homer, even in the Senate.[7] Pliny himself knew Greek well—he also had been a kind of infant prodigy and at the age of fourteen had composed a Greek tragedy.[8] He had done Greek rhetoric under the celebrated Nicetas of Smyrna, and at the same time Latin under Quintilian.[9] He had been to the philosophers,[10] he had listened to the Sophists lecturing,[11] and he knew his classics—in his letters he is always quoting Homer, the comic poets, Thucydides, Demosthenes. In fact we might be back in Cicero's time.

But the resemblance is so perfect that it becomes slightly suspicious, and one begins to wonder whether there is not a trace of affectation in Pliny and his friends. Clearly Pliny wants his correspondence to remind us of Cicero's, and so he imitates it, conscientiously, down to using Greek; but what a vast gulf there is between his laborious efforts, his frequent pedantry,[12] and the spontaneous humour of the letters to Atticus.

Let us proceed further into this second century. In the *Historia Augusta*

---

[1] Quint., I, I, 12; X, 5, 2 *seq.*; X, I, 22 *seq.*

[2] *Ibid.*, X, I, 46 *seq.*

[3] Dessau, 5177.

[4] Pliny, *Ep.*, III, I, 7; VII, 25, 4.

[5] *Ibid.*, IV, 3, 3; IV, 18.

[6] *Ibid.*, VIII, 4, 3.

[7] *Ibid.*, IX, 13, 20.

[8] *Ibid.*, VII, 4, 2.

[9] *Ibid.*, VI, 6, 3.

[10] *Ibid.*, I, 10, 2; III, 11, 5.

[11] *Ibid.*, II, 3.

[12] *Ibid.*, IX, 26, 8–9 (cf. Sen., *Ep.*, 27, 5–6).

we find Marcus Aurelius[1] and Lucius Verus[2] studying grammar and eloquence in both Greek and Latin at the same time, under different masters, and for once we can accept what it says as true, for we know from other sources that they did in fact both study rhetoric under Fronto and Herod Atticus at the same time. Of course they were princes, but it is most unlikely that an age as conservative as that of the Antonines did not do all it could to keep the old traditions going. The change must have come suddenly in the third century, especially as a result of the terrible crisis that shook the Roman world in the year 235. By the following century, as I have said, this change was practically over (15); and nowhere is this seen more clearly than in the state of the Christian Church.

For a long time the language of the Church had been Greek, but by the end of the second century the Church communities first in Africa and then in Italy had begun to adopt Latin for their liturgy and theology. By the fourth century the Eastern and Western Churches were living their own lives and keeping themselves very much to themselves. This is clear in the long-drawn-out Arian crisis. To take one single episode: just think of the inextricable situation that St. Basil's "neo-orthodox" followers got themselves into in the years 368-377. Yet there was nothing really separating them from Pope Damasus and the Latins. But they could not get their opponents to see this[3]—the two sides literally could not understand each other, they had grown so far apart (16).

When the Latins did learn Greek, it was an academic, bookish Greek. St. Jerome made a pathetic appeal to Damasus from the depths of the Syrian desert, refusing to admit the expression "one *ousia*, three *hypostases*"—the expression ultimately adopted as orthodox—because he thought he could sniff some taint of Arianism in it, "for," he said, "in classical Greek οὐσία is the same thing as ὑπόστασις, and both mean 'substance'".[4] Apparently it did not occur to him that Greek was a living language, that there was a Christian Greek being used in theology and that it was developing and changing from day to day.

People at the time,[5] and, following them, the moderns, have tried to explain these difficulties away by referring once again to the limited nature of Latin and the poverty of its vocabulary. This does not seem to me in this instance to be quite justified, for there was a theological Latin which was soon well adapted to what was asked of it. But the two languages developed along their own lines: the Latin words had a life of their own and grew away from the Greek words on which they had originally been modelled: *substantia* is not the same thing as ὑπόστασις; *persona* has a much richer content than πρόσωπον.

Not that the theologians in the Lateran were the only people in the West. There were many different sections of society and culture, and Greek lasted longer in some than in others. Medicine and philosophy in particular remained dependent on Greek—the last of the Hellenists were fervent neo-Platonists: Claudius Mamertinus in fifth-century Gaul, Boethius in sixth-century Italy. But these were exceptional vocations and first-class minds.

[1] S.H.A., *M. Aur.*, 2, 2-4.
[2] *Ibid., Ver.*, 2-5.
[3] Bas., *Ep.*, 214, 789 AC.
[4] Hieron., *Ep.*, 15, 3-4.
[5] Greg. Naz., *Or.*, XXI, 35, 1124 D-1125 A. Bas., *Ep.*, 214, 789.

The last section of society to hold on to the Greek tradition was the high aristocracy in Rome itself—conservative by tradition, deeply attached to the old ways—hence, it seems to me, its stubborn fidelity to paganism—and bound to the East by so many family and economic ties. This was the society formed by the friends of Macrobius, the society that produced St. Ambrose and provided St. Jerome with so many spiritual daughters; and here Greek lasted better than amongst the middle-class people in the provinces—who included St. Jerome himself, and St. Augustine—whose culture was less advanced and possibly more utilitarian.

But even here it was simply a matter of degree: even in these privileged circles the quality of the Hellenism was not particularly high (17)—and then again, of course, it was still an understood thing that everybody should learn Greek and study Homer and Menander: this was still Ausonius' scheme of work for his grandson—Paulinus of Pella or one of his cousins.[1] Ausonius' family in fact gives us a good idea of the state of Greek in fourth-century Gaul. Ausonius himself, who lays his Greek on with a trowel and is an exasperating pedant to boot,[2] was no great Greek scholar.[3] Nor, as we have seen, was Paulinus.[4] And yet they were a highly aristocratic family living in a university town, with estates in Epirus and Greece, able to give their children Greek servants in their cradles. . . . In the West, Greek was gradually dying out. Competent teachers were becoming rare: in the year 376 the Emperor Gratian acknowledged the difficulty of getting one for Trèves.[5] Translations multiplied, but they were no longer literary exercises as they had been in the golden age; they were intended for publication, to supply the Latin public with a foreign literature that they could no longer read in the original.

THE DIRECT METHOD

This gradual decline was reflected in the teaching methods that were used. Originally—and it remained the custom in aristocratic families—education was genuinely bilingual: the study of the two languages went on side by side.

Young children were put in the hands of a Greek servant or slave[6] just as in a good French middle-class family it used to be the custom to give a child a foreign governess, a "Fraülein" or "Miss". Under this nurse or teacher they learned to speak Greek before they knew anything about Latin: this was such a well-established custom that Quintilian had to insist on not waiting too long before a child began on Latin in case he might come to speak it with a foreign accent,[7] and the danger was not just imaginary.[8]

When they reached school age they could therefore start learning both languages at once—reading and writing both, beginning, apparently, with Greek.[9] This seems absurd today, but we must not forget that before the Port Royal schools gained their victory for the priority of French over all other languages,

---

[1] Auson., *Protr.*, 46.
[2] *Ibid.*, *Epigr.*, 21; 47; 49-51; 57.
[3] *Ibid.*, *Prof. Burd.*, 8, 13-16.
[4] P. Pel., 81-84.
[5] *Cod. Theod.*, XIII, 3, 11.
[6] Tac., *Dial.*, 29, 1.
[7] Quint., I, 1, 12-14; Hieron., *Ep.*, 107, 9, 1.
[8] P. Pel., 75-80; cf. 72.
[9] Diehl, 742.

the old French colleges used Latin to teach children to read. Later on, Roman children went to lessons given in Greek by the *grammaticus Graecus* and in Latin by his opposite number, and then on to an *orator Graecus* and an *orator Latinus*.

This method could obviously be very effective, for though it demanded a double effort from the Latin children it put them on the same level as children who were Greek by birth. But it was based on an aristocratic way of life; and this meant that its scope was limited. A lower-middle-class African like St. Augustine was never able to have the luxury of a Greek governess: he had been taught Greek at school, he complained,[1] as though it was a foreign language—*lingua peregrina*—whereas Latin had come to him without effort when he was hardly more than a baby, playing games, blandly unaware that he was learning anything at all.

BILINGUAL SCHOOL MANUALS

It was for this school teaching that at the beginning of the third century those curious bilingual textbooks known to scholars as the *Hermeneumata Pseudo-dositheana* were written (18)—books that inaugurated the method still followed in our own day in so many "practical" books of foreign words and phrases.

Written in the first place probably for Greeks, they were arranged in such a way that they could be used by Latins too—in fact they were to be found all over Western Europe throughout antiquity and into the Middle Ages. We know of at least six different varieties. They begin with a Greek-Latin vocabulary, arranged first in alphabetical order and then under various headings—names of gods and goddesses; vegetables, fishes, birds; maritime and medical words. Then come short, simple passages like the ones used for "narrations" in the Hellenistic schools. Here is one of many anecdotes about the emperor Hadrian:

> Someone asked him to take him on in the army. "What unit do you want to serve in?" asked Hadrian. "In the Praetorian Cohorts," said the other. Hadrian asked him, "What is your height?" "Five foot six." Hadrian said: "To begin with you must go into the Urban Cohorts and after three years if you are a good soldier you will be able to get into the Praetorians."[2]

The passages were given in two columns, the Greek on one side and the Latin opposite:

αἰτοῦντος τινός	*petente quodam*
ἵνα στρατεύηται	*ut militaret*
Ἀδριανὸς εἶπεν	*Adrianus dixit:*
Ποῖ θέλεις	"*Ubi vis*
στρατεύεσθαι	*militare?*" etc.

Many other kinds of subject-matter were presented in the same way—Aesop's fables, a little book on law (*De Manumissionibus*), an elementary book on mythology (Hyginus' *Genealogy*), a brief account of the Trojan War, and, last but not least, a book of everyday conversation—*quotidiana conversatio, ὁμιλία καθημερινή*

[1] *Conf.*, I, 14(23).   [2] *C. Gloss. Lat.*, III, 31, 24 *seq.*

or συναστροφή—made up of little bits of ordinary dialogue genuinely collo-quial in tone and highly instructive about Roman life under the Empire. I shall be using them later. A sample:

And the *paterfamilias* went up to his friend and said, "Good morning, Gaius," and embraced him. The other returned his greeting and said: "How are you, Lucius? Nice to see you![1] . . . Will you come with me?" "Where to?" "To see Lucius. Let's go and call on him." "What is the matter with him?" "He is ill." "How long has he been ill?" "A few days." "Where does he live?" "Not far away." "All right, let's go."[2]

We have no documents showing what went on in the Latin schools, so that we cannot tell how these books were used to teach Greek. On the other hand we do know something about the way the people in the East learned Latin, thanks to papyri discovered in Egypt. We know that they began with the alphabet:

α	βη	κη	δη	ε	ιφφε	γη	δασια
a	b	c	d	e	f	g	h

(i.e., ἡ δασεῖα προσῳδία—hard aspiration)

					ι	κα			
					i	k			

ιλλε	ιμμε	ιννε	ο	πη	κου	ιρρε	ισσε	τη	ου
l	m	n	o	p	q	r	s	t	u[3]

Then came elementary little passages like the ones in the *Hermeneumata*—which, as we have seen, were in some respects at least identical with the first passages for continuous reading in Greek schools. These the children practised translating. There is one papyrus on which an attempt has been made to translate three fables by Babrius, and the result is a word-for-word translation and very bad Latin.[4] Having thus acquired a decent grounding they could then start on the classics (19). The same method was used to "expound" both Virgil's *Aeneid*—for Virgil came first, of course[5]—and Cicero's *Catilinariae*,[6] and it is the method we use today. Greek boys in Egypt were taught to "prepare word by word"; and thus the method used in Hellenistic schools for studying Homer and the other poets was simply adapted to a foreign language: the work was set out in two columns, with the text on the left and its translation into colloquial Greek on the right:

Aen., III, 447:	illa manent	ἐκεῖνα μένει
	immota	ἀκίνητα
	locis	ἐν τοῖς τόποις
	neque ab ordine	οὐδὲ ἀπὸ τῆς τάξεως
	cedunt	εἴκει (20)[7]

[1] *Ibid.*, 647, §4.
[2] *Ibid.*, 649, §6.
[3] *PAntin.*, 1; *POxy.*, 1315.
[4] *PAmh.*, II, 26.
[5] *PMilan.*, 1; *PRyl.*, 478; *PSI*, 756; *POxy.*, 1099.
[6] *PRyl.*, 61; *WS* (1937), LV, 95 *seq.*
[7] *PFouad* I, 5, 12, *seq.*

CHAPTER IV

THE ROMAN SCHOOLS

I. PRIMARY EDUCATION

THE three chapters that follow are in a sense unnecessary, for the general principles, the syllabus and the methods used in Roman schools were simply copied from their Hellenistic prototypes: the change-over to a Latin-speaking society caused no important modifications in teaching. The reader will certainly . be surprised when he discovers how mechanically the change-over was made. It was not even a case of imitating; it was on the whole a pure and simple transfer.

As time went on, Latin education tended more and more to become absolutely identical with the contemporary Greek education, and as generation followed generation the last relics of the archaic tradition through which Rome had asserted her own originality against Greece gradually disappeared. Increasingly the emphasis is on books, and education as a result becomes more and more a matter of schooling—and Roman schools (to say it once again) had, from the very beginning, been entirely modelled on those of Greece.

The real purpose of these chapters will be to prove in detail the truth of this statement. This will lead us to modify many of the judgments made by previous historians of Roman education. Having been insufficiently informed about Hellenistic education, and having, as a result, confined their attentions to the "old" Greek education of the sixth and fifth centuries B.C., they have often attributed to Latin originality what was in fact simply a case of Roman "modernism", a straight copy or a close parallel with the current Greek education.

In Rome, then, as in the Greek-speaking countries, there were three successive stages in education,[1] and usually (1) three corresponding kinds of school run by three different specialists. Children went to the primary school when they were seven,[2] on to the *grammaticus* when they got to the age of eleven[3] or twelve,[4] and, when they were given the toga of manhood—sometimes as early as at fifteen[5]— to the rhetor. This last stage usually lasted till they were about twenty,[6] and might go on longer.

The primary-school teacher was sometimes called the *litterator*,[7] on the model of the Greek γραμματιστής—"one who teaches letters"—but they preferred to call him the *primus magister*[8] and, more generally still, the "schoolmaster"—

---

[1] Apul., *Flor.*, 20, 3; S.H.A., *M. Aur.*, 2, 2-4; *Ver.*, 2, 5; Auson., *Protr.*, 63 *seq.*
[2] Quint., I, 1, 15-18; Juv., XIV, 10.
[3] Suet., *Ner.*, 7.
[4] *V. Pers.*
[5] Dessau, 4976.
[6] *Cod. Theod.*, XIV, 9, 1.
[7] Suet., *Gram.*, 4; S.H.A., *M. Aur.*, 2, 2.
[8] Diehl, 720; August., *Conf.*, I, 13 (20).

magister ludi,[1] *magister ludi literarii*.[2] The preference is instructive: in Rome as in Greece communal school education was the general rule.

PRIVATE EDUCATION

Not that there were no exceptions; on the contrary, education at home under a private tutor—usually a slave or a freedman of the house—was even commoner than in Greek-speaking districts. In Hellenistic States before the Roman conquest private education hardly existed outside the royal families, but after the conquest of the Greek East this royal way of life, and especially its culture, was adopted by all the great senatorial families of the Kingly People (2).

Thus from the beginning—in the third and second centuries B.C.—the aristocracy regarded private education as the normal thing; and they never lost their fondness for it. We can see from Quintilian[3] and Pliny the Younger[4] what tremendous prestige it still had at the end of the first century and the beginning of the second century A.D. The *Confessions* of Paulinus of Pella,[5] who was born in 376, show it still in existence in the "best" families at the end of the fourth century—Paulinus, it will be remembered, was Ausonius' grandson, and Ausonius had amassed great wealth and the highest honours in the Empire.

EDUCATION OF SLAVES

In these great aristocratic families all the young slaves were brought up at home to serve their master, so that they had no need to go to any outside school either. Naturally, in the case of wealthy Romans under the Empire, who owned hundreds or even thousands of slaves (3), there must have been quite a number of children about. These were taught in a school in the house, a *paedagogium* (4). One we know a good deal about was for the Emperor's young slaves; they were under a "teacher of Caesar's [young] servants," who had assistants.[6]

Most of their education, of course, meant learning how to do their particular job, and this usually meant learning how to behave properly so that they would turn out to be good pages—the Romans loved having crowds of pages round them. But the more gifted, at least, were given some sort of intellectual education too: all the great houses had a number of "literate" or "learned" slaves who acted as readers or secretaries, and when they had a master who was fond of literature, like Pliny the Younger, they would often discuss the things they were both interested in.[7]

THE PRIMARY SCHOOL

But apart from these exceptions, most children went to school—the girls, apparently, on the same footing as the boys,[8] with possibly a little more private

[1] Diehl, 718.
[2] Dessau, 7763, 5.
[3] Quint., I, 2.
[4] Pliny, *Ep.*, III, 3, 3.
[5] P. Pell., 60 *seq.*
[6] Dessau, 1825–1836.
[7] *Ep.*, IX, 36, 4; V, 19, 3; VIII, 1, 2.
[8] Mart., IX, 68, 2.

tutoring in their case[1]—though this was not without its dangers: the well-known tutor Q. Caecilius Epirota was suspected of carrying on with his employer's daughter when he was supposed to be teaching her.[2] From the moral point of view, of course, boys ran just as much risk as girls in the street and in school, and so the Romans adopted the Greek custom of providing the child with a slave-companion, whom they also called by his Greek name: *paedagogus* (5).

If this companion turned out all right he might become the assistant master[3] or indeed an out-and-out tutor responsible for the child's moral development; we have a touching epitaph from a grateful pupil to the man who had been "his pedagogue and teacher"—*paedagogo suo*, καὶ καθηγητῇ—and his tutor too: in this case he was a free man, an attendant in the temple of Diana, not the usual slave or freedman of the family.[4]

The pedagogue took his young master to school—the *ludus litterarius* (6), as it was called (ironically, they said).[5] We know a little more about the actual building than we do about Greek schools. Not that it was any more impressive. The Latin *magister* was quite satisfied with a shop—a *pergula*[6]—and he liked to have one that opened out on to the porticos of the forum; this can be seen in Rome[7], as well as Pompeii (7) and Carthage.[8] The class was held practically in the open air, with an improvised hanging—a *velum*[9]—to shield it from the noise and all the interesting things going on in the street. The children sat on backless stools—they wrote on their knees and had no need of tables—round the teacher, who was enthroned on his chair—his *cathedra*[10]—raised up on a dais (8). Sometimes the teacher had an assistant—the *hypodidascalos*.[11]

But we must not be misled by the attractiveness of the setting. In Rome, as in Greece, schoolmastering remained a despised occupation, the lowest of all professions—*rem indignissimam*[12]—tiring, arduous[13] and badly paid (9).[14] In A.D. 301 Diocletian's *Edict* fixed a *magister's* salary at the same level as a pedagogue's, fifty denarii a month for each pupil.[15] As a bushel of wheat cost 100 denarii[16] it was necessary to have a class of thirty pupils to get as much money as a qualified workman like a mason or a carpenter,[17] and in spite of the expansion of collective education it does not seem likely that many classes reached that figure. It is not surprising to find a schoolmaster in Campania trying to make a bit on the side by drafting wills.[18]

[1] Pliny, *Ep.*, V, 16, 3.
[2] Suet., *Gram.*, 16, 1.
[3] Quint., I, 1, 8.
[4] Dessau, 4999.
[5] Festus, s.v. *Schola*, 470.
[6] Suet., *Gram.*, 18, 1.
[7] Livy, III, 44, 6; D.H., XI, 28.
[8] August., *Conf.*, I, 16(26).
[9] *Ibid.*, I, 13(22).
[10] Juv., VII, 203.
[11] Cic., *Fam.*, IX, 18, 4.
[12] Flor., *Virg.*, 3, 2.
[13] Pliny, *Ep.*, I, 8, 11.
[14] Hor., *Sat.*, I, 6, 75; cf. Juv., X, 116; Ovid, *Fast.*, III, 829.
[15] Diocl., *Max.*, 7, 65–66.
[16] *Ibid.*, I, 1.
[17] *Ibid.*, 7, 2–3a.
[18] Dessau, 7763, 7.

Any kind of wage-earning was looked down upon as degrading by the aristocracy. This was as true in Rome as it was in Greece.[1] School-teaching brought no prestige to anyone: it was all right for slaves, freedmen and nonentities—*obscura initia*, said Tacitus of a self-made man who had started as a teacher.[2] It must be added that teachers were often suspect from the moral point of view:[3] there was one who, in the *elogium* of his epitaph, prided himself on having been that rarity—a teacher who was "perfectly proper in his relations with his pupils"—*summa castitate in discipulos suos*.[4]

No school calendars like the Cos one[5] have been found, so that we know very little for certain about the Roman school year. Rome came to have a great many festivals in its calendar, but we cannot say which of these were school holidays (10). On the other hand, it is a well-known fact that they had summer holidays, lasting from the end of July to the middle of October.[6] "In the hot weather children are working quite hard enough if their health remains good," says Martial:

Aestate pueri si valent, satis discunt.[7]

As in Greece, the schoolboy's day began very early in the morning, as soon as the sun was up,[8] and in winter in the smoky lamplight.[9] Fortunately we have a particularly vivid picture of this. The *Hermeneumata Pseudodositheana*, the Graeco-Latin conversation books that I have already referred to, get a young Roman schoolboy to describe his day. This is in the years A.D. 200–210, remember.

When day breaks I wake up,[10] call the slave, and get him to open the window—which he does at once. I sit up, sit on the edge of the bed, and ask for my shoes and stockings because it is cold [otherwise, no doubt, he would have put on his sandals straightaway without bothering about his *hypodesmata* or stockings].

As soon as I have put my shoes on I take a towel—I have been brought a clean one. Water is brought me in a jug so that I can wash. I pour some of it over my hands and face and into my mouth; I rub my teeth and gums; I spit out, blow my nose and wipe it, as any well brought-up child should.[11]

I take off my nightshirt and put on a tunic and girdle; I perfume my head and comb my hair; I put a scarf round my neck (11); I get into my white cloak. I leave my room with my pedagogue and nurse and go and say good morning to my father and mother. I say good morning to them both and kiss them.[12]

---

[1] Sen., *Ep.*, 88, 1; August., *Conf.*, IX, 2(2); 5(13).
[2] *Ann.*, III, 6, 4.
[3] Quint., I, 3, 17; Juv., X, 224.
[4] Dessau, 7763, 6.
[5] Dittenberg., *SIG*, 1028.
[6] Mart., X, 62; August., *Conf.*, IX 2 (2).
[7] Mart., X, 62, 12.
[8] Ov., *Am.*, I, 13, 17; Mart., IX, 68; XII, 57, 5; XIV, 223.
[9] Juv., VII, 222–227.
[10] *C. Gloss. Lat.*, III, 645, §2.
[11] *Ibid.*, 379, 74 *seq.*
[12] *Ibid.*, 645, §2 *seq.*

THE ROMAN SCHOOLS: PRIMARY

I go and find my inkstand and exercise book and give them to the slave.
Then everything is ready, and, followed by my pedagogue, I set off through the
portico that leads to the school.

There is no breakfast. Probably he simply had a sort of *jentaculum*—a little
cake or pie bought as he passed a baker's shop.[1]

My schoolfellows come and meet me; I say hello to them and they say
hello back. I come to the staircase. I go up the stairs quietly, as I should.
In the hall I take off my cloak, run through my hair with my comb,[2] and go
in, saying, "Good morning, master." The master embraces me and returns
my greeting. The slave hands me my writing-boards, my ink-stand and my
ruler.
   "Good morning, everybody. Let me have my place [my seat, my stool].
Squeeze up a bit." "Come here." "This is my place!" "I got it first!"
I sit down and set to work.[3]

Most of the work was done in the morning,[4] but it also went on into the
second half of the day:

I have finished my lesson. I ask the master to let me go home for lunch;
he lets me go; I say goodbye to him, and he returns my farewell.[5] I go home
and change. I have white bread, olives, cheese, dry figs and nuts; I drink
some fresh water. Having finished my lunch, I go off to school again. I find
the master reading; he says to us, "Now to work again!"[6]

There was no longer, as at the beginning of the Hellenistic period, any time
for physical exercise: the child does not seem to have gone to the gymnasium,
but only to the baths; for the day ended with a bath:

I must go and have a bath. Yes, it's time. I go off; I get myself some
towels and I follow my servant. I run and catch up with the others who are
going to the baths and I say to them one and all, "How are you? Have a good
bath! Have a good supper!"[7]

PRIMARY INSTRUCTION

The primary-school syllabus was still very modest in its scope. There was
reading and writing, and that was about all: anything more advanced belonged
to the secondary-school stage.[8] The children began with the alphabet and the
names of the letters, of course, before they learned what they looked like; first
in their right order, from A to X[9] (Y and Z were looked upon as foreign because

[1] Mart., XIV, 223.
[2] C. Gloss. Lat., III, 380, 40 seq.
[3] Ibid., 646, §2; 637, §3 seq.
[4] Auson., Protr., 28; August., Conf., VI, 11(18).
[5] C. Gloss. Lat., III, 377, 70 seq.; 638, §7.
[6] Ibid., 646 seq.
[7] Ibid., 378, 22 seq.
[8] Quint., I, 4, 1.
[9] Ibid., I, 1, 24. P. Pel., 65.

they were only used for Greek words), and then backwards from X to A; then in pairs—AX, BV, CT, DS, ER[1]—then jumbled into different combinations.[2] After the letters came the syllables with all their combinations,[3] and then single names. These stages came one after the other, and there was no hurry to get on to the next. The little schoolboys were known as *abecedarii, syllabarii* and *nominarii*.[4] Before they went on to continuous passages the children practised little sentences, moral sayings one or two lines long:[5] as young Greek boys in Egypt had copied out the monostich sayings attributed to Menander, Roman schoolboys ploughed through (Dionysius) Cato's *Distichs*:

> Plus vigila semper neu somno deditus esto;
> nam diuturna quies vitiis alimenta ministrat.[6]

(It is good to be awake, sleep makes men careless; in long repose, vice receives nourishment.)

These sayings, which first appeared at the beginning of the third century, were constantly in use throughout the latter part of antiquity and the whole of the Middle Ages: as the basis of the elementary teaching of Latin they were copied over and over again and translated into all the languages of Western Europe—Romance, Germanic and Slav (12).

As will be seen, the method is the Greek method right down to the smallest details. There is the same analytical approach, the same wisdom in taking it easy—Quintilian was never tired of saying, "No short cuts, no haste, no missing out anything"[7]—the same lack of interest in child psychology: as in Greece, rare words—$\gamma\lambda\tilde{\omega}\sigma\sigma\alpha\iota$[8]—and the most difficult sayings to pronounce—$\chi\alpha\lambda\iota\nu\upsilon\iota$[9]—were deliberately chosen for these first reading lessons.

Writing went on at the same time as reading. The child wrote the letters[10] or the word or the passage that he had to read[11] on his writing-tablet. For the early stages, two methods were employed alternately. One went back to the beginnings of the Greek school and simply meant guiding the child's hand until he got used to the shape of the letter. The other was more modern and perhaps even entirely Latin in origin: letters were stamped into the waxed surface of a writing-tablet and the child followed their outlines with his pricker.[12] As in the Egyptian schools the child practised with his pricker and with ink alternately. Let us turn to our *Hermeneumata* again:

---

[1] Babelon, *Monn. Rep.*, I, 327; *CIL*, IV, 2541; *BAC* (1881), 132.
[2] Quint., I, 1, 25; Hieron., *Ep.*, 107, 4, 2; *In Jer.*, 25, 26.
[3] Quint., I, 1, 30.
[4] Rufin., transl. of Orig., *In Num.*, 27, 13.
[5] Quint., I, 1, 34–35; Hieron., *Ep.*, 107, 4, 4; 128, 1, 3.
[6] *Dist. Cat.*, I, 2.
[7] Quint., I, 1, 30–34.
[8] *Ibid.*, I, 1, 35.
[9] *Ibid.*, I, 1, 37.
[10] *N.S.* (1912), 451.
[11] *C. Gloss. Lat.*, III, 646.
[12] Quint., I, 1, 27; Hieron., *Ep.*, 107, 4, 3; *CIL*, III, p. 962, XXVII, 1; II, 4967, 31; *BSNAF*, 1883, 139.

I do my copying. When I have finished, I show it to the master, who corrects it and copies it out properly.[1] . . . "I can't copy: copy it out for me, you can do it so well." I rub it out: the wax is hard, it should be soft.[2]

"Do the up-strokes and the down-strokes properly! Put a drop of water in your ink! You see, it is all right now." "Let me see your pen, your knife for sharpening the reed pen."[3] "Let me see it! How have you done it? It's not bad." . . . Or he may easily say: "You deserve to be whipped! All right, I'll let you off this time. . . ."[4]

Recitation was closely associated with reading and writing: the child learnt the little passages he had been practising on by heart, so that he was learning and using his memory both at once.[5]

Finally, arithmetic: as in the Greek countries, this was essentially a matter of learning the names of the numbers, and this was done with the help of small counters—*calculi*—but above all by sign language:[6] it will be remembered that most of the evidence about this finger-counting, which lasted for so many centuries, comes from Roman times. The hardest thing to learn was the complicated language of duodecimal fractions, which was the foundation of the whole metric system of antiquity. Horace has given us an amusing picture of this:

The little Romans are doing long sums to learn how to divide the figure one in about a hundred different ways. "Answer, son of Albinus! If we take $\frac{1}{12}$ from $\frac{5}{12}$, what is left? Come on, what are you waiting for?" "A third? Good, you'll know how to take care of your pennies! If (on the other hand) we add $\frac{1}{12}$, how much is that?" "A half."[7]

In translation we get the wrong impression that the child is working it out in fractions—in Latin it is not $\frac{5}{12}$, $\frac{1}{12}$, $\frac{1}{3}$, $\frac{1}{2}$, but a *quincunx*, an *uncia*, a *triens*, a *semis*; and these are not so much numbers as concrete realities.

Under the Empire, however—and it happened in Greek-speaking countries too—a new kind of arithmetic, in the modern sense of the word, came in. St. Augustine, describing his childhood, remembers the "hateful song", "One and one are two, two and two are four. . . ."[8] It was not on a very high level! Any more advanced arithmetical technique was beyond the powers of the *magister ludi*, and so the matter was left to a specialist, the *calculator*. About this gentleman, unfortunately, we know very little, but he is always referred to as someone quite separate from the *ludi magister*, and classed as a specialist along with the stenographers and calligraphers, so that he would probably be a technical teacher with his own special pupils—not one of the *litterator*'s assistants helping in the general education of all the children (13).

[1] *C. Gloss. Lat.*, III, 646.
[2] *Ibid.*, 377, 55 *seq.*; 638, §6.
[3] *Ibid.*, 640, §7.
[4] *Ibid.*, 640, §10.
[5] Quint., I, 1, 36; 3, 1; Hieron., *Ep.*, 107, 9, 1; 128, 4, 2.
[6] *C. Gloss. Lat.*, III, 382, 36 *seq.*
[7] Hor., *P.*, 325–330; Auson., *Ecl.*, 6.
[8] *Conf.*, I, 13 (22).

K

SEVERITY AND HUMANITY

Roman teaching methods were as Greek as the Roman syllabus. They were entirely passive. The most highly prized qualities were a good memory and powers of imitation.[1] Competition was encouraged; its benefits, according to Quintilian, making up for the moral dangers inherent in communal education[2]. But the main stimulus was by way of coercion, reprimands and punishment. Montaigne's well-known description of "punished children yelling and masters mad with rage" is as true of Latin as it is of Greek schools.[3] When the men of antiquity thought back to their schooldays they immediately remembered the beatings.[4] "To hold out the hand for the cane"—*manum ferulae subducere*—was an elegant Latin way of saying "to study".[5] The cane[6]—the *ferula*—was a very humdrum method of keeping discipline, however; in serious cases recourse was had to a more refined type of punishment, which had to have its proper setting, for the culprit was hoisted on to the shoulders of one of his schoolfellows, specially chosen for the purpose—this was called *catomidiare*,[7] from the Greek κατωμίζειν—and then beaten by the master (14).[8]

A few pricks of conscience began to be felt, however. Ausonius could calmly tell his grandson not to mind the ordeals he was in for—and go on to draw a far from jolly picture of them;[9] St. Augustine trembled at the thought—he could never forget the sufferings he went through at school.[10] Even when he was seventy-two, the old Bishop was still exclaiming, "Who is there who would not recoil in horror and choose death, if he was asked to choose between dying and going back to his childhood!"[11]

At the end of the first century A.D. educational theorists were beginning to evince a few doubts about the legitimacy and efficacy of these brutal methods.[12] They began to rely more on competition and prizes, trying to get their pupils to like their lessons.[13] And their theories undoubtedly affected practice. Teachers began to have recourse to some kindlier tricks for their pupils, especially the very young ones: they gave them wood or ivory letters to play with,[14] and, when they first began to get things right, rewarded them with little cakes, especially cakes[15] in the form of the letters that they were trying to learn (15).

There was thus a general movement towards a relaxation of discipline and greater leniency, a movement towards a "soft" type of education which of course the severer moralists of the old school naturally felt obliged to protest

---

[1] Quint., I, 3, 1.
[2] *Ibid.*, I, 2, 9 *seq.*
[3] Mart., X, 68, 11–12; Juv., XIV, 18–19.
[4] Hor., *Ep.*, II, 1, 70; Suet., *Gram.*, 9, 2; Quint., I, 3, 14.
[5] Juv., I, 15; Hieron., *Ep.*, 32, 33; cf. Ov., *Am.*, I, 13, 17.
[6] Mart., XIV, 80; Prud., *Cath.*, pr. 7–8.
[7] Petron., 132, 2; S.H.A., *Hadr.*, 18, 11.
[8] Mart., X, 62, 8–10; Auson., *Protr.*, 29–30.
[9] *Ibid.*, 12–34.
[10] *Conf.*, I, 9 (14–15).
[11] *De civ. D.*, XXI, 14.
[12] Quint., I, 3, 14–17; Plut., *Lib. Educ.*, 9 A.
[13] Quint., I, 1, 20; Hieron., *Ep.*, 107, 4, 3–4.
[14] Quint., I, 1, 26; Hieron., *Ep.*, 107, 4, 2.
[15] Hor., *Sat.*, I, 25–26; Hieron., *Ep.*, 128, 1, 4–5.

against[1]. *Nunc pueri in scholis ludunt*—"children nowadays play as they learn!"—exclaims the satirical Petronius in Nero's day.[2]

It will be seen that there was nothing specifically Roman about all this. On the contrary, we should expect the grave Latins to insist on the need for severity even more than the Greeks. The truth is that although Latin schools had new features compared with their original Hellenistic models, these were modern, not particularly Western, peculiarities—the same things, except where the evidence is lacking, were to be found in most of the Eastern schools of the time. Roman teaching developed slowly but homogeneously, without altering any of the essential characteristics of the educational system. The school depicted at the end of the fourth century by Ausonius, by St. Jerome and St. Augustine, was still on the whole the school of Quintilian's or even Horace's time. And, with all deference to reactionary moralists, what development there was often meant an advance.

This appeared not only in the increasing humanity of discipline already mentioned, but also in an enrichment of teaching itself: more use began to be made of the resources of communal instruction.[3] With a few exceptions,[4] classes had become large enough to be divided[5] according to the pupils' abilities: the unknown author of the *Hermeneumata Pseudodositheana* is at pains to emphasize the concern "to take into account, in every case, the ability, the stage reached, the circumstances, the age, the different temperaments and varying interests of each of the pupils".[6] In the school he describes there even seem to have been the beginnings of some sort of "student teaching"—the older pupils acting as assistant teachers and showing the younger ones how to do their letters and syllables.[7] The "blackboard", which had been absent from the Greek school, came into existence, and we are shown the class standing in a group around the πίναξ or *titulus*.[8]

[1] Quint., I, 2, 6; Tac., *Dial.*, 28, 2; Epict., III, 19, 4–6; Juv., VII, 158.
[2] Petron., 4, 1.
[3] Quint., I, 2, 9 *seq.*
[4] Cf. Suet., *Gram.*, 16, 1; 24, 2.
[5] *C. Gloss. Lat.*, III, 382, 46 *seq.*
[6] *Ibid.*, 381, 63 *seq.*
[7] *Ibid.*, 646.
[8] *Ibid.*, 382, 32 *seq.*

CHAPTER V

THE ROMAN SCHOOLS

II. SECONDARY SCHOOLS

BUT let us proceed to the second stage. Not every child reached this stage, of course: Roman society was still aristocratic, and advanced education still one of the privileges of the favoured few. Compared with the primary schools, secondary school teaching was much more restricted, and amongst the masses were many who "had not studied geometry or literature or any other daft things like that, but were quite satisfied with being able to read something in big letters and understand fractions and weights and measures".[1] Boys and girls from the more privileged classes still went on studying together[2]—from the Republic[3] to the late Empire[4] there was a constant supply of highly educated aristocratic women,[5] some of them out-and-out blue-stockings, whom the satirists poked a good deal of fun at[6]—but this was not the usual thing: Martial, dreaming of domestic bliss, sighed for a woman who was "not too clever", and St. Augustine imagined the ideal bride as someone who was "literary—or at least easily teachable by her husband."[7] (17).

THE SCHOOL OF THE GRAMMATICUS

We thus go up a step—and undoubtedly there is something a little more exalted about the kind of school we now enter: the grammarian's school. The *grammaticus* is solemnly enveloped in a cloak,[8] and he takes his class in a room adorned with busts of great writers—Virgil, Horace and so on[9]—and even has maps on the wall.[10] But we are still not in very lofty circumstances: the classroom is still a shop shut off from the forum by a kind of curtain, and the assistant-master—the *subdoctor* or *proscholus*[11]—still stands there like an usher.[12]

No doubt the *grammaticus* had more prestige than a mere schoolmaster (18). An edict promulgated by Diocletian in A.D. 301 gave the grammarian 200 denarii per pupil per month,[13]—four times the rate of pay of a primary-school teacher—

[1] Petron., 58, 7.
[2] Ov., *Tr.*, II, 369–370; Mart., VIII, 3, 16.
[3] Cic., *Brut.*, 211; Sall., *Cat.*, 25, 2.
[4] Claud., *Fesc.*, 232 *seq.*
[5] Mart., VII, 69; Pliny, *Ep.*, I, 16, 6; IV, 19, 2–3; V, 16, 3.
[6] Juv., VI, 434–456; Lucian, *M. Cond.*, 36.
[7] Mart., II, 90, 9; August., *Sol.*, I, 10 (17).
[8] August., *Conf.*, I, 16 (25); Sid. Apoll., *Ep.*, II, 2.
[9] Juv., VII, 226–7.
[10] *Pan. Lat.*, IV, 20.
[11] Auson., *Prof. Burd.*, 23.
[12] August., *Serm.*, 178, 7 (8).
[13] Diocl., *Max.*, 7, 70.

but this was still only the equivalent of four days' work by a skilled workman. No doubt the university annals compiled by Suetonius record exceptionally brilliant careers by grammarians like Q. Remmius Palaemon, who got 400,000 sesterces a year out of teaching[1]—which was about the capital demanded of a man of equestrian rank, and meant that he could live like a good upper-middle-class man of property (19): but on the other hand there were all the well-known teachers like L. Orbilius[2] who, according to Suetonius again, were poor all their lives and finally died of want in some garret.[3]

There seems to be no doubt about it: one was the exception, the other the rule. Generally speaking, the grammarian was badly paid,[4] and his meagre salary—*rara merces*—did not even arrive regularly[5]—so little regard had parents for teachers,[6] who had not much in the way of morality to back them up[7] and whose family connections did little to recommend them: often they had been slaves,[8] often they were outcasts—foundlings,[9] ruined men[10] or failures.[11]

The *grammaticus Latinus* had exactly the same teaching methods as his Greek prototype, with the same two features that had been characteristic of Hellenistic grammar—*methodicè, historicè*;[12] i.e. the theory of good speech and the study of the classical poets, *recte loquendi scientiam et poetarum enarrationem*.[13]

LATIN GRAMMAR

Varro during the Republic, and Q. Remmius Palaemon under Tiberius and Claudius (20), had made a Latin adaptation of the newly-born science of philology which had just been created in the schools of Rhodes by the great Dionysius Thrax; and the Latin grammatical tradition, which finally led up to the great classics by Donatus, Servius and Priscian that appeared in the Later Empire (21), remained scrupulously faithful to its Greek model. Grammar still meant essentially the same abstract analysis of the elements of language—letters, syllables, words and parts of speech[14]—and the same meticulous distinctions and classifications: "nouns"—which were still not separate from what we call "adjectives"—were studied according to the six accidents—quality, degree of comparison, gender, number, figure and case; and common nouns were separated into twenty-seven classes—corporeal, incorporeal, primitive, derived, diminutive, etc.[15]

So close was the dependence that Latin grammarians went on talking about

[1] Suet., *Gram.*, 23, 2; 3, 4.
[2] Hor., *Ep.*, II, 1, 70; Macrob., *Sat.*, II, 6, 3.
[3] Suet., *Gram.*, 9, 1; 20.
[4] Juv., VII, 215–242.
[5] *Ibid.*, 157; 203; August., *Conf.*, V, 12 (22).
[6] Suet., *Gram.*, 9, 1.
[7] *Ibid.*, 16, 1; 23, 1; Quint., I, 3, 17 (cf. I, 2, 15).
[8] Suet., *Gram.*, 6, 10–13 (cf. Pliny, *HN*, XXXV, 199); 15–20; 23.
[9] *Ibid.*, 7, 1.
[10] *Ibid.*, 9, 1.
[11] *Ibid.*, 24, 1.
[12] Quint., I, 9, 1.
[13] *Ibid.*, I, 4, 2; *Gramm. Lat.*, IV, 486, 15–16 (Serv.).
[14] Quint., I, 4, 6 *seq.*
[15] *Gramm. Lat.*, IV, 373, 11 *seq.* (Don.).

the article, even though in Latin there was no such thing.[1] The fact was that grammatical science, as Dionysius had taught it, was an entirely logical analysis of the categories of understanding, and the Roman grammarians felt obliged to find a Latin equivalent for the category "article", whose part was played in certain cases by the demonstrative adjective, for instance.[2] For the same reason they were quite ready to distinguish between an optative and a subjunctive mood, though in Latin the same form did for both (22).

No doubt there are many things in the works of the Latin grammarians of the Late Empire that are not to be found in the works of their great originator. Their treatises are as verbose as Dionysius' were concise. But the same thing happened in Greece too: Roman schools simply reflect the progress made in the course of time in the fields of knowledge and teaching. There was indeed genuine progress —and school papyri of Imperial times show that in Greek Egypt, at least, it was intimately bound up with an improvement in teaching methods: grammar slowly descended from the abstract empyrean in which it had been enthroned by Dionysius and came closer to actual practice, approximating more and more to what is fundamentally the modern system, with its emphasis on the child's learning the systematic structure of the language. Thus there were exercises in declension and conjugation, for instance;[3] and the Greek origin behind these exercises appears quite clearly: Roman children would put the "article" *hic*, *haec*, *hoc* before the noun, because the Greeks had put ὁ, ἡ, τό:

nominativo	haec Musa
genitivo	huius Musae
dativo	huic Musae
accusativo	hanc Musam, etc.[4]

There was also an attempt to give the child some idea of the mechanism of the language, and syntax (23), despised by Dionysius, began to appear: whereas he had divided prepositions into mono- and disyllables, Donatus separated them according to the cases they governed.[5] Idioms—*idiomata*—were studied: thus *patiens laboris* and *misereor tui* had to be genitive, whereas *dignus laude* and *utor divitiis* had to have the ablative[6] (24).

Various faults of speech were hunted down and catalogued—barbarisms,[7] solecisms, faults of pronunciation, puns, preciosity, and so on (25). The laws of spelling were studied—the classification of "word-shapes" very quickly reached a state of extreme precision. And metre began to be inquired into.

The progress was real but slow, and it did not cause any deep change in the subject as a whole. Not until the time of Priscian, for example, was there any systematic treatment of syntax, and Priscian (d. 526) was very late—he was teaching in Constantinople in the time of the Emperors Anastasius and Justinian, and his interest in syntax was perhaps a result of the fact that most of his pupils were Greeks, and teaching them Latin was like teaching a foreign language.

[1] *Ibid.*, II, 54, 16 (Prisc.); Quint., I, 4, 19.
[2] *Gramm. Lat.*, V, 135, 5 *seq.*; 210, 38 *seq* (Pomp.).
[3] Quint., I, 4, 22; 27.
[4] *Gramm. Lat.*, IV, 356, 6 *seq.* (Don.).
[5] *Ibid.*, IV, 365, 13 *seq.* (Don.).
[6] *Ibid.*, I, 291 *seq.* (Charis.).
[7] *Ibid.*, IV, 392, 5 *seq.* (Don.).

On the whole, despite the new tendencies, grammar was still essentially theoretical, analytical, and, so to speak, contemplative. The grammarian did not teach people how to use a living language; he took stock of the material that had been used by the great classic writers, the language which in their masterpieces had been hallowed for all eternity. A tyrannical classical ideal dominated this teaching, which ignored the fact that language develops naturally, that words are living things. Latin *was*—it was there for all time in the great writers; the science of correct speaking—*recte loquendi scientia*—was based in the last analysis on *auctoritas*.[1] This was the Latin equivalent of the Atticism of their Greek contemporaries, the Later Sophist rhetors. A glance at the chapters in Latin grammar books on *vitia*, the faults of language, shows that in theory a distinction was made between barbarisms and "metaplasms"—i.e. cases where the verse demanded poetic licence. As Consentius said,[2] "When it is done clumsily, it is a barbarism; but when it is done skilfully and has an authority behind it, it is a metaplasm." But as an example of a "barbarism" Donatus quotes Virgil's *relliquias*[3]—which he had used to lengthen the syllable *re*[4]—and in fact these *vitia* were a collection of anomalies to be found in good authors rather than faults that schoolboys should try to avoid (26).

THE CLASSICS

In short, despite the progress made in the "methodic" teaching of grammar, the grammarian was still mainly concerned with the authors, the poets.[5] We have already seen how the syllabus developed in Roman schools, how for a long time books written by poet-teachers like Livius Andronicus and Ennius were all-important, and how, shortly after 26 B.C., apparently, Q. Caecilius Epirota took the bold step of introducing "Virgil and other modern poets"[6] into his school —Virgil being still alive and the *Aeneid* still unpublished. For a century the Latin grammarians followed this modernist tendency—unlike their Greek colleagues, who, though they did not exclude recent poets completely—especially comic poets like Menander—based the essence of their teaching on Homer and the fifth-century tragedians. In Rome, indeed, every successful poet was studied in the schools in his own lifetime:[7] this happened to Ovid,[8] Nero[9] and Statius;[10] it was to happen to Lucian less than a generation after his death.[11] But towards the end of the first century a reaction began to take place, appearing most characteristically in the person of Quintilian—a reaction in favour of the archaic, a return to old poets—*veteres Latini*[12]—like Ennius, and above all to the classical:

[1] *Gramm. Lat.*, I, 439, 25 *seq.* (Diom.).
[2] *Ibid.*, V, 396, 2 *seq.*; cf. Quint., I, 5, 5.
[3] Ennius, I, 30.
[4] *Gramm. Lat.*, IV, 392, 11 (Don.).
[5] Nep. ap. Suet., *Gramm.*, 4, 1.
[6] *Ibid.*, 16, 2.
[7] Hor., *Sat.*, I., 10, 75; Pers., I, 28–29; Mart., I, 35.
[8] Sen., *Controv.*, III, exc. 7, 2.
[9] *Schol.*, Pers., I, 29.
[10] Stat., *Theb.*, XII, 815.
[11] Tac., *Dial.*, 20, 5–6 (cf. *CIL*, XIII, 3654).
[12] Quint., I, 8 8–11.

an effort was made to fix the syllabus for ever round a few great names whose fame could never be questioned.

First and foremost, of course, came Virgil, the Latin Homer, the poet *par excellence*, study of whom must be the basis of any liberal culture: from Hyginus to Servius and Philargyrius he was to be the subject of a stream of more and more detailed commentaries (27).

Next came Terence—curiously, for critics of Republican times had no such veneration for him: for example, at the end of the second century B.C., Volcacius Sedigitus[1] still rated him no higher than sixth-class, far behind Caecilius, Plautus, etc. Yet under the Empire Terence was studied more than any other dramatic poet,[2] and commentaries on him kept appearing—from Valerius Probus in the middle of the first century to Donatus the Great in the fourth and Evanthius in the fifth (28).

The other great Latin poets, Horace for example,[3] still went on being read in the schools, but far less generally. The prose writers, historians and orators were not supposed to come within the *grammaticus's* sphere but the rhetor's,[4] though the frontier between them, as I have already explained, was fairly fluid, and the grammarians took on themselves the study of the historians.[5]

And here again the choice seems surprising to us for the people it missed out— Caesar and Tacitus, for instance. Despite Quintilian's express wish,[6] Titus Livy does not seem to have "got in". The classic historian *par excellence— historiae maior auctor*[7]—was Sallust, whom the men of letters,[8] scholars[9] and teachers alike[10] regarded as first amongst Roman historians.

Of the orators, the person who, with Virgil, summed up the whole of Latin culture[11] is of course Cicero. Cicero reigned in the schools: there was that golden rule formulated by Titus Livy and repeated by Quintilian[12]—"to study other authors only in so far as they resemble Cicero"—*ut quisque erit Ciceroni simillimus*. Nevertheless, the reaction in favour of the archaic brought attention back to the authors of "antiquity", and sometimes caused quite a fashion for the elder Cato and the Gracchi, for instance;[13] but this was no more than a passing fancy and it never threatened to dislodge the great orator from his place of honour.

In short, the Latin syllabus was contained in the *quadriga*, to adopt the title of the book by Arusianus Messius (29): Virgil, Terence, Sallust and Cicero.

---

[1] Gell., XV, 24.
[2] Auson., *Protr.*, 58–60; August., *Conf.*, I, 16 (26).
[3] Quint., I, 8, 6; Auson., *Protr.*, 56.
[4] Quint., II, 5, 1.
[5] *Ibid.*, II, 1, 4; I, 8, 18.
[6] *Ibid.*, II, 5, 19.
[7] *Ibid.*
[8] Mart., XIV, 191.
[9] Gell., XVIII, 4.
[10] Auson., *Protr.*, 61–65; August., *De civ. D.*, III, 17, 1; *PSI* (I) 110.
[11] Mart., V, 56, 5.
[12] Quint., II, 5, 20.
[13] *Ibid.*, II, 5, 21; Fronto, *M. Caes.*, II, 13; III, 18.

THE EXPOSITION OF THE AUTHORS

There is not much to be said about the actual method of teaching, beyond the fact that it was the Hellenistic method all over again—i.e. it meant reading "with expression"[1] a passage that had been corrected beforehand.[2] This presented the same difficulty as in Greek, because there was usually no punctuation, and there were no gaps between the words.[3] The reading involved a certain amount of preparation both material and intellectual—material, because the passage had to be marked with special signs[4] showing in cases of doubt where words had to be run on or separated, and marking the accents and quantities and pauses (30); intellectual, because in fact it was impossible to read a passage properly if one did not know it or at least understand it.[5] Hence arose the technical expression *praelectio*,[6] which meant the "explanatory reading": the master read the passage, explaining it as he went along, and it was only when he had finished that the pupil made any attempt to read it himself.[7] If the class was not too large,[8] the children read it one after the other.[9] Along with reading went recitation: learning by heart helped to train and store the memory.[10]

The exposition—*enarratio*—which was supposed to end with a criticism of the whole passage from an aesthetic point of view, had two sides to it—a criticism of the form and a criticism of the matter—*verborum interpretatio, historiarum cognitio*.[11] Thanks to the voluminous commentaries that have come down to us in manuscript—Servius on Virgil, Donatus on Terence, etc.—we can get a very clear idea of the way in which the grammarians of the Late Empire conducted their lessons. After a rapid introduction that was clearly made as short as possible, came, line by line and word by word, a long and meticulous *explanatio*. This was supposed[12] to explain the rhythm of the verse, rare or difficult words, *glossemata*, poetic turns of phrase, but in fact to a modern reader this commentary seems finicky and irritating in the minuteness of its detail. Priscian devoted the whole of quite a bulky treatise[13] to explaining the first line of each of the twelve books of the *Aeneid*. Here is his treatment of Book I, line 1. The master asks the following questions one after the other:

Scan the line.
Arma vi/rumque ca/no Tro/iae qui primus ab/oris.
How many caesuras are there?
Two.
What are they?

---

[1] Quint., I, 8, 1; Auson., *Protr.*, 48–50; C. *Gloss. Lat.*, III, 381, 4 *seq.*
[2] *Ibid.*, 381, 61–63.
[3] August., *Doctr. Chr.*, III, 2 (4) *seq.*
[4] *Gramm. Lat.*, V, 132, 1 *seq.* (Pomp.); IV, 372, 15 *seq.* (Don.).
[5] Gell., XIII, 30.
[6] Quint., I, 8, 13; II, 5, 4.
[7] C. *Gloss. Lat.*, III, 381, 61–75.
[8] *Ibid.*, 381, 4–60.
[9] Cf. Quint., II, 5, 3; 6.
[10] *Ibid.*, I, 1, 36; II, 14; XI, 2, 41; August., *Conf.*, I, 13 (20).
[11] Cic., *De Or.*, I, 187.
[12] Quint., I, 8, 13 *seq.*
[13] *Gramm. Lat.*, III, 459–515.

The penthemimera and the hephthemimera [*semiquinaria, semiseptenaria,* Priscian says in his barbarous Latin].

Which is which?

The penthemimera is *Arma virumque cano,* and the hephthemimera *Arma virumque cano Troiae.*

How many "figures" has it?

Ten.

Why has it got ten?

Because it is made up of three dactyls and two spondees.

[Priscianus takes no notice of the final spondee.]

How many words ["parts of speech"] are there?

Nine.

How many nouns?

Six—*Arma, Virum, Troiae, qui* [sic], *primus, oris.*

How many verbs?

One—*cano.*

How many prepositions?

One—*ab.*

How many conjunctions?

One—*que.*

Study each word in turn. Let us begin with *arma.* What part of speech is it?

A noun.

What is its quality?

Appellative.

What kind is it?

General.

What gender?

Neuter.

How do you know?

All nouns ending in -*a* in the plural are neuter.

Why is *arma* not used in the singular?

Because it means many different things. . . .

And so on. The commentary then goes off into a long inquiry, that has nothing to do with the context, about the word *arma*—the way it is used, the words connected with it and so on; and it is only after several pages that we get the second word. And so it goes on.

Whenever the meaning allowed it—as in this case with the word *Troiae*—the teacher gave, side by side with this literal commentary on the actual words, an explanation of the things signified, the matter: this was the *enarratio historiarum.* This hallowed word *historiae*[1] must not be misunderstood: it did not mean "history" in the restricted modern sense of the word, but, in a very general way, everything "that was told" in the passage concerned.

[1] Cic., *De Or.,* I, 187; Quint., I, 8, 18; August., *Ord.,* II, 12 (13).

LITERARY SCHOLARSHIP

The first thing, of course, was to understand the subject, to get to know the people and the events; but very soon the commentary would branch out in all directions, and the grammarian would offer observations and information of the most varied kind, showing off his vast pedantry with a great deal of naïve self-satisfaction.[1] He was not so much interested in aesthetic values and in getting his pupil to appreciate them as in satisfying his own lust for learning. We saw the same thing in the Hellenistic schools, and it was—if possible—even more marked in Rome. All Latin literature which developed within the framework of Hellenistic civilization, had what we have called a "culture complex". For instance, not once in the whole of Virgil do we find the word *panis*. He always calls "bread" *Ceres*.[2] The proper term is always giving way to the pedantic allusion: the *Georgics* are not "a poem in imitation of Hesiod", but an *Ascraeum carmen*,[3] and so on. Naturally, any explaining of such passages tended to encourage mere erudition: a good grammarian was someone who knew "who Anchises' nurse was, the name of Anchemolus' stepmother, and the country she came from [Anchemolus being a hero who makes a fleeting appearance in two lines of the *Aeneid*],[4] how long Acestes lived and how many jars of Sicilian wine he gave the Phrygians."[5]

Mythology, heroic legend, came first, in fact, in all this grammatical erudition, but history, geography and all the other sciences came into it too. It was necessary to know that Achelous was "a river in Aetolia. It is said to have been the first to come out of the earth. It rises in the Pindus, in the country of the Perrhaebi, and it flows into the Maleac sea. It separates Aetolia from Acarnania. . . . The Amphrysus is a river in Thessaly to which, according to legend, Apollo took Admetus' flocks, etc."[3] It is impossible to exaggerate the importance that this erudition had in classical education. I have shown elsewhere (31) that it was a kind of twin pole of liberal culture. A really educated man was not merely a man of letters but a scholar too, a man of learning. But the "learning" was essentially this kind of erudition that could be gained as a sort of by-product from the great classics.

THE SCIENTIFIC SIDE

In theory the Romans, like the Greeks, remained faithful to the traditional ideal, according to which the higher states of culture existed on a basis of the ἐγκύκλιος παιδεία,[7] generally known in Latin as the *artes liberales*,[8] which, it will be remembered, ranged the mathematical "sciences" alongside the liberal "arts". But the former were in fact very much neglected. The theorists—Cicero,[9] Quintilian—took over Plato's and Isocrates' teaching that geometry has an educational value because it "exercises the brain, sharpens the wits,

---

[1] Quint., I, 8, 13 *seq.*
[2] *Aen.*, I, 177; 701.
[3] *G.*, II, 176.
[4] *Aen.*, X, 388-389.
[5] Juv., VII, 232-236.
[6] Vib. Seq., s.v.
[7] Vitr., I, 1 (3-10); Quint., I, 10, 1.
[8] Cic., *De Or.*, I, 72-73; III, 127; Sen., *Ep.*, 88, 1.
[9] Cic., *Resp.*, I, 30.

gives quick intuition . . ."[1] but it is quite clear that they had no illusions about this, and that it was simply an ideal[2] that was hardly ever realized in practice. It is no use Quintilian saying, "No mathematics, no orator"—*ut . . . nullo modo sine geometria esse possit orator*.[3] It is a splendid formula, worthy of Plato; but it turns out to mean very little in practice. Quintilian would not allow scientific subjects any time on the syllabus. That all had to be devoted to grammar. Science was for "odd periods"—*temporum velut subcesiva*.[4]

In actual fact it did not even receive as much attention as that. There were plenty of teachers of mathematics, geometers and "musicians" in the Roman Empire—there is evidence of their existence from the first century to the fourth[5]—but they only taught a small minority who were assumed to have special scientific or technical gifts (32). Generally speaking, secondary-school teaching was given by the grammarian only.

Here again, modern writers, and even the men of antiquity themselves,[6] are fond of talking about the Romans' utilitarian, down-to-earth mentality, incapable of applying itself like the Greek mind to any disinterested scientific investigations. But this sort of crude judgment falsifies any true historical perspective. It is no use comparing a first-century Roman, say, with a fifth-century Greek. As we have seen, Hellenistic education and culture as a whole were dominated by this insistence on literary erudition, whether Greek or Latin.

From the Greeks of their own day, for instance, the Romans developed the habit of studying astronomy with the mythological rather than mathematical work by Aratus, and generally sacrificing science to literature—to be more precise, to commentaries on works of literature (33).

Exercises in Style

To complete our picture of the *grammaticus'* teaching, the only other thing that needs to be mentioned is the practice in acquiring a good style—"preparatory exercises", that led up to the study of eloquence, i.e. the fables, and the sayings—"chria", "ethology", etc.[7] Terminology and technique were both Greek: Roman teachers took their subject-matter from the Greeks and even copied their mistakes. You will remember Isocrates' sentence which was commented on by Aphthonius. The Latins took up this theme—attributing it to the elder Cato—and Latin schoolboys carefully declined it:

Marcus Portius Cato said that the roots of literature were bitter but that its fruit was sweet. Of Cato it is reported that he said . . . It has seemed good to Cato to say that . . . It is reported that Cato said that . . . O Cato, did you not say that . . .

[1] Quint., I, 10, 34.
[2] Cic., *De Or.*, I, 78; *Orat.*, 7–10; 19, 101; Quint., I, 10, 4.
[3] *Ibid.*, I, 10, 49.
[4] *Ibid.*, I, 12, 13.
[5] Colum., I, pr. 1–7; *Dig.*, L, 13, 1; Diocl., *Max.*, 7, 70; *Cod. Just.*, IX, 18, 2; *Cod. Theod.*, XIII, 4, 3.
[6] Cic., *Tusc.*, I, 5; Virg., *Aen.*, VI, 849–850.
[7] Quint., I, 9; Suet., 25, 5; *Rhet. Lat. Min.*, 561 *seq.* (Empor.); 551 *seq.* (Prisc.).

Then in the plural:

The Marci Portii Catones said that the roots of literature were bitter . . .

and so with each case in turn.[1]

But this brings us to the (disputed) frontier between grammar and rhetoric.[2] In Rome as in Greece rhetoric belonged to the sphere of higher education, and was its chief manifestation.

[1] *Gramm. Lat.*, I, 310 (Diom.).
[2] Quint., I, 9, 6; II, 1.

CHAPTER VI

THE ROMAN SCHOOLS

III. Higher Education

THE first thing that had to be learned, then, was the art of oratory, and this too was in the hands of a specialist, known in Latin as a *rhetor*,[1] and sometimes as an *orator*,[2] though strictly speaking the latter word had a wider meaning.[3]

THE RHETOR

In the social and professional hierarchy of values the rhetor had a distinctly higher place than either of his colleagues in the two lower stages. He was better paid. Juvenal, writing at the beginning of the second century, gives a figure of 2,000 sesterces per pupil per year,[4] i.e. four times as much as a mere grammarian got[5]—though he was speaking, it is true, of the great Quintilian, and the rate of pay may not have been so high in the case of ordinary teachers. In Diocletian's time his position was not so outstanding: orator and grammarian received respectively 250 and 200 *denarii* per pupil per month in contrast to the 50 received by the mere schoolmaster.[6] In 376 Gratian passed a law fixing the ratio between a rhetor's pay and a grammarian's. In Trèves he was to receive half as much again, elsewhere in Gaul double.[7] Even in the eyes of the men of antiquity themselves,[8] the rhetor was not particularly well off. And then there were all the familiar difficulties inherent in work open to all comers —competition,[9] and employers who hated paying up.[10]

It was a career that, once again, only attracted the unimportant, freed slaves[11] or senators who had fallen from grace;[12] nevertheless it was far more common for them than for grammarians to make their fortune or gain any honours.[13] In the Late Empire they were entrusted with some of the highest offices of State, and one of them—Eugenius—even reached the throne. But usually, unless they were tutor to a young prince, as Fronto was to Marcus Aurelius and Verus or Ausonius to Gratian, it was not the actual teaching that brought

---

[1] Dessau, 7773; 2951; Diehl, 104.
[2] *Ibid.*, 105ad n.; Auson., *Prof.*, 1; *Cod. Theod.*, XIII, 3, 11.
[3] Sen., *Controv.*, VII, 1, 20.
[4] Juv., VII, 186–187.
[5] *Ibid.*, 243 (*Schol.*).
[6] Diocl., *Max.*, 7, 70–71.
[7] *Cod. Theod.*, XIII, 3, 11.
[8] Juv., VII, 187–188.
[9] Tac., *Dial.*, 29, 7.
[10] Juv., VII, 157–158; 203; August., *Conf.*, V, 15 (22).
[11] Suet., *Gramm.*, 6.
[12] *Ibid.*, 28; Pliny, *Ep.*, IV, 11.
[13] Suet., *Gramm.*, 25, 4.

rhetors to such heights, but their unofficial literary and (in the Late Empire) administrative or political activities.

Like his humble colleague, the *magister ludi*, the rhetor taught within the precincts of the forum, but he was not content with a mere shop. In the Late Empire, and perhaps as early as Hadrian's time, the State supplied him with fine rooms like exedras, arranged like little theatres and opening out on to the forum porticos at the far end: such are the schola in Trajan's forum, the exedra in Augustus' forum in Rome, and the exedras by the north portico of the Capitol in Constantinople (34). The building and fittings were modelled on the kind of halls that, as we have seen, fulfilled a similar function in the Greek gymnasiums.

The *rhetor Latinus*, like the Greek σοφιστής, aimed at teaching his pupil how to master the art of oratory as handed down traditionally in the complex system of rules, methods and customs that had gradually been perfected in Greek schools from the time of the Sophists. It was all laid down in advance: one learned the rules, and then practised how to use them.

Cicero, probably under the influence of the Stoic philosopher Philo of Larissa (35), had tried hard to wean the youth of his day from this naïve, utilitarian idea of rhetoric and to enlarge their conception of the ideal orator, harking back to Isocrates' original ideal in all its noble simplicity. He wanted the orator's training to be based on the widest possible culture,[1] and insisted particularly, even more than Isocrates would have done, on the need for a solid philosophical foundation,[2] to which, as a good Roman, he added law[3] and also history,[4] which could enlarge one's understanding of humanity so much and provide so many lessons for the statesman.

But Cicero convinced neither his young contemporaries nor succeeding generations. Nor was Quintilian listened to either,[5] when, a century later, he taught practically the same doctrine, basing his neo-classicism on Cicero's[6] authority (36). For most Romans of Imperial times law was a speciality and philosophy for those with an exceptional vocation—that is, if it was to be anything more than a superficial veneer or a sort of purveyor of general ideas. Similarly history, apart from supplying models that could be used as samples of good style, was reduced to a list of *exempla*, memorable "words and deeds"[7] that an orator would find it useful to remember, so that he could bring them out on the right occasion. In practice, higher education was reduced to rhetoric, in the strictest sense of the word. Of Cicero's theoretical works it was not the *De Oratore* but the early *De Inventione*, that dry and academic work, that received the most attention and most of the commentaries.[8]

---

[1] Cic., *De Or.*, I, 20; 48–73; II, 5; *Brut.*, 322.
[2] *Ibid.*, *De Or.*, I, 53–57; 68–69; III, 76–80.
[3] *Ibid.*, I, 166–203; *Orat.*, 120.
[4] *De Or.*, I, 158–159; 201; *Orat.*, 120.
[5] Tac., *Dial.*, 28–35.
[6] Quint., I, pr. 13.
[7] Val. Max.
[8] *Rhet. Lat. Min.*, 155 *seq.* (M. Vict.); 596 *seq.* (Grill.).

RHETORIC COMPLETELY GREEK

There was no real Latin rhetoric. It was an art that had been invented and developed and brought nearer and nearer to perfection by the Greeks. The work of the *rhetores Latini* of the first century B.C. and later of Cicero had simply been to develop a technical vocabulary, and this they had done by transposing the Greek vocabulary into their own language, word for word and often quite slavishly—ἔντεχνος, for instance, simply became *artificialis*. The Latin schools never had any teaching tradition of their own: throughout the Empire they remained very closely connected with Greek rhetoric (37). Their "Latinity" indeed shows a certain retrogression from the position taken up by writers of Republican times. Thus Quintilian's technical language includes many Greek terms which are simply written out in Latin and frequently, indeed, in Greek, even though Latin equivalents were to hand in the *Rhetoric for Herennius* or in Cicero. Quintilian wrote ἀναγκαῖον, ἀνακεφαλαίωσις, ἀποσιώπησις, εἰρωνεία, ἐτυμολογία—not, like his predecessors, *necessitudo, enumeratio, reticentia, dissimulatio, notatio*. He seems to have considered these technical terms so rich and so precise in their original tongue that they could not be translated without loss of meaning (38).

In practice, too, Roman teaching closely followed the Greeks' example. As soon as a pupil got to the end of the long series of preparatory exercises he was allowed to make up imaginary speeches. The teacher decided what the subject was to be, laying down the rules and making suggestions. The speeches were then learnt by heart and delivered in public—"action" being an essential part of oratory—with a certain amount of show. The teacher and his fellow-pupils would be there, and sometimes, at least, the speaker's parents and friends.[1] The technical term for this exercise was *declamatio* (*declamare*), corresponding to the Greek μελέτη (μελετᾶν). As in Greek, again, there were two species within the genus—the *suasio* which belonged more to the political sphere and preferred historical subjects ("Hannibal, on the morrow of Cannae, wonders whether he should march on Rome"),[2] and the *controversia*, on the legal side, a pleading for or against a clearly defined case as laid down by law.

And here again I must emphasize the uniformity and longevity of the old teaching practice. We know a great deal about the subjects that budding young Latin rhetoricians had to tackle, thanks particularly to the collections of fair copies that were kept by Seneca the Elder, (Ps.) Quintilian, Calpurnius Flaccus and Ennodius. These collections are spread over six centuries, and yet it is always the same kind of subjects that keep reappearing, and they are the very subjects that we have already come across in Hellenistic schools (39), with the same vein of phantasy, the same taste for paradoxes and improbabilities—the same tyrants and pirates, the same plagues and madness—kidnapping, rape, cruel stepmothers, disinherited sons, ticklish situations, remote questions of conscience, imaginary laws. I will content myself with two examples.

---

[1] Pers., III, 45–47; Quint., II, 2, 9–12; 7, 1; X, 5, 21; Pliny, *Ep.*, II, 18, 1–2.
[2] Juv., VII, 160–164.

The Priestess-Prostitute

Suppose there is a law that a priestess must be chaste and pure, and her parents chaste and pure.

A virgin is captured by pirates and sold to a procurer who lets her out for prostitution. She asks her clients to pay her and yet respect her chastity. A soldier refuses to do this and tries to violate her. She kills him. She is accused of murder, is acquitted, and returns home. She asks to become a priestess. Plead for or against.[1]

The Double Seducer

In this case the law is that if a woman has been seduced she can choose either to have her seducer condemned to death or marry him without bringing him any dowry.

A man violates two women on the same night. One asks for him to be put to death, the other chooses to marry him.[2]

Such charming subjects naturally led to very subtle arguments, much flashing of wit, a great many *concetti*: Latin rhetors were no more averse to them than their Greek colleagues amongst the Later Sophists. The subject, *Fortis sine manibus*, concerns a war hero who has lost both hands and surprises his wife in the act of adultery. Here is the famous rhetor M. Portius Latro's version of the event:

Adulteros meos tantum excitavi . . . They didn't seem to mind whether I had come back or not . . . O, what a cruel reminder of my former prowess! O, what a sad memorial of my victories! . . . Of all deceived husbands I am the first who could neither drive them from the house nor kill them! "Oh, you are laughing, are you?" I said to them. "You'll see that I have got a pair of hands!" And I called my son. . . .[3]

LITERATURE AND THE BAR

Enough has been said—even in antiquity itself[4]—about the absurdity of such an artificial system of teaching, that seems quite gaily to turn its back on life (40). But we must not be in too much of a hurry to condemn it before we are quite sure that we understand it. Historians of the Roman Empire have been far too keen to class academic eloquence as one of the signs of the "decadence" that they seem able to detect all over the place in the "Silver Age". But, as we have already seen, this kind of eloquence was not peculiar to Imperial Rome; it ran through Hellenistic culture as a whole. For a thousand years—possibly two—from Demetrius Phalereus to Ennodius (later still in Byzantium), this was the standard type of teaching in all higher education. Can so many generations be accused of

---

[1] Sen., *Controv.*, I, 2.
[2] *Ibid.*, I, 5; cf. IV, 3; VII, 8.
[3] *Ibid.*, I, 4, 1.
[4] Petron., I, 3; Quint., II, 10; Tac., *Dial.*, 31, 1; 35, 4-5.

blindness? Can a civilization whose vitality and greatness in the things of the mind is on other counts not open to question, be condemned as unimaginative and decadent?

I shall not say anything about the extenuating circumstances. It might be shown, for example, that Latin rhetoric had not entirely forgotten Plotius Gallus, and did in fact have a place for present-day affairs, for concrete political and legal problems (41). But in the first place, as I have already shown in connection with Hellenistic rhetoric, the ancients intentionally chose paradoxical subjects for their exercises because they were more difficult and therefore more profitable than subjects taken from real life.[1]

Secondly, despite what Seneca said,[2] it is not true that the schools were so remote from life—he meant literary life. The coming of the Empire and the loss of political "liberty" from the time of Augustus onwards had caused Roman culture to model itself on Hellenistic culture, and the higher eloquence became, not political eloquence, but the disinterested aesthetic eloquence of the public lecturer. Asinius Pollio had introduced the practice of public recitations[3] under Augustus, and from then on they dominated the whole of literary life, just as they did in Greek-speaking regions.

As time went on, it became more and more difficult to distinguish the features that had once differentiated Latin education from Greek. Under the Empire both were essentially aesthetic in character, and the chief aim of Roman education was to realize through literature and art an ideal of humanism that was unconcerned with, unconstrained by, any sordid technical or utilitarian considerations.

From then on academic eloquence no longer seemed deplorable or absurd. It naturally tended to become focused on the art of lecturing, on the set speech that in the eyes of Latin men of letters under the Empire, as in the eyes of their Greek contemporaries the Later Sophists, was the highest possible form of art. And when they are looked at from the purely literary point of view, the subjects that they treated are not without merit. Real life is not the sole source of inspiration; there is also imagination, there is the great event. And indeed these subjects had a peculiar destiny that in the West took them far beyond the confines of the academic world, for they lie behind the development of the tales or stories that began to appear in the Middle Ages in Latin, like the *Gesta Romanorum* (42), or in the vernacular; they are one of the sources of the romantic tradition in modern European literature.

It should also be realized that, however surprising it may seem, this abstract way of learning oratory did not turn young Romans away from public life. We shall see in the next chapter how the Empire—and this is true of the liberal Empire of the first two centuries, as well as the bureaucratic monarchy of the fourth, fifth and sixth—found the schools of rhetoric a very useful nursery, full of shrewd and active minds that were just the kind it wanted for the higher administrative and governmental posts.

Taking things by and large, it may be said that the teaching of rhetoric was in fact directed towards practical affairs. Normally, it led to the Bar. If we take

[1] Gell., XVII, 12.   [2] Sen., *Ep.*, 106, 12.   [3] Sen., *Controv.*, IV, pr. 2.

Quintilian, for instance, who was writing in the nineties—a good observation point in the middle of the Imperial age—it is clear that the kind of orator he aimed at producing was mainly the advocate[1]—a man whose profession brought him plenty of custom, in view of the enormous development of the legal system in the Roman Empire (43). The training may seem highly untechnical to us: Quintilian, following Cicero's example and trying to persuade his disciples of the need for making a thorough study of the law,[2] seems to have been fighting in vain against a deeply ingrained tendency of the time. It must be realized that the tremendous development of the technical side of Roman law had made it a matter for specialists, and there had developed a kind of division of labour between the jurist and the advocate. The advocate had technical advisers—*pragmatici*—who were in charge of the actual procedure and supplied him with a file of the legal arguments.[3] His own particular task was to present these effectively, passing from the field of law to the larger field of equity, speaking in a way that would move and persuade. In fact his work was more literary than legal.

THE TEACHING OF LAW

The one really great original feature of Latin education was in fact the opportunity it provided of a legal career. On this point alone does the perfect parallel between Greek and Latin schools break down. Having left philosophy and—for a long time, at least—medicine to the Greeks, the Romans created their own original type of higher education with their law schools.

Everyone knows that law was the great creation achieved by the genius of Rome, and in fact it meant the appearance of a whole new form of culture, a new type of mind that the Greeks had never imagined. The *juris prudens* was something absolutely novel. He was a man who knew his law, who knew all the laws, the customs, the rules of procedure, all that was meant by "jurisprudence"—the whole system of precedents that could be referred to in order to support one's cases by analogies from the past, by tradition. He was, moreover, a man who could "cite" the law, who could apply all this vast knowledge, all the material furnished by his erudition and memory, to any individual case—could discern at once what category it belonged to, and suggest the perfect solution, that pierced through the difficulties of the case and the ambiguity of the law. The wisdom of the lawyer was not mere cunning: it was based on an elevated sense of justice, goodness, order. At first, and for a long time, intuitive, it then became conscious and deliberate, drawing on the great intellectual achievement of Greek thought, the sturdy diet of Aristotelian logic, and the rich moral fare of Stoicism.

Thus in Rome there existed a science of law. The knowledge of this science was a precious boon, and many young Romans aspired after it. It was a good way of making a career—it seems to have been even a better way of getting on than by taking up eloquence.[4] Naturally a demand arose for a master of law—*magister juris*[5]—and a system of teaching law (44).

---

[1] Quint., XII, I, 13; 24–26; XII, 3; XII, 6.   [3] *Ibid.*, XII, 3, 4–9; Tac., *Dial.*, 31–32.
[2] *Ibid.*, XII, 3.   [4] Petron., 46.
[5] Dessau, 7748; *CIL*, VI, 1602.

The institutional side of this teaching remained for a long time embryonic: even in Cicero's day it was still being given as part of the practical instruction known as the *tirocinium fori*. If we turn to the passages describing the young Cicero in company with either of the Mucii Scaevolae,[1] for example, it is clear that the master was a practitioner rather than a teacher.[2] But his young disciples were present when he had consultations with his clients and learned by listening to him, for naturally he could use the cases to explain all the legal points that were involved, with their consequences, just like a doctor in a clinic. It was only from the time of Cicero, and largely, apparently, as a result of his energetic propaganda,[3] that the teaching of Roman law began to include, along with this practical instruction—*respondentes audire*—a certain amount of theory—*instituere*. Cicero himself had called one of his works, unfortunately lost, *De jure civili in artem redigendo*;[4] and thereafter Roman law, making full use of all the resources of Greek logic, was presented as far as was possible in the form of a body of doctrine, a system with its own principles, its own divisions and class-ifications, all precisely defined in their own terminology.[5]

Simultaneously with the formulation of its method, the teaching of law was gradually becoming fixed in more clearly defined institutions of an increasingly official character: in fact, it was evolving on the same lines as the function of the jurisconsult, with which it remained closely connected. From the time of Augustus onwards the most recognized of the Prudent Ones are known to have been invested with official authority by being given the *ius publice respondendi*.[6] By the second century whole consulting offices are known to have been in exis-tence, and these were law schools as well—*stationes ius publice docentium aut respondentium*.[7] These were always near a temple, probably so that they could use the special libraries to be found there—for instance, Augustus had endowed the sanctuary of Apollo with one, on the Palatine.[8]

At this time the instruments of Roman law were perfected. In this century Gaius, whose way had been prepared by other similar workers, produced his *Institutes*, a model of systematic treatment of the elements of Roman law for beginners. Many other kinds of books on law were being produced—books on procedure, commentaries on Hadrian's *Perpetual Edict*, systematic collections—*Digesta*—and excerpts from lawyers' works. This creative activity culminated under the Severi in the admirable works by Ulpianus, Papinianus, Paulus, etc.

These works quickly became classical, in the most precise sense of the word: they were recognized authorities, and the teaching of law could be organized round them. The law teacher, making full use of the ripe experience he had gained from studying the poets under the grammaticus, could now devote him-self entirely to explaining and interpreting his own authors.

We know most about the syllabus and methods used in the school at Beirut, which was the most flourishing centre of Roman law in the East. It probably came into existence at the beginning of the third century as a result of the fact that Beirut was a centre for public proclamations, and contained the archives of

[1] Cic., *Lae.*, I.
[2] *Ibid.*, *Brut.*, 306.
[3] *Ibid.*, *De Or.*, I, 166–201.
[4] Gell., I, 22, 7.
[5] Cic., *De Or.*, I, 87–190.
[6] Just., *Inst.*, I, 2, 8; *Dig.*, I, 2, 2, 49.
[7] Gell., XIII, 13, I.
[8] *Schol.*, Juv., I, 128.

imperial laws and constitutions affecting the whole of the East (45). By 239 it was in full swing, attracting students from such far-off provinces as Cappadocia.[1] Its fame lasted throughout the fourth[2] and fifth[3] centuries, and only later did it begin to be rivalled by Constantinople.

When the Empire became Christian this teaching took place in the afternoon in the cathedral of Eustathius—rather as, in Moslem countries, advanced education still takes place in the mosques—and it usually lasted four years.[4] The master read the basic texts, explained them and commented upon them. During the first year, he took Gaius's *Institutes* and Ulpianus' *Libri ad Sabinum* with the novices—*dupondii*: in the second year, Ulpianus' *Libri ad Edictum*; in the third, the *Responsa Papiniani*, and in the fourth, the *Responsa Pauli*. An extra fifth year was introduced for studying the Imperial Constitutions that began to be collected in the Codes between 291 and 295. The first two, the Gregorian Code and the Hermogenian Code, are known to have been the result of private initiative: not until 439 did an Emperor—Theodosius II—promulgate an official Code; so it is not impossible that they may have been compiled in the first place to help teachers. In Beirut and in Constantinople the teaching was done in Latin: Greek was only introduced between 381–382 and 410–420, and even then it did not completely oust Latin, which, though it had various ups and downs, managed to keep some of its positions intact until Justinian's time.

[1] Greg. Thaum., *Pan.*, 5.
[2] Lib., *Or.*, I, 214.
[3] Zach., *V. Sev.*, p. 46.
[4] Just., *Omnem*, 2–6,

CHAPTER VII

THE ROMAN EDUCATIONAL ACHIEVEMENT

THE historical importance of Roman education is not to be found in any slight variations or additions it may have made to classical education of the Hellenistic type, but in the way it managed to spread this education through time and space.

ROMAN GREATNESS

Modern historians have not always done justice to the greatness of the Roman achievement. Inheriting the Romantic attitude, according to which the highest and, in a sense, the only value is originality, pure creation, they have only been able to see Roman civilization as a degenerate, bastard form of the genuine original to be found in Hellas (1).

It is unnecessary to show the inadequacy of this attitude here. It is worth noticing that for a long time the same purist attitude has also led to similarly unfavourable judgments on Hellenistic civilization, which has been condemned for not having equalled the civilization of the sixth, fifth and fourth centuries and also for having followed it too faithfully—for fundamentally what is objected to is its classicism, the fact that it did not get rid of everything it inherited from the preceding age and set off in a new direction.

But on the other hand it is a waste of time for Roman enthusiasts to pursue the phantom of some imaginary Latin originality that either never existed or involved only superficial matters that can be safely neglected. The truth concerns something quite different: Rome's historic function was not to create a new civilization but to take the Hellenistic civilization which had conquered her and establish it firmly on the whole of the Mediterranean world.

ROME AS A CIVILIZING FORCE

Politically, as we have seen, the Roman achievement was "to turn the whole world into a single country"[1]—to unite conquerors and conquered in one community. There is a great deal that testifies to this—I need only mention here the passionate way in which, as spokesman for the aristocracy of Ionia, Aelius Aristides addressed the good emperor Antoninus Pius, extolling the benefits of the *pax Romana*, which had made the whole world one immense choir singing (in unison!) under the baton of the Imperial "coryphaeus"[2]: "As bats in caves cling to rocks and to each other, so all are suspended from Rome, and their greatest fear is to be detached from her"[3] (2).

[1] Rut. Namat., I, 63.   [2] Arstd., XXVI K, 29.   [3] *Ibid.*, 68.

But a community is judged by the values that its members have in common. Now the Roman Empire's ideal values were not confined to politics. Justice, order and peace were not regarded as ends in themselves; they were only means enabling men to spend their days in security and comfort and leisure—in one word, happily—with that happiness that all the Hellenistic thinkers had regarded as the highest value—τέλος—the real point of living. This was the essence—the *Wesen*—of *Romanitas*: to organize the world in such a way that the values of Hellenistic civilization—the civilization of happiness—could blossom forth.

Let us turn to Aelius Aristides again:

> The whole world seems to be on holiday. It has laid aside its garments of iron so that it shall be free to devote itself entirely to beauty and the joy of living. The cities have forgotten their old rivalries—or rather the same spirit of emulation animates them all, the desire to be considered first in beauty and charm. On all sides can be seen gymnasiums, fountains, *propylaea*, temples, workshops, schools.[1]

We must not try to judge the Roman achievement according to the Hegelian category of becoming. Rome's own point of view was entirely classical, and she saw herself *sub specie aeternitatis*, in the unchanging light of an eternal present. She believed herself to be eternal because she had enabled the civilized part of mankind to attain a general standard of maturity, had provided an order so stable that there could never be any reason for disturbing it or changing it.

Once again, a historian does not regard originality as the only claim to glory that a civilization can have. Its historic greatness and its importance for mankind depend not only on the value intrinsic to it but on its extension, its rootedness in time and space. The civilization of the island of Pascua no doubt possessed some very precious values too; but they would have been more fruitful and more enduring if they had not been restricted to an island of forty-five square miles, lost in the middle of the South Pacific. If, to come closer to our subject, Minoan civilization had not spread beyond Crete, there would have been no ripe Mycenean autumn, no fertilizing influence on the Hellenic Middle Ages, no Homer. . . . And if Greek civilization in its turn had remained the jealously guarded preserve of a few Aegean cities, it too would have disappeared long ago, without renewing, as it has, the face of the earth.

And the fact that it thus fulfilled its destiny is largely due to Rome. Rome's historic function was to complete the work begun by Alexander, and plant Hellenistic civilization from the Sahara to the lochs of Scotland, from the Euphrates to the Atlantic; and to give it such deep roots that it could withstand the storms of Teuton and Slav invasions, and the Arab invasion, if not that of the Turks. It is this profound labour, ensuring the renaissances of the future, that constitutes Rome's real honour and imperishable glory.

[1] Arstd., XXVI, K, 97.

POLICY OF ROMANIZATION

"On all sides are gymnasiums . . . schools." It is remarkable to find Aelius Aristides' list ending with this phrase. For him the gymnasium was the symbol of Hellenism in barbarian lands. Rome too introduced her own way of life into these lands—the aristocratic life of luxury and pleasure. Her characteristic buildings seem to be her baths, her theatres, the amphitheatre, the circus. And yet all those were only the outer shell—Rome introduced something more precious still: her schools, and with them her language—her two languages— and her culture.

In all the "barbarian" regions of the West we can see the same signs of a conscious, deliberate policy of Romanization. In Spain, for instance, there was Sertorius, who, though he had broken off from the aristocratic power then in control of the Republic, still looked upon himself as representing the Roman idea. In 79 B.C. he summoned all the sons of the noblest Spanish families to Osca, obviously to make certain of the loyalty of the local leaders. And he had these young hostages brought up as Romans: they are described as being clothed in the *toga praetextata*, with the *bulla* round their necks, starting to learn Greek and Latin literature.[1] By the time of the Empire we can begin to see the results of his policy—the whole network of schools throughout the peninsula: elementary schools, even in little mining centres in southern Lusitania;[2] in any city of the slightest importance there were grammarians[3]—Latin[4] and Greek[5] —and teachers of Latin[6] and Greek[7] rhetoric. Is it surprising, then, to find the Iberian peninsula playing such an active part in Roman life and giving it in return so many great writers—the Senecas, Lucan, Quintilian, Martial: so many administrators and statesmen, and even—beginning with Trajan— emperors (3)?

The same thing could be shown to have happened in all the great regions of the West. In Imperial Africa, where Latin had been introduced in Caesar's time, we are continually coming across grammarians,[8] rhetors,[9] well-educated men like the young man of Setif—*summarum artium liberalium, litterarum studiis utriusque linguae perfecte eruditus, optima facundia praeditus*[10]—or the citizens of Sala, who lived on the edge of the Atlantic, at the south-western tip of the Roman world, and who in 144 produced a decree in honour of one of their prefects that has a most uncommon verbal luxuriance.[11]

Gaul did not lag behind Africa.[12] It too was a chosen land for grammar[13] and

---

[1] Plut., *Sert.*, 14.
[2] Dessau, 6891, 57.
[3] Sen., *Controv.*, I, pr. 2; Dessau, 7765; *CIL*, II, 5079.
[4] *Ibid.*, 2892.
[5] Dessau, 7766.
[6] *CIL*, II, 354.
[7] *Ibid.*, 1738.
[8] Dessau, 7762.
[9] *Ibid.*, 7772.
[10] *Ibid.*, 7761; cf. 7742.
[11] Carcopino, *Maroc*, 200 seq. (= *Aep.*, 1931, 36).
[12] Juv., VII, 148.
[13] Suet., *Gram.*, 3, 4.

eloquence.[1] Here too, on the basis of a system of schools that soon had famous teachers amongst them,[2] Romanization made rapid strides. In A.D. 48 the Emperor Claudius, addressing the Senate in favour of the granting of the *jus honorum* to the notables of Gallia Comata, could maintain that the Gauls were equal to the Romans in their customs and culture—*moribus, artibus*.[3]

The same process went on throughout the whole of the West. In the reign of Tiberius, Velleius Paterculus was writing that "in all the Pannonian provinces, with the coming of the Roman peace the Latin language and in many cases her literary culture too had spread far and wide."[4] Along the Danube, helped by the army, Latin culture reached the Black Sea.

In Dobrogea it spread through the country districts and reached the walls of the old Greek colonies on the coast—Callatis, Tomis, Istros. This province of Scythia Minor, at the extreme corner of the *orbis Romanus*, was to give John Cassian to the Latin Church in the fourth to fifth centuries, and Dionysius the Less in the sixth. There is no clearer proof of the genuineness of Latin culture in this remote province than the episode of the Scythian monks (519–520). It was not only the boldness of their Christology that sounded so strange in Constantinople. The fact was that these Danubians were of a different mould from the Byzantine theologians. They were pure Latins—in touch with Rome, in correspondence with the African bishops who had been exiled to Sardinia. Their master, practically unknown in the East, was St. Augustine (4).

The Roman procedure began in the same way everywhere: Rome took as hostages the children from all the best families in the newly conquered land, and brought them up in Roman schools. The method adopted in Spain by Sertorius was repeated along the Rhine by Caligula[5] and in Britain by Agricola.[6] Even in a province as far north as Britain, the Latin language, and with it the whole classical culture, succeeded in taking root (5). There was a Greek grammarian, a friend of Plutarch's, who went there to seek his fortune,[7] and Juvenal was thinking of Britain when he said, very profoundly and very truly, despite the comic overstatement at the end: "In the time of old Metellus"— Sulla's governor in Outer Spain, and Sertorius' enemy—"could one have imagined a Stoic coming from Cantabria? Today the whole world enjoys Greek culture and Latin culture":

Nunc totus Graias nostrasque habet orbis Athenas

"Gaul has grown eloquent and raises British lawyers, and Thule is already about to hire a rhetor!"[8]

LIMITS OF ROMANIZATION

We must remember, however, that this diffusion of the Latin language and Latin culture had certain limits. In Rome as in all other places in antiquity,

[1] Juv., XV, 11.
[2] Suet., *Gram.*, 3, 4.
[3] Tac., *Ann.*, XI, 24, 13.
[4] II, 110.
[5] Suet., *Calig.*, 45, 3.
[6] Tac., *Agr.*, 21, 2.
[7] Dessau, 8861 (Plut., *Def. Or.*, 422 D; 423 A).
[8] Juv., XV, 108–112.

culture was always the privilege of the governing classes; and in times of great catastrophe, when she was suffering the onslaughts of the barbarian invasions, this aristocratic feature was to prove a formidable source of weakness. There is no doubt that it helped to limit the movement of conquest.

The earliest schools were opened for the benefit of the children of the great families only—for those who came from the highest section of society, or at least from the privileged class of city-dwellers—for cities went on setting the standard in all matters of civilization, and they presupposed a considerable amount of material refinement and spiritual capital. The Romanization of any district was measured by the number and importance of its towns. The lower classes and rural districts were always sacrificed to them, with the result that for a long time they resisted Romanization.

The mining village in Lusitania which I have quoted was not an isolated instance, of course: the lawyer Ulpianus speaks of elementary schools in country boroughs—*vici*[1]—as though they were the normal thing. But there were not enough of them to reach the masses as a whole. "Punic" was still being spoken around Hippo in St. Augustine's time (6), and Celtic in the country districts of Gaul in the third and fourth centuries. It seems to have been the propagation of Christianity that finally caused Latin to be adopted in Gaul as a whole, for just as in Southern France Protestant propaganda in the sixteenth century was done in French and not in the language of Languedoc, so in this earlier age the new religion was preached to the masses in Latin (7)—though it is only fair to add that this would not have been possible without a fairly advanced state of Latinization being in existence already. Celtic could not have been as living a language as Coptic or Syriac, which the Church in Egypt and the East found it advisable or necessary to use, rather than Greek.

THE MAP OF SCHOOL DISTRIBUTION

Granted these limitations, it remains true that the whole of the Empire was covered with a fairly dense network of academic institutions: elementary-school teachers were to be found more or less everywhere, grammarians and rhetors in places of any importance.

Take Cisalpine Italy in Caesar's time, where Virgil was born in a village called Andes, a dependency of the city of Mantua.[2] In Mantua, no doubt, he first went to school. When he was twelve,[3] he went to the grammarian in Cremona. At fifteen or sixteen, having received the *toga virilis*,[4] he went on to Milan to learn rhetoric;[5] then to Rome, to study under the famous rhetor M. Epidius, who later had Mark Antony and Octavian among his pupils.[6] The future poet, whose interests were very wide, also studied the sciences—medicine and above all mathematics.[7] This led him on to philosophy, and, touched by the light of truth, he was converted to the Epicurism that the Roman intellectuals of the time found so congenial—as we can see from Lucretius; he then went to Naples[8]

[1] *Dig.*, V, 5, 2, 8.
[2] *V. Virg.*, Don., 7; Serv., 4.
[3] Hieron., *Chron.*, 59a.
[4] *V. Virg.*, Don., 20 *seq.*; Philarg., 25 *seq.*

[5] *Ibid.*, Don., 24; Serv., 6.
[6] *Ibid.*, Bern., 7.
[7] *Ibid.*, Don., 47 *seq.*
[8] *Ibid.*, Serv., 6.

and joined the philosopher Siro's[1] school and became a member of the Epicurean circle that centred round Philodemus in Herculaneum[2] (8).

More than four hundred years later we find the same thing repeating itself in Africa. St. Augustine was born in a little town in Numidia called Tagaste. He could only do his elementary schooling there, and like Virgil he had to go into a more important city—in this case Madaurus, Apuleius' native town—to study grammar and begin on rhetoric.[3] There was a gap, for material reasons, when he was sixteen, and then for more advanced studies he went on to Carthage.[4] Being fatherless and poor, he was unable to finish these. He too was "converted" to philosophy,[5] when he was eighteen, but he had to be his own teacher—as a philosopher St. Augustine was a self-made man.[6] Others who were better off socially, like his pupil, friend and future colleague, Alypius, continued their studies and went overseas to read law in Rome.[7]

Thus the educational facilities varied greatly from city to city. There were fairly competent grammarians and rhetors in a number of cities—in Gaul, for example, according to the documents, in Limoges,[8] Bordeaux,[9] Toulouse,[10] Narbonne,[11] Marseilles,[12] Arles,[13] Vienne,[14] Lyons,[15] Avenches,[16] Autun,[17] Besançon,[18] Rheims,[19] Trèves,[20] Cologne[21] . . . though this list tends to give a slightly wrong impression, since it covers four centuries. We have not enough evidence to be able to write the history of any single one of these schools. On the other hand it is fairly easy to pick out the great "university" centres, where there was a relatively high number of famous teachers who drew large numbers of students, sometimes from a great distance—and fought as fiercely over them as their Greek colleagues in the East.

In Africa the second capital city—intellectually, and in every other way—was of course Carthage (9).

In Gaul the concentration varied more. At the beginning of the Empire the most famous schools were to be found first in Marseilles, with its Greek heritage, and then in Autun, the capital of the Heduan country that had provided Caesar with his first allies and Gaul with her first Senators after the Claudian senatus-consultum. Already fairly common in the first century,[22] they reappeared in their full splendour in about 297 under Constantius Chlorus.[23] Later, in the fourth century, Bordeaux is the most prominent centre, but this may simply be because Ausonius' personality and work are there to attract our attention (10).

In Italy the main centres were Naples (11) and Milan, whose prestige was enhanced in St. Ambrose's and St. Augustine's time by the fact that the Imperial court of the West was there. But of course for Italy and the whole of the Latin

---

[1] [Virg.] *Epigr.*, V; Serv., *Aen.*, VI, 264.
[2] *PHerc.*,[2] I, 93, XI, 3; VII, 196, XII, 4.
[3] August., *Conf.*, II, 3 (5).
[4] *Ibid.*, III, 1 (1) *seq.*
[5] *Ibid.*, III, 4 (7).
[6] *Ibid.*, IV, 16 (28).
[7] *Ibid.*, VI, 8 (13).
[8] Dessau, 7764.
[9] Auson., *Prof. Burd.*
[10] Hieron., *Chron.*, 56p.
[11] *CIL*, XII, 5074.
[12] *IG*, XIV, 2434.
[13] *CIL*, XII, 714, 12.
[14] *Ibid.*, 1918–1921.
[15] *Ibid.*, XIII, 2038.
[16] *Ibid.*, 5079.
[17] Tac., *Ann.*, III, 43.
[18] Auson., *Grat. Act.*, VII, 31.
[19] *Gramm. Lat.*, V., 349 (Cons.).
[20] Dessau, 7765.
[21] *CIL*, XIII, 8356.
[22] Tac., *Ann.*, III, 43.
[23] *Pan. Lat.*, IV; XI.

Empire the great university centre was Rome, which was far more important than any of the others:

Quantum lenta solent inter viburna cupressi.

Its pre-eminence in all the affairs of the West—including those of the intellect —raised it above any other centre in the eastern part of the Empire. Constantinople only became the outstanding city in the second period of Byzantine history, so lasting was the prestige of Athens, Alexandria, Antioch and (as regards the law) Beirut. To Rome came all the most famous grammarians and rhetors, both Latin and Greek: as we shall see, the emperor did all he could to entice them and to keep them there. Rome was perhaps the only place in the West where there was any organized teaching of philosophy, and, most important of all, where there was an official centre for the teaching of law. Law was in great demand, and great numbers of students came to Rome from the provinces— not only from all parts of Italy, but from Africa,[1] Gaul,[2] the Danubian provinces[3] and even from the Greek lands in the east.[4]

But the history of these various educational centres only becomes clear when we realize the part played by the Roman State in the development of education.

[1] *Cod. Theod.*, XIV, 9, 1; August., *Conf.*, VI, 8 (13).
[2] Rut. Namat., I, 209; *AA. SS.*, Jul., VII, 202; cf. Hieron., *Ep.*, 125, 6, 1.
[3] Diehl, 740.
[4] Dessau, 7742; Lib., *Or.*, I, 214.

CHAPTER VIII

THE ROMAN STATE AND EDUCATION

As long as the Republic lasted there had been no proper scholastic policy. A Greek like Polybius, accustomed to seeing Hellenistic cities take such a close interest in educational matters, was astonished by this "negligence".[1] The Roman State left education to the initiative and activity of its citizens. This was one of the ways in which Roman institutions were relatively archaic, compared with the Hellenistic world. Under the Empire Rome did something to make up lost ground, and made an effort to conform to the standards in force in the Greek world.

THE COLLEGIA IUVENUM

Thus in Augustus' reign a highly characteristic institution like the ephebia found its equivalent in the "youth clubs"—*collegia iuvenum*—that were beginning to flourish, especially in central Italy (1). These seem to have come into existence on the initiative of Augustus himself, as part of his work of national restoration.[2] He is said to have taken in hand the youth of the senatorial and equestrian classes in Rome itself, reviving their taste for military training, for physical exercises on the Field of Mars and especially for horsemanship. These seem to have been given up in Cicero's time,[3] but now the poet laureates[4] vied with each other in praising them. Young aristocrats competed in the *ludi sevirales*;[5] as children, they took part in the sacred tournament, the old *ludus Troiae*.[6] Having been duly enrolled, they were officially reviewed each year at the *transvectio equitum*, a ceremony that took place in the Great Circus.[7]. In about 51 B.C. the organization reached its zenith when Augustus' (grand-) sons were given the characteristic title, *principes iuventutis*—"youth leaders".[8] This was the first appearance of the title in Rome; in the time of the Julio-Claudians it was frequently conferred, always on some young prince of the reigning house,[9] and from the Severi onwards it was used regularly to describe the heir to the throne—a function that had been implicit in its wording from the first.[10]

It is clear that the institution that Augustus had thus created, or revived, was deeply rooted in the nation's past. The actual division of society into two age-

---

[1] Ap. Cic., *Resp.*, IV, 3; cf. [ap. Tyan.] *Ep.* LIV.
[2] Dio Cass., LII, 26, 1 *seq.*
[3] Cic., *Cael.*, 11.
[4] Hor., *Carm.*, I, 8; III, 12, 7 *seq.*; Virg., *Aen.*, VII, 162–165; IX, 606.
[5] Dio Cass., LV, 10, 4, S.H.A., *M. Aur.*, 6, 3.
[6] Suet., *Aug.*, 43, 5.
[7] *Ibid.*, 38, 2.
[8] Aug. Imp., *R.G.*, 14, 2; Tac., *Ann.*, I, 3, 2.
[9] Suet., *Calig.*, 15, 4; Dessau, 222, 4.
[10] Ov., *Ars Am.*, I, 194.

groups, "youths"—*iuvenes*—and *seniores*, may possibly go back further than Rome herself into a remote period of Indo-European pre-history (2). The title "prince of youth" seems to have been in existence amidst the Ausones, an Italic nation, by the end of the fourth century B.C.,[1] and young men's colleges seem to have existed for a long time too, centring round the old sanctuaries that during the Augustan renaissance were piously restored. In Tusculum there was even a young girls' *sodalitas*[2] that ran under the auspices of one of the old city cults (3).

But, as we have already seen in the case of the young men of Pompeii—VEREIIA PVMPAIIANA—even in pre-Roman Italy these youth organizations had been profoundly influenced, in Campania at least, by the Hellenistic ephebia. Under the Empire the resemblance became more noticeable still—either as a result of deliberate imitation, or unconscious influence, or simply through a parallel development. Wherever these *collegia iuvenum* spring up, from the time of Augustus onwards—first in Latium, then in Campania, Umbria, Picenum—and further away still, in the Cisalpine region, the Narbonnaise, even into Spain, they appear as morphologically the equivalent of the ephebic colleges of Hellenistic Greece.

Like the ephebia they were clubs formed of young men from all the best families in town. At first they had favours showered upon them by emperors with leanings towards the aristocracy, and this lasted from the Augustan dynasty to the Gordian;[3] but the Severi rather tended to frown upon them, apparently fearing that they might be used to camouflage an aristocratic opposition[4] (4).

And undoubtedly they had a political side to them, in municipal affairs at least: Pompeian epigraphy shows them playing an active part at election times. Like the ephebia in Hellenistic Athens, they were little miniature republics, with their own elected magistrates, where they could try themselves out at the parliamentary game.

But true to their Italian origins, these clubs were primarily religious. Many of them worshipped a particular divinity, especially Hercules[5]—Herakles was one of the divinities who protected the gymnasiums in Greek-speaking countries but it is quite clear that the religious ceremonies—the processions and sacrifices (which meant banquets) and so on—were at this time chiefly an excuse for feasting and social occasions. In Pompeii the local club building—the *schola*—is said to have been identified: a lovely hall richly decorated with frescoes, trophies, and symbols of victory. Here the *iuvenes* must have gathered, before going out on their official processions (5).

The thing that these clubs, like the ephebes, mostly went in for, was sport. In Rome and in many other cities the young men took part in many different games such as the *ludi iuvenales* and *Iuvenalia* in which, from Nero[6] to Gordianus I,[7] the emperor himself frequently took part. Very occasionally, as for example

---

[1] Livy, IX, 25, 4.
[2] Dessau, 6211–6212.
[3] S.H.A., *Gord.*, 4, 6.
[4] *Dig.*, XLVIII, 19, 28, 3.
[5] Dessau, 7306; *CIL*, IX, 1681; cf. *Aep.* (1911), 67; (1926), 126.
[6] Suet., *Ner.*, 11; Tac., *Ann.*, XIV, 15; *Hist.*, III, 62.
[7] S.H.A., *Gord.*, 4, 6.

at the Quinquatria to Minerva founded in Albano by Domitian,[1] there were literary contests too, as there had sometimes been in Athens; but usually they were sports, as in Greece—with this difference, that they were not the kind of sports that went on in a stadium, but in a circus or amphitheatre: I have already described how the young aristocrats of Imperial times were thus brought up to learn horsemanship and fencing and "hunting"—i.e. fights with wild animals.

Undoubtedly Augustus' main idea, like that of the Athenians between 338–335 B.C., was to use this institution to give a military turn to education. But under the Empire, as previously in Hellenistic Greece, this para- or pre-military aspect soon faded into the background, and the *collegia iuvenum* became for the most part fashionable clubs for the aristocracy, where gilded youths could learn how to live properly and how to enjoy their sport. I am speaking of the *collegia iuvenum* in Italy. What I have said is perhaps less true of the organizations for youth that began to appear in the second century, particularly in districts near the frontier along the Rhine and the Danube; nor is it true to any great extent of those in Africa,[2] which were less exclusive—they were usually called *Iuventus*, not *collegium iuvenum*—and seem to have been far more closely connected with military training and the army; so that they hardly come into the sphere of education.

School Policy

The Roman Empire gradually came to pursue an active policy of intervention and support in the matter of schools (6). Unlike the Hellenistic cities, Rome never had any special supervisor or inspector of schools (7), but, as in the case of the Greek cities, the Roman State granted the teaching body a number of economic privileges, and in certain cases at least paid the teachers directly out of its own coffers. This system, in both its aspects, was inaugurated by Vespasian.

Exemptions from Taxation

The measures that Caesar[3] and Augustus[4] had introduced for the benefit of teachers only applied to foreigners and were really part of the policy of attracting Greek teachers to Rome. Vespasian introduced a whole system of economic privilege: all teachers of secondary-school standard and above were exempted from municipal levies—*munera*—a concession that Augustus had only granted to physicians.[5] At first this only meant exemption from "hospitality", i.e. the duty of providing billets for troops,[6] but, beginning with Hadrian,[7] the emperors re-enacted and confirmed these privileges, and from the time of Antoninus[8] and Commodus[9] onwards gradually extended them to apply to other forms of duty—such as that affecting guardians of children under age, gymnasiarchs, agoranomes (supervisors of markets), priests and so on. The same policy was reaffirmed,

---

[1] Suet., *Dom.*, 4, 11.
[2] *ILA*, 3079 (= *Aep.* 1921, 21).
[3] Suet., *Caes.*, 42, 2.
[4] *Ibid., Aug.*, 42, 3; Oros., VII, 3.
[5] Dio. Cass., LIII, 60 (=Zonar., X, 30).
[6] *Dig.*, L, 4, 18, 30; *SPAW* (1935), 968, 7.
[7] *Dig., ibid.*
[8] *Ibid.*, XXVII, 1, 6, 1.
[9] *Ibid.*, 8.

with a few slight modifications, by the Severi,[1] Gordianus,[2] Diocletian,[3] Constantine,[4] Valentinian,[5] Theodosius II,[6] and finally ratified by the Code of Justinian.[7] It must be added that on the way it lost some of its significance, as, by Caracalla's time,[8] these immunities were also granted to students, and by the time of Constantine[9] to many other professions that were considered equally valuable forms of public service.

The long list of favours granted to the educational world (8) might be construed as a sign of constant solicitude on the part of the emperors, but I am afraid that it rather tends to bring out the obvious ill-will of the municipal authorities, who objected to all these exemptions because, in bringing relief to some of their citizens, they laid heavier burdens on the rest. It is yet another sign of the breakdown of the municipal system, which had been based, it will be remembered, on the rivalry and spontaneous enthusiasm of rich "benefactors" who were delighted to be able to make generous contributions towards the general purse.

And so we find the same emperors trying to limit the number of people who could claim these exemptions. They cut out primary-school teachers,[10] technical teachers,[11] law teachers outside Rome,[12] and sometimes even philosophers.[13] Antoninus, disturbed no doubt by the growing number of eminent men who were trying to dodge the *munera* by getting themselves recognized as teachers—often merely honorary ones—fixed a maximum figure[14] and left the towns free to reduce it[15]—in a statement that incidentally gives us some idea of the number of people who may have been involved in teaching in the Greek parts of Asia in the second century. Antoninus' decision, though subsequently recognized as applying to the whole of the Empire, was originally addressed to the *koinon* of Asia only. He divided the cities into three categories, in ascending order of importance, and these are identified by the jurisconsult Modestinus as provincial capitals, places where the law courts were held, and finally the ordinary cities. These were allowed seven, six or five physicians, five, four or three rhetors, and the same number of grammarians.

The immunities that the students received from Caracalla were open to similar abuses, and this led to the severe regulations enacted by Valentinian I in 370:[16] provincial students coming to study in Rome had to obtain a permit from their native town and to be registered in Rome in the prefect's offices; the prefect checked up on them once a month, kept them under strict supervision, and could expel them and send them home if they were found guilty of repeated offences. They could not stay in Rome after they were twenty—this is pretty severe, when one thinks how customary it was in the Early Empire to spend several years on rhetoric. In Beirut the limit for law students, from Diocletian's time to Justinian's,[17] was twenty-five.

[1] *Ibid.*, 9.
[2] *Cod. Just.*, X, 53, 2.
[3] *Ibid.*, 4.
[4] *Cod. Theod.*, XIII, 3, 1-3.
[5] *Ibid.*, 10.
[6] *Ibid.*, 16-18.
[7] *Cod. Just.*, X, 53.
[8] *Frag. Vat.*, 204.
[9] *Cod. Theod.*, XIII, 4.
[10] *Dig.*, L, 4, 11, 4; 5, 2, 8.
[11] *Cod. Just.*, X, 53, 4.
[12] *Dig.*, XXVII, 1, 6, 12.
[13] *Ibid.*, I, 6, 7; 8; L, 5, 8, 4.
[14] *Ibid.*, XXVII, 1, 6, 2.
[15] *Ibid.*, 3.
[16] *Cod. Theod.*, XIV, 9, 1.
[17] *Cod. Just.*, X, 50, 1.

STATE PROFESSORSHIPS

There was another side to the emperors' educational policy. Again it was Vespasian who was "the first to establish official chairs of Greek and Latin rhetoric, for which the salary was a hundred thousand sesterces a year, to be paid by the Imperial treasury."[1] This shows remarkable initiative, even though its application was somewhat circumscribed—it only affected Rome,[2] not the whole of the Empire, and despite the emphatic plural there were probably only two such chairs, one for Greek rhetoric—mentioned several times by Philostratus (9), describing the teachers who adorned it in the course of the second century—and one for Latin rhetoric, first held by the great Quintilian.[3]

Vespasian's policy for Rome was followed in Athens by Marcus Aurelius,[4] who made a similar endowment, financed by the Imperial funds, of a chair of rhetoric and four (10) chairs of philosophy, one for each of the four great sects —the Platonists, the Aristotelians, the Epicureans and the Stoics. The first holders were chosen by Herod Atticus, one of the Emperor's old tutors; and their successors, by a committee of well-known public figures.[5] The philosophers were to receive sixty thousand sesterces a year,[6] the rhetor, forty thousand.[7] The rhetor's chair was consequently much less sought after than the one in Rome, and Philagros for example went from Athens to Rome;[8] but in the Late Empire the fame of the school at Athens spread far and wide and Prohaeresius had himself transferred from Rome to Athens.[9] And this gives a fair idea of the decline of Greek in the West.

INSTITUTIONS FOR THE SUPPORT OF NEEDY CHILDREN

The emperors of the Antonine dynasty looked after the welfare of the pupils as well as the masters. Here I can only mention briefly Trajan's creation of institutions for the support of needy children[10] (11)—foundations of a highly original type, supported by the interest received by the beneficiaries of a land-bank system and intended to provide education for a fixed number of children, both boys and girls, some legitimate, some illegitimate. Their aim was to put a stop to the economic and demographic decadence that had affected the whole country; and from certain well-known inscriptions[11] we can see how effective they were in doing this.

THE EMPEROR AS EVERGETES

Though the emperors were responsible for all these measures, they did not pretend to take over the whole business of educating and instructing the youth of their country. In the Early Empire there was no such thing as national State-controlled education: the work accomplished by these great emperors always

---

[1] Suet., *Vesp.*, 18.
[2] Zonar., XI, 17.
[3] Hieron., *Chron.*, 88p.
[4] Dio. Cass., LXXXII, 31, 3.
[5] Philstr., *VS*, II, 2, 566; Lucian, *Eun.*, 3, 8.
[6] Tat., 19
[7] Philstr., *VS*, II, 2 566.
[8] *Ibid.*, II, 8, 580.
[9] Eunap., *Proh.*, 492.
[10] Pliny, *Pan.*, 26–28; Dio. Cass., LVIII, 6.
[11] Dessau, 6509, 6675.

L

had behind it the characteristic background of Hellenistic civilization. Within their empire they behaved in rather the same way as, for propaganda purposes, the kings of Pergamus had behaved in Rhodes or Delphi—i.e. not like sovereigns whose duty it was to see that any public service was running properly, but rather as "evergetes", or private benefactors.

The fiction invented by Augustus never died out: the emperor was in theory only a *privatus cum imperio*, the first citizen in the republic, owing it to himself and to the *auctoritas* with which he was invested to set everyone an example of generosity and devotion to the public good.

And in fact the endowments that we have just described were not peculiar to the Imperial munificence. Sometimes private initiative came first. In the matter of the institutions that supported needy pupils, for instance, Trajan had had precursors as far back as Augustus' reign:[1] in 97, under Nerva, Pliny the Younger had conceived the idea—and confirmed it in his will— of leaving his native Como a legacy of five hundred thousand sesterces, the interest on it to be used to support some of the boys and girls of the city *in alimenta*.[2]

Once the example had been given from above, it was followed with alacrity, both by members of the emperor's family—like Matidia, Trajan's niece[3]—and by private individuals in Italy—in Ostia,[4] Terracina,[5] Florence:[6] and in the provinces—in Spain[7] and Africa. . . .[8]

Similarly, when the emperor started endowing professorial chairs he was still acting as an *evergetes*, either in his own city of Rome or in Athens, which every man of letters regarded as his adopted country. Suetonius looks upon the first State-endowed foundations as one aspect of Vespasian's determination to appear as a benefactor, an enlightened patron of literature and the arts.[9] Hadrian, again, is not so much a sovereign concerned with educational reform as another patron, giving pensions to famous rhetors,[10] granting favours and legal assistance to the Epicureans in Athens.[11]

Like the institutions in support of needy children, this founding of professorial chairs found imitators among private *evergetes* too. Pliny the Younger, who did so much for his beloved Como,[12] persuaded the parents of children who had to go all the way to Milan for their higher education—and perhaps their secondary-schooling too—to club together and pay for the teachers to come to Como itself.[13] He offered to pay a third of the cost himself[14]—he tells us that he would have paid it all, but that he wanted the parents to take a personal

---

[1] *Ibid.*, 977.
[2] *Ibid.*, 2927; Pliny, *Ep.*, I, 8, 10; VIII, 18, 2.
[3] Fronto, *Amic.*, I, 14.
[4] *CIL*, XIV, 350.
[5] Dessau, 6278.
[6] *CIL*, XI, 1602.
[7] *Ibid.*, II, 1172.
[8] *Ibid.*, VIII, 960; Dessau, 6818.
[9] Suet., *Vesp.*, 17–18.
[10] Philstr., *VS*, I, 25, 532–533; I, 22, 524; S.H.A., *Hadr.*, 16, 10–11.
[11] *IG*², II, 1099; Dessau, 7784.
[12] Dessau, 2927; *CIL*, V, 5263, 5279, 5667, 5272.
[13] Pliny, *Ep.*, IV, 13, 1 *seq.*
[14] *Ibid.*, 5.

interest in the scheme,[1] and also he did not want it to look as though he was trying to curry favour with his fellow-citizens; "which is what happens," he writes, "whenever teachers are engaged by a city on those terms."[2]

This throws an interesting sidelight on the state of affairs: we see that in spite of the disintegration of the municipal system in other respects, the great days of private munificence, with all their pomp and self-interest, were still going on, and this act of Pliny's in Como repeats the gesture made three centuries earlier by Polythrous in Teos and Eudemus in Miletus.

MUNICIPAL SCHOOLS

But there is more to be got out of this remark. Pliny's actual words are, "*Multis in locis . . . in quibus praeceptores publice conducuntur.*" This means that in his day there were "many cities that had municipal schools". There is a good deal of evidence, indeed, that there were grammarians[3] and rhetors[4] holding municipal chairs—though it is not always clear whether they were financed out of the city funds or privately.

This is true not only of the Latin West but of Greek-speaking regions too.[5] Athens for instance had not waited for Marcus Aurelius: it had instituted a municipal chair of eloquence when Antoninus was emperor, its first occupant being Lollianus of Ephesus[6] (12).

There was a general tendency in the same direction, in fact. It had begun in the Hellenistic age, and it continued under the Roman Empire. People had developed such a lively interest in education that every important city felt increasingly that it should have its own schools, and staff them and maintain them and keep an eye on them at the public expense.

This development seems to have reached its climax in the Christian Empire. In the fourth century we keep coming across these schools more or less everywhere—*schola publica*[7] (or *municipalis*)[8]—in Greek, πολιτικὸς θρόνος[9]— maintained (though not always quite regularly) at the city's expense—*salario publico*.[10] Ausonius mentions them as existing in Gaul, in Lyons, Besançon,[11] and, apparently, Toulouse;[12] St. Augustine mentions them in Carthage[13] and Milan,[14] Libanius in Constantinople,[15] Nicomedia, Nicea,[16] and of course Antioch in the East (13). It can be assumed that by this time every city of the least importance had undertaken to provide one or more teachers at its own expense.

PERSISTENCE OF PRIVATE INSTRUCTION

Not that all education became public. Private teaching still went on, recognized by law,[17] even in cities like Rome, Athens and Constantinople,[18] where

[1] *Ibid.*, 8.
[2] *Ibid.*, 6.
[3] *CIL*, II, 2892.
[4] Gell., XIX, 9, 2; Juv., XV, 112.
[5] Cf. Philstr., *VS*, I, 21, 516.
[6] *Ibid.*, I, 23, 526.
[7] August., *Conf.*, VI, 7 (11).
[8] Auson., *Grat. Act.*, 7, 31.
[9] Philstr., *VS*, II, 20, 600.
[10] August., *De Civ. D.*, I, 3.
[11] Auson., *Grat. Act.*, VII, 31.
[12] *Ibid.*, *Prof. Burd.*, 17, 7.
[13] August., *Conf.*, VI, 7 (11).
[14] *Ibid.*, V, 13 (33).
[15] Lib., *Or.*, I, 35.
[16] *Ibid.*, 48.
[17] *Cod. Theod.*, XIV, 9, 3.
[18] August., *Conf.*, V, 12, (22).

there were official chairs[1]—and as this kind of teaching was a matter of free competition, and very keen competition too, it tended to keep even the best teachers rather too short of money for comfort.[2]

There are some curious bits of evidence about the highly picturesque methods adopted by teachers in fourth-century Athens. The disciples of one master locked up newly arrived "freshers" and forced them to enrol in their school.[3] A ship's captain discharged, in the middle of the night,[4] a whole shipload of Asiatic students into the house of a rhetor who was a friend of his.

MODES OF NOMINATION

The municipal teachers were chosen by the city council—the *ordo*—and so could be dismissed by it—a logical consequence of which Gordianus[5] made use. The law[6]—probably introduced by Marcus Aurelius[7]—encouraged competition by way of examinations: in the final form[8] it assumed under Julian the Apostate in 362[9] the candidates had to submit a specimen of their work—*probatio*—to a board of city notables—*optimorum conspirante consensu*.

There was naturally plenty of competition for the Athens chair, and not only competition but intrigues, plots and disturbances, in which the students really came into their own.[10] Other cities had more difficulty in finding candidates: Milan had to write to the Roman prefect—Symmachus, the orator—for a teacher of rhetoric, and St. Augustine, who was teaching privately at the time, got himself introduced to Symmachus, submitted one of his own discourses to him, and so had his name sent to the people in Milan.[11]

INTERVENTION OF THE IMPERIAL POWER

It is possible that even as far back as Antoninus, the emperor had made some effort to encourage municipal authorities to open schools and fix the rates of teachers' wages, but the only evidence we have about this is the highly suspect *Historia Augusta*,[12] and it is quite likely that its authors were simply reading current practice back into the past.

Intervention by the emperors only became common in the Late Empire. Hellenistic civilization had had its day, and the liberal State, which had to keep centralization down to a minimum and give each city as much responsibility as possible, was finished. The State's hold on the cities became much tighter, their autonomy more precarious daily. The emperor, embodying the general

---

[1] Lib., *Or.*, I, 37.
[2] *Ibid.*, *Or.*, XXXI.
[3] Eunap., *V.L.*, 495; Lib., *Or.*, I, 16, 19; Greg. Naz., *Or.*, XLIII, 15, 3 *seq.*
[4] Eunap., *Proh.*, 485.
[5] *Cod. Just.*, X, 53, 2.
[6] Eunap., *Proh.*, 487.
[7] Philstr., *VS*, II, 2, 566; cf. Lucian, *Eun.*, 3, 8.
[8] Cf. *Cod. Just.*, X, 53, 7.
[9] *Cod. Theod.*, XIII, 3, 5.
[10] Eunap., *Proh.*, 487–488.
[11] August., *Conf.*, 13 (33).
[12] S.H.A., *Ant.*, 12, 3; *Alex. Sev.*, 44, 4–5.

interest, was obliged to intervene to make sure that a form of social service as important as education was functioning properly.

Nominations to teaching posts were no longer left to the municipalities. In Athens the proconsul, representing the emperor, often intervened to settle disputed elections,[1] change the teachers,[2] or suggest his own nominations.[3] The emperor himself kept a close watch on who was chosen, and sometimes took action himself. In 297 Constantius Chlorus sent a high official of his court in Trèves, the rhetor Eumenes,[4] to restore the schools in Autun. Constantius summoned the distinguished Sophist Prohaeresius to Trèves, and then transferred him to Rome before he would allow him to return, loaded with honours, to Athens.[5] Constantius II gave the Senate of "New Rome" a list of several teachers of eloquence and philosophy to choose from; among them were the rhetor Libanius and the philosopher Themistius,[6] and Libanius had to get his permission to leave Constantinople before he could go to Antioch.[7]

Julian made this kind of intervention the general rule: he decided that no one should be allowed to teach until he had been approved by the municipal council and had this properly confirmed by the emperor[8]—who thus assumed the right to inspect all the education in the Empire (14). As we shall see in the following chapter, this decision was part of a whole religious policy, but even when its anti-Christian sting was removed it still remained in force under Julian's successors, as its insertion in the Theodosian Code bears witness: it was not until Justinian came along that the need for the emperor's sanction was abolished as unnecessary.[9]

The emperor also intervened in municipal affairs to remind cities of their duties. A law of Gratian's in 376, probably inspired by Ausonius (15), informed all the big cities that they were supposed to get the best rhetors and grammarians they could for their young people. The emperor did not wish to deprive them of their right to choose their "noble teachers", but he fixed the scale of their salaries—twenty-four annonae for the rhetors and twelve for Latin and Greek grammarians, to be paid out of the city's funds. The capital, Trèves, had these figures increased to thirty for the rhetor and twenty for the Latin grammarian; his Greek colleague—if anyone could be found fit for the post—was to be satisfied with twelve.[10]

THE CONSTANTINOPLE UNIVERSITY

This policy of active intervention reached its climax in the famous constitution of February 27th, 425, by which Theodosius II founded a State University in Constantinople that had a complete monopoly of the city's higher education, only private tutoring remaining free.[11] Its professors were forbidden to give private lessons and had to lecture in rooms arranged in exedra form on the north side of

[1] Eunap., *Proh.*, 488.
[2] Lib., *Or.*, I, 25.
[3] *Ibid.*, 82.
[4] *Pan. Lat.*, IV, 14, 15, 17.
[5] Eunap., *Proh.*, 492.
[6] Lib., *Or.*, I, 25, 37, 74; Them., *Or.*, II.
[7] Lib., *Or.*, I, 94–95.
[8] *Cod. Theod.*, XIII, 3, 5.
[9] *Cod. Just.*, X, 53, 7.
[10] *Cod. Theod.*, XIII, 3, 11.
[11] *Ibid.*, XIV, 9, 3.

Capitol Square.[1] There were three rhetors and ten grammarians for Latin, five rhetors and ten grammarians for Greek, one professor of philosophy and two professors of law[2] (16).

The fragments of this Constitution that found their way into the Codes give no indication of material conditions, but there must have been some desire to honour the teaching body, because a decision was taken on March 15th of the same year 425 conferring the honorary title *comes primi ordinis* on teachers who had completed twenty years' service and given every satisfaction.[3]

HONOURS CONFERRED ON TEACHERS

There was nothing new in this: the emperors often conferred high honours on members of the teaching profession. And here again it is the Flavians who must be given the credit for taking the first step: Domitian was the first to confer consular rank upon a rhetor—Quintilian.[4]

This, it is true, was mainly as a reward for bringing up Domitian's nephews and adopted sons. The same kind of service, rather than their work in the university sphere, led to Fronto and Herod Atticus receiving the consulate in the second century, and two rhetors from Toulouse were honoured in the fourth century for being tutors to Constantine's son and his two nephews.[5] Then there was the well-known case of Ausonius, who was summoned from Bordeaux to Trèves by Valentinian and received from his pupil, the young Emperor Gratian, the highest honours in the Empire—the consulate and prefecture of the praetorium of the Gauls, not to speak of those he obtained for his father, son and son-in-law: indeed, there was a time in the years 378–80 when the whole of the West was governed by the family of this Aquitainian rhetor. The political advancement made by Themistius, on the other hand, was entirely a result of his public teaching: he was made a senator[6] and then archon-proconsul of Constantinople[7] by Constantius II long before Valens, and later Theodosius thought of entrusting him with the education of a prince of the Empire.[8]

Thus in the Late Empire we find the emperors' interest in education becoming more direct, more active and more effective. This was the result of something much more than the general development of State control over all manifestations of public activity; it was the result of a personal concern and genuine interest (17).

PRESTIGE OF CLASSICAL CULTURE IN THE LATE EMPIRE

People have sometimes thought it surprising that schools should have grown more important and teachers developed greater authority when the old culture was sinking deeper and deeper into barbarism.

---

[1] *Ibid.*, XV, 1, 53.
[2] *Ibid.*, XIV, 9, 3 (=*Cod. Just.*, XI, 19, 1).
[3] *Ibid.*, VI, 21, 1.
[4] Auson., *Grat. Act.*, 7, 31; cf. Juv., VII, 198.
[5] Auson., *Prof. Burd.*, 16, 13–15; 7, 9–13.
[6] Them., *Or.*, II.
[7] Lib., *Ep.*, 40.
[8] Them., *Or.*, VIII, 120 A; IX, 123 C; 126 D.

But the concept of decadence is one that needs careful treatment, and in any case merely represents the judgment of later generations. The people who lived under the Late Empire certainly did not think of themselves as the exponents of a culture that was on the way to extinction. They were Romans, servants of an eternal city, and the Empire mobilized all its energies to surmount the internal and external crises that beset it, with the feeling that it was fulfilling its historic mission—to preserve civilization and culture in the face of the barbarians; and their culture came more and more to mean the classical literary tradition.

This essentially aristocratic culture was the special prerogative of the senatorial class of great landed proprietors, and it is remarkable how the delight in the things of the mind and the classical tradition generally remained alive in them, persisting in spite of all the profound changes that took place in the social and economic structure: after each storm, after crises and revolutions that decimated their numbers, this class always revived, and the newly-rich did not rest until they had assimilated the intellectual traditions of which their predecessors had been so proud. It was in vain that the *clarissimi* left the cities at the end of the third century and tried to settle down on their country estates in the *villae*, their country houses which soon became true castles (18); they remained men of letters and intellectuals. The Gallo-Roman aristocracy, as they appear in the pages of Sidonius Apollinaris, who was writing in the fifth century, when Gaul was almost in the hands of the barbarians, was as cultured as Italian aristocracy in Pliny the Younger's day (19).

It mattered little that from the third century onwards the emperor himself did not usually belong to this class. All these self-made men and soldiers of fortune, however humble or vulgar their origin, were as keen as the aristocrats themselves to promote classical culture: they had an inferiority complex about it, not the hatred that modern apostles of "class-consciousness" would anachronistically saddle them with—one only has to think of the highbrow education that they gave their children. It was "the last of the great Pannonians", Valentinian I, who called upon Ausonius to act as tutor to his son Gratian.

The same feeling was shared by the barbarian *condottieri* who, from the end of the fourth century onwards, acted as mayors of the palace to the decadent emperors of the West. The Franks Richomer and Arbogast conferred the purple on a former rhetor called Eugenius; the Vandal Stilicho had his daughter Maria educated in the most polished way imaginable as though she were a Hellenistic princess, and then married her off to his master and protégé, Honorius;[1] Alaric was patron to Attalus, Theodoric II to Avitus, both representatives of the cultured class, aristocratic senators.

The fact was that though they had tried to proletarianize and then barbarize the army, it still remained the Roman army. Whether the emperor or someone else was in power, his first aim was always to serve and preserve the Roman Empire, the Roman idea; and this, I repeat, was inseparable from the old classical ideal of a culture based on great literature.

Never had this ideal been more profoundly venerated than in these latter days. In the minds of the last of the pagans it took on a mystical flavour, and the classics

[1] Claud., *Fesc.*, 232 *seq.*

became even more important than neo-Platonism as the old religion's last line of defence against the invasion of Christianity. What an inspired prophet Virgil seemed to the intellectuals grouped around Macrobius! (20). When Anatolius, the prefect of the praetorium and a fervent pagan, arrived in Athens in the course of his pilgrimage through Greece between 357 and 360, he was as much concerned with organizing a debating match as with offering sacrifices and visiting the temples.[1] And the Christians too, as we shall see in the following chapter, were equally attached to the classical traditions as forming a bond between all mankind.

Is it surprising then that schools should have had such an important position in the State? Roman culture, which was an offshoot of later Hellenism, had always had an "academic" tinge, and this became more marked as time went on. The fact that the aristocracy was so unstable, always being decimated and re-constituted, tended to lessen the importance of the family tradition, and most of the work of preservation fell on the schools as guardians of tradition, and on books as ennobling influences. More than ever, classical education was regarded as the embodiment of the ideal of perfect humanity.

It was only natural that the State, the emperor, should become the patron of literature. This idea was magnificently expressed in 297 by the rhetor Eumenes when the schools in Autun had been restored. He is congratulating Constantius Chlorus on having, like his colleagues in the Tetrarchy, shown such favour to literature, and the fact is, he says, "that he has had the gift to see that the art of elegant speech, which is the art of elegant deeds, comes under the care and fore-sight of His Majesty; the divine intelligence of his undying mind enables him to understand that literature is the foundation of all the virtues."[2]

You may say that this is simply a rhetor's sales-talk. But the legislators said the same. Constantius II and Julian kept "the distinguished order of the *decuriae*" of the city of Rome for educated men who could appreciate literature and eloquence, "for," they said, "it is necessary to reward literary culture, the first of all virtues"—*litteratura quae omnium virtutum maxima est.* . . .[3]

SCHOOLS AND THE RECRUITMENT OF OFFICIALS

Their enthusiasm was not, however, wholly disinterested. In the Late Empire, the State rested on a double foundation—the army, and the civil administration, which was an absolute rabbit-warren of different departments and offices. Since Diocletian the Roman State had been a bureaucratic monarchy, run on the same lines as the old oriental monarchies—government by scribes.

Thus the schools had the practical task of training a competent body of administrators and State servants. There can be no doubt that the fourth-century emperors had this in mind when they were producing their beneficent laws on education.

We have seen how in 370 Valentinian put students in Rome under the strict control of the city prefect.[4] This prefect not only had to keep the students quiet

[1] Eunap., *Proh.*, 491.   [3] *Cod. Theod.*, XIV, 1, 1.
[2] *Pan. Lat.*, IV, 8; 14.   [4] *Ibid.*, XIV, 9, 1.

and see that they did not dodge the responsibilities that were awaiting them at home; he had each year to draw up for the emperor a list of the outstanding students, so that they could have proper places found for them in the administrative services.

The Autun panegyrists insist on the wonderful future awaiting their rhetoricians —in the law courts, the treasury, provincial governments, as heads of ministries (*palatii magisteria*).[1] The same idea was present everywhere: Ausonius encouraged his grandson to study by showing him how eloquence had led his own relatives to the highest positions in the State.[2] Symmachus praised literature as the way to the various magistracies.[3] In Antioch St. John Chrysostom described ambitious parents forcing their children to go in for literature so as to get into the Imperial service.[4]

These were not vain promises or illusory hopes: we see in fact that, apart from a few exceptions, the Imperial government reserved all the highest administrative posts for "old boys".

I used the phrase, "a competent body". This needs explaining. The natural thing to think of is technical competence, acquired in law schools or at the bar. As in the Early Empire, the bar was one of the best careers that an educated man could take up, and it often led on to some administrative post. There was the poet Prudentius, for instance. He was born in 348, and after studying rhetoric[5] became a barrister, then governor of two different provinces and finally a high Court official.[6] And this was normal: a Constitution passed by Theodosius II and re-enacted by Justinian[7] shows that it was usual for provincial governors— whose functions, as we know, had become mainly judicial—to be chosen from amongst distinguished barristers.

But this was not all. What is surprising is to find the key positions being offered quite regularly to men who had never had any legal or administrative training at all, rhetors with a mere gift for words—or, if you prefer, for literature. Once again, there was Ausonius. Knowing as we do his mental limitations and the gaps in his culture, it comes as something of a surprise to find his pupil Gratian entrusting him with such a responsible position as that of prefect of the praetorium. And he was not the only one: one of his colleagues, the rhetor Exuperius of Toulouse, had pupils who became emperors, and they chose him to be a *praeses*, a provincial governor in Spain.[8] When St. Augustine was a rhetor in Milan he had hopes of the same sort of advancement: he describes himself shortly before his conversion haunting the waiting-rooms of the various ministries day after day when he had finished his day's work, hoping to get some such post as *praeses* through influence—which he was careful to foster.[9]

Is all this to be deplored as the blindness of a decadent society desperately clinging to the old values that were supposed to be possessed by formal rhetoric? Did the Empire simply hand over control to incompetent windbags? It would not show much historical sense to think so, for the truth is that the Late Empire

[1] *Pan. Lat.*, IV, 5; 6; VII, 23.
[2] Auson., *Protr.*, 43–44.
[3] Symm., *Ep.*, I, 25.
[4] Chrys., *Adv. Opp.*, III, 12, 369; 13, 371.
[5] Prud., *Cath.*, pr. 8–9.
[6] *Ibid.*, 13–21.
[7] *Cod. Just.*, II, 7, 9.
[8] Auson., *Prof. Burd.*, 17, 13.
[9] August., *Conf.*, VI, 11 (18–19).

was in perfect line with the classical tradition, and when we read Eumenes or Julian we seem to hear the voice of old Isocrates again, sounding over a distance of six or seven centuries in praise of the Logos and saying that the art of rhetoric teaches men not only to write properly, but to think properly and to act properly. The traditional education had always aimed at producing mental clarity and mental agility: anyone could learn to be practical. And even in its disdain for technical ability the Later Empire remained entirely traditional (21).

THE TEACHING OF SHORTHAND

Nevertheless, on a lower level a new kind of technical teaching did develop, and in this case too the moving force was administrative need. I am speaking of shorthand—*notae, ταχυγραφία, σημεῖα* (22).

Some kind of shorthand was already in existence, going back perhaps to the fourth century B.C.,[1] but it did not really appear in all its fullness until Cicero's time.[2] Its invention has often been attributed to his freedman Tiro, but it is difficult in the present state of our knowledge to decide whether he invented an entirely new system or whether the *notae Tironianae* are simply his own adaptation into Latin of a Greek system already in existence. Whatever the truth about this may be, there is no doubt that under the Empire two closely related systems were being used together, one in Greek, the other in Latin.

Quite early on, the Emperor Titus had been able to write as fast as his secretaries.[3] A papyrus from Oxyrhynchus dating from the year 155 tells us of a young slave whom his master put under a shorthand teacher—*σημειογράφος*: the teacher undertook to teach the boy in two years, in return for payment spread over three terms.[4]

But the art—and consequently the teaching of the art—only became really common in the Late Empire. *Notarii*—secretaries expert in the art of the *notae* —were indispensable to the administrative system, accompanying magistrates and other high officials wherever they went.[5] They were particularly important in the central offices. From being at first responsible merely for the minutes of meetings of the consistory, the emperor's notaries gradually, from the middle of the fourth century onwards, became entrusted with missions to the provinces as commissioners invested with extraordinary powers, and were grouped with the higher officials—*tribuni et notarii*.

Shorthand spread from the civil service and passed into general use. Ausonius had a shorthand secretary to take down his works.[6] The Christian Church began to do the same: the reason why so many of the sermons composed by the Fathers of the Church in the fourth and fifth centuries have come down to us is that shorthand secretaries used to sit in the basilica at the feet of the bishop and take down his words as he delivered his homily during the service.

There were so many people wanting to learn the new art that poor parents would do all they could to get their sons training in it, so that they could be sure

[1] D.L., II, 48.
[2] Plut., *Cat. Mai.*, 23.
[3] Suet., *Tit.*, 3, 3.
[4] *POxy.*, 724.
[5] Eunap., *Proh.*, 489.
[6] Auson., *Ephem.*, 7.

of having well-paid work. Even in some remote spot in Upper Egypt a teacher had only to open a school and advertise that he could teach shorthand as well as literature and the people would come flocking to him.[1] Libanius, who did not much like competition, says that in the end parents came to attach more importance to the shorthand than the literature.[2]

The fact was that it meant a safe job and good prospects. Theoretically all the best posts went to the men who had studied under a rhetor, but with an absolute monarch whose favour was law, more than one secretary had reached the highest office, not excepting the prefecture of the praetorium.[3] The same advance could be made in the Church: Eunomius, the great champion of neo-Arianism, was a peasant's son who took up shorthand so that he could get away from the land. He then became secretary to the Arian bishop Acacius—and that was his first step on the ladder.[4]

Thus the education of the Late Empire assumed its final form. Was I mistaken when at the beginning of this history I suggested that the old education was to develop into a culture dominated by scribes?

[1] Theod., *H.E.*, IV, 18, 8 *seq.*
[2] Lib., *Or.*, XXXI, 28; 33.
[3] *Ibid.*, LXII, 51.
[4] Greg. Nys., *C. Eun.*, I, 50.

CHAPTER IX

CHRISTIANITY AND CLASSICAL EDUCATION

THE expression "Christian education"—*ἐν Χριστῷ παιδεία*—was first used in about A.D. 96 by St. Clement of Rome.[1] Before that date St. Paul had been concerned with the way parents should bring up their children.[2] This has in fact always been one of Christianity's main preoccupations.

RELIGIOUS EDUCATION

When we speak of "Christian education" today we usually mean that the child should be brought up in a Christian atmosphere—especially at school. We must remember that the Christians of the early Church meant something much more precise and much deeper by the phrase, something essentially religious. They meant, on the one hand, learning the dogmas—the truths necessary for salvation; and, on the other, moral training—the laws of Christian behaviour. The reader recognises here the scheme on which St. Paul's Epistles were built up, and this scheme was adopted by the whole of the primitive Church. Christian education, in the sacred, transcendent meaning of the word, could not be given at school like any other kind of education, but only in and through the Church on the one hand and the family on the other.

This Christian education of children, through which they learnt to share in the treasury of the faith, to submit to a healthy discipline in the matter of morals, was the parents' fundamental duty. There was more in this than was contained in the Roman tradition; it was essentially a continuation of the Jewish tradition, which emphasised the importance of the family in the development of religious consciousness.[3] And this duty could not be delegated: the early Church would have had sharp words to say about "Christian" parents of today who think that they have done all that is required of them when they have passed their children over to a teacher or an institution.

The natural environment for the development of the Christian soul was the Christian family. As the mainspring of all education is imitation, the most important thing was a good example, but this did not mean that there should be no specifically religious teaching. An essay by St. John Chrysostom, unjustifiably neglected, has some very sound advice "on the way that parents should bring up their children"[4] (1). The obligation of providing a Christian training falls upon the parents—on the father for the boys,[5] and on the mother for the girls.[6] The children should be taught religious history—all the excellent stories about Cain[7] and Abel, and Jacob and Esau,[8] for instance—

[1] Clem. Rom., I Cor. 21, 8; 6 cf. 62, 3.
[2] Eph. vi, 4; Col. iii, 21.
[3] Deut. vi, 2; 7; 20.
[4] Chrys., *Inan. glor.*, 19 seq.
[5] *Ibid.*, 32, 1.
[6] *Ibid.*, 90, 1.
[7] *Ibid.*, 39, 5, seq.
[8] *Ibid.*, 43, 5 seq.

in a homely way, so that their interest is aroused. "When the child really knows the story, wait a few days and then one evening say to him, 'Tell me the story of the two brothers.' And if he begins to tell you about Cain and Abel, stop him and say, 'No, I don't mean that one, I mean the one about the other two brothers, the ones whose father gave a blessing.' Then remind him of a few important little details, without mentioning the brothers' names. When he has told you the whole story properly, go on to the next part. . . ."[1]

Thus the family[2] had a very important part to play in the matter of education. Even more important, however, was the doctrinal teaching given by the Church to the neophyte before he was admitted to baptism. In its form, Christianity is a mystery religion. This is not very clear nowadays because there is still a great deal of mediaeval Christianity left in our paganized world—our churches are open and anyone can go in, people who have never been baptized can be present at the mystery of the Eucharist—but it was very marked in the early days of Christianity (2).

It was the Church herself who, through the medium of a delegate specially appointed for the purpose, instructed her catechumens. The earliest Christian generations had "teachers"—διδάσκαλοι[3] (3)—whose work it was to do this teaching and who had received a special charism. The catechumen system developed gradually as new converts came in, and achieved its final form in Rome in about 180 (4). In this form it involved a long probationary period lasting three years, during which a carefully graded course of instruction was given. This soon seems to have been taken from the specialised *didascali* and handed over to the priests, with the bishop himself having the last word. The courses of instruction that have come down to us from St. Gregory of Nyssa, Cyril of Jerusalem, Theodore of Mopsuestia and others, show that the great bishops of the fourth century attained a remarkably high standard of teaching. St. Augustine, again, in his treatise *De catechizandis rudibus*, written in about 405, produced a theory of "how to begin religious instruction" that was studied for centuries because of the excellence of its method. But this tract, addressed to a mere deacon, Deogratias, cannot be put in the same category as the *Catecheses* of Cyril or Theodore, which were instructions from the bishop himself and aimed at the preparation of candidates for baptism. For such homilies addressed to *competentes* see, among the sermons of St. Augustine, *Serm.* 56–59, 212–216, 363, and *Denis* 8.

Religious training did not end with baptism, of course; in a sense it went on through the whole of life, getting deeper and deeper all the time—witness the importance of readings and preaching in the Church's liturgy.

CHRISTIANITY AN INTELLECTUAL RELIGION

But though Christian education in the strict sense was not the school's concern, the Church could not afford to ignore the schools. If the Christian

---

[1] *Ibid.*, 45, 1–2.
[2] *Ibid.*, 79, 3, 80, 1.
[3] Acts, xiii, 1; I Cor., xii, 28; Eph., iv, 11; *Didache*, 13, 2; 15, 2; Barn., I, 8; 4, 9; Hermas, *Vis.*, III, 5, 1; *Sim.*, IX, 15, 4.

religion was to persist and spread, if it was to continue its teaching activity, or even merely to preserve its form of worship, there was an absolute minimum of literary culture that it could not do without. Christianity is an intellectual religion and cannot exist in a context of barbarism.

In the first place, as Moslems say, it was a religion of the Book, based on a written Revelation—the holy books of the religion of Israel, which it took and claimed as its own, and the books of the New Testament, which were added later as they were composed and recognized as canonical—Γραφή. The Biblical character of the Church's prayers, and the importance of readings from Scripture, made it essential that the Book should always be there on the spot: the wandering Arabs of the Syrian *limes* or frontier had not always an altar amongst their camp equipment; they stood the chalice on the open Gospels.[1] And as time went on, the value of the written word in the daily life of the Church increased: "tradition"—παράδοσις—was constantly growing (5), and it meant not merely a collection of doctrines and explanations and customs handed down by word of mouth, but a whole literature that was soon very rich and varied. There were the disciplinary rules and regulations—everything that later became known as canon law, whose origins go back well beyond the great Councils to the beginning of the second century with the Διδαχή or *Doctrine of the Twelve Apostles*: and the spiritual literature—apologetics, and, after the rise of the heresies, polemics, and the dogmatic theology of the Church.

Thus the most immediate practical necessities and the highest flights of religious thought combined to demand of Christians the kind of culture—and consequently of education—in which the literary side was all-important. One would therefore have expected the early Christians, who were adamant in their determination to break with a pagan world that they were constantly upbraiding for its errors and defects, to develop their own religious type of school as something quite separate from the classical pagan school. But this, surprisingly, they did not do—not, at least, in Graeco-Roman times.

There would have been no great difficulty about creating a religious education with the Bible as its centre. The Christians had something of the sort under their very eyes, in the Jewish schools which had just managed to organize themselves properly under the Empire.

THE RABBINICAL SCHOOL

After the Dispersion, and particularly after the destruction of the Temple, the religious life of Israel became entirely a matter of practising the revealed Law, the *Torah*,[2] and it therefore meant knowing the Law inside out. Now this was a written Law—even the oral tradition that had originally reinforced it and interpreted it was written down and codified in the second century; and thus Jewish religious education was based entirely on the sacred texts. This meant, in the first place, studying the sacred tongue—in the first centuries of the Christian era the Greek Bible was abandoned (6), and Hebrew became the only language in which the Law could be studied.

[1] Bar Hebr., *Nomocan.*, I, 4. [2] Cf. Joseph., *Ap.*, I, 12; II, 19.

The Law ordered that education should be carried on in the family,[1] but a system of communal teaching in organized schools was added to this or took its place. This system reached its full development in the Late Empire, when it was made up of three stages—first, Bible-reading; secondly, the study of the *Mishna*; thirdly, the *Talmud*.[2] The *Mishna* and the *Talmud* were commentaries on the Bible, a mixture of law and exegesis that gradually got more and more complicated and difficult (7).

Schools were set up everywhere.[3] The "house of instruction"—*bêt hami-drâsch*—or the "house of the book"—*bêt sêfer*—existed side by side with the synagogue, the house of prayer—προσευχή; together they were the soul of any Jewish community. "As long as the voice of Jacob is heard in the synagogues and the schools, the hands of Esau [i.e. the persecutor, the Empire] will not prevail."[4] They were the object of loving care; even in the elementary school the teacher was respected, for he was ennobled by the glory of the divine word he could disclose to the child. "A teacher should be venerated as much as God Himself," says the *Talmud*.[5]

CHRISTIAN SCHOOLS IN BARBARIAN LANDS

Except that for Christians there was no sacred language—the Scriptures having from very early times been translated into every language—the same causes might have led Christians to create religious schools on a similar pattern —indeed they did do this whenever the Church was set up in a "barbarian" land, i.e. one that had not assimilated classical culture.

In Egypt, in Syria, in Mesopotamia, Christianity brought new life into Egyptian and Aramaic, which had had no cultural value since Alexander's time. It led to the development of a literature, and thence a system of education, in Coptic and Syriac, both closely bound up with the requirements of the religious life (8).

Further, in countries which had previously had no written culture, Christianity gave birth to a national culture, a national literature, and above all a national script, all for its own purposes. It was primarily so that he could translate the Bible, the source of Christian life, that Frumentius—or his earliest associates—in the fourth to the fifth centuries raised Ethiopian to the level of a written language. Mesrob is traditionally supposed to have done the same for Armenian and Georgian, Qardutsat of Arran probably for Hunnish, Ulfilas, as we know, for the Germanic, and much later, in the ninth century, Cyril and Methodius for the Slav languages. In each case the education was essentially religious from the very beginning.

But, I repeat, there was nothing like this in the original Graeco-Latin cultural area. Never throughout the whole of antiquity, except for a few particular cases, did the Christians set up their own special schools. They simply added their own specifically religious kind of training—which, as we

---

[1] Deut. vi, 2; 7; 20.　　　　　[3] B. Bathra, 21a.
[2] Aboth, 6, 5.　　　　　　　　[4] Pesikta, 121a.
　　　　　　　[5] Aboth, 4, 15.

have seen, came from the Church and the family—on to the classical teaching
that they received along with their non-Christian fellows in the established
schools.

CHRISTIANITY AND CLASSICAL CULTURE

This may seem surprising to us today. We expect a Christian Church to
claim the right to its own schools as an immediate corollary of the Faith. But
it is a fact worth remembering, for it meant that from very early times a connection was established between classicism and Christianity—a connection that
the historian knows to have been very enduring. Theologians sometimes objected to it and denounced any collusion with Hellenism as an infidelity, an
adulteration of the pure essence of primitive Christianity; but whether it is
deplorable or providential the fact is clear: Christianity was born in Hellenistic
Palestine and developed in the midst of Graeco-Roman civilization—and it was
everlastingly affected by it. Even when the Gospel is preached to the Chinese
or the Bantus it is impossible to forget that it was first written in Greek. This is
as inescapable as the fact that Buddhism made its first appearance in India or
that the Koran was first written in Arabic.

Nothing shows the extent of the synthesis achieved in four centuries of
Christianity and Hellenism better than the Christian cultures that sprang up
in barbarian lands. They did not come brand-new into being, from the data
of revelation alone; technically they were simply an adaptation to the local
linguistic medium of Greek Christian culture, itself already thoroughly per-
meated with classical elements.

One has only to open a Coptic book to see what an extraordinary number of
Greek words were introduced into the language used by the Egyptian Christians.
In fact, until the Arab invasion the Coptic schools were bilingual, Greek being
learnt along with the national language.[1] The same is true of Syriac culture.
This, it must be admitted, was very Semitic, not only in expression but in its
spirit: in their form, the Syriac schools were less like the Hellenistic than
the Mohammedan schools—which, incidentally, they very probably helped to
shape. But Syriac culture drew its inspiration from the Greek tradition,
especially from Antioch: the leading spirit of the Nestorian schools was Theodore of Mopsuestia. And through the Fathers of the Greek Church the whole
classical educational tradition made its way into these remote provinces. We
have already come across the extraordinary fact that Dionysius Thrax's grammar, upon which the Hellenistic school was based, was translated word for
word into languages as different from Greek as Armenian and Syriac.

But we must not merely feel surprised: we must try to understand how it is
that Mediterranean Christianity managed to get on so well with the pagan
school. And in the first place it may be observed that Christianity is first and
foremost a religion, something that determines the relationship between God
and man, not essentially, or primarily, a cultural ideal, a way of managing life
on this earth. And though no doubt any profound doctrine about human

[1] O. Lond. Hall, 14222.

beings and human existence gradually, by a natural repercussion, tends to bring out the practical consequences that are implied by its principles, and thus to react on civilization, this is a long process lasting many centuries. The early generations of Christians had not worked out any specifically Christian form of education, any more than they had worked out a Christian system of politics. They put first things first, and they laid the rock-bottom foundations of any Christian civilization to come: a system of dogma, a system of morals, canonical discipline, and the liturgy.

But that is not all. Even a religion that is the prototype of all revolutionary movements whose ultimate aim is some sort of totalitarianism cannot escape the influence—which is all the deeper, the more unconscious it is—of the civilization it grows up in. This is a widespread phenomenon which I have elsewhere suggested might be called "cultural osmosis" (9). The current civilization is like a life-giving fluid, surrounding men and human institutions and permeating them even when they are unaware of it, even against their will.

The Christian adoption of Greek and Latin schools is a remarkable example of this kind of osmosis. Precisely because they were living in a classical world, the Christians of the early centuries accepted the fundamental category of Hellenistic humanism as "natural" and self-evident—the view of man as an unconditioned source of value existing before any particular specification took place in him. It might be said (10) that before one can be a Christian one must first be a man, mature enough on the purely human level to be able to perform an act of faith and acts of morality. It is a fact established by history and by ethnography that Christianity requires a minimum of civilization as a condition of its existence. So, if classical education had developed its own admirable technique for producing a perfectly developed type of human being, what point was there in looking elsewhere for some other kind of education? However that may be, the moment arrives when on to the fully human being it becomes necessary to graft the purely religious shoot of a supernatural Gift. In some way the unchanging technique of classical humanism made it marvellously apt for having the golden branch of the order of grace grafted on to it. A man educated according to classical standards could become an orator or a philosopher, whichever he liked; he could choose the life of action or the life of contemplation. He was now offered a further choice, with the announcement of Good Tidings: besides these things he could now lay himself open to grace, to faith, could receive the sacrament of baptism, could become a Christian.

CHRISTIAN OPPOSITION TO CLASSICAL CULTURE

In practice this involved a certain amount of difficulty. I must here draw attention to an important distinction. Adopting the classical system of education did not mean accepting the culture it subserved.

There was a profound gulf between this culture and Christianity. This was caused, not so much by the long symbiosis that bound classical literature and classical art to the old polytheism, as by the fact that the whole trend of this humanistic culture was to set itself up as a rival to the new religion, for it too in its own way claimed to solve the problem of human existence. This is clearly true of philosophy: each sect imagined that it had unearthed the secret of man's ultimate end—τέλος, happiness. But it is no less true of rhetoric and aesthetics: as I have already tried to explain, the "cult of the muses" had become the educated man's religion. And this is borne out by later Renaissances in East and West: every time there has been a revival of the classical tradition, it has been accompanied by an upsurge of neo-paganism. Before a man of antiquity could be converted to Christianity he had to make an effort of renunciation and self-transcendence; he had to realize the limits,[1] and see the ultimate vanity, of a culture that had previously sustained him.

The Christians of the first centuries were quite aware of this. *Quid Athenae Hierosolymis* . . . "What is there in common between Athens and Jerusalem, the Academy and the Church?"[2] That is not only the rigorous Tertullian's view, as a glance at the literature of the early Fathers will show. Even the most "educated" of them, those who remained most faithful to classical art and classical thought—St. Augustine, for example (11)—share the spontaneous reaction of the simple and the ignorant, and condemn the old culture for being an independent ideal hostile to the Christian revelation.

The number of passages that show this is embarrassingly large. I shall not select the more striking ones—like St. Jerome's dream, in which the Saint found himself before the throne of God, being reproached for being "a Ciceronian instead of a Christian"[3]—but more official passages, in which the Church's own authority was involved. Canon law, in fact, contains regulations that can only be explained as a result of this conflict between classical culture and Christianity.

This is true of the *Didascalia Apostolorum*, a third-century document which for a long time had considerable influence in the East.[4] This says bluntly, "Have nothing to do with pagan books," and gives some rather surprising grounds for this injunction. What connection can any Christian have with all the errors they contain? He has the Word of God—what else does he want? The Bible not only provides for the supernatural life but for all cultural needs too—*nam quid tibi deest in verbo Dei ut ad illas gentiles fabulas pergas*! Is it history he wants? There are the Books of Kings. Eloquence, poetry? The Prophets! Lyrics? The Psalms! Cosmology? Genesis! Laws, morality? The glorious Law of God! But all these outlandish books that come from the Devil —they must be hurled away—*ab omnibus igitur alienis et diabolicis scripturis fortiter te abstine*.[5]

The West could be just as strict—if not towards the rank and file, at least towards the man who possessed all the powers of the priesthood, and was supposed to give an example of perfection—i.e. the bishop. He was not to read any pagan books and was to concern himself solely with heretics *pro necessitate et tempore*—so said the *Statutes of the Early Church*,[6] for long held to contain the canons of a pseudo-Fourth Council of Carthage, but generally

[1] Cf. Ps. cxiii (lxx), 96.
[2] Tert., *Praescr.*, 7.
[3] Hieron., *Ep.*, XXII, XXX.
[4] Cf. *Const. Apost.*, I, 6.
[5] *Didasc. Ap.*, I, 6, 1–6.
[6] *Stat. Eccl. Ant.*, 16.

thought today to have been compiled in Arles in about the year 500. The same ban was reaffirmed by Isidore of Seville[1] and again as late as the twelfth century by Gratian's *Decretum*.[2] In fact it is still part of canon law today (12).

CHRISTIANITY ACCEPTS THE CLASSICAL SCHOOL

There would be no point in discussing all the evidence about this matter here, or in trying to decide how it actually worked out in practice through the centuries. It is more a matter of culture in general, i.e., the intellectual life of the adult, not preparatory culture, education (13).

The Church's attitude towards education was quite different. Being thoroughly awake to the fact that the "scholarly" and "bookish" aspect of Christianity made it essential for the faithful to have some sort of literary culture, she could see no other solution than to allow them to be educated in schools of the traditional Hellenistic type. Theory and practice were here perfectly at one.

The distinction is made quite clear in the writings of the time. We know from Eusebius[3] that Origen considered the rôle of grammarian, which he had at one time adopted, incompatible with the work of catechist which the Bishop of Alexandria had laid upon him. Then again St. Jerome, writing in the spirit of canon law, censures priests who neglect the Gospels and the Prophets and waste their time reading profane authors. He says it is a crime for them to do voluntarily what children are obliged to do for the sake of their education— *id quod in pueris necessitatis est, crimen in se facere voluntatis.*[4]

The criticisms that were made against profane culture undoubtedly applied to the schools too, for they were traditionally bound up with paganism. Children passed from learning their syllables to lists of the names of the gods, and the texts used in the class-room were taken from poems as impious as they were immoral. And yet none of the Christians ever suggested that children should be brought up differently, away from the pagan schools.

Take a controversialist as violent and uncompromising as Tertullian. No one was more deeply aware of the idolatry and immorality of the classical school. He even went to the extent of refusing to allow Christians to teach, because teaching was absolutely incompatible with the Faith, on a level with making idols or being an astrologer. But as profane studies could not be given up without religious studies becoming impossible—it being necessary to learn to read—he allowed the Christian child to go to school as a matter of *necessity*, but he would not allow any Christian adult to go there as a teacher. But the child must know what he was doing and not let himself be affected by the idolatry implicit in the teaching and even in the list of school events: he must behave like someone who knows he is being given poison and takes good care not to drink it.[5]

This solution was not peculiar to Tertullian's time, when Christians were still a submerged minority within a persecuting Empire. Things were just the same

[1] Isid., *Sent.*, III, 3.
[2] I, 37.
[3] *H.E.*, VI, 3, 8.
[4] Hieron., *Ep.* XXI, 13, 9.
[5] Tert., *Idol.*, 10.

in the fourth century when the Emperor was converted, and the mass of people in Asia Minor with him. Christian children were still being brought up with pagans in classical schools, still being given "poison"—Homer, the poets, the long insidious line of mythological figures and the dark passions they symbolized or embodied. Immunity was supposed to come from the antidote of religious training which they received outside school from the Church and their parents: once their religious consciousness had been properly enlightened and developed, they would know how to make the necessary discriminations and adjustments.

This—if it is read aright—is made clear in St. Basil's well-known essay *On the Reading of the Profane Authors*.[1] But we must not try to turn it into a formal treatise on the value of studying the pagan classics (14), as far too many of its readers have tried to do from the Renaissance to our own times. It was more a kind of homily on the danger there is in these authors and the way of avoiding it —either by interpreting the poets in the light of the Gospels or by a careful sorting-out process. This does not mean that St. Basil suggests any expurgation of the curriculum of Christian educators generally. St. Basil was addressing young men, his own nephews, who were coming to the end of their studies; and, like Tertullian, he was simply trying to develop their Christian insight and enable them to get the best out of all they had learned. A Christian upbringing was something superimposed on a humanistic education that had taken place without it, something that had not previously been subjected to the requirements of the Christian religion.

CHRISTIANS IN CLASSICAL EDUCATION

It is worth noting that the Church did not follow Tertullian's advice and ban the teaching profession. In about the year 215—just about the time when Tertullian was writing his *De Idololatria* (211-212)—St. Hippolytus of Rome was composing, probably for his schismatic community, his *Apostolic Tradition*, a work that was to go on being read in Syria, Egypt and even as far as Ethiopia, for such a long time. He too gives a list of professions that are incompatible with the Christian faith, and surprisingly he does not include teachers along with his procurers, actors and makers of idols. "If," he says,[2] "anyone is occupied in teaching children the sciences of this world, he would be well advised to give it up, but if he has no other means of livelihood, he may be excused." The collections of canons deriving from Hippolytus were equally tolerant,[3] or even more so.[4]

There is no doubt that this was the Church's normal attitude, for many Christians taught in classical schools. The first we know about for certain is the great Origen who, in 202-203, when he was seventeen, opened a grammar school to help to maintain the family which had been left destitute as a result of the martyrdom of his father Leonides and the confiscation of all his goods.[5] This can hardly have damaged his prestige in the eyes of the ecclesiastical authorities,

---

[1] Bas., *Hom.*, XXII.   [3] *Test. J.C.*, II, 2; *Can. Hipp.*, 12.
[2] Hipp., *Trad. Ap.*, 16.   [4] Cf. *Const. Ap.*, VIII, 32, 7-13.
[5] Eus., *H.E.*, VI, 2, 15.

for a year later his bishop Demetrius made him the recognized teacher of the catechism.[1]

Fifty years later Christians made their first entry into higher education. In 264 Anatolius, the future bishop of Laodicea, was elected by his fellow-citizens in Alexandria to the ordinary chair of Aristotelian philosophy.[2] At more or less the same time, in 268, there was a priest named Malchion in Antioch who was also in charge of a school of rhetoric run on Hellenic lines.[3]

As time went on such cases became more and more common, until in the fourth century Christians were to be found in all grades of teaching; there were Christians among the lowest schoolteachers[4] and grammarians[5] and Christians occupying the highest chairs of eloquence: in the course of his persecution in 362 Julian the Apostate found Prohaeresius holding the chair in Athens and Marius Victorinus the chair in Rome.[6]

THE SCHOLASTIC LAW OF JULIAN THE APOSTATE

This curious episode deserves a moment's attention. It was the first academic persecution inflicted on the Christians, and its peculiar nature sheds a good deal of light on the question we are studying here. By a law passed on June 17th 362, the Emperor Julian had forbidden Christians to teach.[7] The actual wording simply said that permission to teach had to be obtained in advance from the municipal authorities and the Emperor himself, as a guarantee of the intending teacher's efficiency and morality. But in an accompanying circular[8] Julian made it clear what he meant by "morality": Christians who taught Homer and Hesiod without believing in the gods they described were accused of failing in honesty and candour by teaching something they did not believe. They were ordered either to apostatise or to give up teaching.

It is not paradoxical to say that with this measure Julian created the first real Christian school, with its own particular religious mission. Higher education in this second half of the fourth century had been amazingly neutral. It did not matter whether the teachers were Christians or pagans; the only thing that attracted students was their ability as teachers—religious beliefs did not come into it. A convinced pagan like Eunapius was proud of having been taught by a Christian like Prohaeresius.[9] St. John Chrysostom, despite the fact that he had been brought up in a highly Christian atmosphere by his mother Anthousa, who was a deeply religious woman, still went to lectures by a pagan like Libanius.[10] And in each case neither seems to have run any risk of being converted.

But Julian was determined to inject a new anti-Christian virulence into classical education by laying the greatest possible stress on the original bond

[1] *Ibid.*, VI, 3, 3; 8.
[2] Hieron., *De Vir. ill.*, 73; Eus., *H.E.*, VII, 32, 6.
[3] *Ibid.*, VII, 29, 2.
[4] Diehl, 717–723.
[5] *Ibid.*, 725–726.
[6] Eunap., *Proh.*, 493; Hieron., *Chron.*, 363p. August., *Conf.*, VIII, 5 (10).
[7] *Cod. Theod.*, XIII, 3, 5.
[8] Jul., *Ep.*, LXI.
[9] Eunap., *Proh.*, 485.
[10] Socrates, *H.E.*, III, 11.

between paganism and classicism. I have called it new: there was, however, a precedent; the emperor Maximin Daza had ordered the teachers of primary schools to make their pupils study and learn by heart the *Acts of Pilate*, which were filled with blasphemies against Christ.[1] He decided to describe the religion of the gods, for instance, as "Hellenism", thus identifying civilization with paganism. He regarded Christians as barbarians—that is why he called them "Galileans"[2], and perhaps wanted to force them to adopt that as their official name. Under Julian the schools, which until his time had been open to Christian children—could they now in conscience be allowed to attend?—became an instrument for the return of paganism, and the Christian religion was thrown back into its original "barbarism".

The reaction of the Christians against this measure, which they regarded as annoying and humiliating in the highest degree,[3] was very violent, but also highly ingenious. Having been ordered by the Emperor to be satisfied with "going to their Galilean churches and reading Matthew and Luke",[4] they refused to allow themselves to be thus deprived of their literary inheritance and set to work to produce their own text-books as substitutes for the classics. This was the work of the two Apollinarii—father and son—two teachers from Alexandria who had gone to Laodicea in Syria, and had become so enthusiastic about literature that for a time they had been excommunicated. They set about rewriting the Pentateuch in the style of Homer, the historical books of the Old Testament in the style of the drama, and so on, using every kind of literary form and all manner of metres, from Menander's comedies to Pindaric odes. The New Testament became a series of Platonic dialogues.[5]

Thus, having been in a way obliged to create a strictly Christian type of education, the Christians, paradoxically, refused, and still managed to remain within the classical fold. In any case the efforts of the Apollinarii were short-lived: on January 11th 364[6] Julian's ban was lifted, the Christian teachers went back to their chairs, and everything went on as before, the Church accommodating herself to the classical education without any difficulty whatsoever.

SLIGHT CHRISTIAN INFLUENCE ON THE SCHOOL

It might be imagined that when Christian teachers and pupils came to form a majority the school would find itself Christianized (15). There is indeed a canon, unfortunately difficult to date—is it fourth, fifth or sixth century?—that makes it one of the Christian grammarian's duties to tell his pupils that "the gods of the Gentiles are devils",[7] and that there is no other God but the Father, the Son and the Holy Spirit, and which seems to encourage him—in the modern phrase—"to take part in the lay apostolate". "It is all right to teach the

---

[1] Eus., *H.E.*, IX, 5, 1; 7, 1.
[2] Greg. Naz., *Or.*, IV, 76.
[3] Cf. Jul., *Ep.*, LXIa.
[4] *Ibid.*, LXIc., 423d.
[5] Socrates, *H.E.*, III, 16; Sozom., *H.E.*, V, 18.
[6] *Cod. Theod.*, XIII, 3, 6.
[7] *Can. Hipp.*, 12.

poets, but if he can pass on the deposit of faith to his pupils he will merit even more greatly" (16).

It seems likely that this advice was sometimes followed, for Julian the Apostate accused Christian teachers of misrepresenting poets like Homer by accusing them of impiety, madness and error;[1] but judging by the documents that have been left behind, it does not seem as though the ordinary teaching was affected by the new religion. There is an exercise-book kept by a young Christian schoolboy in fourth-century Egypt,[2] for instance, which has nothing to distinguish it from a Hellenistic book six or seven centuries older[3]—the same lists of mythological names, the same maxims and anecdotes (both moral and the opposite). The only sign of Christianity, apart from the "Blessed be God" at the top of the first page, is the monogrammatic cross which is carefully drawn at the beginning of every page. That is something, of course: we can imagine that while he was drawing it the child would say a short prayer like "Holy Cross, protect me!" (17). But that kind of general consecration was hardly enough to make the general atmosphere of the school Christian. And this is not the only document of its kind: in the fifth and sixth centuries little Christian children in the Fayum were still learning to write by copying out lists of mythological names—Europa, Pasiphae, etc.—and no one seems to have minded.[4]

The Church does not seem to have introduced any teaching of her own—though there were exceptions, as we shall see in the following chapter—even for children for whom she had a special responsibility, like orphans brought up on Church assistance[5] or those young *lectores* with clear voices who took part so effectively in church services and who from at least the fourth century onwards were part of the official hierarchy of the Church (18).

This comes out very clearly in a curious episode in the life of St. Athanasius (19). He was picked out when he was still a child by Bishop Alexander, who came across him when he was playing at being a bishop with a group of his little friends, and doing it with such precocious skill that Alexander determined that he should become a priest. This meant that a certain amount of education was necessary. Now if there had been any church school in existence he would undoubtedly have been sent to it; instead, it was left to his parents "to bring him up for the Church", and they sent him to the elementary school, to learn shorthand, receive a smattering of grammar—and then packed him off to the bishop as an acolyte.[6]

I only know of one case in which there seems to have been any desire to create a proper Christian church school. In about the year 372 the Emperor Valens exiled two orthodox priests of Edessa to Antinoë, a place in the wilds of the Thebaïd, as a punishment for resisting his Arianizing policy. There, they were surprised and shocked to discover that things were very different from what they were used to at home and that the Christians were only a small minority amongst a mass of pagans. How were all these infidels to be converted? One of them, Protogenes, started an elementary school and gave lessons in writing and

---

[1] Jul., *Ep*,. 61c, 423 d,

[2] *PBouriant*, I.

[3] *PGuér. Joug*,

[4] Wessely, *Studien*, II, lvi.

[5] *Didasc. Ap*., IV.

[6] Rufin., *H.E.*, X, 15.

shorthand, but being a missionary as well he carefully selected his passages for dictation or recitation from the Psalms of David or the New Testament. Thus he taught the children a kind of catechism as well, and soon, as a result of his affection for them—as a result too of his fellow-priest Eulogius' miracles—they were all converted to the Faith.[1]

It is clear from the astonished delight with which Theodoret relates this story that it was something unheard of. Protogenes would have to be regarded as the founder of religious education in the modern sense of the word—i.e. education and instruction in religious matters being combined with purely academic work—if he had not in fact come from Edessa, one of the main centres of Syriac culture, where this type of school is known to have been the usual thing. Moreover, his example was confined to a remote district in Upper Egypt, and it seems to have petered out for lack of followers.

HIGHER SCHOOLS OF THEOLOGY

Thus there were not usually any Christian schools at primary- and secondary-school level. More advanced schools for the teaching of Christian theology came into being as early as the middle of the second century, but they did not manage to become deeply rooted in the Church and soon faded away.

The teaching of doctrine had a high place in Christianity, so that it naturally went on developing on a level far above that of the simple catechism, a level on which revealed Truth was investigated far more deeply, presented far more systematically, and dealt with in far greater detail. This longing for a Sacred Science, for a Christian equivalent of the pagan philosophical culture, appears most clearly in Gnosticism.

As a matter of fact the first people to have gone in for this kind of learning seem to have been the great heretics, but the orthodox soon followed suit, as appears from the Apologists—particularly the most famous of them, St. Justin Martyr. These liked to call themselves philosophers,[2] and wore the traditional garb[3]—Eusebius says that Justin taught "dressed like" (or "standing like") "a philosopher"[4]—and they opened a proper school—διδασκαλεῖον[5]—with a proper address.[6] They seem to have been true philosophers, for they were soon being attacked by their pagan colleagues—near-Cynics like Crescens, who caused Justin such a lot of trouble.[7]

Justin's audience included cradle-Catholics like Euelpistes, who is mentioned in the Acts of his martyrdom;[8] thus Justin cannot merely have given propaganda lectures to good pagans—he must have given a more advanced kind of teaching on a higher level. It should be noticed that unlike the people who taught the catechism the Apologists were not commissioned by the hierarchy; they were laymen who taught on their own responsibility, "Christian philosophers", not Doctors of the Church (20).

[1] Theodor., H.E., IV, 18, 7-14.
[2] Just., Dial., I, 1; Tat., 32; Athenag.; Hermias.
[3] Just., Dial., I, 2; Tert., Pall.
[4] Eus., H.E., IV, 11, 8.
[5] Iren., I, 28, 1.
[6] Just., Acts, 3, p. 34.
[7] Just., Ap., II, 3; Tat., 19.
[8] Just., Acts, 4, p. 35.

THE THIRD CENTURY IN ROME AND ALEXANDRIA

This kind of teaching must have gone on into the third century, for it was thus that Clement of Alexandria taught, and Hippolytus of Rome. Hippolytus' followers erected a statue to his memory, showing him in action as a philosopher— i.e. sitting on a throne with a list of his works and his table for reckoning the date of Easter engraved on it. There were other similar monuments (21): Christian tombstones dating from before the Peace of Constantine often represent the deceased person as a "teacher", a philosopher or a man of letters meditating or commenting upon the sacred Book.

But these were all individual affairs. Some historians, on the basis of statements in Eusebius[1] and Philip of Side,[2] have tried to imagine a School of Sacred Literature in Alexandria, with a regular succession—διαδοχή—of qualified teachers, such as the Greek philosophical sects had, lasting over a couple of centuries; but although Alexandria was an outstanding centre of intense doctrinal activity, first Jewish, then Christian, from the days of Philo the Jew to the time of St. Cyril, it only came to have an official school of theology in Origen's time.

As we have seen, Origen was only eighteen when his bishop, Demetrius, put him officially in charge of teaching the catechism, which had been completely disorganized by the persecution.[3] He was a great success, and was obliged to give up his secular teaching so that he could devote himself to his new work entirely.[4] Not only this: with a growing public, and an increasingly high standard, and perhaps influenced by Hippolytus,[5] he divided his school work into two parts: one, the original official teaching of the catechism, he put under Heraclas, one of his first disciples;[6] the other, which he added on to it, was a more advanced class in which he himself taught higher exegesis and theology.[7] From Eusebius again, we can form some idea of what this "School for Advanced Religious Studies" was like. It was an ingenious adaptation of the methods used in the Hellenistic higher education: a solid groundwork of secondary-school knowledge—which meant the liberal arts, literature and mathematics—leading to philosophy, which in its turn led on to specifically religious studies founded on a thorough reading of the Scriptures.[8]

Unfortunately, Origen's work, despite its great originality and promise for the future, did not last long; after fifteen years of it, in about 230–231, he was dismissed from his post and banished from Alexandria as a result of certain differences of opinion about matters of discipline and doctrine with Bishop Demetrius.[9] With his disappearance the School for Advanced Studies disappeared too, and all that remained was the school for teaching the catechism, still run by Heraclas[10] until he became a bishop, when it was taken over by another of Origen's pupils, Dionysius.[11]

---

[1] Eus., *H.E.*, V, 10, 1; VI, 6.
[2] *PG*, 39, 229.
[3] Eus., *H.E.*, VI, 3, 3.
[4] *Ibid.*, VI, 3, 8.
[5] Cf. Hieron., *De Vir. ill.*, 61.
[6] Eus., *H.E.*, VI, 3, 1.
[7] *Ibid.*, VI, 15.
[8] *Ibid.*, VI, 18, 3–4.
[9] *Ibid.*, VI, 19, 15–19; 23; Phot., *Bibl.*, 118.
[10] Eus., *H.E.*, VI, 26, 1.
[11] *Ibid.*, VI, 29, 4; Hieron., *De Vir. ill.*, 69.

Having been driven from Alexandria, Origen finally landed in Caesarea, in Palestine, where his teaching was just as successful as it had been in Alexandria— he prevailed upon St. Gregory Thaumaturgus and his brother to give up law and study under him, for instance.[1] He remained in Caesarea for nearly twenty years, until Decius began his persecution in 250 and he was martyred. He left behind a wonderful library which for a long time was used as a study centre, but not as an actual school in the proper sense (22).

DISAPPEARANCE OF THESE SCHOOLS

The example of Origen and the Apologists was not followed. There was an increasing amount of higher theology and so on, of course, particularly after the Peace of Constantine. Theology and the study of the Bible were beginning to create a new culture, Christian in essence, that was to be the distinguishing feature of the civilization of the Late Empire and Byzantium. Not only the clergy but all really educated Christians had a specifically religious field of interest as well as all their secular activity, and the religious side often took up more of their time. "We are all theologians today," they might have said— —from the Emperor downwards—and the Emperor might be Constantine, Justinian or Chilperic.[2] In fact it became a bit too much of a good thing: the orthodox leaders were sometimes hard put to it to keep the craze within proper bounds, for all the cultural forces of the time seemed to meet in it, and all the worst features of Hellenistic humanism too—the philosopher's logic-chopping, the orator's dubious gift of the gab.

But this Christian culture, it should be noted, though it was helped by this remarkable burst of literature and oratory, had no recognized education underlying it. There were no theological colleges. The only instruction that the faithful received was by way of the simple catechism and preaching. The clergy did not go to college; they learned their theology through personal contact with the bishop and the older priests, whom they often joined when they were quite young children, as lectors.

Thus, as regards actual teaching establishments, far from there being any progress from the third century to the fourth, there was a distinct retrogression. When St. Jerome, for instance, tells us that during his youthful voyages in the East he went to lessons given by Apollinaris in Antioch, Didymus the Blind[3] in Alexandria and Gregory Nazianzen[4] in Constantinople, we must understand that he means private lessons, personal intercourse as between one man and another, not on a teacher-student basis.

Remarkable things were achieved by the great bishops of the fourth and fifth centuries, by St. Basil in Caesarea, St. John Chrysostom in Constantinople, St. Ambrose in Milan, St. Augustine in Hippo; but there is nothing to show that they ever created anything like a Christian school. They managed to reach a remarkable level of personal Christian culture, which they spread abroad by

[1] Eus., H.E., VI, 30, 1; Hieron., De Vir. ill., 65; Greg. Thaum., Pan., 6.
[2] Greg. Tur., Hist. Fr., V, 44.
[3] Hieron., Ep., 84, 3, 1.
[4] Ibid., 50, 1; 52, 8; In Isaiam, III, ad 6, 1.

preaching and example, and, in the case of Augustine anyway (23), developed into a complete system of culture; they defined its ends, its methods, its limits. But they made no attempt to turn it into a real system of education. They themselves had been brought up in classical schools, they knew all about their dangers and deficiencies, and they found it natural to try to make the best of them.

Even in Justinian's time in the sixth century Westerners passing through Constantinople were surprised and delighted to learn that in Nisibis in the land of Syria there were "proper schools where Holy Scripture is taught properly, just like the secular schools in the Roman Empire that teach grammar and rhetoric."[1]

[1] Junil. Pr.; Cassiod., *Inst.*, I, pr. I.

CHAPTER X

APPEARANCE OF CHRISTIAN SCHOOLS OF THE MEDIAEVAL TYPE

In the fourth century, however, there appeared a type of Christian school that was wholly devoted to religion and had none of the features of the old classical school; already mediaeval and not classical in its inspiration, it remained for a long time peculiar to its own environment and had little outside influence. This was the monastic school.

THE MONASTIC SCHOOL IN THE EAST

From the very early days, apparently,[1] the Desert Fathers in Egypt had adopted young boys and even little children, and though no doubt this was exceptional at first, early vocations began to multiply and the large communities that were organized by St. Pachomius generally included a number of children.[2]

Having adopted these children, the monks naturally had to educate them, and each child was treated like a novice and put under one of the older monks, someone respected for his experience and integrity who could be his spiritual father—APA, the Coptic form for "abbot", i.e. "father" (1). From this "father" the child received a kind of training that was ascetic and moral, spiritual rather than intellectual. It will be remembered that St. Anthony, the great founder of monasticism, was an illiterate Coptic peasant[3] who was able to get on quite well without any books, as he soon proved to any philosophers who came and argued with him.[4] This was a fundamental feature of Eastern monasticism and it was never lost: these desert people were less concerned with learning than with forgetting the poetry and secular knowledge they had picked up in the schools[5] before their conversion. Monasticism brought back into the Christian tradition the virtues of the simple and unlettered,[6] as against the intellectual pride fostered by the old culture, which, as is clear from the Gnostics and the Alexandrians, was in the third century threatening to destroy the original simplicity of the Gospels.

But here again the scholarly and "bookish" side of Christianity inevitably asserted itself. Day and night, the monk meditated on the Divine Law, the Word of God—the Scriptures, in fact. He usually knew them by heart. And obviously the best way of learning them was by reading them. Hence, at some time between 320 and 340 St. Pachomius laid it down in his *Rule* that any ignorant man entering the monastery should immediately be given twenty

---

[1] Cassian, *Inst.*, V, 40.
[2] *Reg. Pach.*, pr. 5; 159; 166; 172.
[3] Athan., *V. Ant.*, 72.
[4] *Ibid.*, 73; cf. 20.
[5] Cassian, *Conl.*, XIV, 12.
[6] Luke x, 21 = Matt. xi, 25.

Psalms or two Epistles to learn. If he could not read he was to be given lessons by one of the monks for three hours a day, learning the letters and syllables and nouns . . . *Etiam nolens legere compelletur!* The idea was that everyone in the monastery should be able to read and know by heart at least the Psalter and the New Testament.[1]

St. Basil's *Rule* also allowed for the entry of young boys presented by their parents, and it too saw to it that they were put under an old monk and taught to read so that they could study the Bible. By a single happy intuition St. Basil founded a remarkable system of teaching. It will be remembered that as soon as a child had mastered the syllables he started reading single names, then sayings, and then little stories, all of which were based on characters in Greek mythology. St. Basil substituted the names of people in the Bible, verses of Proverbs and stories from the Bible.[2]

St. Jerome developed what was in effect the same method in the scheme of Christian education that he drew up between 400 and 402 for a child called Paula (whose parents and grandparents and uncles and aunts were amongst his favourite disciples in Rome)[3] and another little girl called Pacatula.[4] Both became nuns, having been consecrated as soon as they were born to the service of Christ.[5] Paula was brought up, not in Rome, but in Bethlehem, in a convent where her aunt Eustochium was the Mother Superior and St. Jerome himself the spiritual director. Her education was entirely ascetic,[6] with no literature[7] or any other of the secular arts,[8] but revolving entirely around the Bible, which she learned systematically from beginning to end.[9] The only other books she read were by the Fathers—Cyprian, Athanasius and Hilary;[10] and as in the case of St. Basil, her very first lessons were based on the Bible—the lists of names by which she learned to read, for example, were taken from the genealogies of Christ in the Gospels.[11]

It is clear that this is the way teaching went on in the monasteries, from some Egyptain *ostraca* we possess of an unusually late date (seventh to eighth centuries). These contain word-lists full of Christian names[12]—for example, all the proper names that occur in the story of Pentecost in the Acts,[13] extracts from the Psalms as subjects for writing exercises,[14] and, most surprising of all, an essay in narrative form on a legendary subject—"Relate the miracle of Christ and the vine".[15] An even better example, perhaps, is the schoolboy's exercise book discovered in the Fayum: it dates back to the fourth or fifth century and contains, among other exercises in writing, verses from Psalm xxxii.[16]

[1] *Reg. Pach.*, 139–140.
[2] Bas., *Reg. fus.*, 15.
[3] Hieron., *Ep.*, 107.
[4] *Ibid.*, *Ep.*, 128.
[5] *Ibid.*, 107, 5, 1; 128, 2, 1.
[6] *Ibid.*, 107, 7, 1; 128, 4, 1.
[7] *Ibid.*, 107, 4, 1.
[8] *Ibid.*, 4, 3.
[9] *Ibid.*, 107, 12; 128, 4, 2.
[10] *Ibid.*, 107, 12, 3.
[11] *Ibid.*, 4, 4.
[12] *O. Lond. Hall*, 21379.
[13] *Ibid.*, 26210.
[14] *Ibid.*, 27426.
[15] *Ibid.*, 148–149.
[16] B. Sanz, *Griechische literarische Papyri christlichen Inhaltes*, I (Biblica Väterschriften und Verwandtes), in *Mitteilungen aus der Papyrussammlung der Nationalbibliothek in Wien*, N.S., IV, Baden, 1946.

ITS LIMITED INFLUENCE

But this education was only for young monks. Sometimes there was talk of extending it to other children. St. Basil raises the matter in another of his *Rules* and agrees, after a certain amount of hesitation, to open the door of the monastery, rather gingerly, to "children of the world"—παῖδες βιωτικοί—if their parents wish to send them there.[1] In about the year 375 St. John Chrysostom, passionately devoted to the ascetic life, tried to prevail upon Christian parents to have their children educated after they were ten by the monks in the "deserts" round Antioch, so that they should be far from the world and its dangers.[2]

The response was small. Chrysostom's words are clearly those of an inspired soul bent on perfection, who will not see that his enthusiasm is not shared by everyone. In point of fact his suggestion was utterly impractical. The boys were to spend ten years, twenty if necessary, in a monastery, to develop their moral strength.[3] But what was to become of them when they went out into the world? No doubt St. John is careful to say that he does not want them to be left without any kind of practical instruction,[4] but there seem to have been singularly few facilities for providing it in the desert.[5] He does on one occasion describe a young man working at some kind of secular study under the direction of a monk,[6] but this, as he himself admits, was quite exceptional: it was precisely because such training was unusual there that he suggested this prolonged stay in the desert.

It seems unlikely that his suggestion was ever generally accepted. Twenty years later he himself, having grown wiser and more experienced, expressly repudiated it.[7] He still insisted, more emphatically than ever, on the parents' duty to bring up their children in a Christian manner, but he now added that it was the parents' mission, not the monks', to develop their children's religious consciousness. And, as we have seen, it was from their life in the family that children did in fact receive their religious training, while they went out to the secular schools for their general education.[8]

As for St. Jerome's scheme, it was never intended as a general rule (incidentally, Paula herself does not seem to have come up to her tutor's expectations),[9] and he does not seem to have applied it in any sort of systematic fashion himself. He is known to have been in charge of the education of a number of young Latin boys in his monastery in Bethlehem, but this followed the classical pattern: grammar, Virgil, the comic and lyric poets, the historians, and so on[10] (2).

St. Basil, as we have seen, was not very keen on admitting children to the cloister unless their religious vocation was assured in advance, and, as time went on, the monasteries' attitude towards any sort of intrusion that tended to disturb their peace and recollection gradually hardened until finally, in 451, the Council

[1] Bas., *Reg. brev.*, 292.
[2] Chrys., *Adv. opp.*, III, 17, 378.
[3] *Ibid.*, III, 18, 380.
[4] *Ibid.*, III, 12, 368.
[5] *Ibid.*, III, 8, 363; 11, 366; 13, 371.
[6] *Ibid.*, III, 12, 369-370.
[7] Chrys., *Inan. gl.*, 19, 2-3.
[8] *Ibid.*, 19, 1 *seq.*; 73, 2-3.
[9] Hieron., *Ep.*, 153, 3.
[10] Rufin., *Apol.*, II, 8, 592 A.

of Chalcedon forbade monasteries to undertake the education of any children who intended to return to secular life—παῖδες κοσμικοί.[1] This ban was never relaxed: in Greek-speaking countries the monastic school is, so to speak, for internal use only.

This is one of the most characteristic features of Eastern monasticism: since the monasteries were part of a society which on the whole always maintained a high standard of education, they were not obliged to adopt an educational rôle for which they had never been designed. Instead of becoming study centres they endeavoured to remain homes of asceticism; instead of trying to influence the world, they tried to get right away from it.

THE MONASTIC SCHOOL IN THE WEST

In the West the Germanic invasions and the general decline of culture led ultimately to an utterly different state of affairs.

In the beginning things had been the same as in the East—except in one small but very important respect: Latin monasticism was imported comparatively late; it was something borrowed from an already well-developed organism. Literature and the cenobitic life were the accepted things in it. It did not have, as the East had, memories and a kind of nostalgia for its first heroes, those cultureless anchorites to whom St. Anthony's deeds counted for more than Pachomius' *Rule*. In the East, in fact, no one has ever been surprised to find that a monk could be both illiterate and holy (3).

In the West it was quite different: there, the *lectio divina*—the reading of Holy Scripture, and above all the Office—seemed essential to any full monastic life. This emphasis on the written word had been strong from the beginning—St. Augustine, who introduced monasticism into Africa, had formed a community round him in Tagaste while he was still a layman, and its general tone was academic (4), while in his *Rule* he took the existence of a library for granted.[2] In Marmoutier, where St. Martin first introduced monasticism into Gaul, the monks copied out manuscripts.[3] There was a kind of automatic association between monks and the written word. Even in an environment as utterly remote from classical culture as Ireland, whenever St. Patrick adopted a boy, or had one brought to him to become a monk, there was the same reaction: "He baptized him and then gave him an alphabet."[4]

When in the sixth century the darkness of barbarism descended, and culture declined in the West and threatened to disappear altogether, we find those in charge of monasticism insisting more than ever on the need for every monk and every nun to be able to read and devote themselves to the Scriptures. The best-known of all the *Rules* for women, that of St. Caesarius of Arles (534), laid it down that children were only to be accepted when they were six or seven years of age and able to learn to read;[5] all the nuns were to learn to read—*omnes litteras*

---

[1] *Rev. Hist. et Phil. Relig.* (Strasbourg), XXI (1941), 63.
[2] August., *Ep.*, 211, 3.
[3] S. Sev., *V. Mart.*, 10, 6.
[4] Stokes, *Tripartite Life*, II, 326, 29; 328, 27; 497, 24.
[5] Caes. Ar., *Virg.*, 7, 104.

discant;[1] they were to devote two hours a day to reading;[2] they were to copy manuscripts.[3]

The same concern for the *lectio divina* appears in many other *Rules*. The *Rule of St. Radegund* is simply copied from St. Caesarius',[4] but there were also those of St. Leander of Seville (d. 601),[5] and St. Donatus of Besançon (d. 650).[6] If all this was so important for women—who naturally did not go in for education to the same extent—it was obviously just as important for men.[7] In the *Tarnatensis Rule* (c. 570) not even working in the fields[8] dispensed a monk from the *lectio*. The *Rule of St. Ferreolus of Uzès*[9] (d. 581) and the *Regula Magistri*[10] (date?) both insisted on the study of the written word and meditation on the written word.[11] The movement culminated of course in the *Rule of St. Benedict* (c. 525), which came to dominate the entire West. The *Rule* goes into great detail about the reading of the Scriptures,[12] and lays down laws about the admission of children into the monastery[13] and how they are to be educated:[14] books, writing-boards and pens are accepted as part of the monastery's general furniture and setting:[15] even in Western Europe's darkest days the monastery remained a true home of culture.

THE EPISCOPAL SCHOOL

The calamities of the time gave rise to a second type of Christian school—the episcopal school. It is not always easy to separate this from the monastic school, at least in the early stages, for we know that many of the great Western bishops, who had been educated as monks and inherited the monastic ideals, were keen to have monastic communities near them. There was St. Eusebius in Vercelli, for instance, and St. Augustine in Hippo, and St. Martin of Tours in Marmoutier.

There had always been a body of ecclesiastics round the bishop, including the many children acting as lectors who were being apprenticed, so to speak, to the clerical life (5). This was the usual way to become a deacon, a priest, a future bishop; as I indicated in the preceding chapter, it was this highly practical and very personal kind of training that supplied the clergy, who had no seminaries or theological schools, with their knowledge of Church dogma and liturgy and Canon Law. The necessary foundation of secular—"humanist"—culture came through the ordinary schools, as it did in the case of St. Athanasius, as described on a previous page.[16]

The whole thing changed when the Roman social and political system collapsed —and the classical school with it. The worse things got, the more difficult it became to find young men who had received the necessary minimum of secular knowledge that would enable them to be trained for the priesthood. This was

---

[1] *Ibid.*, 18, 105.
[2] *Ibid.*, 19, 105; *Ep.*, II, 7, 140.
[3] *Ibid, Vit.*, I, 58, 320.
[4] Greg. Tur., *Hist. Fr.*, IX, 39 *seq.*
[5] *Reg.*, 6–7; *PL*, 72, 883–884.
[6] *Reg.*, 20; *PL*, 87, 281–282.
[7] Caes. Ar., *Mon.*, 151, 25.
[8] *Reg.*, 9; *PL*, 66, 981.
[9] *Reg.*, 11; *PL*, 66, 963–964.
[10] *Ibid.*, 26, 968.
[11] *Reg. Mag.*, 50; *PL*, 88, 1010 D.
[12] Bened., *Reg.*, 48.
[13] *Ibid.*, 59.
[14] *Ibid.*, 30; 37; 39; 45; 63; 70.
[15] *Ibid.*, 33.
[16] Rufin., *H.E.*, X, 15.

why in France in Merovingian times, for example, bishops sometimes had to give children their elementary education themselves (6).

In this connection the case of Gregory of Tours (born in 538) is very significant. His education had been entirely religious, and he had been given it by his (great-) uncle St. Nicetius, Bishop of Lyons, who had himself been brought up "on church literature" and had decided to bring up any children related to him likewise. Young Gregory was brought to him when he was seven, was taught to read and write, and then learned the Psalms.[1]

As a result of the urgent need to ensure the training of the clergy, which was endangered by the increasing barbarism, this type of education became fairly general. There were always the monasteries, of course: Lérins produced most of the bishops in south-east Gaul in the fifth and sixth centuries and Marmoutier did the same for central Gaul.[2] Another of Gregory of Tours' uncles, for instance, St. Gall, was taken to the Cournon monastery near Clermont-Ferrand by his father when he was still a child, received the tonsure, and was immediately put to reading and writing and the chant; the bishop happened to notice that he had a lovely voice, took him on with his own clergy, and eventually St. Gall became bishop himself.[3]

But this was exceptional; usually, to secure a regular supply of candidates for the priesthood it was necessary for the bishop himself to give them a general education as well as their specialized theological training, and thus there came into existence the episcopal school, which was to develop into the mediaeval university of the future.

But we are still very far from that: the only aim at the moment was to teach people how to read. St. Caesarius is an important witness to this development. He was determined that his clergy should be properly educated, and he lived more or less in community with them, and edified them by his example and conversation. He would not ordain a man as deacon unless he had read the whole of the Old and New Testament four times.[4]

The episcopal school of the sixth century should therefore be regarded as a kind of choir school, a group—*schola*—of young lectors under the direction of their *primicerius*, as it existed for example in Mouzon in the time of St. Remigius (d. 533),[5] in Lyons in 551–552,[6] and in Carthage, under the rule of their *magister*, as early as the year 480 or thereabouts.[7]

The system grew up wherever the new barbarism was to be found—even in the Spain of the Visigoths, where the Second Council of Toledo (527) laid it down that children intended for the priesthood should be instructed in the "house of the church" under the direct supervision of the bishop, as soon as they received the tonsure.[8] This rule was re-stated a century later by the Fourth Council of Toledo in 633.[9] We know that it was enforced: the *Lives* of the seventh-century Bishops of Merida describe children belonging to the basilica of St. Eulalia learning to read and write in the basilica under a teacher,[10] whilst a bishop is

---

[1] Greg. Tur., *V. Patr.*, 8, 2.
[2] S. Sev., *V. Mart.*, 10, 9.
[3] Greg. Tur., *V. Patr.*, 6, 1–2.
[4] Caes. Ar., *Vit.*, I, 56, 320.
[5] Rem. Rem., *Ep.*, IV, 115.
[6] Diehl, 1287.
[7] Victor Vitensis, V, 9.
[8] C. 1, *PL*, 84, 335.
[9] C. 24, *id.*, 374.
[10] *V. Patr. Emer.*, II, 14; I, 1.

training his future successor by teaching him *officium ecclesiasticum omnemque bibliothecam scripturarum divinarum*.[1]

THE PRESBYTERIAL SCHOOL

In the sixth century the network of rural parishes was finally organized, or re-organized, after the stormy period of the invasions (7). The masses were converted so successfully that the tight urban structure of the early Church, which centred round the bishop, was forced to expand. And the number of priests was rising rapidly. How, with the surrounding barbarism, were they to be educated?

The answer was to adopt the system already operating in the episcopal schools. In 529 the Second Council of Vaison, probably on the initiative of St. Caesarius, enjoined "all parish priests to gather some boys round them as lectors, so that they may give them a Christian upbringing, teach them the Psalms and the lessons of Scripture and the whole law of the Lord and so prepare worthy successors to themselves".[2]

This decision must be regarded as a memorable one, for it signified the birth of the modern school, the ordinary village school—which not even antiquity had known in any general, systematic form.

The Council of Vaison was not alone in making this move; it mentioned as a precedent "what seems to be the general custom throughout Italy". A century later, in 666, at the Council of Merida, Visigothic Spain followed suit.[3] In Gaul too there is proof that it was not without its effect: we see this in the canons of the Councils forbidding the ordination of the illiterate;[4] in the *Life* of St. Géry of Cambrai (d. 623–626) a bishop inquires on his pastoral tour whether any children are being prepared for the priesthood in a certain village.[5] The hermit St. Patroclus (d. 576), who set himself up in the *vicus* of Néris (near Montluçon, Allier), built a chapel there and consecrated it with some of St. Martin's relics, and then quite as a matter of course began to teach children to read and write—*pueros erudire coepit in studiis litterarum*.[6] The two functions of village priest and teacher were thus intimately associated with each other.

THE BEGINNING OF THE MEDIAEVAL SCHOOLS

We have now described all the various institutions upon which the education of mediaeval times was to be based. In the sixth and seventh centuries the mediaeval system only existed in outline; all the schools, both monastic and secular, had a very limited range—they were, so to speak, merely technical schools designed to produce monks and clerics.

But by force of circumstances, as soon as the secular schools that had carried on the classical tradition finally disappeared, the religious schools became the

[1] *Ibid.*, IV, 4, 1.
[2] *Conc. Merov.*, 56, c. 1.
[3] C. 18, *PL*, 84, 623.
[4] Orleans, 533 (*Conc. Merov.*, p. 63, c. 16), Narbonne, 589 (Mansi, *Amplissima Collectio*, IX, c.1016 E–1017 A, c.11).
[5] *V. SS. Merov.*, I, 652, c. 2.
[6] Greg. Tur., *V. Patr.*, 9, 2.

only medium whereby culture could be acquired and handed on. Theoretically they were open to any member of the Church, but it was a characteristic of the Latin Middle Ages that learning was primarily a matter for the clergy. Nevertheless, even at this date, in the sixth century, they were beginning to affect a wider group.

No doubt the monasteries of Western Europe, like those in the East, were determined to defend themselves against the infiltration of any worldly influences: the Canon of Chalcedon had its equivalent in the *Rule of St. Caesarius*, which strictly—*penitus non accipiantur*—forbade girls, whether rich or poor, to be educated in convents.[1] St. Benedict makes it quite clear in his *Rule* that the children he has in mind are all young oblates. All the children brought up in the cloister were intended to become monks, in fact—whether they were like St. Eucherius' sons, Salonius and Veran, who went to Lérins when they were still quite young, just when their father was making his profession (c. 420),[2] or like St. Benedict's young disciples, Maurus and Placidus, sent by their fathers to be brought up in the service of God.[3] In Ireland at least, however—possibly following Druid tradition dating from pagan times (8)—it was already quite usual for the sons of kings or chieftains to be sent to a monastery to be educated: they remained laymen, and when their education was finished they would return to the world and take up their hereditary position in society.[4]

But when the presbyterial schools came into existence and gave more or less everyone a chance to be educated, many of the pupils who came along were not always quite sure that they had a religious vocation.[5] There were the sons of ordinary peasants, for instance,[6] and, to a far greater extent, the sons of the nobility—for the old aristocratic custom persisted of teaching their children to read and write, as is clear from the *Lives* of St. Leodegar[7] and St. Sequanus.[8] This was partly a survival from Roman times, when culture was one of the marks of the upper class, and partly a matter of practical necessity, for no matter how low the technical level of administration fell there was still a bureaucratic element in the Merovingian monarchy, and it was only in proper schools (9) that the kind of lay servants could be educated who would be of any use to the kings.

The level was on the whole still very low; it was very much a technical education for one particular purpose, involving reading and writing, knowing the Bible, or at least the Psalms,[9] by heart, with a certain basic minimum of doctrinal, canonical[10] and liturgical knowledge. That was all. Western culture had reached its nadir.

It would be an anachronism to see in these first religious schools of the fifth to the seventh centuries any of the rich humanistic aspirations that were to lead to the Carolingian and the twelfth-century Renaissances (10). Far from making the

[1] Caes. Ar., *Virg.*, 7, 104.
[2] Euch., *Instr.*, pr. 773.
[3] Greg. Magn., *Dial.*, II, 3.
[4] *V. SS. Hib.*, I, 250; 252; II, 180–181.
[5] Greg. Tur., *V. Patr.*, 20, I.
[6] *Ibid.*, 9, 2.
[7] *V. SS. Merov.*, III, 283.
[8] *Act. Sanct. Ord. Bened.*, I, 263.
[9] *AA. SS. Hib.*, 166; Ferreol., *Reg.*, 11; *PL*, 66, 963.
[10] *Conc. Merov.*, 88, c. 6.

most of the meagre knowledge still available to them, the schoolmasters in these Dark Ages did their best to keep their pupils away from all contact with a culture which they regarded as being far too sympathetic towards pagan traditions. Western monasticism still had the same atmosphere of cultural asceticism as the East: the monk must flee the world with its vanity and all its riches—and its riches included culture. I return to St. Caesarius, who has left so much valuable evidence about this. St. Caesarius had to leave Lérins for reasons of health, and in Arles he met the African scholar Julian Pomerius. Under him he began to study grammar and philosophy, but soon he had given up his studies and left him, preferring to remain faithful to the ideal of "monastic simplicity".[1] And Pomerius was not particularly secular-minded, judging by his *De Vita contemplativa*! There was the same atmosphere in the episcopal schools: if a bishop took too much trouble over the teaching of grammar he was apt to cause quite a scandal and be brought back to his senses in no uncertain fashion, as Desiderius of Vienne discovered from Gregory the Great[2] (11).

This obscurantism had another cause: the general disintegration of culture in the West. Decadence is not only a matter of ignorance and forgetfulness but of inner degeneration too. The attitude of Caesarius or Gregory can only be properly understood against the background of the secular culture of their time which they rejected with so much horror. It was not the eternal humanistic values that they rejected but the monstrous puerilities that the fag-end intellectuals of their day used to indulge in—as, for instance, in the curious piece of work by Virgil the Grammarian (12), which is full of pedantic mystifications and a pretence of higher learning and ends up in a riddle:

Cicero dicit *RRR-SS-PP-MM-N-T-EE-OO-A-V-I, quod sic solvendum est: Spes Romanorum periit*——[3]

Obviously the Christian school still existed only in seed, and had hardly begun to sprout; but it was a seed, not a mere residue. To vary the metaphor, it was only in the stammering stage, but it was a new creation, with its own new spirit and methods. It was the beginning of a new kind of education, no mere offshoot of the education of classical antiquity.

It still began, of course, with the alphabet;[4] but whereas in classical times this led on to a series of carefully graded stages of an abstract analytical system, it now led straight on to a text, the Text—the Sacred Text. The master would take a writing-board and write out the passage that was to be the subject of the lesson; generally he began with a Psalm,[5] for the main idea behind the teaching was to enable the pupil to master the Psalter, the basis of the Divine Office. The child was supposed to read the passage again and again until he knew it by heart—a sort of crude equivalent of our general method.[6] In the early stages this was less

---

[1] Caes. Ar., *Vit.*, 9, 299.
[2] Greg. Magn., *Reg.*, XI, 34.
[3] Virg. Gram., *Epit.*, 13, 77.
[4] *V. SS. Merov.*, II, 161; Stokes, *Tripartite Life*, I, cliii; II, 328; *V. SS. Hib.*, I, 67; II, 210.
[5] *Ibid.*, I, 165; II, 156–157.
[6] *V. SS. Merov.*, II, 342, c. 6.

a matter of reading the passage properly than of doing it from memory. He did not learn to read like a Greek child; he learned to read the particular passage—the Psalter, the New Testament. And what he learned was the Word of God, the revealed Scripture, the only thing worth knowing. How different from the classical method! It rather reminds one of the Moslem methods still being used today in schools where the Koran is taught. It is more accurate, more historical, to regard such teaching as we have been describing as the Christian equivalent of the Rabbinical school. Nothing is missing to the parallel. Above all, there is a special strain of veneration, of religious respect, for the teacher. The old Greek or Latin teacher, despised by everyone as one of the lowest of the low, is miles away. Now, as amongst the Jews, lessons were requested "with the deepest veneration and a humble prayer"—*cum summa veneratione humilique prece . . .*[1]

This new attitude is no doubt partly to be explained as an effect of decadence and the surrounding barbarism: the school-teacher had become a shadowy figure who had mastered the mysterious secret of how to write. This appears in an episode recounted by Gregory of Tours. A wandering cleric, soon to prove unworthy of his calling, presented himself to Bishop Aetherius of Lisieux (c. 584) as a school-teacher—*litterarum doctorem.* The prelate was overjoyed, for a school-teacher was a rare figure, and immediately got all the children of the city together so that the new arrival could start teaching them at once. Favours, kindnesses were showered upon him by everybody, particularly the parents; and then, inevitably, some kind of scandal cropped up. There was an immediate attempt to suppress it.[2]

But the teacher was far more than someone who knew the secrets of writing; he knew the secrets of Holy Writ. Whether a school was monastic, episcopal or presbyterial, it never separated teaching from religious education, from instruction in Church dogma and morals. Christianity was an intellectual religion but it was a religion for the masses, and the humblest of the faithful, however elementary their intellectual development, received something equivalent to what the culture of antiquity had haughtily reserved for a philosophical élite—a doctrine about being and life, an inner life and spiritual direction. As the old hagiographers used to say, the Christian school trained its pupils *litteris et bonis moribus*—"in letters and in virtue".[3] This close association, even on the most elementary level, between literary learning and religious education, this synthesis of teacher and spiritual father in the person of the school-teacher, seems to me to be the very essence of the Christian school and mediaeval education as contrasted with the education of classical antiquity. Its first appearance must therefore be traced back to the monasteries that arose in Egypt in the fourth century.

[1] *Ibid.*, 161, c. 1.
[2] Greg. Tur., *Hist. Fr.*, VI, 36.
[3] *AA. SS. Feb.*, III, 11; *V. SS. Hib.*, I, 99; 153; 269; II, 77; 107; etc.

THE END OF THE SCHOOL OF ANTIQUITY

ANY historical enquiry which does not take the reader "right up to our own day" ought to end by giving some sort of answer to the question "What came next?" This history of education in antiquity will come to a natural end when we know exactly when and how the religious education of mediaeval days, which I tried to describe in the last chapter, took the place of the old classical education.

BYZANTINE EDUCATION

Surprising as it may seem, there is to begin with a whole area where, strictly speaking, the old classical school never came to an end—in the Greek East; for Byzantine education was a direct continuation of classical education (1). This is in fact simply one particular aspect of the fundamental fact that there was no gap, no difference, even, between the civilization of the Late Roman Empire and the early Byzantine Middle Ages.

This appears most clearly in the history of the higher education of the time, which is more fully documented and has been more closely studied than the rest. From 425 to 1453 the University of Constantinople was a most fruitful centre of study, the main pillar of the classical tradition. Naturally, in the course of a thousand years it had many ups and downs, periods of decline and even temporary disappearances, that were then redeemed by splendid revivals: the most thorough-going reorganizations were made by the Cæsar Bardas in 863, by Constantine Monomachus in 1045, and probably in the thirteenth and early fourteenth centuries by the Paleologi.

Like all living things it underwent many transformations, but it always remained loyal to the spirit of its original foundation in the time of Theodosius II. The education it provided was always governed by classical standards, with the liberal arts supplying the foundation, and rhetoric, philosophy and law the crown. It continued to serve the same function in society—that of training an élite from which the Empire could draw its state officials. It never meddled with religion: the closing of the Neo-Platonic school in Athens by Justinian in 529[1] was part of the struggle against the declining paganism, but did not mean that the Christian Empire had any desire to steer higher education into more religious channels.

We know much less about the lower levels of this education, but it seems certain that here too the ancient tradition must have persisted. It will be found that on the primary level some aspects of Hellenistic teaching lasted right through the period of Turkish ascendancy into modern times. Secondary education was still based on grammar and the classics, and Hellenistic text-books and commentaries went on being used or copied.

[1] Malal., XVIII, 151.

The ideal educated man remained classical. Michael Psellus was born in 1018, and in his funeral oration on his mother, recalling his studious childhood,[1] he tells us that he learned the whole of the *Iliad* by heart, thus, after fourteen centuries, repeating the achievement of Xenophon's Nicoratus. Almost a century later Anna Comnena was being given an education that was entirely classical—humanist in tone and content: the classics, Greek, rhetoric, Aristotle and Plato, the four mathematical disciplines. . . .[2]

Thus there was an unbroken tradition between Hellenistic intellectuals and the highly "modern" humanists who lived in the time of the Paleologi—people like Nicephorus Gregoras (d. c. 1360) (2).

And the surprising fact emerges that this Byzantine society, which was so profoundly Christian, so absorbed in religion, particularly in theology, remained stubbornly faithful to the traditions of the old humanism. This had its dangers: the Byzantine school was so loyal to its pagan masters that there were periodic attempts at pagan revivals—in the ninth century there was Leon the mathematician, in the eleventh John Italos, in the fifteenth Gemistus Plethon—and these were as suspect from the orthodox Christian point of view as our own Western Renaissance was in the fifteenth and sixteenth centuries—which, as we know, was to a great extent a result of Byzantine influences.

There was, of course, besides this classical type of school, another cultural centre entirely Christian in inspiration—the monastic school. Throughout the Middle Ages the monastic schools maintained their original hostility to humanism and "the world" (the *Lives* of Byzantine saints always tend to minimize their heroes' secular culture) and remained exclusively concerned with spiritual and primarily ascetic preoccupations. They were a closed preserve for those who aspired to the religious life: the ban passed by the Council of Chalcedon against accepting children from "the world" remained in full force.

The one slightly disturbing feature is that it seems to have been necessary to renew this ban on several occasions—in 806 and in 1205, for instance (3); which seems to suggest that there was a tendency to infringe it! And indeed it seems clear that this was so: in 1238, for example, the Emperor John III Vatatzes entrusted the archimandrite of St. Gregory of Ephesus, Nicephorus Blemmydes, with the education of five boys, one of whom was the future historian George Acropolites, who had a brilliant career as a high secular official.

But if we are looking for a centre of religious education to counterbalance the highly secular education provided by the Imperial University, this will be found in the special patriarchal schools rather than in the monasteries. The origin of this type of school is still not clear; it may go back to the seventh century but it certainly appears quite clearly and quite fully developed in the eleventh. By this time there was a body called the "Didascali of the Great Church" (or "on the Episcopal List"), which taught near St. Sophia, as opposed to the "Philosophers of the Senate"—i.e. teachers nominated, as in the fourth century, by the Senate. These "didascali" were chosen by the patriarch and they formed what amounted to a theological faculty based on Scripture. They included specialists on the Gospels, the Apostles and the Psalter.

---

[1] *Epit.*, I, 14. [2] Ann. Comn., *Alex.*, I, p. 3.

Whereas the monasteries were strictly ascetic, the patriarchal schools were profoundly affected by the traditional humanism. They did not simply teach religion; they aimed at supplying a foundation of general learning. Besides having a theological faculty they had a faculty of arts, run by a "master— μαΐστωρ—of the rhetors"—who also had grammarians under him—and a "master of the philosophers", who also taught mathematics. Compared with the classical-humanistic University, the patriarchal schools were an attempt to create an attractive and comparatively original type of Christian humanism on the basis of the old models.

Thus, in the middle of the twelfth century Nicephorus Basilikes (who later became Professor of Gospel Exegesis) composed a text-book of *Progymnasmata* in the purest Hellenistic tradition: the only subjects mentioned besides the usual Atlantis, Danaë or Xerxes—and so on—were a few in the chapter on the "ethopoea" taken from religious history: "Samson's words when he was blinded by the Philistines; David's words when he found his enemy Saul asleep in a cavern; the words of the Mother of God when Christ changed the water into wine at the wedding-feast of Cana."[1] Eustathius of Thessalonica, the great commentator on Homer and the other classics, is regarded by people today as having been one of the most representative figures of Byzantine humanism, yet he had been brought up in a monastery and was "master of the rhetors" in the patriarchal school.

Only after the Turkish conquest does the situation resemble that of the Western world a thousand years earlier. The year 1453 broke the tradition and the Greek world found itself in the same situation as Merovingian Gaul: lack of schools endangered the supply of priests and hence the actual maintenance of Christian life. And the Greek Church reacted in exactly the same way as the Council of Vaison had reacted in Gaul in 529: in every village the priest gathered the children together in the shade of the church and did his best to teach them to read—to read the Psalter and the other books used in the liturgy so as to "bring up a competent successor" (5).

But it is an extraordinary thing, showing the depth to which the classical tradition had rooted itself in the East, that even in the eighteenth century little Greek children could be heard chanting the alphabet backwards and forwards at the same time, as in Quintilian's or St. Jerome's day; or repeating this sort of thing:

'Εκκλησία μολυβδοκαντηλορελεκμένη . . .
O my church chiselled and sculptured in lead,
Which was chiselled and sculptured in lead
By the son of the chiseller and sculptor in lead,
If I had also been the son of the chiseller and sculptor in lead,
I should have chiselled and sculptured it in lead more prettily
Than the son of the chiseller and sculptor in lead.

This is a perfectly clear synthesis of two typical exercises that went on in the classical Greek school—"tongue-twisters" and "declension".

[1] *Rhet. Gr.*, I, 566 *et seq.*; 480; 517; 499.

THE MONASTIC SCHOOL IN IRELAND

At the other end of the Christian world, in Ireland, the situation was exactly the opposite. Having remained outside the Empire, Celtic Ireland had not come into contact with classical culture. Remarkable—and in certain respects advanced—though its civilization was, pagan Ireland had remained "barbarian", unaware of the written word. The Book—and as a result the school—came to it by way of Christianity, thanks chiefly to St. Patrick (d. 460–470). Unlike all the other countries of Western Europe, Ireland has never had any written tradition apart from that supplied by its Christian schools.

I say "Christian" schools, but I mean "monastic" for, as is well known, Celtic Christendom developed entirely within the framework of the monastery. As in Egypt and elsewhere, the schools were strictly religious, and the teaching was essentially for boys who intended to be monks (even though as a special favour chieftains' sons were accepted). The basis of the entire education was the Bible, and chiefly the Psalter. It is not necessary to describe the life in these schools here (6)—incidentally it was extremely unusual: children were often taken to the monastery as soon as they were born—there were real monastic nurseries; everything was carried to extremes in an atmosphere of such fierce asceticism. It is sufficient to say that the history of Irish culture is entirely mediaeval. From this "isle of saints", growing constantly stronger and richer, its culture spread gradually throughout the whole of the West, settling and fertilizing wherever it went—beginning in Britain in the sixth century, first colonizing the north, the part of Scotland that like itself had remained outside the sphere of Roman domination, and gradually making its way south, to restore what had been ruined by the Germanic invasions.

THE DESTRUCTION OF THE SCHOOL OF ANTIQUITY BY INVASIONS

For the classical schools and classical culture of Roman Britain had been destroyed by the Anglo-Saxons, who had shattered not only the political structure of the island but its ethnographic structure too. In Britain the first half of the fifth century was a period of violence in which the darkness of barbarism rapidly increased.

It was the same on the Continent: everywhere what had been Roman territory was seized by the Germanic peoples, and the result was a complete breakdown of Roman life and the disappearance of the old schools.

This is perhaps most clearly to be seen in Gaul (7). Long before that fatal day, December 31st 406, after which Roman dominion over Gaul was never to be complete again, cracks had appeared in the structure of the classical system. In 276 the Rhine had been crossed for the first time, and since then the barbarian raids had been multiplying, ravaging the whole of Gaul and causing long periods of insecurity; the cities contracted, withdrew within the narrow confines of their newly-constructed ramparts, and the wealthy country gentlemen entrenched themselves in their *villae*, which thus became *burgi*.

These trials and transformations did not actually break the continuity of the cultural tradition, but they undermined the vitality of academic institutions, which had developed in close association with the brilliant city life, and were bound to wane when it waned. Again, as they, and with them the whole system of classical education, had gradually passed out of private hands and into the sphere of public service, they had come to depend more and more on the State and the local public authorities for money and organization: their fate was bound up with the political structure of the Empire.

And when the Empire collapsed, they collapsed. It seems fairly certain that the generation that came after Ausonius (d. c. 395) was the last to be familiar with the normal system of Roman education, with its three stages—*magister ludi*, grammarian, rhetor. This system must have disappeared with the great invasion and the catastrophes that marked the beginning of the fifth century: Ausonius' grandson Paulinus of Pella has described what occurred round the region of Marseilles, where he took refuge about 422.[1]

Nevertheless, though the official schools, which had been properly organized by the local authorities, disappeared, classical education persisted for another century, thanks mainly to the "senatorial" class of great landowners, who were very much attached to it. Though there were no schools, there were always private teachers to collect a few pupils to teach at home. Sidonius Apollinaris, for instance, who was born in Lyons in about 430, reminds his friend Probus of how they had studied together, probably in Arles, in their teacher Eusebius' house—*inter Eusebianos lares*.[2] But gradually the number of pupils declined, and one is tempted to wonder whether the "professors" who keep on appearing in Sidonius' writings were not really private tutors in the service of some great family (8).

Thus the future of classical education came to depend on the existence of a classical way of life within the ranks of the Gallo-Roman aristocracy. But through contact with its new German masters this aristocracy itself rapidly became barbarised; even in Sidonius' lifetime there were "collaborators" who admired the barbarians and began speaking their language. . . .[3] The Roman way of life may have lasted longer in certain parts like Auvergne, where Sidonius himself came from, and above all Aquitaine—districts which had not been so upset by the invasions and not so directly subjected to the barbarian kings—but gradually the few remaining centres of the old culture faded out, and by the sixth century the only kind of education in existence was that which had been taken over by the Church.

It was much the same over the rest of Europe. The Danubian provinces and the country beyond, which had been forcibly occupied by the Germanic "confederates" at the end of the fourth century and then been at the mercy of all kinds of different tribes and races, had been utterly disorganized since the beginning of the fifth century and, as in Gaul, Roman life had been suffocated by barbarism, as can be seen from Eugippius' *Life of St. Severinus* (d. 482). In Spain, again, the Germanic invasions and occupations, which began with the Suevi, the Alani and the Vandals in 409, destroyed Roman culture and with

[1] P. Pell., 68–69.   [2] Sid. Apoll., *Ep.*, IV, 1, 3.   [3] *Ibid.*, V, 5; IV, 20.

it the Roman school: intellectual life in Visigothic Spain came entirely through the Church (9).

AFRICA AN EXCEPTION

The old education survived for a time in two regions—Vandal Africa, and Italy. However brutal his actual conquest may have been, Genseric's subsequent African kingdom certainly did not deserve the bad reputation which it got from Church chroniclers because of his Arian persecution of the Catholics (10). From the intellectual point of view Carthage in particular was extremely active under the "Vandal peace", as can be seen particularly from the compilation known as the *Anthologia Latina,* which reveals the existence of a teaching circle in the genuine classical tradition. After the victories by Belisarius, the Emperor Justinian determined to give this teaching official recognition and passed a Constitution in 533–534 providing for the upkeep of two grammarians and two rhetors in Carthage.[1]

The number of teachers seems to have been very much reduced, however, and it is also to be noticed that Justinian did nothing of the same kind anywhere else outside Carthage. There is known to have been a great territorial decrease in the occupation of African soil between the Early Empire and Byzantine times: Vandal domination had been obliged to come to terms with the surge of independence that had come from the Berber tribes in the African interior. Some traces of Roman culture—Christianity, the use of Latin, certain municipal traditions—do indeed seem to have survived in Morocco and Orania until the time of the Arab invasion (11), but the classical educational tradition had clearly become extremely tenuous and was only really to be found near the capital, Carthage. There at least it lasted until the collapse of the Byzantine domination: its end came with the capture of Carthage (695–697). Christianity went on existing there until the eleventh century and, with Christianity, Latin —written Latin, hence education in Latin; but the culture of these later "Roumi" was essentially and strictly religious (12).

This relatively long survival of classicism in Africa was not without its effect on European culture. In the fifth, sixth and seventh centuries Africa produced a number of scholars who went bearing precious manuscripts into Southern Gaul, and still more into Spain and Southern Italy, and thus helped to build up the reserves from which mediaeval humanism was later to draw its strength.

ITALY ALSO AN EXCEPTION

The part played by Italy was even more important. In Italy more than anywhere else the twilight of classicism was long-drawn-out, and the way prepared unconsciously for the future. In Italy, naturally, the classical tradition had struck its deepest roots, and the result was that it managed to resist the ravages caused by the invasions which, probably from 401 onwards, descended upon it. The Germanic occupation did not lead to the disappearance of the old way of

[1] *Cod. Just.,* I, 27, i, 42.

life; Italy was even more successful than Vandal Africa in her efforts to go on living according to the traditional standards under the Ostrogoth domination, especially during the long reign of their first king, the great Theodoric (493–526). Theodoric really did reign "for the good of Rome"—*Bono Romae*[1]—as the motto said that was stamped on the bricks he used to restore the old city's monuments.

Without education himself, he nevertheless appreciated the greatness of classical culture, and like Stilicho he was determined that his daughter Amalaswinthe should get the best education she could. Latin literature and Latin thought had their last brief spell of glory—it was a real renaissance, ultimately to prove of great value to the Middle Ages, thanks to the great work of Boethius and Cassiodorus (whose services, incidentally, Theodoric did not fail to make full use of).

Through Cassiodorus—appointed *magister officiorum*, chief of the chancellery, in 523—Theodoric encouraged learning[2] and maintained the State professorships that drew students from the provinces to Rome. Theodoric died in 533 and his daughter Amalaswinthe became regent. Cassiodorus was made prefect of the praetorium and managed to get the teachers' salaries put on a proper footing—a matter which had been neglected for a time[3]—and when the Emperor Justinian reorganized Italy on the basis of his Pragmatic Sanction after the reconquest (535), all he had to do was to ordain that the practices should be followed that had been in use in Theodoric's time.[4]

Thus it is clear that the old academic life lasted on in Rome until the middle of the sixth century. There were still men teaching grammar, rhetoric, law and medicine,[5] with salaries paid by the State—one of the last holders of the chair of eloquence, which had been inaugurated so long before by Quintilian, was a certain Felix, who in 534 prepared a critical edition of Martianus Capella (13) and they were still teaching in rooms arranged around Trajan's Forum,[6] which were also used for public recitations[7]—for Imperial Rome hung on to its literary customs as long as it did to its schools.

Rome was still the main university town[8] but academic life was just as active in the other big Italian cities. Ennodius of Arles, the future Bishop of Pavia (473/474–521), has described the school—*auditorium*—run by the grammarian and rhetor Deuterius in Milan.[9] The pupils did all the usual classical subjects —Latin, Greek, grammar and rhetoric[10]—and, as in the great days of Seneca the Elder, they "declaimed" in their *controversiae* and their *suasoriae* on the same eternal subjects—the ungrateful son, tyrannicide, Diomedes, Thetis. . . .[11] Even Ennodius himself, lawyer as he was,[12] was not above composing model copies—his *Dictiones*—for the edification of the young friends whose studies he was supervising.

Besides Milan there was Ravenna, where one of Ennodius' disciples, the future poet Arator, studied law.[13] The schools were still flourishing there thirty

[1] Diehl, 37.
[2] Cassiod., *Var.*, I, 39.
[3] *Ibid.*, IX, 21.
[4] Just., *Nov.*, *Ap.* 7, 22.
[5] *Ibid.*
[6] Fort., *Carm.*, VII, 8, 26.
[7] *Ibid.*, III, 18, 8.
[8] Ennod., *Ep.*, V, 9; VIII, 33; IX, 2.
[9] *Ibid.*, *Dict.*, VII; IX–X; *Carm.*, I, 2; II, 104.
[10] *Ibid.*, *Ep.*, I, 5, 10.
[11] *Ibid.*, *Dict.*, XVII–XVIII; XXIV–XXV.
[12] *Ibid.*, *Ep.*, II, 27, 4.
[13] Cassiod., *Var.*, VIII, 12.

years later, as we can tell from Fortunatus, who studied there some time after 552 (14).

THE LOMBARD INVASION

But Italian prosperity had been shattered by the long and gruelling Gothic resistance to reconquest by Byzantium (535–555), and it was finally destroyed by the invasion of a late-comer among the German peoples, the Lombards, who entered Italy in 568, conquered the plain of the Po, infiltrated along the Apennine backbone, and reached Beneventum in 572. Under the Lombards the peninsula experienced the horrors that Gaul and the rest of Europe had gone through a hundred and fifty years earlier. Barbarism spread over the whole of the country, and for nearly a hundred years, from the end of the sixth century to the end of the seventh, the land which had been for so long the guardian of the classical tradition was forced to watch its intellectual standard decline to Merovingian level. This period was a kind of watershed, beyond which the only education that remained was almost entirely religious.

As long as the classical tradition had lasted, sixth-century Italy had presented a picture of the same strict dualism as had been manifest in the Late Empire and the Byzantine period, between a secular education faithful to the humanism it had inherited from paganism and an ascetic religious education, violently at odds with it, supplied not by proper schools but by the clergy or the monasteries.

Ennodius, Cassiodorus and St. Gregory the Great all had a double career, first in the world and then in the Church, and in his own way each illustrates the antagonism between the two kinds of education. As soon as Ennodius took Holy Orders, and while he was still merely a deacon to Bishop Epiphanius of Pavia, his spiritual master, whom he later succeeded, he solemnly broke with all the pomp of secular eloquence,[1] and refused with horror to concern himself as he had done so often before with the literary studies of one of his young nephews, whose mother had thought it would be a good idea for him to be ordained priest. "I should be ashamed," he said, "to give any secular instruction to a man of the Church"[2] (15).

Cassiodorus, who, as we know, was so keen to keep the chairs of secular learning filled in Rome, was disturbed to find sacred learning so completely without its own institutions. In 534 he was involved in Pope Agapetus' curious endeavour to create a great scholar's library in Rome itself and build up Christian schools, like the ones in Nisibis, round it (16). Then he retired from the world, and some years later he founded a double monastery on his estate in Vivarium, in the most sheltered part of Italy on the Ionian coast of Calabria. Here he set up a vast library, with a whole team of translators and copyists, in the effort to create a centre of purely religious studies based on the Bible, and integrating the traditional humanism in a Christian synthesis. The scheme set out in his two volumes of *Institutiones* gives an outline of this remarkable attempt at monastic culture (17).

[1] Ennod., *Ep.*, III, 24; IX, 1.　　　　　[2] *Ibid.*, IX, 9.

More radical in his attitude, and from the beginning less deeply attached to the old culture, St. Gregory the Great broke entirely with classical culture as soon as he was converted to the monastic life. He had been born in about 540, so that he had been able to receive his education in Rome along more or less traditional lines,[1] but the tradition had been emptied of all its content by the prevailing decadence. Hence St. Gregory had never known the real depth of classical humanism, and, as we have seen, in his religious culture he reacted violently against it. It was in his monastery of the Clivus Scauri that he first received this culture from the first abbots he put in charge there, Hilarion and Maximianus.[2]

Then came the dark days of the Lombard conquest: the secular school, and with it all the old tradition, collapsed. As the only organized force in existence, the Church lived through the upheaval and preserved her own kind of education too. The educational centres that survived were first, and essentially, the monasteries: in Calabria there was Vivarium—after Cassiodorus' death it seems to have played rather a passive rôle, but it managed to hold on to, and later hand on, all its treasures, and that was something. In Naples there was the monastery of Pizzofalcone, famous for having, in earlier days, sheltered Eugippius; further to the north were St. Vincent of Volturno, Monte Cassino, the monastery in Bobbio which St. Columba had come from Great Britain and founded in 612—the influence of Celtic monasticism was now beginning to be felt on the continent. . . .

Along with the monastic schools there developed episcopal schools, as had happened earlier in Gaul: if any active teaching seems to have been going on in decadent Rome in St. Gregory's time, it was the kind that needed to be given —as in Gaul, again—to the choir of young clerics—the *schola cantorum*— which, according to tradition, the great Pope himself, to his everlasting fame, had reorganized. Everywhere in Italy we come across signs of this kind of ecclesiastical education, which centred round the bishop, was given within the actual cathedral, and was clearly intended primarily as a means of ensuring a constant supply of educated priests. In 678–679 a bishop of Fiesole declared that this was the way he had been brought up in the church in Arezzo: *per plures annos in ecclesia Sancti Donati notritus et litteras edoctus sum.*[3]

But it should be emphasized that the change over from the old Italy to a mediaeval Italy was not as radical as in the rest of Europe. The barbarism of the Lombards was appalling, but it never entirely put a stop to the literary tradition, primarily because it never covered the whole of the peninsula: the coastal regions were protected by the Byzantine fleet and put up a long resistance—Ravenna lasted out until 751. Naples, Salerno, the far south and Rome in particular were never really barbarized: there was always something of the Byzantine continuity in these special centres.

When after a century the situation became comparatively stable, and, very diffidently, the Lombard Court in Pavia tried to link up with the literary

---

[1] Greg. Tur., *Hist. Fr.*, X, 1; Paul Diac., *V. Greg.*, 2.
[2] Joh. Diac., *V. Greg.*, I, 6.
[3] Schiaparelli, *C. dipl. Long.*, I, p. 71, 1, 29–30.

tradition initiated by Theodoric, King Cunincpert (678–700) found a "magister" called Etienne who was prepared, probably rather dubiously, to play the part of court poet.[1] In 680 the same king presented the grammarian Felix with a walking-stick decorated with gold and silver.[2] There were already signs of a Lombard renaissance (18).

Possible though it may have been, there is no reason to suppose that the slightest thread of the old academic tradition lasted through this iron century; the education that went on in the home was sufficient to ensure the transmission of the necessary minimum of knowledge and love of letters through several generations. Thus we are told that before he entered the religious life Attala of Bobbio, successor to St. Columba, had received his secular education from his own father, though this was in Burgundy and not in Italy.[3] Something of this domestic tradition still went on: the grammarian mentioned above, Felix of Pavia, brought up his own nephew Flavian, who was later to be tutor to the great Paul the Deacon.[4]

PRELUDES TO THE CAROLINGIAN RENAISSANCE

But these circumstances, which put Italy in a separate category amongst the nations of the West, not only gave rise to the Lombard Renaissance; they also led to a remarkable development of culture and education in the schools of Britain.

From the first Irish schools to those of the *Scoti* and Anglo-Saxons of Charlemagne's time there is a straight line. This was not a purely native development; it was helped by the almost continuous influence of former Roman districts in which fragments of the classical heritage had persisted. Thus the first generations of Irish priests were probably indebted to Britain and Gaul, and later there was a surprising Spanish influence on them. But the moving force in this early pre-Carolingian mediaeval culture was Italy, as appeared in the famous mission sent by St. Gregory the Great to the English in 597 under the leadership of St. Augustine, the first Archbishop of Canterbury, one of whose successors was a Greek, Theodore of Tarsus (669–690). Rome was now a province of Byzantium, and it is not difficult to imagine what a combination of cultural influences this meant. After 597 there was continuous intercourse between Italy and Great Britain. Pilgrims passed from one country to the other, often bringing back with them books or old and new manuscripts—books connected with the liturgy—which the old Roman libraries still possessed in abundance despite all the pillage that had taken place. Benedict Biscop, for instance, who founded the abbeys in Wearmouth and Jarrow, went to Rome six times during the second half of the seventh century, and each time he returned with a great number of books.[5]

Thus the long Italian twilight mingled with the early dawn that had broken beyond the Channel, and this affected the future of the whole of Western civilization. The Scots and their Anglo-Saxon pupils and imitators were not left entirely

[1] *Poet. lat. med.*, IV, 731.
[2] Paul Diac., *Hist. Long.*, VI, 7.
[3] *AA. SS. Mart.*, II, 42.
[4] Paul Diac., *loc. cit.*
[5] Bede, *H. Abb.*; *PL*, 94, 716 A; 717 B, 720 B, 721 C.

to their own resources: they did not have to re-invent grammar and science, or rediscover Greek: all these things and more—the marvellous heritage of the classics—were there waiting for them in the Mediterranean culture as soon as they had developed the intelligence and wisdom to realize it.

In this double way the material components of the classical tradition were enabled to survive the destruction of the classical Form and be used again in a new synthesis that appeared as mediaeval culture, with its Christian inspiration. This first began to manifest its own distinctive Form in the Carolingian Renaissance, which indeed developed from the combination of Lombard and British cultural factors. There is something highly symbolic in the meeting at the court of Charlemagne between the English Alcuin and the Lombard Paul the Deacon (with Alcuin were the *Scoti*, Clement, Joseph, Dungal; accompanying Paul were Peter of Pisa and Paulinus of Aquileia).

Hence arose one of the characteristic features of mediaeval Christianity, of the whole of Western civilization in fact: however original its first inspiration may have been, however much opposed to the spirit of the old humanism, it was not fundamentally different from it. It was not an absolutely new beginning, a fresh start. From the beginning and throughout its subsequent history it drew so much from the old classical sources that it seems to appear as a continual Renaissance. Despite the barbarian interlude there was a certain continuity of matter, if not of form, that made Western man the heir to the old Classicism.

ADDITIONAL NOTES

ADDITIONAL NOTES

INTRODUCTION

I

Bibliography. For Education in Antiquity as a whole the basic work is still:

L. GRASBERGER, *Erziehung und Unterricht im klassischen Alterthum, mit besonderer Rücksicht auf die Bedürfnisse der Gegenwart, nach den Quellen dargestellt*; vol. I, *Die leibliche Erziehung bei den Griechen und Römern*, 1, *Die Knabenspiele*, Würzburg, 1864; 2, *Die Turnschule der Knaben*, 1866; vol. II, *Die musische Unterricht oder die Elementarschule bei den Griechen und Römern*, 1875; vol. III, *Die Ephebenbildung oder die musische und militärische Ausbildung der Griechischen und Römischen Jünglinge*, 1880.

This is a very old book and very much of its time—very long, very heavy, and very cumbersome, especially since, like Fustel de Coulanges in *La Cité antique*, Grasberger mixes up evidence from the most diverse sources and ages. He studies the education of antiquity as though it were all of a piece, without dividing it up into separate historical stages. On the other hand, despite his title he does not always quote the original sources in support of his opinions, but refers to the works of earlier scholars, works which are today quite unknown and very difficult to come by.

Nevertheless, despite these flaws, this highly erudite work makes it pretty well unnecessary to bother about any of the earlier books by F. H. C. SCHWARZ (Leipzig, 1829), J. NAUDET (Paris, 1831), F. CRAMER (Elberfeld, 1833), J. H. KRAUSE (Halle, 1851); but the following little book may still be found useful:

J. L. USSING, *Erziehung und Jugendunterricht bei den Griechen und Römern*[2] (Berlin, 1885), the German translation of two Copenhagen "Programmes", the first edition of which (Altona, 1870) appeared under the title: *Darstellung des Erziehung- und Unterrichtswesen bei den Griechen und Römern.*

I have no direct knowledge of the large volume (530 pp.) by:

P. MONROE, *Source Book of the History of Education for the Greek and Roman Period* (London, 1902).

DAREMBERG and SAGLIO, *Dictionnaire des Antiquités grecques et romaines*, contains an excellent article, "Educatio", brilliant but not always very reliable, by E. POTTIER: vol. II, 1 (1892), pp. 462 a–490 b. On the other hand the PAULY-WISSOWA *Real-encyclopädie der Altertumswissenschaft* contains only a brief article, "Schulen", by E. ZIEBARTH: II R., II, 1 (1923), c. 763–768; the bulk of the matter will no doubt appear in the article "Unterricht", which has not yet been published. The treatment is also rather sketchy in the pages which are devoted to this subject in the volumes of the series:

I. VON MÜLLER, *Handbuch der [klassischen] Altertumswissenschaft*: vol. IV, 1, 2; I. VON MÜLLER-A. BAUER, *Die Griechischen Privat- und Kriegsaltertümer*, Munich, 1893 (the revised work promised from E. PERNICE has not appeared), pp. 312–342; 11, 2, H. BLÜMNER, *Die Römischen Privataltertümer* (1911), pp. 312–342.

The need for the publication of a work summarising recent research has also been felt abroad:

J. F. DOBSON, *Ancient Education and its Meaning to Us, Our Debt to Greece and Rome*, London, 1932.

M. LECHNER, *Erziehung und Bildung in der Griechische-römischen Antike*, Münich, 1933.

H. FRANZ, "Die Erziehung bei den Griechen und den Römern", in J. SCHROETELER, *Die Pädagogik der nichtchristlichen Kulturvölker*, Munich, 1934.

On Greek Education an excellent book is:

P. GIRARD, *L'Education athénienne*[2], Paris, 1891.

See also (though this book largely derives from Grasberger and Girard):

K. J. FREEMAN, *Schools of Hellas, an Essay on the Practice and Theory of Ancient Greek Education from 600 to 300 B.C.*, [2] London, 1912; and:

J. DREVER, *Greek Education, Its Practice and Principles*, Cambridge, 1912.

To these must be added, for its tremendous insight into Greek cultural ideals and consequently Greek education, the great work:

W. JÄGER, *Paideia: The Ideals of Greek Culture*, trans. Gilbert Highet, 3 vols., Blackwell, Oxford. Vol. I, 1936; II, 1944; III, 1945.

Our documentation may be completed by mentioning the works on decorated monuments, especially vase-paintings:

F. WINTER, "Schulunterricht auf griechischen Vasenbildern", *Bonner Jahrbücher* (1916), CXXIII, pp. 275–285; and on physical education:

E. NORMAN GARDINER, *Greek Athletic Sports and Festivals*, London, 1910, pp. 511–517 (Bibliography), and the illustrations to his:

Athletics of the Ancient World, Oxford, 1930. Cf. also:

C. A. FORBES, *Greek Physical Education*, New York, 1929.

For Roman Education two fundamental works are:

E. JULLIEN, *Les Professeurs de littérature dans l'ancienne Rome*, Paris, 1885.

A. GWYNN, *Roman Education from Cicero to Quintilian*, Oxford, 1926.

There is a brief account in:

J. MARQUARDT, "La Vie privée des Romains" (in T. MOMMSEN and J. MARQUARDT, *Manuel des Antiquités romaines*, French trans., XIV, 1), Paris, 1892, pp. 96–157.

L. FRIEDLÄNDER, 10th ed. taken by G. WISSOWA from: *Darstellungen aus der Sittengeschichte Roms in der Zeit von August bis zum Ausgang der Antonine*, Leipzig, 1921, vol. I, pp. 175–188; II, pp. 191–214.

For archaeological documentation:

H. I. MARROU, Μουσικὸς ἀνήρ, *Etude sur les Scènes de la Vie intellectuelle figurant sur les Monuments funéraires romains*, Grenoble, 1937.

The schools of the Late Empire have been the subject of special works:

G. RAUSCHEN, *Das griechische-römische Schulwesen zur Zeit des ausgehenden Heidentums*, Bonn, 1900.

P. R. COLE, *Later Roman Education in Ausonius, Capella, and the Theodosian Code*, New York, 1902.

P. HAARHOFF, *Schools of Gaul, a Study of Pagan and Christian Education in the Last Century of the Western Empire*, Oxford, 1920.

There is little of lasting value in M. PAVAN'S *La Crisi della scuola nel IV secolo d.C.*, Bari, 1952.

There is a great deal of material in the article "Ecoles" by Dom H. Leclercq in F. CABROL-H. LECLERCQ, *Dictionnaire d'Archéologie chrétienne et de Liturgie*, vol. IV, 2 (1921), c. 1730–1883.

2

For the history of education in the Middle Ages in Western Europe, it will be sufficient to mention:

M. ROGER, *L'Enseignement des Lettres classiques d'Ausone à Alcuin, introduction à l'Histoire des écoles carolingiennes*, Paris, 1905.

L. MAITRE, *Les Ecoles épiscopales et monastiques en Occident avant les Universités (768–1180)*, Paris, 1924 (2nd ed. of *Les Ecoles épiscopales et monastiques de l'Occident depuis Charlemagne jusqu'à Philippe Auguste*, Paris, 1866).

E. LESNE, *Histoire de la propriété ecclésiastique en France*, vol. V, *Les Ecoles de la fin du VIIIe siècle à la fin du XIIe*, Lille, 1940.

G. PARÉ, A. BRUNET, P. TREMBLAY: *La Renaissance du XIIe siècle, les Ecoles et l'Enseignement*, refonte complète de l'ouvrage de G. Robert (1909), Paris-Ottawa, 1933.

L. J. PAETOW, *The Arts Course at Mediaeval Universities, with Special Reference to Grammar and Rhetoric*, Champaign, 1910.

M. GRABMANN, *Geschichte der scholastischen Methode*, Freiburg-im-Breisgau, 1909–1911.

S. D'IRSAY, *Histoire des Universités françaises et étrangères depuis les origines jusqu'à 1860*, vol. I, *Moyen-Age et Renaissance*, Paris, 1933.

3

For the neo-classical character of French classical teaching:

F. DE DAINVILLE, *Les Jésuites et l'éducation de la Société française, la naissance de l'humanisme moderne*, vol. I, Paris, 1942.

P. D. BOURCHENIN, *Etude sur les académies protestantes en France au XVIe et au XVIIe siècle*, Paris, 1882.

4

The word *culture:* this must be understood in its specifically French sense as "a *personal* form of the life of the mind", and not, as some ethnographers wrongly interpret it, in the sense of the German *Kultur*, which means *civilisation.* Cf. my essay "Culture, Civilisation, Decadence", *Revue de Synthèse*, XV (=*Revue de Synthèse Historique*, LVII), 1938, pp. 133–160.

5

For the Book of Proverbs as a "Mirror of the Scribes", it will be sufficient to refer to the brief remarks by A. MORET, *Histoire de l'Orient* (=G. GLOTZ, *Histoire Générale*, I), 2, Paris, 1936, p. 786, rather than to the wordy and exhausting work by Dom H. DUESBERG, *Les Scribes inspirés* (I), *Le Livre des Proverbes*, Paris, 1938.

6

For the oldest known Sumerian writing-tablets (level IV in the Uruk excavations): J. JORDAN, *Abhandlungen* of the Berlin Academy of Sciences, *Phil.-hist. Kl.*, 1932, 2, pp. 11–12; A. FALKENSTEIN, *Archaische Texte aus Uruk*, Berlin, 1936; V. GORDON CHILDE, *The Prehistoric East.*
These seem to refer to the administration of the Temple.

7

The *Teachings of Akhthoy*—this title is merely one of convenience: the same text is also called by J. MASPERO in *Du Genre épistolaire chez les Egyptiens de l'époque pharaonique* (Paris, 1872), the *Satire des métiers*—have been translated by A. ERMAN, *Die*

Literatur der Aegypter, Leipzig, 1923, pp. 100–105 (Eng. trans. by A. H. Blackman, London, 1927) under the title "Die Lehre des Duauf". The author's full name is sometimes taken to be "Douaouf son of Kheti" (or Akhti, Akhthoy), and sometimes "Akhthoy son of Douaouf".

The scribe Amenemope's *Satire on the Countryman* is also translated by ERMAN, *ibid.*, pp. 246–247.

8

For the scribes' divine guardians: G. CONTENAU, *Manuel d'Archéologie orientale*, Paris, 1927, I, p. 232; A. ERMAN, *La Religion des Egyptiens*, French trans., Paris, 1937, p. 81. With Thoth is associated the goddess Seshat. The scribes' veneration was also to be directed to "heroes", i.e. divinised scribes, like the celebrated Imhotep, minister and architect to the old king Djezer who built the pyramid with steps in Saqqarah (twenty-eighth century) and the later Amenhotep, the son of Hapu, a scribe under Amenophis III (1405–1370): ERMAN, *ibid.*, pp. 372–373; P. GILBERT, *La Naissance et la carrière du dieu Asclépios-Imouthès*, Brussels, 1929; W. R. DAWSON, "Amenophis, the Son of Hapu", *Aegyptus*, VII (1926), pp. 122–138.

R. LABAT has drawn my attention to an interesting cuneiform text (*Vorderasiatische Bibliothek*, VII, 256, 18) in which Assurbanipal prides himself on his abilities as a scribe as much as on his victories. He claims "on this point to surpass all previous kings and to be able to read stones dating from the time of the deluge and understand writing tablets in obscure Sumerian and the Accadian which is so difficult to master". He says that he himself wrote the books in his library. On bas-reliefs he had himself portrayed with a style in his belt.

9

For the school in the palace at Mari: A. PARROT, *Syria*, XVII (1936), p. 21; pl. III, 3–4.

10

For education in ancient Mesopotamia: B. MEISSNER, *Babylonien und Assyrien* (*Kulturgeschichtliche Bibliothek herausgegeben von* W. FOY), Heidelberg, 1925, II, pp. 324 *et seq.*; S. LANDESDORFER, *Schule und Unterricht in alten Babylonien*, *Blätter f.d. Gym.-Schulwesen*, XLV, pp. 577–624.

For its parallel in Jewry: L. DURR, *Das Erziehungswesen in Alten Testament und in antiken Orient*, Leipzig, 1932.

For Egypt the classical work is the essay by A. ERMAN, "Die Aegyptischen Schuler-handschriften", *Abhandlungen* of the Berlin Academy of Sciences, *Phil.-hist. Kl.*, 1925, 2; cf. B. VAN DE WALLE, "Les Exercices d'écoliers dans l'ancienne Egypte", *Revue des Questions scientifiques* (Louvain), 4, XXIV (1933), pp. 219–247.

11

The passages concerning the Egyptians' severe way of teaching (*Papyrus Anastasi* V, 3, 9, and IV, 8, 7) have been translated by A. ERMAN, *Literatur der Aegypter*, pp. 243 and 267.

12

Of the oral teaching which is reflected in Mesopotamia in the texts known as "Commentaries" (cf. R. LABAT, *Commentaires Assyro-Babyloniens sur les présages*, Bordeaux, 1933, pp. 9 *et seq.*), there is an excellent example in the literary conversation between a teacher and his pupil in *Keilschrifttexte aus Assur religiösen Inhalts*, No. 111 (partly translated by B. MEISSNER, *Babylonien und Assyrien*, II, pp. 326–327).

13

For the Egyptian sapiential literature, which has often been analysed on the lines of A. ERMAN'S *Literatur der Aegypter*, see for example the work already mentioned: H. DUESBERG, *Les Scribes inspirés*, I, pp. 59–68.

14

For its influence on Jewish Wisdom: A. ERMAN, *Sitzungsberichte* of the Berlin Academy of Sciences, 1924, pp. 86–93; P. HUMBERT, *Recherches sur les sources égyptiennes de la littérature sapientiale des Hébreux*, Neuchâtel, 1929.

15

For the Wisdom of Mesopotamia: B. MEISSNER, *Babylonien und Assyrien*, II, pp. 419 *et seq.*; S. LANGDON, "Babylonian Wisdom", *Babyloniaca*, VII (1923), pp. 137 *et seq.*; E. EBELING, "Reste akkadischen Weisheitsliteratur", *Mitteilungen altorient Gesellschaft*, IV, pp. 21–29; a brief description in E. DHORME, *La Littérature babylonienne et assyrienne*, Paris, 1937, pp. 85–90.

16

The scribe culture of the first two Egyptian dynasties is proved by the official seals bearing characteristic titles like "Chancellor of all the Writings" (J. PIRENNE, *Histoire des Institutions et de Droit privé de l'ancienne Egypte*, I, Brussels, 1932, pp. 121–125, 301–304). Naturally, as time goes on the documents become more explicit: from the third dynasty (twenty-eighth century) we find biographical inscriptions which enable us to recreate the administrative system and the various grades in the Civil Service (J. PIRENNE, *ibid.*, pp. 139–144).

17

For the Jemdet-nasr tablets, S. LANGDON, *Oxford Editions of Cuneiform Texts*, VII (1928), *Pictographic Inscriptions from Jemdet-nasr*. For the Uruk III tablets cf. the books mentioned above, n. 6, and GORDON CHILDE, *The Prehistoric East*.

18

For the administration of the Minoan monarchy at the time of the Cnossos hegemony: G. GLOTZ, *La Civilisation égéenne*, Paris, 1923, pp. 174–182. For the hieroglyphic writings and the linear writings of Crete, *ibid.*, pp. 421–438, and a number of articles by J. SUNDWALL, particularly in M. EBERT, *Reallexikon der Vorgeschichte*, vol. III, pp. 95a–101a, in *Kretische Schrift*; to which should be added F. CHAPOUTHIER, "Les Ecritures minoennes au palais de Mallia", *Etudes Crétoises*, II, Paris, 1930; G. P. CARATELLI, "Le Iscrizione preelleniche di Hagia Triada", in *Monumenti Antichi* of the Italian Academy, vol. XL, 4, Milan, 1945, pp. 420–610; and, finally, B. BROZNY'S bold attempt at deciphering in *Archivum Orientale*, XIV, 1943, pp. 1–117; *Archiv Orientalni*, XV, pp. 158–302. For Cypriot writing: S. CASSON, *Ancient Cyprus*, Methuen, 1937; *Iraq*, VI (1939), pp. 39–44; J. F. DANIEL in *American Journal of Archeology*, XLV (1941), pp. 249–282.

19

Nothing definite is known so far about Minoan schools. The "classroom" in the palace at Cnossus is simply an ingenious nickname given by Evans to a room (or shop?) in the north-west wing (*The Palace of Minos*, I, pp. 365–366). F. CHAPOUTHIER found a tablet in Mallia which had the graffito of a child on it, but this does not mean that it was necessarily a child's slate—see "Une Ardoise d'écolier à l'époque minoenne", *Revue des Etudes Grecques*, XXXIII (1925), pp. 427–432.

20

The excavations by Kourouniotis and Blegen at Pylos in 1939 brought to light hundreds of tablets bearing Minoan linear writing of the "B" type in a palace that was burned down in about 1200, i.e. in the middle of the Mycenean epoch: see C. W. BLEGEN, K. KOUROUNIOTIS, "Excavations at Pylos", *American Journal of Archeology*, XLIII, 1939, pp. 564–570; P. M. MERIGGI, "Zu den neuentdeckter minoischen Inschrifter aus Pylos", *Die Antike*, XVII, 1941, pp. 170–176; G. P. CARRATELLI, *op. cit.*, n. 18. The deciphering of this "B-linear" writing is now well under way, and we know that the language it noted down was Greek.

PART ONE

CHAPTER I

I

Homeric education. On this subject, of course, as on all others, there is the inevitable German *Inaugural Dissertation*: R. F. KLÖTZER, *Die Griechische Erziehung in Homers Iliad und Odyssee, ein Beitrag zur Geschichte der Erziehung im Altertum*, Leipzig, 1911; but the most illuminating pages I know are to be found in W. JÄGER, *Paideia*, I, pp. 46–105. The book by V. BENETTI-BRUNELLI, *L'Educazione in Grecia*, I, *L'Educazione della Grecia eroica. Il problema* (*Publicazioni della Scuola di filosofia della R. Università di Roma*, XIII), Florence, 1939, is simply an introduction to the subject and makes no attempt to deal with it properly.

2

The problem of Homer. It would be ridiculous to attempt here to introduce the reader to the maze of books on this subject, but I should like to refer him to P. MAZON, *Introduction à l'Iliade*, Paris, 1942, a relatively recent work, well informed, sensible, and, I must admit, a great relief after the orgies of conjecture which erudite romantics, especially of the German variety, have gone in for; an interesting example of which is still the *Odyssée* by V. BÉRARD, Paris, 1924.

3

There can never be any *consensus omnium* in matters of philology. There will always be some hardy scholars who want to go in for daring hypotheses—what chemists call "look and see" experiments; but there is no need to remember any of these or to bother to refute them at any great length. There was for example E. SCHWARTZ in 1924 and U. VON WILAMOWITZ in 1927, who tried to make out that the latest parts of the *Odyssey* were written as late as 550. For the arguments against this see JÄGER, *Paideia*, I, p. 48.

4

I am here following, and I refer the reader to, P. MAZON, *Introduction à l'Iliade*, p. 266.

5

The Ancients were unable to decide whether this date should be from 1159 B.C. (Hellanicos) to 686 B.C. (Theopompus): PAULY-WISSOWA, VIII, c. 2207–2210, s.v. "Homeros".

6

Homer's historical value. For a summary of the arguments about this see H. JEANMAIRE, *Couroi et Courètes, essai sur l'Education spartiate et sur les Rites d'adolescence dans l'Antiquité héllénique* (*Travaux et Mémoires de l'Université de Lille*, No. XXI, Lille, 1939, p. 12, n. 1); to which should be added MAZON, Introduction, pp. 288–292.

7

Homeric chivalry. I have adopted the conclusions to the first chapter (which bears this title) of the essay by H. JEANMAIRE: *Couroi et Courètes*, pp. 11–111.

8

Sport as a Homeric pastime: cf. again B 773–775 (Achilles' warriors amuse themselves while they are resting on the beach by throwing the discus and the javelin and
by shooting arrows).

9

Debates? This is so, at least, if one accepts—which I hesitate to do—the interpretation by H. JEANMAIRE, who gives the most forceful meaning to the lines O 283–284,
in which the poet says of Thoas:

ἀγορῇ δέ ἑ παῦροι Ἀχαιῶν
νίκων, ὁππότε κοῦροι ἐρίσσειαν περὶ μύθων,

"and in the market-place few Achaeans triumph over him when the young warriors
have contests about the myths" (for ". . . take counsel in the assembly") (ibid., p. 42).

10

Minoan boxing: E. N. GARDINER, Athletics of the Ancient World, pp. 11–14. I can
here do no more than mention the difficult problem of the survivals of Creto-Mycenean
civilization in the athletic and musical games of classical Greece: cf. PAUS., XVIII,
4, 1; 23, 2; HES., Op., 655 (GARDINER, ibid., p. 30; W. D. RIDINGTON, The Minoan-
Mycaenian Background of Greek Athletics, Philadelphia thesis, 1935).

11

Chiron as Achilles' tutor: cf. V. SYBEL, s.v. "Cheiron", in W. H. ROSCHER,
Ausf. Lexikon der gr. u. röm. Mythologie, I, c. 888–892; DE RONCHAUD, s.v. "Chiron"
in DAREMBERG-SAGLIO, I, 2, pp. 1105a–1106a. The most interesting passages are to
be found in PINDAR, who was a privileged observer of the aristocratic tradition:
Pyth., III, 1–5 (cf. IV, 101–115); VI, 20–27; Nem., III, 43–48. Of the decorated
monuments those most worth remembering are a fine stamnos with red figures in the
Louvre, which represents Peleus leading the child Achilles to Chiron (C. V. A.,
Louvre, fasc. 2, III, 1c, pl. XX, fig. 1), a Herculaneum painting in the Naples Museum
which is often reproduced, of Chiron teaching Achilles to play the lyre (O. ELIA,
Pitture murali e mosaici nel Museo Nazionale di Napoli, Rome, 1932, No. 25 (9019),
fig. 5, p. 25) and the reliefs of the tensa capitolina, of Chiron teaching Achilles how to
hunt and throw the javelin (S. REINACH, RPGR, I, 377, II, a).

There was an archaic poem, "The Teachings of Chiron"—Χίρωνος Ὑποθῆκαι
—of which a few Gnomic fragments remain which have been handed down as
Hesiod's (see, for example, Didot's edition of Hesiod, pp. 61–69).

12

A certain amount of skill may be necessary to combine the respective roles of
Phoenix and Chiron. The Ancients, to judge by LUCIAN, Dial. Mort., XV, 1, saw no
difficulty in this, however, and simply referred to Achilles' "two masters"—τοῖν
διδασκάλοιν ἀμφοῖν. J. A. SCOTT, American Journal of Philology, XXXIII (1912),
p. 76, has endeavoured to show that Achilles could have had Phoenix as his tutor
when he was a baby and then studied under Chiron afterwards, but Homer does
not describe Phoenix as having been merely a "dry nurse" (cf. 438 et seq., 485). In
the opinion of W. JÄGER, Paideia, I, pp. 60–65, Phoenix is a humanized double of the
mythical Chiron, whom the poet could not decently bring on to the stage because of
the realism of this epic. The song may have been composed separately and added

later—not without a certain incongruity—to the rest of the *Iliad* (cf., for another statement of this view, MAZON, Introduction, p. 178).

13

Homer as a non-religious poet, noble-minded, secular, anti-sacerdotal: cf. on this
point the stimulating remarks by O. SPENGLER, *The Decline of the West*—a monumental
work of murky error shot through with dazzling sparks of illumination. As against this
see the bold and badly supported theory of C. AUTRAN, *Homère et les Origines sacer-
dotales de l'Epopée grecque*, vols. I–III, Paris, 1938–1944. Cf. M. P. NILSSON *et contra*
E. EHNMARK in A. PASSERINI, *IX° Congrès intern. des Sciences Historiques*, Paris, 1950,
vol. I, p. 125, n. 28: see p. 126 for Passerini's own opinion.

14

"La Tristesse d'Achille": cf. the rather disappointing article with this title by
G. MÉAUTIS, in *Revue des Etudes Grecques*, XLIII (1930), pp. 9–20.

15

The Homeric ethic. Here more than anywhere else I am simply repeating the
powerful ideas of W. JÄGER, *Paideia*, I, pp. 76 *et seq.* Cf. also, in a minor key, P. MAZON,
Introduction, pp. 296 *et seq.*: *La Morale de l'Iliade*, and a rather nice page or so by
A. J. FESTUGIÈRE, "L'Enfant d'Agrigente", pp. 13–14.

16

The Agonistic ideal: J. BURCKHARDT, *Griechische Kulturgeschichte, passim* (likewise
II, pp. 365 *et seq.*; IV, pp. 89 *et seq.*) and, for a brief résumé, C. ANDLER, *Nietzsche*,
I, pp. 299 *et seq.*

CHAPTER II

1

Sparta as a semi-illiterate town: E. BOURGUET, "Le Dialecte laconien", *Collection
linguistique publiée par la Société linguistique de Paris*, XXIII, Paris, 1927, pp. 13 *et
seq.* This is a remarkable piece of work, in which the study of linguistic facts leads to
a whole history of civilization.

2

The education of Crete and its analogies with Spartan education: "Les Lois de
Gortyne", in DARESTE-HAUSSOULIER-T. REINACH, *Inscriptions juridiques grecques*,
I, 3, pp. 406–408; cf. STRABO, X, 483; JEANMAIRE, *Couroi et Courètes*, pp. 421–444.

3

The chronology of archaic civilization in Sparta: R. M. DAWKINS, "The Sanctuary
of Artemis Orthia at Sparta", *Journal of Hellenic Studies, Supplementary Paper* No. 5,
London 1929, particularly p. 49, fig. 28.

4

The originality of Sparta was bound up with its conservative archaism. The racial
theory which attempts to explain this quite differently as a result of Sparta's Dorian
character was formulated by K. O. MÜLLER in his well-known work *Die Dorier*
(1st. ed. Breslau, 1824), and has always been favoured in Germany: cf. V. EHRENBERG,

"Spartiaten und Lakedaimonier", *Hermes*, LIX, 1924, pp. 23–72; H. BERVE, *Sparta*, Leipzig, 1939; T. MEIER, "Wesen der Spartanischen Staatsordnung", *Klio, Beiheft* XLII, 1939. It has nevertheless been strongly attacked, even in Germany; K. J. BELOCH even denies there ever having been a Dorian invasion: *Griechische Geschichte*, I, 2, Berlin-Leipzig, 1926, pp. 76–93; U. KAHRSTEDT, *Greichisches Staatsrecht*, I, *Sparta und seine Symmachie*, Göttingen, 1922, pp. 369 *et seq.*, and, in France: P. ROUSSEL, *Sparte*, Paris, 1939, pp. 19–22; H. JEANMAIRE, *Couroi et Courètes*, pp. 422, 474 *et seq.*

5

The revival of nationalist spirit in Sparta in Roman times: cf. again BOURGUET, "Le Dialecte laconien", pp. 20 *et seq.*

6

The Spartan hoplite in archaic art. A battle scene on a magnificent *pithos* dating from 600 to 550, decorated with reliefs in the style of metal vases: DAWKINS, "Artemis Orthia", pl. XV–XVI, p. 92; a bronze statuette of the hoplite "Carmos": C. PICARD, *Manuel d'Archéologie grecque*, I, p. 464, fig. 136. Nearer to classical art, a fine helmeted head of Leonidas (a little later than 480): *ibid.*, II, I, pp. 163–164, fig. 75.

7

The political consequences of the new tactics of heavy infantry: J. HASEBROEK, *Griechische Wirtschafts-und Gesellschaftsgeschichte bis zur Perserzeit*, Tübingen, 1931, p. 158; H. JEANMAIRE, *Couroi et Courètes*, pp. 130–131.

8

Tyrtaeus as a representative of the city's new ideal: cf. the fundamental study by W. JÄGER, *Tyrtaios, über die wahre Arete, Sitzungsberichte* of the Berlin Academy of Sciences, *Phil.-hist. Klasse*, 1932, pp. 537–568; *Paideia*, I, pp. 146–164.

9

Tyrtaeus's patriotic military ethics seem to me to reflect a significant moment in the evolution of Greek political consciousness rather than the temperament of the Dorian race. We shall discover the same kind of inspiration in the heart of Ionia, in the person of Callinus of Ephesus at the period of the Cimmerian invasion, shortly before Tyrtaeus's time, in the first half of the seventh century.

10

Spartan champions in the Olympic Games: E. NORMAN GARDINER, G. DICKINS, *Journal of Hellenic Studies*, XXXII (1912), p. 19, n. 106; *Athletics of the Ancient World*, p. 34.

11

Women athletes in Sparta: small archaic bronzes (600–530): C. PICARD, *Manuel d'Archéologie grecque*, I, fig. 135, p. 460, distant prototypes of the famous Barberini Runner, whose dubious charm is nevertheless very attractive—a Roman copy of a bronze dating from about 460: *ibid.*, II, I, pp. 161–162.

12

The earliest known Spartan texts are brief votive inscriptions on vases dating from the end of the seventh century: DAWKINS, "Artemis Orthia", p. 76, fig. 54; p. 111, fig. 86, 3.

13

Glaucos of Rhegium (latter half of the fifth century) as a source of Plutarch's history of music: T. REINACH, in WEIL-REINACH'S edition of PLUTARCH, *De Musica*, Introduction, pp. XI-XII, 37, *ad* §89.

14

The calendar of feasts in Sparta: ZIEHEN, in PAULY-WISSOWA, II R, III, 2, c. 1508–1520, s.v. "Sparta".

15

On the votive masks found in profusion—more than six hundred of them—in the excavations of the sanctuary to Artemis Orthia: DAWKINS, "Artemis Orthia", pp. 163–185, pl. XLVII–LII. The oldest of them date back to the beginning of the seventh century; *akmè*, about 600.

16

On the interpretation, which is difficult, of Alcman's *Partheneion*, cf. the bibliography collected by E. DIEHL, *Anthologia Lyrica Graeca*², II, 1942, pp. 7–8, and particularly D. A. VAN GRONINGEN, *The Enigma of Alcman's Partheneion, Mnemosyne*, 3, III (1936), pp. 241–261; add: D. L. PAGE, *Alcman, the Partheneion*, Oxford, 1951.

17

The reactionary revolution in the middle of the sixth century: G. GLOTZ, *Histoire grecque*, I, pp. 349, 372–373; EHRENBERG, in PAULY-WISSOWA, s.v. "Sparta", c. 1381; H. JEANMAIRE, *Couroi et Courètes*, p. 548.

18

After 576, Spartan victories in the Olympic Games end abruptly. There was only one in 552 and then between 548 and 400 no more than a dozen, with one to finish with in 316. These victories were mainly won by entrants from the royal stables of King Demaratus and Cynisca, the daughter of Archidamus: cf. GARDINER and DICKINS, *supra*, n. 10.

19

For a picture of classical education in Sparta: W. KNAUTH, "Die spartanische Knabenerziehung im Lichte der Völkerkunde", *Zeitschrift für Geschichte der Erziehung und des Unterrichts*, XXIII (1933), pp. 151–185; T. R. HARLEY, "The Public Schools of Sparta", in *Greece and Rome*, 1934, III, pp. 124–139; P. ROUSSEL, *Sparte*, pp. 59–65. But nothing can take the place of XENOPHON, *Lac.*, 2; PLUTARCH, *Lyc.*, 16–17; PLATO, *Leg.*, I, 633 ac.

20

Iphicrates' tactical innovations: R. COHEN, *La Grèce et l'hellénisation du Monde antique* (*Klio* series), pp. 309–310; for those introduced by Gorgias, Epaminondas and Pelopidas, cf. s.vv. PAULY-WISSOWA, VIII, c. 1619–1620; V, c. 2678–2679, 2683–2684 (SWOBODA); XIX, I, c. 380 (G. REINCKE).

21

For the right to claim the city-law in Sparta it was certainly necessary to have received the state's education: XEN., *Lac.*, 10, 7; PLUT., *Inst. Lac.*, 238 F, 21. But was this all that was required? Jeanmaire believes that it was (*Couroi et Courètes*, p. 490), but does not prove his case: PLUT., *ibid.*, 22.

22

The age-groups of Spartan children—see, besides the classic essay by M. P. NILSSON, "Grundlagen des spartanischen Lebens", *Klio*, 1912, pp. 308–340, my essay under the above title in *Revue des Etudes anciennes*, XLVIII, 1946, pp. 216–230.

23

Βοναγός, patrol leader. Votive inscriptions commemorating the victories won by young boys in the games of Artemis Orthia never fail to mention this rank, saying either that the winner bore it, or that he had some family connection with it—or, perhaps, as I think, some friendly connection, using the word "friendly" in its most Greekish meaning: A. M. WOODWARD, in DAWKINS, "Artemis Orthia", pp. 290–291.

24

The *ephores* condemned the musicians who had added strings to Terpander's classical lyre, which had seven strings: C. DEL GRANDE, *Espressione musicale dei poeti greci*, Naples, 1932, pp. 89–100; K. SCHLESINGER, *The Greek Aulos*, London, 1939, p. 143; L. DÜRING, "Studies in Musical Terminology in Fifth-Century Literature", *Eranos*, XLIII (1945), 176 *et seq.*, esp. 190–192. The adventure is supposed to have happened to Phrynis of Mitylene, according to PLUTARCH, *Prof. in virt.*, 84 A; *Agis*, 10; to Timotheus of Miletus, according to PAUSANIAS, XII, 10; CICERO, *Leg.*, II, 39, and BOETHIUS, *De Mus.*, I, 1. The latter preserved the Greek text of the decree pronounced against the unfortunate musician. But on closer examination the language of this document seems to prove that it is a forgery by a grammarian in Trajan's or Hadrian's time: BOURGUET, "Dialecte laconien", pp. 154–159.

25

The "aulos" kept the rhythm not only for the Spartan army but also for the Athenian navy, in which the crew rowed to the sound of the instrument played by the τριηραύλης (PAULY-WISSOWA, s.v. "Nautae", XVI, 2, c. 2031).

26

Spartan Machiavellianism in the fourth century—cases will be remembered like that of Phoibidas taking the Cadmea by surprise in 382 under the cover of one of the city's festivals, and Sphodrias's raid on the Piraeus during peacetime in 378: XEN., *Hell.*, V, 2, 25–36; 4, 20–33.

27

For the Krypteïa: H. JEANMAIRE, lastly, in *Couroi et Courètes*, pp. 550–588.

28

Spartan dancing-girls: reliefs in the Berlin Museum, after a work by the sculptor Callimachus (end of the fifth century): C. PICARD, *Manuel d'Archéologie grecque*, II, ii, pp. 624–626, figs. 252, 253.

29

Philolaconism as a part of the Greek tradition: F. OLLIER, *Le Mirage spartiate*, 2 vols., Paris, 1932–1943.

30

Timaia, wife to Agis II: EHRENBERG, in PAULY-WISSOWA, II R, VI, 1, c. 1074–1075. Spartan business-women in the third century: the people I have in mind are Agis's mother Agesicrates and his grandmother Archidamia, "who were richer than all the rest of the Lacedaemonians put together"; his wife Agiatis, and Cratesilea, mother to Cleomenes: PLUT., *Agis*, 5, 23, 29.

31

For the gymnopedia the classic passage is to be found in PLATO, *Leg.*, I, 633c; cf. BÖLTE and ZIEHEN, in PAULY-WISSOWA, II R, III, 2, c. 1372, 1510. That flagellation in front of the altar to Orthia was not the "primitive" rite imagined by our morbid modern sociologists is now well established: JEANMAIRE, *Couroi et Courètes*, pp. 513–523; the "cheese-battle" did not take the place of the flagellation except according to CICERO, *Tusc.*, II, 34. The ceremony was still attracting tourists in the middle of the fourth century A.D.: LIBANIUS, *Or.*, I, 23. I stand by this, in spite of the criticism of W. den BOER (*Laconian Studies*, Amsterdam, 1954, pp. 269–270), who assigns me to "the clique of younger, too self-confident historians". My certainty is based on the chronological data of JEANMAIRE, which W. den BOER leaves out of account. On all this see, in addition to this book (pp. 233–298, "Aspects of the Spartan *Agoge*", and especially pp. 248–261 against my interpretation of the age groups), the work of K. M. T. CHRIMES, *Ancient Sparta, A Re-Examination of the Evidence* (Publications of the University of Manchester, Historical Series, LXXXIV, Manchester, 1949).

CHAPTER III

I

Greek love. The most fundamental works on this subject are still K. O. MÜLLER, *Die Dorier*[2], Breslau, 1844, pp. 289–298, and M. H. E. MEIER, J. S. ERSCH, J. G. GRUBER, *Encyclopädie der Wissenschaften und Künsten*, IX, Leipzig, 1837 (French trans. L. R. DE POGEY-CASTRIES, *Histoire de l'Amour grec dans l'Antiquité, par M. H. E. Meier, augmentée d'un choix de documents originaux*—a valuable anthology of literary and historical passages—*et de plusieurs dissertations complémentaires*, Paris, 1930). It has often been studied since, of course: L. DUGAS, *L'Amitié antique d'après les Moeurs populaires et les Théories des Philosophes*, Paris, 1894; H. HOESSLI, *Eros, die Männerliebe der Griechen*[3], Münster-Berlin, 1924; D. H. ROBINSON, E. J. FLUCK, *A Study of Greek Love-Names, Including a Discussion of Paederasty*, Johns Hopkins University Studies in Archaeology, XXIII, Baltimore, 1937; S. WIKANDER, *Der arische Männerbund*, Lund, 1938. But I have found nothing more instructive than the teaching of Prof. L. MASSIGNON.

2

The Greek language reflects an explicit condemnation of inversion. It is described in terms that mean "to dishonour", "to outrage", "a shameful act", "infamous conduct", "impurity", "despicable habits". The contempt is more explicitly directed against the passive partner: someone who submits to shameful and abominable things: DE POGEY-CASTRIES, pp. 176, 307–311.

3

Homosexuality and the law. It does not seem to have been legal except in Elis: XEN., *Lac.*, 2, 12; PLUT., *Pel.*, 19. Elsewhere—even in Crete and Sparta, where there was no attempt to conceal it—any violation of an ephebe and any sort of carnal relationship was forbidden and theoretically a punishable offence: STRAB., X, 483; DARESTE, HAUSSOULIER, REINACH, *Inscriptions juridiques grecques*, I, pp. 358–359, 451; XEN., *Lac.*, 2, 13; *Conv.*, 8, 35; AEL., *V.H.*, III, 12. In Athens the slave-pederast was punishable by law, as were also, amongst the citizens, prostitution, "white slave traffic", and the violation of an adolescent. Police laws attributed to Solon forbade adults to enter schools (of literature or gymnastics?) attended by young boys: cf. the passages in DE POGEY-CASTRIES, pp. 284–290.

4

Pure pederasty. Even in ancient times there was an attempt to justify the customs of Crete and Sparta by saying that they only approved of relationships that were chaste (see the passages quoted in the note above); but the allowed limits were pretty wide and this kind of "purity" seems to be as dubious and "shady" as that of the courtly love codified in the thirteenth century by André le Chapelain: pure love— σώφρων—allowed many favours: kisses, caresses—in a word, says CICERO, *Omnia praeter stuprum*, . . . *complexus enim concubitusque permittunt palliis interjectis* (*De Rep.*, IV, 4). There is no need to have a Jansenist conception of human nature to realise that such frail barriers would not put up much resistance against carnal passion. The tradition of antiquity has many stories that refute this attempt at an apology—for instance, the story of Aristodemus, the "harmoste" of Oreos, who took an adolescent away by force (PLUT., *Amat. narr.*, 773–774).

5

There seems to be no pederasty in Homer: Ganymede is Zeus's cup-bearer, not his favourite; between Achilles and Patrocles there is simply a boyish friendship and a comradeship in arms. It may be wondered whether or not their friendship concealed a more carnal kind of passion: some moderns seem inclined to think so, for instance J. A. SYMONS, *The Greek Poets*, III, p. 80, quoted by A. GIDE, *Corydon, Œ. C.*, IX, p. 299; and the Ancients were in no doubt about it even as far back as Aeschylus in his *Myrmidons* (fr. 128; cf. LUCIAN, *Am.*, 54).

It is quite possible that Homer decided to ignore a well-known institution of the day—his picture of the heroic life is not without some omissions, particularly about religion; but his silence on this point, whether intentional or not, has been explained in two different ways, either as a survival from the Minoan civilization which, it is thought, would have rejected with horror the brutality of these warlike habits imported into Aegeum by the nordic invaders, or as the effect of a more precocious development of conscience in Asiatic Greece, in which, in the classical age, pederasty was judged more severely than in the rest of the Hellenic world (cf. PLATO, *Conv.*, 182bc). The first theory is maintained by S. WIKANDER, *Der arische Männerbund*, Lund, 1938, who traces the origin of our fighting brotherhoods back to the remotest European past.

6

Inversion was canonized in myths: the love of Zeus and Ganymede, Heracles and Iolaus (or Hylas), Apollo and Hyacinth, etc. But it is difficult to say when these first appeared. The epic about Heracles which is attributed to Pisander and described the violation of the young Chrysippes by Laius cannot be, as according to an ancient tradition it was supposed to be, earlier than Hesiod (KEYDELL, in PAULY-WISSOWA, XIX, I, c. 144, s.v. "Peisandros"). Pederasty is celebrated as something quite normal by the great lyrical writers from the end of the seventh century, from Alceus to Pindar.

7

Pederasty as specially Dorian: cf. K. O. MÜLLER, *Die Dorier* (*supra* n. 1); E. BETHE, "Die dorische Knabenliebe, ihre Ethik, ihre Idee", *Rheinisches Museum*, LXII (1907), pp. 438–475.

8

Pederasty as magical initiation. The work that first went into this curious question is E. CARPENTER, "Beziehungen zwischen Homosexualität und Prophetentum", in *Jahrbuch für sexuelle Zwischenstufen unter besonderer Berücksichtung der Homosexualität, Suppl.*, 1911.

9

The Greek city as a man's club: BARKER, *Greek Political Theory*, p. 218. Pederasty and comradeship in arms: L. DUGAS, *L'Amitié antique*, p. 87; in Crete (STRAB., X, 483) and in Thebes (PLUT., *Amat.*, 930) it was customary for the lover to offer his beloved a suit of armour, his entire fighting equipment.

10

Pederasty as an initiatory rite. The fundamental work is BETHE (quoted in n. 7) whose thesis, which has however been severely criticized since it first appeared—A. SEMENOV, *Zur dorischen Knabenliebe, Philologus*, N. F., XXIV (1911), pp. 146–150; A. RUPPERSBERG, Εἰσπνήλας, *ibid.*, pp. 151–154—has recently been taken up again by H. JEANMAIRE, *Couroi et Courètes*, particularly pp. 456–460, "Forerunners of the Platonic Theory of Love".

Bethe and Jeanmaire make a great deal of the archaic rupestral inscriptions (seventh century) brought to light in Thera by HILLER VON GÄRTHRINGEN: *IG*, XII, 3, 536 *et seq.*; alternatively, in PAULY-WISSOWA, II R, V, 2, c. 2289. Amongst these are sayings such as, "Krimon was here with Amotion" (*IG*, XII, 3, 538). "By Apollo, it was at this very spot that Krimon was with his friend, Bathykles's brother" (*ibid.*, 537; for the insertion of the punctuation see HILLER VON GÄRTHRINGEN, PAULY-WISSOWA, *loc. cit.*). These seem to me to be no more than the kind of indecent wall-scratchings to be found in Pompeii: *Hic ego cum veni futui; fututa sum hic . . .* (cf. No. 536: added in a later hand is πόρνος). None of the arguments that have been used seems to me to be sufficient to transform affairs like these into religious ceremonies marking the ephebe's entry into the brotherhood of men. The fact that the letters are so large does not mean to say that these *graffitti* are votive inscriptions. The rock on which they are to be found is in any case more than sixty yards west of the sanctuary to Apollo Carneius and south-west of the site of the religious dedications (*IG*, XII, 3, 351–373) with which Jeanmaire quite arbitrarily connects them, and though it may overlook the site of the ephebes' gymnasium, this was only built five or six hundred years later!

11

Pederasty and attempts to take the lives of tyrants: see the whole list of facts collected by MEIER-DE POGEY-CASTRIES, *Histoire de l'Amour grec*, pp. 160–168.

12

The cultural significance of Theognis of Megara has been strikingly brought out by W. JÄGER, *Paideia*, I, pp. 291–317; also by J. CARRIÈRE, *Théognis*, pp. 177–240.

13

On the love of Theognis for Cyrnus, see the extracts from the *Elegies* collected by DE POGEY-CASTRIES, *Histoire de l'Amour grec*, pp. 235–237.

14

"Philosophical" pederasty, or the passionate relationship between master and pupil: the evidence will be found in MEIER-DE POGEY-CASTRIES, *ibid.*, p. 84.

N

15

On Baudelaire's Lesbians, his contemporaries (Gautier, de Banville, etc.) and romantic predecessors, cf. the critical edition of the *Fleurs du Mal* by J. CREPET-G. BLIN, Paris, 1942, pp. 271–275.

16

For a description and defence of Sappho: U. VON WILAMOWITZ-MÖLLENDORF, *Sappho und Simonides*, Berlin, 1913; T. REINACH's edition (posthumous, edited by A. Puech) of *Alcée et Sapho*, Paris, 1937, pp. 168–176; and of course the works of RENÉE VIVIEN.

CHAPTER IV

1

When was the Attic ephebia first instituted? There has been a great deal of argument about this question. As we shall see later (Part II, Ch. II), the ephebia in its classical form as a two-year period of compulsory military service, is only known to have existed from 337 or 335. U. VON WILAMOWITZ–MÖLLENDORF, *Aristoteles und Athen*, I, Berlin, 1893, pp. 193–194, and, following him, A. BRENOT, "Recherches sur l'Ephébie attique et en particulier sur la date de l'Institution", *BEHE*, CCIX, Paris, 1920, maintain that it did not exist before this date. But this theory cannot be accepted; it makes an unfair use of the argument *a silentio* and through being too critical minimizes the importance of a piece of evidence like that found in ÆSCHINES, *Amb.*, 167, who tells us that upon emerging from childhood in about the year 370 he served as a "militia-man" for two years: cf. V. CHAPOT, "Quand fut instituée l'Ephébie attique", *Revue de Synthèse historique*, XXXIV (1922), pp. 105–111; J. O. LOFBERG, "The Date of the Athenian Ephebia", *Classical Philology*, XX (1925), pp. 330–335. The question came up again when L. ROBERT published an epigraphical text of the ephebic oath, which we had previously known only through Stobaeus and Pollux: "Etudes épigraphiques et archéologiques", *BEHE*, CCLXXII, Paris, 1938, pp. 296–307. This oath is given in the name of a series of divinities who are archaic in character, which seems to take us a very long way back indeed. H. JEANMAIRE, *Couroi et Courètes*, pp. 464–507, believes that the oath is in fact very old and that therefore the ephebia is very old too but that it was at the beginning a mere "initiatory rite" which only took on its ultimate character during the Peloponnesian War in imitation of the Spartan ἀγωγή. A pseudo rather than a genuinely archaic oath, retorts A. PIGANIOL, "Les Origines de l'Ephébie attique", *Annales d'Histoire [économique et] sociale*, XI, 1939, pp. 212–213, criticizing G. MATHIEU ("Remarques sur l'Ephébie attique", *Mélanges Desrousseaux*, Paris, 1937, pp. 311–318), in whose opinion "ephebia" was a general term for the organization that came into existence in the fifth century for war orphans, "the nation's wards"; this, he says, was indeed imitated from Sparta, but only after the defeat in 404, and it only became obligatory after 338.

2

Theognis and Pindar as mouthpieces of the aristocratic ideal: as usual, I follow W. JÄGER, *Paideia*, I, pp. 291–342.

3

Sports events for children: the difficulty is to decide the age of these "children"—were they fully grown youths of seventeen and over or "juniors" from twelve to sixteen? NORMAN GARDINER plumps for the former in the case of the Olympic Games and for the latter in the Nemean, Isthmic and pan-Athenian Games: *Athletics of the Ancient World*, p. 41. It is worth noting that the expressions Ἰσθμικοί and Πυθικοί παῖδες were commonly used in Graeco-Roman times to denote age-groups in Agonistic catalogues or lists of winners: cf., for instance, the passages collected by L. ROBERT in *Revue de Philologie*, 1930, p. 46, n. 1; *BEHE*, 272, p. 24.

4

The "skolion" as a typical literary genre of the old aristocratic culture: W. JÄGER, *Paideia*, I, pp. 294 *et seq.*, following R. REITZENSTEIN, *Epigramm und Skolion, ein Beitrag zur Geschichte der alexandrinischen Dichtung*, Giessen, 1893, and F. JACOBY, "Theognis", *Sitzungsberichte* of the Berlin Academy of Sciences, *Phil.-hist. Klasse*, 1931, pp. 90–180.

5

The educational significance of Solon's elegies: the fundamental work is again by W. JÄGER: "Solons Eunomie", in the same *Sitzungsberichte*, 1926, pp. 69–94.

6

Ostracophoria by writing: J. CARCOPINO, *L'Ostracisme athénien*[2], Paris, 1935, pp. 78–87; pl. I–III.

7

The date of the first appearance of schools. Outside Athens the following pieces of evidence have been found: in Chios shortly before the battle of Lade in 496 a school roof caved in and buried a hundred and nineteen children (HDT., VI, 27); in Astypalaea in 492 the pugilist Cleomedes went mad and massacred sixty children in a school (PAUS., VI, 9, 6).

8

With regard to the anti-Christian myth of a Hellas that founded its spiritual culture on an exaltation of the corporal virtues, it will be sufficient to refer the reader to the work of one of our French vulgarizers of Nazi "thought": J. E. SPENLE, *Nietzsche et le Problème européen*, Paris, 1943, p. 239.

CHAPTER V

1

The elementary nature of Attic education at the time of Pericles: O. NAVARRE, *Essai sur la rhétorique grecque avant Aristote*, Paris, 1900, pp. 25–26; M. DELCOURT, *Périclès*, Paris, 1939, pp. 65–69.

2

The oldest schools of medicine: R. FUCHS, T. PUSCHMANN, M. NEUNBURGER, J. PAGEL, *Handbuch der Geschichte der Medizin*, I, Jena, 1902, pp. 191–193.

3

No proper "school" of the old Physicians in Miletus: A. J. FESTUGIERE, *Contemplation et Vie contemplative selon Platon*, Paris, 1936, pp. 32–33, and App. I, pp. 461–463.
The school of philosophy as a religious brotherhood: this was first pointed out by G. LUMBROSO, "Ricerche alessandrine", in *Memorie* of the Turin Academy, 1873,

p. 268, and has since been the subject of a penetrating study by P. BOYANCE, "Le Culte des Muses chez les Philosophes grecs", *Etudes d'Histoire et de Psychologie religieuses*, Paris, 1936, pp. 232–241 (Pythagorean School), 261–267 (the Academy), 299–300, 310–322 (the Lyceum), 322–327 (Epicurean School).

4

I do not pretend to decide whether Antiphon of Rhamnus, the author of fifteen legal speeches and a right-wing politician, is the same person as Antiphon the Sophist, who left behind some important fragments of political philosophy (DIELS, *Vorsokratiker*, §80, or, better still, GERNET, following the former's *Discours*, collection "Budé", Paris, 1923); it is enough that the former was a practitioner of rhetoric. The question whether these two people were or were not one person seems to me pointless—there is not enough evidence to make the argument worth while: holders of each hypothesis throw the *onus probandi* upon their opponents.

5

The chronology and various careers of the Sophists: the data about this will be found, for example, in K. PRAECHTER, in F. UEBERWEG, *Grundriss der Geschichte der Philosophie*, I [12], pp. 112–129.

Protagoras, born in Abdera in Thrace c. 485, *akmè* c. 446–440; frequently stayed in Athens; died *c*. 411.

Gorgias of Leontini in Sicily, born c. 483; went to Athens for the first time in 427 as ambassador; died in 376 (at the court of the tyrant Jason of Pheres?) in Thessaly.

Antiphon, son of Sophilus of the "deme" of Rhamnus, born c. 480, logographer and rhetorician, condemned to death in 411 for his extremist oligarchic politics and for treason under the reactionary government of the Four Hundred.

Prodicus of Ceos in the Cyclades, born c. 465; according to Plato, Socrates was his pupil: *Men.*, 96d; *Prot.*, 341a; *Charm.*, 163d.

Hippias of Elis in the Peloponnesus clearly seems to have been of the same time as Prodicus.

6

For the Sophists cf. in the general histories of Greek thought: E. ZELLER, W. NESTLE, *Die Philosophie der Griechen in ihre geschichtliche Entwicklung dargestellt*, I, II[6], Leipzig, 1920, pp. 1278, 1441; T. GOMPERZ, *Les Penseurs de la Grèce* (French trans.)[3], I, Paris, 1928, pp. 452–536. The fundamental work for our present purpose is H. GOMPERZ, *Sophistik und Rhetorik, das Bildungsideal des EY ΛEΓEIN in seinem Verhältnis zur Philosophie des V. Jahrhunderts*, Leipzig-Berlin, 1912, with the first pages of H. VON ARNIM, *Sophistik, Rhetorik, Philosophie in ihrem Kampf um die Jugendbildung*, the introduction to his book *Leben und Werke des Dio von Prusa*, Berlin, 1898, pp. 4 *et seq.*

From the point of view of the history of science: A. REY, *La Science dans l'Antiquité* (III), *la Maturité de la pensée scientifique en Grèce*, Paris, 1939, pp. 46–67; and of the history of education: W. JÄGER, *Paideia*, I, pp. 425–489.

7

For Protagoras' phenomenological relativism: P. NATORP, *Forschungen zur Geschichte der Erkenntnissproblems im Alterthum: Protagoras* . . ., Berlin, 1844, and partly (as objective relativism, no subjectivism) in V. BROCHARD, *Etudes de Philosophie ancienne et de Philosophie moderne*, Paris, 1912, pp. 23–29, in spite of T. GOMPERZ, *Penseurs de la Grèce*, pp. 494–505.

For Gorgias' philosophical nihilism, UEBERWEG-PRAECHTER, p. 89, and the criticism by H. GOMPERZ, *Sophistik und Rhetorik*, pp. 1–35.
For a similar over-estimation of Hippias' thought, cf. *infra*, n. 11.

8

The dissertation by O. NAVARRE, *Essai sur la Rhétorique grecque avant Aristote*, Paris, 1900, is necessary as a completion on the technical level of the analysis by H. GOMPERZ, *Sophistik und Rhetorik*.

9

Gorgias' dependence upon Empedocles: H. DIELS, "Gorgias und Empedokles", *Sitzungsberichte* of the Berlin Academy of Sciences, *Phil.-hist. Kl.*, 1884, pp. 343–368; E. GRIMAL, "A propos d'un passage du Ménon: une définition tragique de la couleur", *Revue des Etudes grecques*, LV (1942), pp. 1–13.

10

Gorgias' figures of speech may have been studied by St. Augustine and Sidonius Apollinaris; for example: M. COMEAU, *La Rhétorique de saint Augustin d'après les Tractatus in Johannem*, Paris, 1930, pp. 46–70; A. LOYEN, *Sidoine Apollinaire et l'esprit précieux en Gaule aux derniers jours de l'Empire*, Paris, 1943, pp. viii, 133–134.

11

Hippias' seriousness: this is generally contested: e.g. by L. ROBIN, *La Pensée grecque et les Origines de l'Esprit scientifique*, Paris, 1923, p. 172. In any case, the attempt made by E. DUPREEL, *La Légende socratique et les sources de Platon*, Brussels, 1922, to puff him up into a first-class mind, a kind of Pico della Mirandola or even Leibnitz, seems far-fetched: e.g. the harsh criticism by A. DIES, *Autour de Platon*, Paris, 1927, I, pp. 229–237.

12

Acoustics: I have adopted this word, for reasons of space, to translate the μουσικήν of *Prot.* 318e. When it is used in conjunction with λογισμοί (problems of arithmetic), astronomy and geometry, this word no longer means the "things of the Muses", intellectual culture as a whole, but the science of mathematics introduced by Pythagoras, the study of the numerical structure of intervals and rhythm: cf. my *Saint Augustin et la Fin de la Culture antique*, Paris, 1937, pp. 40–44.

13

For the Sophists' literary studies cf. again NAVARRE, *Essai sur la Rhétorique grecque*, pp. 40–44.

14

Scientific research and education: for the present state of the problem see the book which appeared in French under this title, J. STRZYGOWSKI, *Les Documents bleus*, V, Paris, 1932, and my note: "Manque de tradition et erreur de méthode", in *Foyers de notre Culture*, Rencontres, IX, Paris, 1942, pp. 134–140.

15

Passages from the comedians against Socrates: E. CAVAIGNAC, *Musée Belge*, XXVII, 1923, pp. 157–167.

16

The problem of Socrates: a concentrated discussion of his ups-and-downs from J. JOËLL (1893) to E. DUPREEL (1922), H. VON ARNIM (1923) and H. GOMPERZ (1924,) will be found in the work already mentioned by A. DIES, *Autour de Platon, Essais de critique et d'histoire*, Paris, 1927, I, pp. 127–143. This question has since been taken up again and again: see esp. W. D. ROSS, "The Problem of Socrates", *Proceedings of the Classical Association*, London, 1933, pp. 7–24; A. E. TAYLOR, *Socrates*, London, 1932; H. KUHN, *Sokrates, ein Versuch über den Ursprung der Metaphysik*, Berlin, 1934; G. BASTIDE, *Le Moment historique de Socrate*, Paris, 1939; T. DEMAN, *Le Témoignage d'Aristote sur Socrate*, Paris, 1943; W. JÄGER, *Paideia*, II, London, 1945, pp. 13–76; V. DE MAGALHÃES-VILHERA, *Le problème de Socrate, le Socrate historique et le Socrate de Platon*, Paris, 1952.

I quote in passing a remark by A. E. TAYLOR, *Varia Socratica*, Oxford, 1911, p. 30.

17

The School of Socrates as an ascetic community of scholars: H. GOMPERZ, "Die Sokratische Frage als geschichtliches Problem", *Historische Zeitschrift*, CXXIX, 3 (1924), pp. 377–423, discussed by A. DIES, *Autour de Platon*, I, pp. 229–237.

18

The development of professionalism in sport: Norman GARDINER, *Athletics of the Ancient World*, pp. 99–106; A. H. GILBERT, "Olympic Decadence", *Classical Journal*, XXI (1925–1926), pp. 587–598.

CHAPTER VI

I

The significance of the Lesser Socratics from the point of view of the history of education: I have summarized the weighty pages on this subject which are to be found in the Introduction already mentioned to H. VON ARNIM, *Dio von Prusa*: pp. 21 (Aeschines), 21–25 (Schools of Megara and Elis-Eretrea), 25–32 (essential: Aristippus) 32–43 (Antisthenes and the Cynics).

2

Publicity shows: Aristippus had published six books of Debates—Διατριβαί— (D.L., II, 84–85); VON ARNIM (*ibid.*, p. 30) shows that they marked the transition between the self-advertising exhibitions given by the first Sophists and the popular sermons by the third-century Cyrenaics and Cynics, Theodorus, Bion, etc., who were to have so many imitators.

3

The price of Aristippus' lessons: the evidence seems to vary between 1,000 drachmas (PLUT., *Lib. educ.*, 4 F) and 500 (D.L., II, 72); the comedian Alexis mentions 6,000 but this is a comic exaggeration (ATH., XII, 544 E): VON ARNIM, *ibid.*, p. 25.

4

Plato as educator: J. A. ADAMSON, *The Theory of Education in Plato's Republic*, London, 1903; R. L. NETTLESHIP, *The Theory of Education in the Republic of Plato*, Chicago, 1906; P. FRIEDLÄNDER, *Plato*, I, *Eidos, Paideia, Dialogos*, Leipzig, 1928; II. *Die Platonischen Schriften*, Leipzig, 1930, pp. 363 *et seq.*; 670 *et seq.*; J. STENZEL, *Plato der Erzieher*, Leipzig, 1928; W. JÄGER, *Paideia*, II–III, London, 1945.

5

I accept Plato's Letters VII and VIII as authentic: cf. the remarks in the SOUILHE edition, *Collection Budé*, Paris, 1926, in which the historical facts of this disputed question will be found: cf. the bibliography given by G. GLOTZ (-R. COHEN), *Histoire Grecque*, III, Paris, 1936, p. 409, n. 102; to which should be added: G. R. MORROW, "Studies in the Platonic Epistles", *Illinois Studies in Language and Literature*, XVIII, University of Illinois, 1935; G. PASQUALI, *Le Lettere di Platone*, Florence, 1938; E. DES PLACES, "Un Livre nouveau sur les Lettres de Platon", *Revue de Philologie*, 1940, pp. 127-135.

6

Plato versus Tyrtaeus (*Leg.*, I, 628e–630e): this passage has been excellently reinstated and commented on by E. DES PLACES, "Platon et Tyrtée", *Revue des Etudes grecques*, LV (1942), pp. 14–24.

7

Fourth-century mercenaries: H. W. PARKE, *Greek Mercenary Soldiers from the Earliest Times to the Battle of Ipsus*, Oxford, 1933.

8

What the Academy was: P. BOYANCE, *Le Culte des Muses chez les Philosophes grecs*, p. 261, gives a summary of the discussion: was it an association of scholars (U. VON WILAMOWITZ-MÖLLENDORF, *Platon*², Berlin, 1920, pp. 270 *et seq.*; *Antigonos von Karystos*, *Philologische Untersuchungen*, IV, Berlin, 1881, pp. 279 *et seq.*; H. USENER, *Organisation der Wissenschaftlichen Arbeit*, *Vorträge und Aufsätze*, Leipzig-Berlin, 1907, pp. 67 *et seq.*), or a proper University (E. HOWALD, *Die Platonische Akademie und die moderne Universitas litterarum*, Berne, 1921)?

9

The Academy as the "thiasos" of the Muses: P. BOYANCE, *ibid.*, pp. 261–267; for the apotheosization of Plato, *ibid.*, pp. 259–261, 267–275, and O. REVERDIN, *La Religion de la Cité platonicienne*, Paris, 1945.

10

For *Les Procès d'impiété intentés aux Philosophes à Athènes aux Vᵉ-IVᵉ siècles*, cf. the work which appeared under this title by E. DERENNE, in *Bibliothèque de la Faculté de Philosophie et Lettres de l'Université de Liége*, XLV, Liége, 1930.

11

The sacred character of the site of the Academy: C. PICARD, "Dans les Jardins du héros Academos" (*Institut de France, Séance publique annuelle des cinq Académies du jeudi 25 octobre 1934, Discours*, Paris, 1934). On the initiative and under the patronage of P. ARISTOPHRON (*L'Académie de Platon*, Paris, 1933), the Academy of Athens began to undertake the work of excavation, but this was unfortunately broken off just when it was beginning to prove fruitful: see the reports in *Bulletin de Correspondance hellénique*, from 1930 (vol. LIV, pp. 459–460) to 1937 (vol. LXII, pp. 458–459), or *Jahrbuch des deutschen archäologischen Instituts, Archäologischer Anzeiger*, esp. 1934, c. 137–140 (map: *Abb.* 8).

12

Plato's "exedra": as a help to the modern reader to make a "composition of place", I recommend the mosaics—they are Roman, but copies of Greek originals—in Naples Museum and in Villa Torlonia-Albani, showing a meeting of philosophers (the Seven Sages?): G. W. ELDERKIN, *American Journal of Archaeology*, XXXIX (1935), pp. 92–111; O. BRENDEL, *Römische Mitteilungen*, LI (1936), pp. 1–22, and again ELDERKIN, *ibid.*, LII (1937), pp. 223–226.

13

Wall-pictures used in the Academy for practical exercises in classification (cf. ARIST., *Part. An.*, I, 639a): A. DIES, *Notice* to his edition of the *Politics*, Collection Budé, Paris, 1935, p. xxvii.

14

The influence of medicine and particularly the science of hygiene on Plato's thought: W. JÄGER in the admirable opening chapter to Vol. III of his *Paideia*, pp. 3–45, "Greek Medicine as a form of Paideia".

15

Elementary arithmetical problems: Plato only indicates these by one word: τὸ λογισμόν (*Resp.*, VII, 522c), λογιστική (525a), λογισμοί (*Leg.*, VII, 809c, 817e). There is a slightly more detailed description in *Leg.*, VII, 819c, of the arithmetical games which he says were played in Egyptian schools and which, though they were intended as pure arithmetic, also "involved indispensable practical applications" —τὰς τῶν ἀναγκαίων ἀριθμῶν χρήσεις.

In *Leg.*, VII, 809c, he includes counting among all the other kinds of knowledge that are necessary for warfare, domestic affairs and the administration of the city. This concrete practical attitude appears more clearly *e contrario* in the passages in which, describing the abstract, scientific, disinterested character which it is necessary for his introductory mathematical teaching to have, he contrasts this with accepted exoteric usage—which he himself admits to be necessary in the early stages for the masses: *Leg.*, VII, 818a: budding philosophers will not use arithmetic like shopkeepers and business men to calculate their profit and loss (*Resp.*, VII, 525c), will not introduce into their reasoning any numbers representing visible, material objects (525e), will eliminate anything grasping or illiberal from their treatment of practical problems (*Leg.*, VII, 747b).

16

Egyptian mathematical papyri: A. REY, *La Science dans l'antiquité* (I), *la Science orientale avant les Grecs*, Paris, 1930, pp. 201–287.

17

Plato's rational, geometric idea of astronomy: cf. with the classic pages from P. DUHEM, *Le Système du monde, Histoire des doctrines cosmologiques de Platon à Copernic*, vol. I, Paris, 1913, pp. 94–95; II, pp. 59 *et seq.* (see the bibliography, p. 67, n. 1); A. RIVAUD, "Le Système astronomique de Platon", *Revue d'Histoire de la Philosophie*, II (1928), pp. 1–26. It is useful to compare this with the equally *a priori* idea of acoustics: A. RIVAUD, "Platon et la Musique", in the same *Revue*, III (1929), pp. 1–30.

18

Plato's course of study. I must here attempt a brief justification of the solution which I have adopted, which may seem at first sight to be more dogmatic than the evidence warrants.

There is indeed some difficulty in getting the two pictures of education—as found on the one hand in *The Republic* (II–III and VII) and on the other in *The Laws* (II and VII)—to agree. I know how careful one must be not to succumb to the tendency to establish an artificial harmony between Plato's different works: each of them is in a sense a whole which cannot be reduced to any of the others. Nevertheless, it seems to me that despite their different viewpoints these two pictures are indeed complementary. *The Laws* describe in detail the more elementary and in a sense more "popular" education which is only sketched very briefly in books II–III of *The Republic* and which was intended for the aristocratic class of the φύλακες as a whole. This "minor education"—σμικρὰ παιδεία (*Leg.*, V, 735a)—is contrasted in *The Laws* itself with a "more elaborate education"—ἀκριβεστέρα παιδεία (*Leg.*, XII, 965b)—intended only for the members of the Nocturnal Council (*Leg.*, XII, 961a *et seq.*)—the Chiefs of State, i.e. the equivalent of the statesmen-philosophers of *The Republic*, in which book indeed their higher studies are described in these very words: παιδεία ἡ ἀκριβεστάτη (*Resp.*, VII, 503d). This higher course of study is not analysed explicitly in *The Laws*, but it is assumed to follow later, and it is emphasized that more advanced study of the mathematical sciences as a whole is to be reserved for a few specially gifted intellects—τινες ὀλίγοι—which brings us back to the selection suggested in *Resp.*, VII, 537ac. The course of study mentioned in *The Laws* was to end, to judge by *Leg.*, VII, 818d, with the same general view of the whole, the same comparative study, as is suggested as the final aim in *The Republic* (VII, 537bc).

Once the equation has been made—the education in *The Laws*=the education of the φύλακες in *The Republic*—a few apparent discrepancies remain to be overcome and the chronological sequence needs to be defined. According to *The Republic*, II, 376e–377a, education was to begin with μουσική (including the γράμματα) before gymnastics, which were to occupy two or three years of compulsory service ending at the age of twenty (VIII, 537b). *The Laws* (VII, 795d), on the other hand, put gymnastics before music. As *The Laws* say that children were to leave the "kindergarten" when they were six (VII, 794c) and then (809e) go on to say that they should begin to study literature when they are ten, it might be concluded that *The Laws*, unlike *The Republic*, put the period for gymnastics between the ages of seven and nine and not at the end of the school period.

But this would not follow, because:

(1) The account of gymnastics (in *Leg.*, VII, 795d *et seq.*) is shown later (797e) as coming after the account given in Books I–II (641c–673e), which has already been devoted (in connection with the banqueting rules) to the part played by the μουσική in education.

(2) In *The Laws*, after returning to the study of the γράμματα (809a *et seq.*) and music (812b *et seq.*), Plato returns to the matter of physical education (813a *et seq.*), thus following the order in *The Republic* again.

(3) When gymnastics are first mentioned in *The Laws* (VII, 795d *et seq.*), troops of infantry and cavalry are referred to as taking part in the religious processions (796e), and this for Plato, as for Athens itself at the time, meant that fully grown ephebes would be taking part, not children between the ages of seven and nine.

(4) It seems highly likely that if, in both *The Laws* and *The Republic*, Plato means primarily the ephebia when he is talking about gymnastics (I have noted the emphasis that is put on military preparation, as in *Leg.*, VII, 795c, 804c . . .), then gymnastics, in the sense of physical education, was to accompany the whole of education from childhood onwards and not simply occupy one special period—unless, again, it was for two or three years' military service. This is proved by the fact that the games programme (*Leg.*, VIII, 832d *et seq.*) allows for three categories of masculine competitors (833 *et seq.*)—children, boys and grown men—and two of feminine (833cd)—over thirteen and under thirteen (excluding married women).

It can therefore be taken as certain that *The Laws* want athletics to be practised at "secondary-school age" (from ten to seventeen) as well as at "primary-school age". The question is whether this latter period was to be devoted to physical education exclusively. *The Laws* expressly say that three years, from ten to thirteen, should be devoted to the study of the γράμματα, and since this word means the study of literature (the argument in *Leg.*, VII, 810c *et seq.* repeats, as we have seen in the text, the argument in *Resp.*, II, 377a *et seq.*; X, 595a *et seq.*)—which was entirely a matter for the secondary school—it is assumed that reading and writing had already been learned.

Three years (from seven to ten) were not too long a period for this, considering the backward state of primary-school teaching in those days. Plato alludes to the teaching methods in use: first the letters were learned, then the syllables, in every possible kind of combination (*Resp.*, III, 402ab; *Pol.*, 227e-278b).

I have explained in the actual text the way secondary-school studies were to be divided into three stages: (1) from ten to thirteen, mainly literary; (2) from thirteen to sixteen, mainly artistic; (3) from sixteen to seventeen or eighteen, mainly mathematical. But, as we have already seen, Plato wanted children to learn mathematics from their earliest days (*Resp.*, VII, 536d; 537a; *Leg.*, VII, 819b), and the part which he wanted mathematics to play in the selection of pupils makes it quite certain that this subject was not to be broken off after the first rudiments had been learned at the primary school. It is therefore highly probable, as I have said, that the dividing line between these three different stages was not as precise as it seems to be at first sight: it is a question all the time of more or less, of the way three different branches of study, which were going on at more or less the same time, were to be divided up.

19

Μακροτέρα ὁδός: see the note in WILAMOWITZ: *Platon*², II, pp. 218-220.

20

In my attempt to show how Plato's philosophy ultimately ends up in a contemplative Wisdom of a personal not a collective kind, I have done no more than repeat for my own purposes the profound observations by W. JÄGER, *Paideia*, II, pp. 271-278, 353-357; cf. III, pp. 197-212.

CHAPTER VII

1

On Isocrates: G. BLASS, *Die attische Beredsamkeit*², II, Leipzig, 1892; MÜNSCHNER, in PAULY-WISSOWA, IX, 2, c. 2146-2227, s.v. "Isokrates", 2; G. MATHIEU, *Les Idées politiques d'Isocrate*, Paris, 1925; A. BURK (a pupil of E. DRERUP), "Die Pädagogie des Isokrates, als Grundlegung des humanistischen Bildungsideals im Vergleich mit den zeitgenössischen und den modernen Theorien", in *Studien zur Geschichte und Kultur des Altertums*, XIV, 3/4, Würtzburg, 1932; W. JÄGER, *Paideia*, III, pp. 46-155.

2

Isocrates sacrificed to Plato: this is my one complaint against W. JÄGER, as I have explained in my note, "Le Siècle de Platon, à propos d'un livre récent", *Revue Historique*, CXCVI (1946), pp. 142-149.

3

Isocrates as the father of humanism: see the authors quoted and criticized by W. JÄGER, *Paideia*, III, p. 300, n. 2.

4

Φιλοσοφία and φιλοσοφεῖν in Isocrates: cf. the passages collected by A. PREUSS, *Index Isocrateus*, Leipzig, 1904, p. 104.

5

The composition of the *Panegyric*: the evidence will be found in G. MATHIEU, E. BREMOND, *Notice* to their edition, II, p. 5, n. 7.

6

Isocrates and Socrates: H. GOMPERZ, "Isokrates and Sokratik," *Wiener Studien*, XXVII (1905), pp. 163 *et seq.*; XXVIII (1906), p. 1 *et seq.*

7

The dates of Isocrates' stay with Gorgias in Thessaly: *see* G. MATHIEU, *Introduction* to the Budé edition, *Isocrate*, vol. I, p. 11, n. 1.

8

The Life of Isocrates by the Pseudo-Plutarch (837B) relates that "some say that he first opened a school ἐπὶ Χίου". This is usually translated as "in Chios" (cf. *ibid.*, 837 C: he is supposed to have granted a constitution to the island); but this expression ἐπὶ Χίου seems queer (should it be ἐν Χίῳ?): might it not hide a date supplied by the name of an archon that accidentally got changed? Cf. W. JÄGER, *Paideia*, III, p. 302, n. 32.

9

Did Isocrates compose a treatise on the theory of the art of oratory? The answer would seem to be no. The one which circulated under his name could not have been genuinely his. [PLUT.] *Isoc.*, 838 E; *V. Isoc.*, 148, 151; CIC., *Inv.*, II, 7; QUINT., II, 15, 4; O. NAVARRE, *Essai sur la Rhétorique grecque avant Aristote*, p. 117.

10

Alcidamas: J. VAHLEN, "Der Rhetor Alkidamas", *Gesammelte Schriften*, I, pp. 117 *et seq.* (=*Sitzungsberichte* of the Vienna Academy of Sciences, *Phil.-Hist. Kl.*, XLIII (1863), pp. 491–528); C. REINHARDT, *De Isocratis aemulis*, Bonn Dissertation, 1873, pp. 6–24.

11

The average number of pupils in Isocrates' school. He had in all about a hundred ([PLUT.] *Isoc.*, 837 C). A course of study could last up to three or four years (ISOC. *Ant.*, 87: ". . . of so many pupils, and there are some of them who have spent three years with me and others who have spent four"); let us say three, which is probably above the average. Isocrates taught for fifty-five years (393–338). This gives an average of: 100 × 3 ÷ 55 = 5.45 pupils per year.

Nine is given as the maximum for his first attempt at teaching ἐπι Χίου ([PLUT.] *Isoc.*, 837 B). Isocrates himself speaks of "three or four" specially chosen pupils working in his "seminary" (*Panath.*, 200).

12

Isocrates' political ideas; see the theory put forward by G. MATHIEU, quoted above, n. 1, and W. JÄGER, *Paideia*, III, pp. 46–155.

13

Isocrates leaves Athens because democracy is ruining its culture, and goes over to Philip, the champion of Hellenism: I have summarized the rather optimistic judgment expressed by W. JÄGER, *ibid.*, pp. 152–155.

14

The relationship between Isocrates and Plato has been the subject of a number of conflicting works, a list of which will be found in A. DIES, *Autour de Platon*, II, p. 407, n. 1; MATHIEU, BREMOND, *Introduction* to their edition, *Isocrate*, vol. I, p. ix, n. 3 (cf. pp. 155–157); G. MERIDIER, in his edition, *Euthydème*, pp. 133 *et seq.*, p. 137, n. 1; DIES, *Introduction* to *La République*, pp. lvi *et seq.*; L. ROBIN in his edition of the *Phaedrus*, pp. xxii *et seq.*, clxi *et seq.*; to which should be added: R. FLACELIERE, "L'Eloge d'Isocrate à la fin du Phèdre", *Revue des Etudes grecques*, XLVI (1933), pp. 224–232; G. MATHIEU, "Les Premiers Conflits entre Platon et Isocrate et la date de l'Euthydème", *Mélanges G. Glotz*, Paris, 1932, II, pp. 555–564; *Notice* to his edition of the *Antidosis*, the Budé edition, *Isocrate*, III, Paris, 1942, pp. 90–94; and finally W. JÄGER, *Paideia*, III, London, 1945, *passim*, (cf. p. 364), s.v. "Isocrates and Plato"; R. SCHAERER, *La question platonicienne*, Neuchâtel, 1938.

I cannot regard any of the conclusions reached by these experts as certain. There are a number of factors that make research difficult, and, until new evidence appears, condemn it to failure:

(1) The vagueness of the chronology as regards the works of the two different authors. Whatever progress may have been made, especially as regards Plato's *Dialogues*, since the time of Campbell and Lutoslawski, many uncertainties still remain: does the *Busiris*, for instance, come before *The Republic* or after it? Cf. A. DIES, *Autour de Platon*, II, p. 247.

(2) The vagueness of Isocrates' allusions: it is one of the characteristic features of his aesthetics—and he has all too often been imitated by those who have come after him!—that he simply will not make any precise references. When he mentions his opponents he uses vague expressions like "those who take part in discussions" and "in philosophy". Does this mean Plato? or Antisthenes? or both at once? The odds are even. It may also be that Isocrates was drawing a composite portrait whose features he took first from one group of philosophers and then from another, composed perhaps of Sophists like Alcidamas.

(3) Finally, doubt as to what value is to be attributed to Plato's judgments. Thus at the end of the *Phaedrus* (287d–279b) he makes Socrates deliver a eulogy on Isocra.es. Is this to be taken seriously (FLACELIERE, and Isocrates himself, *Ep.*, V)? But supposing it is ironic (ROBIN)? And even if we take it at its face value, what exactly does it mean? Is it a eulogy on what Isocrates had become when Plato was writing (WILAMOWITZ, "Platon"[2], II, p. 212), or a regret for the splendid promise given by Isocrates in his youth, i.e. when Socrates was supposed to be speaking (about 410), and which he had not fulfilled (T. GOMPERZ, *Penseurs de la Grèce*, II, p. 438)?

15

Aristotle and the teaching of rhetoric in the Academy: cf. finally W. JÄGER, *Paideia*, III, pp. 147, 185–186, who refers to the work of his disciple, F. SOLMSEN, "Die Entwicklung der aristotelischen Logik und Rhetorik", *Neue Philologische Untersuchungen*, IV, Berlin, 1929.

PART TWO

CHAPTER I

1

The fundamental work on Hellenistic education is still the little book by E. ZIE-BARTH, *Aus dem griechischen Schulwesen, Eudemos von Milet und Verwandtes*[2], Leipzig, 1914; cf. also the highly concentrated but necessarily brief pages in P. WENDLAND, "Die hellenistisch-römische Kultur in ihren Beziehungen zu Judentum Christentum"[2-3], *Handbuch zum Neuen Testament*, I, 2, Tübingen, 1912, and in A. J. FESTU-GIERE, *Le Monde gréco-romain au temps de Notre-Seigneur*, I. *Le cadre temporel*, Paris, 1935, pp. 64–94. The clearest and most detailed information is to be found in the work by M. ROSTOVTSEFF mentioned *infra*, n. 4, and in M. NILSSON, *Die hellenistische Schule*, Munich 1955.

2

School documents of Egyptian origin (most of them date from the time of the Roman Empire but there are enough from the time of the Ptolemies to prove the point advanced here of a perfectly homogeneous teaching tradition from the period of Alexander's conquests up to Byzantine times): a convenient collection has been made by E. ZIEBARTH, *Aus der antiken Schule, Sammlung griechischer Texte auf Papyrus, Holztafeln, Ostraka*[2], *Kleine Texte für Vorlesungen und Uebungen herausgegeben von H. Lietzmann*, No. 65, Bonn, 1913; for an early treatment: P. BEUDEL, *Qua ratione Graeci liberos docuerint, papyris, ostracis, tabulis in Aegypto inventis, illustrantur*, Münster Dissertation, 1911. These findings need to be brought up to date. A list, which was complete when it was composed (it tends to sin by excess, accepting documents as school documents which seem to be scientific rather than educational, especially in the matter of mathematics), was compiled by P. COLLART, "Les Papyrus scolaires", *Mélanges Desrousseaux*, Paris, 1937, pp. 69–80. To this should be added the recent discoveries: O. GUERAUD-P. JOUGUET, "Un livre d'écolier du IIIe siècle avant Jésus-Christ", *Publications de la Société Royale Egyptienne de Papyrologie, Textes et Documents*, II, Cairo, 1938, which includes a very valuable commentary referring to a number of important texts. (The details in the account by A. KORTE, *Archiv für Papyrusforschung*, XIII (1938–1939), pp. 104–109, should not be forgotten, particularly for the date: 217 to 200.)

3

I make this confession and these excuses to L. ROBERT, who is more qualified than anyone else to supply the first-hand study which we still lack on Greek education in the Graeco-Roman period: cf. meanwhile the research which he has already done in the adjacent field of games, esp. in *Etudes épigraphiques et philologiques, Bibliothèque de l'Ecole pratique des Hautes-Etudes (Sciences historiques et philologiques)*, vol. 272, pp. 7–112: "Fêtes, musiciens et athlètes."

J. OEHLER has long been the recognized specialist in this field (see his many contributions to PAULY-WISSOWA, his *Epigraphische Beiträge zur Geschichte der Bildung im Altertum*, Vienna Syllabus, 1909, etc.); but he has never managed to develop his material to the point of writing a real history of the subject.

4

Recent summaries of Hellenistic civilization: I am not thinking so much of the compilation by A. H. M. JONES, *The Greek City from Alexander to Justinian*, Oxford, 1940 (for education see amongst others pp. 220–225, 285, with the corresponding notes, pp. 351–353, 365), as of the great book by M. ROSTOVTSEFF, *The Social and Economic History of the Hellenistic World*, 3 vols., Oxford, 1942: cf. pp. 1084–1095, 1058–1060 and *passim.*; the notes, pp. 1588–1590, 1596–1600. The books which existed before this appeared were far too superficial, especially as regards education, and in any case were no longer up to date: F. BAUMGARTEN, F. POLAND, R. WAGNER, *Die hellenistisch-römische Kultur*, Leipzig-Berlin, 1913 (cf. pp. 57–63); W. TARN, *La Civilisation hellénistique*, French trans., Paris, 1936, pp. 94–95.

For the hellenisation of the East, cf. the note by E. BIKERMAN, " Sur une Inscription grecque de Sidon" (in honour of one of the sons of a "suffete" who won the chariot race in the Nemean Games in about the year 200 B.C.), in *Mélanges syriens offerts à M. R. Dussaud*, Paris, 1939, I, pp. 91–99.

5

The idea of the "citizen of the world", which was to have such a tremendous future, especially in Stoic thought, appears at the very beginning of Hellenistic times in Diogenes of Sinope and had been prepared for by Antiphon and Theophrastes: cf. J. MEWALDT, "Das Weltbürgertum in der Antike", *Die Antike*, II (1926), pp. 177–190.

6

Παιδεία=*humanitas*=culture: cf. my note in *Saint Augustin et la Fin de la Culture antique*, Paris, 1938, pp. 552–554, in which I quote from P. DE LABRIOLLE, "Pour l'Histoire du mot Humanitas", *Les Humanités, Classes de Lettres*, VIII (1931–1932), pp. 478–479.

7

Παιδεία and the life beyond the grave: I have here summarized the thesis established (with a few discrepancies) by researches carried out jointly by P. BOYANCE, " Le Culte des Muses chez les Philosophes grecs," *Etudes d'Histoire et de Psychologie Religieuses*, Paris, 1936; F. CUMONT, *Recherches sur le Symbolisme funéraire des Romains*, Paris, 1942; and myself, Μουσικὸς Ἀνήρ, *Etude sur les scènes de la Vie intellectuelle figurant sur les Monuments funéraires romains*, Grenoble, 1938 (not forgetting the valuable supplementary data supplied by A. J. FESTUGIÈRE in his account in the *Revue des Etudes Grecques*, LII (1939), pp. 241–243); "Le Symbolisme funéraire des Romains", *Journal des Savants*, 1944, pp. 23–37, 77–86. The available documentation is growing day by day: see for example the inscription in the Fitzwilliam Museum recently published by F. M. HEICHELHEIM, *Journal of Hellenic Studies*, LXII (1942), p. 30, No. XII, 2. Nor do I consider that the thesis has been disproved by the suggestion of C. PICARD, who believes that "the mousikos aner is not just—as has been supposed—some ordinary reader interested in learning, but the immortal and beneficient image of one of those whose works are read" ("Le Pindare de l'exèdre des poètes et des sages au Serapeion de Memphis", in *Monuments Piot*, 1952, vol. 46, p. 24; cf. *Revue Archéologique*, 1954, I, p. 103). It seems quite certain that in most cases the person represented on funeral monuments—the exedra at Memphis was not, of course, a funeral monument—as a doctor, lector, orator or musician, is the dead man himself and not his master or the source of his inspiration. Everything points to this—inscriptions, portraits, styles of hair-dressing, unfinished faces: cf. my note in *Revue Archéologique*, 1939, vol. XIV, pp. 200–202.

CHAPTER II

I

The education of Greek slaves has not, so far as I know, been the subject of any systematic enquiry: cf. the few pieces of information supplied by E. ZIEBARTH, *Aus dem griechischen Schulwesen*[2], p. 39, n. 1; M. ROSTOVTSEFF, *The Social and Economic History of the Hellenistic World* (II), p. 1106 (III), p. 1600, n. 51.

Aristotle had advised masters to have their slaves educated if they wanted them to perform the same work as free men (*Œc.*, A, 1344, a 23 *et seq.*); he knew that there were real "domestic" schools for slaves in Syracuse (*Pol.*, A, 1255, b 22 *et seq.*): a comedy by PHERECRATES (second half of the fifth century) had as its title Δουλοδιδάσκαλος—"The Slaves' Teacher" (ATH., VI, 262b).

According to Zeno's correspondence (third century B.C.), young slaves seem to have been given a sporting education in the palestras to enable them to become professional champions: *PSI*, 418, 340, and on this subject: M. ROSTOVTSEFF, *A Large Estate in Egypt in the Third Century B.C.*, Madison, 1922, pp. 60, 172–173; C. PRÉAUX, "Lettres privées grecques relatives à l'Education", in *Revue belge de Philologie et d'Histoire*, VIII (1929), pp. 577–800. In Doryleia at the time of the Roman Empire there was a "gymnasiarch for free men and slaves" (DITTENBERG., *Or.*, 479, 9) which proves that the latter went to the gymnasium and shared in the free distribution of oil. A rescript by Vespasian (*SPAW*, 1935, p. 968, l. 25) seems to forbid the teaching of medicine to slaves (cf. R. HERZOG, *ibid.*, p. 1013), so that they must have been taught it until then.

But there is something better than amassing all these indirect inferences, and that would be to collect all the positive evidence. This exists: cf. the essay in *Ægyptus*, XV (1935), pp. 1–66, which A. ZAMBON devotes to the Διδασκαλικαί—"teaching contracts" in Greek Egypt which have been preserved on papyri: some of these were entered into by masters for the benefit of their young slaves, and they were not always meant to lead to "servile" work only: thus No. 29 (*BGU*, 1125) is for a year's instruction in learning to play the double oboe, διαυλεῖν (13 B.C.), No. 30 (*POxy.*, 724) for two years' instruction in shorthand (A.D. 155).

2

Aristotle and education. The reader may be rather surprised to find that in this *History* so little attention is paid to the great philosopher and that he should be mentioned only in passing. The fact is that Aristotle's educational work does not seem to me to have the same kind of creative originality as Plato's and Isocrates'. His ideas and his actual practice as the founder of a school, a brotherhood of philosophers supported financially by the generous benefactions of Philip and Alexander, simply reflect the ideas and practice of his age; and though in more than one case they may seem to prefigure those of the Hellenistic age, the reason for this is that Aristotle lived at a time which was a kind of watershed between the two separate phases of Greek history.

The best work on this subject is still: M. DEFOURNY, "Aristote et l'Education" (*Annales de l'Institut supérieur de Philosophie*, Louvain, IV (1920), pp. 1–176).

3

Legislation about compulsory schooling. What Aristotle (*loc. cit.*) regarded as characteristic of aristocratic cities, i.e. the existence of a kind of magistracy known as παιδονομία, was only to be met with in Sparta and Crete, but this symbolized and implied the whole of the State control of education. The absence of this special magistracy in the other Greek cities, particularly Athens, meant—since the State was deprived of any regular control over education, and therefore any means of coercion—absolute freedom of education.

I remain sceptical about the attempts that have been made to establish the fact that the Athenians had legislation about compulsory schooling (see P. GIRARD, *L'Education athénienne*, pp. 39–41): the basic text that is always being referred to is the Prosopopeia of the Laws in *Crito*, in which Plato makes them say (50d): "Speak, have you any criticisms to make about those laws of ours . . . concerning how children should be brought up and educated? is it not a fact that they were good laws, those which were enacted about this, ordering your father to educate you in music and gymnastics?" But leaving aside the oratorical tone of the passage, it is sufficient to remember that Plato is thinking here of unwritten Laws—Custom—so that there is no need to assume the existence of any actual written law saying that there was an obligation (under what penalty?) for a father to send his son to the schools of letters and gymnastics.

The force of custom is also sufficient to explain how, in DEMOSTHENES, *Aph.*, I, 46, a careless tutor could be reprimanded for having deprived his pupils' teachers of their wages.

As for Solon's laws about schools—quoted by AESCHINES, *Tim.*, 9–12—if they are not entirely imaginary, they simply concern the supervision of behaviour, and their only object is to prevent any development of pederasty; they have no positive educational aim.

As regards the magistrates, only the "strategus" was able to play any part in the supervision of education, and then only as an official of the ephebia, this being a military institution. The famous inscription (DITTENBERG., *Syll.*, 956) in which the deme of Eleusis honours the strategus Derkylus for "the generosity he has shown in connection with children's education", does not prove that primary-school teaching was a normal part of the strategus's functions: it may be thanking Derkylus for an act of evergetism which he performed for the demus not as a magistrate but as a private person (date: 350? 320? Cf. DITTENBERG., *ad loc.*; P. GIRARD, *L'Education athénienne*, 51–53). The only legislative act which seems to have any direct connection with teaching in Athens is a decree famous in the annals of epigraphy, taken on the initiative of Archinus under Euclid's archonship (403/2), ordering the adoption of the Ionian alphabet (EPHOR., fr. 169, *Didot*): this included teaching, as we learn from one of the scholiasts of Dionysius Thrax (E. BEKKER, *Anecdota Graeca*, II, p. 783, where παρὰ Θηβαίοις needs to be corrected to Ἀθηναίοις).

4

On the gymnasiums in Hellenistic Egypt: P. JOUGUET, *La Vie municipale dans l'Egypte romaine*, Paris, 1911, pp. 67–68; T. A. BRADY, "The Gymnasium in Ptolemaic Egypt," *Philological Studies in Honour of Walter Miller* (= *The University of Missouri Studies*, XI, 3), Columbia (Miss.), 1936, pp. 9–20; M. ROSTOVTSEFF, *The Social and Economic History of the Hellenistic World* (III), pp. 1395, 1588, n. 23.

5

On the Attic ephebia, the fundamental work is still A. DUMONT, *Essai sur l'Ephébie attique*, 2 vols., Paris, 1875–1876, although it becomes more and more difficult to use;

its documentation, its system of references and its chronology are none of them up to date. The article by THALHEIM in PAULY-WISSOWA, which is in any case far too short, has not worn well either. See P. GRAINDOR, "Etudes sur l'Ephébie attique sous l'Empire", in *Musée Belge*, XXVI (1912), pp. 165–208; M. ROSTOVTSEFF, *Hellenistic World* (III), p. 1505, n. 12.

"Les Chlamydes noires des Ephèbes athéniens": cf. the note by P. ROUSSEL, in *Revue des Etudes anciennes*, XLIII (1941), pp. 163–165.

6

The total complement of the Attic ephebia: I say at most 500 to 600 for the period 334–326, as does A. W. GOMME, *The Population of Athens in the Fifth and Fourth Centuries* (Glasgow University Publications, XXVIII, Oxford, 1933, pp. 8–10, 67–70). From the inscription IG^2, II, 1156, it is often taken to have been between 800 and 1,000 in round figures (e.g. P. GIRARD, *L'Education athénienne*, p. 288; W. S. FERGUSON, *Hellenistic Athens*, London, 1911, p. 128, which refers to SUNDWALL in *Acta* of the Finnish Society of Sciences, XXXIV, 2, pp. 24 *et seq.*), but this is based on faulty reasoning. From the marble, which is damaged, we are led to believe that six small "demes" of the Cecropis tribe had supplied forty-four ephebes; as there were twelve demes to a tribe and ten tribes in Attica, it is calculated that the ephebe class in the year 334/3 must have been $44 \times 2 \times 10 = 880$.

But this ignores the fact that the demes were not all of the same importance. The five that are still well preserved on the stone supplied respectively five, twelve, seven, two and two ephebes. By taking into account the way the demes were distributed geographically A. W. GOMME concludes that the Cecropis tribe supplied either forty-three or forty-five ephebes altogether.

For the year 327/6, the inscription Ἐφημερὶς Ἀρχαιολογική, 1918, p. 75, No. 95, gives sixty-five ephebes for the Leontis tribe; for 305/4, IG^2, 478, suggests that the Erechteis tribe provided about thirty-three ephebes.

We must pass from the tribe to the city. We can hardly do anything else except multiply by ten, though this is a purely hypothetical number as there is no guarantee that the ten tribes were equal in number. This gives us 450 for the year 334, 630 for the year 327, 400 for the year 305. C. A. FORBES, *Greek Physical Education*, New York-London, 1929, p. 152, reaches a similar figure of 450–500 for the year 334, but rather amusingly he arrives at this result by making two mistakes which cancel each other out: he adopts Girard's wrong figure of 900–1,000, and then divides it by two on the assumption that two classes of ephebes were doing their service in that year, which is another error, the text making it quite clear, l. 37, 46, that the reference is to the ephebes stationed in Eleusis, i.e. sophomores only.

For the next period we possess a considerable amount of data, thanks to the lists of names that are to be found on inscriptions. Ignoring those that are too badly damaged to be of any use, we obtain the following table (cf. a similar table in L. W. REINMUTH, "The Foreigners in the Athenian Ephebia", in *University of Nebraska Studies in Language, Literature and Criticism*, IX, Lincoln, 1929, p. 18. I have corrected the references and the chronology which are quite arbitrary and in any case out of date). For the Hellenistic period I follow W. K. PRITCHETT-B. D. MERITT, *The Chronology of Hellenistic Athens*, Cambridge (Mass.), 1940, who bring up to date the work by W. B. DINSMOOR, *The Archons of Athens in the Hellenistic Age*, ibid., 1938, and as a result I have changed the dates of the IG^2. For the period of the Empire the dates (cf. their table of Archons, IG^2, II, 2, Berlin, 1931, pp. 789–796), based on P. GRAINDOR, "Chronologie des Archontes athéniens sous l'Empire", in *Mémoires de l'Académie de*

Belgique, 2, VIII, 1921, have not been changed, for the years with which we are concerned, by the more recent studies of S. H. OLIVER, "Athenian Archons under the Roman Empire", in *Hesperia*, 1942, pp. 81–89; NOTOPOULOS, "Ferguson's Law in Athens under the Empire", in the *American Journal of Philology*, 1933, pp. 44–55; "The Method of Choosing Archons in Athens under the Empire", *ibid.*, 1944, pp. 149–166.

| *IG²*, II, No. | Date | Ephebes | | Total |
		Athenian	Foreign	
665	269/8	33	0	33
681	249/8	29	0	29
766	244/3	23	0	23
(*Hesperia*, IV, p. 74)	128/7	107	0	107
1,008	119/8	124	17	141
1,009	117/6	162	12	174
1,011	107/6	116	24	140
1,028	102/1	102	36	138
1,039	83–73	105	5+x	110+x
1,043	39/8 B.C.	53	66	119
1,996	84/5–92/3 A.D.	80	151	231
2,024	111/2	21	79	100
2,026	116/7	4	48	52
2,065	150/1	70	7	77
2,086	163/4	95	41	136
2,097	169/70	80	154	234
2,103	172/3+x	106	109	215
2,130	192/3	85	39	124
2,128	c. 190–200	94	104	198
2,191	c. 200/1	70	61	131
2,193	200+x	76	27	103
2,199	200+y	61	32	93
2,245	262/3 or 266/7	313	52	365

7

Foreigners in the Attic ephebia: cf. note *supra* and the pamphlet by REINMUTH; M. ROSTOVTSEFF, *Hellenistic World* (III), p. 1505, n. 12, assumes that their admission was imposed upon the narrowly nationalistic Athenian aristocracy by the pressure of rich Syrian and Italian merchants living in Delos. Whatever the cause may be, it seems quite certain (cf. REINMUTH, pp. 46–48) that the great majority of these foreign ephebes were not the sons of foreigners who had settled in Attica or its dependencies but students who came to Athens for the particular purpose of completing their education; most of them came from Asia Minor—the majority of them were Milesians in the years A.D. 80–90 to 115, but there were also quite a few from Syria-Palestine; those who came from the West came chiefly from Sicily, Tarento, and above all Roman Italy.

These foreign ephebes are listed separately under the heading ξένοι—"foreigners", (in the oldest inscriptions), "Milesians" (in 84/5–92/3, 111/2 and 115/6), ἐπέγγραφοι —"listed lower down" (from 141/2). For the problem raised by this word "Milesians", cf. finally L. ROBERT, *Hellenica*, II, p. 76, n. 6.

8

The eclipse of the army instructors: the javelin and archery teachers had disappeared by 39/8 B.C. (*IG²*, II, 1043); the catapult teachers by the end of the century. The "hoplomachos" still remained, but his prestige was going down—he began by being ranked third, and then he gave way to the hegemon, the pedotribe and even to the secretary, e.g. on *IG²*, II, 1973 (40/1–53/4 A.D.)

9

For the *Paidotribes* of the Athenian ephebes cf. J. JÜLICHER, PAULY-WISSOWA, s.v., XVIII, 2, 2390–2391. He had already appeared by 269/8 B.C. (*IG²*, II, 665, 25): unlike the "cosmete"—a yearly magistrate who was chosen particularly for his moral standing (cf. *IG²*, II, 1106, 25 *et seq.*)—he was a professional who remained in service for several years at a stretch (e.g.: *IG²*, II, 1969, 4: A.D. 45/6); from the second century onwards he was chosen "for life"—διὰ βίου. We know for instance the career of a certain Aristo, son of Aphrodeisias, probably the grandson of somebody of the same name who had already been pedotribe to the ephebes in 61/2 (*IG²*, II, 1990): he took on the job shortly after the year 102 (*IG²*, II, 2017), had it extended "for life" in 118/9 (*IG²*, II, 2030), and was still in service in 125/6 (*IG²*, II, 2037). Even more remarkable was the career of Abascantus, son of Eumolpes: in the beginning—125/6— he was simply an "instructor"—παιδευτής—under the preceding pedotribe (*IG²*, II, 2037); was promoted to be pedotribe in 136/7, and only died after having filled the position for at least thirty-four years (*IG²*, II, 2097, 190; cf. his epitaph, *IG²*, II, 6397).

A "hypopedotribe" appeared in A.D. 36/7 (*IG²*, II, 1967). His prestige was comparatively low at first, but went up, and from the end of the second century he too was nominated for life (*IG²*, II, 2113, 30: *c.* 183/4–191/2).

10

This introduction to a life made up of sport, high society and civic affairs went on, in addition to the ephebia, in the young men's clubs—νέοι—which are known to have existed (though not in Athens), particularly in Asia Minor: cf. F. POLAND, PAULY-WISSOWA, s.v. *Neoi*, XVI, c. 2401–2409; C. A. FORBES, *Neoi, A Contribution to the Study of Greek Associations* (*Philological Monographs Published by the American Philological Association*, Middleton, 1933). They often had a proper gymnasium and did a great deal in the way of quasi-parliamentary activities by means of assemblies, councils, and magistrates.

11

The ephebia outside Attica: cf. the old Latin thesis by M. COLLIGNON, *Quid de collegiis epheborum apud Graecos, excepta Attica* ... Paris, 1877; the article by OEHLER, PAULY-WISSOWA, V, 2741–2746; A. H. M. JONES, *The Greek City*, pp. 220–225, 351–353; C. A. FORBES, *Greek Physical Education*, pp. 179–257; in Cyprus, T. B. MITFORD, *Opuscula Archeologica VI* (Skrifter Svenska Institut, Rom, XV, 1950), n. 12; in Cyrenaica, S. APPLEBAUM, *Journal of Roman Studies* (1950), p. 90.

12

The ephebes' participation in religious festivals: A. H. M. JONES, *op. cit.*, p. 354, n. 35, has not sorted out the documents concerning children in the lower schools from those about the ephebes.

13

Was the ephebia organised in Hellenistic kingdoms with a view to recruiting people for the army? M. ROSTOVTSEFF says that it was, in the kingdom of Pergamus (*The Social and Economic History of the Hellenistic World*, pp. 809–810, 1524, n. 82), but the passages he quotes are not sufficient to establish that there was any particular emphasis on preparation for the army (cf. for a view agreeing with mine, L. ROBERT, in *Revue des Etudes grecques*, 1935, p. 332): we know that warlike exercises went on in Athens, for instance—javelin throwing and archery (DITTENBERG., *Or.*, 339, 37; L. ROBERT, *Etudes anatoliennes*, Paris, 1937, pp. 201–202), but I do not see that this has any more significance in Pergamus than in Attica. As for the οἱ διὰ τῶν ὅπλων ἀγῶνες of DITTENBERG., *Or.*, 764, 24, this may simply have been a flat race "armed" rather than fencing bouts: cf. for Athens P. GRAINDOR, *Musée Belge*, XXVI (1922), p. 166.

14

The indirect but close association between the ephebia and the army in the time of the Ptolemies: cf. the facts collected by T. A. BRADY, in the volume quoted *supra*, n. 4, pp. 15–16, and M. ROSTOVTSEFF, *Hellenistic World* (III), p. 1688, n. 23; and, generally, M. LAUNEY, *Recherches sur les armeés hellénistiques*, vol. II, Paris, 1950. Officers often used to do the gymnasiarch's job; for instance, PREISIGKE, *SB*, 2264; 7456 ... Similarly in Cyrene: *Africa Italiana*, III (1930), p. 189.

15

The Egyptian ephebia: P. JOUGUET, *La Vie municipale dans l'Egypte romaine*, Paris, 1911, pp. 67–68, 150–160 (a repeat of *Revue de Philologie*, 1910, pp. 43–56); E. BICKERMANN, in the same *Revue*, 1927, pp. 367–368; T. A. BRADY, *art. cit.*, n. 4; M. ROSTOVTSEFF, *Hellenistic World*, III, p. 1395.

16

I have intentionally chosen the ambiguous word "class" to translate the technical term αἵρεσις. Papyrologists hesitate between two meanings (cf. P. JOUGUET, *Vie municipale*, p. 155)—"class" in the military sense of yearly promotion (thus M. ROSTOVTSEFF, *Hellenistic World*, p. 1059: and "class" in the educational sense, "small groups in order to facilitate instruction" (T. A. BRADY, *op. cit.*, pp. 12–13). The passages which we have are obscure: WILCKEN, *Chrest.*, I, 141, 142; *Bulletin de la Société Archéologique d'Alexandrie*, XXIV (1929), p. 277, n. 3.

17

For the "ἀπὸ γυμνασίου" of Roman Egypt, cf. P. JOUGUET, *La Vie municipale*, pp. 79–86. I admit that in practice this term is the equivalent of ἀπὸ ἐφηβείας (*BGU*, 1903, 2)—although Jouguet (p. 83) does not omit the possibility of a difference in meaning (but who would go to the gymnasium, if not the ephebes?)—and also that it is synonymous with the expression οἱ ἐκ τοῦ γυμνασίου (cf. ROSTOVTSEFF, *Hellenistic World*, p. 1059): BRADY (*Mélanges Miller*, p. 11) was in doubt as to whether to equate them, but the recent publication of *POxy.*, 2186, gets over the difficulty, for the expression ἐκ τοῦ γ seemed to be limited to the time of the Lagids (*APF*, II, 548, 26; V, 415–416, 13, 17; *SEG*, VIII, 504, 531, 641, 694); but here is *POxy.*, 2196, in A.D. 260, giving a list of nine generations of ἐκ τοῦ γυμνασίου.

18

Ephebes who had their names put down well in advance. We must not jump to the conclusion that parents behaved just like English parents who get their sons' names put down in advance for the famous public schools; it may have been, as P. JOUGUET suggests, nothing more than a generous gesture performed voluntarily or on the school's suggestion; the parents sharing the ephebia's expenses in their boy's name so that he became a kind of honorary ephebe (*Vie municipale*, p. 152).

19

The Hellenistic magistrates who controlled education: see the material assembled in the articles in DAREMBERG-SAGLIO and PAULY-WISSOWA on the words: *gymnasiarchia* (G. GLOTZ, *D. S.*, II, 2, pp. 1675*a*–1684*b*), γυμνασίαρχος (J. OEHLER, *P. W.*, VII, c. 1969–2004), *kosmetes* (P. GIRARD, *D. S.*, III, 2, p. 865ab), κοσμητής (PREISIGKE, *P. W.*, XI, c. 1490–1495), *sophronistes* (P. GIRARD, *D. S.*, IV, 2, pp. 1399*b*–1400*b*), σωφρονισταί (J. OEHLER, *P. W.*, II R., III, c. 1104–1106), ἐφήβαρχος (*Ibid.*, *P. W.*, V., 2, c. 2735–2736), *paidonomos* (P. GIRARD, *D.S.*, IV, I, pp. 276*b*–277a), παιδονόμοι (O. SCHULTHESS, *P. W.*, XVIII, 2, c. 2387–2389), γυναικονόμοι (BOERNER, *P. W.*, VII, 2, c. 2089–2090).

20

The gymnasiarchy as the supreme magistracy in Egypt: cf. P. JOUGUET, *La Vie municipale*, pp. 68, 83, 167. Nothing of the same kind in Greece: it is true that inscriptions have been found in twenty-nine cities dated with the gymnasiarch's name (J. OEHLER, in PAULY-WISSOWA, VII, 2, c. 1981), but all that this means is a kind of eponymy relating to the magistrate's sphere of action; whatever G. GLOTZ (in DAREMBERG-SAGLIO, II, 2, 1676*b*) may think, there is no definite example of any "absolute" eponymy making the gymnasiarch the eponym of the official acts of the city as a whole: thus in Larissa (*IG*, IX, 2, 517) and in Krannon (*ibid.*, 460–461) the gymnasiarch took second place after the *tagoi*, the real eponyms.

21

Gymnasiums and gymnasiarchs in the villages of Egypt: F. ZUCKER, Γυμνασίαρχος κώμης, *Aegyptus*, XI (1930–1931), pp. 485–496.

22

The gymnasiarch-general: he had various titles—"gymnasiarch of the four gymnasiums", which meant, no doubt, the children's, the ephebes', the νέοι's and the adults' (in Iasos: *Revue des Etudes grecques*, VI (1893), p. 175, No. 9), "gymnasiarch of all the gymnasiums" or "of all" (in Miletus, *CIG*, 2885; DITTENBERG., *Or.*, 472, 6; in Pergamus: *Athenische Mitteilungen*, XXXII, p. 330, No. 61). It should be noted that the title "city gymnasiarch"—τῆς πόλεως (in Cos, for example: PATON-HICKS, *Inscriptions of Cos*, No. 108, 9) seems to mean "gymnasiarch τῶν πολιτῶν"— "of the adults"—as distinguished from "gymnasiarch of the ephebes" or "of the νέοι" —and not "gymnasiarch-general".

23

The *gyneconome* seems to have been obliged mainly to apply the sumptuary laws and to keep an eye on the "behaviour", and no doubt, as a result of this, the morals of the grown women (cf. BOERNER, PAULY-WISSOWA, s.v.). But the edict promulgated in

Magnesia in 196 B.C. with regard to the festivals in honour of Zeus Sosipolis gives the gyneconomes exactly the same rôle as the pedonomes, from which it can be concluded that their job included looking after girls as well (they were each to choose nine girls and nine boys "with both parents living" to take part in the ceremony): DITTENBERG., *SIG*, 589, 15–20.

24

Charondas' school law: DIODORUS SICULUS (XII, 12 to the end) claims that the founders of Thourioi chose Charondas of Locres (*sic*) as the legislator for their colony, and seems to think that he was present at the foundation (445), whereas Charondas and Zaleucus lived in the seventh century: "He enacted that all citizens' children should learn their letters, the city bearing the cost of the teachers' salaries." The aim of the law was to establish the equality of all citizens, no matter how much money they had, in the matter of access to literary culture, which Diodorus (c. 13) eulogised above. Modern historians seem to agree that this is an anachronism: if such a law had come into existence, it would have been so extraordinary at the time that it would have been bound to attract Aristotle's attention; the silence of the *Politics* is disturbing (G. BUSOLT, *Griechische Staatskunde*, I³, pp. 378–379; E. ZIEBARTH, *Aus dem griechischen Schulwesen²*, p. 33).

25

Gymnasiums were also founded by patrons, either private individuals or sovereigns: this at least is what is suggested by names like "Philip's Gymnasium" in Halicarnassus (E. ZIEBARTH, *ibid.*, pp. 49–50).

26

Foundations in Graeco-Roman cities: cf. the study and record—which is far from complete, however—by B. LAUM, *Stiftungen in der griechischen und römischen Antike, ein Beitrag zur antiken Kulturgeschichte*, 2 vols., Leipzig-Berlin, 1914; cf. on this subject F. POLAND, *Berliner Philologische Wochenschrift*, 1915, c. 427–435.

27

The date of Eumenes' donation has been settled by G. DAUX, "Craton, Eumène II et Attale II" (*Bulletin de Correspondance hellénique*, LIX (1935), pp. 222–224).

28

For the Athenian Diogeneion cf. DITTENBERG., *SIG*, 497, n. 5; WACHSMUTH, PAULY-WISSOWA, V, c. 734–735, and, especially, P. GRAINDOR, "Etudes sur l'Ephébie attique sous l'Empire", II, in *Musée belge*, XXVI (1922), pp. 220–228. The name "Diogeneion" seems to have been chosen in honour of a man called Diogenes, probably in charge of the Macedonian garrison, to whom Aratus had given 500 talents so that he would get out of Attica without causing any trouble in 229 B.C., on the death of Demetrius II.

29

The gymnasiarchy as a "liturgy": G. GLOTZ tried (DAREMBERG-SAGLIO, II, 2, p. 1678d) to distinguish between two kinds of gymnasiarchies, the magistrate's (equivalent to the Athenian cosmete's office) and the liturgy's. But this is one of those legal constructions that sociologists looking for hard and fast "laws" have been far too fond of: there is no such difference for the historian. J. OEHLER (PAULY-WISSOWA, VII, c. 1976) has shown quite clearly that these two aspects were in fact inseparable. For the gymnasiarchy as filled by women or children who inherited the charge of it cf. GLOTZ, *D.S.*, 1681b; OEHLER, *P. W.*, c. 1983.

30

Foundations devoted to financing the gymnasiarchy: B. Laum, *Stiftungen*, vol. I, p. 97; vol. II, i, No. 49, 102, 114, 127, 162; and for distributions of oil for athletics: *ibid.*, I, pp. 88–90; II, i, No. 9, 16, 23, 25, 61, 68, 71–73a, 121–125, 136, 177; II, 11, No. 87, 94, 109; L. Robert, *Etudes Anatoliennes*, pp. 317, 381; *Bull. Epigr.*, *REG*, 61 (1948), p. 169, no. 112.

31

The young people's share in religious festivals: see the material collected by E. Ziebarth, *Aus dem griechischen Schulwesen*[2], pp. 42 *et seq.*, 147 *et seq.*; A. J. Festugiere, *Le Monde gréco-romain*, I, pp. 87–92; L. Robert, *Etudes anatoliennes*, pp. 9–20; A. H. M. Jones, *The Greek City*, p. 354, n. 35; M. Nilsson, *Die hellen. Schule*, pp. 61 *seq.*

CHAPTER III

1

Did physical education begin as early as seven or eight? I have hesitated about adopting this view, which is not generally accepted: P. Girard, for example (*L'Education athénienne*, pp. 127–128, 194), puts it at from twelve to fourteen years and there are a lot of passages to support him (e.g. Gal., *San. tu.*, II, i, p. 81; II, 12, p. 162). The truth is that the custom must have varied according to the time and the place, especially the time. If, as I endeavour to prove at the end of this chapter, the importance of gymnastics in education slowly declined during the Graeco-Roman period and finally disappeared in about the fourth century A.D., there must have come a time when the age for beginning began to retreat as a result of the growing indifference to this kind of instruction.

2

The games played by the Spartan *mikkikhizomenes*: A. M. Woodward in R. M. Dawkins, "The Sanctuary of Artemis Orthia", p. 288; cf. p. 318, No. 41.

3

We possess a series of magnificent children's sarcophagi of the Roman period which show the child who had died—who could not have been more than seven, judging by his size—as a victorious athlete: F. Cumont, *Recherches sur le Symbolisme funéraire des Romains*, Paris, 1942, pp. 469–473; Pl. XVLI, 2–3. It is not an easy matter to interpret reliefs like these because of the amount of symbolism that may be involved: cf. similar receptacles showing young children apotheosized as quadriga-drivers; during their lives they could never have driven more than a goat-cart! (F. Cumont, *ibid.*, pp. 461–465).

4

For doctors' and hygienists' writings about gymnastics see the account by J. Jüthner in the introduction to his edition of Philostratus, *Über Gymnastik*, Leipzig-Berlin, 1909, pp. 3–60.

5

For the importance of riding in the education of the young: G. Lafaye, s. v. "Equitatio", in Daremberg-Saglio, II, 1, pp. 750b–751a.

6

Greek nautical sports: in Hermione, cf. K. SCHUTZE, "Warum kannten die Griechen keine Schwimmwettkämpfe?" in *Hermes*, 73 (1938), pp. 355–357, which rectifies the dubious hypotheses in M. AURIGA, "Gedanken über das Fehlen des Schwimmwett-kampfes bei den Griechen", in *Leibesübungen und körperliche Erziehung*, 1938, 8, pp. 206–211; but I in my turn have a couple of objections to make against Schutze—first, that the connection he establishes between these games and fishing for purple does not seem to me to be proved, and secondly that in the passage from Pausanias, κόλυμβος seems to mean "diving", not "swimming".

7

In Corcyra and elsewhere: P. GARDNER, "Boat Races among the Greeks", in the *Journal of Hellenic Studies*, 2 (1881), pp. 90–97; cf. in general MEHL, s. v. "Schwim-men", in PAULY-WISSOWA, *Suppl.*, V, c. 847–864; M. A. SANDERS "Swimming Among the Greeks and the Romans", in the *Classical Journal*, 20 (1924–1925), pp. 566–568.

In Athens: P. GARDNER, "Boat Races at Athens", in the *Journal of Hellenic Studies*, 2 (1881), pp. 315–317, and especially P. GRAINDOR, in *Musée belge*, XXVI (1922), pp. 217–219. Inscriptions of the Roman period use the term ναυμαχία to signify these games, but I am not sure that this must be understood to mean "water-tourna-ments", a mock battle, in the Roman sense of the word *naumachia*. The bas-reliefs (unfortunately damaged) that appear as decorations to many of these inscriptions do not make it absolutely certain that they are about regattas as in Hellenistic times: cf. E. NORMAN GARDINER, *Athletics of the Ancient World*, figs. 66–69.

8

"Hockey": cf. one of the reliefs discovered in Athens in 1922; see, for example, L. GRUNDEL, "Griechische Ballspiele", in *Archäologischer Anzeiger*, 1925, c. 80–95; finally, C. PICARD, *Manuel d'Archéologie grecque*, I, pp. 628–632. Galen's tract "On the Little Ball" has been translated with a critical analysis by F. A. WRIGHT, *Greek Athletics*, London, 1925, pp. 108–122.

9

Greek athletics: I apologise to the reader for giving so few references in support of the rapid sketch I have attempted to make of the various branches of Greek athletics. There are a certain number of references scattered throughout the whole of the literature of antiquity, often obscure and comparatively insignificant in themselves, but they begin to take on their true value when they are studied in connection with various kinds of picture—most of which (sixth- and fifth-century vase-paintings) date back long before the Hellenistic period, but sporting technique evidently changed very little. It is only modern scholarship that has thought of collecting and comparing these two different kinds of evidence; the work which began quite a long time ago (cf. J. H. KRAUSE, *Die Gymnastik und die Agonistik der Hellenen*, Leipzig, 1841) has been completed in our own day by J. JÜTHNER and E. NORMAN GARDINER.

I have already mentioned the latter's two great works, *Greek Athletic Sports and Festivals*, London, 1910; *Athletics of the Ancient World*, Oxford, 1930 (for further works of the same order see: B. SCHRÖDER, *Der Sport im Altertum*, Berlin, 1927, and C. A. FORBES, *Greek Physical Education*, New York-London, 1929); but for erudition the best things to look up are the excellent series of articles he did for the *Journal of Hellenic Studies*: 23 (1903), pp. 54–70, "The Method of Deciding the Pentathlon";

ibid., pp. 261–291, "Notes on the Greek Foot Race"; 24 (1904), pp. 70–80, "Phayllus and his Record Jump"; *ibid.*, pp. 179–194, "Further Notes on the Greek Jump"; 25 (1905), pp. 14–31; 263–293, "Wrestling"; 26 (1906), pp. 4–22, "The Pancration" (cf. *ibid.*, K. T. FROST, "Greek Boxing"); 27 (1907), pp. 1–36, "Throwing the Diskos"; *ibid.*, pp. 249–273, "Throwing the Javelin"; 45 (1925), pp. 132–134 (with L. PIHKALA), "The System of the Pentathlon".

Of the writings of J. JÜTHNER the following should be consulted: *Ueber antike Turngeräte*, Vienna, 1896, and his excellent edition, including both a translation and a critical comment, of PHILOSTRATOS, *Ueber Gymnastik*, Leipzig-Berlin, 1909, and the many articles he has contributed to PAULY-WISSOWA, particularly: "Diskobolia", V, 1, 1187–1189; "Dolichos" (4), V, 1, 1282–1283; "Dromos" (2), V, 2, 1717–1720; "Gymnastik", VII, 2, 2030–2085; "Gymnastes", VII, 2, 2026–2030; "Halma", VII, 2, 2273–2276; "Halter", VII, 2, 2284–2285; "Hippios" (5), VIII, 2, 1719–1720; "Hoplites" (3), VIII, 2, 2297–2298; "Skamma", II R., III, 1, 435–437; "Stadion" (3) II R., III, 2, 1963–1966; and, in vol. III, "Pale" and "Pankration". Cf. also, still in PAULY-WISSOWA, the articles in the first few volumes by REISCH: "Akontion" (2), I, 1183–1185; "Balbis", II, 2819, and of course the corresponding articles in DAREMBERG-SAGLIO, for example A. DE RIDDER, III, 2, pp. 1340a–1347b, s. v. "Lucta".

10

The interpretation of *POxy.* (III), 466, second century A.D. Certain words are used (for example, verbs made up from βάλλω and τίθημι) which, though they were ambiguous or imprecise in everyday speech, had undoubtedly acquired a technical meaning as sporting terms. I have made use of the paraphrase and analysis by J. JÜTHNER in PHILOSTRATOS, *Ueber Gymnastik*, pp. 26–30; most of the technical terms in question had already been dealt with in great detail by E. NORMAN GARDINER in the *Journal of Hellenic Studies*, 25 (1905), pp. 262 *et seq.*, esp. pp. 244–246, 280, 287; cf. also the *Classical Review*, 1929, pp. 210–212. Whenever the two interpretations have differed, I have almost always, for good reasons, adopted Norman Gardiner's against Jüthner's. Thus as regards the first command; παράθες τὸ μέσον, Jüthner translates, *Stemme die Mitte an*—"Straighten the trunk"—but it is difficult to see how this can be a preparation for the next movement, whereas Norman Gardiner's translation, "Turn your body sideways", leads quite naturally to the next movement, a head grip with the right arm; moreover it is supported by a passage in PLUTARCH, *Quaest. Conv.*, 638 F, in which παραθέσεις seems to be the opposite of συστάσεις.

11

The part played by the aulos-player in gymnastics: cf. the quotations and decorated sculpture collected by J. JÜTHNER in PHILOSTRATUS, *Ueber Gymnastik*, p. 301, n. ad p. 180, 18. It will be remembered that he played a similar part in the army and the navy: *supra*, Part I.

12

The athlete's complete nudity: the Greeks did not go in for any belts. The practice known as κυνοδέσμη, which meant fastening the end of the prepuce with a string attached to a belt, was introduced for other reasons, both hygienic and moral, and was not suitable for violent physical effort: cf. for this practice, JÜTHNER in PAULY-WISSOWA, IX, 2, c. 2545, s. v. "Infibulatio" (but the κυνοδέσμη is not the *infibulatio*—in Greek, κρίκωσις—which was a much more brutal method that involved fastening the prepuce with a metal brooch).

13

For the athletes' stringed cap, cf. P. GIRARD, *L'Education Athénienne*, pp. 210–211; but this must not be confused, as Girard seems to confuse it (p. 211, n. 2) with the ear-protector—ἀμφωτίδες or ἐπωτίδες—which was worn for boxing (cf. E. SAGLIO in DAREMBERG-SAGLIO, I, 1, p. 521a).

14

The pedotribe's chastisement of the athlete: cf. e.g. HDT., VIII, 59 (the runner who sets off before the starting signal has gone); LUCIAN, *Asin.*, 10 ("Watch out—you'll get a lot more punishment if you don't do what you're told!"); and especially pieces of decorated ceramics like the beautiful fragment with red figures in the British Museum (E. 78), in which the master is using his birch to give a hefty clout to a pancratist who is trying to gouge his opponent's eye out with his finger and thumb. This was against the rules!

15

For the argument about γυμνάσιον and παλαίστρα, cf. G. FOUGÈRES, in DAREMBERG-SAGLIO, s. v. "Gymnasium", II, 2, pp. 1685b–1686a; J. OEHLER in PAULY-WISSOWA, s.v., VII, 2, c. 2009–2011; K. SCHNEIDER, *ibid.*, s. v. "Palaistra", XVIII, 2, c. 2473, 2490–2492; J. JANNORAY, in *Bulletin de Correspondance hellénique*, 61 (1937), pp. 55–56. Other words that originally referred to a particular part of the gymnasium also sometimes came to mean the sporting facilities as a whole—like ξυστός in Elis (PAUS., VI, 23, 1), δρόμος in Crete (SUID., s. v.).

16

The lower gymnasium in Priene (the "higher gymnasium" is Roman): cf. T. WIEGAND-H. SCHRADER, *Priene, Ergebnisse der Ausgrabungen und Untersuchungen in den Jahren 1895–1898*, Berlin, 1904, pp. 259–275; plates XIX–XX; M. SCHEDE, *Die Ruinen von Priene, kurze Beschreibung*, Berlin-Leipzig, 1934, pp. 80–90 (excellent restorations: figs. 96–100).

On the various gymnasiums and palestras dating from Hellenic times that have been found in the Greek world, cf. the three articles by FOUGÈRES, OEHLER and SCHNEIDER, mentioned in the previous note. For the palestras in Delos see (while awaiting the promised works by J. DELORME) R. VALLOIS, "L'Architecture hellénique et hellénistique à Délos jusqu'à l'éviction des Déliens" (166 B.C.), Part I, *Les Monuments*, Paris, 1944, pp. 176 *et seq.* For the latest excavations of the gymnasium in Delphos, which were carried out by J. JANNORAY, cf. *Bulletin de Correspondance hellénique*, 60 (1936), pp. 463–465, 64–65 (1940–1941), p. 288.

As typical of the gymnasiums of Roman times, with the hypertrophy induced by the hot baths, and the general impression of luxury, the sumptuous gymnasiums in Ephesus will be remembered particularly: see the accounts by S. KEIL in the *Jahreshefte* of the Austrian Archaeological Institute, *Beiblatt*, vol. 24 (1929), c. 25 *et seq.*; 25 (1929), c. 21 *et seq.*; 26 (1930), c. 17 *et seq.*; 27 (1932), c. 16 *et seq.*; 28 (1933), c. 6 *et seq.*; 29 (1934), c. 148; cf. also, though in essentials it takes us back to the Hellenistic age, the big gymnasium in Pergamus: P. SCHAZMANN, "Das Gymnasion" (*Altertümer von Pergamon*, VI, Berlin-Leipzig, 1923).

17

Hermes in gymnasiums and palestras—mainly busts of Hermes and Heracles, who were the guardians of sport—cf. C. MICHALOWSKI, "Les Hermès du gymnase de Délos", *Bulletin de Correspondance hellénique*, 54 (1930), pp. 131–146. The inventory which is mentioned (*ibid.*, p. 98, l. 146–147) refers to forty-one marble Hermes in the same gymnasium.

18

School sports in Termessus under the Empire: it will suffice to mention R. HEBERDEY, in PAULY-WISSOWA, II R., V, 1, c. 767–768, s. v. "Termessos, Schulagone".

19

Athletes who came from the aristocracy and were honoured under the Empire: cf. L. ROBERT, "Notes de Numismatique et d'Epigraphie grecques", in *Revue archéologique*, 1934, I, pp. 55–56 (cf. 52–54), 56–58.

20

O. A. SAWHILL, *The Use of Athletic Metaphors in the Biblical Homilies of St. John Chrysostom*, Princeton Dissertation, 1928; C. SPICQ, "L'Image sportive de II Cor. iv, 7–9", in *Ephemerides Theologicae Lovanienses*, 1937, pp. 209–229; "Gymnastique et Morale, d'après I Tim. iv, 7–8", in *Revue biblique*, 1947, 229–242 (reprinted in *Les Epîtres pastorales*, Paris, 1947, pp. 151–162).

CHAPTER IV

1

For the teaching of drawing, cf. the few facts collected by L. GRASBERGER, *Erziehung und Unterricht im klassichen Altertum*, vol. II, pp. 343–350. W. JÄGER, *Paideia*, vol. II, p. 228, seems to me to be wrong in excluding the plastic arts from the Greek paideia: the generally recognised interpretation of the passage from ARISTOTLE, *Pol.*, H, 1337b 25, which he rejects, seems to be illustrated in the epigraphical winners' lists in Teos and Magnesium, not to speak of the evidence in TEL., in STOB., 98, 72.

2

The joint teaching of aulos and lyre as illustrated by painted vases: cf. e.g. P. GIRARD, *L'Education athénienne*, figs. 6, 8, 13, 14, 15, pp. 105, 111, 165, 169, 171.

3

For the aulos and the part it played in Greek music—which has not been sufficiently recognised—cf. the wordy and often debatable book by K. SCHLESINGER, *The Greek Aulos, a Study of its Mechanism and of its Relation to the Modal System of Ancient Greek Music*, London, 1939 (and my account of this in *Revue des Etudes grecques*, LIII (1940), pp. 87–92); N. B. BODLEY, "The Auloï of Meroë", in the *American Journal of Archaeology*, L (1946), pp. 217–240, follows Schlesinger rather uncritically.

4

On the disputed harmony of the seven-stringed lyre, cf. finally I. DÜRING, "Studies in Musical Terminology in Fifth-Century Literature", in *Eranos*, XLIII (1945), pp. 190–193. Passages relating to the history of the gradual addition of more strings to the lyre are arranged by (H. WEIL)-T. REINACH, in their edition of PLUTARCH, *De la Musique*, Paris, 1900, pp. 119–129, ad §303.

5

Greek theory of music: the best treatment is still the excellent essay by L. LALOY, *Aristoxène de Tarente et la Musique de l'Antiquité*, Paris, 1904; for a brief sketch cf. the *Introduction* by J. F. MOUNTFORD to the book mentioned in n. 3 by K. SCHLESINGER, pp. xv–xxxvii.

6

On the double meaning of the word *music*, which in antiquity sometimes meant the art of music and sometimes the mathematical science of intervals and rhythm, cf. my *Saint Augustin et la Fin du Monde antique*, Paris, 1937, pp. 197–210; usually, this science—harmonics—was the province of mathematicians and, if any specialising went on, of a ἁρμονικός (cf. TEL., in STOB., 98, 72), not of a cithern player. There is a doubt, however, about the schools in Teos: their charter, DITTENBERGER, *SIG.*, 578, l. 18–19, prescribes that the cithern player shall teach the children not only how to play the lyre but "music" too—τὰ μουσικά: as it was children of secondary-school age or higher that were involved this may very well have meant the science, but if so, why did they not simply say τὴν μουσικήν? Occasionally τὰ μουσικά is translated as "sol-fa" (thus T. Reinach in *La Musique grecque*, Paris, 1926, p. 135), but (cf. the following note) is it quite certain that Hellenistic teaching included anything like our solfeggio system? Τὰ μουσικά may have meant practising the various songs that the older pupils in Teos had to perform at festivals and civic ceremonies.

7

It is generally considered that the teaching of music in Hellenistic times included musical dictation, hence musical notation too, but this view depends on what I consider to be a faulty interpretation of the words μελογραφία and ῥυθμογραφία, which appear in the winners' list of the school competitions held in Teos and Magnesia (MICHEL, 913, 12, 9; DITTENBERGER, *SIG.*, 960, 4): cf. my note entitled "*ΜΕΛΟΓΡΑΦΙΑ*" in *L'Antiquité classique*, XV, 1946, pp. 289–296.

8

The teaching of the lyre *ad orecchio* according to the vase-paintings: P. GIRARD, *L'Education athénienne*, figs. 5, 7, 9, 16, pp. 103, 119, 120, 173.

9

For the choir cf. e.g. G. BUSOLT-H. SWOBODA, *Griechische Staatskunde*³, pp. 975 *et seq.*; 1086 *et seq.*, or the articles *ad hoc* in PAULY-WISSOWA and DAREMBERG-SAGLIO (in the latter, e.g. s. v. "Cyclicus chorus", vol. II, 1, pp. 1691a–1693b, etc.); A. BRINCK, "Inscriptiones Graecae ad choregiam pertinentes", in *Dissertationes philologicae Halenses*, VII (1886), pp. 71–274.

10

For the Pythaïdes, A. BOËTHIUS, *Die Pythaïs, Studien zur Geschichte der Verbindungen zwischen Athen und Delphi*, Upsala Dissertation, 1918; C. DAUX, *Delphes aux II*ᵉ *et I*ᵉʳ *siècles*, Paris, 1936, pp. 521–583, 708–729.

11

The inscription *F. Eph.*, II, No. 21, l. 53 *et seq.* informs us how, in the year A.D. 44, as a result of the intervention of the pro-consul Paulus Fabius Persicus, the professional hymn-singers who had been in service until then were to be replaced by a choir of ephebes. The motive was supposed to be economy—it would have taken most of the city revenues to support a choir—but it is not beyond the bounds of possibility that there was some sort of political motive behind it too: cf. C. PICARD, *Ephèse et Claros, Recherches sur les Sanctuaires et les Cultes de l'Ionie du Nord*, Paris, 1922, pp. 252–254; or F. K. DÖRNER, *Der Erlass des Staathalters von Asien Paullus Fabius Persicus*, Greifswald Dissertation, 1935, pp. 38–39.

12

On dancing in Greek education, cf. the Latin essay by M. EMMANUEL, *De Saltationis disciplina apud Graecos*, Paris, 1896, pp. 15, 73, n. 9, 74. . . .

13

The real musician's education included actual playing: I have adopted for my own purposes and for our own times this Aristotelian doctrine, from [H. DAVENSON], *Traité de la Musique selon l'esprit de saint Augustin*, Baudry, 1942, pp. 59–63.

14

On the ethos of the Greek modes, cf. the classic work by H. ABERT, *Die Lehre vom Ethos in der griechischen Musik*, Leipzig, 1899. A corresponding doctrine had also been developed about the ethos of rhythm; cf. G. AMSEL, "De Vi atque indole rhythmorum quid veteres judicaverint" (*Breslauer philologische Abhandlungen*, I, 3, Breslau, 1887). For a few brief remarks on each, cf. T. REINACH, *La Musique grecque*, pp. 44–46, 113–114.

15

On the profound significance of the "nomos" in archaic times, cf. L. LALOY, *Aristoxène de Tarente*, pp. 104–105; the thing would be more understandable still if, as K. SCHLESINGER maintains (*op. cit. supra*, n. 3), the Greek modes were originally a succession of entirely different intervals which could easily be played on *auloi* that had equidistant holes: their originality would then have been striking. This disappears entirely however if the various modes were simply taken from a standard scale, "the one perfect system".

CHAPTER V

1

Nurses and nurse-maids: G. HERZOG-HAUSER, in PAULY-WISSOWA, XVII, c. 1491–1500, s. v. "Nutrix"; A. WILHELM, in *Glotta*, XVI (1928), pp. 274–279; L. ROBERT, "Etudes épigraphiques" (*BEHE*, 272), p. 187.

2

On primary education up to the age of seven, there is a good chapter by P. GIRARD, "L'Education athénienne aux Vᵉ et IVᵉ siècles avant Jésus-Christ", pp. 65–99, which is also useful for the Hellenistic period; cf. also L. GRASBERGER, *Erziehung und Unterricht*, I, pp. 221–235, and especially, for the children's games, the whole of the first part, I, pp. 1–163.

3

The term "école maternelle" was only adopted in France in 1881 to describe what until then had been known as "salles d'asile", which had appeared in Paris in 1828 (cf. from 1801 onwards, Mme. de Pastoret's "salles d'hospitalité"), modelled on the "infants' schools" which had existed since 1819, if not earlier, in industrialised England.

4

Paidagogos: cf. E. Schuppe, s. v. in Pauly-Wissowa, XVIII, 2, c. 2375–2385. The pedagogue carrying his young master on his shoulder with a lantern in his hand: cf. e.g. the terra-cotta reproduced by M. Rostovtseff, . . . *Hellenistic World* (I), pl. XXX, 2.

5

On the military colonisation of the Fayum, cf. M. Rostovtseff, *The Social and Economic History of the Hellenistic World, passim*, (cf. *Index*, I, s. v. p. 1691a). In the villages of this Nome of Arsinoë we find a pedotribe (*PCair.Zen.*, III, 59326, 28), a gymnasiarch (*BGU*, VI, 1256), a gymnasium (*PSI*, IV, 391a), a small palestra (*PSI*, IV, 418, 7) and school papyri (*PGuer.Joug.*, *O. Michigan*, 656, 657, 658, 661, 662, 693; *PVarsovie*, 7; *PGrenf.*, II, 84; *PFayûm*, 19; Wessely, *Stud.*, II, lviii; *PIand.*, 83; Ziebarth, *Ant. Sch.*, 29).

6

The knowledge of writing in the papyri: E. Majer-Leonhard, *Appammatoi, In Ægypto qui litteras sciverint, qui nesciverint, ex papyris Graecis quantum potest exploratur*, Frankfurt, 1913, esp. pp. 35 *et seq.*, the *Index* II (*qui homines in Aegypto litteras sciverint*) and the classification by period and social rank, p. 74. Also R. Calderini, "Ἀγράμματοι nell' Egitto greco-romano", in *Ægyptus*, vol. 30, 1950, pp. 14–41.

7

Terra-cottas showing schoolgirls: E. Pottier-S. Reinach, *Myrina*, pl. XXXIII, 4; P. Graindor, "Terres cuites de l'Egypte gréco-romaine" (*Werken* of the Faculty of Letters of the University of Ghent, 86), No. 54, pp. 135–136, pl. XX; C. Lécuyer, *Terres cuites antiques*, I, pl. II, 4, No. 5; A. Cartault, *Deuxième collection Lécuyer*, pl. LIX, ii; F. Winter, *Die antiken Terrakoten*, I, ii, p. 123, Nos. 6–7; 124, No. 1, etc.

8

Παιδαγωγεῖον (Dem., *De Cor.*, 258): a pedagogues' waiting-room (K. F. Hermann, Cramer)? No, merely a synonym for διδασκαλεῖον—a classroom (cf. Poll., IX, 41): P. Girard, *L'Education athénienne*, p. 102.

9

For the assistant—ὑποδιδάσκαλος—cf. L. Grasberger, *Erziehung und Unterricht*, II, pp. 144–145.

10

For teachers' salaries, cf. C. A. Forbes, *Teachers' Pay in Ancient Greece*, Lincoln (Nebraska), 1942.

11

The foundation by Polythrous (Dittenberg., *SIG.*, 578) allowed for three classes, whose masters were to receive 600, 550 and 500 drachmas respectively a year. I have assumed the last figure to represent the primary school teacher's salary, the other two classes belonging, as we shall see, to the secondary school.

12

The primary school teacher only needed a character reference; nobody bothered about his teaching ability: for the same point of view, L. Grasberger, *Erziehung und*

Unterricht, II, pp. 162, 85; M. ROSTOVTSEFF, *The Social and Economic History of the Hellenistic World*, pp. 1087–1088.

13

IG, XII, 1, 141: there is no proof that the school-teacher in question was the Hieronymus son of Simylinus to whom the lovely funeral bas-relief was dedicated that has been published by F. HILLER VON GAERTRINGEN in *Bulletin de Correspondance hellénique*, 36 (1912), pp. 236–239—though he tries to make this out.

14

On PLUTARCH'S *De liberis educandis*, cf. F. GLAESER, *De Pseudo-Plutarchi libro περὶ παίδων ἀγωγῆς*, *Dissertationes philologicae Vindobonenses*, XII (Vienna, Leipzig, 1918), 1. It does not seem to me to be quite certain that this tract is apocryphal, though no one has questioned this opinion since WYTTENBACH (1820).

15

The school calendar and time-table: L. GRASBERGER, *Erziehung und Unterricht*, I, pp. 239–240, 242, 291–295; II, pp. 244–252; P. GIRARD, *L'Education athénienne*, pp. 249–250; E. ZIEBARTH, *Schulwesen*, pp. 153–155; K. FREEMAN, *Schools of Hellas*, pp. 80–81.

The knotty point is, how exactly was the day divided up between the school and the gymnasium? Such was Grasberger's authority that his final conclusion has usually been accepted by his successors, but they do not seem to have noticed that Grasberger himself only came to his conclusion after a good deal of doubt and hesitancy, and that it is based on evidence that is neither explicit nor homogeneous enough.

What exactly is the problem? (1) It is quite clear that under the Roman Empire in both the Greek East and the Latin West the school day was organised as follows: in the morning, as soon as it was light, the child would set off to school—the school of letters: cf. the terra-cotta showing a child being carried on the shoulders of a pedagogue with a lantern in his hand: M. ROSTOVTSEFF, . . . *Hellenistic World* (I), pl. XXX, 2. When gymnastics was included in his syllabus the child would then go on to the palestra for his lesson in physical training. Then he would have a bath, go back home and have his lunch. In the afternoon he would go back to school for a second reading and writing lesson: see e.g. the perfectly clear passages in LUCIAN, *Am.*, 44–45; *Paras.*, 61.

(2) But was this the usual time-table in actual Hellenistic times, i.e. third to first centuries B.C.? Apparently not, judging by some lines in the *Bacchides* which bring in the evidence in PLAUTUS or rather MENANDER (who died in 292 B.C.). The *Bacchides* seems to have been merely a transposition of the latter's *Double Deceiver*, if not a translation—in so far as can be conjectured from the line quoted by STOBAEUS, 120, 8, which is exactly rendered in *Bacch.*, 816–817. The critics (cf. E. ERNOUT, *Notice* to his edition, p. 11) have not been able to find any trace of re-writing or "contamination".

Picturing his studious and virtuous youth, one of the characters says, "If you had not arrived at the palestra before the sun had risen the gymnasium master gave you a severe punishment":

> *Ante solem exorientem nisi in palaestram veneras,*
> *Gymnasi praefecto haud mediocris poenae penderes*
>
> (v. 424–425)

After a description of the exercises in the gymnasium comes:

> *Inde de hippodromo et palaestra ubi revenisses domum,*
> *Cincticulo praecinctus in sella apud magistrum adsideres:*
> *Cum librum legeres, si unam peccavisses syllabam*
> *Fieret corium tam maculosum quam est nutricis pallium*
>
> (431–434)

Thus the day *began* with the palestra and the reading lesson *came later*.

How are these two different pieces of evidence to be reconciled? It must not be assumed that Plautus (Menander) is here describing the life of the fully grown youths at the ephebia, who were anything from eighteen to twenty and who, having become sports- rather than intellectually-minded, spent the whole morning in the gymnasium and only went to one language lesson in the evening: lines 431–434 are not only highly descriptive, they are quite precise as well, and they can only be taken to refer to the primary school, where the little boy, dressed in his short tunic, would sit at his master's feet on a stool and stumble through his syllables under the threat of the rod.

It seems difficult to dismiss this evidence from the *Bacchides*. The passage in PLATO, *Prot.*, 326d, does not contradict it: here it is said that the child was sent to the pedotribe after having been to the language and music teachers, but this refers to the date (which may indeed have been later) at which physical education began, not the time of day that the boy went to the various teachers. This leads to the solution that I suggest in the text: in the third century B.C., Greek education, still faithful to its warlike origins, put gymnastics first, and the boy's day began with gymnastics, the whole morning being devoted to it. Language had to be satisfied with a single lesson in the afternoon.

Then, as a result of the growing importance of language and literature in teaching, an additional lesson was introduced first thing in the morning. This transition may have been effected by way of a lesson given at home by the pedagogue—as has been shrewdly conjectured by GRASBERGER (II, p. 248). Such a scene seems to be evoked by those delightful terra-cottas that show a bearded fellow giving a child a lesson in reading or writing (cf. e.g. E. POTTIER-S. REINACH, *La Nécropole de Myrina*, pl. XXIX, 3, No. 287; A. CARTAULT, "Terres cuites antiques . . .", 2ᵉ *Collection Lécuyer*, pl. XIX, No. 12). Then this very early additional morning lesson (cf. MART., XII, 57, 5; IX, 68; JUV., VII, 222–225) was transferred to the school itself and gradually became the most important lesson of all.

It would be useful if we could date this innovation, which gives a typical sidelight on the advance of language and literature at the expense of gymnastics. Gymnastics kept on getting less and less important as time went by. In the second century A.D., in Greek districts at least, it still took place in the second half of the morning: LUCIAN describes a child doing exercises under the hot sun in the middle of the day (*Am.*, 44–45); in the third century, in Latin districts, it has disappeared: the child is with the school-teacher until dinner time and comes back to him after dinner, his bath, in accordance with the Roman custom, being put back to the end of the day's work, before the *cena* (*Colloquia* of the *Hermeneumata Ps. Dositheana, C. Gloss. Lat.*, III, pp. 378, 22 et seq.).

16

The Cos school calendar: the column that was used for the month of Artemision ends with the following words (DITTENBERG., *SIG.*, 1028, 43–45):

π(ϱ)ο(τριακάδι) ἀπόδειξι[ς]/διδασκάλων/καὶ κεφαλ(α)ὶ γʹ.

The last mention remains baffling. I have boldly translated ἀπόδειξις διδασκάλων as "school examination": the meaning of ἀπόδειξις—an examination passed by the pupils—is well attested: PLUT., *Quaest. Conv.*, IX, 376; DITTENBERG., *SIG.*, 578, 32–34; 717, 41; cf. 1028, n. 16; *Ins. Priene*, 114, 20; 113, 30. The genitive διδασκάλων does not mean that this examination was taken by the teachers themselves: in Athens in imperial times these tests were taken by the pupils before the βουλή, and they were therefore like an inspection, a test of the school-teaching—hence the term used here. Assuming that διδάσκαλος has the specifically intellectual meaning that it took on in Hellenistic Greek, I reckon that these tests differ from the ἀγωνάρια mentioned as occurring on the 5th, 7th, 11th and 25th of the same month, which must have been sports tests.

17

No "blackboard" (as a matter of fact, if such a thing had been used it would have been a "whiteboard"—λεύκωμα—an "album"): see the small amount of data collected by GRASBERGER, *Erziehung und Unterricht*, II, pp. 223–224. There are some scholars, by the way, who refer to "boards with a hole in them so that they could be hung on the wall" (thus P. BEUDEL, *Qua ratione Graeci . . . p.* 40): it is worth noticing that these were little boards belonging to the pupils, and the hole was in such a position that when the board was hung up it would show the vertical lines of writing (e.g. *Journal of Hellenic Studies*, 29 [1909], pp. 39 *et seq*).

CHAPTER VI

1

Teaching methods in primary schools: the most detailed investigation will be found in P. BEUDEL, *Qua ratione Graeci liberos docuerint, papyris, ostracis, tabulis in Ægypto inventis, illustretur*, Munster Dissertation, 1911, pp. 6–29.

2

Astrological and magical beliefs about the alphabet: DIETERICH, "ABC Denkmäler", *Rheinisches Museum* LVI (1901), pp. 77 *et seq.*; F. DORNSEIFF, *Das Alphabet in Mystik und Magik²*, Leipzig, 1925. The alphabet in church dedication ceremonies: H. LECLERCQ, in *Dictionnaire d'Archéologie chrétienne et de Liturgie*, I, 1, c. 56–58; IV, 1, c. 389–290.

3

History of Hellenistic school anthologies: O. GUERAUD-P. JOUGUET, *Un Livre d'écolier . . .*, pp. xxiv–xxxi.

4

Reading aloud and silent reading: a bibliography will be found in H. I. MARROU, *Saint Augustin et la Fin de la Culture antique*, p. 89, n. 3; to which should be added: G. L. HENDRICKSON, in the *Classical Journal*, 23 (1929–1930), p. 182; W. J. CLARK, *ibid.*, 26 (1931), pp. 698–700.

5

"Codices et Volumina dans les bibliothèques juives et chrétiennes": see "Notes d'iconographie", by R. VIELLIARD, in *Rivista di Archeologia cristiana*, XVII (1940), pp. 143–148; and for a more general treatment: F. G. KENYON, *Books and Readers in Ancient Greece and Rome*, 2nd. ed., Oxford, 1951.

o

6

The length of the *Papyrus Guéraud-Jouguet*. It is damaged at the beginning and in the middle (between lines 57 and 58). By a great feat of ingenuity the editors have managed to calculate the extent of the second gap—$2\frac{1}{2}''$—which brings the length of the whole roll to 3 yds. $1\frac{4}{5}$ ins. plus the first gap. The length of this can also be worked out. There are either 14 or 15 columns missing on the left, to make up the list of syllables (according to whether or not this was preceded by a column of vowels)—i.e. $7\frac{4}{5}''$ or $8\frac{1}{2}''$—plus 3 or 4 columns for the alphabet which I reckon was there—i.e. $1\frac{3}{5}''$ to $2\frac{2}{5}''$—then a blank space where the roll could be attached to the roller at the end and so be rolled up, as at the end of the book, where it takes up $5\frac{1}{2}''$. What is missing therefore is a length which could be anything from a little more than $9''$ $(7\frac{4}{5}'' + 1\frac{3}{5}'' + x)$ to $16\frac{1}{2}''$ $(8\frac{1}{2}'' + 2\frac{2}{5}'' + 5\frac{1}{2}'')$. The average length of the sheets which are put together end to end ($\kappa o\lambda\lambda\eta\mu\alpha\tau\alpha$) is $6\frac{1}{10}''$ and the first one we have—it is in a mutilated condition —is only $3\frac{1}{8}''$. Therefore one or more probably two sheets are missing (more probably, because one sheet added to what is missing from the first gives rather too small a length: $6\frac{1}{10}'' + 2\frac{9}{10}'' = 9''$), i.e. a length of $2\frac{9}{10}'' + (6\frac{1}{10}'' \times 2) = 15\frac{1}{10}''$ for the first gap, and for the whole roll a total length of 3 yds. $1\frac{4}{5}$ ins.$+ 1$ in. $= 3$ yds. $2\frac{4}{5}$ ins.

7

The price of papyrus: see N. Lewis, *L'Industrie du Papyrus dans l'Egypte gréco-romaine*, Paris, 1934, pp. 152–157, who in my opinion has reacted too violently against the over-pessimistic opinion (the price was twenty times too high as the result of a confusion between a sheet and the usual roll, which was made up of twenty sheets) of G. Glotz, "Le Prix du Papyrus dans l'Antiquité grecque", *Bulletin de la Société Archéologique d'Alexandrie*, 25 (1930), pp. 83–96: the custom, which Oldfather has investigated so thoroughly, of using the backs of old documents from the archives for copying school exercises on, makes it quite clear that they used to look twice before they bought any new paper!

8

The use of "monostich" sayings in schools: selected sayings appear in papyri dating from the time of the Ptolemies: *PHibeh*, 17 (the sayings of Simonides, third century B.C.); Wessely in *Festschrift Gomperz*, pp. 67–74 (the "chries" of Diogenes, first century B.C.); but it is not absolutely certain that these early documents came from schools. Nevertheless I should hesitate to say, because their evidence is ambiguous, that the use of these sayings was the result of a progress in educational methods that only took place in Imperial times.

9

Counting on the fingers: cf. D. E. Smith, *History of Mathematics*, Boston, 1925, vol. II, pp. 196–202; E. A. Bechtel, "Finger Counting among the Romans", in *Classical Philology*, IV (1909), pp. 25 *et seq.*; Froehner, in *Annuaire de la Société française de Numismatique et d'Archéologie*, VIII (1884), pp. 232–238; J. G. Lemoine, "Les Anciens procédés de calcul sur les doigts en Orient et en Occident", in *Revue des Etudes Islamiques*, VI (1932), pp. 1–60; A. Cordoliani, "Etudes de comput", I, in *Bibliothèque de l'Ecole des Chartes*, CIII (1942), pp. 62–65.

Two problems arise: (1) the date when this first appeared. The only account that we have *ex professo* about the West is the treatise by the Venerable Bede (eighth century; *PL*, vol. 90, c. 685–693: the manuscripts are accompanied by curious illustrated plates), and in the East a few pages by Rhabdas (*alias* Nicolas Artavasdos of Smyrna, fourteenth century), text and translation in P. Tannery, *Mémoires scientifiques*,

IV, pp. 90–97. But there are allusions which are quite precise from the technical point of view that show that the method was in use in Imperial Rome from the first century:

PLINY (*HN*, XXXIV, 33) mentions a statue of Janus dedicated by King Numa (?), and says that its fingers represent the number 365. Whatever the truth may be about the real date of the dedication, and the intentions of the person who had the statue put up, this shows that contemporaries of the elder Pliny regarded the pose adopted by this Janus as an expression of the rules of counting. See also JUVENAL (X, 248: a centenarian is counting the number of years he has lived on his right hand) and esp. APULEIUS (*Apol.*, 89, 6–7), St. JEROME (*Adv. Jovinian.*, I, 3), St. AUGUSTINE (*Serm.*, 175, 1), MARTIANUS CAPELLA (VII, 746). The custom did not properly belong to Latin districts: there is a story by PLUTARCH (*Reg. Imp. Apopht.*, 174 B); AELIUS ARISTIDES (XLVI D, 257) and SUIDAS (Vol. I, p. 339, 3752) that shows that it was at least known in his day (second century A.D.) and, if the story has any historical basis, in the fourth century B.C. Orontes, the nephew of King Artaxerxes II (404–358), compared the friends of kings, who are powerful or wretched according to whether they are in favour or in disgrace, to the fingers of the hands, which signify now ten thousands (when the left hand is resting against a certain part of the body) and now mere units (when the left hand is stretched out in front of the body); cf. also *Anth. Pal.*, XI, 72.

PLINY (*HN*, XXXIV, 88) also knew of the existence of a statue of a man (it may have been Chrysippus) counting on his fingers; it was the work of the sculptor Euboulides (II: cf. C. ROBERT, in PAULY-WISSOWA, VI, c. 871–875, s.v. "Eubulides" No. 10; it is reckoned to have been done *c.* 204 B.C.). HERODOTUS even mentions the matter (VI, 63; 65) but it seems doubtful whether his system was the same as the one codified by Bede. And the vases with red figures that seem to represent people playing *morra* do not seem to contain the kind of mimicry that could accord with these rules (G. LAFAYE, in DAREMBERG-SAGLIO, III, 2, pp. 1889b–1890b, s.v. "Micatio"; K. SCHNEIDER, in PAULY-WISSOWA, XV, 2, c. 1516–1517, s.v. "Micare"). Cf. however, perhaps, one of the vase-paintings depicting the "Representation of the Sale of Oil in Athens" (under this title: F. J. M. De WAELE, *Revue Archéologique*, 5, XXIII (1926), pp. 282–295): it shows a *pelikè* with black figures (E. PERNICE, *ΣΙΦΩΝ*, in *Jahrbuch d. deutsch. archaeolog. Instituts* VIII (1893), p. 181) showing a woman shop-keeper whose left-hand fingers seem to represent the number 31; cf. again AR., *Vesp.*, 656.

The only figurative monuments dating from antiquity that give any proof that the Bede-Rhabdas system was in use are the curious tesserae in the Medal Room of the Bibliothèque Nationale, which were first pointed out by Froehner (*art. cit.*, in default of the unpublished catalogue by J. Babelon, *Coll. Froehner*, II, No. 316–327). They must be some kind of counters; nothing has been found that denotes any number higher than 16. From the way they are made it seems likely that they came from the toy business that went on in Alexandria under the Empire (as a matter of fact most of the known examples come from Egypt, and a few from Rome). Unfortunately it seems difficult to give the precise date: numismatists are divided. I have consulted J. Babelon and P. Le Gentilhomme: the first inclines towards the Early Empire, the latter towards a somewhat later date, after Constantine.

(2) Where and when was this way of counting learned? It is clear from the writings of Roman times that its use was quite habitual (lawyers used it for example in the law-courts: QUINT., XI, 3, 117). I do not see why it cannot have been taught in the primary schools: by its qualitative character—one sign for each whole number—it seems to go quite naturally with the teaching of numbers.

10

Arithmetic in the primary schools: the classification of mathematical papyri needs to be done very carefully. There is no point in shoving anything into the category of "school papyri" simply because it looks highly elementary—as P. COLLART does for instance in *Mélanges Desrousseaux*, pp. 79–80. It is very instructive that even in the fourth century A.D. an educated man, an official like the Hermesion of the *PSI*, 22, 958, 959, had to copy down a multiplication table in his own hand in the same book as he used for doing horoscopes and keeping his accounts. Cf. the same thing in the sixth century in the long metrological tables in the *PLondon*, V, 1718, which go into great detail in "converting" the *artabe* and each of its sub-divisions into lower units: one is tempted to look upon this as a primary school textbook—converting one thing to another is so important in our schools!—but these tables are in the hand of Fl. Dioscorus, a curious gentleman of a type very familiar to us, "a typical Byzantine country gentleman, a great landed proprietor in Aphrodito-Kom Ishqaw, a 'proto-comete', a lawyer and a poet in his spare time" (so I have described him in *Mélanges d'Archéologie et d'Histoire*, LVII (1940), p. 129). The reason why such highly educated men found it necessary to make up *aide-mémoires* like this for themselves was because this kind of elementary mathematical knowledge was not really acquired at school. There is no reason to suppose that it was an effect of "decadence": the fact that XENOPHON's Socrates (*Mem.*, IV, 4, 7) asks Hippias whether $2 \times 2 = 5$ does not necessarily tell us anything about the way arithmetic was taught in the primary schools.

To return to the papyri: though many of them are very difficult to classify and supply somewhat ambiguous evidence (e.g.: *PLondon*, III, 737, adding tables; *POxy.*, 9 (vol. I, p. 77) *verso*; 669, metrological tables), some are highly informative: PLAU-MANN (*ABKK*, XXXIV [1913], c. 223) notes, with reference to PREISIGKE, *Sammel-buch*, 6220–6222, that as soon as the exercises in arithmetic rise above the most elementary stage (e.g. tables of fractions, $\frac{1}{2}$ or $\frac{1}{3}$ of whole numbers; multiplications like $19 \times 55 = 4,005$; $78 \times 76 = 5,928$; the adding up of fractions), the writing, which in this case dates from the seventh century, is an adult's, not a child's.

11

Calculations done on the abacus: cf. E. GUILLAUME, in DAREMBERG-SAGLIO, I, pp. 1b–3b, s.v. "Abacus", II; HULTSCH in PAULY-WISSOWA, I, c. 5–10, s.v. "Abacus", 9; A. NAGL, *ibid.*, *Suppl.*, III, c. 4–13; 1305.

12

Children's musical games. I have mentioned the epigraphic winners' lists that refer to them, but it must not be assumed too readily that they concern children of primary school age. The writing test in Pergamus is to be found on a fragment that has no context to it and is ambiguous (*AM*, 35 (1910), p. 436, No. 20); "reading" appears on another inscription along with epic, elegy and μέλος (song? lyric poetry? *AM*, 37 (1912), p. 277, 1, 2–7): secondary context; the "reading" in question may have been the reading with expression which, as we shall see, was part of the art taught by the grammarian, i.e. the secondary school teacher. The same may have been true in Chios (DITTENBERG., *SIG.*, 959): reading (l. 8) in this case comes immediately in front of the "Homer recitation"—ῥαψῳδία—a secondary exercise, as music probably was too, that came directly afterwards; the παῖδες in question may have been children who were anything from twelve to sixteen years of age—the term is elastic. The evidence is much clearer as regards the competitions held in Teos (MICHEL, 913): the list is damaged but it nevertheless shows quite clearly that the winners belonged to three different age-groups: reading figured in all three, writing in the youngest, but these were not primary-school children, for amongst the examinations that they had to take we find not only poetry—tragic, comic and lyric—but also instrumental music. Now the epigraphic charter of the schools in Teos (DITTENBERG., *SIG.*, 578: end of the third century; the MICHEL winners' list is second-century) explicitly states that the teaching of the lyre was to be limited to children who were not more than two years less than ephebia age (l. 17–18): the "junior class" in our winners' list —"junior" compared with the children in the ephebia—was therefore actually one of the two upper classes of the three mentioned in the charter (l. 9).

Cf. however *Anth.*, VI, 308: the writing test which had a prize of eighty knuckle-bones, but it was not only the young children who were interested in this game: cf. the admirable "Astragal Players" in Herculaneum, a cameo painting on marble in the Naples Museum: O. ELIA, *Pitture murali e mosaici nel Museo Nazionale di Napoli*, p. 40, No. 49 (9562).

13

The Spartan μῶα: A. M. WOODWARD, in R. M. DAWKINS, "The Sanctuary of Artemis Orthia at Sparta" (*Journal of Hellenic Studies, Supplementary Paper*, No. 5), London, 1929, p. 288: of the twenty-two inscriptions that mention them six give the winners' ages and four of these are *mikkikhizomenes*: No. 2, p. 297 (second century B.C.); 43, p. 319; 67, p. 332; 68, p. 333.

CHAPTER VII

1

Teachers' two subjects (grammar and rhetoric) in Rhodes: F. MARX, *Berliner Philologische Wochenschrift*, 1890, c. 1007.

2

The classic "canons" of writers and artists: J. COUSIN, "Etudes sur Quintilien", vol. I, *Contribution à la Recherche des Sources de l'Institution oratoire*, Paris, 1935, pp. 565–570; this summarizes all the material in the many works devoted to this subject by German scholars, esp. the Dissertations by J. BRZOSKA, *De Canone decem oratorum atticorum quaestiones*, Breslau, 1883, and O. KROEHNERT, *Canonesne poetarum, scriptorum, artificum per antiquitatem fuerunt*, Koenigsberg, 1897. On the lists of inventors, cf. M. KREMNER, *De Catalogis heurematum*, Leipzig Dissertation, 1890; A. KLEIGUENTHER, ΠΡΩΤΟΣ ΕΥΡΗΤΗΣ, Leipzig, 1933.

3

The influence of school editions on the transmission of Greek classical drama by way of manuscripts: see the *Introduction* to their editions (*Collection Budé*): V. COULON, *Aristophane* (pp. x–xi); P. MAZON, *Eschyle* (pp. xiv–xv); P. MASQUERAY, *Sophocle* (p. xiii); L. MERIDIER, *Euripide* (p. xx. Euripides was luckier: the "Selected Plays" that appeared in the time of Hadrian only contained ten plays; our manuscripts L and P have preserved nine others as well).

4

The Seven Wise Men had been known ever since PLATO's time (*Prot.*, 343a), but they were only popularized in Hellenistic times, particularly by the Apophthegms of Demetrius Phalereus (H. DIELS, *Fragmente der Vorsokratiker*, §73a).

On the history and function of anthologies I have already referred the reader to O. GUERAUD-P. JOUGUET, *Un Livre d'Ecolier* . . ., pp. xxiv–xxxi.

5

On the "political" editions of Homer, cf. finally P. CHANTRAINE, in P. MAZON, *Introduction à l'Iliade*, Paris, 1942, pp. 23–25: they are only supposed to date from 200 B.C. according to BOLLING, *External Evidence of Interpolation in Homer*, p. 41. The best known (twenty-seven fragments) is that of Marseilles, which has been studied by S. GAMBER, *L'Edition massaliotique de l'Iliade d'Homère*, Paris, 1888.

6

School papyri of Homer: C. H. OLDFATHER, *The Greek Literary Texts from Graeco-Roman Egypt, A Study in the History of Civilisation* (University of Wisconsin Studies in the Social Sciences and History, 9, Madison, 1923, pp. 66–70); P. COLLART, in *Mélanges Desrousseaux*, pp. 76–79, Nos. 141–143, 145–162 (No. 144 is not a school copy); and in P. MAZON, *Introduction à l'Iliade*, pp. 59–60; cf. J. SCHWARTZ, "Papyrus homériques" in *BIFAO*, vol. XLVI, pp. 29–71, esp. Nos. 6, 8, 9.

7

Statistics about Homeric papyri: P. COLLART, in *Introduction à l'Iliade*, p. 62 and n. 1: in 1941, 372 papyri of the *Iliad* had been collected, as against 104 of the *Odyssey*, and they represented almost the whole poem, 13,542 lines out of 15,693, whereas the *Odyssey* papyri only have 5,171 lines out of 12,110. J. SCHWARTZ, *art. cit.*, has published twenty-three new papyri, containing 600 lines from Homer. About 500 of these "are from the *Iliad*, and most of them are from the first eight cantos".

8

Writers included in the school syllabuses: C. H. OLDFATHER, *The Greek Literary Texts from Graeco-Roman Egypt*, pp. 62 *et seq.*, and his *Catalogue*, pp. 4 *et seq.*, of the names of the various writers. But his list, which is now fairly old (1923), needs to be revised: many new discoveries have been made and these have slightly altered his conclusions—in the case of Aeschylus, for instance, who appeared more frequently than he thought, and the epigrams: O. GUERAUD-P. JOUGUET, *Un Livre d'Ecolier*, p. xxiii, n. 1, n. 6. See also W. N. BATES, "The Euripides Papyri," *AJPhil.*, 1941, vol. 62, pp. 469–475; P. COLLART, "Les fragments des tragiques grecs sur papyrus", *R.Ph.*, vol. 17, pp. 5–36; R. A. PACK, *The Greek and Latin Literary Texts from Graeco-Roman Egypt*, Ann Arbor—not to mention the more ambitious though not wholly successful research carried out by E. REGGERS and L. GIABBANI (cf. *Chronique d'-Egypte*, 1943, vol. 18, pp. 312–315; 1948, vol. 24, pp. 211–212). Again, Egypt was not the whole of the Greek world, nor are papyri our only evidence for school libraries: we must remember the epigraphical catalogues—like the one in Athens, IG^2, II, 2363 —which include Sophocles (who does not appear very frequently in Oldfather's book), Aeschylus, Aeschines, Hellanicus. . . . The Rhodes Catalogue (N. SERGE, *Rivista di Filologia*, 1935, 214–222) was only for advanced students.

9

Alexandrian criticisms of the Homer "Vulgate": P. CHANTRAINE and P. COLLART, in P. MAZON, *Introduction à l'Iliade*, p. 13 (of the 874 lessons that Aristarchus is known to have given on the *Iliad*, only 80 appear in all our manuscripts, 160 in most of them, 76 in half of them, 181 in a minority of them, 245 in less than ten, and 132 in none at all); 16, 73. On the "scholia", P. CHANTRAINE and R. LANGUMIER, *ibid.*, pp. 15–16, 73–88.

10

The Stoics' work in grammar: J. STERN, *Homerstudien der Stoiker*, Lonach, 1893; C. WACHSMUTH, *De Cratete Mallota*, Leipzig, 1860; J. HELCK, *De Cratetis Mallotae studiis criticis quae ad Odysseam spectant*, Dresden, 1914.

11

Iliac tables: L. COUVE, in DAREMBERG-SAGLIO, III, 1, pp. 372a–383a, s.v. "Iliacae (tabulae)"; LIPPOLD, in PAULY-WISSOWA, II R., IV, 2, 1886–1896; K. BULAS, in *Eos*, *Suppl.*, III (1929), pp. 124 *et seq.* They all come from Italy, but there is nothing to prove that they were made up by Roman teachers or that they were specially intended to introduce Latin children to Greek legends. It has been questioned whether they were used in schools, because they are so small, but the old style of teaching was more individualistic than ours, and it was not necessary for these tables to be looked at from a distance by the whole class like our wall charts. It seems to me to be proved that they were used in schools because of the inscription on the famous Capitoline Table (*IG*, XIV, 1284: Θεοδ] ὥρον μάθε τάξιν Ὁμήρου), which looks as though it was composed by an unknown grammarian of the name of Theodore. If, as is often stated, these reliefs were votive or decorative, they could give us some idea of actual school tables, less luxuriously carried out.

12

Textual criticism (διόρθωσις, *emendatio*) in the old schools: H. I. MARROU, *Saint Augustin et la Fin de la Culture antique*, pp. 21–23.

13

Passages prepared for reading: a wooden tablet (*PBerlin*, 13839) has on its verso side lines B 146–162 of the *Iliad* in a schoolboy's handwriting; the lines are separated by an "obelus" and the words by an accent: photograph in W. SCHUBART, *Einführung in die Papyruskunde*, pl. III, 3; transcription in P. BEUDEL, *Qua ratione Graeci liberos docuerint*, p. 41.

14

The allegorical explanation of Homer: P. DECHARME, *La Critique des Traditions religieuses chez les Grecs*, Paris, 1904, pp. 270–354; K. MUELLER, in PAULY-WISSOWA, *Suppl.*, IV, c. 16–20, s.v. "Allegorische Dichtererklärung".

15

The interpolation of moral tags in Homer's accepted text: see at least the theories— they are no more—in V. BERARD, *Introduction à l'Odyssée*, II, pp. 237–291, "La Grosse Sagesse".

CHAPTER VIII

I

What date does Plutarch's evidence about the teaching of science in the *Diogeneion* go back to (*Quaest. Conv.*, IX, 736 D)? It seems impossible to say with certainty. Plutarch simply says: "Ammonius, who was then 'strategus', had introduced an examination into the Diogeneion for the ephebes" (*sic*: in fact, as we have seen, the college took "mellephebes", i.e. young men who were to go into the ephebia the following year) "who were learning letters, geometry, rhetoric and music." We know of many people called Ammonius, and we cannot say of any in particular that he was a strategus, but as Plutarch does not seem to think it necessary to be more precise about him, one is tempted to assume that he is writing of the Ammonius he knew best, the twelfth mentioned in the article "Ammonius" in PAULY-WISSOWA (I, c. 1862)—i.e. the Platonic philosopher under whom Plutarch studied in Athens; he is often mentioned by Plutarch and his words are frequently quoted (cf. the *Introduction* by R. FLACE-LIÈRE to his edition of the treatise *Sur l'E de Delphes, Annales de l'Université de Lyon*, 3, Letters, ii, pp. 8–10); which would take us back to the time of Nero. But this is no more than a suggestion.

2

There is a whole chapter on the history of the ἐγκύκλιος παιδεία in my book *Saint Augustin et la Fin de la Culture antique*, Paris, 1937, pp. 211–235. I should like to take this opportunity to mention two points on which it seems to me to be necessary to correct the views I put forward in that book: (1) The first appearance of this educational ideal should not be put back, as I thought then, to the generation that came after Aristotle. As we have seen, it was to all intents and purposes put forward by both Plato and Isocrates, who agreed in combining mathematics and literature. It is not therefore necessary to discard (*op. cit.*, p. 221, n. 1) the evidence of DIOGENES LAERTIUS (II, 79) about Aristippes, who compared people who neglect philosophy after having studied the ἐγκύκλια μαθήματα to Penelope's lovers; (2) I am no longer quite so certain that the idea of the ἐγκύκλιος παιδεία as a sort of "general culture" as opposed to "preliminary culture" was the result of a "degeneration" that was due to the decadence of secondary-school teaching in Roman times (*op. cit.*, pp. 226–227). Since it included rhetoric, the ἐγκύκλιος παιδεία syllabus encroached upon the field of secondary-school teaching proper from the very beginning, and any of Isocrates' pupils would have been quite satisfied with it; only the philosophers, who followed Plato, were obliged to regard it as being merely preliminary. On the other hand, I still maintain, despite the criticisms of A. J. FESTUGIERE (in *Revue des Etudes grecques*, LII [1939], p. 239), that such a syllabus was hardly more than an ideal, and was only rarely and imperfectly realized in practice.

3

"Encyclopaedia" a modern idea: cf. again my *Saint Augustin*, pp. 228–229. The only Greek word was ἐγκύκλιος παιδεία; in the form ἐγκυκλιοπαιδεία it is only to be met with in the writings of QUINTILIAN (I, 10, i) and this was probably a mistake made by copyists. The word "encyclopaedia" first appears in the sixteenth century —in English, in Elyot, 1531; in French, in Rabelais, 1532—and was re-created, or at least used to express a new idea, by being connected etymologically with κύκλος—i.e. the complete circle of human knowledge: whereas in Hellenistic Greek the adjective ἐγκύκλιος had a much weaker derivative meaning—"in circulation", hence "current", "common", or something that "happens periodically", thus "daily", "everyday".

4

The varying contents of the ἐγκύκλιος παιδεία syllabus: see the evidence quoted in my *Saint Augustin* . . ., p. 227, n. 1: VITR., I, i, 3–10; GAL., *Prot.*, 14, pp. 38–39; MAR. VICTOR., in KEIL, *Grammatici Latini*, VI, p. 187; *Schol.* to DION. THRAX, in HILGARD, *Grammatici Graeci*, III, p. 112; PHILSTR., *Gym.*, I.

5

The ἐγκύκλιος παιδεία syllabus as followed by Graeco-Roman philosophers: see the table drawn up in *Saint Augustin* . . ., pp. 216–217: Heraclides Ponticus (D.L., V, 86–88), Arcesilaus (D.L., IV, 29–33), Ps. Cebes (*Pinax*), Philo (*De Congr., pass.*), Seneca (*Ep.*, 88, 3–14), Sextus Empiricus (plan of the *Contra Mathematicos*), Origen (*Ep. ad Greg.*, I; cf. EUS., *H. E.*, VI, 18, 3–4), Anatolius of Laodicea (EUS., *H. E.*, VII, 32, 6; HIER., *De Vir. Ill.*, 73), Porphyry (TZETZ., *Chil.*, XI, 532), Lactantius (*Inst.*, III, 25, I); cf. *ibid.*, p. 189 for St. Augustine (*De Ord.*, II, 12, 35 *et seq.*; II, 4, 13 *et seq.*; *De Quant. an.*, 23, 72; *Retract.*, I, 6; *Conf.*, IV, 16, 30.)

For the date of the first appearance of the liberal arts "septenary" between Dionysius Thrax and Varro, I follow F. MARX, *Prolegomena* to his edition of CELSUS, in *Corpus Medicorum Latinorum*, I, Leipzig, 1915, p. x (cf. my *Saint Augustin*, p. 220, n. 2).

6

The history of Greek geometry and arithmetic: there are several elementary books on this subject, of which the best seems to me to be D. E. SMITH, *History of Mathematics*, 2 vols., Boston, 1925; but a book that is always worth returning to is that of J. GOW, *A Short History of Greek Mathematics*, Cambridge, 1884, which many more recent works seem content to ignore. Anybody wishing to study the subject more deeply would of course need to consult the classic works by M. CANTOR, *Vorlesungen über Geschichte der Mathematik*, I⁴, Leipzig, 1922, and P. TANNERY, *La Géométrie grecque: Comment son histoire nous est parvenue, ce que nous en savons*, I, Paris, 1887, and the articles collected in the posthumous edition of his *Mémoires scientifiques*, I–IV, Paris-Toulouse, 1912–1920.

7

On the Greek science of music, cf. besides L. LALOY, *Aristoxène de Tarente*, and T. REINACH, *La Musique grecque*, to which I have already referred: M. EMMANUEL, *Histoire de la Langue musicale*, I, Paris, 1911, pp. 61–165; "Grèce (Art gréco-romain)", in H. LAVIGNAC, *Encyclopédie de la Musique*, 1, I, pp. 377–537.

8

R. G. H. WESTPHAL has studied Greek rhythms in conjunction with the rhythms of our own classical music: cf. his well-known books: *Die Fragmente und Lehrsätze der griechischen Rhythmiker* (1861) and *Allgemeine Theorie der musikalischen Rhythmik seit J. S. Bach* (1881).

9

On Greek astronomy: it is always interesting to return to J. B. DELAMBRE, *Histoire de l'Astronomie ancienne*, Paris, 1817. See amongst later works: P. TANNERY, *Recherches sur l'Histoire de l'Astronomie ancienne*, Paris, 1893; J. HARTMANN, "Astronomie", in *Die Kultur der Gegenwart*, III, 3, 3, Leipzig, 1921.

10

On teaching science in the neo-Platonic schools: F. SCHEMMEL, "Die Hochschule von Konstantinopel im IV. Jahrhundert", in *Neue Jahrbücher der klassischen Alter-tumsgeschichte und deutscher Literatur*, 22 (1908), pp. 147–168; "Die Hochschule von Alexandreia im IV und V Jahrundert," *ibid.*, 24 (1909), pp. 438–457; O. SCHISSEL VON FLESCHENBERG, *Marinos von Neapolis und die neuplatonischen Tugendgrade*, Athens, 1928 (and the account by E. BREHIER, in *Revue d'Histoire de la Philosophie*, 1929, pp. 226–227); and C. LACOMBRADE, *Synesios de Cyrène, hellène et chrétien*, Paris, 1951, pp. 39–46, 64–71.

11

The teaching of astronomy: cf. H. WEINHOLD, *Die Astronomie in der antiken Schule*, Münich Dissertation, 1912: an excellent piece of work, but the author has not drawn the conclusions that emerge from the facts so admirably presented. To this should be added L. ROBERT, in *Etudes Epigraphiques et Philologiques* (BEHE, 272), Paris, 1938, p. 15.

12

Aratus of Soli portrayed in company with the Muse Urania to symbolize the science of astronomy: on a silver "skyphos", for example, in the Berthouville collection: C. PICARD, in *Monuments Piot*, vol. XLIV (1950), pp. 55–60, pl. V; and for a general treatment: K. SCHEFOLD, *Die Bildnisse der antiken Dichter, Redner und Denker*, Basle, 1943.

For the life and work of Aratus, see finally V. BUESCU's edition of CICERO, *Les Aratea* (a collection of critical editions published by the Rumanian Institute of Latin Studies, I), Paris-Bucharest, 1941, pp. 15 *et seq*.

CHAPTERS IX–XI

1

Σχολαι, ἐπιδείξεις, ἀκροάσεις: it is difficult to give a proper precise meaning to each of these three words which were used at one time or another, and sometimes all together, to denote lectures given in the gymnasium. Ἐπίδειξις (cf. s.v. W. SCHMID, in PAULY-WISSOWA, VI, I, c. 53–56) means in a very general way a "lecture" as distinct from a "competition"; in Hellenistic times the word had long since lost its technical meaning of a "demonstration, exhibition, specimen lecture", which, as we have seen, it had in the days of the Early Sophists. The rhetors regarded the epideictic style as being opposed to political and legal eloquence. Cf. the evolution of the word ἀπαρχή (ἀπάρχεσθαι), which first meant a lecture or "hearing" offered as a kind of first-fruits to the god of a sanctuary like the one in Delphi, and ended up by meaning an ordinary lecture or concert (L. ROBERT, in *Bibliothèque de l'Ecole pratique des Hautes-Etudes (Sciences historiques et philologiques)*, fasc. 272, pp. 38–45).

Ἀκρόασις was, strictly speaking, a "hearing", but it was used to describe a lecturer as well as a musician (see L. ROBERT, *ibid.*, pp. 14–15; *Hellenica*, II, pp. 35–36). Σχολή may have already begun to have a more "academic" tinge about it: cf. *infra*, n. 5.

2

Lecture halls in gymnasiums of the Roman period: L. ROBERT, "Etudes anatoliennes" (*Etudes orientales publiées par l'Institut français d'Archéologie de Stamboul*, V), pp. 79–81; P. Schazmann, *Altertümer von Pergamon*, VI, *Das Gymnasion*, pp. 61–63; pl. IV–V; J. Keil, "Ausgrabungen in Ephesos 1931", in *Jarheshefte des österreichen archäologischen Instituts*, XXVIII (1933), *Beiblatt*, 9–10; Cawadias, Tὸ ἱερὸν τοῦ Ἀσκληπίου, pp. 150–154; P. Lemerle, "Palestre romaine à Philippes", in *Bulletin de Correspondance hellénique*, LXI (1937), pp. 86–102; pl. IX–XIII, and finally in *Philippes et la Macédoine orientale à l'époque chrétienne et byzantine*, Paris, 1945, pp. 421–423.

3

"Secondary" teaching in the gymnasiums: too much emphasis must not be placed on the distinction I have made between "secondary school" and "higher" education. This distinction is useful as a way of classifying subject matter, but it does not always correspond in practice to the division of work that obtained in the various educational centres. Here we find the "higher" education of the ephebia still going on with the classics at a "secondary school" level; on the other hand, if I understand Plutarch's evidence properly, he shows us pupils in the Diogeneion, i.e. boys who were preparing to go to the ephebia, starting on the "higher" syllabus with rhetoric (n. 1 of the previous chapter).

To prove the existence of the teaching of mathematics, reference is often made (e.g. Oehler, in Pauly-Wissowa, VII, 2, c. 2014) to an inscription copied in Gallipoli (in A. Dumont, *Mélanges d'Epigraphie et d'Archéologie*, Paris, 1892, p. 435, No. 100*x*: sic, not 100*a*) in honour of a geometrician called Asklepiades, crowned by ephebes—both the children and their teachers—"because of his worth and his devotion to their interests". There is nothing here to say that Asklepiades taught geometry: he may simply have been a benefactor who had been good to the city's schools and gymnasium, like Polythrous in Teos and Eudemus in Miletus.

4

Wandering lecturers: cf. the classic essay by M. Guarducci, "Poeti vaganti e conferenzieri dell' età ellenistica, ricerche di epigrafia greca nel campo della letteratura e del costume", in *Memorie* of the Academy of the Lincei, Moral Sciences, 6, II, ix (Rome, 1929), pp. 629–665. Of course the account given here would have to be completed with the help of documents that have been published or studied since, e.g. by L. Robert, in *Bibliothèque de l'Ecole pratique des Hautes-Etudes*, 272, pp. 7 et seq.

5

Odd lectures or whole courses? It seems to be quite clear what happened in Eretrea: Dittenberg., *SIG.*, 714, 8–10, congratulates the gymnasiarch Elpinikus "on having performed his functions so effectively throughout the year, and on having supplied at his own expense a rhetor and a fencing master, who gave their lessons in the ephebes' gymnasium and to the children, not to mention the citizens": ἐμμονεύσας ἐν τῷ γυμνασίῳ δι' ἐνιαυτοῦ, καὶ παρέσχεν ἐκ τοῦ ἰδίου ῥήτορά τε καὶ ὁπλομάχον, οἵτινες ἐσχόλαζον ἐν τῷ γυμνασίῳ τοῖς τε παισὶν καὶ ἐφήβοις καὶ τοῖς ἄλλοις τοῖς βουλομένοις . . .

I know that it is said in Athens that the people congratulated the ephebes on having gone to lectures on philosophy for a whole year—e.g. the inscription *IG²*, II, 1030, 31; but this inscription has been restored. The idea of conscientiousness, which is not quite so prominent, is nevertheless expressed quite clearly in the inscriptions mentioned in the text. It should also be noted that the expression usually employed seems to draw a distinction between the "lessons—σχολαί—given by the grammarians, rhetors and philosophers" and "what are called ἀκροάσεις". I am quite prepared to agree that the first category could be described as "whole courses" and the second as additional "lectures", given more or less on their own.

6

Libraries in Hellenistic gymnasiums: cf. E. ZIEBARTH, *Aus dem griechischen Schulwesen*[2], pp. 131–132: Athens, Halicarnassos, Corinth, Pergamus; L. ROBERT, in *Bulletin de Correspondance hellénique*, XLIX (1935), p. 425; "Etudes anatoliennes", p. 72, n. 7. M. ROSTOVTSEFF has collected the documents relating to the libraries that existed in Egypt in *Social and Economic History of the Hellenistic World*, p. 1589, n. 24, but he does not seem to me to have established that they were school libraries.

7

Literary competitions for Athenian ephebes in the years A.D. 180/181–191/192: cf. P. GRAINDOR, "Etudes sur l'Ephébie attique sous l'Empire, I. Les concours éphébiques," in *Musée belge*, XXVI (1922), pp. 166–168. The inscriptions also mention ephebes who distinguished themselves in the "exhortation speech"—λόγος προτρεπτικός—which was delivered to the competitors at the beginning of the examination: *IG*[2], II, 2119, 231, 234; we even have the text of one of these speeches, which was considered worth "printing": (*IG*[2], II, 2291a; cf. l. 4). This was another kind of literary activity that went on in the ephebia, but it does not seem to have formed part of any competition.

8

Character tests: see the inscriptions collected together by J. OEHLER, in PAULY-WISSOWA, VII, 2, c. 2014.

9

On the subject of the Alexandria Museum, which has been so thoroughly studied, it will be enough here if I refer the reader to the summary by MÜLLER-GRAUPA, s.v. "Μουσεῖον", in PAULY-WISSOWA, XVI, c. 801–821. Finally, M. ROSTOVTSEFF, *The Social and Economic History of the Hellenistic World*, pp. 1084–1085, 1596, n. 39, and G. FAIDER-FEYTMANS, "ΜΟΥΣΕΙΟΝ, Musée", in *Hommages à Joseph Bidez et à Franz Cumont* (Brussels), pp. 97–106.

10

For a list of librarians of the Museum, and their dates of service, cf. *POxy.*, 1241, and the article by G. PERROTTA in *Athenaeum*, 1928, pp. 125–156.

11

We have precious little information about the kind of teaching that went on in the Museum: cf. the inferences drawn by MÜLLER-GRAUPA, *art. cit.*, *supra*, c. 809–810.

12

For the dates and the career and works of the curious person known as Anatolius of Laodicea, cf. all the information that I have collected in my *Saint Augustin et la Fin de la Culture antique*, p. 217, n. 8.

13

The destruction of the Serapeum: see the texts in G. RAUSCHEN, *Jahrbücher der christlichen Kirche unter dem Kaiser Theodosius dem Grossen*, pp. 301–303; the date has been rectified by O. SEECK, *Geschichte des Untergangs der antiken Welt*, V, p. 534.

14

Museums outside Alexandria: R. HERZOG, in *Urkunden zur Hochschulpolitik der römischen Kaiser, Sitzungsberichte* of the Berlin Academy, *Phil.-hist. Klasse*, 1935, xxxii, pp. 1005–1006. On the Ephesus Museum cf. esp. J. KEIL, "Aertzeinschriften aus Ephesos", in *Jahreshefte* of the Austrian Archeological Institute, VIII (1905), pp. 128 *et seq.*, and P. WOLTERS, *ibid.*, IX (1906), pp. 295 *et seq.* On the Smyrna Museum, L. ROBERT, "Etudes anatoliennes", pp. 146–148. Of course there are other inscriptions to be found elsewhere about "members of the Museum"—ἀπὸ Μουσείου —(cf. the collection of passages in P. LEMERLE, "Inscriptions de Philippes", *Bulletin de Correspondance hellénique*, XLIX (1935), pp. 131–140, brought up to date by L. ROBERT, "Etudes anatoliennes", p. 146), but they are not about local museums: the people concerned were attached in either a working or honorary capacity to the great Museum of Alexandria; this is especially the case as regards several inscriptions in Athens. J. H. OLIVER, who has edited them, believes that they reveal the name of the Athens "University": "The Mouseion in Late Attic Inscriptions", in *Hesperia*, III (1934), pp. 191–196; cf. *ibid.*, IV (1935), p. 63, No. 26; but this has been refuted by P. GRAINDOR, "Le Nom de l'Université d'Athènes sous l'Empire", in *Revue belge de Philologie et d'Histoire*, 1938, pp. 207–212. On the site and architecture of the Museums, see the invaluable remarks of G. ROUX, "Le Val des Muses et les Musées chez les auteurs anciens", in *Bulletin de Correspondence Hellénique*, 1954, vol. 78, I, pp. 38–45.

15

On Hellenistic lawyers and the absence of any organized teaching of law, cf. M. ROSTOVTSEFF, *The Social and Economic History of the Hellenistic World*, p. 1095; 1600, n. 49 (which emphasizes the need for a more detailed study of the question).

16

On the place of medicine in Hellenistic civilization, cf. M. ROSTOVTSEFF, *ibid.*, pp. 1088–1094; and the wealth of bibliographical material gathered together on pp. 1597–1600, n. 45–48.

17

On the history of the school in Cnidus: cf. J. ILBERG, "Die Aertzschule von Knidos", in *Berichte* of the Leipzig Academy of Sciences, *Philol.-hist. Kl.*, 76 (1924), 3. On the Cos school see the notes by R. HERZOG in the *Jahrbuch* of the German Archeological Institute, 47 (1932), "Arch. Anz.", c. 274–276, and his old book, *Koische Forschungen und Funde*, Leipzig, 1889, pp. 199–208.

18

The history of Greek medicine has been studied very thoroughly: to the books mentioned by ROSTOVTSEFF (n. 16, *supra*), may be added, so far as France is concerned, A. CASTIGLIONI, *Histoire de la Médicine*, French trans., Paris, 1931, and, for its wonderful illustrations, [M.] LAIGNEL-LAVASTINE, *Histoire générale de la Médicine, de la Pharmacie, de l'Art dentaire et de l'Art vétérinaire*, I, Paris, 1936. The history of the actual *teaching* of medicine has not been so fortunate: there are not so many actual facts in the old work by T. PUSCHMANN, *Geschichte des medizinischen Unterrichts*, Leipzig, 1889, pp. 61–70, as in the article by S. REINACH in DAREMBERG-SAGLIO, III, 2, c. 1673a–1676b, s.v. "Medicus".

On the teacher's little manuals in the *Hippocratic Corpus* (which are only supposed to date from the first to the second century A.D., with the exception of the π. ἰητροῦ, which is supposed to go back to the third century) cf. U. Fleischer, "Untersuchungen zu den pseudohippokratischen Schriften Παραγγελίαι, περὶ ἰητροῦ und περὶ εὐσχημοσύνης" (Neue deutsche Forschungen, Abt. klassischer Philologie, X), Berlin, 1939.

19

Galen's studies: the autobiographical passages in Galen's works will be found collected in their chronological order by R. Fuchs, in T. Puschmann, Handbuch der Geschichte der Medizin, I, Jena, 1902, pp. 374-378.

20

Choosing ambassadors: the orators and the Sophists were not the only people to be elected—cities were glad to be able to send philosophers too. In the year 154 the Athenians sent the heads of three of their four schools of philosophy to Rome—the Stoic Diogenes, the Peripatetic Critolaus and the Academician Carneades. We know of more surprising choices still: Thyatira sent an athlete to the Emperor Elagabalus (IG Rom., IV, 1251): L. Robert makes the ingenious suggestion that it was probably because of the connections he had made with members of the Imperial court when he was a high dignitary in the "xystus", i.e. the general association of professional athletes (in Etudes anatoliennes, pp. 119-123). Like causes produce like effects: it was only natural that Cos should send one of its doctors on an embassy to Crete when it was so famous for medicine.

21

Rhetors as ambassadors. When Sulla was dictator the celebrated rhetor Molon was sent by his city of Rhodes to discuss with the Roman Senate the question of compensation due to the people of Rhodes (Cic., Brut., 312). Again, under the Republic Xenocles was sent to defend, before the Senate, the province of Asia against charges of Mithridatism (Strab., XIII, 614). Under Domitian, Scopelianus was deputed by the same province to protest against the Imperial edict forbidding the growing of vines outside Italy (Philstr., VS, I, 21, 520). Aelius Aristides got help from Marcus Aurelius for the reconstruction of Smyrna after the earthquake that took place there in the year 178 (Arstd., XIX-XX K.; cf. A. Boulanger, Aelius Aristide, pp. 387-389). And these of course are only a few examples. In the fifth century again, Synesius of Cyrene was elected Bishop of Ptolemais (c. 410) although he was a dubious Christian and as a good pupil of Hypatia and a convinced neo-Platonist had many objections against the Faith. Surely this would be chiefly because his fellow-citizens felt sure that his prestige and talent as an orator meant that he would serve them well in interceding with the governors and the Emperor?

22

Greek eloquence in Graeco-Roman times: F. Blass, Die Griechische Beredsamkeit in dem Zeitraum von Alexander bis Augustus, Berlin, 1865 (which is a good deal less accurate than his great Attische Beredsamkeit², 4 vols., Leipzig, 1887-1898); E. Norden, Die Antike Kunstprosa³·⁴, Leipzig, 1915-1923; A. Boulanger, Aelius Aristide, et la Sophistique dans la Province d'Asie au IIᵉ siècle de notre ère, Paris, 1923, pp. 37-108; W. Kroll, in Pauly-Wissowa, Suppl., VII, c. 1039-1138, s.v. "Rhetorik"; and the two "Berichte" by E. Richtsteig, in C. Bursian, Jahresbericht über die Fortschritte der klassischen Altertumswissenschaft, 234 (1932), pp. 1-66; 238 (1933), pp. 1-104.

23

Is the "academic" nature of Greek (and Graeco-Roman) culture a sign of decadence? I once believed it was, like many others (cf. my *Saint Augustin et la Fin de la Culture antique*, pp. 89–94), but I am not quite so sure nowadays. . . .

24

The terms "rhetor" and "sophist" are not interchangeable theoretically (although in fact they ended up by meaning pretty well the same thing): the ῥήτωρ was originally (from Aristophanes to Strabo) an orator in the full sense of the word, someone who addressed the assembly and the tribunal. The σοφιστής, on the other hand, was a technician, a teacher whose words were only heard inside school. Under the influence of Plato's attacks, the name rather went down in meaning; then at the time of the Empire the Later Sophists did something to redeem its prestige, infusing into the Sophists' "epideictic" eloquence a certain political content and significance. The rhetor, faced with this, tended to become a teacher and nothing more, someone whose only interest was in the formal rules of his art. Cf. for this development, which is rather complicated, the suggestions made by LIDDELL-SCOTT-ST.-JONES, s.vv.; A. BOULANGER, *Aelius Aristide*, p. 76, n. 3; W. KROLL, in PAULY-WISSOWA, *Suppl.*, VII, c. 1040; H. VON ARNIM, *Leben und Werke des Dio von Prusa*, p. 67.

25

"Chorus, Thiasos, Phratria" as applied to the pupils who gathered round one teacher: cf. L. GRASBERGER, *Erziehung und Unterricht im klassischen Alterthum*, III, pp. 409–410.

26

We have not had any French account of rhetoric since A. E. CHAIGNET wrote *La Rhétorique et son Histoire*, Paris, 1888 (written after the reform of 1885, which the author deplored: cf. his Preface, p. vii); for further details: R. VOLKMANN, *Die Rhetorik der Griechen und Römer in systematischer Uebersicht dargestellt*[2], Leipzig, 1885; W. KROLL, in PAULY-WISSOWA, *Suppl.*, VII, c. 1039–1138, s.v. "Rhetorik".

27

The eulogy in music exams: J. FREI, *De Certaminibus thymelicis*, Basle Dissertation, 1900, pp. 34–41, brought up to date by L. ROBERT, *Bibliothèque de l'Ecole des Hautes-Etudes*, fasc. 272, pp. 17 *et seq.*, esp. 21–23.

28

For "chironomy", or sign-language, cf. J. COUSIN, *Etudes sur Quinttilien*, I, "Contribution à la recherche des sources de l'Institution oratoire" (Paris, 1935, pp. 625–627), and the classic by C. SITTL, *Die Gebärden der Griechen und Römer*, Leipzig, 1890, *passim*.

29

The "canon" of orators: cf. *supra*, n. 2 of Chap. VII of Part Two.

30

Atticism. The basic work is still the powerful study by W. SCHMID, *Der Atticismus in seinen Hauptvertretern*, 4 vols., Stuttgart, 1887–1896. In Germany between the years 1880 and 1900 the problem of Atticism, its history and its nature, gave rise to one of those magnificent controversies between the learned that are important in philological circles: E. RHODE, W. SCHMID, E. NORDEN, U. VON WILAMOWITZ-MÖLLENDORF all took part in it. The final balance-sheet will be found in A. BOULANGER, *Aelius Aristide*, pp. 58–108; W. KROLL, in PAULY-WISSOWA, *Suppl.*, VII, c. 1105–1108. The final result was not all on the credit side. . . .

31

On Demetrius Phalereus, cf. finally E. BAYER, "Demetrios Phalereus der Athener", *Tübinger Beiträge zur Altertumswissenschaft*, XXXVI, Tübingen, 1942.

32

For the subjects used for the "controversies" and "suasions", cf. the classic by H. BORNECQUE, *Les Déclamations et les Déclamateurs d'après Sénèque le Père*, Lille, 1902; "Les Sujets de Suasoria chez les Romains", in *Revue d'Histoire de la Philosophie et d'Histoire générale de la Civilisation*, 1934, pp. 1 et seq.; W. MOREL, in PAULY-WISSOWA, XV, I, c. 496–499, s.v. "Melete"; *ibid.*, II R., IV, 1, c. 469–471, s.v. "Suasoria"; W. KROLL, *ibid.*, *Suppl.*, VII, c. 1119–1124.

33

St. Basil and St. Gregory Nazianzen's stay in Athens: cf. S. GIET, *Sasimes, une méprise de saint Basile*, Paris, 1941, p. 31, n. 1 (Basil, 351–355; Gregory, 351– [apparently] 356); P. GALLAY, *La Vie de saint Grégoire de Nazianze*, Lyons, 1943, pp. 36–37: "in about the year 350", "between 358 and 359". It seems to have been quite the usual thing to spend eight years on rhetoric, according to LIBANIUS: *Or.*, I, 26.

34

For the eulogies known as "paradoxal" (the technical term would be "adoxal", for the old theory, with its usual talent for hair-splitting, distinguished between different kinds of eulogy—ἔνδοξα, ἄδοξα, ἀμφίδοξα, παράδοξα: *Rhet. Gr.*, III, 346, 9–19, MEN.): cf. A. STANLEY-PEASE, "Things without Honor", in *Classical Philology*, XXI (1926), pp. 27–42; hence J. COUSIN, *Etudes sur Quintilien*, I, p. 192.

35

Rhetoric's formal beauty: I have already given a brief sketch of this opinion in *Saint Augustin et la Fin de la Culture antique*, p. 83, following NIETZSCHE and many others, e.g. L. PETIT DE JULLEVILLE, *L'Ecole d'Athènes au IVᵉ siècle après Jésus-Christ*, Paris, 1868 (there is no point in turning up one's nose at these old books), pp. 104–107.

36

On the cynics, see D. R. DUDLEY, *A History of Cynicism from Diogenes to the Sixth Century A.D.*, London, 1937, esp. pp. 26 et seq., 59, 122.

37

For the origins and constituents of this ideal of the "philosophic life", cf. the essay by W. JÄGER, "Ueber Ursprung und Kreislauf des philosophischen Lebensideals", in *Sitzungsberichte* of the Berlin Academy of Sciences, *Philos.-hist. Klasse*, 1928, xxv. pp. 390–421.

38

On the subject of the women philosophers of antiquity the old work by G. MENAGE should always be read: *Historia Mulierum philosopharum* (translated into French in

Vie des plus illustres philosophes de l'Antiquité, Paris, 1796, II, pp. 379–469); cf. M. MEUNIER, *Prolégomènes* to his *Femmes pythagoriciennes, Fragments et Lettres*, Paris, 1932.

39

Conversion to philosophy: cf. the remarks in my *Saint Augustin et la Fin de la Culture antique*, pp. 161 *et seq.*, esp. 169–173; A. D. NOCK, *Conversion, the Old and New in Religion from Alexander the Great to Augustine of Hippo*, Oxford, 1933, pp. 164–186.

40

For the conversion of Dionysus of Prusa, see the classic by H. VON ARNIM, *Leben und Werke des Dio von Prusa*, Berlin, 1898, pp. 223 *et seq.*; L. FRANÇOIS, *Essai sur Dion Chrysostome*, Paris, 1921, pp. 5 *et seq.*

41

The succession of "scholiarchs" in the Athenian schools of philosophy: cf. the table given by K. PRÄCHTER in F. UEBERWEG, *Grundriss der Geschichte der Philosophie*,[11] I, pp. 663–666.

42

Epictetus in Nicopolis: see finally, for a brief account: J. SOUILHE in the Introduction to his edition, *Entretiens*, coll. Budé, I, Paris, 1943, pp. viii *et seq.*

43

Modern scholarship has done a great deal of work on the diatribe, and has not always avoided the danger of giving too static an idea of something that was essentially fluid in form: cf. P. WENDLAND, "Philo und die kynisch-stoische Diatribe", *Beiträge zur Geschichte der griechischen Philosophie und Religion*, Berlin, 1895; R. BULTMANN, *Der Stil der Paulinischen Predigt und die kynisch-stoische Diatribe*, Göttingen, 1910; A. OLTRAMARE, *Les Origines de la Diatribe romaine*, Geneva thesis, 1926.

44

The history of the Hellenistic "doxographical" tradition has been admirably dealt with by H. DIELS in the *Prolegomena* to his edition of the *Doxographi Graeci*[2], Berlin, 1929.

45

The philosopher's expounding of texts, e.g. by Epictetus: cf. I. BRUNS, *Die Schola Epicteti*, Kiel Dissertation, 1897, pp. 3 *et seq.*; J. SOUILHE, Introduction, *cit. supra*, pp. xxxiii *et seq.*

46

We know far less—the evidence is less direct, less precise and less factual—about the daily life in the schools of philosophy than about the grammarians' and rhetors' schools: cf. the interesting inferences drawn by W. BOUSSET, *Jüdisch-christlicher Schulbetrieb in Alexandria und Rom*, pp. 1–7, and A. J. FESTUGIERE, "Le Logos hermétique d'enseignement," in *Revue des Etudes grecques*, LV (1942), pp. 77–108.

47

The struggle between philosophers and rhetors for control over the education of the young has been most felicitously analysed by H. VON ARNIM in the Introduction to *Leben und Werke des Dio von Prusa*, pp. 1–114: *Sophistik, Rhetorik, Philosophie, in ihrem Kampf um die Jugendbildung*; for the period with which we are concerned here, pp. 37 *et seq.*

48

The persistence of the conflict between philosophical and oratorical culture in the Middle Ages, cf. the material in my *Saint Augustin et la Fin de la Culture antique*, p. 173, and in *Revue du Moyen Age Latin*, I, 1945, p. 201, in which, in connection with Sidonius and Cl. Mamert., I refer readers of A. LOYEN, *Sidoine Apollinaire et l'Esprit précieux en Gaule*, Paris, 1943, to P. COURCELLE, *Les Lettres grecques en Occident*, Paris, 1943, pp. 223 *et seq.*

49

On the interesting and subtle position of Dionysius of Halicarnassus, cf. e.g. G. KAIBEL, "Dionysios von Halikarnassos und die Sophistik," in *Hermes*, XX (1885), pp. 497–513; W. R. ROBERTS's critical edition of *Dionysius of Halicarnassus on Literary Composition*, London, 1910.

50

The argument between philosophers and rhetors about the "theses" has been treated by H. VON ARNIM in the Introduction already mentioned to his *Dio von Prusa*, pp. 93–96.

51

Rhetoric annexed by the Stoics to philosophy: cf. VON ARNIM, *ibid.*, pp. 78–79; the clearest passage is D. L. VII, 41: "The Stoics teach that logic is divided into two parts, rhetoric and dialectics."

52

For Philo of Larissa, whose philosophy is so favourable to rhetoric that he seems like a typical Sophist of the old school, cf. once again VON ARNIM, *ibid.*, pp. 97 *et seq.*

53

The establishment of schools of philosophy in Athens at the end of the fourth century: cf. the subtle observations by W. S. FERGUSON, *Hellenistic Athens, An Historical Essay*, London, 1911, pp. 60–61, 104–107, 129, 214–216.

54

On Herod Atticus, P. GRAINDOR, "Un Milliardaire antique, Hérode Atticus et sa Famille", *Recueil des Travaux de l'Université égyptienne*, VII, Cairo, 1930.

55

Asianism has usually been studied in connection with Atticism (cf. the books referred to in n. 30): here again criticism has occasionally tended to harden concepts that should not be treated as though they were chemical substances with fixed properties.

56

The kings of Pergamus as patrons of learning outside their own kingdom: in Chapter II (Part Two) we have discussed their generosity towards the schools in Delphi and Rhodes; W. S. FERGUSON, *Hellenistic Athens*, pp. 234–236, describes the Attalides showering favours upon the Athenian philosophers instead of trying to attract them into their own capital in the way that other Hellenistic kings were doing at the time.

57

For the Rhodes schools and their fame: F. DELLA CORTE, "Rodi e l'istituzione dei pubblici studi nel II secolo a. C.", in *Atti* of the Turin Academy, 74, 2 (1939), pp. 255–272.

As regards Posidonius (canonized by K. GRONAU, *Poseidonios*, Leipzig, 1914; K. REINHARDT, *Poseidonios*, Munich, 1931; J. HEINEMANN, *Poseidonios*, Breslau, 1921–1928), I have shown how, in connection with the origin of the subjects included in the seven liberal arts, the fascination that this great Rhodian philosopher exerted on our learned contemporaries could lead to error (see my *Saint Augustin et la Fin de la Culture antique*, p. 215); I am not the only person to react against the "Posidonius myth": cf. J. F. DOBSON, "The Poseidonios Myth", in the *Classical Quarterly*, 1918, pp. 179 *et seq.*, esp. p. 181; P. BOYANCE, *Etudes sur le Songe de Scipion*, Paris, 1936, p. 87; K. PRÜMM, *Religionsgeschichtliches Handbuch für den Raum der altchristlichen Umwelt*, Freiburg-im-Breisgau, 1943, pp. 158–159; and M. CROISET in his account of Reinhardt in *Journal des Savants*, 1922, pp. 145–152.

58

The middle position of Rhodian eloquence between Asianism and Atticism: cf. A. BOULANGER, *Aelius Aristide*, p. 61.

As a matter of interest it is worth mentioning the Marseilles schools that existed at the other end of the Greek world; their fame, although it was much more limited in character, reached as far as Rome. In the first century B.C. many Roman families sent their sons there to learn about Greek culture because it was quieter and less expensive and better morally than the big schools on the Aegean: cf. M. CLERC, *Massalia, Histoire de Marseille dans l'Antiquité*, II, Marseilles, 1929, pp. 314 *et seq.*; I, 1927, p. 463.

59

For "La Sophistique dans la Province d'Asie au IIe siècle de notre ère", I must refer once again to the excellent essay by A. BOULANGER, *Aelius Aristide*, Paris, 1923, which has this as its sub-title; cf. esp. pp. 74–108, 16–19, 37–57.

60

On the student life in the "universities" of the Later Empire, see A. MÜLLER, "Studentenleben im 4. Jahrhundert n. Chr.", in *Philologus*, LXIX (1910), pp. 292–317; it can always be studied in L. PETIT DE JULLEVILLE, *L'Ecole d'Athènes au IVe siècle*, Paris, 1868: through the swollen oratorical style fashionable at the time one can discern a real effort to think out the subject and develop the material. F. SCHEMMEL, on the other hand, in an effort to be objective, restricts himself to a depressing list of data in the series of articles to which I have already referred *supra*, Chap. VIII, n. 10.

PART THREE

CHAPTER I

1

The essential facts about the earliest kind of education in Rome have been collected by E. JULLIEN in *Les Professeurs de Littérature dans l'ancienne Rome*, pp. 11-33, and A. GWYNN, *Roman Education from Cicero to Quintilian*, pp. 11-33 (*sic*).

2

A history of Roman education thus has no need to venture out on to the hazardous ground of proto-history. For G. DUMEZIL, for example, in *Naissance de Rome* (*Jupiter, Mars, Quirinus*, II) Paris, 1944, pp. 47-58, Rome was not *originally* a society of peasants and shepherds but a threefold community ruled in Indo-European fashion by a dual aristocracy of warriors and priests, the peasants being reduced to the level of a sort of third estate. But this theory takes us well beyond the bounds of history proper, into a kind of fabulous prologue which we may safely ignore here.

3

The expulsion of the kings as the Latin aristocracy's revenge on the Etruscan "tyrants": I have adopted the modern interpretation of this revolution: cf. e.g. E. PAIS–J. BAYET, "Histoire Romaine" (in G. GLOTZ, *Histoire générale*, III), I², pp. 54-55; and finally S. MAZZARINO, *Della Monarchia allo stato Repubblicano*, Catania, 1945.

4

"Le Latin, langue de Paysans": see the very illuminating essay under this title by J. MAROUZEAU in *Mélanges linguistiques offerts à M. J. Vendryès, Collection Linguistique publiée par la Société linguistique de Paris*, 17, Paris, 1925, pp. 251-264, which refers to the classic work by A. ERNOUT, "Les Eléments dialectaux du Vocabulaire latin", in the same collection, 3, Paris, 1909, and the valuable pages in A. MEILLET, "Esquisse d'une Histoire de la Langue latine"⁴, pp. 94-118, and the chronological details in G. DEVOTO, *Storia della lingua di Roma* (*Storia di Roma*), Rome, XXIII, 1940, pp. 101-103.

5

The development of Roman houses: I have adopted the theory developed, with slight differences of emphasis, by G. PATRONI, A. BOETHIUS and P. GRIMAL: see finally the latter's *Les Jardins romains à la fin de la République et aux deux premiers siècles de l'Empire, Essai sur le Naturalisme romain*, Paris, 1943, pp. 216 *et seq.*

6

Tirocinium fori: to JULLIEN and GWYNN should be added the short article, s. v. § a by J. REGNER, in PAULY-WISSOWA, II R., VI, 2, c. 1450. For the age when the toga of manhood could be worn—it varied—*id., b*, c. 1452.

7

There were in fact two kinds of *tribuni militum*—the *comitiati*, elected each year by the people, and the *rufuli* whose choice was left to the general commander-in-chief: FEST., p. 260; but cf. LENGLE, in PAULY-WISSOWA II R., VI, 2, c. 2439-2442, s. v. "Tribunus", 9.

8

The influence of family traditions on Roman historiography: see esp. E. PAIS in his first *Storia di Roma*, "Critica della tradizione" . . . I, 1, Turin, 1898, pp. 117-126, and finally, E. PAIS-J. BAYET, *Histoire romaine*, I², pp. 25-26; F. MÜNZER, *Römische Adelsparteien und Adelsfamilien*, Stuttgart, 1920, pp. 4 and *passim* (cf. p. 432, s. v. "Familienüberlieferung und Fälschungen der Ueberlieferung").

9

On the *devotio*, cf. s. v. the slightly outmoded article by A. BOUCHE-LECLERCQ, in DAREMBERG-SAGLIO, II, i, pp. 113a-119b; G. STÜBLER, "Die Religiosität des Livius" (*Tübinger Beiträge zur Altertumswissenschaft*, XXXV), Tübingen, 1941, pp. 173-204, and esp. the discussion by J. HEURGON, *Recherches sur l'Histoire, la Religion et la Civilisation de Capoue préromaine*, pp. 260-270. For the identification of the three Decii, cf. MÜNZER, in PAULY-WISSOWA, IV, 2, c. 2279-2285, s. v. "Decius", Nos. 15-17.

10

For the story about Regulus being taken prisoner by the Carthaginians and then sent back to Rome with peace proposals, cf. the whole collection of texts examined by E. PAIS, *Ricerche sulla storia e sul diritto pubblico di Roma*, IV, pp. 411 *et seq*.

11

The feeling for religion in the Roman political ideal: I have summarised the excellent analysis by F. ALTHEIM, *A History of Roman Religion*, London, 1938, pp. 411-432 ("The Causes of the Greatness of Rome").

12

Luxury and "softness" as classic symptoms of decadence: cf. A. PASSERINI, "La τρυφή nella storiografia ellenistica", in *Studi italiani di filologia classica*, 1934, pp. 3-56; J. PERRET, *Siris, Recherches critiques sur l'Histoire de la Siritide avant 433-432*, Paris, 1941, p. 267.

13

For a comparison of Roman and Greek physical training, cf. E. Norman GARDINER, *Athletics of the Ancient World*, pp. 117-119, and E. MEHL, "Die Ueberlieferung über das Turn im römischen Heere" (with reference to Vegetius, I, 6-18), in *Mitteilungen des Vereins klassischer Philologen in Wien*, 1928, pp. 21-27. On the *ludus Troiae*, cf. s. v. J. TOUTAIN, in DAREMBERG-SAGLIO, V, pp. 493a-496b; K. SCHNEIDER, in PAULY-WISSOWA, XIII, 2, c. 2059-2067, and E. GIGLIOLI, "L'oinochoe di Tragliatella", in *Studi Etruschi*, III (1929), pp. 121-134, pl. XXIV.

14

On Roman "encyclopaedism", cf. O. JAHN, "Ueber römische Encyclopädien", in *Berichte* of the Leipzig Academy of Sciences, *Ph.-hist. Klasse*, III, 4 (1850), pp. 263-287; F. DELLA CORTE, *Enciclopedisti Latini*, Genoa, 1946.

15

On Celsus's encyclopaedia, cf. F. MARX's prolegomena to his edition in *Corpus Medicorum Latinorum*, I, Leipzig, 1915, pp. v–cxiv.

16

Pliny makes Q. Metellus Macedonicus, Lucius's son, but he was only his grandson: cf. MÜNZER, in PAULY-WISSOWA, III, I, c. 1203, s. v. "Caecilius", No. 72 (for Lucius), and c. 1213, No. 94 (for Macedonicus).

CHAPTER II

1

The introduction of Greek education into Rome: I have followed throughout E. JULLIEN, *Les Professeurs de Littérature* (pp. 34–111), and A. GWYNN, *Roman Education* (pp. 34–69), but the subject is so obviously important that it has been tackled by all the historians of Roman culture, no matter what their point of view: cf. e.g. A. GRENIER, *Le Génie romain dans la Religion, la Pensée et l'Art* (from the earliest times to Augustus), Paris, 1925, pp. 136–185, 199–320; J. CARCOPINO, "Histoire romaine" (in G. GLOTZ, *Histoire générale*, III), II, 1, pp. 47–58; P. GRIMAL, *Les Jardins romains à la fin de la République et aux deux premiers siècles de l'Empire*, Paris, 1943, pp. 23–26, from whom I have borrowed the phrase, "the spiritual revolution of the second century".

2

The date of the foundation of Cumae has been neatly settled by J. BERARD, *La Colonisation grecque de l'Italie méridionale et de la Sicile dans l'Antiquité: l'Histoire et la Légende*, Paris, 1941, p. 62.

3

I still insist on the possibility of a period of Etruscan education in Rome anterior to any Greek influence, in spite of the objections made by JULLIEN, *Les Professeurs de Littérature*, pp. 29–33: Jullien was writing in 1885, and today we know more about the greatness and expansion of the Etruscan civilisation in Italy in the fifth and fourth centuries B.C.: cf. the remarks by A. PIGANIOL, "Clio", III, *Histoire de Rome*[2], Paris, 1946, pp. 58, 70; and for a general treatment of the Etruscan question the remarkable work of synthesis by J. BERARD, *La Colonisation grecque*, pp. 492–524.

4

The extent of the civilisation of Campania before the Roman Conquest: cf. the influence of Capuan decorative art on Rome, Satricum, Veii, Caere: J. HEURGON, *Recherches sur l'Histoire, la Religion et la Civilisation de Capoue préromaine des origines à la deuxième guerre punique*, Paris, 1942, p. 351.

5

The Greek influence on Roman religion: here again all historians of Rome have had to take this phenomenon into account; as specialist works, cf. e.g. J. BAYET, *Les Origines de l'Hercule romain*, Paris, 1926; F. ALTHEIM, "Griechische Götter im alten Rom", in *Religionsgeschichtliche Versuche und Vorarbeiten*, XXII, 1, Giessen, 1930.

6

The influence of Syracuse on the building of the so-called "Servius' Wall": G. SAEFLUND, "Le Mura di Roma repubblicana" (*Skrifter* of the Swedish Institute in Rome, I), Lund, 1932, pp. 169–174 (though G. LUGLI supports in part the traditional date—the sixth century. Cf. *I monumenti antichi di Roma*, II, Rome, 1934, pp. 99–138). For the friendly relations between Rome and Syracuse in the time of the Elder Dionysius, cf. *ibid.*, p. 172, n. 3, and for a more general view E. PAIS, "Gli Elementi sicelioti nella più antica storia Romana", in *Italia antica, Ricerche di storie e di geografia storica*, I, Bologna, 1922, pp. 61–132. For the ancient relationship between Rome and Marseilles, cf. M. CLERC, *Massalia*, I, Marseilles, 1927, pp. 178–184.

7

On the "Hellenistic" civilisation of pre-Roman Campania—a civilisation which had its own particular flavour, of course: it was a kind of Hellenistic civilisation, but an original kind—cf. the highly revealing book by J. HEURGON, mentioned in n. 4: cf. esp. the very far-reaching stylistic analysis of the architectonic terra-cottas, pp. 337, 352, and the conclusion, p. 443; for its influence on Rome, cf. E. PAIS, "Gl, Elementi italioti, sannitici e campani nella più antica civiltà romana", in *Italia antica*, I, pp. 133–177. As for Pompeii, cf. the typical title of the book by F. VON DUHN, *Pompeii, eine hellenistische Stadt in Italien* (*Aus Natur und Geisteswelt*, 114)[3], Leipzigi 1918.

8

For the VEREIIA PUMPAIIANA and the Hellenistic palestra in Pompeii, cf. M. DELLA CORTE, *Juventus*, Arpino, 1924, pp. 44–60.

9

The Latin vocabulary, which is studded with Hellenisms, shows how far Greek influence had penetrated into popular life: cf. A. MEILLET, *Esquisse d'une Histoire de la Langue latine*[4], pp. 106–117; cf. 87–94. G. DEVOTO, *Storia della lingua di Roma*, pp. 88–91, 127–131.

10

For the identification of the Crassus mentioned by VALERIUS MAXIMUS, VIII, 7, 6, and QUINTILIAN, XI, 2, 50, cf. MÜNZER, in PAULY-WISSOWA, XIII, I, c. 334–338, s. v. "Licinius", No. 72.

11

The Roman aristocracy open to Greek influence: a protest must be made against the narrow and unnecessarily harsh judgment expressed by M. HOLLEAUX, *Rome, la Grèce et les Monarchies hellénistiques au IIIe siècle avant Jésus-Christ*, Paris, 1921, pp. 170–171; cf. the drastic criticism—hidden perhaps by the intentional sobriety of the style—by J. CARCOPINO, *Points de vue sur l'Impérialisme romain*, Paris, 1934, pp. 58 *et seq.*

There is far more historical understanding in the slightly out-of-date, wordy, but still valuable book by G. COLIN, *Rome et la Grèce de 200 à 146 avant Jésus-Christ*, Paris, 1905, pp. 97–171, 242–372 (esp. 348 *et seq.*), 524–606 (esp. 540 *et seq.*).

12

Scipio Aemilianus' "circle": cf. A. GRENIER, *Le Génie romain*, pp. 199–214; I. LANA, in *RF*, 75 (1947), pp. 44–80, 155–175.

13

The date of Crates of Mallus's embassy to Rome: I have adopted the conclusion reached by JULLIEN, in *Les Professeurs de Littérature*, pp. 369–371. The passage from Suetonius (*Gram.*, 2, 1) contains two statements that cannot be reconciled: Crates is said to have been sent to Rome by King Attalus (II, 159–138) *sub ipsam Ennii mortem* (169). One of these must be sacrificed—in my opinion, the second, which is expressed very vaguely, rather than the first. For the opposite point of view cf. e.g. H. FUNAIOLI, *Grammaticae Romanae fragmenta*, I, Leipzig, 1907, p. xi.

14

Music in Roman life and Roman education: cf. L. FRIEDLÄNDER-G. WISSOWA, *Darstellungen aus der Sittengeschichte Roms in der Zeit von Augustus bis zum Ausgang der Antonine*[10], II, pp. 163–190; and in girls' education, I, pp. 271–272.

15

For the Emperor as the ideal man, cf. finally A. PIGANIOL, "L'Empire chrétien" (in G. GLOTZ, *Histoire générale*, III, *Histoire romaine*, IV, 2), Paris, 1947, pp. 309–310, and the authors referred to in this book. The last word has not yet been said on this highly interesting subject: in my opinion another title could be thrown in—that of a lost book by Origen, *That the King Alone is a Poet* (PORPH., *Vit. Plot.*, 3), despite the view of R. CADIOU (*La Jeunesse d'Origène*, Paris, 1926, pp. 253–255), who, along with many others, takes this to mean "that the King [of heaven] alone is the Creator [of the world]". For the Early Empire cf. also H. BARDON, *Les Empereurs romains et les Lettres latines, d'Auguste à Hadrien*, Paris, 1940.

16

Stadium-games in Rome: L. FRIEDLANDER-G. WISSOWA, *Sittengeschichte Roms*[10], II, pp. 147–162.

17

The degeneration of palestras and gymnasiums amongst the Romans: cf. finally P. GRIMAL, *Les Jardins romains*, pp. 262 *et seq.* Palestras tacked on to the hot baths: cf. the classic example of the "Stabies" baths in Pompeii (H. THEDENAT-A. PIGANIOL, *Pompei*[3], Paris, 1928, II, p. 109) and those in Herculaneum (A. MAIURI, *Ercolano*, Rome, 1936, pp. 30–33).

18

For "L'Alphabet de Marsiliana et les origines de l'écriture à Rome", cf. the excellent article under this title by A. GRENIER, in *Mélanges d'Archéologie et d'Histoire* of the French School in Rome, XLI (1924), pp. 1–42. The question has often been treated since, of course: cf. D. DIRINGER, *L'Alfabeto nella storia della civiltà*, Florence, 1937, pp. 371–400.

19

The Etruscan syllabary: D. ANZIANI, "Le Vase Galassi", in *Mélanges Cagnat*, Paris, 1912, pp. 17–30, and, more recently, as also for the other "model alphabets", D. DIRINGER, *L'Alfabeto*, pp. 378–379.

20

Livius Andronicus created not only the Roman epic for teaching purposes, but also Latin lyric and dramatic poetry: his works were composed at the Senate's request for religious ceremonies copied from Greece—there was a terrific crisis during the Second Punic War, and the Senate was trying to get protection from the gods by whatever means it could: stage plays (Andronicus's first tragedy was performed in the year 240: CIC., *Brut.*, 72), hymns sung in solemn supplication (like the one that he composed in 207 when Hasdrubal was descending upon Italy: LIV., XXVII, 37, 7).

21

History of the *grammatici Latini*: cf. SUET., *Gram.*, 5 *et seq.*, and the passages collected by H. FUNAIOLI, *Grammaticae Romanae Fragmenta*, I, Leipzig, 1907.

For Varro's *De Grammatica*, cf. *ibid.*, pp. 205-206. For a treatise in two books, *De litteris syllabisque, item de metris*, attributed to a certain ENNIUS, a different person from the poet of Rudiae, and later, cf. SUET., *Gram.*, 1, 2, and FUNAIOLI, *op. cit.*, pp. 101-102.

22

In my interpretation of the edict of the year 92 against the Latin rhetors I have followed J. CARCOPINO, *Histoire romaine*, I, 1, p. 347; cf. also, and for the *Rhetoric to Herennius*, F. MARX, *Prolegomena* to his edition, Leipzig, 1894, pp. 141-156, and A. GWYNN, *Roman Education*, pp. 59-69.

23

For Cicero's education, which was fundamentally that of an aristocrat, cf. my "Défense de Ciceron", *Revue historique*, CLXXVII (1936), pp. 58-59, in which I follow GWYNN, *op. cit.*, pp. 69 *et seq.*

24

In the passage from the *De Grammaticis et Rhetoribus* (16, 2) already mentioned in connection with the introduction of Virgil into school syllabuses, SUETONIUS says that Q. Caecilius Epirota *"primus dicitur Latine ex tempore disputasse"*—"is reckoned to have been the first person to improvise Latin declamations".

25

Latin philosophers' Greek education: cf. my *Saint Augustin et la Fin de la Culture antique*, p. 42, and: E. ALBERTINI, *La Composition dans les ouvrages philosophiques de Sénèque*, Paris, 1923, pp. 206-215.

26

For the place of architecture in Roman culture, cf. VARRO'S essays on architecture (F. W. RITSCHL, "De M. Varronis disciplinarum libris", in *Opuscula philologica*, III, Leipzig, 1877, pp. 352 *et seq.*) and VITRUVIUS.

For the *Agrimensores*, cf. M. SCHANZ, "Geschichte der römischen Literatur" (in I. VON MUELLER, *Handbuch der klassischen Altertumswissenschaft*, VIII), II, 2, §501-502; IV, 2, §1138, 1141; M. CANTOR, *Die römische Agrimensoren*, Leipzig, 1875, and the brief account by R. DE CATERINI, "Gromatici veteres", in *Rivista del Catasto e dei servizi tecnici erariali*, II (1935), pp. 261-358.

27

For the *archiatri* in Latin countries, cf. S. REINACH, in DAREMBERG-SAGLIO, III, 2, p. 1674b, s.v. "Medicus"; WELLMANN, in PAULY-WISSOWA, II, 1, c. 464-466, s.v., and for a general treatment of medicine in Rome: T. Clifford ALLBUTT, *Greek Medicine in Rome*, London, 1921.

28

Roman writings on medicine and the veterinary art in the fourth to the fifth centuries, cf. SCHANZ, *Geschichte der Römischen Literatur*, IV, 1, §845, 847–849; 2, §1126–1137.

CHAPTER III

1

For the expression *utraque lingua*, cf. the authorities collected by L. LAFOSCADE, *Influence du latin sur le grec*, in J. PSICHARI, "Etudes de philologie néo-grecque", *Bibliothèque de l'Ecole des Hautes-Etudes, Sciences philologiques et historiques*, 92nd fasc., Paris, 1892, pp. 117–118. Before Horace, cf. CICERO, *De Off.*, I, i, 1: *ut par sis in utriusque orationis facultate.*

2

The comparative study of Latin and Greek: this was one of the few original features of Roman culture. No doubt there were Greek grammarians practising too, but they were teaching in Rome and they had Latin pupils, e.g. Claudius Didymus, the author of a περὶ τῆς παρὰ ʿΡωμαίοις ἀναλογίας (cf. COHN, in PAULY-WISSOWA, V, 1, c. 473, s.v. "Didymos", No. 10) and probably of a commentary on CICERO'S *Republic* wrongly attributed by Ammianus Marcellinus to the famous Didymus Chalcenterius (COHN, *ibid.*, c. 471, 2, "Didymos", No. 8); cf. however ATH., XV, 680 D: a περὶ ʿΡωμαϊκῆς διαλέκτου by Apion: was this the Alexandrian grammarian Apion Plistonices?

Comparisons of Greek and Latin authors: cf. W. KROLL, *Studien zum Verständnis der römischen Literatur*, Stuttgart, 1924, pp. 14–16.

3

The hatred of Rome in Greek literature: G. SCHNAYDER, "De infenso alienigenarum in Romanos animo", in *Eos*, XXX (1927), pp. 113–149; to this should be added, amongst other evidence, HIPPOLYTUS of Rome, *In Danielem*, IV, 8, 7; 9, 2.

4

The linguistic frontier between Greek and Latin: the map which accompanies the text has been drawn up by my pupil C. R. AGERON, who has used and completed the works by: A. BUDINSKY, *Die Ausbreitung der lateinischen Sprache über Italien und die Provinzen des römischen Reiches*, Berlin, 1881; C. JIRECEK, "Die Romanen in den Städten Dalmatiens", in *Denkschriften* of the Vienna Academy, *Phil.-hist. Kl.*, 1902; G. SEURE, "Nicopolis ad Istrum", in *Revue archéologique*, 1907, II, pp. 266–271, 414; D. P. DIMITROV, "Ueber die römischen Grabsteine in Bulgarien", in *Jahrbuch* of the German Archaeological Institute, *Arch. Anzeiger*, 1937, c. 511–526 (which proves that Greek gave way to Latin in that part of Thrace which became part of the Mediterranean districts of Dacia in 275: this seems to have been the only noticeable change in the Balkans); R. VULPE, *Histoire ancienne de la Dobroudja*, the Rumanian Academy, "Connaissance de la Terre et de la Pensée roumaines", IV, *La Dobroudja*, Bucharest, 1938, pp. 35–454; D. TSONTCHEV, *Annales du Musée de Plovdiv*, vol. II, pp. 69–83; I. STEFANOVA, *ibid.*, pp. 85–92.

5

P. Collart has made a thorough study of the fate of Latin in the Roman colonies of Macedonia: *Philippes, ville de Macédoine, depuis ses origines jusqu'à la fin de l'Epoque romaine* (*Travaux et Memoires*, published by foreign members of the French School in Athens, V), Paris, 1937, pp. 300-316: "Serta Kazaroviana", *Bulletin de l'Institut archéologique bulgare*, XVI, 1950, pp. 7-16.

6

Greek translations of official government acts: T. Mommsen, "Le Droit public romain", in Mommsen-Marquardt, *Manuel des Antiquités romaines*, VII, French trans., Paris, 1891, pp. 201-202; Lafoscade, *art. cit.*, in n. 1, pp. 96-97; G. Collin, *Rome et la Grèce de 200 à 146 avant Jésus-Christ*, Paris, 1905, pp. 142-143; L. Hahn, *Rom und Romanismus im griechisch-römischen Osten*, Leipzig, 1906, pp. 37-40, 82-85, 111-119, 211-213, 223-232.

7

"De l'Etude de la Langue latine chez les Grecs dans l'Antiquité": see the article under this title by E. Egger, in *Mémoires d'Histoire ancienne et de Philologie*, Paris, 1863, pp. 259-276, and the article by Lafoscade already mentioned, in J. Psichari, *Etudes de Philologie néo-grecque*, pp. 83-158; W. Kroll, *Studien zum Verständnis der römischen Literatur*, I, *Römer und Griechen*, pp. 1-23, esp. 8-10. cf. also L. Hahn, "Zum Sprachenkampf im römischen Reich", in *Philologus*, Suppl. X, 1907, 4, pp. 675-718; H. Zilliacus, *Zum Kampf der Weltsprachen im oströmischen Reich*, Helsinki, 1935, and Dölger's review, *Byzantinische Zeitschrift*, 1936, vol. 36, pp. 108-117.

For the careers of officials of Greek origin, see H. G. Pflaum, *Essai sur les Procurateurs équestres sous le haut-empire romain*, Paris, 1950; *Corpus des cursus procuratoriens équestres*, soon to appear.

8

Latin in Constantinople: high society, especially the court, remained Latin for a long time here. We have to wait for the accession of Tiberius II (578) before we find an Emperor of Greek origin on the throne in Byzantium.

The highly conservative ceremonial at the Byzantine court preserved Latin traces for a long time: even in the days of Constantine VII Porphyrogenetes (944-959), as can be seen from his *Book of Ceremonies*, Latin motets were sung when the Emperor entered Hagia Sophia on the great feast days (II, 83 [74]); at feasts every gesture by the Emperor was received with Latin acclamations, acclamations which the Porphyrogenetes wrote down phonetically—κωνσέϱβεθ Δέους ἠμπέϱιουμ βέστϱουμ—and translated into Greek (II, 84 [75])—when he understood the meaning, at least, which was not always the case: in the military acclamation τούμβηϰας, for instance, he did not recognize the original *Tu vincas!*—"May you win!"

Again, at the end of the sixth century, commands in the Byzantine army—"Forward! Halt! Into line!"—were always given in Latin—*Move! Sta! Aequaliter ambula!*—as can be seen in the *Strategicon* attributed to the Emperor Maurice: cf. F. Lot, "La Langue de commandement dans les Armées romaines", in *Mélanges Félix Grat*, I, Paris, 1946, pp. 203-209.

9

The Hellenism of Sidonius Apollinaris and his circle: cf. A. Loyen, *Sidoine Apollinaire et l'Esprit précieux en Gaule aux derniers jours de l'Empire*, Paris, 1943, pp.

26–30; P. COURCELLE, *Les Lettres grecques en Occident de Macrobe à Cassiodore*, Paris, 1943, pp. 221–246.

10

The disappearance of Greek in the West: I have repeated, with a few slight differences of emphasis, the arguments in my *Saint Augustin et la Fin de la Culture antique*, Paris, 1937, pp. 38–46, in spite of the criticisms to which it has been subjected by my master, J. CARCOPINO, in *La Vie quotidienne à Rome à l'Apogée de l'Empire*, Paris, 1939, pp. 135–136. The evidence mentioned on p. 327, n. 32, about the Greekish "beauties" ridiculed by JUVENAL, VI, 186–196, and MARTIAL, X, 68, 10–12, does not seem to me to be very important: it is not a case of blue-stockings but of courtesans and one of the technical aspects of Greek was that it was the language of love-making, as it was of medicine and philosophy: cf. E. JULLIEN, *Les Professeurs de Littératur dans l'ancienne Rome*, p. 102. In spite, too, of the criticisms of P. BOYANCE, who has been kind enough to send me the script of a course given in 1945–1946. To their arguments I oppose, with GWYNN (*infra*, n. 13), the evidence in QUINTILIAN, which seems to me to be decisive. In any case the argument only concerns a subordinate matter: we are agreed that Roman education never gave up "basing the teaching of Latin literature on Greek" and that Greek did not begin to decline until after the third century. The only question is how to determine the date when the first symptoms of this decline appeared, and it is a very difficult matter to decide when anything actually begins in history.

On the other hand I must confess that I am unable to accept the conclusions reached in *Les Empereurs et les Lettres latines d'Auguste à Hadrien* (Paris, 1940), whose author, H. BARDON, believes he can discern (p. 127) a "movement which, from Augustus to Hadrian, increasingly inclined the Emperors to prefer Greek to Latin". Here the point of view is at fault, for it is a mistake to study the emperors apart from the cultural history of Rome as a whole, and also to study the line from Augustus to Hadrian apart from the emperors who came before and after. Cf. again pp. 196, 266, 394, 427, 452. Moreover, as regards the history of education, especially the question of languages, this book is badly informed and far too uncritical. It uses "Spartan" without giving any reasons for its confidence in a text that is so late and so full of difficulties; it reckons (pp. 127, 196) that Greek became an official language under Claudian—and yet it was Claudian who deprived a Lycian of his citizen's rights for the simple reason that he did not know any Latin, as any self-respecting citizen should: DIONYSIUS CASSIUS, LX, 17, 4; SUETONIUS, *Cl.*, 16, 2.

11

Cicero's Greek: H. S. SCRIBNER, "Cicero as a Hellenist", in the *Classical Journal*, XVI (1920), pp. 81–92 (superficial); H. J. ROSE, "The Greek of Cicero", in the *Journal of Hellenic Studies*, 41 (1921), pp. 91–146 (a valuable list: it was Rose who first noticed that many of the Greek words used by Cicero only came down to us through him). For his translations: B. FARRINGTON, *Primum Graius Homo, an Anthology of Latin Translations from the Greek*, Cambridge, 1927, pp. 27–32, 41–46, 51–59; G. CUENDET, "Cicéron et saint Jérome traducteurs", in *Revue des Etudes latines*, XI (1933), pp. 380–400; V. BUESCU's edition of the *Aratea* (a collection of critical editions by the Rumanian Institute of Latin Studies, I), Paris-Bucharest, 1941; MAROUZEAU, *Stylistique*, pp. 161–162.

W. KROLL, "Die griechische Bildung im ciceronischen Rom", in *Forschungen und Fortschritte*, 1933, pp. 200b–201b (or in *Investigacion y Progreso*, VII (1933), pp. 212–215), has strangely under-estimated the significance of the facts which he has so admirably collected in *Die Kultur der Ciceronischen Zeit*, vol. II, Leipzig, 1933, pp. 117–134: "Die griechische Bildung." If we are to believe him, Cicero was a solitary exception and the Greek culture of most of his contemporaries never went very deep, and was in fact a mere superficial veneer. This may very well have been so, but it was not only Greek culture, it was culture as a whole that, in its higher forms at least, was exceptional in Roman society. In any society a high degree of culture is the privilege of the favoured few, and in all ancient societies, which were highly aristocratic in form, these favoured few were very few indeed. But that does not affect the fundamental identity that I say existed between Greek culture and culture as a whole in Cicero's Rome.

12

A South African scholar, T. HAARHOFF, has very acutely compared the problem of Greek in Roman times to the problem of the "second language" in modern countries, inhabited, like his own, by a society in which bilingualism has been officially sanctioned: *Schools of Gaul, a Study of Pagan and Christian Education in the Last Century of the Western Empire*, Oxford, 1920, pp. 230–231.

13

A very thorough study of Quintilian's Greek, backed up by statistics, has been made by A. GWYNN in *Roman Education from Cicero to Quintilian*, pp. 226–230; though he only deals with the classics. For an understanding of the Greek technique of oratory, cf. the two books by J. COUSIN, *Etudes sur Quintilien*, I, *Contribution à la Recherche des Sources de l'Institution oratoire*, Paris, 1935; II, *Vocabulaire grec de la Terminologie rhétorique dans l'Institution oratoire*, Paris, 1936.

14

The evidence in Pliny the Younger: I owe it to P. Boyancé that I have had my attention drawn to these important passages: cf. however (and for the same point of view as ours) A. GUILLEMIN, "La Culture de Pline le Jeune", in *Mélanges Félix Grat*, Paris, 1946, pp. 78–79, 86.

15

Greek in the Late Empire: See particularly the exhaustive enquiry made by P. COURCELLE in *Les Lettres grecques en Occident, de Macrobe à Cassiodore*, Paris, 1943, whose conclusions (with a few slight changes that are not important here) I have adopted for my own purposes, transposing them, of course, according to the more general perspective which I have assumed here. The relics or revivals of Western Hellenism that he records are only relative, slight oscillations on the main curve of a general decadence—as for instance, the third-century "revival" of Hellenism under Gallienus, which has been so well covered by A. ALFÖLDI in *Fünfundzwanzig Jahre römische-germanische Kommission*, Berlin, 1930, pp. 11–51.

Cf. also G. BARDY, "La Culture grecque dans l'Occident chrétien au IVᵉ siècle" in *Recherches de Science religieuse*, XXIX (1939), pp. 5–58, the foundation-stone of a complete work of synthesis which has been announced on *La question des langues dans l'Eglise ancienne*, of which Vol. I, Paris, 1948, has so far appeared.

16

The language question in the time of St. Basil and St. Damasus: A. MICHEL in VACANT-MANGENOT-AMANN, *Dictionnaire de Théologie catholique*, s. v. "Hypostase", vol. VII, 1, c. 377–385. For the vocabulary of the Trinity: G. L. PRESTIGE, *God in Patristic Thought*, London, 1936.

17

The mediocre quality of what was left of Hellenism in Rome in the fourth century: cf. P. COURCELLE, *Les Lettres grecques en Occident*, pp. 4–5 (Symmachus was no great Greek scholar), 37–115 (St. Jerome only really learned Greek after his conversion, and then he was in the East: his Greek culture always, apparently, had "big gaps in it").

18

On the *Hermeneumata Pseudodositheana*—the attribution of this work to the grammarian DOSITHEUS, suggested by CUJAS, has now been abandoned—cf. esp. Vol. I of the *Corpus Glossariorum Latinorum* by G. GOETZ, Leipzig–Berlin, 1923, pp. 17–23; the *Hermeneumata* appear in Vol. III, 1892.

To the editions published by Goetz should be added the Latin-Greek-Coptic version—edited by W. SCHUBART in *Klio*, XIII (1913), pp. 27–38—in fifth- or more probably fourth-century papyrus which includes a fragment of colloquial dialogue very similar to the passage in the Montpellier Text (cf. G. ESAU in *Philologus*, 73, 1914–1916, pp. 157–158).

The sixth section of these *Hermeneumata*, "Hyginus' genealogy", can be dated by its *explicit* of September 11th 207 (III, 56, 30–34), and we can agree with Goetz, I, 18, that the whole thing dates from more or less the same time. The question is whether these books were written in Greek- or Latin-speaking countries. Authors who refer to them have often solved this problem one way or the other without giving it very much attention. Goetz (cf. I, 18) adopts the first alternative (*in usum Graecorum qui Latine scire vellent compositus*), and I am inclined to agree with him: the language seems rather more natural in the Greek rendering, the Latin seems more like a translation, and the little book on law, *De Manumissionibus*, and a vocabulary of legal terms (Montpellier text: III, 336, 29 *et seq.*) are more easily explained on this assumption.

Krumbacher (*De codicibus quibus Interpretamenta Pseudodositheana nobis tradita sunt*, Munich, 1883) assumes that the Munich text might have been published in Antioch, or for Antioch—because it includes a list of the names of the months current in Antioch.

But the Leyden text seems to be the only one that was intended for a purely Greek public (III, 30, 31 *et seq.*: "useful for lovers of the Latin language ..."). The others might have been for either—they were addressed to "all who wish to speak Greek and Latin" (III, 94, 21; 223, 5; 644, §1; 654, §1). The Vatican text only mentions pupils as wanting to learn Greek, III, 421, 11, but L. TRAUBE has shown in *Byzantinische Zeitschrift*, III, p. 605, that it is a later work by an Irish monk (the fact that we have in our libraries many manuscripts going back to the ninth and tenth centuries proves that these books circulated in the West).

19

The study of Latin classics in Egyptian schools in the fourth and fifth centuries: C. H. MOORE, "Latin Exercises from a Greek Schoolroom" in *Classical Philology*, XIX (1924), pp. 317–328; H. GERSTINGER in *Wiener Studien*, LV (1937), pp. 95–106 and the account of the *Chronique d'Égypte*, 27 (1939), pp. 181–182; to which should be added O. GUERAUD–P. JOUGUET, *Papyrus Fouad* I, 5: R. REMONDON, "A propos d'un papyrus de l'Enéide", in *The Journal of Juristic Papyrology* (1950) IV, pp. 239–251, and P. COLLART, *Les papyrus littéraires latins*, in *R. Ph.*, 1941, vol. 15, pp. 112–128.

20

I should like to mention, just as a reminder until better treatments of this subject appear—it has been grossly neglected so far—another technique that was to have a splendid future in the Middle Ages: in about the year 300 Dositheus translated a Latin grammar, line by line, into Greek, no doubt as a basic text-book for Latins who wanted to learn Greek; KEIL, *Grammatici Latini*, vol. VII, pp. 95 *et seq.*; cf. SCHANZ, *Geschischte der römischen Literatur*, vol. IV, i, §836. That such bi-lingual grammars were used, and used effectively, in teaching, is proved by such papyri as *PLouvre*, Eg. 7332: see E. A. LOWE, *Codices Latini Antiquiores*, V, n. 697: C. WESSELY, *Wiener Studien*, 8, 1886, 218-221. It would be interesting to discover whether this kind of thing helped to bring grammar down out of the theoretical empyrean in which it had been enthroned by its founder, Dionysius Thrax, and concentrate it on a more concrete account of the use of the language: this might help to explain why Priscianus in about the year 500, teaching Latin in Constantinople—which at that time was bilingual—should have devoted two books (L. 17-18) of his great *Grammar* to the study of syntax, which is so essential for any foreigner learning a language and so curiously left out by the first practitioners of the old science of language. The fact that these bilingual grammars were made good use of for educational purposes is proved by papyri such as *PLouvre*, Eg., 733a. cf. E. A. LOWE, *Codices Latini Antiquiores*, V. n. 697; C. WESSELY, *Wiener Studien*, 8, 1886, 218-221.

CHAPTERS IV–VI

I

This splitting-up of teaching into three different stages was not always done very rigorously: (1) in the beginning (SUET., *Gram.*, 4, 3), and even in Cicero's time (*ibid.*, 7, 2), the higher stages were still not separated very clearly, and, as in the Hellenistic schools in Rhodes, the same teacher taught both grammar and rhetoric; (2) the same confusion seems to have obtained in Gaul at the end of the fourth century, when the social structure of the Empire began to peter out: the obituary of Ausonius's Bordeaux teachers gives us a very clear idea of the teaching staff that existed when the poet was young; and one of the teachers was a certain Nepotianus, who was both grammarian and rhetor (AUSON., *Prof. Burd.*, 15). Sometimes there was even a certain amount of confusion between the schoolmaster and the grammarian (*ibid.*, 21, 4-6). Ausonius himself says that he went through the three stages one after the other—primary (*Protrept.*, 67-69), secondary (*ibid.*, 70-72) and higher (*ibid.*, 73 *et seq.*).

2

The Roman aristocracy's way of life imitated that of Hellenistic princes: cf. P. GRIMAL, *Les Jardins romains*, pp. 226-229, commenting on VITR., VI, 7, 10: the vast peristyles and the parks imitating the royal gardens of the East form part of the setting in which the Roman aristocracy chose to live.

3

The number of slaves in big Roman houses: see the conclusions arrived at by J. CARCOPINO in *La Vie quotidienne à Rome à l'apogée de l'Empire*, pp. 89-93, 323 (n. 23-26). In the first century B.C. there was the case of a self-made man—a freed slave—

who had 4,116 slaves (Pliny, *HN*, XXXIII, 135).   The Emperor may have had as many as 20,000—this figure is supplied by ATH., VI, 104 and referred by Carcopino to the Imperial house; cf. also L. FRIEDLÄNDER, *Sittengeschichte Roms*[10], II, pp. 369–372; IV, pp. 16–17.

4

The education of Roman slaves: S. L. MOHLER, "Slave Education in the Roman Empire", *Transactions of the American Philological Association*, 1940, pp. 262–280; but all the essential points are to be found in the article by O. NAVARRE, "Paedagogium", in DAREMBERG-SAGLIO, IV, i, pp. 271b–272a; cf. also W. ENSSLIN, in PAULY-WISSOWA, XVIII, 2, c. 2204–2205, s. v. "Paedagogiani", and for an interpretation of the excavations of the "Paedagogium Palatini," which is rather more complicated than Navarre imagined, cf. *ibid.*, s. v. c. 2205–2224 (H. RIEMANN).

5

The pedagogue in Rome, cf. s. v. the articles by O. NAVARRE in DAREMBERG-SAGLIO, IV, 1, p. 273ab, s. v. "Paedagogus", and by E. SCHUPPE in PAULY-WISSOWA, XVIII, 2, c. 2380–2385, s. v. "Paidagogus": BOULOGNE, *De plaats van de paedagogus in de romeinse cultur*; Gröningen Dissertation (1951) and my remarks (*Gnomon*, 1951, pp. 460–461).

6

"A propos du latin Ludus": see the note under this title by A. YON in *Mélanges Alfred Ernout* (Paris, 1940), pp. 389–395. It is not, as Festus claims, certain that this word was chosen jokingly "so as not to frighten the children": *ludus* originally meant "a kind of activity that has no practical end", no matter whether it was free (i.e. a game) or controlled (i.e. an exercise done at school or anywhere else).

7

Schools in the shops on the Forum: in Rome the Basilica of the Argentarii in Caesar's forum: cf. M. DELLA CORTE, "Le Iscrizioni graffite della basilica degli Argentari sul foro di Giulio Cesare", *Bulletino della Commissione Archeologica Comunale di Roma*, LXI (1933), pp. 111–130—whose theories, which become more and more dangerous as the work goes on, I cannot entirely subscribe to: the *graffiti*, especially the ones about Virgil, undoubtedly tend to show that the shop in which they appear was used as a classroom, but they do not enable us to identify the master who taught there.

In Pompeii: the well-known painting in the Naples Museum (REINACH, *RPGR*, 255, 3), showing a boy being flogged in school, is one of a whole series (*ibid.*, 249, 253, 255, 5) devoted to scenes in the forum: the portico leading on to the forum can be seen in the background (O. ELIA, *Pitture murali e mosaici nel Museo Nazionale di Napoli*, Nos. 282–286, 291).

8

The master's seat raised up on a dais: cf. the fine "stele" belonging to the *magister ludi litterari*, Philocalus (DESSAU, 7763) in the Naples Museum, which I have reproduced in my thesis, Μουσικὸς ᾽Ανήρ, *Etude sur les Scènes de la Vie intellectuelle figurant sur les Monuments funéraires romains*, Grenoble, 1937, pl. II. In the text, p. 47, I have dated this monument as being second-century—wrongly, as has been pointed out to me by A. Piganiol: the hair style of the feminine figure who appears on the right reminds one of certain portraits of Julia, and undoubtedly takes us back to the time of Augustus.

9

Schoolmasters' pay: the article by R. P. ROBINSON, "The Roman Schoolteacher and his Reward", *Classical Weekly*, XV (1921), pp. 57–61, deals mainly with the position of grammarians and rhetors. As regards the *ludi magister*, the only precise evidence that we have seems rather difficult to interpret. When Horace was young the pay seems to have been eight *as* per pupil per month (*Sat.*, I, 6, 75), if *octonos referentes Idibus aeris* is taken to mean, as the DERay manuscripts take it to mean, "paying eight bronze pieces to the Ides". Other manuscripts (MFLou) have *octonis referentes Idibus aera*, "paying an *as* to the Ides eight times a year" (cf. MART., X, 61, 6–11: the Roman school year lasted in fact eight months). This is the figure provided by Juvenal in the second century: *Uno parcam colit asse Mineruam* (X, 116). But surely this is a comic exaggeration? The normal wage received by a Roman workman was one *denarius* (ten *asses*) a day. Even if he got eight *asses* per pupil per month, a teacher would have needed a class of more than thirty children to get a decent income (T. FRANK is mistaken when he says eighty in *An Economic Survey of Ancient Rome*, Vol. I, *Rome and Italy of the Republic*, Baltimore, 1933, p. 382): even this was perhaps rather too high a figure to expect under the old system of teaching; a figure eight times as high goes beyond the limits of probability.

10

L. HALKIN, "Le Congé des Nundines dans les Ecoles romaines", *Revue belge de Philologie et d'Histoire*, 1932, pp. 121–130, says that the *nundinae* were not holidays and that as a result school-children did not get the day off for them.

11

I have translated the words "palla, ἀναβόλαιον", as "scarf". If this passage came from the first or second century and not the third it would be more likely to mean "I wrap my cloak round my neck", but as the child in this case goes on to put another piece of clothing on—his *paenula*—I am inclined to wonder whether the *palla* had not already become a "long muffler", like the *pallium* worn by Christian bishops in the sixth century (cf. my note, "Les Deux Palliums de saint Césaire", *Revue archéologique*, 1946, I, pp. 231–233).

12

For the Pseudo-Cato's *Disticha* cf. SCHANZ, *Geschichte der römischen Literatur* (vol. III), §519–520, the posthumous edition by M. BOAS, and the previous studies listed in *Année philologique*. For their popularity in the Middle Ages, *ibid.*, §521. The old French translations have been published by ULRICH in *Romanische Forschungen*, XV (1903).

13

It is difficult to get any clear idea of either the *calculator* or his public. The most detailed information we have about him is the funeral *elogium* on the *calculator* Melior, who died in Ostia in A.D. 144. In this, his great memory and knowledge are praised, and he is said to have written a number of text-books—*commentarios*—on his art (DESSAU, 7755); which is all pretty vague. When the calculator is mentioned in any actual laws (*Cod. Just.*, X, 53, 4; *Dig.*, XXVII, 1, 15, 5; XXXVIII, 1, 7, 5; L, 13, 1, 6) it is only so that he shall be excluded from concessions granted to teachers of secondary schools and higher education. This puts him on the same level as the schoolmaster, but it also connects him even more closely with the out-and-out technicians—*librarii* (who copied out books) and *notarii* (stenographers). Similarly MART., X, 62,

4; Diocl., VII, 66–69; Isid., *Etym.*, I, 3, 1 (=Aug., *Ord.*, II, 12 (35), in which the manuscripts have *calculonum* or *calculorum*). In Rufinus (translating Origen *In Num.*, 27, 13, p. 279, Baehrens), *calculatores* does not mean the teachers but primary-school pupils who had got to the stage of learning their numbers.

14

Catomidiare: I have already referred (*supra*, n. 7) to the fresco in Pompeii that shows a schoolboy being flogged. The same technique may have gone on for many centuries, judging by the fresco by Benozzo Gozzoli in Sant' Agostino de San Gimi-niano, illustrating St. Augustine's childhood.

15

For the wooden model letters cf. F. S. Dölger in *Antike und Christentum*, III (1932), pp. 62–72.

For the "alphabetical cakes" cf. the note by H. Gaidoz in *Mélanges Rénier* (*Bibliothèque de l'Ecole pratique des Hautes-Etudes*, fasc. 73), pp. 1–8. As regards this custom in the Talmudic schools in France in the Middle Ages, T. Perlow, *L'Education et l'Enseignement chez les Juifs*, Paris, 1931, p. 47, n. 3.

16

The relaxation—or humanisation—of discipline in Roman education under the Empire: O. E. Nybakken, "Progressive Education in the Roman Empire", *Classical Journal*, 34 (1938–1939), pp. 38–42, which really gives the same facts as H. E. Burton, "The Elective System in the Roman Schools", in the same *Journal*, 16 (1920–1921), pp. 532–535.

17

Women intellectuals and blue-stockings in Roman society: L. Friedländer, *Darstellungen aus der Sittengeschichte Roms*[10], I, pp. 270–271, 296–302.

18

The grammarian's salary: cf. the article by Robinson *cit. supra*, n. 9, and the rather laborious lines of reasoning in E. Jullien, *Les Professeurs de Littérature dans l'ancienne Rome*, pp. 178. Suetonius, besides mentioning the 400,000 sesterces which he says Remmius Palaemon and L. Appuleius received as their annual income (*Gram.*, 23, 2; 3, 4), also informs us that Augustus gave M. Verrius Flaccus 100,000 sesterces a year for the lessons he gave his grandchildren, but there were other pupils there too, for *transiit in Palatium cum tota schola* (*Id.*, 17, 1). Juvenal (VII, 243, helped by the *Scholia ad loc.*) gives 500 sesterces per pupil per month as the figure for his own day.

19

The property qualification of 400,000 sesterces expected from those of equestrian rank represented a capital that produced enough income to live on: cf. the brilliant discussion by J. Carcopino, *La Vie quotidienne à Rome*, p. 87, based on Juv., XIV, 322–329; IX, 140.

20

For Remmius Palaemon, cf. the slightly rash speculations in the work by K. Barwick, "Remmius Palaemon und die römische Ars grammatica" (*Philologus, Suppl.*, XV, 2), Leipzig, 1922.

21

C. LAMBERT, "La Grammaire latine selon les Grammairiens latins du IVe et du Ve siècle", *Revue bourguignonne publiée par l'Université de Dijon*, XVIII (1908), 1–2, and the brief account, which I have repeated here with a few slight changes of emphasis, in my *Saint Augustin et la Fin de la Culture antique*, pp. 11–17.

22

The optative and the subjunctive only had different forms in the future tense. The optative future, for instance, was *utinam legam*; the subjunctive future (our future anterior), *cum legero* (LAMBERT, *op. cit.*, pp. 130, 138–139).

23

Latin syntax before Priscianus: LAMBERT, pp. 181 *et seq.*; MARROU, *Saint Augustin*, p. 14, n. 3.

24

For a treatment of idioms see again LAMBERT, pp. 189–192; for a treatment of orthography, *ibid.*, pp. 222–226 (and QUINTILIAN, I, 7; J. COUSIN, *Etudes sur Quintilien*, I, *Sources*, pp. 65–69); for tropes and figures of speech, LAMBERT, pp. 216–219.

25

For a treatment of the *vitia*, LAMBERT, pp. 205–214.

26

Nevertheless it must not be assumed—as I tended to assume too broadly in my *Saint Augustin*, pp. 13–14—that the *vitia* can be reduced to a series of poetic licences: the grammarian certainly taught his pupil how to make his language "correct" and treated any solecism or barbarism as a horror—*foeditas*—to be avoided (QUINTILIAN, I, 5, 5 *et seq.*; COUSIN, *Etudes sur Quintilien*, I, pp. 60–65).

27

On the classics: A. VERGEEST, *Poetarum enarratio, Leraren en schoolauteurs to Rome van Cicero tot Quintilianus:* Dissert. at Nijmegen, 1950, with my review in the *Revue des Etudes Latines*, 1951, pp. 445–448.

Commentaries on Virgil: cf. the old book by E. THOMAS, *Scoliastes de Virgile, essai sur Servius et son Commentaire*, Paris, 1879, and all the literature referred to by N. I. HERESCU, *Bibliographie de la Littérature latine*, Paris, 1943, pp. 141–142 (to which should be added PHILARGYRIUS, and, about him: G. FUNAIOLI, *Esegesi virgiliana antica, prolegomeni all'edizione del commento di G. Filargirio e di T. Gallo*, Milan, 1930).

28

The commentary on Terence: cf. the information collected by J. MAROUZEAU in the Introduction to his edition of Terence (Coll. Budé), Vol. 1, pp. 19–20.

29

The rhetor ARUSIANUS MESSIUS dedicated to the consuls of 395 his collection of *Exempla elocutionum* (=grammatical constructions) *ex Virgilio, Sallustio, Terentio, Cicerone digesta per litteras* (KEIL, *Grammatici Latini*, vol. VII, p. 449 *et seq.*): CASSIODORUS quotes this under the title *Quadriga Messii* (*Insti.*, I, 15, 7).

30

Signs used in preparation for reading: LAMBERT, *Grammaire* ... pp. 42–44: accents, quantity, running on (*hyphen*) or separating (*diastole*) syllables that might get joined up or separated wrongly, punctuation (*positurae*: a full stop above or below or in the middle to show three pauses of decreasing length).

There has been a great deal of discussion about the Roman use of punctuation: cf. finally J. ANDRIEU, "Problèmes d'Histoire des Textes", III, in *Revue des Etudes Latines*, XXIV (1946), pp. 293-305. The author ends by asking for further views on this subject, and I shall therefore endeavour to give my own particular theory as a starting point. Punctuation (and other diacritical signs) were not used for publication purposes but as a preparation for reading passages aloud in schools. Putting these signs into a passage was known as *codicem distinguere* (KEIL, *Gramm. Lat.*, V, 132, I, POMP.). A manuscript which had been "prepared" in this way was called a *codex distinctus* (*Id.*, IV, 484, 26–27: *cum sit codex emendatus distinctione, media distinctione, subdistinctione, dicitur tamen codex esse distinctus:* SER[V]IUS). But I do not believe that there were any such *codices distincti* in any libraries—none has been found, anyway. The punctuation in the manuscripts we possess is quite recent and does not correspond to anything in antiquity; at the earliest it is Carolingian: (J. ANDRIEU, *art. cit.*, p. 296, ad n. 1). It will be remembered that at least one papyrus has been found in Egypt "prepared" by a schoolboy, with the words cut up and the lines separated (Part II, Chap. VII, n. 13).

Besides punctuation, the Latins also used *interpunctio*—which was Etruscan in origin: G. NICOLAU, *Revue des Etudes Indo-Européennes*, Bucharest, 1938, pp. 85–88—the custom of separating words by means of full stops. In more artistic inscriptions the full stop developed into a *hedera distinguens*. But this never came into general use, either in cursive writing—as can be seen from the papyri, only *a few* of which are *interpuncti*—or in epigraphy; and never seems to have extended to proper literary editions, which, as can be seen from the manuscripts we possess, were always in *scriptio continua*.

31

Roman erudition split up when grammatical explanation began: see the two chapters of my *Saint Augustin et la Fin de la Culture antique*, pp. 105–157.

32

The geometers, whose existence is proved by their being mentioned in certain laws —valid in both the Greek- and Latin-speaking parts of the Empire—may have been teachers of pure mathematics, addressing themselves to a small minority of specially gifted minds who never lost their interest in science either for its own sake or as a preparation for philosophy—as well as technical teachers preparing their pupils for particular professions like surveying. (This means a slight change in my note in *Saint Augustin* ... p. 111, n. 1.)

33

ARATUS in Roman culture: cf. the *Aratea* by CICERO, GERMANICUS, AVIENUS, not to mention the anonymous translations: cf. M. SCHANZ, *Geschichte der römischen Literatur*, IV, I, p. 302; V. BUESCU's edition of CICERO, *Aratea* (*Collection d'Editions Critiques de l'Institut Roumain d'Etudes Latines*, I, Paris-Bucharest, 1941). The author has announced his intention of producing a full-scale work, *La fortune d' Aratos à Rome*.

Except for future scholars and philosophers, there was usually no specialised teaching of science in liberal education (cf. again my *Saint Augustin*, pp. 109–113, 226–227, 232). The only evidence pointing the other way is to be found in the biographies in the *Historia Augusta*, which inform us for example that when Marcus Aurelius was young he had lessons in "music" and geometry from Andronicus (*M. Aur.*, 2, 2. We are also told the names of his other teachers—the *litterator*—his diction master—Latin and Greek grammarians, rhetors and so on), and that Hadrian was very good at arithmetic and geometry and Severus Alexander good at geometry (S.H.A., *Hadr.*, 14, 8; *Alex. Sev.*, 27, 7). Assuming that this evidence is to be trusted, a prince's education—Marcus Aurelius was singled out by Hadrian when he was still quite young and promoted to the Salian College when he was seven; thus he was brought up like an hereditary prince—was somewhat unusual. It was assumed that the Emperor, being a perfect example of humanity, should realise the cultural ideal in all its fullness (*supra*, Chap. II, n. 15). On the other hand, if this teaching existed it could only have been given in Greek: science, as I have said, was written entirely in Greek under the Empire. Amongst the scientific books written in Latin, we only have works on mathematics by Varro, Appuleius, Martianus Capella, Boethius and Cassiodorus.

34

Lecture halls like *exedras* in the Roman forums: cf. my article, "La Vie intellectuelle au Forum de Trajan et au Forum d'Auguste", in *Mélanges d'Archéologie et d'Histoire*, Vol. XLIX (1932), pp. 93–110. There is evidence that these halls were used for academic purposes in Rome in the fourth, fifth and sixth centuries, and the custom may possibly have gone back to Hadrian's time, if the *Athenaeum, ludus ingenuarum artium*, that Aurelius Victor tells us (xiv, 3) was founded by that emperor, can be identified with the *Schola fori Traiani*. But we know very little about this. See the passages collected by F. SCHEMMEL, in *Wochenschrift für klassische Philologie* (Vienna), 1919, c. 91 *et seq.*; *Philologische Wochenschrift* (Berlin), 1921, c. 982 *et seq.*; A. PAZZINI, "L'Atheneum di Adriano e il 'Capitolii Auditorium'" ("*L'Università romana de l'-Impero*"), in *Capitolium*, IX, 1933, pp. 137–149.

35

The orator's cultural ideal in Cicero: A. GWYNN, *Roman Education from Cicero to Quintilian*, pp. 79–122; H. K. SCHULTE, "Orator, Untersuchungen über das Ciceronianische Bildungsideal", *Frankfurter Studien zur Religion und Kultur der Antike herausgegeben von W. F. OTTO*, Vol. XI, Frankfurt, 1935. For the influence of Philo of Larissa, who tried to create a synthesis that would fill the gap between philosophical and oratorical culture, cf. H. VON ARNIM, *Leben und Werke des Dio von Prusa*, pp. 97 *et seq.*

36

Quintilian's return to the Ciceronian ideal: cf. again GWYNN, *Roman Education*, pp. 185–200; J. COUSIN, *Etudes sur Quintilien*, I, *Contribution à la Recherche des Sources de l'Institution oratoire*, pp. 685 *et seq.*

37

Latin rhetoric as a derivative of Greek rhetoric: see the detailed proof of this assertion in the voluminous work by J. COUSIN quoted above—a good example is to be found on pp. 191–195, where there is a discussion of the subject matter used in eulogies, which we have already studied in connection with the Greek rhetors.

P

38

Quintilian's terminology more Greek than the language in the *Rhetoric to Herennius* or in Cicero: cf. again J. COUSIN, Vol. II of his *Etudes sur Quintilien: Vocabulaire grec de la Terminologie rhétorique dans l'Institution oratoire*, Paris, 1936, s.vv.

39

The same subjects are simply transferred from the Greek schools to Latin schools: cf. J. COUSIN, *Etudes sur Quintilien*, I, *Sources*, p. 727, n. 1 (subjects used by both Quintilian and Hermogenes—but what is the source? Hermagoras?); *ibid.*, pp. 709–713 (subjects taken from Greek law); H. BORNECQUE, "Les Déclamations et les Déclamateurs d'après Sénèque le Père" (*Travaux et Mémoires de l'Université de Lille*, N. S., I, 1, Lille, 1902, pp. 75–76. On twenty-four of his *Controversies* the Elder Seneca collected *sententiae* or *colores* by Greek rhetors who had treated the same subjects). See also S. F. BONNER, *Roman Declamations*, Liverpool, 1945.

40

I have already undertaken to defend the ancient pedagogies in *Saint Augustin et la Fin de la Culture antique*, Paris, 1937, pp. 53–54, 83, reacting against the usual opinion, which has always been very harsh (thus: G. BOISSIER, *La Fin du Paganisme*, *Etudes sur les dernières Luttes en Occident au IVe siècle^3*, Paris, 1896, pp. 213–231). My arguments have not been sufficiently powerful to convince J. CARCOPINO, *La Vie quotidienne à Rome à l'Apogée de l' Empire*, Paris, 1939, pp. 145–146: *Perseverare diabolicum. . . .* But I shall go on trying!

41

Topics for declamation purposes taken from actual Roman law: J. COUSIN, *Etudes sur Quintilien*, I, *Sources*, pp. 685–709; SUET., *Gram.*, 25, 6–7; from Roman history: SEN., *Controv.*, IV, 2; VII, 2; *Suas.*, 6–7; I have already referred in the text to JUV., VII, 160–164. No doubt even on such topics there was often a certain amount of imagination (cf. J. CARCOPINO, *La Vie quotidienne*, pp. 143–144), but this does not mean that there were no hidden references to actual events: declaiming for or against Cicero or Anthony—e.g. (SALL.) *Inv.*—was often a way of expressing "opposition to Caesar" (cf. the old book by G. BOISSIER, *Opposition sous les Césars*, Paris, 1875, which was founded upon his experience of the Second Empire—a collection of articles that appeared in the *Revue des Deux Mondes* from 1867 to 1871). The Imperial police were quite aware of this: cf. the fate of Secundus Carrinas, exiled by Caligula for having declaimed against tyrants: DIO. CASS., LIX, 20; JUV., VII, 204–205. See however also N. DERETANI, "Le Réalisme dans les Déclamations", *Revue de Philologie*, LV (1929), pp. 184–189.

42

H. BORNECQUE (*Les Déclamations et les Déclamateurs d'après Sénèque le Père*, Lille, 1902, p. 32) has discovered that the subjects lying behind fifteen of Seneca's declamations appear again in the collection of the *Gesta Romanorum* (fourteenth century).

43

Rhetoric as a stepping-stone to the law: cf. the thesis—which is perfectly accurate, even though the arguments are not always what they might be—maintained by E. J. PARKS, *The Roman Rhetorical Schools as a Preparation for the Courts under the Early*

Empire (the *Johns Hopkins University Studies in Historical and Practical Science*, 62, 2), Baltimore, 1945, or, better still, P. LANFRANCHI, *Il Diritto nei Retori Romani*, Milan, 1938.

44

The teaching of law: F. P. BREMER, *Rechtslehrer und Rechtsschulen*, 1868; P. COLLINET, *Etudes historiques sur le Droit de Justinien*, II, *Histoire de l'Ecole de Droit de Beyrouth*, Paris, 1925; M. VILLEY, *Recherches sur la Littérature didactique du Droit romain*, Paris, 1945.

45

"Beyrouth, centre d'Affichage et de Dépôt des Constitutions impériales": cf. under this title the article by P. COLLINET, in *Syria*, 1924, pp. 359-372.

CHAPTER VII

1

The depreciation of the Roman Empire's achievement: cf. e.g. S. PETREMENT, *Essai sur le Dualisme chez Platon, les Gnostiques et les Manichéens*, Paris, 1947, p. 158: " ... The Roman power had finally triumphed over all other nations, had laid upon them a burden that could not be shaken off, an administration that was utterly inflexible, and the whole world was without hope, without future. ... The Empire was like a vast extinguisher that had been laid upon the world, and in the end it put everything out. ... The Roman Empire was like a sickness falling upon the world, and it took the world more than a thousand years to get over it." I have not quoted these words because of the author's authority, which in the matter of history is not particularly great, but because they are characteristic of a widespread state of mind, particularly in France, where the anti-Roman point of view has been considerably strengthened by C. JULLIAN—the foundations of whose thought have been clearly brought out by A. GRENIER in his book *Camille Jullian, un demi-siècle de science historique et de progrès français*, Paris, 1944.

The point of view which I have presented here, on the other hand, has been acutely defended by C. N. COCHRANE, basing his arguments mainly on the thought of the Latin classical writers in Augustan times, in *Christianity and Classical Culture*,[2] London, 1944, pp. 1-176.

2

The eulogy of Rome in Aelius Aristides' twenty-sixth Discourse (Keil): cf. the very valuable analysis made by A. BOULANGER, *Aelius Aristide et la Sophistique dans la Province d'Asie au IIe siècle de notre ère*, Paris, 1923, pp. 347-362; 1-2; and the edition and study by J H. OLIVER, Philadelphia 1953.

3

The Latinisation of the Western provinces: for Spain, cf. M. TORRES, in R. MENENDEZ PIDAL, *Historia de España*, vol. II, *España Romana*, pp. 287 et seq.; R. THOUVENOT, *Essai sur la Province romaine de Bettique*, Paris, 1940, pp. 188, 667-686.

For Africa: S. GSELL, *Histoire ancienne de l'Afrique du Nord*, vol. VI, Paris, 1927, pp. 117-118; VII, 1928, pp. 115-116; VIII, 1928, pp. 239-241.

For Gaul: C. JULLIAN, *Histoire de la Gaule*, vol. VI, Paris, 1920, pp. 104-115, 123-128, VIII, 1926, pp. 246-264.

For Rhetia, F. STAEHELIN, *Die Schweiz in römischer Zeit*.

For Pannonia: the works analysed by A. ALFÖLDI, "Studi Ungheresi sulla Romanizzazione della Pannonia", in *Gli Studi Romani nel mondo* (published by the Istituto di Studi Romani), Bologna, 1935, vol. II, pp. 265–283, and the brief sketch by the same author in *Cambridge Ancient History*, vol. XI, pp. 540–554.

4

The Latinity of Scythia Minor: R. VULPE, "Histoire ancienne de la Dobroudja", in the Rumanian Academy's publication, *Connaissance de la Terre et de la Pensée roumaines*, vol. IV, *La Dobroudja*, Bucharest, 1938, passim.; H. I. MARROU, in *Revue du Moyen-Age latin*, vol. I (1945), pp. 11–12; and, for a special treatment of the Scythian monks, E. SCHWARTZ, *Acta conciliorum oecumenicorum*, IV, vol. 2, pp. v–xii.

5

For the classical culture of Britain, cf. R. G. COLLINGWOOD, in T. FRANK, *An Economical Survey of Ancient Rome*, vol. III, pp. 65–70; H. DESSAU, "Ein Freund Plutarchs in England", in *Hermes*, 1011, pp. 156–160. (Cf. R. FLACELIÈRE, in his edition of PLUTARCH, *Sur la Disparition des Oracles*, Paris, 1947, pp. 26–30; the grammarian Demetrius was sent on a mission of scientific investigation to Britain.)

6

The survival of "Punic" (is it always clearly distinguished from Berber in the old sources?) in Roman Africa: cf. C. FRIEND, "A Note on the Berber Background in the Life of Augustine", in the *Journal of Theological Studies*, 1942, vol. 43, pp. 188–189; C. COURTOIS, "Saint Augustine et la survivance du punique", in *Revue Africaine*, XCIV, 1950, pp. 259–282, criticized by J. LECERF in *Augustinus Magister*, vol. I, Paris, 1954, and M. SIMON in *Mélanges Isidore Lévy*, 1955. S. GSELL, *Histoire ancienne de l'Afrique du Nord, les siècles obscurs*,[2] Paris 1937, pp. 123–157.

7

Latinisation of the people in Gaul under the influence of Christianity: C. JULLIAN, *Histoire de la Gaule*, vol. VIII, p. 267.

There is an interesting comparison in the spread of Oïl-French into Oc-speaking territory (the parallel has been drawn by C. JULLIAN, who regards the position of Celtic at the end of the Empire as analogous with the position of Gascon in the seventeenth century). Protestant propaganda, which in most countries relied on the popular language, used French in southern France, and so indirectly helped the spread of this language: cf. A. BRUN, *Recherches historiques sur l'Introduction du français dans les Provinces du Midi*, Paris, 1923, p. 426.

8

Studies of Virgil, cf. e.g. E. de SAINT-DENIS, *Vie de Virgile*, at the front of his edition of the *Eclogues* (*Bucoliques*, Paris, 1942, pp. vii–xii), which, however, does not take into account the data furnished by the papyri in Herculaneum about the relation between Virgil and the Epicurean school in Campania: cf. G. DELLA VALLE, *Tito Lucrezio Caro e l'epicureismo campano*, I², Naples, 1935, pp. 185 *et seq.*, 254 *et seq.*

9

Carthage as an educational centre: cf. the short note by F. SCHEMMEL, "Die Schule von Karthago", in *Philologische Wochenschrift*, Vol. 47 (1927), c. 1342–1344, and above all A. AUDOLLENT, *Carthage romaine*, Paris, 1901, pp. 692–700; also LAPEYRE-FERRON's article entitled "Carthage" in the *Dictionnaire d'Histoire et de Géographie ecclésiastiques*.

10

C. JULLIAN, inspired by local patriotism—a very dangerous feeling for any historian to harbour (he was a teacher in Bordeaux from 1883 to 1905)—over-estimated the importance of the schools in Bordeaux in the fourth century: cf., besides his *Histoire de la Gaule*, vol. VIII, pp. 260–263, his article, "Les Premières Universités françaises, l'Ecole de Bordeaux au IVe siècle", in the *Revue Internationale de l'Enseignement*, XXV (1893), pp. 21–50, or *Ausone et Bordeaux, Etude sur les derniers temps de la Gaule romaine*, Bordeaux, 1893.

In actual fact the picture we get in AUSONIUS (*Prof.*) gives the impression of a mainly regional influence. The fact that Bordeaux exported teachers to Constantinople (*Prof. Burd.*, I, 4) or imported a teacher from Sicily (*ibid.*, 13) has nothing unusual about it, as under the Early Empire teachers moved about a great deal from one end of the Mediterranean to the other. Besides Ausonius, cf. SYMMACHUS, *Ep.*, XI, 88, who had as his teacher (probably in Rome) a *senex olim Garumnae alumnus*, IV, 34.

II

For Naples: M. di MARTINO FUSCO, *Le Scuole e l'istruzione in Napoli dall' epoca greco-romana al Generale Studium*, ΜΟΥΣΕΙΟΝ (Naples), II (1924), pp. 65–99, 155–171 —an uncritical and altogether unfortunate piece of work: it accepts the extraordinary inscription on the Lago Fusaro without making any attempt to discuss its authenticity or restoration: *Aep.*, 1925, 119 (=*RIGI*, 1924, 152 *et seq.*), *Eruditioni publicae, religionum contemptrici, gymnasia, collegia*.

CHAPTER VIII

I

Young men's clubs in the Latin West in Imperial times: see in the first place M. ROSTOVTSEFF, "Römische Bleitesserae, ein Beitrag zur Sozial- und Wirtschaftsgeschichte der römischen Kaiserzeit", in *Klio, Beiheft*, III, 1905, pp. 59–93; "Storia economica e sociale dell' impero romano", pp. 54, n. 4; 120, 125, 148, 268, 352; 379, n. 11; 501, and the works based on it: L. R. TAYLOR, "Seviri Equitum Romanorum and Municipal Seviri, a Study in Pre-Military Training among the Romans", in the *Journal of Roman Studies*, vol. 14, 1924, pp. 158–171; S. L. MOHLER, "The Juvenes and Roman Education", in *Transactions of the American Philological Society*, vol. 68 (1937), pp. 442–479, and also M. DELLA CORTE, *Juventus, un nuovo aspetto della vita pubblica di Pompei finora inesplorato, studiato e ricostruito con la scorta dei relativi documenti epigrafici, topografici, demografici, artistici e religiosi*, Arpino, 1924; [H. G. PFLAUM], "Essai sur le Cursus Publicus sous le Haut-Empire romain", in *Mémoires présentés par divers Savants à l'Académie des Inscriptions et Belles-Lettres*, XIV, Paris, 1940, pp. 214–217. I have also benefited from a still unpublished work by my pupil P. GINESTET, which has led me, despite Rostovtseff's and della Corte's opinion, to minimise the pre-military character of the institution, as far as the Italian *collegia* are concerned. For the history of the *Iuventus* in Africa, cf. L. LESCHI, "Les 'Juvenes' de Saldae d'après une inscription métrique", in *Revue Africaine*, 1927, No. 333, and the recent discoveries in Maktar which G. PICARD has announced are shortly to be published.

2

Indo-European origin of the Roman category, *"Juvenes"*: G. DUMEZIL, "Jeunesse, Eternité, Aube: Linguistique comparée et Mythologie comparée indo-européenne", in *Annales d'Histoire Economique et Sociale*, X (1938), pp. 289 *et seq.*, esp. 290–298.

3

For the girls' *sodalitas* in Tusculum, cf. the argument between A. ROSEMBERG, "Nochmals Aedilis Lustralis und die Sacra von Tusculum", in *Hermes*, 49 (1914), pp. 253–272, and O. LEUZE, *ibid.*, pp. 116–118.

4

Dig., XLVIII, 19, 28, 3 (Callistratus): this was an attempt to suppress the disturbances caused by the *Iuvenes'* games. We know of course that Italian crowds could get very excited on festive occasions—there was the murderous fighting that took place in 59 in the amphitheatre in Pompeii between the Pompeians and the Nucerians (TAC., *Ann.*, XIV, 17). Nevertheless, in this case the extreme harshness of the penalties —a second offence meant death—and an allusion to "seeking popularity" seem to indicate that the Severi had something else in mind besides the mere maintenance of order: this law must have had a political significance.

5

For the *schola* for the *Iuventus* in Pompeii (Pompeii, *Reg.* III, *Inst.* 3, No. 6) cf. DELLA CORTE, *Juventus*, pp. 60–71. A bas-relief in the Klagenfurt Museum has preserved a picture of an equestrian procession of the *Iuventus* in Virunum: R. EGGER, "Eine Darstellung des Lusus juvenalis" in *Jahreshefte* of the Austrian Archaeological Institute, vol. XVIII (1915), pp. 115–119.

6

For the school policy of the Roman Empire the fundamental work—though it is fairly out of date by now—is still that of C. BARBAGALLO, *Lo Stato e l'istruzione pubblica nell' impero romano*, Catania, 1911; cf. also: H. E. HADLEY, "Ueber das Verhältnis von Staat und Schule in der römischen Kaiserzeit", in *Philologus*, 1920, pp. 176–191; R. HERZOG, "Urkunden zur Hochschulpolitik der römischen Kaiser", in *Sitzungsberichte* of the Berlin Academy of Sciences, *Phil.-Hist. Klasse*, 1935, pp. 967–1,019. His interpretation of an inscription in Pergamus, *ibid.*, p. 968, which is the basis for this study, has been contested by H. BARDON, *Les Empereurs et les Lettres latines d'Auguste à Hadrien*, Paris, 1940, p. 301; cf. again M. A. LEVI, "Gli Studi Superiori nella politica di Vespasiano", in *Romana* (*Rivista dell' Istituto Inter-universitario Italiano*), I, 1937, pp. 361–367.

7

No special school inspector. The most that happened was that occasionally the Emperor, taking advantage of his powers of censorship, took measures against the teachers. In 72 for instance Vespasian (DIO. CASS., LXVI, 13) and in 93–95 Domitian (SUET., *Dom.*, 10, 5; TAC., *Agr.*, 2) banished from Rome philosophers suspected of indulging in subversive propaganda—and this was not mere imagination either, considering the part played by Cynic-Stoic ideas in the Senate's opposition—but this was not so much the result of the actual teaching of philosophy as of the part played by domestic philosophers as moral counsellors and private advisers to the great.

There is no point in wasting any time over the mis-reading made by C. BARBAGALLO (*Lo Stato e l'istruzione pubblica*, p. 32) who imagined that the procurator *a studiis* was a kind of minister of national education. O. HIRSCHFELD (*Verwaltungsbeamten bis auf Diokletian*[2], Berlin, 1905, pp. 332–334) has shown quite clearly that the *a studiis* was in charge of the office in which the preliminary studies took place for the central administration. Barbagallo's mistake can be explained, if not excused, on two counts: (1) the title *a studiis* is written in Greek ἐπὶ παιδείας: *IG Rom.*, I, 136; *IG*, XIV, 1085; *Aep.*, 1915, 51; (2) before he received the procuratorship *a studiis*, the same official had often been in charge of the libraries: *IG Rom.*, I, 136; *IG*, XIV, 1085.

8

Besides these municipal immunities, teachers received other privileges; for instance any lawsuits they went in for, to get money that had not been paid to them for services rendered, were to be evoked by the provincial governor himself: *Dig.*, L., 13, 1.

9

The number of chairs created by Vespasian in Rome: Philostratus refers several times to the chair of Greek rhetoric, and he always mentions it in the singular—"the chair of Rome", ὁ κατὰ ῾Ρώμην Θρόνος (*V.S.*, II, 8, 580; II, 33, 627); "the highest chair", ὁ ἄνω Θρόνος (*ibid.*, II, 10, 589).

This expression seems to me to shed some light on another expression, *procurator centenarius primae cathedrae*, which is to be found in a Latin inscription (DESSAU, 9020): *prima cathedra* seems to me to distinguish this chair from all the other chairs in the Empire, not from others in Rome, which are never mentioned. The inscription is dedicated by the town council of Sicca Veneria in Africa, and it seems to date from the beginning of the third century—an interesting fact, which shows that salaries had not changed since Vespasian's time. I do not know what to think of the title *trecenarius, a declamationibus Latinus* which was given to another African, a lawyer contemporary with Papinian at the end of his career (*Année épigraphique*, 1932, 34); but I do not think that it can have meant a teacher of rhetoric.

10

How many chairs of philosophy did Marcus Aurelius found in Athens? People often say eight (following H. AHRENS, *De Atheniensium statu politico*, p. 70), two per sect, because of a passage in LUCIAN which speaks of the "second" teacher of the peripatetic philosophy (*Eun.*, 3, 8), but this is a lot to make out of a single passage, which in any case may have a different meaning—"second", in point of time. By the same reasoning a passage in EUNAPIUS (*Proh.*, p. 487) could be made to prove that there were six official chairs of rhetoric in Athens in the fourth century—which there were certainly not.

11

For the institutions for needy children, see F. DE PACHTERE, "La Table hypothé-caire de Veleia", *Bibliothèque de l'Ecole des Hautes-Etudes*, fasc. 228, Paris 1920 (and for a discussion of this work, J. CARCOPINO, *Revue des Etudes anciennes*, vol. 23, 1921, pp. 287 *et seq.*; M. BESNIER, *ibid.*, vol. 24, 1922, pp. 118 *et seq.*); M. ROSTOVTSEFF, *Storia economica e sociale dell'impero romano*, pp. 412–413, pl. LXVIII, 3; LXX (from W. SESTON, "Les Anaglypha Traiani du Forum romain et la politique d'Hadrien en 118", in *Mélanges d'Archéologie et d'Histoire*, vol. 44, 1927, pp. 154–183).

12

Were there two official chairs of rhetoric in Athens from the time of Marcus Aurelius onwards, one a municipal foundation—with Lollianus as its first holder: PHILSTR., *V.S.*, I, 23, 526—and the other founded by the Emperor, with its first holder Theodotes? I do not think so. The simplest explanation is that the source of the money, and perhaps the amount paid out in salaries too, had changed (Philostrates, speaking of Theodotes, simply says (*V.S.*, II, 2, 566), that he was "the first to get the Emperor's 10,000 drachmas"). The way people were nominated meant that the chair was in the hands of the city, and it would thus be possible for Philostratus, speaking of a certain Apollonius, who lived in the time of Septimus Severus, to refer to "*the* municipal chair"—ὁ πολιτικὸς Θρόνος—(*V.S.*, II, 20, 600), without necessarily distinguishing it from any possible "Imperial" chair—of whose separate existence there is, incidentally, no proof.

13

For Libanius's teaching career, which was so varied and hence is so informative for us, it will be sufficient to refer to the article by FÖRSTER and MÜNSCHER, in PAULY-WISSOWA, Vol. XII, 2, c. 2485 *et seq.*, esp. 2489–2498. The fundamental source is Libanius's own autobiography (*Or.*, I), translated into French by L. PETIT, *Essai sur la Vie et la Correspondance du sophiste Libanios*, Paris, 1886, pp. 171–273.

14

Cod. Theod., XIII, 3, 5: this law of Julian's seems to have had a very wide reference, for it was not only those who held municipal chairs but all the teachers who were to be approved by the local curia. Thus the curia not only had the task of choosing, they were empowered to give what was in fact a *licentia docendi*.

15

Gratian's law about the payment of teachers in Gaul (*Cod. Theod.*, XIII, 3, 11): this may easily have been inspired by Ausonius, even though he had not yet become Pretorian prefect. A. PIGANIOL in G. GLOTZ, *Histoire générale*, 3, *Histoire romaine*, Vol. IV, 2, Paris, 1947, p. 325, n. 156, thinks it rather risky to do as SCALIGER and J. R. PALANQUE (*Essai sur la Préfecture du Prétoire du Bas-Empire*, Paris, 1933, p. 49) have done, in correcting the address *Antonio ppo. Galliarum* in this law to *Ausonius*.

It is laid down in the text that salaries shall be paid *e fisco*: what follows (*nec vero judicemus liberum ut sit cuique ciuitati suos doctores et magistro placito sibi iuvare compendio*) shows that this expression must be taken to mean the city's funds, not the Imperial treasury, which it might seem to mean at first sight (cf. for the same interpretation, C. JULLIAN, *Histoire de la Gaule*, Vol. VIII, p. 249, n. 1, and GODEFROY, *ad loc.*).

16

Did the constitution of February 27th 425 create a State University in Rome as well as Constantinople? The answer would seem to be No. The fact that it was signed by the two Emperors Theodosius II and Valentinian III was simply in conformity with the legal fiction of the unity of the Imperial college and did not mean that Valentinian III, who was governor in the West, intended to apply it in his part of the Empire. The fact that it appears in the *Justinian Code* (XI, 19) under the heading "De studiis liberalibus urbis Romae et Constantinopolis", can be explained as a survival of the *Theodosian Code*, whose section XIV, 9, which has the same heading, combines this constitution of 427 (XIV, 9, 2) with Valentinian I's law of 370 (XIV, 9, 1) about supervising students in Rome. The only reference in the law of 427 is to the Constantinople university, which is described in precise topographical terms as *Capitolii auditorium*, which makes no sense unless it is applied to Constantinople (cf. *Cod. Theod.*, XV, 1, 53).

The Pragmatic Sanction, furthermore, shows that under Justinian at least the officially recognised advanced education in Rome was quite different from that in Constantinople—it included medical professors and had no philosophers: JUST., *Nov., Ap.*, 7, 22.

It was the law about granting the title of "Count" to the Emeritus professors (the law of March 15th 425: *Cod. Theod.*, VI, 21, 1=*Cod. Just.*, XII, 15, 1) that applied to Rome as well as the East, as is clear from the inscription on the sarcophagus of the *rhetor urbis aeternae* Fl. Magnus (DESSAU, 2951) *cui tantum ob meritum suum detulit, senatus amplissimus ut sat idoneum iudicaret a quo lex dignitatis inciperet*—that is to say, if one accepts the interpretation of this vague passage that has been suggested by DE ROSSI, in *Bulletino di archeologia cristiana*, Vol. I (1863), p. 15.

17

The increasing interest shown by the Emperors of the Late Empire in educational matters, cf. e.g. the remarks made by A. ALFÖLDI about the policy pursued by Valentinian I in *A Conflict of Ideas in the Late Roman Empire, the Clash between the Senate and Valentinian I*, Oxford 1952.

18

For aristocratic country houses in the Late Empire, cf. R. PARIBENI, "Le Dimore dei Potentiores nel Basso Impero", in *Römische Mitteilungen*, 1940, pp. 131–148. The continuity of the aristocratic tradition is particularly evident in Africa, where there are lovely mosaics depicting the country life of the rich landed gentry from the second century to the time of the Vandal invasions: cf. e.g. the plates in M. ROSTOVTSEFF, *Storia . . . dell'Impero romano*, pl. LXII, 1; LXVIII, 1; LXXX.

19

Literary society in fifth-century Gaul: cf. A. LOYEN, *Sidoine Apollinaire et l'esprit précieux en Gaule aux derniers jours de l'Empire*, Paris, 1943, and my observations in the *Revue du Moyen Age Latin*, vol. I (1945), pp. 198–204.

20

Virgil in the Late Empire, particularly in the Macrobius circle: D. COMPARETTI, *Virgilio nel medio evo*, I^2, Florence, 1937, pp. 66 (in the first edition), *et seq.*, esp. 84–93.

21

Humanism versus technology: there was undoubtedly a certain movement towards a more technical kind of culture in the Late Empire, but it was suffocated by the dominant traditional humanism: cf. a curious piece of evidence like the *Anonymus de rebus bellicis*: E. A. THOMPSON, *A Roman Reformer and Inventor*, Oxford 1952, which at times makes one think of Leonardo da Vinci; and more generally the facts brought out, perhaps rather too complacently, by A. PIGANIOL, *Histoire romaine*, vol. IV, 2, p. 390, "Progrès des techniques".

22

The history of the ancient stenography has still not been satisfactorily written: cf. WEINBERGER in PAULY-WISSOWA, XI, 2, c. 2217–2231, s.v. "Kurzschrift". The other articles in PAULY-WISSOWA on the subject are most unsatisfactory: s.vv. "Exceptor" (VI 2, 1565–1566, FIEBERGER), Ταχυγραφία (II R., IV, 2, c. 1926; WEINBERGER), "Tribunus No. 11" (*tribunus et notarius*, II R., VI, 2, c. 2453–2455; LENGLE), *Notarius* (*Suppl.*, VII, c. 586, W. MOREL). The same is true of the article "Notarius" in DAREMBERG-SAGLIO, IV, 1, pp. 105b—106a (C. LECRIVAIN).

For Greek shorthand, H. I. M. MILNE, *Greek Shorthand Manuals, Syllabary and Commentary, edited from Papyri and Waxed Tablets in the British Museum and from the Antinoë Papyri in the Possession of the Egypt Exploration Society*, London, 1934: A. MENTZ, "Zwei Tachygraphische Papyri der Sammlung Ibscher", in *Byzantinische Zeitschrift*, vol. 43, 1950.

Latin shorthand (Tironian Notes) is technically better known: W. SCHMITZ, *Commentarii Notarum Tironianarum*, 1893; E. CHATELAIN, *Introduction à la lecture des Notes tironiennes*, Paris, 1900. A. MENTZ, "Die Enstehungsgeschichte der römischen Stenographie", in *Hermes*, Vol. LXVI (1936), pp. 369–386; *Drei Homilien aus der Karolingerzeit in tironischen Noten* (*Quellen zur Geschichte der Kurzschrift*, II, Bayreuth, 1942).

But the chief thing we lack is a history of the part played by shorthand and shorthand-writers in the administrative, literary and ecclesiastical life of the Roman Empire. Such a history would make a fascinating study. Meanwhile there is plenty to lure one on to further research in the many notes to the *Archiv für Stenographie*— for instance, for the part played by shorthand in the Church, D. OHLMANN, "Die Stenographie im Leben des hl. Augustin", Vol. 56 (1905), pp. 273–279, 312–319; E. PREUSCHEN, "Die Stenographie im Leben des Origenes", *ibid.*, pp. 6–14; A. WICKENHAUSER, "Beiträge zur Geschichte der Stenographie auf den Synoden des vierten Jahrhunderts n. Chr.", Vol. 59 (1908), pp. 4–9, 33–39; "Kleine Beiträge zur Geschichte der antiken Stenographie", Vol. 62 (1911), pp. 1–6, 57–64; cf. also R. DEFERRARI, "The Presence of Notarii in the Churches to take down Sermons when they were being Delivered", in the *American Journal of Philology*, 1922, pp. 106–110; A. COMEAU, "Sur la transmission des Sermons de saint Augustin", in *Revue des Etudes latines*, X (1932), p. 422; A. MENTZ, *Ein Schülerschrift mit altgriechischer Kurzschrift: neue Wachstafeln des Instituts für Altertumswissenschaft Robertinum zu Halle (Saale)* (*Quellen zur Geschichte der Kurzschrift*, I), Bayreuth, 1940 (Egypt, sixth to seventh century; it contains a transcription of several passages from St. Paul).

CHAPTER IX

I

St. John Chrysostom, *On Vainglory: and on how Parents should bring up their Children:* the genuineness of this essay, which was questioned without valid grounds by C. OUDIN, *Commentarius de scriptoribus ecclesiae antiquis*, Leipzig, 1722, I, 740, was reinstated by S. HAIDACHER, *Des heiligen Johannes Chrysostomus Büchlein über Hoffart und Kindererziehung . . .* Fribourg, 1907, and seems to me to have been established beyond any doubt by J. HILLARD, in a Paris thesis which unfortunately the author's death prevented from being sustained, and, so far, from being published; cf., meanwhile, the edition by F. SCHULTE, Münster, 1914, and the English translation by

M. L. W. LAISTNER, in *Christianity and Pagan Culture in the Later Roman Empire*, Ithaca, 1951.

2

Christianity as a mystery religion: here the discipline of the *arcanum* should be mentioned—the truths of the faith were not to be divulged without proper precautions, only initiates were allowed to take part in the ceremonies—but this is a delicate matter which has not yet been absolutely satisfactorily explained. See the suggestions by O. PERLER in T. KLAUSER's *Reallexikon für Antike und Christentum*, vol. 1, c. 667–676. As the Rev. G. HOCQUARD suggests, in a work so far unpublished which he has had the kindness to lend me, it was less a case of a "discipline" introduced for educational reasons or reasons of prudence than a particular kind of practice based upon the actual doctrinal teaching of the Church: "Only the illumination that came from baptism could initiate anyone into the mysteries which were thus hidden, inaccessibly—which indeed they were, literally—and yet nevertheless not secret."

3

For the "*didascali*" in the Primitive Church, cf. A. HARNACK, *Die Mission und Ausbreitung des Christentums in den ersten drei Jahrhunderten*, I[4], Leipzig, 1923, pp. 332–377.

4

For the development of the catechumen system cf. especially B. CAPELLE, "L'Introduction du catéchuménat à Rome", in *Recherches de Théologie ancienne et médiévale*, V (1933), pp. 129–154; J. LEBRETON, "Le Développement des Institutions ecclésiastiques à la fin du IIe et au début du IIIe siècle", in *Recherches de Science religieuse*, XXIV (1934), pp. 129–164.

5

For the idea of "tradition" in the Early Church, cf. D. VAN DEN EYNDE, *Les Normes de l'Enseignement chrétien dans la Littérature chretienne des trois premiers siècles*, Louvain thesis, 1933.

6

The Jews in Alexandria in the time of Philo kept a festival to commemorate the translation of the Septuagint (PHILO, *V. Moys.*, II, 7, 41). Later, according to the Babylonian Talmud (gloss of *Megillat Ta'anith*, 50), this day became a day of mourning and fasting, "to expiate the sin that was committed when the Torah was divulged in the language of the Goyims".
Nevertheless, the turn of events that took place soon afterwards (JUST., *Tryph.*, 68, 71) did not happen quite as quickly as might be thought: M. SIMON (in his thesis *Verus Israel*) has collected various pieces of evidence showing that the Greek Bible survived amongst the Jews in the first centuries of the Empire.

7

For the Rabbinical education, cf. T. PERLOW, *L'Education et l'Enseignement chez les Juifs à l'époque talmudique*, Paris thesis, 1931, to which little is added by N. DRAZIN, *History of Jewish Education from 515 B.C.E. to 220 C.E.* (*during the Periods of the Second Commonwealth and the Tannaim*), the Johns Hopkins University Studies in Education, 29, Baltimore, 1940.

8

For the Syriac schools: J. B. CHABOT, "L'Ecole de Nisibe, son Histoire, ses Statuts", in *Journal Asiatique*, 9, VIII (1896), pp. 43–93; "Narsai le Docteur et les Origines de l'Ecole de Nisibe", *ibid.*, 10, VI, (1905), pp. 157–177; E. R. Hayes, *L'Ecole d'Edesse*, Paris thesis, 1930 (mediocre); H. Kihn, *Theodor von Mopsuestia und Junilius Africanus als Exegeten*, Fribourg, 1880.

9

Cultural osmosis: H. Davenson, *Fondements d'une Culture chrétienne*, Paris, 1934, pp. 82–83, 57–68.

10

I am quite aware, of course, that there is an anachronism here: the distinction between nature and supernature does not belong to early Christian thought; it was only developed much later by the mediaeval theologians: cf. H. De Lubac, *Surnaturel, Etudes Historiques*, Paris, 1946.

11

The Fathers of the Church's opposition to classical culture: there have been many attempts to describe this—see esp.: H. Fuchs, "Die frühe Kirche und die antike Bildung", in *Die Antike* (1929) V, pp. 107 *et seq.* P. De Labriolle, *Histoire de la Littérature latine chrétienne*[3], 1947, pp. 14 *et seq.*; F. Boulenger, Introduction to his edition of St. Basil, *Aux Jeunes Gens . . .* Paris, 1935, pp. 16–23; H. I. Marrou, *Saint Augustin et la Fin de la Culture antique*, pp. 339–356; C. L. Ellspermann, *The Attitude of the Early Christian Fathers Towards Pagan Literature and Learning* (the Catholic University of American, *Patristic Studies*, vol. LXXXII, Washington, 1949).

12

The prohibition of the bishop (and the other members of the clergy too) from attending secular lectures: cf. B. Dolhagaray, in Vacant-Mangenot-Amann, *Dictionnaire de Théologie Catholique*, vol., III, 1 c. 607–608, s. v. "Compétente (Science)". I uphold this view despite the criticisms of Dom B. Botte in his account of the first edition of this work (see *Bulletin de Théologie ancienne et médiévale*, vol. VI, n. 283).

13

For the distinction between culture in the general sense and the "preparatory" culture that may be subdivided into "perfective" culture and "formal" culture, cf. my *Saint Augustin et la Fin de la Culture antique*, pp. vi-viii.

14

For the real significance of St. Basil's *Hom. XXII*, cf. again my *Saint Augustin*, p. 396, n. 2, and more recently: S. Giet, *Les Idées et les Doctrines sociales de saint Basile*, Paris, 1941, pp. 217–232.

15

There is a charming passage in one of St. Basil's writings describing the joy of the children in Caesarea in 368 on being allowed to forget school and writing tablets for a day so that they could take part in the prayers ordered by the bishop on the occasion of a famine caused by drought, thus in their innocence turning a time of general sorrow into a holiday (*Hom. VIII*, 72, *PG*, 31, 309); this suggests an atmosphere of confidence and co-operation between parents and teachers and the Church.

16

The Arab text of the *Canons of Hippolytus* published by D. B. Von Haneberg, Münich, 1870 (Chap. XII, with which we are concerned here, also appears in the *Sitzungsberichte* of the Münich Academy of Sciences, 1869, 2, pp. 43–44), on the basis of two Roman manuscripts, is very corrupt. The Latin translation followed by H. ACHELIS in HARNACK-GEBHARDT, *Texte und Untersuchungen*, VI, 4, pp. 80–81, is not satisfactory. Prof. L. MASSIGNON has very kindly helped me to deal with this difficult passage. We availed ourselves of the German translation given by W. RIEDEL in *Die Kirchenrechtsquellen des Patriarchats Alexandrien*, Leipzig, 1900, p. 206, using a collection of Berlin manuscripts that has unfortunately not been published.

17

Under Turkish rule Greek children said the invocation Σταυρέ, βοήθει μοι by "reading" the cross drawn at the head of their alphabet: G. CHASSIOTIS, *L'Instruction publique chez les Grecs depuis la prise de Constantinople par les Turcs*, Paris, 1881, p. 16.

18

For the *lectores infantuli*, see the material collected by J. QUASTEN, "Musik und Gesang in den Kulten der heidnischen Antiken und christlichen Frühzeit" (*Liturgiege-schichtliche Quellen und Forschungen*, XXV), Münster, 1930, pp. 133–141.

19

RUFINUS, *H.E.*, X, 15: it must be made clear that this episode may have been purely legendary. There is the difficulty of chronology—the bishop in question can only have been Alexander, who did not become Bishop of Alexandria until 312: Athanasius, who was born between 293 and 295, would already have been too old—but it is not important: it is the moral of the story that interests us, not the historical truth of the event.

20

For the theological schools of the second to the third centuries, cf. esp. the articles by G. BARDY, "Les Ecoles romaines au IIe siècle", in *Revue d'Histoire ecclésiastique*, XXVIII (1932), pp. 501–532; "Aux origines de l'Ecole d'Alexandrie", in *Recherches de Science religieuse*, XXVII (1937), pp. 65–90; "Pour l'Histoire de l'Ecole d'Alexandrie" in *Vivre et Penser*, II (1942), pp. 80–109.

21

For the Roman statue of Hippolytus, cf. H. LECLERCQ, in *Dictionnaire d'Archéologie chrétienne et de Liturgie*, vol. VI, 2, c. 2419–2460; G. DE JERPHANION, *La Voix des Monuments*, p. 303, n. 1. For the Christian tombstones on which the dead person is represented as a "philosopher", cf. my Μουσικὸς Ἀνήρ, Grenoble, 1937, pp. 296–299.

22

F. SCHEMMEL, "Die Schule von Caesarea in Palaestina", in *Philologische Wochenschrift*, 1925, c. 1277–1280.

23

St. Augustine as the theorist of a Christian culture: cf. my *Saint Augustinte la Fin de la Culture antique*, pp. 331 *et seq*.

CHAPTER X

1

For the name "Abbot" as used by the solitaries in Egypt, cf. the article by J. DUPONT, in *La Vie Spirituelle*, 1947, No. 321, pp. 216–230.

2

RUFINUS, *Apol.*, II, 8: it was Rufinus who accused St. Jerome of being unfaithful to his vow in the "Dream" by teaching the pagan classics to his pupils in Bethlehem. But as F. CAVALLERA notes acutely in his *St. Jerome*, vol. I, p. 202, n. 1, St. Jerome, contrary to his custom, did not refute the accusation, and his silence may be taken as acquiescence.

3

Illiterate monks in Byzantium: see the data collected by L. BREHIER in *Revue d'Histoire et de Philosophie religieuses*, XXI (1941), p. 60, n. 86.

4

St. Augustine's learned monastery in Tagaste: M. MELLET, *L'Itinéraire et l'Idéal monastiques de saint Augustin*, Paris, 1934, pp. 19–29; P. MONCEAUX in *Miscellanea Agostiniana*, II, Rome, 1931, pp. 70–75.

5

Young *lectores*: cf. the preceding chapter, n. 18. For its place in the career of ecclesiastics, cf. L. DUCHESNE, *Origines du culte chrétien*[5], pp. 366–367: "Most of the ecclesiastics' careers that are known in any detail began with being *lectors*. This is true of St. Felix of Nola, St. Eusebius of Vercelli, Pope Damasus's father, Popes Liberius and Siricius, the deacon of Fiesole, Romulus, St. Epiphanius of Pavia, and many others. . . ." The inscriptions quoted come from DIEHL, 967, 970, 972.

6

Origins of the episcopal school. It is difficult to decide when this first appeared: our sources, especially the *Lives* of the Saints, need to be used with care. According to a *Life* of Saints Victor and Victeur of Le Mans in the fourth century, St. Martin of Tours is supposed to have educated a child of ten for the priesthood: *AA. SS.*, Jul. V, 146, C, F. But this Life has no historic value whatever—even the very existence of its two heroes is imaginary: cf. H. LECLERCQ in *Dictionnaire d'Archéologie chrétienne et de Liturgie*, vol. X, 2, c. 1478–1480.

7

For the history of the country parishes in Gaul, cf. the classic work by P. IMBART DE LA TOUR, *Les Paroisses rurales du IVe au XIe siècle*, Paris, 1900, and the additions or corrections to his teaching in W. SESTON, "Note sur les origines religieuses des Paroisses rurales" in *Revue d'Histoire et de Philosophie religieuses*, 1935, pp. 243–254. The two points of view are complementary rather than contradictory: cf. F. CHATILLON, *Locus cui nomen Theopoli est*, Gap, 1943, pp. 125–126, 135, n. 57.

8

The Druids as the educators of pagan Ireland: H. HUBERT, *Les Celtes depuis l'époque de La Tène*, Paris, 1932, pp. 279–281, and for ancient Gaul, CAESAR, G., VI, 14, 2–6: C. JULLIAN, *Histoire de la Gaule*, vol. II, p. 106.

9

Merovingian schools were religious schools: H. PIRENNE maintained exactly the opposite point of view in his article "De l'Etat de l'Instruction des Laïques à l'époque mérovingienne" in *Revue bénédictine*, XLVI (1934), pp. 165–177. I leave it to any impartial reader to decide between our different points of view. Pirenne systematically over-estimates and distorts the significance of the texts: I do not see how, as he maintains, there can be any question of there being lay *schools* in Gaul in Merovingian times—all the *schools* that we know to have existed are religious, monastic, episcopal and (generally speaking) presbyterial schools. No doubt there are a few cases of lay *teaching* as regards the alphabet, grammar, rhetoric and law, but this was always given privately at home under a tutor, as in the days of Sidonius Apollinaris.

10

The anachronism has been committed: the Romantic approach to the Church, which followed Chateaubriand in glorifying the Church's positive cultural rôle, has systematically over-emphasised the value of the evidence about Christian schools in the fifth to the sixth centuries: see e.g. A. F. OZANAM, *La civilisation chrétienne chez les Francs*, Paris, 1849. To M. ROGER goes the credit for having cleared this question up in his thesis, which is absolutely fundamental to our subject, *L'Enseignement des lettres classiques d'Ausone à Alcuin*, Paris, 1905.

11

GREG. MAGN., *Reg.*, XI, 34: there has been a great deal of argument about the interpretation of this letter: cf. the old work by H. J. LEBLANC, *Utrum B. Gregorius Magnus litteras humaniores et ingenuas artes odio persecutus sit*, Paris, 1852. Here again it is wise to follow the sensible views of M. ROGER, *op. cit.*, pp. 156–157.

12

For Virgil the Grammarian, alias Virgil of Toulouse, cf. the very useful translation —for the Latin text by itself, as edited by HUEMER, is absolutely unintelligible—by D. TARDI, *Les Epitomae de Virgile de Toulouse, essai de traduction critique avec une bibliographie, une introduction et des notes*, Paris, 1928.

EPILOGUE

1

For Byzantine education, especially the higher education: F. FUCHS, "Die höheren Schulen von Konstantinopel im Mittelalter, Byzantinisches Archiv" (Supplement to the *Byzantinische Zeitschrift*), VIII, Leipzig, 1926; J. M. HUSSEY, *Church and Learning in the Byzantine Empire*, 867–1185, Oxford-London, 1937; L. BREHIER, "L'Enseigne-ment classique et l'Enseignement religieux à Byzance", in *Revue d'Histoire et de Philosophie religieuses*, XXI (1941), pp. 34–69 (and now Vols. II–III of his *Monde Byzantin* in the collection "L'Evolution de l'Humanité").

There is one point to which the attention of Byzantine scholars should be drawn. They are very keen on drawing a parallel between the Byzantine syllabus and the syllabus of the neo-Platonic schools of philosophy (cf.: O. SCHISSEL VON FLESCHEN-BERG, *Marinos von Neapolis und die neuplatonischen Tugendgrade*, Athens, 1928). Does this mean to say that philosophical culture had become the rule, that Plato had finally defeated Isocrates? Or was philosophy the crown reserved for an élite? To answer these questions it would be necessary to find out what happened in Byzantine times to the dialectical tension between these two poles of classical culture which I have shown to be so fundamental during the Graeco-Roman period.

For the elementary-school teaching, about which little is still known, cf. the few suggestions in F. DVORNIK, *Les Légendes de Constantin et de Méthode vues de Byzance*, *Byzantinoslavica*, Supplement I, Prague, 1933, pp. 25–33. There is an excellent treatment of the subject, under the title "Byzantine Education", by G. BUCKLER, in *Byzantium, an Introduction to East Roman Civilization*, ed. N. H. BAYNES and H. St. L. B. MOSS, Oxford, 1948, pp. 200–220. The reader is warned, however, to accept with caution the somewhat uncritical work of P. KOUKOULES, written in Greek (English title, *Byzantine Life and Civilization*), vol. I, fasc. 1, Athens, 1948 (*Coll. de l'Institut fr. d'Athènes*, vol. 10), pp. 35–137.

2

For humanism in the time of the Palaeologi cf. R. GUILLAND, *Essai sur Nicéphone Grégoras, l'Homme et l'Oeuvre*, Paris, 1926, pp. 55 *et seq.*, 111 *et seq.*

3

The law against receiving "children of the world" into the monasteries in Byzantium: cf. the data presented by L. BREHIER, *art. cit.* in *Revue d'Histoire et de Philosophie religieuses*, 1941, pp. 63–64.

4

Origins of the patriarchal school in Constantinople: cf. again BREHIER, *ibid.*, pp. 42–44, which mentions the evidence in the *Autobiography* by ANANIAS of SCHIRAG (c. 600–650), trans. by CONYBEARE, in *Byzantinische Zeitschrift*, VI (1897), pp. 572–573.

5

For Greek schools after 1453: G. CHASSIOTIS, *L'Instruction publique chez les Grecs depuis la prise de Constantinople par les Turcs jusqu'à nos jours*, Paris, 1881, pp. 14 *et seq.* It will be observed that higher education never disappeared in the East as it did in the West, because immediately after Constantinople was taken Mehmed II re-established the office of Patriarch for the benefit of Gennadius Scholarius, who immediately revived the patriarchal school in the Phanar: CHASSIOTIS, *op. cit.*, p. 4; 34–42. For school exercises, still bearing the character they bore in antiquity, the same author refers to F. POUQUEVILLE, *Voyage de Morée*, Paris, 1805, pp. 267–270.

6

For school life in Irish monasteries in the fifth to the seventh centuries it will be sufficient if I mention the article by my pupil, A. LORCIN, in *Revue du Moyen-Age latin*, vol. I, 1945, pp. 221–236; despite the criticisms that have been made against it by Fr. GROSJEAN in *Analecta Bollandiana*, Vol. LXIV (1946), p. 323. The account by J. RYAN, *Irish Monasticism, Origins and Early Development*, Dublin, 1931, pp. 200–216, 360–383, referred to by Fr. Grosjean, is very summary.

7

The end of the old schools in Gaul: the fundamental work still remains that already mentioned in the preceding chapter (n. 10) by M. ROGER, *L'Enseignement des Lettres classiques d'Ausone à Alcuin, introduction à l'histoire des écoles carolingiennes*, Paris, 1905.

8

Were teachers in the time of Sidonius Apollinaris anything more than private tutors? Cf. A. LOYEN, *Sidoine Apollinaire et l'esprit précieux en Gaule*, Paris, 1943, p. 93.

9

For the end of "Romanitas" in the Danubian provinces, cf. A. ALFÖLDI, *Der Unter-gang der Römerherrschaft in Pannorien*, II (Ungarische Bibliothek, I R., 12), Berlin, 1926, p. 575.

For schools in Spain under the Visigoths: R. MENENDEZ PIDAL, *Historia de España*, Vol. III, *España Visigoda*, Madrid, 1940, pp. 343 (M. TORRES), 391, 397 (n. 88), 398, 416, 418–423 (J. PEREZ DE URBEL).

10

For the *Vandal Peace*, cf. the article—which has a certain tendencious bias—by C. SAUMAGNE in *Revue Tunisienne*, 1930, and a book which is again rather paradoxical in places by COURTOIS, *Les Vandales et l'Afrique*, Paris, 1955. For intellectual and university life in Carthage at the time of the Vandals, cf. the material collected by A. AUDOLLENT, *Carthage romaine*, Paris, 1901, pp. 749–766.

11

Vestiges of Christianity and Latinity in Morocco and Oran, J. CARCOPINO, *Le Maroc antique*, Paris, 1943, pp. 288–301.

12

For the end of Christianity in Africa, cf. the excellent essay by W. SESTON, in *Mélanges d'Archéologie et d'Histoire*, LIII (1936), pp. 101–124, and also: C. COURTOIS, "Grégoire VII et l'Afrique du Nord, remarques sur les communautés chrétiennes d'Afrique au XIᵉ siècle", in *Revue historique*, CXCV (1943), pp. 97–122, 193–226.

13

The last classical schools in Rome: for Felix, the last person known to have occupied the official chair of rhetoric in Rome, cf. my article "Autour de la Bibliothèque du pape Agapit", in *Mélanges d'Archéologie et d'Histoire*, XLVIII (1931), pp. 157–165. We find that he was already pensioned off in 534. For a more general treatment, F. ERMINI, "La Scuola in Roma nel VI secolo", in *Archivum Romanicum*, 1934, pp. 143–154.

14

Fortunatus's studies in Ravenna: D. TARDI, *Fortunat*, Paris, 1928, p. 62.

15

The same conflict between classical and Christian culture lasted in Gaul as long as anything remained of the old classical tradition: cf. c. 408, the satire by St. PAULINUS (of Béziers?), *Ad Salmonem* (*CSEL*, XVI, 1), 76–79.

16

For the centre for advanced religious studies that the Pope Agapetus and Cassiodorus tried to set up in Rome, cf. again the article mentioned *supra* n. 13, pp. 124 *et seq.*

17

For Cassiodorus's work cf. primarily P. COURCELLE, *Les Lettres grecques en Occident*, *de Macrobe à Cassiodore*, Paris, 1943, pp. 313–388; cf. also A. VAN DE VYVER, "Cassiodore et son oeuvre", in *Speculum*, VI (1931), pp. 244–292; "Les Institutiones de Cassiodore et sa fondation à Vivarium", in *Revue Bénédictine*, LXIII (1941), pp. 59–88.

18

For the Lombard "Renaissance", cf. A. Viscardi in the "Storia Letteraria d'Italia", ed. Vallardi, vol. I, *Le Origini*, Milan, 1939, *passim*, and especially: R. Bezzola, "Les Origines et la Formation de la littérature courtoise en Occident" (500–1200), I, "La Tradition impériale de la fin de l'antiquité au XIe siècle" (*BEHE*, fasc. 286), pp. 24–33. The author only describes one aspect of it but it is the most interesting. He shows that a slender thread of the *profane* academic tradition managed on the whole to persist through the Dark Ages, thus joining the old classical culture with the secular side of mediaeval culture, which it would be a mistake to confine to its religious side only.

REFERENCES

Apocryphal works are given under the name, enclosed in square brackets, of the author to whom tradition ascribes them. Thus, [Pl.] *Ax.* =Pseudo-Plato, *Axiochos*.

AA.SS. Acta Sanctorum (ed. Bollandists)
AA.SS. Hib. Acta Sanctorum Hiberniae ex codice Salmanticensi, Bruges-Edinburgh, 1888, ed. C. de Smedt and J. de Backer
ABAW Abhandlungen der bayerischen Akademie der Wissenschaften, Munich
ABKK Amtliche Berichte aus den königlichen Kunstsammlungen, monatlich erscheinendes Beiblatt zum Jahrbuch der kgl. preuszischen Kunstsammlungen, Berlin
Aboth Pirke Aboth Treatise in the Babylonian Talmud (IV, 9)
ABSA Annual of the British School at Athens
Aeg. Aegyptus, Rivista di Egittologia e di Papirologia
AEL. Aelianus of Preneste
  N.A. *On the Nature of Animals*
  V.H. *Various Stories*
Aep. L'Année Epigraphique (offprint of the Revue des Publications épigraphiques relatives à l'antiquité romaine, pub. in connection with the Revue Archéologique)
AESCHIN. Aeschines
  Amb. *On the False Embassy*
  Tim. *Against Timarchus*
AI Africa Italiana
AJPhil. American Journal of Philology
ALBIN. Albinus
  Isag. Introduction to Plato's Philosophy
  Epit. Summing-up of Plato's Philosophy
ALCID. Alcidamas
  Soph. *Against the Sophists*
ALCM. Alcman
  Fr. Fragments, in *Poetae Latini Graeci*, ed. Bergck
AM Mitteilungen des deutschen archaeologischen Instituts, Athenische Abteilung
AMM. MARC. Ammianus Marcellinus
ANAT. Anatolius of Laodicaea (P. Tannery, *Mémoires scientifiques*, III, pp. 12–25)
ANN. COMN. Anna Comnena, *Alexias*
ANTYLL. Antyllus
Anth. Pal. Anthologia Palatina
APAW Abhandlungen der preussischen Akademie der Wissenschaften, Class of History and Philosophy, Berlin
APP. Appian
[AP. TYAN] Pseudo-Apollonius of Tyana
  Ep. *Letters*
APUL. Apuleius
  Flor. *Florida*
  Mund. *Treatise on the World*
  De dog. Plat. *On the Teaching of Plato*
AR. Aristophanes
  Ach. *Acharnians*, ed. Starkie, 1909
  Nub. *Clouds*, ed. Starkie, 1911
ARAT. (AR. SOL.) Aratus of Soli
  Ph. *Phaenomena*

AR. BYZ. Aristophanes of Byzantium
  Onom. *On the Age-Names*. Page references from ed. E. Miller, *Mélanges de littérature grecque*, Paris, 1868
Arch. Pap. Archiv für Papyrusforschung und verwandte Gebiete
ARCHYT. Archytas of Tarentum
  Fr. Fragments in Diels, *Fragmente der Vorsokratiker*, §47 (35)
ARISTOX. Aristoxenus of Tarentum
ARIST. Aristotle
  Ath. Pol. *Athenaion Politeia. The Constitution of Athens* (chapter and paragraph from the Kenyon edition)
  Fr. Fragments (number according to the Rose edition). For his other works, see book, page, column and line of the Bekker edition
  Eth. Nic. *Nichomachean Ethics*
  Metaph. *Metaphysics*
  OEc. *Oeconomica*
  Part. An. *De Partibus Animalium*
  Poet. *Poetics*
  Pol. *Politics*
  Pr. *Problems*
  Rh. *Rhetoric*
ARSTD. Aelius Aristides
  D: Number of Discourse according to the Dindorf edition
  K: ditto, Keil edition
  Rhet. *Rhetoric*
ASFNA Annuaire de la Société française de Numismatique et d'Archéologie
ATH. Athenaeus. *The Sophists' Banquet* (page references from the Casaubon edition)
ATHAN. St. Athanasius of Alexandria
  V. Ant. *Life of St. Anthony*
ATHENAG. Athenagoras, *Apology for the Christians*
AUGUST. St. Augustine of Hippo
  De civ. D. *The City of God*
  Conf. *Confessions*
  Ep. *Letters*
  Mus. *On Music*
  Ord. *On Order*
  Serm. *Sermons*
  Sol. *Soliloquies*
AUG. IMP. Augustus, emperor
  R.G. *Res Gestae*
AUSON. Ausonius
  Ecl. *Eclogues*
  Ep. *Letters*
  Epigr. *Epigrams*
  Grat. Act. *Gratiarum actio*
  Prof. Burd. *Commemoratio Professorum Burdigalensium*
  Protr. *Exhortation to his Grandson* (=Epistles, XXII, *Idylls*, IV)

454   A HISTORY OF EDUCATION IN ANTIQUITY

BABR. Babrius: *Fables* (page references from Crusius ed.)
  English ed. W. G. Rutherford (1883)
BABELON E. Babelon
  Monn. Rep. Description historique et chronologique des Monnaies de la République romaine, vulgairement appelées Monnaies consulaires, Paris, 1885–6
BAC G. B. de Rossi, *Bulletino di Archeologia cristiana*
BAR HEBR. Bar Hebraeus
  Nomocan. Nomocanon, see A. Mai, *Scriptorum Veterum Nova Collectio*, X, Rome, 1838
BARN. Epistle of Barnabas
BAS. St. Basil of Caesarea
  Ep. Letters (no. of order and column according to *PG*, vol. 32)
  Hom. Sermons (*Hom.* XXII = *To Young Men, on Reading Profane Authors*)
  Reg. Brev. The Shorter Monastic Rules
  Reg. fus. The Longer Monastic Rules
B. BATHRA *Baba Bathra* Treatise in the Babylonian *Talmud*
BCH *Bulletin de Correspondance hellénique*
BEDE St. Bede the Venerable
  H. Abb. History of the Abbots of Wearmouth and Jarrow (col. ref. from *PL*, vol. 94)
BEHE *Bibliothèque de l'Ecole pratique des Hautes-Etudes* (*Section des Sciences historiques et philologiques*)
BENED. St. Benedict of Nursia
  Reg. Monastic Rule
BGU *Aegyptische Urkunden aus den königlichen* (or *staatlichen*) *Museen zu Berlin: Griechische Urkunden*
BIFAO *Bulletin de l'institut Français d'Archéologie Orientale*, Cairo
BKT *Berliner Klassikertexte herausgegeben von der Generalverwaltung der* [*königlichen*] *Museen zu Berlin*
BSA *Bulletin de la Société archéologique d'Alexandrie*
BSNAF *Bulletin de la Société nationale des Antiquaires de France*

C Canon (of the Council referred to)
CAES. AR. St. Caesarius of Arles (page ref. from vol. II of the Morin ed.)
  Ep. Letters
  Mon. Rule for Monks
  Virg. Rule for Nuns
  Vit. Life of St. Caesarius by his disciples
CALLIM. Callimachus
  Epigr. Epigrams (numbered according to the Cahen ed.)
CALLINUS OF EPHESUS. Fr. Fragments: see *Poetae Lyrici Graeci*, ed. Bergck
Can. Hipp. Canons (Arabic) of the Pseudo-Hippolytus
CARCOPINO J. Carcopino
  Maroc. Le Maroc antique, Paris, 1943
CASSIAN John Cassian
  Conl. Conferences with the Desert Fathers
  Inst. Monastic Institutions
CASSIOD. Cassiodorus
  Inst. Institutions
  Var. Variae

CATO Cato the Censor
  Agr. Treatise on Agriculture
CATULL. Catullus
[CEB.] Pseudo-Cebes
CENSOR. Censorinus
  D.N. On the Anniversary Day
CHRYS. St. John Chrysostom
  Adv. Opp. Against the Detractors of the Monastic Life (book, chapter and column from *PG*, vol. 47)
  Inan. gl. On Vain Glory, and how Parents should bring up their Children (chapter and paragraph)
CIC. Cicero (book, paragraph, but not chapter)
  Arat. Translation of Aratus
  Att. Letters to Atticus
  Brut. Brutus
  Coel. For Coelius
  De Or. Orator
  Div. On Divination
  Fam. Letters to his Friends
  Har. Resp. De Haruspicum responso
  Her. Auctor ad Herennium
  Inv. On Invention
  Leg. Laws
  Off. De Officiis
  Orat. The Orator
  Pis. Against L. Piso
  Resp. The Republic
  Sen. On Old Age
  Tim. Translation of Plato's *Timaeus*
  Tusc. Tusculans
  Verr. Against Verres
C. Gloss Lat. *Corpus Glossariorum Latinorum*
CIG *Corpus Inscriptionum Graecarum*
CIL *Corpus Inscriptionum Latinarum*
CLAUD. Claudian
  Carm. min. Minor Poems
  Fesc. Epithalamium of Honorius and Maria
CLEM. Clement of Alexandria
  Strom. Stromata (book, paragraph and section from the Stählin ed.)
CLEM. ROM. St. Clement of Rome
Cod. Just. Codex Justinianus
Cod. Theod. Codex Theodosianus
Conc. Merov. *Concilia Merovingici Aevi*, ed. Maassen (*Monumenta Germaniae Historica, Leges*, III, *Concilia*, I)
Const. apost. *Apostolic Constitutions* (ed. Funk, *Didascalia et Constitutiones apostolorum*)
CONWAY R. S. Conway, *The Italic Dialects*, edited with a Grammar and Glossary, Cambridge, 1897
CRUM W. E. Crum (with H. E. Winlock and H. G. Evelyn White)
  Epiph. The Monastery of Epiphanius at Thebes, II, *Coptic, Greek Ostraca and Papyri*, New York, 1926
CSEL *Corpus Scriptorum Ecclesiasticorum Latinorum*, edited by the Vienna Academy of Sciences
[CYPR.] Pseudo-St. Cyprian of Carthage
  Spect. On Spectacles

DIO CASS. Dio Cassius, *History of Rome*
DIO CHRYS. Dio Chrysostom
  Orat. Speeches

DEM. Demosthenes
Aph. Against Aphobus
Cor. On the Crown
Euerg. Against Euergus
DESSAU H. Dessau, *Inscriptiones Latinae Selectae (ILS)*
D.H. Dionysius of Halicarnassus
(where there is no indication of the title)
Roman Antiquities
Comp. On Literary Composition
Dem. On the Eloquence of Demosthenes
Isoc. Life of Isocrates
Didach. Didache. The Teaching of the Twelve Apostles
Didasc. Ap. The Teaching of the Apostles (Didascalia et Constitutiones Apostolorum, ed. Funk)
DIDYM. Didymus Chalcenterius
DIEHL E. Diehl, *Inscriptiones Latinae Christianae Veteres*
Dig. See Just. (2)
DIOCL. Diocletian
Max. Edict of Maximum, ed. Mommsen
Dialexeis Δισσοί Λόγοι, in H. Diels, *Fragmente der Vorsokratiker,* §90 (83)
DIOD. SIC. Diodorus Siculus, *Historical Library* (C. H. Oldfather, 1933–   , Loeb)
DION. THRAX Dionysius Thrax, *Grammar* (paragraph from the Uhlig ed.)
DIONYS. PER. Dionysius Periegetes, "Description of Greece" (page reference from Bernhardy ed.)
Dist. Cat. Distichs attributed to Cato, ed. Boas
Dittenberg. W. Dittenberger
Or. Orientis Graeci Inscriptiones Selectae
SIG Sylloge Inscriptionum Graecarum, 3rd ed.
D.L. Diogenes Laertius, *Lives of the Philosophers* (book, paragraph, but not chapter)
DURRBACH F. Durrbach
Choix. Choix d'Inscriptions de Délos avec traduction et commentaire, I, *Textes Historiques,* Paris, 1921

ENN. Ennius (quoted, usually, from citations)
Fr. Sc. Scenic Fragments, from the Vahlen ed.
ENNOD. Ennodius of Pavia
Carm. Poems
Dict. Declamations
Ep. Letters
EPHOR. Ephorus of Cyme
Fr. Fragments: order taken from Didot, *Fragmenta Historicorum Graecorum*
EPICR. Epicrates
EPICT. Epictetes, *Lectures Collected by Arrianus*
EUC. Euclid
Elem. Elements of Geometry
EUCH. St. Eucherius of Lyons
Instr. Instruction
De Laud. Er. In Praise of Solitude
EUNAP. Eunapius
V.S. Lives of the Sophists (page refs. from the Boissonade edition)
V.L. Life of Libanius
Proh. Life of Prohairesius

EUP. Eupolis, fragments. See *Fragmenta Comicorum Graecorum,* ed. Meinecke
EUR. Euripides
EUS. Eusebius of Caesarea
H.E. Ecclesiastical History
EUST. Eustathius of Thessalonica
Commentary on the Iliad (quoted according to the lemma)

F. Delph. Fouilles de Delphes, published by the Ecole Française d'Athènes
F. Eph. Forschungen in Ephesos, published by the Austrian Archaeological Institute
FERRAND. Ferrandus of Carthage, *Life of St. Fulgentius of Ruspe* (ed. Lapeyre)
FERREOL. St. Ferreolus of Uzès
Reg. Monastic Rule (in *PL,* vol. 66)
FESTUS Festus, *On the Meaning of Words* (page and line ref. from the Lindsay ed.)
FCG Fragmente Comicorum Graecorum, ed. A. Meinecke
FLOR. L. Annaeus Florus
Virg. Was Virgil an Orator or a Poet? (chapter and paragraph from the edition of H. Malcovati, Rome, 1938)
FORT. Venantius Fortunatus
Carm. Poems
Frag. Vat. Fragmenta Vaticana (paragraph ref. from the Mommsen edition)
FRONTO Fronto (ed. Naber)
Amic. Letters to his Friends
M. Caes. Correspondence with Marcus Aurelius (Eng. text, with translation, ed. C. R. Haines, Loeb, 1919–20)

GAL. Galen (pagination of the Kuhn edition)
Libr. propr. On his Own Writings
Med. Phil. That the Doctor is Also a Philosopher (vol. I, pp. 53 *seq.*)
Met. Med. Of Medical Method (vol. X, pp. 1 *seq.*)
Parv. pil. On the Little Ball (vol. V, pp. 899 *seq.*)
Plat. On the Opinions of Plato and Hippocrates (vol. I, pp. 181 *seq.*)
Protr. Speech of exhortation
San. tu. Advice on Hygiene (vol. VI, pp. 1 *seq.*)
GELL. Aulus Gelius, *NA (Attic Nights)*
Gramm. Lat. Grammatici Latini (ed. Keil)
CHAR. Charisius
CONS. Consentius
DIOM. Diomedes
DON. Donatus
M. VICT. Marius Victorinus
POMP. Pompeius
PRISC. Priscian
SERV. Servius (*sic:* I identify as Servius the Sergius of the MSS.)
GREG. MAGN. St. Gregory the Great
Dial. Dialogues
Reg. Letters (classified according to the Ewald-Hartmann edition, *Monumenta Germaniae Historica, Epistulae,* I–II)
GREG. NAZ. St. Gregory of Nazianzus
Carm. Poems
Or. Speeches (number, chapter, paragraph or column according to *PG,* vols. 35–8)

GREG. NYS. St. Gregory of Nyssa
C. Eun. Against Eunomius (book and paragraph according to the edition of W. Jäger)
GREG. TH. St. Gregory the Thaumaturge
Pan. Panegyric of Origen (paragraph and column of PG, vol. 10)
GREG. TUR. St. Gregory of Tours
Hist. Fr. History of the Franks
V. Patr. Lives of the Fathers

HARP. Harpocration, Lexicon
HDT. Herodotus, History
HER. Herondas, Mimes
Did. The Schoolmaster (Mime III)
HERM. TR. Corpus Hermeticum
HERM. Hermas, The Shepherd
Sim. Comparisons
Vis. Visions
HERMIAS Irrisio of the Pagan Philosophers
HES. Hesiod, Works and Days
Hesp. Hesperia, Journal of the American School of Archeology at Athens
HESYCH. Hesychius of Alexandria, Lexicon
HIERON Hieron of Alexandria
Geom. Geometry
Geod. Geodesy
Stereom. Stereometry
HIERON. St. Jerome
Chron. Chronicle (years before or after Christ)
Ep. Correspondence
In. Is. Commentary on Isias (PL, vol. 24)
In Jer. Commentary on Jeremias (ibid.)
De Vir Ill. Of Illustrious Men
HIMER. Himerius
Or. Speeches (page refs. according to the Dübner edition)
HIPP. St. Hippolytus of Rome
Trad. Ap. The Apostolic Tradition
HIPPARCHUS In Arat. Commentary on the Phenomena of Aratus
HIPPIAS Fr. Fragments. See Fragmente der Vorsokratiker, ed. Diels, §86 (79)
HOM. Homer
Il. Iliad
Od. Odyssey
HOR. Horace
Carm. Odes
Carm. Saec. Secular Ode
Epist. Letters
Sat. Satires
HPC Corpus of Works attributed to Hippocrates (vol. and page of the Littré edition)
Hab. On Wellbeing
Praec. Rules

IAMBL. Iamblichus
Theol. arith. The Theology of Numbers
IG Inscriptiones Graecae
IG², II Inscriptiones Graecae, editio minor, vols. II–III
IG Rom. Inscriptiones Graecae ad Res Romanes pertinentes, ed. R. Cagnat
ILA Inscriptions Latines de l'Algérie
Ins. Perg. M. Fraenkel, Inschriften von Pergamon (Altertümer von Pergamon, vol. VIII)
Ins. Priene. F. Hiller von Gaerthringen, Inschriften von Priene, Berlin, 1906
IOSPE B. Latyschev, E. Pridik, Inscriptiones antiquae orae septentrionalis Ponti Euxeni Graecae et Latinae

IREN. St. Irenaeus of Lyons, Against Heresies
ISID. Isidore of Seville
Sent. Book of Sentences
ISOC. Isocrates
Ad Nic. To Nicocles
Ant. On Exchange
Arch. Archidamus
Areop. Areopagiticus
Bus. Busiris
Evag. Evagoras
Hel. Encomium of Helen
Nic. Nicocles
Pan. Panegyricus
Panath. Panathenaicus
Phil. Philippus
Soph. Against the Sophists

JHS Journal of Hellenic Studies
JÖAI Jahreshefte des oesterreichen archaeologischen Instituts in Wien
JOH. DIAC. John the Deacon
V. Greg. Life of St. Gregory the Great
JOSEPH. Josephus
Ap. Against Apion
JUL. Julian the Apostate
C. Gal. Against the Galileans (page and page section from the Spanheim edition of St. Cyril of Alexandria)
Ep. (order number according to the Bidez-Cumont edition, page refs. according to the Spanheim edition)
JUNIL. Junillus Africanus, Instituta regularia divinae legis
JUST. (1) St. Justin Martyr
Acts. Acts of his Martyrdom (ed. Franchi de' Cavalieri, Studi e Testi, vol. VIII, 2)
Ap. Apologies
Dial. Dialogue with Tryphon
(2) Justinian
Cod. Just. Code of Justinian
Dig. Digesta
Inst. Institutiones
Nov. Novellae
Omnem. Omnem Constitution at the beginning of the Digesta
JUV. Juvenal, Satires

L. & S. Liddell and Scott. H. G. Liddell, R. Scott, H. Stuart Jones, R. Mackenzie, A Greek-English Lexicon, new edition
LIB. Libanius
Ep. Letters (order number from the Förster ed.)
Or. Speeches (number and paragraph from the Förster ed.: I have restored the order number of speeches in vol. I)
LUCIAN
Abd. The Disinherited Son
Am. Loves
Anach. Anacharsis
As. Lucius or the Donkey
Eun. The Eunuch
Herm. Hermotimus
Lex. Lexiphanes
M. cond. On Those in the Pay of the Great
Mnsc. The Fly
Paras. The Parasite
Rh. Pr. The Master of Rhetoric
Salt. On Dancing

LUCR.   Lucretius, *De Natura Rerum*
LYD.   Lydus
   Mag. Of Roman Magistratures

MACROB.   Macrobius
   Diff. Comparison of Greek and Latin Verbs
   Sat. Saturnalia
MALAL.   Malalas, *Chronicle* (book and page
   from the Dindorf edition, vol. XV of the
   Bonn Byzantine Collection)
MARIN.   Marinus of Neapolis
   V. Procl. Life of Proclus
MART.   Martial, *Epigrams*
MAXIMUS OF TYRE   *Dissertations*
MENANDER   *Monost. Monosticha* (number
   of verse according to the Meinecke edition)
MICHEL   C. Michel, *Recueil d'Inscriptions
   Grecques*

NEMBN   *Notices et Extraits des manuscrits de
   la Bibliothèque* [*Impériale*, then] *Nationale*
NEP.   Cornelius Nepos
   Epam. Life of Epaminondas
NICOM.   Nicomachus of Gerasa, *Introduc-
   tion to Arithmetic*
NON.   Nonius Marcellus, *De Compendiosa
   Doctrina* (pagination of the minor edition
   of Lindsay, coll. Teubner)
Not. Dign. Notitia Dignitatum
   Or. In partibus Orientis
N.S.   Notizie degli Scavi di Antichità, pub-
   lished by the Academia dei Lincei

O. Ostraca
O. Lond. Hall   H. R. Hall, *Coptic and Greek
   Texts of the Christian Period from Ostraka,
   Stelae, etc., in the British Museum*
ORIB.   *Oribases: Medical Miscellany*
ORIG.   Origen
   Greg. Letter to St. Gregory Thaumaturge
   In Num.   Homilies on Numbers, in Rufinus'
   translation.
OROS.   Orosius Paulus, *History against the
   Pagans*
OV.   Ovid
   Ars Am. Ars amatoria
   Am.   Amores
   F.   Fasti
   Tr.   Tristia
U. Wilcken   U. Wilcken, *Griechische Ostraka
   aus Egypten und Nubien*

P   Papyrus (the volume is not indicated in
   cases where the numbering is carried on
   throughout)
PAchmim   P. Collart, *Les Papyrus grecs
   d' Achmim* (from the *Bulletin de l'Institut
   Français d'Archéologie Orientale de Caire*,
   vol. 31, 1930, pp. 35–111)
PAmh.   Amherst Papyri, B. P. Grenfell and
   A. S. Hunt
PAntin.   Antinoë Papyrus, in H. J. M. Milne,
   Greek Shorthand Manuals
PBerl.   Berlin Papyri, ed. A. Erman and F.
   Krebs. *Aus den Papyrus der königlichen
   Museen* (*Handbücher der königlichen Mu-
   seen zu Berlin*)
PBouriant   P. Collart, *Les Papyrus Bouriant*,
   Paris, 1926

*PCairo Zenon   Catalogue Général des Anti-
   quités Egyptiennes du Musée du Caire*.
   C. C. Edgar, *Zenon Papyri*
PFay.   B. P. Grenfell, A. S. Hunt, D. G.
   Hogarth, *Fayûm Towns and Their Papyri*
PFior.   G. Vitelli, D. Comparetti, *Papiri
   greco-egizii, Papiri Fiorentini*
*PFouad I   Publications de la Société Fouad
   Ier de Papyrologie,Textes et documents*, III,
   Les Papyrus Fouad Ier, vol. I
PFreid.   W. Aly, M. Gelzer, *Mittheilungen aus
   der Freiburger Papyrussammlung*, I–II, in
   *Sitzungsberichte der Heidelberger Akademie
   der Wissenshaften* (philos.-hist. Klasse),
   1914, 2
PGen.   *Geneva Papyri* (quoted from special
   editions)
PGiess.   E. Kornemann, O. Eger, P. M. Meyer.
   *Griechische Papyri im Museum des ober-
   hessischen Geschichtevereins zu Giessen*
PGuér.Joug.   *Publications de la Société Royale
   Egyptienne de Papyrologie, Textes et
   Documents*, II. O. Guéraud, P. Jouguet,
   *Un Livre d'Ecolier du IIIe Siècle avant
   Jésus-Christ*
PHal.   *Dikaiomata, Auszüge aus alexandrini-
   schen Gesetzen und Verordnungen in einem
   Papyrus des philologischen Seminars der
   Universität Halle*, Berlin, 1913
PHerc.[2]   *Herculanensium Voluminum quae
   supersunt collectio altera.*
PHombert-Préaux   M Hombert, C. Préaux,
   "Une tablette homérique de la Bibliothèque
   Bodleienne", in *Mélanges Henri Grégoire*,
   Brussells, 1951, vol. III, pp. 161–8.
PIand.   C. Kalbfleisch, *Papyri Iandanae*
PLetronne   Papyrus Letronne, in *Notes et
   Extraits des Manuscrits de la Bibliothèque
   Nationale*, vol. XVIII, 2, pp. 25 *seq.*
*PMilan   Papiri Milanesi per cura della Scuola
   di Papirologie dell'Universita del Sacro
   Cuore*
POsl.   S. Eitrem, L. Amundsen, *Papyri
   Osloenses*
POxy.   B. P. Grenfell, A. S. Hunt, H. I. Bell,
   etc., *The Oxyrhynchus Papyri*
PReinach   T. Reinach, *Papyrus Grecs et
   Démotiques*, Paris, 1905
PRyl.   A. S. Hunt, J. de M. Johnson, V.
   Martin, *Catalogue of the Greek Papyri in
   the John Rylands Library at Manchester*
PSchwartz   I have given this provisional title
   to papyrus no. 320 in the collections of the
   Institut Français d'Archéologie Orientale,
   published by J. Schwartz in *Etudes de
   Papyrologie de la Société Fouad Ier de
   Papyrologie*, vol. VII (1948), pp. 93–
   109, under the title *Un Manuel scolaire de
   l'époque byzantine*
PTebt.   B. P. Grenfell, A. S. Hunt, J. G.
   Symly, E. J. Goodspeed, *The Tebtunis
   Papyri*
PG   Migne, *Patrologiae Cursus, series Graeca*
PL   Migne, *Patrologiae Cursus, series Latina*
Pan. Lat.   Latin Panegyrics (numbered accord-
   ing to the Baehrens ed.)
PAUL DIAC.   Paul the Deacon
   Hist. Long. History of the Lombards
   V. Greg. Life of St. Gregory the Great

PAUS. Pausanias, *Description of Greece*
PERS. Persius, *Satires*
Pesikta Folio of the Sal. Buber ed., Lyck, 1868
PETRON. Petronius, *Satyricon*
Ph. Philologus
PHILO Philo of Alexandria
  Congr. On Preparatory Studies (ed. Cohn, vol. III, pp. 72 seq.)
  V. Moys. Life of Moses (ibid., pp. 118 *seq.)*
PHILSTR. Philostratus
  Gym. On Gymnastics
  Im. The Statues
  VA Life of Apollonius of Tyana
  V.S. Lives of the Sophists (book, chapter and page according to the Olearius ed.)
PHOT. Photius the Patriarch
  Bibl. Biblioteca (number of codex and column from vol. 103 or 104 of *PG*)
PIND. Pindar
  Nem. Nemeans
  Ol. Olympics
  Pyth. Pythian Odes
PL. Plato (page and section of page according to the edition of H. Estienne)
  Ax. Axiochus
  Chrm. Charmides
  Cra. Cratylus
  Ep. Epistulae
  Grg. Gorgias
  Hipp. Ma. Hippias Major
  Hipp. Mi. Hippias Minor
  Hipparch. Hipparchus
  Lach. Laches
  Leg. Leges
  Lys. Lysis
  Menex. Menexenus
  Phdr. Phaedrus
  Pol. Politica
  Prot. Protogoras
  Resp. The Republic
  Soph. The Sophists
  Tht. Theaetetus
PLAUT. Plautonius
  Bacch. Bacchides
PLINY (1) Pliny the Elder
  HN Natural History (book and paragraph, not chapter)
  (2) Pliny the Younger
  Ep. Letters
  Pan. Panegyric of Trajan
PLOT. Plotinus
  Enn. Enneads
PLUT. Plutarch
  (1) *Vitae Parallelae* (chapter)
  Alc. Alcibiades
  Aem. Aemilius Paulus
  Ag. Cleom. Agis and Cleomenes
  Cat. Mai. Cato the Censor
  Cat. Min. Cato of Utica
  C. Grach. Caius Gracchus
  Cim. Cimon
  Dion. Dion
  Lyc. Lycurgus
  Pel. Pelopidas
  Pomp. Pompeius
  Rom. Romulus
  Sert. Sertorius

Them. Themistocles
Ti. Gracch. Tiberius Gracchus
  (2) *Moralia* (page and section of page from the Estienne-Xylander edition, 1599)
  Adv. Col. Against Colotes
  Amat. Amatorius
  Amat. narr. Love Tales
  Aud. poet. On the Manner of Studying the Poets
  Isocr. Life of Isocrates (Lives of the Ten Orators, IV)
  Lib. educ. On the Education of Children
  Non posse suav. That it is not possible to live pleasantly while imitating Epicurus
  Plac. Opinions of the Philosophers
  Prof. in virt. On Progress in Virtue
  Quaest. conv. The Banquet
  Qu. Rom. Roman Questions
  San. tu. Advice on Hygiene
Poet. Lat. Med. Monumenta Germaniae Historica, Antiquitates, Poetae Latini medii aevi
POLEM. Polemon of Laodicea, *Declamations* (order of numbers and pages from the Hinck edition)
POLYB. Polybius, *History of Rome*
POLL. Pollux, *Onomasticon* (s.v. or: book and paragraph from the Bethe edition, *Lexicographi Graeci,* vol. IX)
PORPH. Porphyry
  Abst. On Abstinence
  V. Pyth. Life of Pythagoras
P. PELL. Paulinus of Pella, *Eucharisticon*
PREISIGKE F. Preisigke (cont. by F. Bilabel, etc.)
  SB Sammelbuch griechischer Urkunden aus Aegypten
PROTAGORAS Fr. Fragments in Diels, *Die Fragmente der Vorsokratiker,* §74
PRUD. Prudentius
  Cath. Book of Hours
Ps. *Book of Psalms*
PSELLUS Michael Psellus
  Epit. Funeral Speeches (page ref. from the ed. of K. N. Sathas, *Bibliotheca Graeca medii aevi,* vol. V)
PSI Papiri greci e latini, Pubblicazioni della Società Italiana per la ricerca dei Papiri greci et latini in Egitto
[PYTH.] Pseudo-Pythagoras
  V. Aur. Golden Verses

QUINT. Quintilian, *Institutio oratoria*

REG Revue des Etudes grecques
Reg. Rule (monastic). See under the various authors cited.
Reg. Mag. The Rule of the Master (ed. Masai-Corbett)
Reg. Pach. The Rule of St. Pachomius (ed. A. Boon, T. Lefort, *Pachomiana Latina*)
REM. REM. St. Remy of Rheims
  Ep. Letters (page refs. from the edition of *Monumenta Germaniae Historica, Epistulae,* III, *Epistulae Merovingici aevi*)
RF Rivista di Filologia e d'Istruzione classica, Turin

Rhet. Gr. *Rhetores Graeci* (volume, page and line from the Spengel edition)
APHT. Aphtonius
HERM. Hermogenes
MEN. Menander
THEON. Theon of Alexandria
Rhet. Lat. Min. *Rhetores Latini Minores*, ed. Halm
GRILL. Grillius
M. VICT. Marius Victorinus
PRISC. Priscian
RIGI *Rivista Indo-greco-italica di Filologia, Lingua, Antichità*
ROBERT L. Robert
Et. Anat. *Etudes Anatoliennes* (*Etudes Orientales* published by the Institut Français of Stamboul, vol. V, Paris, 1937)
RPGR S. Reinach, *Repertoire de Peintures grecques et romaines*
RUFIN. Rufinus of Aquileia
Apol. Apology
H.E. Ecclesiastical History
RUT. NAMAT. Rutilius Namatianus, *Poem on his Return*

SALL. Sallust
Cat. Catilina
Inv. Invectives
SAPH. Sappho
Fr. Fragments, ed. Diehl
SAWW *Sitzungsberichte der philosophisch-historischen Klasse der Akademie der Wissenschaften*, Vienna (volume, year, fascicule, page)
SBAW *Sitzungsberichte der bayerischen Akademie der Wissenschaften*, Munich
SCHIAPARELLI L. Schiaparelli, "Codice diplomatico longobardo" in *Fonti per la Storia d'Italia*, vol. 62
Schol. Scholia (lemma)
AR. *Scholia* of Aristophanes
DION. THRAX *Scholia* of Dionysius Thrax (page ref. from the Hilgard ed., *Grammatici Graeci*, vol. III)
HERMOG. *Scholia* of Hermogenes
SEG J. Hondius, etc., *Supplementum Epigraphicum Graecum*
SEN. (1) Seneca the Rhetor
Controv. Controversiae
Suas. Suasoriae
(2) Seneca the Philosopher
Ep. Letters to Lucilius
Ir. On Anger
SERV. Servius, *Commentary on the Aeneid* (*lemma*)
SEXT. EMP. Sextus Empiricus
Math. Against Mathematicians
S.H.A. Authors of the Augustan History
Alex. S. Alexander Severus
Ant. Antoninus Pius
Gord. The Gordians
Hadr. Hadrian
Helag. Helagabalus
M. Aur. Marcus Aurelius
Ver. Lucius Verus
SID. APOLL. Sidonius Apollinaris
Ep. Letters

SIG *Sylloge Inscriptionum Graecarum*, 3rd ed·
SIMPL. Simplicius
In Coel. Commentary on Aristotle's "De Coelo," page references from the Heiberg edition (*Commentaria in Aristotelem Graeca*, vol. VIII)
SOCR. Socrates the Scholastic
H.E. Ecclesiastical History
SOLON *Fr.* Fragments, in Bergck, *Poetae Lyrici Graeci*
SOZOM. Sozomen
H.E. Ecclesiastical History
SPAW *Sitzungsberichte der preussischen Akademie der Wissenschaften*, Berlin
S. SEV. Sulpicius Severus
V. Mart. Life of St. Martin of Tours
STAT. Statius
Theb. Thebais
Stat. Eccl. Ant. Statutes of the Early Church (Morin edition of St. Caesarius of Arles, vol. II)
STEPH. BYZ. Stephanus Byzantius, *Geographical Dictionary*
STOB. Stobaeus, *Extracts* (book and paragraph)
STOKES W. Stokes
Tr. Life. The Tripartite Life of Patrick, with Other Documents Relating to that Saint (*Rerum Britannicarum medii aevi Scriptores*, vol. 89), London, 1887
STRAB. Strabo, *Geography* (book and page from the Casaubon edition)
SUET. Suetonius
Aug. Life of Augustus
Caes. Life of Julius Caesar
Calig. Life of Caligula Caesar
Dom. Life of Domitian
Gram. Of Grammarians and Rhetors (the chapters from *De Rhetoribus*, sometimes regarded as a separate book, are numbered after the preceding ones)
Ner. Life of Nero
Tib. Life of Tiberias
Tit. Life of Titus
Vesp. Life of Vespasian
SUID. Suidas, *Lexicon* (s.v., volume and page, or, letter and article from the Adler edition, *Lexicographi Graeci*, I)
SYN. Synesius of Cyrene
Ep. Letters (number)
Regn. On Royalty (column from *PG*, vol. 66)

TAC. Tacitus
Agr. Life of Agricola
Ann. Annals
Dial. Dialogue of the Orators
Hist. Histories
Talmud Babylonian Talmud (title of treatise and column from the 3rd Bomberg edition)
TAM *Tituli Asiae Minoris*
TAT. Tatian, *Apologia*
TEL. Teles (from extracts in Stobaeus)
TER. Terence
Andr. Andria
TERPANDER *Fr.* Fragments in Bergck, *Poetae Lyrici Graeci*

TERT. Tertullian
  Idol. On Idolatry
  Pall. On the Cloak
  Praescr. On the Argument of Prescription
  Spect. On Spectacles
TH. Theophrastus
  Char. Characters
THEM. Themistius
  Or. Speeches (page reference from the Hardouin edition)
THEOC. Theocritus, *Idylls*
THEODOR. Theodoret
  H.E. Ecclesiastical History
THEOG. Theognis, *Elegies*, in Bergck, *Poetae Lyrici Graeci*
THEON SM. Theon of Smyrna, *Of the Mathematical Knowledge Necessary in Order to read Plato*
  Arith. Arithmetic
THUC. Thucydides
TROG. POMP. Trogus Pompeius, *Abridgment* (made by Justin) of the *Philippic History*
TYRT. Tyrtaeus
  Fr. Fragments, in Bergck, *Poetae Lyrici Graeci*
TZTZ. John Tzetzes
  Chil. Chiliades

UPZ U. Wilcken, *Urkunden der Ptolemäerzeit, ältere Funde*

VAL. MAX. Valerius Maximus, *Memorable Sayings and Doings*
VARR. Varro
  L.L. On the Latin Language
  R.R. On Agriculture
VEG. Vegetius, *Study of the Art of War*
VIB. SEQ. Vibius Sequester, *Names of Rivers, Streams, etc., Mentioned by the Poets*
VIRG. Virgil
  Aen. Aeneid
  Epig. Epigrams from the *Appendix Vergiliana*
  G. Georgics
VIRG. GRAM. Virgil the Grammarian
  Epit. Epitomae
V. Isoc. Anonymous *Life of Isocrates* (line references from G. Mathieu and E. Brémond, vol. I of their edition of Isocrates)

VITR. Vitruvius, *On Architecture*
V. Patr. Emer. J. N. Garvin, *Vitas Sanctorum Patrum Emeritensium*, Washington, 1946
V. Pers. Anonymous *Life of Persius* (at the beginning of Cartault's edition)
V.SS. Hib. C. Plummer, *Vitae Sanctorum Hiberniae partim hactenus ineditae*, Oxford, 1910
V. SS. Merov. Passiones Vitaeque sanctorum merovingici aevi, in *Monumenta Germaniae Historica, Scriptores rerum merovingicarum*, vols. III–V
V. Virg. Ancient biographies of Virgil, ed. Brummer (line reference according to the several biographies)
Bern. Life, from the manuscripts of Berne
DON. Donatus
PHIL. Philargyrius, *Vita Prima*
SERV. Servius

WESSELY C. Wessely
  Stud. Studien zur Palaeographie und Papyruskunde
WILCKEN L. Mitteis, U. Wilcken
  Chrest. Grundzüge und Chrestomathie der Papyruskunde, part I, vol. II (number of papyrus and line)
WS Wiener Studien

XEN. Xenophon
  Ath. The Constitution of the Athenians
  Conv. The Banquet
  Cyn. On Hunting
  Lac. The Constitution of Sparta
  Mem. Memorabilia
  Oec. Oeconomicus
XENOPHANES OF COLOPHON. Fr. Fragments in Diels, *Die Fragmente der Vorsokratiker*, §24 (11)

ZACH. Zacharius the Scholastic
  V. Sev. The Life of Severus of Antioch, in *Patrologia Orientalis*, vol. II, fasc. I
ZIEBARTH E. Ziebarth, *Aus der antiken Schule*, 2nd edition (in H. Lietzmann, *Kleine Texte für Vorlesungen und Uebungen*, no. 65), Leipzig, 1913: the reader is referred to this collection only for such documents as are there published for the first time
ZONAR. Zonaras, abbreviated version of the *Roman History* of Dionysius Cassius

It has been thought advisable, for purposes of classification and pagination, to use standard works (H. Estienne for Plato, etc.), but it goes without saying that the text followed is that of the most recent, or the best, critical edition, which the reader is asked to consult. Thus, although Teles is quoted following Stobaeus, his text will be found in the Hense edition; and the same principle applies throughout.

ANALYTICAL INDEX

I

RES NOVAE

Texts, terms and questions forming the subject of critical discussion or of a new interpretation.

Aep., 1925, 119: 439 (11)
αἵρεσις: 386 (16)
ἀκρόανις: 408 (1)
AM, 37, 1912, 277b, 1, 2–7: 402 (12)
Antiphon of Rhamnus and Antiphon the Sophist: 370 (4)
Attic ephebia, total complement of: 383–4 (6)
Attic legislation on compulsory schooling: 382 (3)

BARDON, H., thesis: 426 (10)

C. Gloss. Lat., III, 645, §2: 431 (11)
CHAPOUTHIER, F., *REG*, 1925, 427 *seq.*: 357 (19)
Cod. Just., XI, 19: 442 (16)
Cnossos, education at the palace of: 357 (19)
counting on fingers: 400 (9)
Crates of Mallus in Rome: 422 (13)
Cod. Theod., XIV, 9, 2: 442–3 (16)

Dig., XLVIII, 19, 28, 3: 440 (4)
distinguere codicem: 434 (30)
DITTENBERG., *SIG*, 959: 402–3 (12); 1028, 43–45: 398–9 (16)
DUMONT, A., *Mél. d'Epigr.*, 435, 100x: 409 (3)

ἐγκύκλιος παιδεία: 406 (2)
ἐπίδειξις: 408 (1)
Etruscan education in Rome: 420 (3)

Geometers in the Late Empire: 434 (32)
γυμνασίου (οἱ ἀπὸ or ἐκ τοῦ): 386 (17)
gymnastics, age at which first practised: 389 (1)
gyneconome: 387 (23)

Hermeneumata Pseudodositheana: 428 (18)
HOLLEAUX, M., thesis: 421 (11)
HOMER, *Il.*, XV, 284: 360 (9)
— and pederasty: 366 (5)
— Phoenix and Chiron: 360 (12)
HOR., *Sat.*, I, 6, 75: 431 (9)
hypodesmata: 268

IG, XII, 1, 141: 397 (13)
Iliac tables: 405 (11)
Isocrates, relations with Plato: 378 (14)
— number of pupils: 377 (11)

jentaculum: 269
JUV., X, 116: 431 (9)

KROLL, W., on Greek culture in the days of Cicero: 426–7 (11)

legislation on compulsory schooling: 382 (3)

mathematical papyri, for school use and otherwise: 402 (10)
MICHEL, 913: 403 (12)
monostich sayings: 400 (8)

Ναυμαχία: 390 (7)

O. Lond. Hall, 26210: 331

PETREMENT, S., thesis: 437 (1)
PGuér.Joug.: 154–5, 400 (6)
PIRENNE, H., *Revue Bénédictine*, 1934, 165 *seq.*: 448–9 (9)
PLATO, *Prot.*, 318e: 371 (12)
— course of study of: 374 (18). *See* Isocrates
PLUTARCH, *Lib. educ.*: 397 (14)
— *Quaest. conv.*, IX, 736 D: 406 (1)
Posidonius: 417 (57)
POxy., 466: 124, 391 (10)

ῥήτωρ: 413 (24)
Roman teachers, specialisation of: 429 (1)

σχολή: 408 (1)
σοφιστής: 413 (24)
Synesius (election as bishop): 412 (21)

time-tables, school: 397–8 (15)

Vorderasiatische Bibliotek, VII, 256, 18: 356 (8)

Remarks concerning historical method: 48, 95, 217, 353–4 (1), 359 (3), 379 (3), 388 (29), 415 (43), 417 (60), 439 (10)

Suggestions for further studies: 95–6 (Hellenistic education), 379 (school papyri), 381 (education of slaves), 413 (rhetoric), 429 (teaching of Greek to Latins), 444 (stenography in antiquity), 449–50 (Byzantine education)

II

NOTABILIA VARIA

Where the development of a subject extends over several consecutive pages, only the first is mentioned: the notes are in general to be understood as included with the text.